Tennessee
grade 8

HOLT SCIENCE & TECHNOLOGY

HOLT McDOUGAL
a division of Houghton Mifflin Harcourt

Acknowledgments

Contributing Authors

Katy Z. Allen
Science Writer
Wayland, Massachusetts

Linda Ruth Berg, Ph.D.
Adjunct Professor of Natural Sciences
St. Petersburg College
St. Petersburg, Florida

Christie Borgford, Ph.D.
Assistant Professor of Chemistry (retired)
Department of Chemistry
The University of Alabama
Birmingham, Alabama

Andrew Champagne
Former Physics Teacher
Ashland, Massachusetts

Mapi Cuevas, Ph.D.
Professor of Chemistry
Department of Natural Sciences
Santa Fe Community College
Gainesville, Florida

Leila Dumas, MA
Former Physics Teacher
Lago Vista, Texas

Jennie Dusheck, MA
Science Writer
Santa Cruz, California

Robert H. Fronk, Ph.D.
Chair of Science and Mathematics Education
Florida Institute of Technology
West Melbourne, Florida

Karen J. Meech, Ph.D.
Associate Astronomer
Institute for Astronomy
University of Hawaii
Honolulu, Hawaii

Lee Summerlin, Ph.D.
Professor of Chemistry (retired)
University of Alabama
Birmingham, Alabama

Sally Ann Vonderbrink, Ph.D.
Chemistry Teacher (retired)
Cincinnati, Ohio

Safety Reviewer

Jack Gerlovich, Ph.D.
Associate Professor
School of Education
Drake University
Des Moines, Iowa

Inclusion Specialist

Karen Clay
Inclusion Consultant
Boston, Massachusetts

Ellen McPeek Glisan
Special Needs Consultant
San Antonio, Texas

Tennessee Advisory Board

Lucy Bonds
Science Teacher
Houston Middle School
Germantown, Tennessee

Linda M. Brown
Science Teacher
Rucker-Stewart Middle School
Gallatin, Tennessee

Benjamin L. Bruce, M.Ed.
Science Teacher
TW Hunter Middle School
Hendersonville, Tennessee

Anne Faulks
Science Teacher
Appling Middle School
Bartlett, Tennessee

Lois Finney
Science Teacher
Joe Shafer Middle School
Gallatin, Tennessee

Anthony Goad
Science Teacher
Tyner Middle Academy
Chattanooga, Tennessee

Mark Jones
Science Teacher
Gresham Middle School
Knoxville, Tennessee

Barbara Greer King
Science Teacher
John P. Freeman Optional School
Memphis, Tennessee

Zach Martin
Science Teacher
Rockvale Middle School
Rockvale, Tennessee

Melissa Onek
Science Teacher
Shadowlawn Middle School
Memphis, Tennessee

Carrie A. Scurlock
Science Teacher
East Literature Magnet School
Nashville, Tennessee

June Anderson Stevens
Science Teacher
Bellevue Middle School
Nashville, Tennessee

Acknowledgments
continued on page 571

ISBN-13: 978-0-55-400939-1
ISBN-10: 0-55-400939-0

2 3 4 5 6   0868   12 11 10 09

Tennessee

As you read the following pages and work through the Tennessee Science Standards and the Tennessee Academic Vocabulary, you will discover the big ideas and key concepts that your teacher expects you to learn and understand.

You will see three things:

1 >
what the standard actually says

2 **Review Question**
a typical standards Review Question

3 *TN VOCAB* **Academic Vocabulary**
definitions of important terms and phrases

Tennessee
Volunteer State

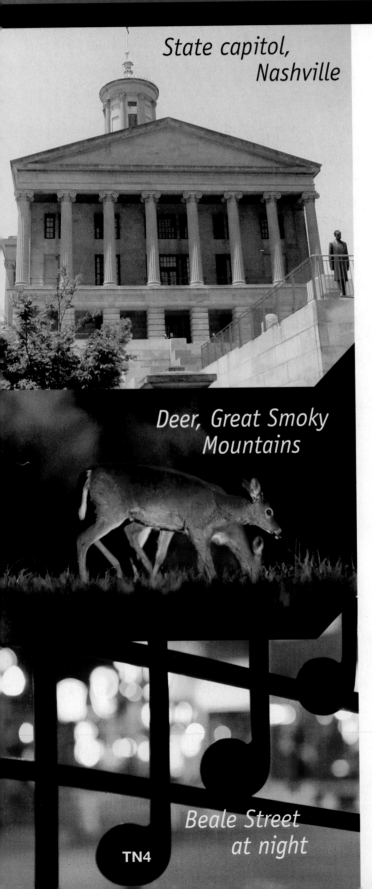

State capitol, Nashville

Deer, Great Smoky Mountains

Beale Street at night

Inquiry

Conceptual Strand
Understandings about scientific inquiry and the ability to conduct inquiry are essential for living in the 21st century.

Guiding Question
What tools, skills, knowledge, and dispositions are needed to conduct scientific inquiry?

>GLE 0807.Inq.1 Design and conduct open-ended scientific investigations.

Review Question The steps of scientific methods
A must all be used in every scientific investigation.
B must always be used in the same order.
C often start with a question.
D always result in the development of a theory.

>GLE 0807.Inq.2 Use appropriate tools and techniques to gather, organize, analyze, and interpret data.

Review Question A scientist is going to measure how quickly a rocket can reach an altitude of 100 meters. She would most likely use which of the following tools to measure the time precisely?
F a stopwatch
G a wrist watch
H a wall clock
J a sun dial

Mockingbird

Iris

>GLE 0807.Inq.3 Synthesize information to determine cause and effect relationships between evidence and explanations.

Review Question The seasons are caused by the tilt of Earth as it orbits the sun. This tilt causes the number of daylight hours to change depending on the time of year. Daylight hours are shortest during which season?
A spring
B summer
C fall
D winter

>GLE 0807.Inq.4 Recognize possible sources of bias and error, alternative explanations, and questions for further exploration.

Review Question Which of the following helps ensure that evidence published in scientific journals is unbiased?
F The journals are very expensive.
G The articles in the journal are subject to peer review.
H The scientists who publish the articles all work for free.
J The institutions that purchase the journals review every article for accuracy.

>GLE 0807.Inq.5 Communicate scientific understanding using descriptions, explanations, and models.

Review Question Which of the following helps you communicate the results of your experiment?
A developing a hypothesis
B making observations
C analyzing your data
D sharing your conclusion with the class

Technology & Engineering

Conceptual Strand
Society benefits when engineers apply scientific discoveries to design materials and processes that develop into enabling technologies.

Guiding Question
How do science concepts, engineering skills, and applications of technology improve the quality of life?

>GLE 0807.T/E.1 Explore how technology responds to social, political, and economic needs.

Review Question Which of the following inventions will most likely have the greatest positive effect on the people of a developing country that has little rainfall?
F an efficient, low-cost, human-powered water pump
G an expensive gas-powered water pump
H a community-wide rain collection system
J bottled water imported from Europe

>GLE 0807.T/E.2 Know that the engineering design process involves an ongoing series of events that incorporate design constraints, model building, testing, evaluating, modifying, and retesting.

Review Question Which is an example of how engineers use models?
A An engineer writes a manual to explain how to use a chainsaw.
B An engineer writes new software enable a machine to count money.
C An engineer uses crash-test dummies to evaluate how a car protects passengers.
D An engineer calls a peer to brainstorm ideas.

Tennessee
Volunteer State

>GLE 0807.T/E.3 Compare the intended benefits with the unintended consequences of a new technology.

Review Question Off-shore oil drilling has many positive benefits. Which of the following is an unintended consequence of this technology?
- F More oil is available than without off-shore drilling.
- G Some oil spills from the well and pollutes the surrounding water.
- H Workers have to live on the off-shore rigs.
- J The rigs create holes in the sea floor.

>GLE 0807.T/E.4 Describe and explain adaptive and assistive bioengineered products.

Review Question Which of the following is an example of integrated pest management?
- A A town sprays insecticides on wetlands to kill mosquitoes.
- B A snake eats a frog in a pond.
- C A child receives a vaccine against measles.
- D A farmer releases ladybugs to eat the aphids that would destroy his crops.

Biodiversity and Change

Conceptual Strand 5
A rich variety of complex organisms have developed in response to a continually changing environment.

Guiding Question 5
How does natural selection explain how organisms have changed over time?

>GLE 0807.5.1 Identify various criteria used to classify organisms into groups.

Review Question How do scientists classify organisms?
- F by grouping the organisms by their characteristics
- G by giving the organisms many common names
- H by deciding whether the organisms are useful
- J by using only existing categories of classification

The Mississippi and Memphis

>GLE 0807.5.2 Use a simple classification key to identify a specific organism.

Review Question In the woods, Chen saw an interesting animal that was brown, with white on its belly. It also had a long furry tail with a black tip. Chen used this dichotomous key to figure out what he saw.

DICHOTOMOUS KEY TO 10 COMMON MAMMALS IN THE EASTERN UNITED STATES

1. a. This mammal flies. Its "hand" forms a wing. **b.** This mammal does not fly. Its "hand" does not form a wing.	Little Brown Bat Go to step 2.
2. a. This mammal has no hair on its tail. **b.** This mammal has hair on its tail.	Go to step 3. Go to step 4.
3. a. This mammal has a short, naked tail. **b.** This mammal has a long, naked tail.	Eastern Mole Go to step 5.
4. a. This mammal has a black mask across its face. **b.** This mammal does not have a black mask across its face.	Raccoon Go to step 6.
5. a. This mammal has a tail that is flat and paddle shaped. **b.** This mammal has a tail that is not flat or paddle shaped.	Beaver Opossum
6. a. This mammal is brown and has a white underbelly. **b.** This mammal is not brown and does not have a white underbelly.	Go to step 7. Striped Skunk
7. a. This mammal has a long, furry tail that is black on the tip. **b.** This mammal has a long tail that has little fur.	Longtail Weasel White-Footed Mouse

Which of the following animals do you think Chen saw?

    A a striped skunk
    B a little brown bat
    C a long-tail weasel
    D a white-footed mouse

>GLE 0807.5.3 Analyze how structural, behavioral, and physiological adaptations within a population enable it to survive in a given environment.

Review Question Darwin puzzled over the various species of Galápagos finches. He eventually concluded that over time, the finches adapted to various environments on the islands. On which of the following traits did Darwin base his conclusions?

    F eye color
    G flight patterns
    H beak size and shape
    J bone structure of the wings

>GLE 0807.5.4 Explain why variation within a population can enhance the chances for group survival.

Review Question In a population of frogs, male frogs croak to scare off predators. However, a few male frogs cannot croak as loudly as other male frogs do. Why are the louder male frogs more likely to survive?

    A They will attract more mates.
    B They will catch more insects.
    C They will jump higher.
    D They will escape predators.

Answers: T/E.3) G; T/E.4) D; 5.1) F; 5.2) C; 5.3) H; 5.4) D

*Ruby Falls,
Chattanooga*

>GLE 0807.5.5 Describe the importance of maintaining the earth's biodiversity.

Review Question Which of the following environments is likely to be most ecologically stable over time?

F an environment with one abundant species

G an environment with two abundant species

H an environment without predators

J a biologically diverse environment

>GLE 0807.5.6 Investigate fossils in sedimentary rock layers to gather evidence of changing life forms.

Review Question The diagram below shows the layers of sedimentary rock exposed during an archaeological dig. These layers of rock have formed over hundreds of millions of years. Archaeologists discovered the fossil of a *Pakicetus*, a mammal that lived around 50 million years ago. They uncovered these remains from layer 2 in the diagram.

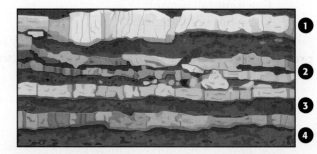

In what layer would you expect to find the remains of an *Ambulocetus,* which existed after the *Pakicetus*?

A layer 1

B layer 2

C layer 3

D layer 4

Matter

Conceptual Strand 9
The composition and structure of matter is known, and it behaves according to principles that are generally understood.

Guiding Question 9
How does the structure of matter influence its physical and chemical behavior?

>GLE 0807.9.1 Understand that all matter is made up of atoms.

Review Question Which sentence correctly describes atoms?
F   All substances are made of the same atoms.
G   Atoms are the smallest particle of a nucleus.
H   An atom is the smallest particle of an element.
J   An atom is a substance that has been cut in half.

>GLE 0807.9.2 Explain that matter has properties that are determined by the structure and arrangement of its atoms.

Review Question Which of the following best describes the properties of metals?
A   hard, brittle, and unconductive
B   liquid, dark, and conductive
C   shiny, malleable, and conductive
D   soft, oily, and very reactive

>GLE 0807.9.3 Interpret data from an investigation to differentiate between physical and chemical changes.

Review Question Which of the following describes signs that a chemical change is occurring?
F   A substance changes shape or state.
G   A substance gives off or absorbs heat.
H   A substance is dense and malleable.
J   A substance is flammable and reactive.

>GLE 0807.9.4 Distinguish among elements, compounds, and mixtures.

Review Question Which of the following best describes chicken noodle soup?
A   element
B   mixture
C   compound
D   solution

>GLE 0807.9.5 Apply the chemical properties of the atmosphere to illustrate a mixture of gases.

Review Question What is the most abundant gas in the atmosphere?
F   oxygen
G   hydrogen
H   nitrogen
J   carbon dioxide

>GLE 0807.9.6 Use the periodic table to determine the characteristics of an element.

Review Question An element that is very reactive is most likely a member of the
A   noble gases.
B   alkali metals.
C   transition metals.
D   actinides.

>GLE 0807.9.7 Explain the Law of Conservation of Mass.

Review Question Balancing a chemical equation so that the same number of atoms of each element is found in both the reactants and the products is an example of

F activation energy.

G the law of conservation of energy.

H the law of conservation of mass.

J a double-displacement reaction.

>GLE 0807.9.8 Interpret the events represented by a chemical equation.

Review Question Which chemical equation correctly shows the formation of water from hydrogen and oxygen?

A $H_2 + O_2 \longrightarrow H_2O$

B $2H_2 + O_2 \longrightarrow 2H_2O$

C $H_2 + 2O \longrightarrow H_2O$

D $H + O_2 \longrightarrow H_2O$

>GLE 0807.9.9 Explain the basic difference between acids and bases.

Review Question What type of compound increases the number of hydronium ions when dissolved in water?

F an acid

G a base

H an indicator

J hydrogen gas

Forces in Nature

Conceptual Strand 12
Everything in the universe exerts a gravitational force on everything else; there is an interplay between magnetic fields and electrical currents.

Guiding Question 12
What are the scientific principles that explain gravity and electromagnetism?

Nashville music scene

>GLE 0807.12.1 Investigate the relationship between magnetism and electricity.

Review Question An electric fan has an electric motor inside to change
- A mechanical energy into electrical energy.
- B thermal energy into electrical energy.
- C electrical energy into thermal energy.
- D electrical energy into mechanical energy.

>GLE 0807.12.2 Design an investigation to change the strength of an electromagnet.

Review Question The magnetic field of a solenoid can be increased by
- F adding more loops per meter.
- G increasing the current.
- H putting an iron core inside the coil to make an electromagnet.
- J All of the above

>GLE 0807.12.3 Compare and contrast the earth's magnetic field to that of a magnet and an electromagnet.

Review Question Which property of Earth enables you to use a compass?
- A Earth's mass
- B Earth's volume
- C Earth's magnetism
- D Earth's density

>GLE 0807.12.4 Identify factors that influence the amount of gravitational force between objects.

Review Question The magnitude of the gravitational force between two bodies depends upon
- F the velocity of the bodies and the friction between them.
- G the size of the bodies and their position relative to Earth.
- H the weight of the bodies and how quickly they are moving.
- J the mass of the bodies and the distance between them.

>GLE 0807.12.5 Recognize that gravity is the force that controls the motion of objects in the solar system.

Review Question The universe contains galaxies, stars, and planets. How does gravity affect these bodies in space?
- A Gravity pulls bodies away from each other.
- B Gravity organizes bodies into nebulas, galaxies, and planetary systems.
- C Gravity attracts bodies with similar compositions to each other.
- D Gravity causes bodies to be scattered randomly throughout the universe.

Answers: 9.7) H; 9.8) B; 9.9) F; 12.1) D; 12.2) J; 12.3) C; 12.4) J; 12.5) B

Memphis

Tennessee Academic Vocabulary

Follow this link to the updated list of Tennessee Academic Vocabulary

http://my.hrw.com/nsmedia/hst/tn_vocab.pdf

Grade 6

TN▶VOCAB absorption in optics, the transfer of light energy to particles of matter

TN▶VOCAB amplitude the maximum distance that the particles of a wave's medium vibrate from their rest position

TN▶VOCAB classification the division of organisms into groups, or classes, based on specific characteristics

TN▶VOCAB commensalism a relationship between two organisms in which one organism benefits and the other is unaffected

TN▶VOCAB consumer an organism that eats other organisms or organic matter

TN▶VOCAB decomposer an organism that gets energy by breaking down the remains of dead organisms or animal wastes and consuming or absorbing the nutrients

TN▶VOCAB eclipse an event in which the shadow of one celestial body falls on another

TN▶VOCAB energy transformations changes from one form of energy to another

TN▶VOCAB extinction the death of every member of a species

TN▶VOCAB food web a diagram that shows the feeding relationships between organisms in an ecosystem

TN▶VOCAB forms of energy energy is the capacity to do work; this capacity can exist in many ways, including thermal energy, potential energy, and kinetic energy

TN▶VOCAB fossil the trace or remains of an organism that lived long ago, most commonly preserved in sedimentary rock

TN▶VOCAB frequency the number of waves produced in a given amount of time

TN▶VOCAB heat flow the transfer of thermal energy between objects of different temperatures

TN▶VOCAB lunar eclipse an event in which the shadow of Earth falls on the moon

TN▶VOCAB mutualism a relationship between two species in which both species benefit

TN▶VOCAB nuclear power controlled nuclear reactions, such as fission, used to make electricity

TN▶VOCAB parasitism a relationship between two species in which one species, the parasite, benefits from the other species, the host, which is harmed

Tennessee river

TN▸VOCAB **producer** an organism that can make its own food by using energy from its surroundings

TN▸VOCAB **reflection** the bouncing back of a ray of light, sound, or heat when the ray hits a surface that it does not go through

TN▸VOCAB **refraction** the bending of a wave as the wave passes between two substances in which the speed of the wave differs

TN▸VOCAB **relative age** the approximate age of fossils or other objects in rock layers determined by comparing whether the surrounding rock layers are younger or older

TN▸VOCAB **seasons** predictable, annual changes in weather due to the tilt of Earth on its axis and the rotation of Earth around the sun

TN▸VOCAB **sedimentary rocks** rocks formed when particles of rock are pressed and cemented together by surrounding minerals, or fused together by pressure from overlying layers of rock

TN▸VOCAB **solar eclipse** an event in which the shadow of the moon falls on Earth

TN▸VOCAB **tide** the periodic rise and fall of the water level in the oceans and other large bodies of water

TN▸VOCAB **universe components** bodies and systems, such as stars, galaxies, planets, and black holes, that make up all of space

TN▸VOCAB **wave** a periodic disturbance in a solid, liquid, or gas as energy is transmitted through a medium

TN▸VOCAB **wavelength** the distance from any point on a wave to an identical point on the next wave

Grade 7

TN▸VOCAB **asexual reproduction** reproduction that does not involve the union of sex cells and in which one parent produces offspring that are genetically identical to the parent

TN▸VOCAB **carbon cycle** the exchange of carbon between the environment and living things

TN▸VOCAB **cell organelles** the small bodies in a cell's cytoplasm that are specialized to perform specific functions

TN▸VOCAB **chloroplast** the organelle that uses the energy of sunlight to make food

TN▸VOCAB **chromosome** in a eukaryotic cell, one of the structures in the nucleus that are made up of DNA and protein; in a prokaryotic cell, the main ring of DNA

TN▸VOCAB **compound** a substance made up of atoms of two or more different elements joined by chemical bonds

TN▸VOCAB **concentration** the amount of a particular substance in a given quantity of a mixture, solution, or ore

TN *VOCAB* **cytoplasm** the fluid and almost all the contents inside a cell

TN *VOCAB* **density** the ratio of the mass of a substance to the volume of the substance

TN *VOCAB* **diffusion** the movement of particles from regions of higher density to regions of lower density

TN *VOCAB* **element** a substance that cannot be separated or broken down into simpler substances by chemical means

TN *VOCAB* **gene** one set of instructions for an inherited trait

TN *VOCAB* **inorganic compound** a compound that does not contain covalently bonded carbon

TN *VOCAB* **lysosome** the organelle that digests food particles, wastes, cell parts, and foreign invaders

TN *VOCAB* **mitochondria** in eukaryotic cells, the cell organelles that are surrounded by two membranes and that are the site of cellular respiration

TN *VOCAB* **mitosis** in eukaryotic cells, a process of cell division that forms two new nuclei, each of which has the same number of chromosomes

TN *VOCAB* **molecule** the smallest unit of a substance that keeps all of the physical and chemical properties of that substance

TN *VOCAB* **nano-technology** science and technology operating at the molecular or atomic scale

TN *VOCAB* **nucleus** in physical science, an atom's central region, which is made up of protons and neutrons

TN *VOCAB* **organ** a collection of tissues that carry out a specialized function of the body

TN *VOCAB* **organ system** a group of organs that work together to perform body functions

TN *VOCAB* **organic compound** a covalently bonded compound that contains carbon

TN *VOCAB* **osmosis** the diffusion of water through a semipermeable membrane

TN *VOCAB* **product** a substance that forms in a chemical reaction

TN *VOCAB* **reactant** a substance or molecule that participates in a chemical reaction

TN *VOCAB* **respiration** in biology, the exchange of oxygen and carbon dioxide between living cells and their environment; includes breathing and cellular respiration

TN *VOCAB* **ribosome** the organelle in which amino acids are hooked together to make proteins

TN *VOCAB* **run-off** water moving over the land surface

TN *VOCAB* **sexual reproduction** reproduction in which the sex cells from two parents unite to produce offspring that share traits from both parents

TN *VOCAB* **tissue** a group of similar cells that perform a common function

TN *VOCAB* **transpiration** the process by which plants release water vapor into the air through stomata; also the release of water vapor into the air by other organisms

TN *VOCAB* **vacuole** a vesicle in a cell

TN *VOCAB* **volume** a measure of the size of a body or region in three-dimensional space

TN *VOCAB* **weather data** information about the short-term state of the atmosphere, including temperature, humidity, precipitation, wind, and visibility

TN *VOCAB* **weight** a measure of the gravitational force exerted on an object; its value can change with the location of the object in the universe. The SI unit of force is the Newton.

Grade 8

TN *VOCAB* **abiotic** describes the nonliving part of the environment, including water, rocks, light, and temperature

TN *VOCAB* **acceleration** the rate at which velocity changes over time; an object accelerates if its speed, direction, or both change

TN *VOCAB* **biome** a large region characterized by a specific type of climate and certain types of plant and animal communities

TN *VOCAB* **biotic** describes living factors in the environment

TN14

TN VOCAB chemical equation a representation of a chemical reaction that uses symbols to show the relationship between the reactants and the products

TN VOCAB continental drift the hypothesis that a single large landmass broke up into smaller landmasses to form the continents, which then drifted to their present locations; the movement of continents

TN VOCAB dichotomous key an aid that is used to identify organisms and that consists of the answers to a series of questions

TN VOCAB DNA deoxyribonucleic acid, a molecule that is present in all living cells and that contains the information that determines the traits that a living thing inherits and needs to live

TN VOCAB dominant trait the trait observed in the first generation when parents that have different traits are bred

TN VOCAB earthquake a movement or trembling of the ground that is caused by a sudden release of energy when rocks along a fault move

TN VOCAB endothermic describes a chemical reaction that requires heat

TN VOCAB energy resources natural resources that humans use to generate energy

TN VOCAB exothermic describes a chemical reaction in which heat is released to the surroundings

TN VOCAB genetic engineering manipulating individual genes within organisms

TN VOCAB genotype the entire genetic makeup of an organism; also the combination of genes for one or more specific traits

TN VOCAB genus a subgroup of a family in biological classification

TN VOCAB gravitation (universal law) All objects in the universe attract each other through gravitational force; the size of the force depends on the masses of the objects and the distance between the objects

TN VOCAB igneous rocks rocks that form when hot, liquid rock, or *magma,* cools and solidifies

*Sun Sphere,
Knoxville*

TN VOCAB inertia the tendency of an object to resist being moved or, if the object is moving, to resist a change in speed or direction until an outside force acts on the object

TN VOCAB law of conservation of mass the law that states that mass cannot be created or destroyed in ordinary chemical and physical changes

TN VOCAB metamorphic rocks rocks in which the structure, texture, or composition of the rock have changed

TN VOCAB minerals a naturally formed, inorganic solid that has a definite chemical structure

TN VOCAB momentum a quantity defined as the product of the mass and velocity of an object

TN VOCAB monohybrid cross a genetic cross between individuals that involves one pair of contrasting traits

TN VOCAB mutation a change in the nucleotide-base sequence of a gene or DNA molecule

TN VOCAB Newton's 3 laws of motion Sir Isaac Newton's laws that explain the relationship between force and the motion of an object.

TN VOCAB Newton's First Law of Motion: An object at rest remains at rest, and an object in motion remains in motion at constant speed and in a straight line, unless acted on by an unbalanced force.

TN VOCAB Newton's Second Law of Motion: The acceleration of an object depends on the mass of the object and the amount of force applied.

TN VOCAB Newton's Third Law of Motion: Whenever one object exerts a force on a second object, the second object exerts an equal and opposite force on the first.

TN VOCAB plate tectonics the theory that explains how large pieces of Earth's outermost layer, called *tectonic plates,* move and change shape

TN VOCAB pH a value that is used to express the acidity or basicity (alkalinity) of a system

TN VOCAB phenotype an organism's appearance or other detectable characteristic

TN VOCAB Punnett square a tool used to organize all the possible combinations of offspring from particular parents

TN VOCAB recessive trait a trait that is apparent only when two recessive alleles for the same characteristic are inherited

TN VOCAB rock cycle the series of processes in which a rock forms, changes from one type to another, is destroyed, and forms again by geological processes

TN VOCAB species a group of organisms that are closely related and can mate to produce fertile offspring

TN VOCAB speed the distance traveled divided by the time interval during which the motion occurred

TN VOCAB velocity the speed of an object in a particular direction

TN VOCAB volcano a vent or fissure in Earth's surface through which magma and gases are expelled

Tennessee farmland

Tennessee
grade 8

HOLT SCIENCE & TECHNOLOGY

HOLT McDOUGAL
a division of Houghton Mifflin Harcourt

Acknowledgments

Contributing Authors

Katy Z. Allen
Science Writer
Wayland, Massachusetts

Linda Ruth Berg, Ph.D.
Adjunct Professor of Natural Sciences
St. Petersburg College
St. Petersburg, Florida

Christie Borgford, Ph.D.
Assistant Professor of Chemistry (retired)
Department of Chemistry
The University of Alabama
Birmingham, Alabama

Andrew Champagne
Former Physics Teacher
Ashland, Massachusetts

Mapi Cuevas, Ph.D.
Professor of Chemistry
Department of Natural Sciences
Santa Fe Community College
Gainesville, Florida

Leila Dumas, MA
Former Physics Teacher
Lago Vista, Texas

Jennie Dusheck, MA
Science Writer
Santa Cruz, California

Robert H. Fronk, Ph.D.
Chair of Science and Mathematics Education
Florida Institute of Technology
West Melbourne, Florida

Karen J. Meech, Ph.D.
Associate Astronomer
Institute for Astronomy
University of Hawaii
Honolulu, Hawaii

Lee Summerlin, Ph.D.
Professor of Chemistry (retired)
University of Alabama
Birmingham, Alabama

Sally Ann Vonderbrink, Ph.D.
Chemistry Teacher (retired)
Cincinnati, Ohio

Safety Reviewer

Jack Gerlovich, Ph.D.
Associate Professor
School of Education
Drake University
Des Moines, Iowa

Inclusion Specialist

Karen Clay
Inclusion Consultant
Boston, Massachusetts

Ellen McPeek Glisan
Special Needs Consultant
San Antonio, Texas

Tennessee Advisory Board

Lucy Bonds
Science Teacher
Houston Middle School
Germantown, Tennessee

Linda M. Brown
Science Teacher
Rucker-Stewart Middle School
Gallatin, Tennessee

Benjamin L. Bruce, M.Ed.
Science Teacher
TW Hunter Middle School
Hendersonville, Tennessee

Anne Faulks
Science Teacher
Appling Middle School
Bartlett, Tennessee

Lois Finney
Science Teacher
Joe Shafer Middle School
Gallatin, Tennessee

Anthony Goad
Science Teacher
Tyner Middle Academy
Chattanooga, Tennessee

Mark Jones
Science Teacher
Gresham Middle School
Knoxville, Tennessee

Barbara Greer King
Science Teacher
John P. Freeman Optional School
Memphis, Tennessee

Zach Martin
Science Teacher
Rockvale Middle School
Rockvale, Tennessee

Melissa Onek
Science Teacher
Shadowlawn Middle School
Memphis, Tennessee

Carrie A. Scurlock
Science Teacher
East Literature Magnet School
Nashville, Tennessee

June Anderson Stevens
Science Teacher
Bellevue Middle School
Nashville, Tennessee

Acknowledgments
continued on page 571

ISBN-13: 978-0-55-400939-1
ISBN-10: 0-55-400939-0

2 3 4 5 6   0868   12 11 10 09

Contents in Brief

Contents

TN Tennessee Science Standards

UNIT 1 ····Life Science

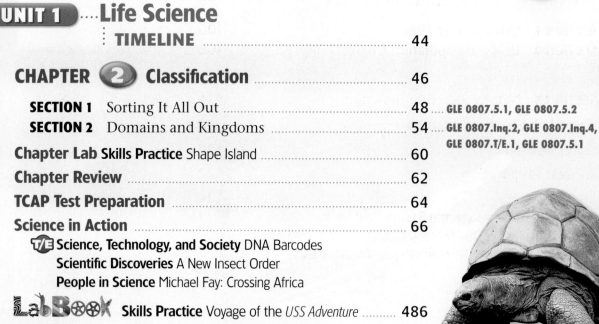

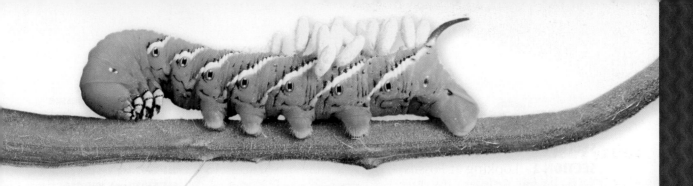

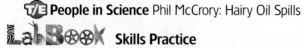

TN Tennessee Science Standards

GLE 0807.Inq.2, GLE 0807.Inq.5,
GLE 0807.T/E.2, GLE 0807.9.1,
GLE 0807.9.2, GLE 0807.9.6

GLE 0807.Inq.3, GLE 0807.Inq.5,
GLE 0807.T/E.1, GLE 0807.T/E.2,
GLE 0807.T/E.3, GLE 0807.9.1,
GLE 0807.9.2, GLE 0807.9.6

GLE 0807.T/E.1, GLE 0807.T/E.2,
GLE 0807.T/E.3, GLE 0807.9.1,
GLE 0807.9.2, GLE 0807.9.6

GLE 0807.T/E.1, GLE 0807.9.2,
GLE 0807.9.4

GLE 0807.Inq.2, GLE 0807.Inq.5,
GLE 0807.T/E.1, GLE 0807.T/E.2,
GLE 0807.9.2, GLE 0807.9.4,
GLE 0807.9.6

TN Tennessee
Science Standards

GLE 0807.Inq.2, GLE 0807.Inq.3,
GLE 0807.T/E.1, GLE 0807.9.2,
GLE 0807.9.4

GLE 0807.Inq.2, GLE 0807.Inq.3,
GLE 0807.Inq.5, GLE 0807.T/E.1,
GLE 0807.9.2, GLE 0807.9.8,
GLE 0807.9.9

GLE 0807.Inq.2, GLE 0807.Inq.5,
GLE 0807.T/E.1, GLE 0807.9.2,
GLE 0807.9.4, GLE 0807.9.9

GLE 0807.Inq.2, GLE 0807.Inq.3,
GLE 0807.Inq.5, GLE 0807.T/E.1,
GLE 0807.T/E.3, GLE 0807.9.2,
GLE 0807.9.4, GLE 0807.9.8

GLE 0807.Inq.3, GLE 0807.Inq.5,
GLE 0807.12.4

GLE 0807.Inq.3, GLE 0807.Inq.5,
GLE 0807.9.1, GLE 0807.9.6

GLE 0807.Inq.2, GLE 0807.Inq.3,
GLE 0807.Inq.5, GLE 0807.9.5

GLE 0807.Inq.2, GLE 0807.Inq.3,
GLE 0807.Inq.5, GLE 0807.12.4,
GLE 0807.12.5

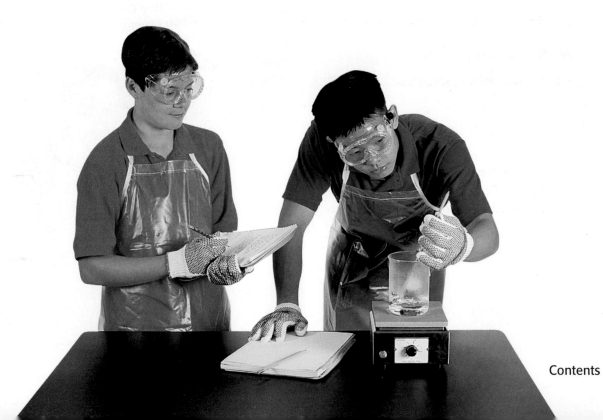

Chapter Labs

Make science a "hands-on" experience.

Each chapter ends with a **Chapter Lab** designed to help you experience science firsthand. But please don't forget to be safe. Read the **Safety First!** section before starting any of the labs.

LabBook Labs

The more labs, the better!

Take a minute to browse the variety of exciting labs in this textbook. Additional chapter labs appear in a special **LabBook** in the back of the textbook. **Quick Labs** appear within each chapter and are designed to require only a small amount of time and limited equipment. Don't forget to read the **Safety First!** section before starting any of the labs.

Quick Labs

Contents **xv**

Pre-Reading Activities

FOLDNOTES

Graphic Organizer

Start your engines with an activity!

Get motivated to learn by doing the two activities at the beginning of each chapter. The **Pre-Reading Activity** helps you organize information as you read the chapter. The **Start-Up Activity** helps you gain scientific understanding of the topic through hands-on experience.

Start-Up Activities

Reading Strategies

Remembering what you read doesn't have to be hard!

A **Reading Strategy** at the beginning of every section provides tips to help you remember and/or organize the information covered in the section.

Internet Activities

Get caught in the Web!

Go to **go.hrw.com** for **Internet Activities** related to each chapter. To find the Internet Activity for a particular chapter, just type in the keyword listed above.

School to Home

Math Practice

Science and math go hand in hand.

Each **Math Practice** activity contains a word problem related to the topic at hand. **Math Focus** activities provide step-by-step instructions and practice questions designed to help you apply math directly to science.

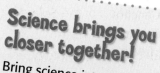

Science brings you closer together!

Bring science into your home by doing **School-to-Home Activities** with a family member or another adult in your household.

Math Focus

Connection to...

One subject leads to another.

You may not realize it at first, but different subjects are related to each other in many ways. Each **Connection** explores a topic from the viewpoint of another discipline. In this way, all of the subjects you learn about in school merge to improve your understanding of the world around you.

Science In Action

T/E Technology and Engineering

Science, technology, and engineering outside the classroom!

Read Science in Action to learn more about science, technology, and engineering in the real world. At the end of each chapter, you will find three short articles that give you an idea of how interesting, useful, and action-packed science and technology are. And for more in-depth coverage, go to go.hrw.com.

How to Use Your Textbook

Your Roadmap for Success with Holt Science and Technology

What You Will Learn

At the beginning of every section you will find the section's objectives, vocabulary terms, and the Tennessee Science Standards that will be covered. The objectives tell you what you'll need to know after you finish reading the section.

Vocabulary terms are listed for each section. Learn the definitions of these terms because you will most likely be tested on them. Each term is highlighted in the text and is defined at point of use and in the margin. You can also use the glossary to locate definitions quickly.

STUDY TIP Reread the objectives and the definitions to the terms when studying for a test to be sure you know the material.

Get Organized

A Reading Strategy at the beginning of every section provides tips to help you organize and remember the information covered in the section. Standards Checks help you see if you are understanding the standard. Keep a science notebook so that you are ready to take notes when your teacher reviews the material in class. Keep your assignments in this notebook so that you can review them when studying for the chapter test.

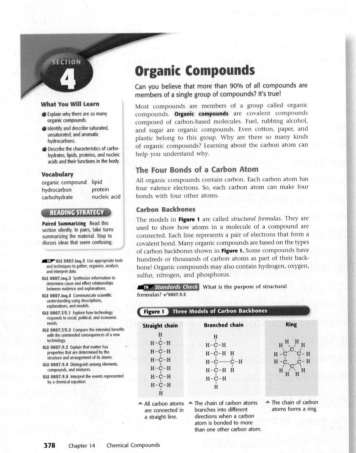

SECTION 4

Organic Compounds

Can you believe that more than 90% of all compounds are members of a single group of compounds? It's true!

Most compounds are members of a group called organic compounds. **Organic compounds** are covalent compounds composed of carbon-based molecules. Fuel, rubbing alcohol, and sugar are organic compounds. Even cotton, paper, and plastic belong to this group. Why are there so many kinds of organic compounds? Learning about the carbon atom can help you understand why.

What You Will Learn

- Explain why there are so many organic compounds.
- Identify and describe saturated, unsaturated, and aromatic hydrocarbons.
- Describe the characteristics of carbohydrates, lipids, proteins, and nucleic acids and their functions in the body.

Vocabulary
organic compound   lipid
hydrocarbon   protein
carbohydrate   nucleic acid

READING STRATEGY

Paired Summarizing Read this section silently. In pairs, take turns summarizing the material. Stop to discuss ideas that seem confusing.

The Four Bonds of a Carbon Atom

All organic compounds contain carbon. Each carbon atom has four valence electrons. So, each carbon atom can make four bonds with four other atoms.

Carbon Backbones

The models in **Figure 1** are called *structural formulas*. They are used to show how atoms in a molecule of a compound are connected. Each line represents a pair of electrons that form a covalent bond. Many organic compounds are based on the types of carbon backbones shown in **Figure 1**. Some compounds have hundreds or thousands of carbon atoms as part of their backbone! Organic compounds may also contain hydrogen, oxygen, sulfur, nitrogen, and phosphorus.

Standards Check What is the purpose of structural formulas? ✓0807.9.5

Figure 1 Three Models of Carbon Backbones

Straight chain — All carbon atoms are connected in a straight line.

Branched chain — The chain of carbon atoms branches into different directions when a carbon atom is bonded to more than one other carbon atom.

Ring — The chain of carbon atoms forms a ring.

378 Chapter 14 Chemical Compounds

Be Resourceful—Use the Web

SciLinks boxes in your textbook take you to resources that you can use for science projects, reports, and research papers. Go to **scilinks.org** and type in the **SciLinks code** to find information on a topic.

Visit go.hrw.com
Check out the **Current Science®** magazine articles and other materials that go with your textbook at **go.hrw.com**. Click on the textbook icon and the table of contents to see all of the resources for each chapter.

Figure 6 Spider webs are made up of proteins that are shaped like long fibers.

nucleic acid a molecule made up of subunits called *nucleotides*

Examples of Proteins

Proteins have many roles in your body and in living things. Enzymes (EN ZIEMZ) are proteins that are catalysts. *Catalysts* regulate chemical reactions in the body by increasing the rate at which the reactions occur. Some hormones are proteins. For example, insulin is a protein hormone that helps regulate your blood-sugar level. Another kind of protein, called *hemoglobin*, is found in red blood cells and delivers oxygen throughout the body. There are also large proteins that extend through cell membranes. These proteins help control the transport of materials into and out of cells. Some proteins, such as those in your hair, provide structural support. The structural proteins of silk fibers make the spider web shown in **Figure 6** strong and lightweight.

Nucleic Acids

The largest molecules made by living organisms are nucleic acids. **Nucleic acids** are biochemicals made up of *nucleotides* (NOO klee oh TIEDZ). Nucleotides are molecules made of carbon, hydrogen, oxygen, nitrogen, and phosphorus atoms. There are only five kinds of nucleotides. But nucleic acids may have millions of nucleotides bonded together. The only reason living things differ from each other is that each living thing has a different order of nucleotides.

Nucleic acids have several functions. One function of nucleic acids is to store genetic information. They also help build proteins and other nucleic acids. Nucleic acids are sometimes called *the blueprints of life*, because they contain all the information needed for a cell to make all of its proteins.

✔ **Reading Check** What are two functions of nucleic acids?

GLE 0807.Inq.2, GLE 0807.Inq.3, GLE 0807.T/E.1, GLE 0807.T/E.3

CONNECTION TO Engineering

Bioengineering Developments in bioengineering enable scientists and engineers to add genetic material to food crops. However, some people think that bioengineering of food crops may have unintended consequences. Research the debate over bioengineering of food crops. List one benefit and one possible unintended consequence of the bioengineering of food crops. Decide whether bioengineering of food crops is adaptive or assistive and explain your reasoning. Write your findings in your **science journal**.
✔0807.Inq.2, ✔0807.Inq.3, ✔0807.T/E.3, ✔0807.T/E.4

ACTIVITY

the second type of nucleic acid, RNA (ribonucleic acid). RNA is involved in the actual building of proteins.

7 Two strands of DNA are twisted in a spiral shape. Four different nucleotides make up the rungs of the DNA ladder.

SECTION Review

GLE 0807.Inq.3, GLE 0807.T/E.1, GLE 0807.9.2, GLE 0807.9.4

Summary

- Organic compounds contain carbon, which can form four bonds.
- Hydrocarbons are composed of only carbon and hydrogen.
- Hydrocarbons may be saturated, unsaturated, or aromatic hydrocarbons.
- Carbohydrates are made of simple sugars.
- Lipids store energy and make up cell membranes.
- Proteins are composed of amino acids.
- Nucleic acids store genetic information and help cells make proteins.

Using Key Terms

1. Use the following terms in the same sentence: *organic compound, hydrocarbon,* and *biochemical.*

2. In your own words, write a definition for each of the following terms: *carbohydrate, lipid, protein,* and *nucleic acid.* ✔0807.9.7

Understanding Key Ideas

3. A saturated hydrocarbon has
   a. only single bonds.
   b. double bonds.
   c. triple bonds.
   d. double and triple bonds.

4. List two functions of proteins.

5. What is an aromatic hydrocarbon?

Critical Thinking

6. **Identifying Relationships** Hemoglobin is a protein that is in blood and that transports oxygen to the tissues of the body. Information stored in nucleic acids tells a cell how to make proteins. What might happen if there is a mistake in the information needed to make hemoglobin? ✔0807.Inq.3

7. **Making Comparisons** Compare saturated hydrocarbons with unsaturated hydrocarbons.

Interpreting Graphics

Use the structural formula of this organic compound to answer the questions that follow.

$$\begin{array}{ccc} H & H & H \\ | & | & | \\ H-C-C-C-H \\ | & | & | \\ H & H & H \end{array}$$

8. What type of bonds are present in this molecule?

9. Can you determine the shape of the molecule from this structural formula? Explain your answer.

10. What elements make up this compound? ✔0807.9.5

Internet Resources

For a variety of links related to this chapter, go to www.scilinks.org
Topic: Aromatic Compounds; Organic Compounds
SciLinks code: HSM0095; HSM1078

383

Illustrations, Photos, and Activities

Art shows complex ideas and processes. Learn to analyze the art so that you better understand the material you read in the text.

Tables and graphs display important information in an organized way to help you see relationships.

A picture is worth a thousand words. Look at the photographs to see relevant examples of science concepts that you are reading about.

Activities and Quick Labs reinforce key science concepts. Activities with the **T/E** icon help you master the Technology and Engineering Standards.

Answer the Section Reviews

Section Reviews test your knowledge of the main points of the section. Critical Thinking items challenge you to think about the material in greater depth and to find connections that you infer from the text. Checks for Understanding assess your mastery of the Tennessee Science Standards.

STUDY TIP When you can't answer a question, reread the section. The answer is usually there.

Do Your Homework

Your teacher may assign worksheets to help you understand and remember the material in the chapter.

STUDY TIP Don't try to answer the questions without reading the text and reviewing your class notes. A little preparation up front will make your homework assignments a lot easier. Answering the items in the Chapter Review will help prepare you for the chapter test.

Holt Online Learning

Visit Holt Online Learning

If your teacher gives you a special password to log onto the **Holt Online Learning** site, you'll find your complete textbook on the Web. In addition, you'll find some great learning tools and practice quizzes. You'll be able to see how well you know the material from your textbook.

SAFETY FIRST!

Exploring, inventing, and investigating are essential to the study of science. However, these activities can also be dangerous. To make sure that your experiments and explorations are safe, you must be aware of a variety of safety guidelines. You have probably heard of the saying, "It is better to be safe than sorry." This is particularly true in a science classroom where experiments and explorations are being performed. Being uninformed and careless can result in serious injuries. Don't take chances with your own safety or with anyone else's.

The following pages describe important guidelines for staying safe in the science classroom. Your teacher may also have safety guidelines and tips that are specific to your classroom and laboratory. Take the time to be safe.

Safety Rules!

Start Out Right

Always get your teacher's permission before attempting any laboratory exploration. Read the procedures carefully, and pay particular attention to safety information and caution statements. If you are unsure about what a safety symbol means, look it up or ask your teacher. You cannot be too careful when it comes to safety. If an accident does occur, inform your teacher immediately regardless of how minor you think the accident is.

Safety Symbols

All of the experiments and investigations in this book and their related worksheets include important safety symbols to alert you to particular safety concerns. Become familiar with these symbols so that when you see them, you will know what they mean and what to do. It is important that you read this entire safety section to learn about specific dangers in the laboratory.

If you are instructed to note the odor of a substance, wave the fumes toward your nose with your hand. Never put your nose close to the source.

Eye protection

Clothing protection

Hand safety

Heating safety

Electric safety

Chemical safety

Animal safety

Sharp object

Plant safety

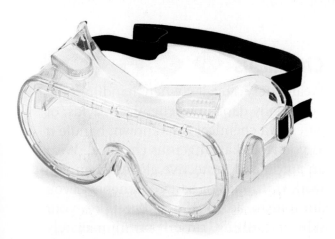

Eye Safety

Wear safety goggles when working around chemicals, acids, bases, or any type of flame or heating device. Wear safety goggles any time there is even the slightest chance that harm could come to your eyes. If any substance gets into your eyes, notify your teacher immediately and flush your eyes with running water for at least 15 minutes. Treat any unknown chemical as if it were a dangerous chemical. Never look directly into the sun. Doing so could cause permanent blindness.

Avoid wearing contact lenses in a laboratory situation. Even if you are wearing safety goggles, chemicals can get between the contact lenses and your eyes. If your doctor requires that you wear contact lenses instead of glasses, wear eye-cup safety goggles in the lab.

Safety Equipment

Know the locations of the nearest fire alarms and any other safety equipment, such as fire blankets and eyewash fountains, as identified by your teacher, and know the procedures for using the equipment.

Neatness

Keep your work area free of all unnecessary books and papers. Tie back long hair, and secure loose sleeves or other loose articles of clothing, such as ties and bows. Remove dangling jewelry. Don't wear open-toed shoes or sandals in the laboratory. Never eat, drink, or apply cosmetics in a laboratory setting. Food, drink, and cosmetics can easily become contaminated with dangerous materials.

Certain hair products (such as aerosol hair spray) are flammable and should not be worn while working near an open flame. Avoid wearing hair spray or hair gel on lab days.

Sharp/Pointed Objects

Use knives and other sharp instruments with extreme care. Never cut objects while holding them in your hands. Place objects on a suitable work surface for cutting.

Be extra careful when using any glassware. When adding a heavy object to a graduated cylinder, tilt the cylinder so that the object slides slowly to the bottom.

Chemicals

Wear safety goggles when handling any potentially dangerous chemicals, acids, or bases. If a chemical is unknown, handle it as you would a dangerous chemical. Wear an apron and protective gloves when you work with acids or bases or whenever you are told to do so. If a spill gets on your skin or clothing, rinse it off immediately with water for at least 5 minutes while calling to your teacher.

Never mix chemicals unless your teacher tells you to do so. Never taste, touch, or smell chemicals unless you are specifically directed to do so. Before working with a flammable liquid or gas, check for the presence of any source of flame, spark, or heat.

Heat

Wear safety goggles when using a heating device or a flame. Whenever possible, use an electric hot plate as a heat source instead of using an open flame. When heating materials in a test tube, always angle the test tube away from yourself and others. To avoid burns, wear heat-resistant gloves whenever instructed to do so.

Electricity

Be careful with electrical cords. When using a microscope with a lamp, do not place the cord where it could trip someone. Do not let cords hang over a table edge in a way that could cause equipment to fall if the cord is accidentally pulled. Do not use equipment with damaged cords. Be sure that your hands are dry and that the electrical equipment is in the "off" position before plugging it in. Turn off and unplug electrical equipment when you are finished.

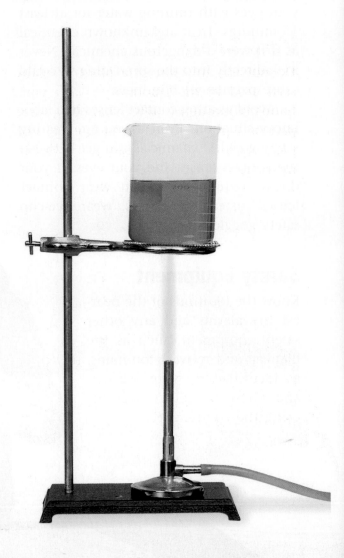

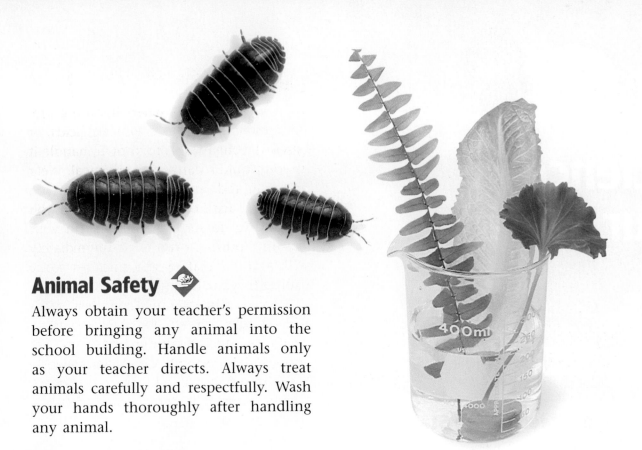

Animal Safety

Always obtain your teacher's permission before bringing any animal into the school building. Handle animals only as your teacher directs. Always treat animals carefully and respectfully. Wash your hands thoroughly after handling any animal.

Plant Safety

Do not eat any part of a plant or plant seed used in the laboratory. Wash your hands thoroughly after handling any part of a plant. When in nature, do not pick any wild plants unless your teacher instructs you to do so.

Glassware

Examine all glassware before use. Be sure that glassware is clean and free of chips and cracks. Report damaged glassware to your teacher. Glass containers used for heating should be made of heat-resistant glass.

1

Science in Our World

The Big Idea

Scientific progress is made by asking meaningful questions and conducting careful investigations.

TN Tennessee Science Standards

Embedded Inquiry

GLE 0807.Inq.1 Design and conduct open-ended scientific investigations.

GLE 0807.Inq.2 Use appropriate tools and techniques to gather, organize, analyze, and interpret data.

GLE 0807.Inq.3 Synthesize information to determine cause and effect relationships between evidence and explanations.

GLE 0807.Inq.4 Recognize possible sources of bias and error, alternative explanations, and questions for further exploration.

GLE 0807.Inq.5 Communicate scientific understanding using descriptions, explanations, and models

✔**0807.Inq 1** Design and conduct an open-ended scientific investigation to answer a question that includes a control and appropriate variables.

✔**0807.Inq.2** Identify tools and techniques needed to gather, organize, analyze, and interpret data collected from a moderately complex scientific investigation.

✔**0807.Inq.3** Use evidence from a dataset to determine cause and effect relationships that explain a phenomenon.

✔**0807.Inq.4** Review an experimental design to determine possible sources of bias or error, state alternative explanations, and identify questions for further investigation.

✔**0807.Inq.5** Design a method to explain the results of an investigation using descriptions, explanations, or models.

Embedded Technology and Engineering

GLE 0807.T/E.1 Explore how technology responds to social, political, and economic needs.

GLE 0807.T/E.2 Know that the engineering design process involves an ongoing series of events that incorporate design constraints, model building, testing, evaluation, modifying, and retesting.

GLE 0807.T/E.3 Compare the intended benefits with the unintended consequences of a new technology.

GLE 0807.T/E.4 Describe and explain adaptive and assistive bio-engineered products.

✔**0807.T/E.2** Apply the engineering design process to construct a prototype that meets certain specifications.

✔**0807.T/E.3** Explore how the unintended consequences of new technologies can impact society.

✔**0807.T/E.4** Research bioengineering technologies that advance health and contribute to improvements in our daily lives.

✔**0807.T/E.5** Develop an adaptive design and test its effectiveness.

PRE-READING ACTIVITY

Graphic Organizer

Spider Map Before you read the chapter, create the graphic organizer entitled "Spider Map" described in the **Study Skills** section of the Appendix. Label the circle "Scientific Models." Create a leg for each type of scientific model. As you read the chapter, fill in the map with details about each type of scientific model.

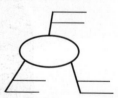

About the Photo

Flippers work great to help penguins move through the water. But could flippers help ships, too? Two scientists have been trying to find out. By using scientific methods, they are asking questions such as, "Would flippers use less energy than propellers do?" As a result of these investigations, ships may have flippers like those of penguins someday!

START-UP ACTIVITY

Figure It Out

In this activity, you will make observations and use them to solve a puzzle, just as scientists do.

Procedure

1. Get the **five shapes** shown here from your teacher.

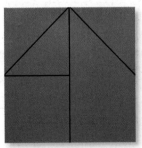

2. Observe the drawing at right. Predict how the five shapes could be arranged to make the fish.

3. Test your idea. You may have to try several times. (Hint: Shapes can be turned over.)

Analysis

1. Did you solve the puzzle just by making observations? What observations helped the most?

2. How did testing your ideas help?

Science and Scientists

You're eating breakfast. You look down and notice your reflection in your spoon is upside down! You wonder, Why is my reflection upside down even though I'm holding the spoon right side up?

Congratulations! You just completed the first steps of being a scientist. How did you do it? You observed the world around you. Then you asked questions about your observations. And that's part of what science is all about.

Science Starts with a Question

The process of gathering knowledge about the natural world is called **science**. Asking a question is often the first step in the process of gathering knowledge. The world around you is full of amazing things that can lead you to ask questions, such as those in **Figure 1.**

In Your Own Neighborhood

Take a look around your school and around your neighborhood. Most of the time, you take things that you use or see every day for granted. However, one day you might look at something in a new way. That's when a question hits you! The student in **Figure 1** didn't have to look very far to realize that she had some questions to ask.

The World and Beyond

Do you think you might get tired asking questions about things in your neighborhood? Then just remember that the world is made up of many different places. You could ask questions about deserts, forests, or sandy beaches. Many different plants and animals live in each of these places. And then there are the rocks, soil, and flowing water in the environment.

But Earth is not the final place to look for questions. You can look outward to the moon, sun, and planets in our solar system. And beyond that, you have the rest of the universe! There seem to be enough questions to keep scientists busy for a long time.

What You Will Learn

- Describe three methods of investigation.
- Identify benefits of science in the world around you.
- Describe jobs that use science.

Vocabulary

science

READING STRATEGY

Reading Organizer As you read this section, create an outline of the section. Use the headings from the section in your outline.

TN **GLE 0807.Inq.2** Use appropriate tools and techniques to gather, organize, analyze, and interpret data.
GLE 0807.Inq.5 Communicate scientific understanding using descriptions, explanations, and models.
GLE 0807.T/E.1 Explore how technology responds to social, political, and economic needs.

Why do I feel pain when I stub my toe?

What causes high and low tides?

Why can I see a reflection in a spoon?

Figure 1 *Part of science is asking questions about the world around you.*

Investigation: The Search for Answers

Once you ask a question, it's time to find an answer. There are several different methods that you can use to start your investigation.

Research

You can find answers to some of your questions by doing research, as shown in **Figure 2.** You can ask someone who knows a lot about the subject of your question, or you can look up information in textbooks, encyclopedias, and magazines. You can also search on the Internet for information. You can find information by reading about an experiment that someone did. But be sure to think about where the information you find comes from. You want to use information only from reliable sources.

Observation

You can find answers to questions by making careful observations. For example, if you want to know if cloud type and weather are associated, you could make daily observations. By daily recording the types of clouds that you see and the day's weather, you may find associations between the two.

Experimentation

You can answer some of your questions by doing an experiment, as shown in **Figure 3.** Your research might help you plan your experiment. And, you'll need to make careful observations. What do you do if your experiment needs materials or conditions that are hard to get? For example, what do you do if you want to see how a rat runs through a maze in space? Don't give up! Do more research, and try to find the results from someone else's experiment!

✓ *Reading Check* What do you do if materials for your experiment are hard to find?

Figure 2 *A library is a good place to begin your search for answers.*

science the knowledge obtained by observing natural events and conditions in order to discover facts and formulate laws or principles that can be verified or tested

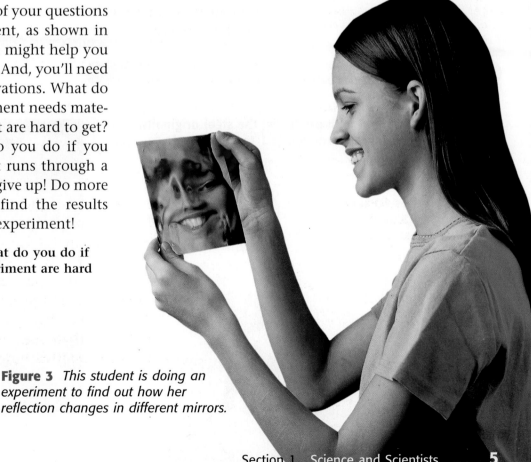

Figure 3 *This student is doing an experiment to find out how her reflection changes in different mirrors.*

Figure 4 *The results of this test are used to improve air bags.*

Why Ask Why?

Although people cannot use science to answer every question, they do find some interesting answers. But do any of the answers really matter? Absolutely! As you study science, you will see how it affects you and everything around you.

Saving Lives

Using science, people have come up with several answers to the question "How can people be protected during an automobile accident?" One answer is to require people to wear seat belts. Other answers include designing and building cars that are made of stronger materials and that have air bags. **Figure 4** shows how air bags are tested under scientific conditions. In this way, science helps make cars safer.

Saving Resources

Science and technology have helped respond to the need to make resources last longer. Recycling is one answer. Science has helped engineers invent ways to recycle a variety of materials. For example, when a car becomes worn out or is wrecked, its steel can be recycled and used to make new products. And recycling steel saves more than just the steel, as shown in **Figure 5.** Using science, engineers develop more-efficient methods and better equipment for recycling steel, aluminum, paper, glass, and even some plastics. As a result, man-made resources such as steel last longer and natural resources from the environment are conserved.

| **Figure 5** | **Resources Saved Through Recycling** |

Compared with producing the steel originally, recycling 1 metric ton (1.1 tons) of steel:

 uses 60 kg (132 lb) less limestone

 uses 1.25 metric tons (1.38 tons) less ore

 uses 0.70 metric tons (0.77 tons) less coal

 uses 2,700,000 kcal less energy

 produces 76 percent less water pollution

 produces 86 percent less air pollution

Saving the Environment

Science has helped answer the question, "How can the ozone layer be protected?" Substances called *chlorofluorocarbons* (KLAWR oh FLUR uh KAHR buhnz) (CFCs), which can be found in aerosols, have had a role in damaging the ozone layer. But using science, people have made other substances that can take the place of CFCs. These substances do not harm the ozone layer.

Why does the loss of this layer matter? The ozone that makes up this layer protects everything on the planet from a harmful type of light called *ultraviolet* (UV) light. Without the protection of the ozone layer, higher levels of UV light will reach the ground. Higher rates of skin cancer could result. By finding ways to reduce the use of these chemicals, we can help protect the environment and make the world a healthier place.

Scientists Are All Around You

Believe it or not, scientists work in many different places. If you think about it, any person who asks questions and looks for answers could be called a scientist! Keep reading to learn about just a few jobs that use science.

Meteorologist

A *meteorologist* (MEET ee uhr AHL uh jist) is a person who studies the atmosphere. One of the most common careers that meteorologists have is that of weather forecaster. But some meteorologists specialize in—and even chase—tornadoes! These meteorologists predict where a tornado is likely to form. Then, they drive very near the site to gather data, as shown in **Figure 6.** These data help meteorologists and other scientists understand tornadoes better. A better understanding of tornadoes enables scientists to more accurately predict the behavior of these violent storms. The ability to make more-accurate predictions allows scientists to give earlier warnings of storms, which helps reduce injuries and deaths caused by storms.

✓ Reading Check What is a meteorologist?

Challenging Topics
Although science can be used to explain or answer many questions about the world around us, there are some topics that cannot be examined usefully in a scientific way. With a parent, list several questions and determine if you could gather, organize, analyze, and interpret data to answer the questions. If you could not for some questions, do you think that these questions cannot be explained by science? ✓0807.Inq.2.

Figure 6 *These meteorologists are risking their lives to gather data about tornadoes.*

Figure 7 *This geochemist takes rock samples from the field. Then she studies them in her laboratory.*

Figure 8 *Volcanologists study volcanoes. Many volcanologists study volcanic patterns in order to predict when a volcano will erupt.*

Geochemist

Look at **Figure 7**. A *geochemist* (JEE oh KEM ist) is a person who specializes in the chemistry of rocks, minerals, and soil. Geochemists determine the economic value of these materials. They also try to find out what the environment was like when these materials formed and what has happened to the materials since they first formed.

Ecologist

To understand the behavior of living things, you also need to know about the surroundings. An *ecologist* (ee KAHL uh jist) is a person who studies communities of organisms and their nonliving environments. Ecologists work in many fields, such as wildlife management, agriculture, forestry, and conservation.

Volcanologist

Imagine that your workplace was at the edge of 1,000°C pool of lava, as seen in **Figure 8**. That's where you might work if you were a volcanologist! A *volcanologist* (VAHL kuh NAHL uh jist) is a scientist who studies volcanoes. Volcanologists must know the structure and the chemistry of Earth and its rocks. They must also understand how volcanic materials interact with air and water. This knowledge helps volcanologists learn how and why volcanoes erupt. If volcanologists can predict when a volcano will erupt, they can help save lives.

Science Illustrator

You may be surprised to learn that there is a career that uses both art and science skills. *Science illustrators* draw scientific diagrams, such as the one in **Figure 9.**

Science illustrators often have a background in art and a variety of sciences. However, some science illustrators focus on one area of science. For example, some science illustrators draw only medical diagrams. These diagrams are used in medical textbooks, or in brochures that patients receive from their doctors.

✓ **Reading Check** What does a science illustrator do?

Figure 9 *A science illustrator drew this diagram so students can learn about the digestive system in birds.*

SECTION Review

TN GLE 0807.Inq.2, GLE 0807.Inq.5, GLE 0807.T/E.1

Summary

- Science is the process of gathering knowledge about the natural world.
- Science begins by asking a question.
- Three methods of investigation are research, observation, and experimentation.
- Science affects people's daily lives. Science can help save lives, save resources, and improve the environment.
- There are several types of scientists and many jobs that use science.

Using Key Terms

1. In your own words, write a definition for the term *science*.

Understanding Key Ideas

2. Which of the following items describes what volcanologists must know in order to help them predict the eruption of a volcano?
   a. the structure of Earth
   b. the chemistry of Earth's rocks
   c. the interaction between volcanic material and air
   d. All of the above.

3. Describe three jobs that use science.

4. What are three methods of investigation?

5. Describe how science and technology can help people save resources such as coal.

Math Skills

6. A slow flow of lava is traveling at a rate of 3 m per day. How far will the lava have traveled at the end of 30 days?

Critical Thinking

7. **Applying Concepts** Your friend wants to know the average amount of salt added to her favorite fast-food French fries. How could she design an experiment that would help her gather, analyze, and interpret the data to answer her question? ✓0807.Inq.2

8. **Making Inferences** The slogan for a package delivery service is "For the fastest shipping from port to port, call Holt Speedy Transport!" What inferences about the service can you make from this slogan? Design an experiment with a control and appropriate variables to see if this service is faster than other services. Tell how you would explain your findings. ✓0807.Inq.2, ✓0807.Inq.5

Internet Resources

For a variety of links related to this chapter, go to www.scilinks.org

Topic: Scientific Inquiry; Careers in Science

SciLinks code: HSM1357; HSM0225

Scientific Methods

Imagine that you are trying to improve ships. Would you study the history of shipbuilding? Would you investigate different types of fuel? Would you observe creatures that move easily through the water, such as dolphins and penguins?

Two scientists from the Massachusetts Institute of Technology (MIT) thought that studying penguins was a great way to improve ships! In the next few pages, you'll learn about James Czarnowski (zahr NOW SKEE) and Michael Triantafyllou (tree AHN ti FEE loo). These two scientists from MIT used scientific methods to develop *Proteus* (PROH tee uhs), the penguin boat.

What Are Scientific Methods?

The ways in which scientists answer questions and solve problems are called **scientific methods**. As scientists look for answers, they often use the same steps. But there is more than one way to use the steps. Look at **Figure 1.** Scientists may use all of the steps or just some of the steps during an investigation. They may even repeat some of the steps or do them in a different order. It all depends on what works best to answer their question.

What You Will Learn

- Identify the steps used in scientific methods.
- Formulate testable hypotheses.
- Explain how scientific methods are used to answer questions and solve problems.

Vocabulary

scientific methods
observation
hypothesis
data

READING STRATEGY

Mnemonics As you read this section, create a mnemonic device to help you remember scientific methods.

TN **GLE 0807.Inq.1** Design and conduct open-ended scientific investigations.

GLE 0807.Inq.2 Use appropriate tools and techniques to gather, organize, analyze, and interpret data.

GLE 0807.Inq.3 Synthesize information to determine cause and effect relationships between evidence and explanations.

GLE 0807.Inq.4 Recognize possible sources of bias and error, alternative explanations, and questions for further exploration.

GLE 0807.Inq.5 Communicate scientific understanding using descriptions, explanations, and models.

GLE 0807.T/E.1 Explore how technology responds to social, political, and economic needs.

GLE 0807.T/E.3 Compare the intended benefits with the unintended consequences of a new technology.

Figure 1 Scientific Methods

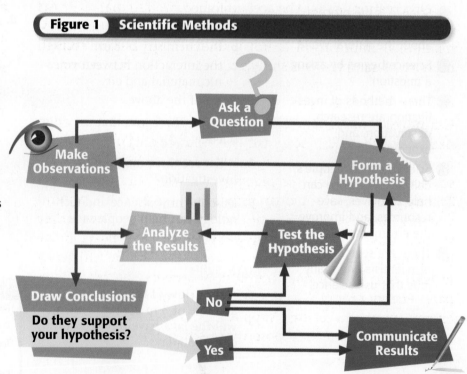

Ask a Question

Asking a question helps focus the purpose of an investigation. Scientists often ask a question after making observations. An **observation** is any use of the senses to gather information. Noting that the sky is blue or that a cotton ball feels soft is an observation. Measurements are observations that are made with tools such as metersticks and stopwatches.

Observations should be accurately recorded so that scientists can use the information in future investigations. In an investigation, if information is not gathered from a large enough number of samples, the study's results may be misleading.

A Real-World Question

Czarnowski and Triantafyllou, shown in **Figure 2,** are engineers (EN juh NIRZ), scientists who put scientific knowledge to practical human use. Engineers create technology or use science to make tools for practical purposes. Czarnowski and Triantafyllou observed boat propulsion (proh PUHL shuhn) systems, which are what make boats move. Then, they studied ways to improve these systems. Most boats move by using propellers. These engineers studied the efficiency (e FISH uhn see) of boat propulsion systems. *Efficiency* compares energy output (the energy used to move the boat) with energy input (the energy supplied by the engine). The engineers learned from their observations that boat propellers are not very efficient.

Reading Check How do engineers use technology?

scientific methods a series of steps followed to solve problems, including collecting data, formulating a hypothesis, testing the hypothesis, and stating conclusions

observation the process of obtaining information by using the senses

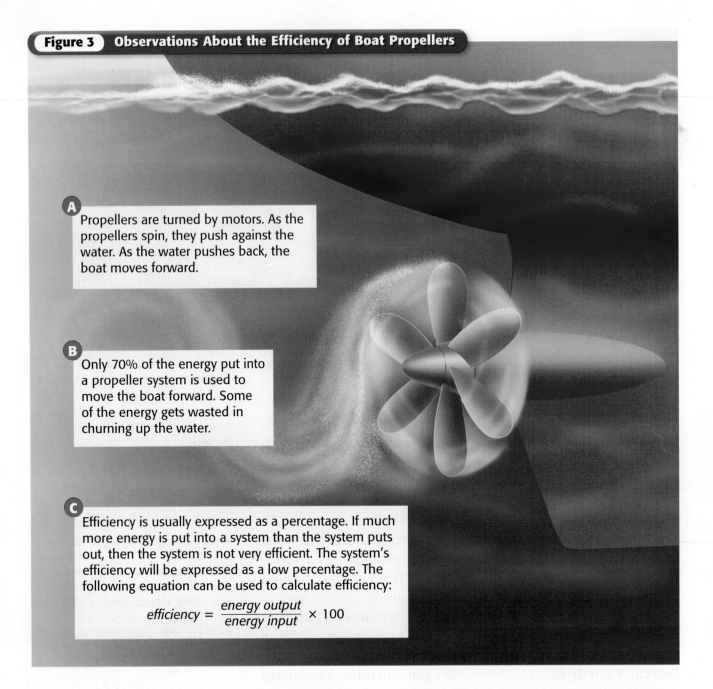

Figure 3 Observations About the Efficiency of Boat Propellers

A Propellers are turned by motors. As the propellers spin, they push against the water. As the water pushes back, the boat moves forward.

B Only 70% of the energy put into a propeller system is used to move the boat forward. Some of the energy gets wasted in churning up the water.

C Efficiency is usually expressed as a percentage. If much more energy is put into a system than the system puts out, then the system is not very efficient. The system's efficiency will be expressed as a low percentage. The following equation can be used to calculate efficiency:

$$efficiency = \frac{energy\ output}{energy\ input} \times 100$$

The Importance of Boat Efficiency

Look at **Figure 3.** Czarnowski and Triantafyllou found that only 70% of the energy put into a propeller system is used to move the boat forward. Why is boat efficiency important? Making only a small fraction of the United States' boats and ships just 10% more efficient would save millions of liters of fuel per year. Saving fuel means saving money. It also means using less of Earth's supply of fossil fuels. Based on their observations and all of this information, Czarnowski and Triantafyllou were ready to ask the following question: How can boat propulsion systems be made more efficient?

Form a Hypothesis

Once you've asked your question and made observations, you are ready to form a *hypothesis*. A **hypothesis** is a possible explanation or answer to a question. You can use what you already know and what you have observed in order to form a hypothesis. A good hypothesis is testable. This means that information can be gathered or an experiment can be designed to test it. A hypothesis that is not testable is not necessarily wrong. But there is no way to support the hypothesis or to show that it is wrong.

hypothesis an explanation that is based on prior scientific research or observations and that can be tested

Nature Provides a Possible Answer

Czarnowski observed how quickly and easily penguins at the New England Aquarium moved through the water. **Figure 4** shows how penguins propel themselves. Czarnowski also observed that penguins have a rigid body, similar to a boat. These observations led to a hypothesis: A propulsion system that mimics the way a penguin swims will be more efficient than a propulsion system that uses propellers.

Make Predictions

Before scientists test a hypothesis, they often make predictions that state what they think will happen during the actual test of the hypothesis. Scientists usually state predictions in an if-then format. The engineers at MIT might have made the following prediction: *If* two flippers are attached to a boat, *then* the boat will be more efficient than a boat powered by propellers.

✓ Reading Check What is a prediction?

TN GLE.0807.T/E.3

CONNECTION TO Biology

T/E **Not Tested on Humans?** When scientists use people as subjects for some investigations, these humans have to agree to participate. Research and describe some investigations that use people. What are the possible intended benefits and unintended consequences of an investigation and why must the people be informed of them? ✓**0807.T/E.4**

TN GLE 0807.Inq.1, GLE 0807.Inq.2, GLE 0807.Inq.3, GLE 0807.Inq.5

Quick Lab

That's Swingin'!

1. Make a pendulum. Tie a **piece of string** to a **ring stand.** Hang a **small weight** from the string.

2. Form a testable hypothesis about one factor (such as the mass of the weight) that may affect the rate at which the pendulum swings.

3. Predict the results as you change this factor (the variable).

4. Test your hypothesis. Record the number of swings made in 10 seconds for each trial.

5. Was your hypothesis supported? Analyze your results. ✓**0807.Inq.1,** ✓**0807.Inq.2,** ✓**0807.Inq.3,** ✓**0807.Inq.5**

Number of Observations

Making several observations during an experiment is important because if you based your conclusions on a small number of observations, you may reach the wrong conclusion. Imagine you flipped a coin 3 times, and each time the coin landed heads-up. You might make the generalization, "Every time I flip a quarter, it will land heads-up." But this generalization is dangerous, because if the coin lands tails up even once, your generalization is incorrect. Now, flip a coin 30 times. Can you make a more accurate generalization now? Why?

✔0807.Inq.2, ✔0807.Inq.3, ✔0807.Inq.4, ✔0807.Inq.5

Test the Hypothesis

After you form a hypothesis, you must test it. You must find out whether it is a reasonable answer to your question. Testing helps you find out if your hypothesis is pointing you in the right direction or if it is way off the mark. Often, a scientist will test a prediction that is based on the hypothesis.

Keep It Under Control

One way to test a hypothesis is to do a controlled experiment. A *controlled experiment* compares the results from a control group with the results from one or more experimental groups. The control group and the experimental groups are the same except for one factor. This factor is called a *variable*. The experiment will then show the effect of the variable. If your experiment has more than one variable, determining which variable is responsible for the experiment's results will be difficult or impossible.

Sometimes, such as in a study of the stars, doing a controlled experiment is not possible. In such cases, you can make more observations or do research. Or you may have to build technology that you want to test as a model or model system. That's just what Czarnowski and Triantafyllou did. They built *Proteus*, the penguin boat, shown in **Figure 5.** *Proteus* is 3.4 m long and 50 cm wide, too narrow for even a single passenger.

Figure 5 *Proteus*

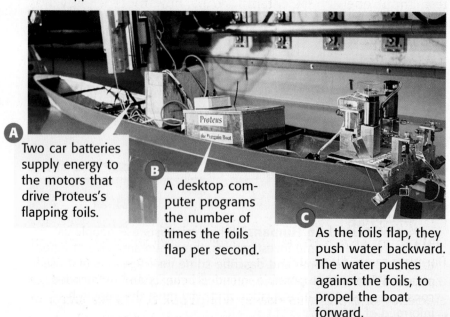

Proteus has two flipperlike paddles, called *foils*. Both foils move out and then in, much as a penguin uses its flippers underwater.

A Two car batteries supply energy to the motors that drive Proteus's flapping foils.

B A desktop computer programs the number of times the foils flap per second.

C As the foils flap, they push water backward. The water pushes against the foils, to propel the boat forward.

Figure 6 Graphs of the Test Results

This line graph shows that *Proteus* was most efficient when its foils were flapping about 1.7 times per second.

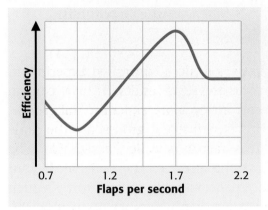

This bar graph shows that the *Proteus* has 17 percent more efficiency than the propeller-driven boat.

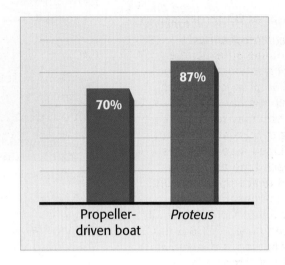

Testing *Proteus*

The engineers took *Proteus* into open water when they were ready to collect data. **Data** are pieces of information acquired through experimentation. The number of data samples in an experiment is important. The sample number must be large enough for scientists to be sure that the experiment's results are due to the variable and not to normal variation between samples. The engineers did several tests. Only the flapping rate varied between tests. Data such as the flapping rate, the energy used by the motor, and the boat's speed were recorded for each test. Input energy was determined by how much energy was used. Output energy was determined from *Proteus*'s speed.

data any pieces of information acquired through observation or experimentation

Analyze the Results

Once you have your data, you must analyze them. You must find out whether the results of your test support the hypothesis. You can analyze your results by doing calculations, or by organizing data into tables and graphs.

✓ *Reading Check* What must you do after you have your data?

Analyzing *Proteus*

Czarnowski and Triantafyllou used the data for input energy and output energy to calculate *Proteus*'s efficiency for different flapping rates. These data are graphed in **Figure 6.** The scientists compared *Proteus*'s highest level of efficiency with the average efficiency of a propeller-driven boat. Look at the bar graph in **Figure 6.** Do the data support the original hypothesis?

Figure 7 *Could a penguin propulsion system be used on large ships, such as oil tankers? The research continues!*

Draw Conclusions

At the end of an investigation, you must draw a conclusion. You could conclude that your results support your hypothesis. Or you could conclude that your results do *not* support your hypothesis. Or you might even conclude that you need more information. Your conclusion can help guide what you do next. You could ask new questions or gather more information. You could change the procedure or check your calculations for errors. Or you could do another investigation.

The *Proteus* Conclusion

After analyzing their data, Czarnowski and Triantafyllou did many more trials. Each time they found that the penguin propulsion system was more efficient than a propeller propulsion system. So they concluded that their hypothesis was supported. But this conclusion led to more questions, as you can see in **Figure 7.**

Communicate Results

One of the most important steps in any investigation is to communicate your results accurately and honestly. Accurate reporting ensures the credibility of a scientist. You can communicate your results in a report or on a Web site. People who read your report can reproduce your experiment and verify your data.

Communicating About *Proteus*

Czarnowski and Triantafyllou published their results in academic papers. They also displayed their project and its results on the Internet. In addition, science magazines and newspapers have reported their work. These reports allow you to conduct some research of your own about *Proteus.*

TN GLE 0807.Inq.4, GLE 0807.Inq.5

CONNECTION TO
Social Studies

Biased Samples Sometimes, the samples of data collected during an investigation may be biased. Information shows bias when it is not objective. For example, in the presidential election of 1936, a polling publication determined that Franklin Roosevelt's opponent, Alf Landon, would win the election by a landslide. The pollsters did not realize that their sample had a greater percentage of supporters of Alf Landon than were in the general population. Their information was biased. When President Roosevelt won the election, the pollsters were very surprised. Research the dangers of biased samples and make a poster about what you have learned. ✔0807.Inq.4, ✔0807.Inq.5

ACTIVITY

TN GLE 0807.Inq.1, GLE 0807.Inq.2, GLE 0807.Inq.3, GLE 0807.Inq.4, GLE 0807.Inq.5

Summary

- Scientific methods are the ways in which scientists answer questions and solve problems.
- Asking a question helps you focus the purpose of an investigation.
- A hypothesis is a possible answer to a question. A good hypothesis is testable.
- Testing a hypothesis helps you find out if the hypothesis is a reasonable answer to your question.

- Analyzing the data collected during an investigation will help you find out whether the results of your test support your hypothesis.
- Conclusions that you draw from your results will show you if your test supported your hypothesis.
- Communicating your results will allow other scientists to use your investigation for research or conduct an investigation of their own.

Using Key Terms

In each of the following sentences, replace the incorrect term with the correct term from the word bank.

        scientific methods   observations
        hypotheses   data

1. Hypotheses are any use of the senses to gather information.

2. Data are possible explanations or answers to a question.

Understanding Key Ideas

3. The statement, "If I don't study for this test, then I will not get a good grade," is an example of a(n)

    a. law.   **c.** observation.

    b. theory.   **d.** prediction.

4. How do scientists and engineers use scientific methods?

5. Name the steps that can be used in scientific methods.

Critical Thinking

6. **Analyzing Methods** Use an example to explain how a small amount of data cannot prove that a prediction is always correct but can prove that a prediction is NOT always correct. ✔0807.Inq.4, ✔0807.Inq.5

7. **Applying Concepts** You want to test different shapes of kites to see which shape produces the strongest lift. What are some factors that need to be the same for each trial so that the only variable is the shape of the kite? ✔0807.Inq.1, ✔0807.Inq.2, ✔0807.Inq.4

Interpreting Graphics

Use the graph below to answer the question that follows.

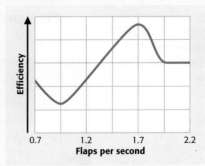

8. What is the flapping rate at the point of lowest efficiency? ✔0807.Inq.3

Internet Resources

For a variety of links related to this chapter, go to www.scilinks.org

Topic: Scientific Methods

SciLinks code: HSM1359

Scientific Models

How much like a penguin was *Proteus*? Well, *Proteus* didn't have feathers and wasn't a living thing. But its "flippers" were designed to create the same kind of motion as a penguin's flippers.

The MIT engineers built *Proteus* to mimic the way a penguin swims. They wanted to get a greater understanding about boat propulsion. In other words, they made a *model*.

Types of Scientific Models

A representation of an object or system is called a **model** or **prototype**. Models often use familiar objects or ideas that stand for other things. That's how a model can be a tool for understanding the natural world. A model uses something familiar to help you understand something that is not familiar. Models can be used to explain the past and the present. They can even be used to predict future events. However, keep in mind that models have limitations. Three major kinds of scientific models are physical, mathematical, and conceptual models.

Physical Models

Model airplanes, dolls, and even many drawings are all physical models. Some physical models, such as the model flower in **Figure 1,** look like the thing they model. However, a limitation of the model flower is that it does not grow like a real flower. Other physical models, such as *Proteus*, act somewhat like the thing they model. *Proteus* was a model of how penguins swim. Of course, *Proteus* doesn't eat fish like penguins do!

What You Will Learn

- Describe how models are used to represent the natural world.
- Identify three types of scientific models.
- Describe theories and laws.

Vocabulary

model
prototype
theory
law

READING STRATEGY

Prediction Guide Before reading this section, write the title of each heading in this section. Next, under each heading, write what you think you will learn.

TN GLE 0807.Inq.2 Use appropriate tools and techniques to gather, organize, analyze, and interpret data.

GLE 0807.Inq.3 Synthesize information to determine cause and effect relationships between evidence and explanations.

GLE 0807.Inq.4 Recognize possible sources of bias and error, alternative explanations, and questions for further exploration.

GLE 0807.Inq.5 Communicate scientific understanding using descriptions, explanations, and models.

model or **prototype** a pattern, plan, representation, or description designed to show the structure or workings of an object, system, or concept

Figure 1 *The model flower makes learning the different parts of a flower much easier. But the model does not smell as sweet!*

Mathematical Models

Every day, people try to predict the weather. One way that they predict the weather is to use mathematical models. **Figure 2** shows a mathematical model that is expressed as a weather map. A mathematical model is made up of mathematical equations and data. Some mathematical models are simple. These models allow you to calculate things such as forces and acceleration. Others are so complex that only computers can handle them. Some of these very complex models have many variables. Using the most correct data does not make the prediction correct. A change in a variable that was not thought of could cause the model to fail.

Figure 2 *Weather maps that you see on the evening news are mathematical models.*

Conceptual Models

The third kind of model is a conceptual model. Some conceptual models are systems of ideas. Others are based on making comparisons with familiar things to help illustrate or explain an idea. The big bang theory, illustrated in **Figure 3,** is a conceptual model. This model says that the universe was once a small, hot, and dense volume of matter. Although the big bang theory is widely accepted by astronomers, some data do not quite fit the model. For example, scientists have calculated the ages of some old, nearby stars. If the calculations are right, then some of these stars are older than the universe itself.

Reading Check What is a conceptual model?

TN GLE 0807.Inq.2, GLE 0807.Inq.5

SCHOOL to HOME

Models and Scale

Models are often built to scale. This means that the size of the parts of the model are proportional to the parts of the real object. Make a scale drawing of a room in your home, including some of the objects in the room. Then, exchange drawings with a classmate. Can you determine the actual size of the room and its objects from your classmate's drawing? ✔0807.Inq.2, ✔0807.Inq.5

ACTIVITY

Figure 3 *The big bang theory says that 12 billion to 15 billion years ago, an event called the big bang sent matter in all directions to eventually form the galaxies and planets.*

Models Are Just the Right Size

Models are often used to represent things that are very small or very large. Particles of matter are too small to see. The Earth or the solar system is too large to see completely. In these cases, a model can help you picture the thing in your mind. How can you learn about the parts of a cell? That's not an easy thing to do because you can't see inside a cell with just your eyes. But you can look at a model, such as the one being used by the student in **Figure 4.**

Figure 4 *Looking at a model of a cell can show you what is inside an actual cell.*

For another activity related to this chapter, go to **go.hrw.com** and type in the keyword **HP5WPSW.**

theory an explanation for some phenomenon that is based on observation, experimentation, and reasoning

law a summary of many experimental results and observations; a law tells how things work.

Models Build Scientific Knowledge

Models are often used to help illustrate and explain scientific theories. In science, a **theory** is a unifying explanation for a broad range of hypotheses and observations that have been supported by testing. A theory not only can explain an observation you've made but also can predict what might happen in the future.

Scientists use models to help guide their search for new information. This information can help support a theory or show it to be wrong. Keep in mind that models can be changed or replaced. These changes happen because new observations that cause scientists to change their theories are made. You can compare an old model with a current one in **Figure 5.**

✓ **Reading Check** What is a theory?

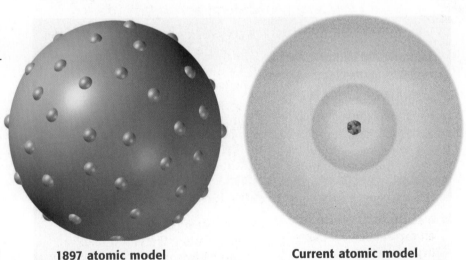

1897 atomic model   **Current atomic model**

Figure 5 *These models show the way scientists' idea of the atom has changed over time as new information was gathered.*

Scientific Laws

What happens when a theory and its models correctly predict the results of many different experiments? A scientific law could be formed. In science, a **law** is a summary of many experimental results and observations. A law tells you how things work. Laws are not the same as theories. Laws tell you only what happens, not why it happens.

A law tells you to expect the same thing to happen every time. Look at **Figure 6.** A chemical change took place when the flask was turned over. A light-blue solid and a dark-blue solution formed. Notice that the mass did not change. This is a demonstration of the *law of conservation of mass*. This law says that during a chemical change, the total mass of the materials formed is the same as the total mass of the starting materials. The law describes every single chemical change! However, the law doesn't explain why this happens. It says only that you can be sure that it will happen.

Figure 6 *The total mass before the change is always the same as the total mass after the change.*

TN GLE 0807.Inq.2, GLE 0807.Inq.4, GLE 0807.Inq.5

SECTION Review

Summary

- A model uses familiar things to describe unfamiliar things.
- Physical, mathematical, and conceptual models are commonly used in science.
- A scientific theory is an explanation for many hypotheses and observations.
- A scientific law summarizes experimental results and observations. It describes what happens, but not why.

Using Key Terms

1. In your own words, write a definition for the term *model*.

Understanding Key Ideas

2. Which kind of model would you use to represent a human heart?
   a. a mathematical model
   b. a physical model
   c. a conceptual model
   d. a natural model

3. Explain the difference between a theory and a law.

Critical Thinking

4. **Analyzing Methods** Both a globe and a flat world map can model features of Earth. Give an example of when and why you would use each of the models. Be sure to tell if the use of one of the models could lead to bias or error. ✔ 0807.Inq.4

5. **Applying Concepts** Identify two limitations of physical models.

Math Skills

6. For a science fair, you want to make a model of the moon orbiting Earth by using a ball. The diameter of the ball that will represent Earth will be about 62 cm. You want your model to be to scale. If the moon is about 4 times smaller than Earth, what should the diameter of the ball that represents the moon be?

Internet Resources

For a variety of links related to this chapter, go to www.scilinks.org
Topic: Using Models
SciLinks code: HSM1588

What You Will Learn

- Explain how science, technology, engineering, and mathematics are related.
- Identify ways that technology responds to social, political, and economic needs.
- Explain the engineering design process for developing new technologies.
- Describe technology in terms of its intended benefits and unintended consequences.

Vocabulary

technology
engineering
engineering design process
prototype
cost-benefit analysis
bioengineering
assistive bioengineering
adaptive bioengineering

READING STRATEGY

Reading Organizer As you read this section, make a concept map by using the terms above.

TN GLE 0807.T/E.1 Explore how technology responds to social, political, and economic needs.

GLE 0807.T/E.2 Know that the engineering design process involves an ongoing series of events that incorporate design constraints, model building, testing, evaluating, modifying, and retesting.

GLE 0807.T/E.3 Compare the intended benefits with the unintended consequences of a new technology.

GLE 0807.T/E.4 Describe and explain adaptive and assistive bioengineered products.

Science and Engineering

Imagine that you are in a car that has broken down on a remote country road. At one time, you would have had to walk to the nearest house with a phone to find help. With the invention of the cellular telephone, it became possible to call for help without ever leaving your disabled vehicle.

Some of today's cell phones allow for even more availability by including a global positioning system (GPS) that can pinpoint your actual location. These improvements are the result of scientists' and engineers' problem-solving efforts to create a new technology. **Figure 1** shows examples of how telephones have advanced over time.

What Is Technology?

Technology refers to the products and processes that are designed to serve our needs. But this is only part of the definition. Technology also refers to the tools and methods for creating these products and processes. For example, a cell phone with GPS is a technology. The tools and processes used to make these telephones are also technologies.

The example of a cell phone with GPS might imply that technology relates only to new products and processes. This is not true. Technology applies to any product, process, or knowledge that is developed to meet a need. Compared with a computer, a typewriter is old technology. However, compared with a pencil, a typewriter is advanced technology.

Figure 1 *Telephones have changed over the years, becoming smaller and more mobile.*

How Does Science Relate to Technology?

You learned that science is knowledge of the natural world. Engineering is closely related to science, but it is not the same. Engineering uses scientific knowledge to develop technologies. A famous engineer explained the difference: "Scientists discover the world that exists; engineers create the world that never was." In other words, engineers use science and mathematics to create new technologies that serve human needs.

When you think of an engineer, you might think of a person who designs bridges or skyscrapers. But there are many different types of engineers who develop a variety of very different products. Hybrid cars, cellular telephones, and disease-resistant corn were all developed by engineers. Engineers also designed the tools and processes needed to make these new products. For example, engineers not only created cell phones but also designed the machines used in making cell phones and the processes used to transmit the microwaves that make cell phones work.

Engineering is the process of creating technology. Although professional engineers have produced a great deal of technology, you don't have to be an engineer to engage in engineering. **Figure 2** shows two children who have built a telephone for their play. Scientists, inventors, business owners, artists, and even students have also engineered new technologies. Anyone can follow the engineering design process to solve a problem or address a need.

✔ Reading Check How are science and mathematics used in engineering?

technology the products and processes that are designed to serve our needs

engineering the process of creating technology

TN GLE 0807.T/E.1

CONNECTION TO Engineering

Shoe Technology Did you know that a shoe could be considered a technology? Shoes are an important technology that has allowed people more freedom in travel by protecting their feet. Shoes have changed over time, from sandals to closed-toe boots to specialized shoes such as running shoes. There have been benefits from being able to protect and support feet with shoes. Research the technology of the shoe and how it has affected society. ✔ 0807.T/E.3

ACTIVITY

engineering design process the process engineers use to develop a new technology

prototype a test model of a product

cost-benefit analysis the process of determining whether the cost of doing something is worth the benefit provided

What Is the Engineering Design Process?

The **engineering design process** has similarities to the scientific process. Like the scientific process, some steps may require repeating or modifying to fit different needs. Learning the process will help you understand how new technology is created.

Step 1
ASK: Identifying and Researching a Need

The first step in the engineering design process is identifying a need. Engineers define and describe the need or problem they are trying to solve. For example, the problem may be to make a phone that will work even in the middle of a desert. Researching travelers' needs, environmental conditions, and existing telephone technology provides engineers with information for problem solving.

Step 2
IMAGINE: Developing Possible Solutions

Once the need has been identified and researched, the second step is to think about possible solutions. This can include the brainstorming of ideas. Brainstorming is the process in which a group of people share ideas quickly to promote additional ideas. Sometimes a possible solution to the problem comes from these ideas. Or it may take more time and thought. Occasionally, as in **Figure 3,** one product may spark an idea for another product.

Step 3
PLAN: Making a Prototype

After the best idea is chosen, the third step is building a **prototype.** A prototype is a test model of the product. Prototypes allow engineers to see if their design works the way they expect it to. **Figure 4** shows different types of cell phones that, at one time, started as prototypes.

Step 4
CREATE: Testing and Evaluating

Testing and evaluating, the fourth step, helps determine whether the technology does the job it was designed to do. Prototypes are tested and evaluated. Engineers make sure that the cost of designing and producing the new product is worth its benefit. This is called a **cost-benefit analysis.** Adding new abilities and styles for cell phones might be useful for most people, but it only makes sense to do so if it is not too expensive to produce.

Figure 3 *Communication radios inspired engineers to develop technologies to make cellular telephones.*

Step 5
IMPROVE: Modifying and Retesting the Solution

If a prototype were not successful or did not work well, the engineers would follow the fifth step in the engineering design process. They would either modify their prototype or try a new solution. It is important that the engineers consider what was learned from the first prototype. They would begin the design process again with their new knowledge and continue working on the problem.

Scientists and engineers also look for other possible uses for the new product. For example, satellite tracking, e-mail, and text messaging features have been added to many cell phones. Also emergency relays have been created to allow the elderly to remain independent by pushing a button on a device worn around the neck if they need assistance. **Figure 5** shows the five steps in the engineering design process.

✓ Reading Check Describe the steps of the engineering design process.

Communication

Engineers often need to share their successes, failures, and reasoning with others. They may explain and promote the technology to customers, or they may communicate with the public through news releases or advertisements. Engineers may also publish details of the design process in journals so that other engineers can build on their work.

Figure 4 *Prototypes helped engineers make new, sleeker cell phones.*

Figure 5 The Engineering Design Process

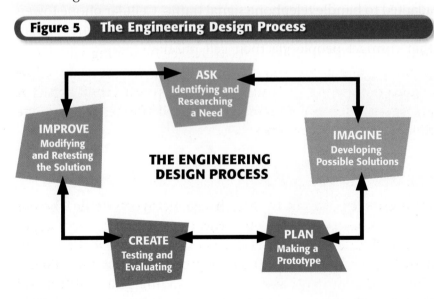

Technology and Society

Now that you have learned about how the engineering design process can use technology to solve one particular problem, you can start to see how technology can affect society. Technology provides solutions for many types of social, political, and economic needs.

For example, engineers fulfill a social need by designing emergency call buttons for the elderly living alone. Political needs include a city government's need for information to improve police, firefighting, and medical services. For this purpose, computer engineers write software that makes data collection from emergency calls accurate and efficient. When electrical engineers develop new materials for building more durable, less expensive telephone and radio towers, they satisfy an economic need.

Intended Benefits

Think about how the cell phone has affected the way we live. With cell phones, people can keep in touch more easily with family and friends both nearby and far away. Cell phones provide their intended benefit—to provide an extremely convenient way to communicate with others, as shown in **Figure 6.** An intended benefit is the positive purpose for which a technology is designed to be used.

Society recognizes that the intended benefit of using cellular telephones has improved people's lives, and communities have adapted to handle telephone signal traffic. Cellular phone towers have been built to receive and transmit radio frequency signals that connect people via their cell phones.

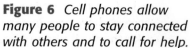

Figure 6 *Cell phones allow many people to stay connected with others and to call for help.*

Unintended Consequences

Cell phones provide the intended benefit of ease of communication, but they have both positive and negative unintended consequences. Unintended consequences are uses or results that engineers do not purposely include in the design of products. An unintended consequence can be beneficial. For example, the cell phone industry has provided many people with new jobs.

Unintended consequences can have a negative impact on society. Cell phones require towers to relay signals. These towers can be seen throughout landscapes and on buildings. **Figure 7** shows how towers can dominate a landscape. These towers can sometimes detract from the beauty of the landscape. For this reason, locations often try to prevent new towers from being built. To combat this objection to the appearance of the cell towers, engineers have designed towers that are camouflaged to look like other objects, such as trees. An example of a camouflaged tower is shown in **Figure 8.**

These are just some of the effects of the use of cell phones on our society. Some effects are positive, while some are negative. Not all technologies introduced into society have had such impact on society, but many have. Think about how society has been changed by automobiles, airplanes, computers, and television.

TN *Standards Check* Identify two positive and two negative effects that airplanes have had on society. ✔0807.T/E.3

Figure 7 *Cell phone and radio towers can be seen in many landscapes.*

TN GLE 0807.T/E.1, GLE 0807.T/E.3

CONNECTION TO Engineering

T/E Noise Pollution and Cell Phones Most noise pollution comes from machines, but many people consider loud cell phone conversations in public places as noise pollution. People have access to cell phones in a great number of places, such as on the bus or train, at a restaurant, in the movie theater, or at a sporting event. There are times when a cell phone ring or a loud conversation can be annoying or disruptive to others. Some engineers have worked on this problem. Research how people can make their cell phone transfer a call to another phone when they do not want their cell phone to ring.

ACTIVITY

Figure 8 *These towers have been disguised as trees to minimize their detracting from the landscape.*

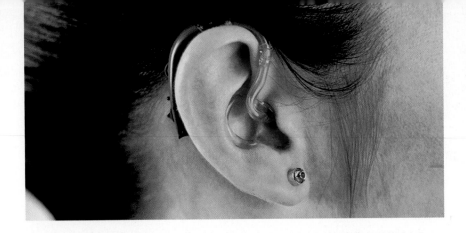

Figure 9 *The hearing aid pictured helps to amplify sounds for people with hearing loss. This is an example of assistive bioengineered technology.*

bioengineering the application of engineering to living things, such as humans and plants

assistive bioengineering engineering that results in a product or process that helps living organisms but does not change them permanently

adaptive bioengineering engineering that results in a product or process that changes living organisms

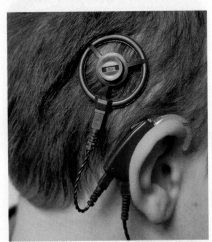

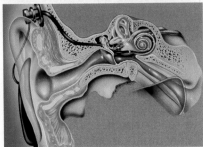

Figure 10 *Cochlear implants are an adaptive bioengineered technology.*

Bioengineering

The engineering design process can even be applied to living things. **Bioengineering** is the application of engineering to living things, such as humans and plants. Bioengineers and scientists study problems that occur in living organisms and their environments. They use their skills, knowledge, and technology to develop solutions to these problems.

Do you know someone who has had a heart bypass? This procedure restructures the blood vessels in a heart to bypass clogged arteries. This surgery is a biotechnology that has improved the lives of many people.

Assistive Bioengineering

Bioengineered technologies can be classified as either **assistive** or **adaptive**. **Figure 9** shows an assistive bioengineered technology.

Assistive technologies are developed to help organisms without changing them. For example, a hearing aid is an assistive technology that helps the hearing-impaired by amplifying sounds. Eyeglasses and prosthetic limbs are two more examples of the many assistive bioengineered products that can improve lives. Sterilized bandages are an assistive technology that has changed medicine. They protect wounds from bacteria and help prevent infection.

Adaptive Bioengineering

Adaptive bioengineered products differ from assistive ones in that they actually change the living organism. Adaptive bioengineering has been used for many exciting new technologies. One of these technologies in the medical field is the cochlear implant, an example of which is shown in **Figure 10.** These implants are permanent and allow individuals who are severely hearing impaired to hear sound. Another kind of adaptive biotechnology is the development of the artificial heart. Engineers are working to develop other artificial organs to help people whose body organs are affected by deformities or disease.

✓ **Reading Check** What is the difference between adaptive and assistive bioengineered products?

TN GLE 0807.Inq.5, GLE 0807.T/E.1,
GLE 0807.T/E.2, GLE 0807.T/E.3,
GLE 0807.T/E.4

Summary

- Science, technology, engineering, and mathematics are closely related.
- Engineers develop technologies to meet social, political, and economic needs.
- The engineering design process describes the steps for developing new technologies.
- Technology has intended benefits and unintended consequences.

- Bioengineering is engineering that develops technology for living things.
- Assistive bioengineering develops technologies that assist but do not change living things.
- Adaptive bioengineering develops technologies that help living things by changing them.

Using Key Terms

Complete each of the following sentences by choosing the correct term from the word bank.

bioengineering   adaptive
technology   prototype

1. ___ bioengineered products change the organism.

2. ___ is the application of engineering to living things.

3. A ___ is a model used to test new technologies.

Understanding Key Ideas

4. Which of the following steps of the engineering design process can be repeated?
   a. identifying and researching a need
   b. modifying and retesting the solution
   c. making a prototype
   d. all of the above

5. Which of the following is an assistive bioengineered product or process?
   a. a pair of crutches
   b. an artificial heart
   c. a blood transfusion
   d. cataract surgery

6. What is cost-benefit analysis, and why is it important in the engineering design process?

Math Skills

7. Engineers are working on a cost-benefit analysis for a feature on a cell phone. The new feature would cost a cell phone user $0.25 for each use. If the user tried the feature 15 times, what would the extra cost for the use of the feature be on the cell phone bill?

Critical Thinking

8. **Applying Concepts** Think about the technology of computers. How have the benefits of computers changed society? What are some of the unintended consequences of computers, and how have they impacted society? ✔0807.T/E.3

9. **Applying Concepts** In the engineering design process, explain how each step may need to be carried out more than once.

10. **Applying Concepts** Think of a need that could be solved with an adaptive bioengineered technology. Tell how you would design an adaptive product to solve this need and how you would test it. ✔0807.T/E.5

Internet Resources

For a variety of links related to this chapter, go to www.scilinks.org

Topic: Scientific Investigations
SciLinks code: HSM1358

Tools, Measurement, and Safety

Would you use a spoon to dig a hole to plant a tree? You wouldn't if you had a shovel!

To dig a hole, you need the correct tools. Scientists use many different tools to help them in their experiments. A *tool* is anything that helps you do a task.

Tools for Measuring

You might remember that one way to collect data is to take measurements. To get the best measurements, you need the proper tools. Stopwatches, metersticks, and balances are some of the tools you can use to make measurements. Thermometers, spring scales, and graduated cylinders are also helpful tools. Some of the uses of these tools are shown in **Figure 1.**

✓ **Reading Check** What kinds of tools are used to make measurements?

Tools for Analyzing

After you collect data, you need to analyze them. Perhaps you need to find the average of your data. Calculators are handy tools to help you do calculations quickly. Or you might show your data in a graph or a figure. You may use a pencil and graph paper or even a computer to graph your data.

Figure 1 **Measurement Tools**

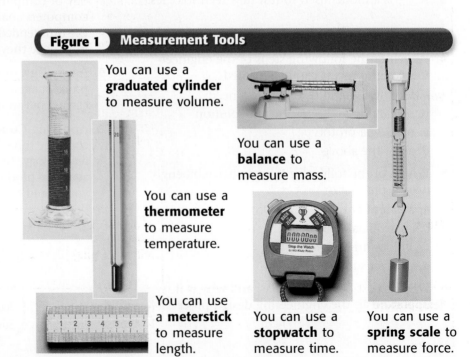

You can use a **graduated cylinder** to measure volume.

You can use a **balance** to measure mass.

You can use a **thermometer** to measure temperature.

You can use a **meterstick** to measure length.

You can use a **stopwatch** to measure time.

You can use a **spring scale** to measure force.

Measurement

Hundreds of years ago, different countries used different systems of measurement. In England, the standard for an inch used to be three grains of barley placed end to end. Other modern standardized units were originally based on parts of the body, such as the foot. Such systems were not very reliable. Their units were based on objects that had different sizes.

The International System of Units

In time, people saw that they needed a simple and reliable measurement system. In the late 1700s, the French Academy of Sciences set out to make that system. Over the next 200 years, the metric system was formed. This system is now called the International System of Units (SI).

Today, most scientists and almost all countries use the International System of Units. One advantage of using SI measurements is that they help all scientists share and compare their observations and results. Another advantage of SI is that all units are based on the number 10. This makes changing from one unit to another easier. **Table 1** shows SI units for length, volume, mass, and temperature.

TN GLE 0807.Inq.4

Units of Measure

Pick an object to use as a unit of measure. You can pick a pencil, your hand, or anything else. Find out how many units wide your desk is, and compare your measurement with those of your classmates. What were some of the units used? What were some of the problems you encountered when comparing measurements? Now, choose two of the units that were used in your class, and make a conversion factor. For example, 1.5 pencils equal 1 board eraser. ✔0807.Inq.4

Table 1 Common SI Units and Conversions

Length		**meter (m)** kilometer (km) decimeter (dm) centimeter (cm) millimeter (mm) micrometer (μm) nanometer (nm)	1 km = 1,000 m 1 dm = 0.1 m 1 cm = 0.01 m 1 mm = 0.001 m 1 μm = 0.000001 m 1 nm = 0.000000001 m
Volume		**cubic meter (m^3)** cubic centimeter (cm^3) liter (L) milliliter (mL)	$1 cm^3 = 0.000001 m^3$ $1 L = 1 dm^3 = 0.001 m^3$ $1 mL = 0.001 L = 1 cm^3$
Mass		**kilogram (kg)** gram (g) milligram (mg)	1 g = 0.001 kg 1 mg = 0.000001 kg
Temperature		**Kelvin (K)** **Celsius (°C)**	0°C = 273 K 100°C = 373 K

Figure 2 *This scientist is measuring the thickness of an ice sheet.*

meter the basic unit of length in the SI (symbol, m)

area a measure of the size of a surface or a region

mass a measure of the amount of matter in an object; a fundamental property of an object that is not affected by the forces that act on the object, such as the gravitational force

Length

How thick is the ice sheet in **Figure 2**? To describe this length, a scientist would probably use meters (m). A **meter** is the basic SI unit of length. Other SI units of length are larger or smaller than the meter by multiples of 10. For example, if you divide 1 m into 1,000 parts, each part equals 1 mm. This means that 1 mm is one-thousandth of a meter. To describe the length of a grain of salt, scientists use micrometers (μm) or nanometers (nm).

Area

How much wallpaper would you need to cover the walls of your classroom? To answer this question, you must find the area of the walls. **Area** is a measure of how much surface an object has. Area is based on two measurements. To calculate the area of a square or a rectangle, first measure the length and width. Then, use the following equation:

$$area = length \times width$$

The units for area are square units, such as square kilometers (km^2), square meters (m^2), and square centimeters (cm^2).

Mass

How many cars can a bridge support? The answer depends on the strength of the bridge and the mass of the cars. **Mass** is the amount of matter that something is made of. The kilogram (kg) is the basic SI unit for mass. The kilogram is used to describe the mass of a car. The gram is used to describe the mass of small objects. One thousand grams equals 1 kg. A medium-sized apple has a mass of about 100 g. Masses of very large objects are given in metric tons. A metric ton equals 1,000 kg.

Volume

Look at **Figure 3.** Think about moving some bones to a museum. How big would your box need to be? To answer that question, you need to understand volume. **Volume** is the amount of space that something occupies or, as in the case of the box, the amount of space that something contains.

The volume of a liquid is often given in liters (L). Liters are based on the meter. A cubic meter (1 m³) is equal to 1,000 L. So 1,000 L will fit into a box measuring 1 m on each side. A milliliter (mL) will fit into a box measuring 1 cm on each side. So 1 mL = 1 cm³. Graduated cylinders are used to measure the volume of liquids.

The volume of a large, solid object is given in cubic meters (m³). The volumes of smaller objects can be given in cubic centimeters (cm³) or cubic millimeters (mm³). To calculate the volume of a box-shaped object, multiply the object's length by its width and then by its height. To find the volume of an irregularly shaped object, measure the volume of liquid that the object displaces. **Figure 4** shows how this method works.

Figure 3 *The box has a volume, so it can hold only a limited number of bones.*

Density

If you measure the mass and the volume of an object, you have the information that you need in order to find the density of the object. **Density** is the amount of matter in a given volume. You cannot measure the density directly. But you can calculate density using the following equation:

$$density = \frac{mass}{volume}$$

Because mass is expressed in grams and volume is expressed in milliliters or cubic centimeters, density can be expressed in grams per milliliter or grams per cubic centimeter.

volume a measure of the size of a body or region in three-dimensional space ◾ TN➤ *VOCAB*

density the ratio of the mass of a substance to the volume of the substance; often expressed as grams per cubic centimeter for solids and liquids and as grams per liter for gases ◾ TN➤ *VOCAB*

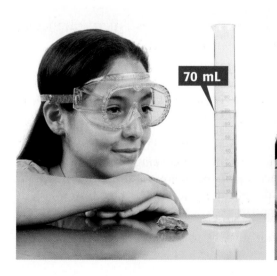

70 mL

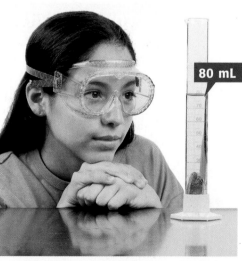

80 mL

Figure 4 *Adding the rock changes the water level from 70 mL to 80 mL. So, the rock displaces 10 mL of water. Because 1 mL = 1 cm³, the volume of the rock is 10 cm³.*

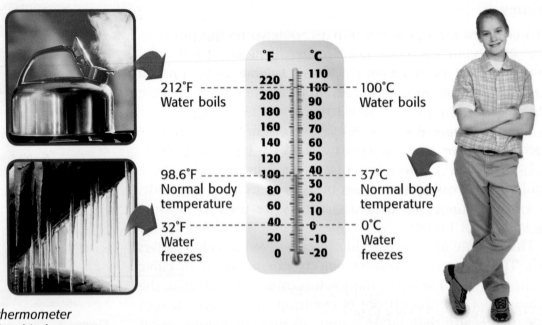

Figure 5 *This thermometer shows the relationship between degrees Fahrenheit and degrees Celsius.*

212°F
Water boils — 100°C Water boils

98.6°F
Normal body temperature — 37°C Normal body temperature

32°F
Water freezes — 0°C Water freezes

temperature a measure of how hot (or cold) something is; specifically, a measure of the average kinetic energy of the particles in an object

Temperature

How hot does it need to be to kill bacteria? How cold does it have to be before mercury freezes? To answer these questions, a scientist would measure the temperature at which bacteria die, or the temperature of the air at which mercury freezes. **Temperature** is a measure of how hot (or cold) something is. You are probably used to describing temperature with degrees Fahrenheit (°F). Scientists often use degrees Celsius (°C). However, kelvins (K), the SI base unit for temperature, is also used. The thermometer in **Figure 5** shows how the Fahrenheit scale compares with the Celsius scale. Degrees Celsius is the unit you will see most often in this book.

✓ **Reading Check** What is the SI base unit for temperature?

TN GLE 0807.Inq.3, GLE 0807.Inq.5, GLE 0807.T/E1

CONNECTION TO Social Studies

Thermal Pollution Factories are often built along the banks of rivers. The factories use the river water to cool the engines of their machinery. Then, the hot water is poured back into the river. Energy, in the form of heat, is transferred from this water to the river water. The increase in temperature results in the death of many living things. Research how thermal pollution causes fish to die. Also, find out what many factories are doing to prevent thermal pollution. Make a brochure that explains what thermal pollution is and what is being done to prevent it. ✓0807.Inq.3, ✓0807.Inq.5

Safety Rules!

Science is exciting and fun, but it can also be dangerous. Always follow your teacher's instructions. Don't take shortcuts, even when you think that there is no danger. Read lab procedures carefully and thoroughly. Pay special attention to safety information and caution statements. **Figure 6** shows the safety symbols used in this book. Learn these symbols and their meanings by reading the safety information at the start of the book. **Knowing the safety information is important!** If you are still not sure about what a safety symbol means, ask your teacher.

Figure 6 Safety Symbols

 Eye Protection
 Clothing Protection
 Hand Safety

 Heating Safety
 Electric Safety
 Sharp Object

 Chemical Safety
 Animal Safety
 Plant Safety

SECTION Review

TN GLE 0807.Inq.2, GLE 0807.Inq.4, GLE 0807.Inq.5

Summary

- Tools are used to make observations, take measurements, and analyze data.
- The International System of Units (SI) is the standard system of measurement.
- Length, volume, mass, and temperature are quantities of measurement.
- Density is the amount of matter in a given volume.
- Safety symbols are for your protection.

Using Key Terms

The statements below are false. For each statement, replace the underlined term to make a true statement.

1. The length multiplied by the width of an object is the <u>density</u> of the object.

2. The measure of the amount of matter in an object is the <u>area</u>.

Understanding Key Ideas

3. Which SI unit would you use to express the height of your desk?
   a. kilogram
   b. gram
   c. meter
   d. inch

4. Explain the relationship between mass and density.

5. What is normal body temperature in degrees Fahrenheit and degrees Celsius?

6. What tools would you select to find the force needed to move a 1 kg object 1 m in 30 seconds?
   ✔0807.Inq.2

7. Explain the importance of having a standard method of measurement such as the SI system.

Math Skills

8. A certain bacterial cell has a diameter of 0.50 μm. The tip of a pin is about 1,100 μm in diameter. How many of these bacterial cells would fit on the tip of the pin?

9. What is the density of lead if a cube measuring 2 cm per side has a mass of 90.8 g?

Critical Thinking

10. **Analyzing Ideas** What safety icons would you see on a lab that asks you to pour acid into a beaker?

11. **Applying Concepts** To find the area of a rectangle, multiply the length by the width. Why is area called a *derived quantity*?

Internet Resources

For a variety of links related to this chapter, go to www.scilinks.org

Topic: SI Units
SciLinks code: HSM1390

Skills Practice Lab

OBJECTIVES

Measure accurately different volumes of liquids with a graduated cylinder.

Transfer exact amounts of liquids from a graduated cylinder to a test tube.

MATERIALS

- beakers, filled with colored liquid (3)
- funnel, small
- graduated cylinder, 10 mL
- marker
- tape, masking
- test-tube rack
- test tubes, large (6)

SAFETY

Measuring Liquid Volume

In this lab, you will use a graduated cylinder to measure and transfer precise amounts of liquids. Remember that, to accurately measure liquids in a graduated cylinder, you should first place the graduated cylinder flat on the lab table. Then, at eye level, read the volume of the liquid at the bottom of the meniscus, which is the curved surface of the liquid.

Procedure

1. Using the masking tape and marker, label the test tubes A, B, C, D, E, and F. Place them in the test-tube rack.

2. Make a data table as shown on the next page.

3. Using the graduated cylinder and the funnel, pour 14 mL of the red liquid into test tube A. (To do this, first measure out 10 mL of the liquid in the graduated cylinder, and pour it into the test tube. Then, measure an additional 4 mL of liquid in the graduated cylinder, and add this liquid to the test tube.)

4. Rinse the graduated cylinder and funnel with water each time you measure a different liquid.

5. Measure 13 mL of the yellow liquid, and pour it into test tube C.

6. Measure 13 mL of the blue liquid, and pour it into test tube E. Record the initial color and the volume of the liquid in each test tube.

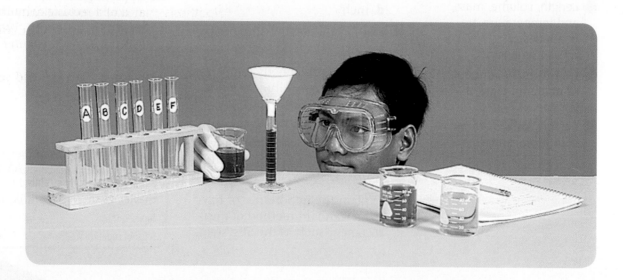

GLE 0807.Inq.2 Use appropriate tools and techniques to gather, organize, analyze, and interpret data.

GLE 0807.Inq.3 Synthesize information to determine cause and effect relationships between evidence and explanations.

GLE 0807.Inq.4 Recognize possible sources of bias and error, alternative explanations, and questions for further exploration.

GLE 0807.Inq.5 Communicate scientific understanding using descriptions, explanations, and models

Data Table

Test tube	Initial color	Initial volume	Final color	Final volume
A				
B				
C				
D				
E				
F				

DO NOT WRITE IN BOOK

7 Transfer 4 mL of liquid from test tube C into test tube D. Transfer 7 mL of liquid from test tube E into test tube D.

8 Measure 4 mL of blue liquid from the beaker, and pour it into test tube F. Measure 7 mL of red liquid from the beaker, and pour it into test tube F.

9 Transfer 8 mL of liquid from test tube A into test tube B. Transfer 3 mL of liquid from test tube C into test tube B.

Analyze the Results

1 **Analyzing Data** Record your final color observations in your data table.

2 **Examining Data** What is the final volume of all of the liquids? Use the graduated cylinder to measure the volume of liquid in each test tube. Record the volumes in your data table.

3 **Organizing Data** Record your final color observations and final volumes in a table of class data prepared by your teacher.

Draw Conclusions

4 **Interpreting Information** Did all of your classmates report the same colors? Form a hypothesis that could explain why the colors were the same or different after the liquids were combined. ✔0807.Inq.3

5 **Evaluating Methods** Why should you not fill the graduated cylinder to the top? ✔0807.Inq.4

Chapter Review

TN GLE 0807.Inq.1, GLE 0807.Inq.2, GLE 0807.Inq.3, GLE 0807.Inq.4, GLE 0807.Inq.5, GLE 0807.T/E.1, GLE 0807.T/E.2, GLE 0807.T/E.3, GLE 0807.T/E.4

USING KEY TERMS

1 In your own words, write a definition for each of the following terms: *meter*, *temperature*, and *density*.

For each pair of terms, explain how the meanings of the terms differ.

2 *science* and *scientific methods*

3 *observation* and *hypothesis*

4 *theory* and *law*

5 *model* and *theory*

6 *volume* and *mass*

UNDERSTANDING KEY IDEAS

Multiple Choice

7 Which of the following are methods of investigation?
  a. research
  b. observation
  c. experimentation
  d. all of the above

8 The statement "Sheila has a stain on her shirt" is an example of a(n)
  a. law.
  b. hypothesis.
  c. observation.
  d. prediction.

9 A hypothesis
  a. may or may not be testable.
  b. is supported by evidence.
  c. is a possible answer to a question.
  d. all of the above

10 You want to see which of three catapults will launch a baseball the farthest. Which is the variable? ✔0807.Inq.1
  a. the type of baseball used
  b. the different catapults
  c. the field where the catapults launch the baseball
  d. the time of day

11 Organizing data into a graph is an example of
  a. collecting data.
  b. forming a hypothesis.
  c. asking a question.
  d. analyzing data.

12 How many milliliters are in 3.5 kL?
  a. 0.0035   c. 35,000
  b. 3,500   d. 3,500,000

13 Sleep apnea is a medical condition in which the sleeper stops breathing for many short periods of time. Which treatment is adaptive? ✔0807.T/E.4
  a. pillow that positions the sleeper on his/her side
  b. surgery that creates more open airways
  c. continuous positive airway pressure (CPAP) machine that forces air into the sleeper
  d. a mouth guard that helps the sleeper continue to breathe

Short Answer

14 Describe three kinds of models used in science. Give an example of each and explain the limitation and possible bias or error each could cause. ✔0807.Inq.4

15 Name two SI units that can be used to describe the volume of an object and two SI units that can be used to describe the mass of an object. ✔0807.Inq.2

16 Engineers are working on developing features that use radar in cars to sense when the car is about to crash. These new features include lights that flash, a brake pedal that is primed, and a gas pedal that pushes back. What need is this technology attempting to meet? Explain.

Math Skills

17 The cereal box on the right has a mass of 340 g. Its dimensions are 27 cm × 19 cm × 6 cm. What is the volume of the box? What is its density?

CRITICAL THINKING

18 Concept Mapping Use the following terms to create a concept map: *science, scientific methods, hypothesis, problems, questions, experiments,* and *observations.*

19 Applying Concepts A tailor is someone who makes or alters items of clothing. Why might a standard system of measurement be helpful to a tailor? ✔0807.Inq.3, ✔0807.Inq.4

20 Analyzing Ideas Imagine that you are conducting an experiment. You are testing the effects of the height of a ramp on the speed at which a toy car goes down the ramp. What is the variable in this experiment? What factors must be controlled? ✔0807.Inq.1

21 Evaluating Assumptions The technology of indoor electric lighting has had a major impact on society. Two results are that people work longer and sleep less. Which is an intended benefit and which is an unintended consequence? How have they impacted society? ✔0807.T/E.3

22 Making Inferences You build a model boat that you predict will float. However, your tests show that the boat sinks. What part of the engineering design process would you use next? Why? ✔0807.T/E.2

INTERPRETING GRAPHICS

Use the picture below to answer the questions that follow.

23 How similar is this model to a real object?

24 What are some of the limitations of this model?

25 How might this model be useful?

TN SPI 0607.Inq.1 Design a simple experimental procedure with an identified control and appropriate variables. SPI 0607.Inq.2 Select tools and procedures needed to conduct a moderately complex experiment. SPI 0607.Inq.3 Interpret and translate data into a table, graph, or diagram. SPI 0607.Inq.4 Draw a conclusion that establishes a cause and effect relationship supported by evidence. SPI 0607.Inq.5 Identify a faulty interpretation of data that is due to bias or experimental error. SPI 0607.T/E.1 Identify the tools and procedures needed to test the design features of a prototype.

Multiple Choice

Use the picture below to answer question 1.

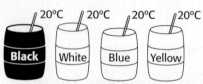

Beginning of Experiment
Cans placed outside

End of Experiment
After 3 hours in the sun

1. **A student set up the experiment shown above to determine what color absorbs the most energy from sunlight. Which of the following would make this a better-designed experiment?**

   A. Use larger thermometers.

   B. Use same-sized containers for each color.

   C. Use glass containers instead of metal containers.

   D. Place the containers in the shade instead of in direct sunlight.

2. **You have been asked to join a team of engineers that is working on a new pesticide. The prototype has been tested, and it works on only one of the pests it was designed for. What step would you suggest the group do next?**

   A. Ask: Identifying and Researching a Need

   B. Imagine: Developing Possible Prototypes

   C. Create: Testing and Evaluating

   D. Improve: Modifying and Retesting the Solution

3. **After swimming in the ocean, Jorge sits in the sun to dry off. After a while, he notices that he has small white crystals on his skin. Analyze the explanations below as to their strengths and weaknesses based on this evidence. Which is the most reasonable explanation of what happened?**

   A. The water evaporated and attracted dust to Jorge's skin.

   B. The white crystals are dead skin cells that are being shed.

   C. Jorge has developed a rare skin disorder.

   D. Salt that is dissolved in the water remained on Jorge's skin after the water evaporated.

4. **Which of the following is an unintended consequence of the cell phone?**

   A. Cell phone rings can interrupt others.

   B. People can take phones in cars to communicate in emergencies.

   C. Business people can keep in better touch with their customers.

   D. Long-distance calling can be more affordable.

5. **Which factor is most likely to introduce bias or error into an experiment designed to determine which brand of bar soap kills bacteria most effectively?**

   A. using different types of soap

   B. using different amounts of soap

   C. using the same amount of bacteria for each trial

   D. having the bacteria on identical surfaces

SPI 0607.T/E.2 Evaluate a protocol to determine if the engineering design process was successfully applied.   SPI 0607.T/E.3 Distinguish between the intended benefits and the unintended consequences of a new technology.   SPI 0607.T/E.4 Differentiate between adaptive and assistive bioengineered products (e.g., food, biofuels, medicines, integrated pest management).

6. A group of environmental scientists suspects that acid precipitation is beginning to affect certain lakes in Tennessee. What tools and procedures could they use to test their hypothesis?

    A. Use research studies and research the harmful effects of acid precipitation in lakes.

    B. Collect acid precipitation in containers and experiment on water plants native to Tennessee.

    C. Use a field guide and count the number of water plant species found in a Tennessee lake.

    D. Use sterile containers and equipment, collect lake water samples, and test the pH of each sample.

7. Which of the following is an adaptive bioengineered product?

    A. liquid pesticide spray for plants

    B. fertilizer that can be put in the soil for plants

    C. gene introduced into a plant that helps it control the pest when the pest tries to eat the plant

    D. pesticide dust for plants

8. Katie wants to learn about the effect that different amounts of sunlight have on plants. Which of the following is the only variable that she should change?

    A. the type of plant

    B. the amount of light

    C. the volume of water

    D. the amount of nutrients

Open Response

9. What tools and procedures would you choose to test a prototype of a new ball that is designed to bounce well when dropped?

10. Lucia is measuring how fast bacteria grow in a Petri dish by measuring the area the bacteria cover. On day 1 the bacteria cover 0.25 cm². On day 2 they cover 0.50 cm². On day 3 they cover 1.00 cm². If you extrapolate from this information, what is the best prediction for the area covered on day 4? Present all the data in a chart or graph, including your prediction for day 4.

TCAP Test Preparation

Science in Action

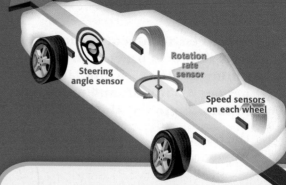

Steering angle sensor

Rotation rate sensor

Speed sensors on each wheel

HOLT ANTHOLOGY OF
Science Fiction
HOLT, RINEHART AND WINSTON

Science Fiction

"Inspiration" by Ben Bova

What if you were able to leap back and forth through time? Novelist H. G. Wells imagined such a possibility in his 1895 novelette *The Time Machine*. Most physicists said that time travel was against all the laws of physics. But what if Albert Einstein, then 16 and not a very good student, had met Wells and had an inspiration? Ben Bova's story "Inspiration" describes such a possibility. Young Einstein meets Wells and the great physicist of the time, Lord Kelvin. But was the meeting just a lucky coincidence or something else entirely? Escape to the *Holt Anthology of Science Fiction*, and read "Inspiration."

Science, Technology, and Society

Crash Prevention

T/E Statistics clearly show that automobile safety increases if the driver is attentive and experienced. But what happens if a driver of any skill level becomes unconscious due to fatigue or illness? or swerves suddenly to avoid a pothole? Engineers have developed an electronic system that allows the car to drive itself for a short time if the driver becomes disabled and the car behaves abnormally. Known as electronic stability control, or ESC, this system uses a computer to record information about the car's speed and direction. The computer works with existing systems, such as anti-lock brakes. If the car changes direction suddenly, the computer sends a signal to the throttle and brakes on the appropriate wheels. The car slows down and the brakes alter the speed of certain wheels, returning the car to its original course. Despite some questions about the reliability of ESCs, especially low-cost systems, all new vehicles will be equipped with them by 2012.

TN GLE 0807.T/E.1, GLE 0807.T/E.2, GLE 0807.T/E.3

Social Studies ACTIViTy

Research the life of Albert Einstein from high school through college. Make a poster that describes some of his experiences during this time. Include information about how he matured as a student.

Math ACTIViTy

Studies have shown that 10,000 fatal collisions each year might be prevented by ESC systems. This number represents 43 percent of all fatal collisions in a year. Without the benefit of ESC systems, how many fatal collisions would occur in a year?

Julie Williams-Byrd

Electronics Engineer Julie Williams-Byrd uses her knowledge of physics to develop better lasers. She started working with lasers when she was a graduate student at Hampton University in Virginia. Today, Williams-Byrd works as an electronics engineer in the Laser Systems Branch (LSB) of NASA. She designs and builds lasers that are used to study wind and ozone in the atmosphere. Williams-Byrd uses scientific models to predict the nature of different aspects of laser design. For example, laser models are used to predict output energy, wavelength, and efficiency of the laser system.

Her most challenging project has been building a laser transmitter that will be used to measure winds in the atmosphere. This system, called *Lidar,* is very much like radar except that it uses light waves instead of sound waves to bounce off objects. Although Williams-Byrd works with high-tech lasers, she points out that lasers are a part of daily life for many people. For example, lasers are used in scanners at many retail stores. Ophthalmologists use lasers to correct vision problems. Some metal workers use them to cut metal. And lasers are even used to create spectacular light shows!

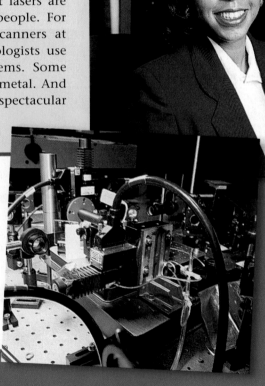

Language Arts
ACTIVITY

WRITING SKILL Research lasers and how they can be used in everyday life. Then, write a one-page essay on how lasers have made life easier for people.

go.hrw.com

To learn more about these Science in Action topics, visit go.hrw.com and type in the keyword HP5WPSF.

Current Science

Check out Current Science® articles related to this chapter by visiting go.hrw.com. Just type in the keyword HP5CS01.

Life Science

The differences and similarities between living things are the subject of this unit. You will learn how living things are classified based on their characteristics, and how these characteristics help living things survive. You will learn how populations of organisms adapt to changes in the environment. You will also learn how fossils provide information about living things of the past. This timeline will give you an idea of what scientists have learned about classification and change so far.

1753
Carolus Linnaeus publishes the first of two volumes containing the classification of all known species.

1905
Nettie Stevens describes how human gender is determined by the X and Y chromosomes.

1930
Pluto is discovered.

1969
Apollo 11 lands on the moon. Neil Armstrong becomes the first person to walk on the lunar surface.

1859

Charles Darwin suggests that natural selection is a mechanism of change over time.

1860

Abraham Lincoln is elected the 16th president of the United States.

1865

Gregor Mendel publishes the results of his studies of genetic inheritance in pea plants.

1951

Rosalind Franklin photographs DNA.

1953

James Watson and Francis Crick figure out the structure of DNA.

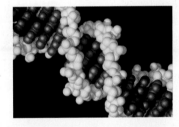

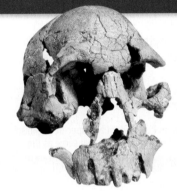

1960

Mary and Jonathan Leakey discover fossil bones of the human ancestor *Homo habilis* in Olduvai Gorge, Tanzania.

1974

Donald Johanson discovers a fossilized skeleton of one of the first hominids, *Australopithecus afarensis,* also called "Lucy."

1990

Ashanti DeSilva's white blood cells are genetically engineered to treat her immune deficiency disease.

2003

The Human Genome Project is completed. Scientists spent 13 years mapping out the 3 billion DNA subunits of chromosomes.

2

Classification

The Big Idea

Organisms are classified into groups based on their characteristics.

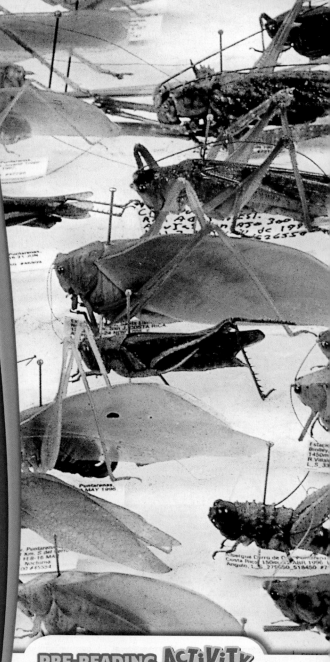

TN Tennessee Science Standards

Embedded Inquiry

GLE 0807.Inq.2 Use appropriate tools and techniques to gather, organize, analyze, and interpret data.
GLE 0807.Inq.4 Recognize possible sources of bias and error, alternative explanations, and questions for further exploration.

Embedded Technology and Engineering

GLE 0807.T/E.1 Explore how technology responds to social, political, and economic needs.

Life Science

GLE 0807.5.1 Identify various criteria used to classify organisms into groups.
GLE 0807.5.2 Use a simple classification key to identify a specific organism.
✔**0807.5.1** Select characteristics of plants and animals that serve as the basis for developing a classification key.
✔**0807.5.2** Create and apply a simple classification key to identify an organism.

PRE-READING ACTIVITY

Booklet Before you read the chapter, create the FoldNote entitled "Booklet" described in the **Study Skills** section of the Appendix. Label each page of the booklet with a main idea from the chapter. As you read the chapter, write what you learn about each main idea on the appropriate page of the booklet.

About the Photo

Look at the katy-dids, grasshoppers, and mantids in the photo. A scientist is classifying these insects. Every insect has a label describing the insect. These descriptions will help the scientist know if each insect has already been discovered and named. When scientists discover a new insect or other organism, they have to give the organism a name. The name chosen is unique and should help other scientists understand some basic facts about the organism.

START-UP ACTIVITY

TN GLE 0807.Inq.2

Classifying Shoes

In this group activity, each group will develop a system of classification for shoes.

Procedure

1. Gather **10 shoes.** Number pieces of **masking tape** from 1 to 10. Label the sole of each shoe with a numbered piece of tape.

2. Make a list of shoe features. Make a table that has a column for each feature. Complete the table by describing each shoe.

3. Use the data in the table to make a shoe identification key.

4. The key should be a list of steps. Each step should have two contrasting statements about the shoes. The statements will lead you either to the next step or to a specific shoe.

5. If your shoe is not identified in one step, go on to the next step or steps until the shoe is identified.

6. Trade keys with another group. How did the other group's key help you identify the shoes?

Analysis

1. How was listing the shoe features before making the key helpful?

2. Were you able to identify the shoes using another group's key? Explain.

Sorting It All Out

Imagine that you live in a tropical rain forest and must get your own food, shelter, and clothing from the forest. What do you need to know to survive in the forest?

To survive in the rain forest, you need to know which plants are safe to eat and which are not. You need to know which animals you can eat and which might eat you. In other words, you need to study the living things around you and organize them into categories, or classify them. **Classification** is putting things into orderly groups based on similar characteristics.

Why Classify?

For thousands of years, humans have classified living things based on usefulness. The Chácabo people of Bolivia know of 360 types of plants that grow in the forest where they live. Of these 360 plant types, 305 are useful to the Chácabo.

Some biologists, such as those shown in **Figure 1,** classify living and extinct organisms. Scientists classify organisms to help make sense and order of the many kinds of living things in the world. Biologists use a system to classify living things. This system groups organisms according to the characteristics they share. The classification of living things makes it easier for biologists to answer many important questions, such as the following:

- How many known species are there?
- What are the defining characteristics of each species?
- What are the relationships between these species?

✓ **Reading Check** What are three questions that classifying organisms can help answer?

Figure 1 *These biologists are sorting rain-forest plant material.*

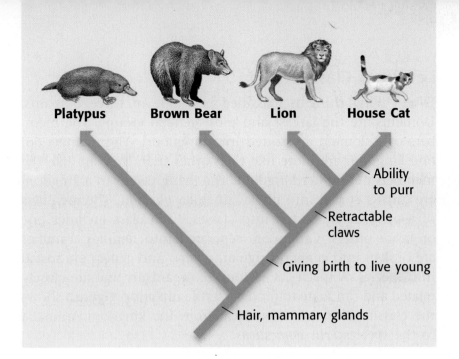

Figure 2 *This branching diagram shows the similarities and differences between four mammals.*

Platypus   Brown Bear   Lion   House Cat

Ability to purr

Retractable claws

Giving birth to live young

Hair, mammary glands

How Do Scientists Classify Organisms?

Before the 1600s, many scientists divided organisms into two groups: plants and animals. But as more organisms were discovered, some did not fit into either group. In the 1700s, Carolus Linnaeus (KAR uh luhs li NAY uhs), a Swedish scientist, founded modern taxonomy. **Taxonomy** (taks AHN uh mee) is the science of describing, classifying, and naming living things. Linnaeus tried to classify all living things based on their shape and structure. Today, scientists use a system of classification that is very similar to the one that Linnaeus developed.

taxonomy the science of describing, naming, and classifying organisms

Classification Today

Taxonomists use an eight-level system to classify living things based on shared characteristics. Scientists also use shared characteristics to hypothesize how closely related living things are. The more characteristics the organisms share, the more closely related the organisms may be. For example, the platypus, brown bear, lion, and house cat are thought to be related because they share many characteristics. These animals have hair and mammary glands, so they are grouped together as mammals. But they can be further classified into more-specific groups.

Branching Diagrams

Look at the branching diagram in **Figure 2.** Several characteristics are listed along the line that points to the right. Each characteristic is shared by the animals to the right of it. All of the animals shown have hair and mammary glands. But only the bear, lion, and house cat give birth to live young. The lion and the house cat have retractable claws, but the other animals do not. Thus, the lion and the house cat are more closely related to each other than to the other animals.

TN GLE 0807.5.2

A Branching Diagram

1. Construct a diagram similar to the one in **Figure 2.**

2. Use a frog, a snake, a kangaroo, and a rabbit in your diagram.

3. Think of one major change that happened before the frog appeared.

4. For the last three organisms, think of a change that happened between one of these organisms and the other two. Write all of these changes in your diagram. ✔0807.5.1, ✔0807.5.2

Levels of Classification

Every living thing is classified into one of three domains. Domains are the largest and most general groups. The members of a domain are sorted into kingdoms. The members of one kingdom are more like each other than they are like the members of another kingdom. The living things in a kingdom are further sorted into phyla (singular, *phylum*). The members of a phylum are sorted into classes. Each class includes one or more orders. Orders are separated into families. Families are broken into genera (singular, *genus*). And genera are sorted into species. A species is a group of organisms that are closely related and can mate to produce fertile offspring. **Figure 3** shows the classification of a house cat from the kingdom Animalia to the species *Felis domesticus*.

Scientific Names

By classifying organisms, biologists can give organisms scientific names. A scientific name remains the same for a specific kind of organism even if the organism has many common names. Before Linnaeus's time, scholars used names that were as long as 12 words to identify species. This system was hard to work with because the names were so long. The system was also hard to use because individual scientists named organisms differently. So, an organism could have more than one name.

INTERNET ACTIVITY

For another activity related to this chapter, go to **go.hrw.com** and type in the keyword **HL5CLSW**.

Figure 3 *The eight levels of classification are domain, kingdom, phylum, class, order, family, genus, and species.*

Kingdom Animalia	Phylum Chordata	Class Mammalia	Order Carnivora
All animals are in the **kingdom Animalia.**	All animals in the **phylum Chordata** have a hollow nerve cord. Most have a backbone.	Animals in the **class Mammalia** have a backbone. They also nurse their young.	Animals in the **order Carnivora** have a backbone and nurse their young. They also have special teeth for tearing meat.

Two-Part Names

Linnaeus simplified the naming of living things by giving each species a two-part scientific name. For example, the scientific name for the Asian elephant is *Elephas maximus* (EL uh fuhs MAK suh muhs). The first part of the name, *Elephas*, is the genus name. The second part, *maximus*, is the specific name. No other species has the name *Elephas maximus*. Naming rules help scientists communicate clearly about living things.

All genus names begin with a capital letter. All specific names begin with a lowercase letter. Usually, both words are underlined or italicized. But if the surrounding text is italicized, the scientific name is not, as **Figure 4** shows. These printing styles show a reader which words are the scientific name.

Scientific names, which are usually in Latin or Greek, contain information about an organism. The name of the animal shown in **Figure 4** is *Tyrannosaurus rex*. *Tyrannosaurus* is a combination of two Greek words and means "tyrant lizard." The word *rex* is Latin for "king." The name tells you that this animal was probably not a passive grass eater! Sometimes, *Tyrannosaurus rex* is referred to as *T. rex*. To be correct, the scientific name must consist of the genus name (or its abbreviation) and the specific name.

Figure 4 *You would never call* Tyrannosaurus rex *just* rex!

✓ Reading Check What are the two parts of a scientific name?

Family Felidae	Genus *Felis*	Species *Felis domesticus*
Animals in the **family Felidae** are cats. They have a backbone, nurse their young, have special teeth for tearing meat, and have retractable claws.	Animals in the **genus Felis** have traits of other animals in the same family. However, these cats cannot roar; they can only purr.	The **species Felis domesticus** is the common house cat. The house cat shares traits with all of the organisms in the levels above the species level, but it also has unique traits.

Dichotomous Keys

You might someday turn over a rock and find an organism that you don't recognize. How would you identify the organism? Taxonomists have developed special guides to help scientists identify organisms. A **dichotomous key** (die KAHT uh muhs KEE) is an identification aid that uses sequential pairs of descriptive statements. There are only two alternative responses for each statement. From each pair of statements, the person trying to identify the organism chooses the statement that describes the organism. Either the chosen statement identifies the organism or the person is directed to another pair of statements. By working through the statements in the key in order, the person can eventually identify the organism. Using the simple dichotomous key in **Figure 5,** try to identify the two animals shown.

dichotomous key an aid that is used to identify organisms and that consists of the answers to a series of questions ▬TN▶VOCAB

✓ **Reading Check** What is a dichotomous key?

Figure 5 *A dichotomous key can help you identify organisms.*

Dichotomous Key to 10 Common Mammals in the Eastern United States

1. a. This mammal flies. Its "hand" forms a wing. **b.** This mammal does not fly. It's "hand" does not form a wing.	**little brown bat** Go to step 2.
2. a. This mammal has no hair on its tail. **b.** This mammal has hair on its tail.	Go to step 3. Go to step 4.
3. a. This mammal has a short, naked tail. **b.** This mammal has a long, naked tail.	**eastern mole** Go to step 5.
4. a. This mammal has a black mask across its face. **b.** This mammal does not have a black mask across its face.	**raccoon** Go to step 6.
5. a. This mammal has a tail that is flat and paddle shaped. **b.** This mammal has a tail that is not flat or paddle shaped.	**beaver** **opossum**
6. a. This mammal is brown and has a white underbelly. **b.** This mammal is not brown and does not have a white underbelly.	Go to step 7. Go to step 8.
7. a. This mammal has a long, furry tail that is black on the tip. **b.** This mammal has a long tail that has little fur.	**longtail weasel** **white-footed mouse**
8. a. This mammal is black and has a narrow white stripe on its forehead and broad white stripes on its back. **b.** This mammal is not black and does not have white stripes.	**striped skunk** Go to step 9.
9. a. This mammal has long ears and a short, cottony tail. **b.** This mammal has short ears and a medium-length tail.	**eastern cottontail** **woodchuck**

A Growing System

You may think that all of the organisms on Earth have already been classified. But people are still discovering and classifying organisms. Some newly discovered organisms fit into existing categories. But sometimes, someone discovers new evidence or an organism that is so different from other organisms that it does not fit existing categories. For example, about 50 years ago, a new organism was found in the Baltic Sea. It looked like a tiny, light-colored blob. Scientists knew it belonged in kingdom Animalia. But it didn't fit in any of the animal phyla. In 2006, after looking at the DNA of the organism, scientists put it in its own phylum. The organism's genus is *Xenoturbella* (ZEE noh tuhr BEL uh).

SECTION Review

TN GLE 0807.5.1, GLE 0807.5.2

Summary

- In classification, organisms are grouped according to the characteristics the organisms share. Classification lets scientists answer important questions about the relationships between organisms.

- The eight levels of classification are domain, kingdom, phylum, class, order, family, genus, and species.

- An organism has one two-part scientific name.

- A dichotomous key is a tool for identifying organisms that uses a series of paired descriptive statements.

Using Key Terms

1. In your own words, write a definition for each of the following terms: *classification* and *taxonomy*.

Understanding Key Ideas

2. The two parts of a scientific name are the names of the genus and the
   a. specific name.
   b. phylum name.
   c. family name.
   d. order name.

3. Why do scientists use scientific names for organisms?

4. List the eight levels of classification.

5. Describe how a dichotomous key helps scientists identify organisms.

Critical Thinking

6. **Analyzing Processes** Biologists think that millions of species are not classified yet. Why do you think so many species have not been classified yet?

7. **Applying Concepts** Select characteristics of the following animals that you could use to develop a classification key for these animals: horse, frog, and chicken. ✔0807.5.1

Interpreting Graphics

Use the figure below to answer the questions that follow.

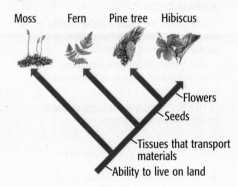

Moss   Fern   Pine tree   Hibiscus

Flowers
Seeds
Tissues that transport materials
Ability to live on land

8. Which plant is most similar to the hibiscus?

9. Which plant is least similar to the hibiscus?

Domains and Kingdoms

What do you call an organism that is green, makes its own food, lives in pond water, and moves? Is it a plant, an animal, or something in between?

For hundreds of years, all living things were classified as either plants or animals. But over time, scientists discovered species that did not fit easily into these two kingdoms. For example, an organism of the genus *Euglena,* such as the one shown in **Figure 1,** has characteristics of both plants and animals. How would you classify such an organism?

What Is It?

Organisms are classified by their characteristics. For example, euglenoids, which include members of the genus *Euglena,* have the following characteristics:

- Euglenoids are single celled and live in pond water.
- Euglenoids are green and make their own food by photosynthesis.

These characteristics might lead you to conclude that euglenoids are plants. However, you should consider the following characteristics of euglenoids:

- Euglenoids move by whipping their "tails," which are called *flagella.*
- Euglenoids can feed on other organisms.

Plants do not move around, and most plants do not eat other organisms. So, are euglenoids animals? As you can see, euglenoids do not fit into plant or animal kingdoms. Scientists solved this problem by adding another kingdom —kingdom Protista—to classify organisms such as euglenoids.

As scientists learned more about living things, they changed the classification system. Today, there are three domains in the classification system. Domains represent the largest differences between organisms. These domains are divided into several kingdoms.

What You Will Learn

- Explain how classification developed as greater numbers of organisms became known.
- Describe the three domains.
- Describe four kingdoms in the domain Eukarya.

Vocabulary

Archaea	Fungi
Bacteria	Plantae
Eukarya	Animalia
Protista	

READING STRATEGY

Discussion Read this section silently. Write down questions that you have about this section. Discuss your questions in a small group.

TN GLE 0807.Inq.2 Use appropriate tools and techniques to gather, organize, analyze, and interpret data.

GLE 0807.Inq.4 Recognize possible sources of bias and error, alternative explanations, and questions for further exploration.

GLE 0807.T/E.1 Explore how technology responds to social, political, and economic needs.

GLE 0807.5.1 Identify various criteria used to classify organisms into groups.

Figure 1 *How would you classify this organism? This member of the genus* Euglena, *which is shown here highly magnified, has characteristics of both plants and animals.*

Figure 2 *The Grand Prismatic Spring in Yellowstone National Park contains water that is about 90°C (194°F). The spring is home to archaea that thrive in its hot water.*

Archaea in a modern taxonomic system, a domain made up of prokaryotes (most of which are known to live in extreme environments) that are distinguished from other prokaryotes by differences in their genetics and in the makeup of their cell wall; this domain aligns with the traditional kingdom Archaebacteria

Bacteria in a modern taxonomic system, a domain made up of prokaryotes that usually have a cell wall and that usually reproduce by cell division; this domain aligns with the traditional kingdom Eubacteria

Domain Archaea

The domain **Archaea** (ahr KEE uh) is made up entirely of archaea. Archaea are one of two kinds of prokaryotes (proh KAR ee OHTS). *Prokaryotes* are single-celled organisms that do not have a nucleus. Archaea were first discovered living in extreme environments, where other organisms could not survive. **Figure 2** shows a hot spring in Yellowstone National Park. The yellow and orange rings around the edge of the hot spring are made up of billions of archaea. Some archaea can also be found in moderate environments, such as the open ocean.

TN *Standards Check* What are some characteristics of archaea that could be used in a classification key to identify an organism as a member of the domain Archaea? ✔0807.5.1

Domain Bacteria

All bacteria (bak TEER ee uh) belong to the domain **Bacteria.** Bacteria are another kind of prokaryote. Bacteria can be found in soil, water, and even on and inside the human body! For example, *Escherichia coli* (ESH uh RIK ee uh KOH LIE), shown in **Figure 3,** is present in large numbers in human intestines, where it produces vitamin K. One kind of bacterium converts milk into yogurt. Some bacteria cause diseases, such as pneumonia. Other bacteria make chemicals that help humans fight disease-causing bacteria.

Figure 3 *Specimens of* E. coli *are shown on the point of a pin under a scanning electron microscope. These bacteria live in the intestines of animals and decompose undigested food.*

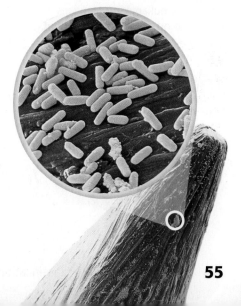

Figure 4 *This slime mold is a protist.*

Domain Eukarya

All organisms whose cells have a nucleus and membrane-bound organelles are called *eukaryotes*. Eukaryotes belong to the domain **Eukarya.** Four kingdoms currently make up the domain Eukarya: Protista, Fungi, Plantae, and Animalia.

Kingdom Protista

Members of the kingdom **Protista** (proh TIST uh), commonly called *protists,* are single-celled or simple multicellular organisms. Scientists think that the first protists arose from ancient bacteria about 2 billion years ago. Eventually, ancient protists gave rise to fungi, plants, and animals. The kingdom Protista contains many kinds of organisms. Some animal-like protists are called *protozoans.* Some plantlike protists are called *algae.* Protists also include slime molds, such as the one shown in **Figure 4,** and euglenoids.

Kingdom Fungi

Molds and mushrooms are examples of the complex, multicellular members of the kingdom **Fungi** (FUHN JIE). Unlike plants, fungi do not perform photosynthesis. Unlike animals, fungi do not eat food. Instead, fungi absorb nutrients from substances in their surroundings. They use digestive juices to break down the substances. **Figure 5** shows a very poisonous fungus. Even though some fungi are edible, you should never eat wild fungi.

Eukarya in a modern taxonomic system, a domain made up of all eukaryotes; this domain aligns with the traditional kingdoms Protista, Fungi, Plantae, and Animalia

Protista a kingdom of mostly one-celled eukaryotic organisms that are different from plants, animals, bacteria, and fungi

Fungi a kingdom made up of nongreen, eukaryotic organisms that have no means of movement, reproduce by using spores, and get food by breaking down substances in their surroundings and absorbing the nutrients

Figure 5 *This beautiful fungus of the genus* Amanita *is poisonous.*

Figure 6 *Giant sequoias can measure 30 m around at the base and can grow to more than 91.5 m tall.*

▲ Figure 7 *Plants such as these are common in the Tropics.*

Kingdom Plantae

Although plants vary remarkably in size and form, most people easily recognize the members of the kingdom Plantae. **Plantae** consist of organisms that are eukaryotic, have cell walls, and make food through photosynthesis. For photosynthesis to occur, plants must be exposed to sunlight. Plants can therefore be found on land and in water that light can penetrate.

The food that plants make is important not only for the plants but also for all of the organisms that get nutrients from plants. Most life on Earth is dependent on plants. For example, some fungi, protists, and bacteria consume plants. When these organisms digest the plant material, they get energy and nutrients made by the plants.

Plants also provide habitat for other organisms. The giant sequoias in **Figure 6** and the flowering plants in **Figure 7** provide birds, insects, and other animals with a place to live.

✓ *Reading Check* How do plants provide energy and nutrients to other organisms?

Plantae a kingdom made up of complex, multicellular organisms that are usually green, have cell walls made of cellulose, cannot move around, and use the sun's energy to make sugar by photosynthesis

MATH PRACTICE

Ring-Around-the-Sequoia

How many students would have to join hands to form a human chain around a giant sequoia that is 30 m in circumference? Assume for this calculation that the average student can extend his or her arms about 1.3 m.

Kingdom Animalia

The kingdom **Animalia** contains complex, multicellular organisms that don't have cell walls, are usually able to move around, and have specialized sense organs. These sense organs help most of these living things to quickly respond to their environment. Organisms in the kingdom Animalia are commonly called *animals*. You probably recognize many of the organisms in the kingdom Animalia. All of the organisms in **Figure 8** are animals.

Animals depend on the organisms from other kingdoms. For example, animals depend on plants for food. Animals also depend on bacteria and fungi to recycle the nutrients found in dead organisms.

Animalia a kingdom made up of complex, multicellular organisms that lack cell walls, can usually move around, and quickly respond to their environment

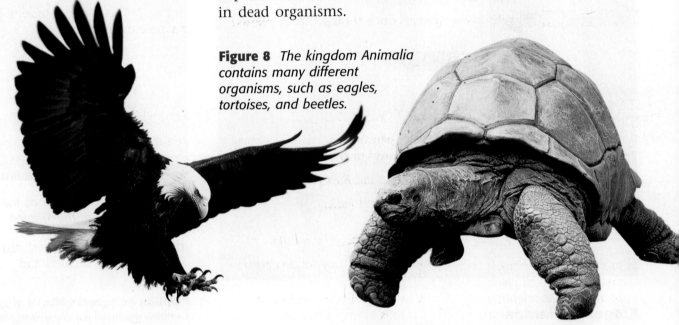

Figure 8 *The kingdom Animalia contains many different organisms, such as eagles, tortoises, and beetles.*

GLE 0807.Inq.2, GLE 0807.Inq.4, GLE 0807.T/E.1

CONNECTION TO Technology

Using Classification Web Sites The Internet can be a powerful research tool. You can use it to find a great deal of information, but much of this information may not be correct. You need to recognize reliable sources for information when using the Internet. You can find Web sites on the Internet dedicated to taxonomy and classification. Use a search engine to look up various words related to classification. When you find a Web site about classification, answer the following questions: What is the source of the information? When was the information last updated? Who was the author of the information? Come up with more questions of your own to evaluate Web sites. Then make a table comparing three Web sites. Identify which of the Web sites is most likely accurate and which of them may be inaccurate. Then evaluate whether the Internet is a reliable tool for classification.

ACTIVITY

Strange Organisms

Classifying organisms is often not easy. Like animals, some plants can eat other organisms to obtain nutrients. Some protists can use photosynthesis as plants do and can move around as animals do. The kingdom Animalia also includes members that might surprise you, such as worms, insects, and corals.

The red cup sponge in **Figure 9** is also an animal. Sponges are usually considered the simplest animals. They lack sense organs, and most of them cannot move. Scientists used to classify sponges as plants. But sponges cannot make their own food. They must eat other organisms to get nutrients, which is one reason that sponges are now classified as animals.

Reading Check Why were sponges once thought to be plants?

Figure 9 *This red cup sponge is a simple animal.*

SECTION Review

TN GLE 0807.5.1

Summary

- In the past, organisms were classified as plants or animals. As scientists discovered more species, they found that organisms did not always fit into one of these two categories, so they changed the classification system.

- Today, domains are the largest groups of related organisms. The three domains are Archaea and Bacteria, both of which consist of prokaryotes, and Eukarya, which consists of eukaryotes.

- The kingdoms of the domain Eukarya are Protista, Fungi, Plantae, and Animalia.

Using Key Terms

For each pair of terms, explain how the meanings of the terms differ.

1. *Archaea* and *Bacteria*

2. *Plantae* and *Fungi*

Understanding Key Ideas

3. Biological classification schemes change
   a. as new evidence and more kinds of organisms are discovered.
   b. every 100 years.
   c. when scientists disagree.
   d. only once.

4. Describe the characteristics of each of the three domains.

5. Describe the four kingdoms of domain Eukarya.

Math Skills

6. A certain bacterium can divide every 30 min. If you begin with 1 bacterium, when will you have more than 1,000 bacteria?

Critical Thinking

7. **Identifying Relationships** How are bacteria similar to fungi? How are fungi similar to animals?

8. **Analyzing Methods** Why do you think Linnaeus did not include classification kingdoms for categories of archaea and bacteria?

9. **Applying Concepts** The Venus' flytrap does not move around. It can make its own food by using photosynthesis. It can also trap insects and digest the insects to get nutrients. The cells of the flytrap also have cell walls. Into which kingdom would you place the Venus' flytrap? What makes this organism unusual in the kingdom you chose?

Internet Resources

For a variety of links related to this chapter, go to www.scilinks.org

Topic: Kingdoms
SciLinks code: HSM1397

Skills Practice Lab

Shape Island

You are a biologist exploring uncharted parts of the world to look for new animal species. You sailed for days across the ocean and finally found Shape Island hundreds of miles south of Hawaii. Shape Island has some very unusual organisms. The shape of each organism is a variation of a geometric shape. You have spent more than a year collecting and classifying specimens. You have been able to assign a two-part scientific name to most of the species that you have collected. Now, you must assign a two-part scientific name to each of the last 12 specimens collected before you begin your journey home.

OBJECTIVES

Classify organisms.

Name organisms.

Procedure

1 Draw each of the organisms pictured on the facing page. Beside each organism, draw a line for its name, as shown on the top left of the following page. The first organism pictured has already been named, but you must name the remaining 12. Use the glossary of Greek and Latin prefixes, suffixes, and root words in the table to help you name the organisms.

Greek and Latin roots, prefixes, and suffixes	Meaning
ankylos	angle
antennae	external sense organs
bi-	two
cyclo-	circular
macro-	large
micro-	small
mono-	one
peri-	around
-plast	body
-pod	foot
quad-	four
stoma	mouth
tri-	three
uro-	tail

Analyze Results

1 **Analyzing Results** If you gave species 1 a common name, such as *round-face-no-nose,* would any other scientist know which of the newly discovered organisms you were referring to? Explain. How many others have a round face and no nose?

2 **Organizing Data** Describe two characteristics that are shared by all of your newly discovered specimens. ✔0807.5.1

3 **Making Inferences** Choose four specimens. Make a branching diagram that classifies the specimens. ✔0807.5.2

TN GLE 0807.Inq.2 Use appropriate tools and techniques to gather, organize, analyze, and interpret data.

GLE 0807.5.1 Identify various criteria used to classify organisms into groups.

GLE 0807.5.2 Use a simple classification key to identify a specific organism.

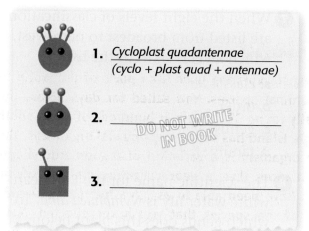

1. *Cycloplast quadantennae*
   (cyclo + plast quad + antennae)

2. _____
   DO NOT WRITE IN BOOK

3. _____

Draw Conclusions

④ **Applying Conclusions** One more organism exists on Shape Island, but you have not been able to capture it. However, your supplies are running out, and you must start sailing for home. You have had a good look at the unusual animal and can draw it in detail. Draw an animal that is different from all of the others, and give it a two-part scientific name.

Applying Your Data

Look up the scientific names *Mertensia virginica* and *Porcellio scaber*. Answer the following questions as they apply to each organism: Is the organism a plant or an animal? How many common names does the organism have? How many scientific names does it have?

Think of the name of your favorite fruit or vegetable. Find out if it has other common names, and find out its two-part scientific name.

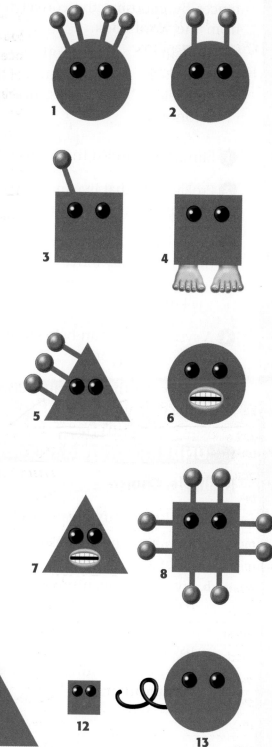

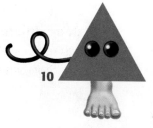

Chapter Review

USING KEY TERMS

Complete each of the following sentences by choosing the correct term from the word bank.

Animalia   Protista
Bacteria   Plantae
Archaea   classification
taxonomy

1 Linnaeus founded the science of ___.

2 Prokaryotes that live in extreme environments are in the domain ___.

3 Complex multicellular organisms that can usually move around and respond to their environment are in the kingdom ___.

4 A system of ___ can help group animals into categories.

5 Prokaryotes that can cause diseases are in the domain ___.

UNDERSTANDING KEY IDEAS

Multiple Choice

6 Scientists classify organisms by

  a. arranging the organisms in orderly groups.

  b. giving the organisms many common names.

  c. deciding whether the organisms are useful.

  d. using only existing categories of classification.

7 When the eight levels of classification are listed from broadest to narrowest, which level is sixth in the list?

  a. class

  b. order

  c. genus

  d. family

8 The scientific name for the European white water lily is *Nymphaea alba*. To which genus does this plant belong?

  a. *Nymphaea*   **c.** water lily

  b. *alba*   **d.** alba lily

9 *Animalia, Protista, Fungi,* and *Plantae* are the

  a. scientific names of different organisms.

  b. names of kingdoms.

  c. levels of classification.

  d. scientists who organized taxonomy.

10 The simple, single-celled organisms that live in your intestines are classified in the domain

  a. Protista.   **c.** Archaea.

  b. Bacteria.   **d.** Eukarya.

11 What kind of organism thrives in hot springs and other extreme environments?

  a. fungus   **c.** archaean

  b. bacterium   **d.** protist

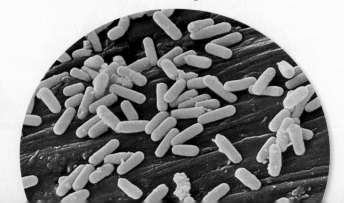

Short Answer

12 Why is the use of scientific names important in biology?

13 What kind of evidence is used by modern taxonomists to classify organisms based on how their relationships changed over time?

14 Is a bacterium a type of eukaryote? Explain your answer

15 Scientists once classified organisms as either plants or animals. Why doesn't that classification system work?

CRITICAL THINKING

16 Concept Mapping Use the following terms to create a concept map: *kingdom, fern, lizard, Animalia, Fungi, algae, Protista, Plantae,* and *mushroom*.

17 Analyzing Methods Explain how the levels of classification depend on the similarities and differences between organisms.

18 Making Inferences Explain why two species that belong to the same genus, such as white oak (*Quercus alba*) and cork oak (*Quercus suber*), also belong to the same family.

19 Identifying Relationships What characteristics do the members of the four kingdoms of the domain Eukarya have in common? Where would this information appear on a branching diagram for the four kingdoms and why?

✔0807.5.1

INTERPRETING GRAPHICS

Use the branching diagram of selected primates below to answer the questions that follow.

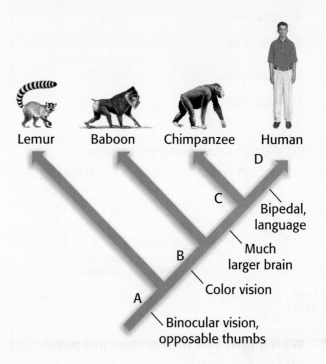

20 Which primate is the closest relative to the common ancestor of all primates?

✔0807.5.2

21 Which primate shares the most traits with humans?

✔0807.5.2

22 Do both lemurs and humans have the characteristics listed at point D? Explain your answer.

✔0807.5.2

23 What characteristic do baboons have that lemurs do not have? Explain your answer.

✔0807.5.2

TN SPI 0807.5.1 Use a simple classification key to identify an unknown organism.

GLE 0807.5.1 Identify various criteria used to classify organisms into groups.

Multiple Choice

1. The genus name of the rose Ryan is looking for is *rosa*. Its specific name is *alba*. What will it say on the tag identifying the plant?

   A. *alba rosa*

   B. *Alba rosa*

   C. *Rosa alba*

   D. *rosa alba*

Use the diagram below to answer question 2.

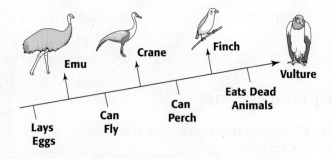

2. Which bird can fly but does not perch on trees or roost?

   A. crane

   B. emu

   C. finch

   D. vulture

3. Kim is studying two types of chimpanzees: *Pan troglodytes* and *Pan paniscus*. Based on their names, Kim can conclude that they

   A. are not similar.

   B. have many common characteristics.

   C. belong to different kingdoms.

   D. have a few common characteristics, but they are not related.

4. What should Elliot do to find out where a new organism fits in the classification system used today?

   A. He should call a scientist to ask what to name the new organism.

   B. He should examine the organism directly.

   C. He should find other organisms that live in the same area.

   D. He should compare it with known organisms.

5. At one time, scientists classified bacteria and protists together in one kingdom, but now they are in two separate domains. What evidence supported putting bacteria in a separate domain?

   A. Protists have cytoplasm, but bacteria do not.

   B. Bacteria have cell walls, but protists do not.

   C. Bacteria consist of only one cell, but protists consist of many cells.

   D. Protist cells have a nucleus and membrane-bound organelles, but bacteria cells do not.

6. Fungi were once classified as plants. Now they are placed in their own kingdom. Why were fungi removed from the plant kingdom?

   A. Fungi live only on land, but plants live on land and in water.

   B. Plants are made of many cells, but fungi consist of one cell.

   C. Fungi can move around on their own, but plants cannot move.

   D. Plants make their own food, but fungi absorb food from their surroundings.

Use the key below to answer questions 7 and 8.

Dichotomous Key for Domains and Kingdoms	
1. a. one cell	Go to Step 2.
b. many cells	Go to Step 4.
2. a. no membrane-bound organelles	Go to Step 3.
b. membrane-bound organelles	Go to Step 5.
3. a. extreme environments	domain Archaea
b. throughout the environment and within larger living things	domain Bacteria
4. a. all the same kind of cell or few different kinds of cells in organism	Go to Step 5. Go to Step 6.
b. many different kinds of cells in organism	
5. a. plantlike characteristics	kingdom Protista
b. absorbs nutrients from surroundings	kingdom Fungi
6. a. uses photosynthesis	kingdom Plantae
b. consumes other organisms	kingdom Animalia

7. **An organism has a few different kinds of cells and has mitochondria. It does not eat food, but cannot perform photosynthesis either. Using the dichotomous key above, determine the kingdom to which the organism belongs.**

   A. kingdom Fungi

   B. kingdom Plantae

   C. kingdom Protista

   D. kingdom Animalia

8. **An organism appears to be made up of one cell, doesn't move, and has mitochondria and chloroplasts. Using the dichotomous key above, determine the group to which the organism belongs.**

   A. domain Archaea

   B. domain Bacteria

   C. kingdom Plantae

   D. kingdom Protista

9. **Drea is comparing three organisms. Two have many of the same characteristics. But they have very few characteristics in common with the third organism. What can Drea infer about the relatedness of these three organisms?**

   A. The first two are equally related to the third.

   B. The first two are unrelated, but each is related to the third.

   C. Relatedness of the three organisms depends on the characteristics the first two share.

   D. The first two are more closely related to each other than they are to the third.

Open Response

10. **Compare kingdoms Plantae and Animalia.**

11. **Why are organisms such as sponges part of kingdom Animalia?**

TCAP Test Preparation

Science in Action

Science, Technology, and Society

DNA Barcodes

T/E Classifying organisms by their physical characteristics can be difficult, especially for organisms that have odd characteristics. For example, where would you classify an organism that has stems and leaves, as a plant does, but that cannot make its own food? Also, the large number of organisms on Earth makes classification difficult. Imagine trying to organize millions of different living things! As a result, some scientists are working on ways to use DNA to classify organisms. These scientists hope to use DNA in the same way that a barcode is used in a store. Since a "DNA barcode" is unique to each species, it can be used to identify them. The scientists also believe the information in the DNA barcode can be used to describe characteristics of the organism.

TN GLE 0807.T/E.1

Math ACTiViTy

Many organisms have not been identified and classified. If scientists have identified 26,000 species in a phylum they believe has 1.5 million species, what percentage of organisms have been identified?

Scientific Discoveries

A New Insect Order

In 2001, Oliver Zompro was studying a fossil insect preserved in amber. Although the fossil insect resembled a grasshopper or a walking stick, it was unique and could not be classified in the same group as either one. Zompro wondered if he might be seeing a new type of insect or an insect that was now thought to be extinct. The fossil insect was less than 4 cm long. Its spiny appearance earned the insect the nickname "gladiator." The gladiator bug that Zompro discovered is so unusual that it cannot be classified in any of the 30 existing orders of insects. Instead, the gladiator bug constitutes its own new order, which has been named *Mantophasmatodea*.

Language Arts ACTiViTy

WRITING SKILL Give the gladiator bug a new nickname. Write a short essay about why you chose that particular name for the insect.

Michael Fay

Crossing Africa Finding and classifying wild animals takes a great deal of perseverance. Just ask Michael Fay, who spent 15 months crossing 2,000 miles of uninhabited rain forest in the Congo River Basin of West Africa. He used video, photography, and old-fashioned note taking to record the types of animals and vegetation that he encountered along the way.

To find and classify wild animals, Fay often had to think like an animal. When coming across a group of monkeys swinging high above him in the emerald green canopy, Fay would greet the monkeys with his imitation of the crowned eagle's high-pitched, whistling cry. When the monkeys responded with their own distinctive call, Fay could identify exactly what species they were and would jot it down in one of his 87 waterproof notebooks. Fay also learned other tricks, such as staying downwind of an elephant to get as close to the elephant as possible. He could then identify its size, its age, and the length of its tusks.

Social Studies ACTiViTY

WRITING SKILL Many organizations around the world are committed to helping preserve biodiversity. Conduct some Internet and library research to find out about an organization that works to keep species safe from extinction. Create a poster that describes the organization and some of the species that the organization protects.

go.hrw.com

To learn more about these Science in Action topics, visit go.hrw.com and type in the keyword **HL5CLSF**.

Current Science

Check out Current Science® articles related to this chapter by visiting go.hrw.com. Just type in the keyword **HL5CS09**.

3

Adapting to the Environment

The Big Idea
Adaptations improve an organism's ability to survive and reproduce.

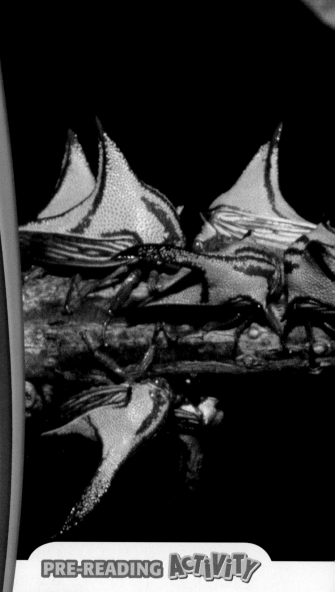

TN Tennessee Science Standards

Embedded Inquiry

GLE 0807.Inq.2 Use appropriate tools and techniques to gather, organize, analyze, and interpret data.

GLE 0807.Inq.3 Synthesize information to determine cause and effect relationships between evidence and explanations.

GLE 0807.Inq.5 Communicate scientific understanding using descriptions, explanations, and models.

✓0807.Inq.3 Use evidence from a dataset to determine cause and effect relationships that explain a phenomenon.

✓0807.Inq.5 Design a method to explain the results of an investigation using descriptions, explanations, or models.

Embedded Technology and Engineering

GLE 0807.T/E.1 Explore how technology responds to social, political, and economic needs.

✓0807.T/E.4 Research bioengineering technologies that advance health and contribute to improvements in our daily lives.

Life Science

GLE 0807.5.3 Analyze how structural, behavioral, and physiological adaptations within a population enable it to survive in a given environment.

GLE 0807.5.4 Explain why variation within a population can enhance the chances for group survival.

✓0807.5.3 Compare and contrast the ability of an organism to survive under different environmental conditions.

✓0807.5.4 Collect and analyze data relating to variation within a population of organisms.

PRE-READING ACTIVITY

Graphic Organizer

Spider Map Before you read the chapter, create the graphic organizer entitled "Spider Map" described in the **Study Skills** section of the Appendix. Label the circle "Adaptations." Create a leg for each type of plant or animal adaptation. As you read the chapter, fill in the map with details about each type of adaptation.

About the Photo

No, this thorny branch isn't part of a rose bush. The thorns on this tree branch are actually insects! Commonly known as thorn bugs, these insects are camouflaged as green thorns and are hard to notice unless they jump to another branch. These thorn bugs were photographed on Sanibel Island, Florida.

START-UP ACTIVITY

TN GLE 0807.Inq.2, GLE 0807.Inq.5

Go on a Safari!

You don't have to travel far to see interesting animals. If you look closely, you can find many animals, nearby. **Caution:** Always be careful around wild or unfamiliar animals, because they may bite or sting. Do not handle wild animals or any animals that are unfamiliar to you.

Procedure

1. Go outside, and find **two different kinds of animals** to observe.

2. Without disturbing the animals, watch them quietly for a few minutes from a distance. You may want to use **binoculars** or a **magnifying lens.**

3. Write down everything you notice about each animal. Do you know what kind of animal each is? Where did you find them? What do they look like? How big are they? What are they doing? You may want to draw a picture of them.

Analysis

1. Compare the two animals that you studied. Do they look alike? Do they have similar behaviors? Explain.

2. How do the animals move? Did you see them communicating with other animals or defending themselves? Explain.

3. Can you tell what each animal eats? What characteristics of each animal help it find or catch food?

Adapting to the Environment   **69**

Animal Reproduction

How can an animal find a mate when it is "glued" to one spot? Do animals in different environments produce offspring in the same way?

For a species to survive, some members of the species must reproduce. Over time, animals have developed different methods of reproduction to suit their environments.

Asexual Reproduction

Some animals reproduce asexually. In **asexual reproduction,** a single parent has offspring that are genetically identical to the parent. This allows organisms that are successful in an environment to produce offspring that will also be successful in the same environment. Organisms that reproduce asexually can produce many offspring in a short amount of time.

One pattern of asexual reproduction is called budding. *Budding* happens when a part of the parent organism pinches off and forms a new organism. The hydra, shown in **Figure 1,** reproduces by budding. The new hydra is genetically identical to its parent. Fragmentation is a second kind of asexual reproduction. In *fragmentation,* part of an organism breaks off and then new parts regenerate to form a new individual. Some organisms also have the ability to regenerate body parts. If an organism loses a body part, that part may develop into a new individual. A sea star, as shown in **Figure 2,** can regenerate body parts.

✓ **Reading Check** What is an advantage of budding?

What You Will Learn

● Describe the patterns and advantages of asexual reproduction in animals.
● Describe the patterns and advantages of sexual reproduction in animals.
● Explain how sexual reproduction is related to variation within a species.
● Explain the difference between external and internal fertilization.
● Identify the three different types of mammalian reproduction.

Vocabulary

asexual reproduction
sexual reproduction
external fertilization
internal fertilization

READING STRATEGY

Prediction Guide Before reading this section, write the title of each heading in this section. Next, under each heading, write what you think you will learn.

TN GLE 0807.Inq.5 Communicate scientific understanding using descriptions, explanations, and models.

asexual reproduction reproduction that does not involve the union of sex cells and in which a single parent produces offspring that are genetically identical to the parent
TN *VOCAB*

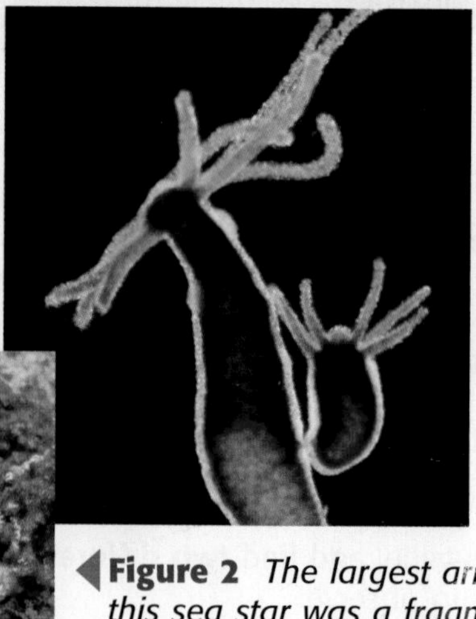

Figure 1 *The hydra bud will separate from its parent. Buds from other organisms, such as certain corals, remain attached to the parent.*

Figure 2 *The largest arm on this sea star was a fragment, from which a new sea star is forming. In time, all of the sea star's arms will grow to the same size.*

Sexual Reproduction

Most animals reproduce sexually. In **sexual reproduction,** offspring are formed when genetic information from more than one parent combines. Sexual reproduction in animals usually requires two parents—a male and a female. The female parent produces sex cells called *eggs*. The male parent produces sex cells called *sperm*. When an egg's nucleus and a sperm's nucleus join, a fertilized egg, called a *zygote* (ZIE GOHT), is created. This joining of an egg and sperm is known as *fertilization*.

Genetic information is found in *genes*. Genes are located on *chromosomes* (KROH muh SOHMZ) made of proteins and DNA. During fertilization, the egg and sperm each contribute chromosomes to the zygote. The combination of genes from the two parents results in a zygote that grows into a unique individual. This individual is not genetically identical to either of its parents. **Figure 3** shows how genes mix through three generations.

The combination of genes during sexual reproduction allows for variation within a population. Variation is an advantage of sexual reproduction and occurs in both plants and animals. The variation of genes allows a population to adapt to changes in the environment over time.

✔ Reading Check How does variation occur during sexual reproduction?

sexual reproduction reproduction in which sex cells from two parents unite to produce offspring that share traits from both parents ◢ TN VOCAB

CONNECTION TO Language Arts

WRITING SKILL **Nature or Nurture?** Scientists debate whether genetics or upbringing is more important in shaping people. Use the Internet or library to research the issue of "nature versus nurture." Find information about identical twins who were raised apart. When you finish your research, write a persuasive essay supporting one side of the debate. Include evidence to support your argument.

Figure 3 Inheriting Genes

Eggs and sperm contain chromosomes. You inherit chromosomes—and the genes on them—from both of your parents.

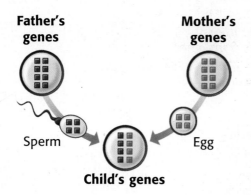

Father's genes

Mother's genes

Sperm

Egg

Child's genes

Figure 4 *Some fish, such as these angelfish, fertilize their eggs externally. The eggs are the orange mass next to the fish.*

external fertilization the union of sex cells outside the bodies of the parents

internal fertilization fertilization of an egg by sperm that occurs inside the body of a female

Figure 5 *Within minutes of birth, this zebra foal is already able to stand. Within an hour of birth, it will be able to run fast enough to keep up with its mother's herd.*

Internal and External Fertilization

Fertilization can happen either outside or inside the female's body. When the sperm fertilizes the eggs outside the female's body, the process is called **external fertilization.** External fertilization must take place in a moist environment so that the delicate zygotes will not dry out. Some fishes, such as those in **Figure 4,** reproduce by external fertilization.

Many amphibians, such as frogs, reproduce by external fertilization. For example, the female frog releases her eggs. At the same time, the male frog releases his sperm over the eggs to fertilize them. Frogs usually leave the zygotes to develop on their own. In about two weeks, the fertilized eggs hatch into tadpoles.

Internal Fertilization

When the egg and sperm join inside the female's body, the process is called **internal fertilization.** Internal fertilization allows the female animal to protect the developing zygote inside her body. For animals that live in dry environments, internal fertilization also provides a moist place for the zygote to develop safely.

Reptiles, birds, mammals, and some fishes reproduce by internal fertilization. Many animals that reproduce by internal fertilization can lay fertilized eggs. Female chickens, for example, usually lay one or two eggs after internal fertilization has taken place. In most mammals, one or more fertilized eggs develop inside the mother's body. Many mammals give birth to young that are well developed. Young zebras, such as this foal in **Figure 5,** can stand up and nurse almost immediately after birth.

✓ Reading Check What is the difference between external and internal fertilization?

Mammals

All mammals reproduce sexually. All mammals nurture their young with milk. The following describes how monotremes, marsupials, and placental mammals reproduce:

- **Monotreme** *Monotremes* (MAHN oh TREEMZ) are mammals that lay eggs. After the eggs are incubated and hatch, the young are nourished by milk that oozes from pores on the mother's belly. Echidnas and platypuses are monotremes.

- **Marsupial** Mammals that give birth to partially developed live young, such as the opossum in **Figure 6,** are *marsupials* (mahr SOO pee uhlz). Most marsupials have pouches where their young continue to develop after birth. Kangaroos, koalas, wombats, and Tasmanian devils are marsupials.

- **Placental Mammal** There are more than 4,000 species of placental mammals, including armadillos, humans, and bats. Placental mammals are nourished inside their mother's body before birth. Newborn placental mammals are more developed than newborn monotremes or marsupials are.

Figure 6 *The Virginia opossum is the only marsupial native to North America. When babies grow too big for their mother's pouch, they ride on her back.*

SECTION Review

TN GLE 0807.Inq.5

Summary

- In asexual reproduction, a single parent's offspring are genetically identical to the parent.
- In sexual reproduction, offspring receive a combination of genes from two parents, allowing variation. Variation allows a population to adapt to changes.
- Fertilization can be external or internal.
- All mammals reproduce sexually.

Using Key Terms

1. In your own words, write definitions for the following terms: *asexual reproduction, sexual reproduction, internal fertilization,* and *external fertilization.*

2. Describe one advantage of asexual reproduction and one advantage of sexual reproduction.

3. List two patterns of asexual reproduction in animals.

4. How does sexual reproduction allow for variation to occur among a species?

5. Female frogs release their eggs in water. Male frogs release their sperm over the eggs to fertilize them. What is this process called?

    a. budding

    b. internal fertilization

    c. external fertilization

    d. regeneration

Math Skills

6. A female largemouth bass can lay 900 to 3,200 eggs per kilogram of body weight each season. If a female fish has a mass of 3.8 kg, what is the maximum number of eggs she can lay in one season?

Critical Thinking

7. **Making Comparisons** Compare the genetic information offspring receive as a result of asexual reproduction with the genetic information offspring receive as result of sexual reproduction.

8. **Applying Concepts** Describe one advantage of internal fertilization over external fertilization.

Internet Resources

For a variety of links related to this chapter, go to www.scilinks.org

Topic: Reproduction
SciLinks code: HSM1293

Plant Reproduction

TN GLE 0807.Inq.2 Use appropriate tools and techniques to gather, organize, analyze, and interpret data.

GLE 0807.Inq.3 Synthesize information to determine cause and effect relationships between evidence and explanations.

GLE 0807.Inq.5 Communicate scientific understanding using descriptions, explanations, and models.

GLE 0807.5.3 Analyze how structural, behavioral, and physiological adaptations within a population enable it to survive in a given environment.

Look outside and you will probably see many different kinds of plants. How do plants reproduce? Like animals, plants can reproduce either asexually or sexually. Some plants can even use both methods! The way a type of plant reproduces is dependent on the plant's environment.

Plants have two stages in their life cycle—the sporophyte (SPAWR uh FIET) stage and the gametophyte (guh MEET uh FIET) stage. During the sporophyte stage, plants make spores. A spore is a reproductive cell, which can grow into a gametophyte. During the gametophyte stage, female gametophytes produce eggs and male gametophytes produce sperm. For plants to reproduce sexually, a sperm must fertilize an egg.

Reproduction in Nonvascular Plants

Nonvascular plants include mosses, liverworts, and hornworts. During the sporophyte stage, nonvascular plants produce a large number of spores. This is an advantage because the greater the number of spores produced is, the greater the chance that some will grow into gametophytes. Spores can be carried by wind or water. Gametophytes of nonvascular plants must be covered by a film of water for fertilization to occur. Eggs and sperm form in separate structures, which are often on separate plants. Gametophytes of nonvascular plants grow very close together in clumps. The green parts of the moss in **Figure 1** are gametophytes. When water covers the gametophytes, sperm swim to the female gametophytes and fertilize the eggs.

✓ Reading Check Explain how nonvascular plants reproduce.

Reproduction in Seedless Vascular Plants

Vascular plants have tissues that deliver materials from one part of the plant to another part of the plant. Some vascular plants are seedless. Seedless vascular plants also produce a lot of spores and need water in order to reproduce. However, in most species of seedless vascular plants, both eggs and sperm are produced on the same plant. Gametophytes of seedless vascular plants are usually very small and develop on or below the surface of soil, on rocks, or on tree bark.

Figure 1 *Moss is an example of a nonvascular plant.*

Reproduction in Seed Plants

The two types of seed plants are *gymnosperms* and *angiosperms*. Gymnosperms are trees and shrubs that do not have flowers or fruit. Angiosperms have flowers and seeds that are protected by fruit. Most seed plants can reproduce sexually without water, which allows them to live in many environments.

Reproduction in Gymnosperms

Most gymnosperms have reproductive structures called *cones*. A cone-bearing gymnosperm, as shown in **Figure 2,** has two kinds of cones—male cones and female cones. Male gametophytes are *pollen*. Pollen contain sperm. Female gametophytes produce eggs. Wind transfers pollen from the male cone to the female cone during **pollination.** Sperm from pollen fertilize the eggs of the female cone. The fertilized egg develops into a seed, and eventually develops into a young plant.

Reproduction in Angiosperms

In angiosperms, gametophytes develop within flowers. Pollen is produced in the male reproductive structures called *anthers*. Pollination happens when pollen is moved from anthers to stigmas. *Stigmas* are the female reproductive structures in flowers. Usually, wind or animals move pollen from one flower to another flower. After pollen lands on the stigma, a tube grows from each pollen grain. The pollen tube grows through the style to an ovule. Ovules are found inside the ovary. Each ovule contains an egg. Sperm from the pollen grain move down the pollen tube and into an ovule. Fertilization happens when a sperm fuses with the egg inside an ovule. **Figure 3** shows the process of pollination and fertilization in angiosperms.

Figure 2 *A gymnosperm, such as the spruce shown in the photo above, has reproductive structures called cones.*

pollination the transfer of pollen from the male reproductive structures to the female structures of seed plants

Figure 3 Pollination and Fertilization in Angiosperms

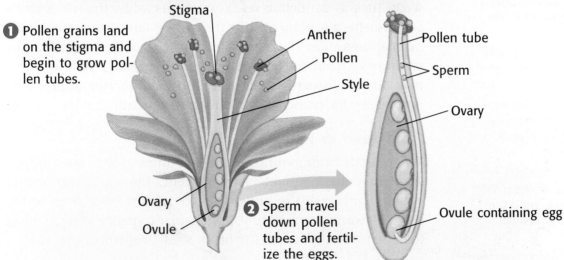

1 Pollen grains land on the stigma and begin to grow pollen tubes.

Stigma

Anther

Pollen

Style

Ovary

Ovule

2 Sperm travel down pollen tubes and fertilize the eggs.

Pollen tube

Sperm

Ovary

Ovule containing egg

Figure 4 Seed Production in Angiosperms

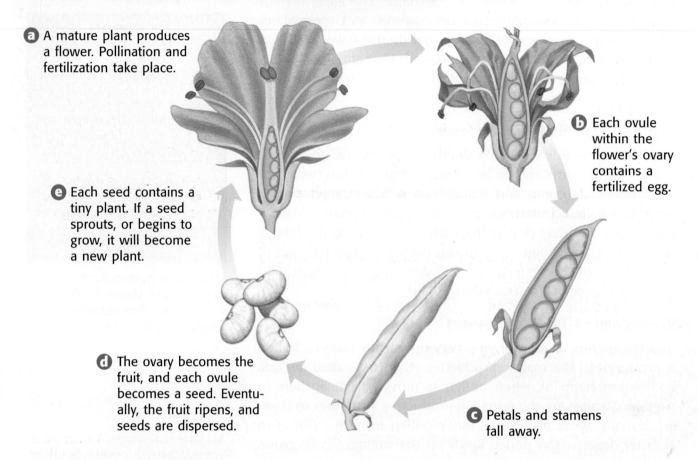

a A mature plant produces a flower. Pollination and fertilization take place.

b Each ovule within the flower's ovary contains a fertilized egg.

e Each seed contains a tiny plant. If a seed sprouts, or begins to grow, it will become a new plant.

d The ovary becomes the fruit, and each ovule becomes a seed. Eventually, the fruit ripens, and seeds are dispersed.

c Petals and stamens fall away.

TN GLE 0807.Inq.2, GLE 0807.Inq.3, GLE 0807.Inq.5

Thirsty Seeds

1. Fill a **Petri dish** two-thirds full of **water,** and add **six dry bean seeds.** Using a **wax pencil,** label the dish "Water."

2. Add **six dry bean seeds** to a dry **Petri dish.** Label this dish "Control."

3. The next day, compare the size of the two sets of seeds. Record your observations.

4. What caused the size of the seeds to change? Why is this change important to the seed's survival?
✔ 0807.Inq.3

From Flower to Fruit

After fertilization takes place in angiosperms, the ovule develops into a seed. The seed contains a young plant. The ovary surrounding the ovule becomes a fruit, as shown in **Figure 4.** As a fruit swells and ripens, it protects the developing seeds. Some seeds, such as dandelion seeds, are dispersed by the wind. Fruits can also help a plant spread its seeds. Many fruits are edible. Animals may eat these fruits. Then, the animals discard the seeds away from the parent plant. Other fruits, such as burrs, may become caught in an animal's fur. And the animal may drop these fruits away from the parent plant.

From Seed to Plant

When seeds from gymnosperms and angiosperms are dropped or planted in a suitable environment, the seeds sprout and young plants begin to grow. To sprout, most seeds need water, air, and warm temperatures. Each plant species has an ideal temperature at which most of its seeds begin to grow.

Other Methods of Reproduction

Angiosperms may also reproduce asexually. The advantage of asexual reproduction is that these plants do not depend on other plants to reproduce. Instead, part of a plant produces a new plant. The following are three structures plants use to reproduce asexually:

- **Plantlets** Tiny plants grow along the edges of a plant's leaves. These plantlets fall off and grow on their own.
- **Tubers** Underground stems, or tubers, can produce new plants after a dormant season.
- **Runners** Above-ground stems from which new plants can grow are called *runners*.

The potato in **Figure 5** is an example of a tuber. A strawberry plant produces runners, or stems that grow horizontally along the ground. Buds along the runners grow into new plants.

Figure 5 *A potato is a tuber, or underground stem. The "eyes" of potatoes are buds that can grow into new plants.*

✓ Reading Check List the advantage of asexual reproduction, and list three kinds of asexual reproduction in plants.

SECTION Review

TN GLE 0807.Inq.5, GLE 0807.5.3

Summary

- Most gametophytes of nonvascular plants and seedless vascular plants need water to reproduce.
- Some seed plants do not need water to reproduce. During fertilization, wind and animals can transfer pollen.
- Some plants use plantlets, tubers, or runners to reproduce asexually.

Using Key Terms

1. Use the term *pollination* in a sentence.

2. Describe one kind of asexual reproduction in plants. What is an advantage of this kind of asexual reproduction?

3. Which part of a flower develops into a fruit? into a seed?

4. One type of asexual reproduction produces stems that grow horizontally along the ground, take root, and grow into new plants. What are these stems called?

   a. runners   **c.** plantlets
   b. tubers   **d.** spores

Math Skills

5. Avocado trees need bees to pollinate their flowers. Scientists have counted an average of 8 grains of pollen per flower stigma when 20 or more bees are present around a single avocado tree. If 80% of the stigmas on the tree are pollinated, how many total grains of pollen would be found on a tree that has 150 flowers?

Critical Thinking

6. **Making Inferences** Under what environmental conditions might asexual reproduction be important for the survival of some angiosperms? ✔0807.5.3

7. **Analyzing Ideas** Sexual reproduction results in more genetic variation than asexual reproduction does. Why is variation important?

Internet Resources

For a variety of links related to this chapter, go to www.scilinks.org
Topic: Reproduction of Plants
SciLinks code: HSM1295

What You Will Learn

● Explain the difference between learned and innate behavior.
● Describe five kinds of behaviors that help animals survive.
● Identify seasonal behaviors that help animals adapt to the environment.

Vocabulary

innate behavior
learned behavior
territory
hibernation
estivation

READING STRATEGY

Discussion Read this section silently. Write down questions that you have about this section. Discuss your questions in a small group.

TN GLE 0807.Inq.5 Communicate scientific understanding using descriptions, explanations, and models.
GLE 0807.T/E.1 Explore how technology responds to social, political, and economic needs.
GLE 0807.5.3 Analyze how structural, behavioral, and physiological adaptations within a population enable it to survive in a given environment.

Animal Behavior

Suppose that you look out a window and see a bird flying away from a tree. Is the bird leaving a nest in search of food? Or is the bird escaping from danger?

Though the bird's purpose may not be clear, the bird is flying away for a specific reason. Animals run from enemies, search for food, battle for territory, and build homes. All of these activities are known as *behavior.*

Kinds of Behavior

How do animals know when a situation is dangerous? How do they know where to find food? Sometimes, animals instinctively know how to behave, but sometimes they learn how.

Innate Behavior

Behavior that does not depend on learning or experience is known as **innate behavior.** Innate behaviors are inherited through genes. Puppies inherit the tendency to chew, and bees inherit the tendency to fly. The male bird in **Figure 1** inherited the tendency to collect colorful objects for its nest. Some innate behaviors are present at birth. Newborn whales have the innate ability to swim. Other innate behaviors develop months or years after birth. For example, walking is innate for humans. But we do not walk until we are about one year old.

Learned Behavior

Innate behaviors can be modified. Animals can use learning to change a behavior. **Learned behavior** is behavior that has been learned from experience or from observing other animals. Humans inherit the tendency to speak. But the language we use is not inherited. We might learn English, Spanish, or sign language. Humans are not the only animals that change behaviors through learning. All animals can learn.

Figure 1 *The male bowerbird collects colorful objects for its nest to attract a female bowerbird to be his mate.*

Figure 2 *Chimpanzees make and use tools to get ants and other food out of hard-to-reach places.*

innate behavior an inherited behavior that does not depend on the environment or experience

learned behavior a behavior that has been learned from experience

territory an area that is occupied by one animal or a group of animals that do not allow other members of the species to enter

Survival Behavior

Animals use their behaviors to survive. To stay alive, an animal has to do many things. It must avoid being eaten, and it must find food, water, and a place to live.

Finding Food

Animals find food in many ways. Bees fly from flower to flower collecting nectar. Koala bears climb trees to get eucalyptus leaves. Some animals, such as the chimpanzee shown in **Figure 2,** use tools to get food. Many animals hunt for their food. For example, owls hunt mice.

Animals that eat other animals are known as *predators*. The animal being eaten is the *prey*. Animals that are predators can also be the prey for another animal. For example, a frog eats insects. So, the frog is a predator. But a frog may be eaten by a snake. In this case, the frog is the prey.

Marking Territory

Sometimes, members of the same species must compete for food and mates. Some animals claim territories to save energy by avoiding this competition. A **territory** is an area that is occupied by one animal or by a group of animals that do not allow other members of the species to enter. Some birds mark a territory by singing. The song lets other birds know not to enter the area. If other birds do enter the area, the bird that has marked the territory may chase them away. Animals use their territories for mating, raising young, and finding food.

✓ Reading Check Explain how marking territory is a survival behavior.

TN GLE 0807.T/E.1

CONNECTION TO Technology

T/E Speak Up! Have you talked with your computer lately? Cell phones, computers, and even cars can recognize and respond to voice commands. These devices can even learn your words and repeat them back to you! Most important, this new technology helps people with disabilities be more self-sufficient. Do you think voice recognition software is similar to innate or learned behavior? Use the Internet to research voice recognition software. Write a report on how this technology allows individuals with disabilities to function more easily in their daily lives.
✓0807.T/E.4

ACTIVITY

Defensive Action

Defensive behavior allows animals to protect resources, including territories, from other animals. Animals defend food, mates, and offspring. Have you ever heard a pet dog growl when a person approached while it was eating? Many male animals, such as lions, fight violently to defend mates. Some birds use distraction to defend their young. When a predator is near, a mother killdeer may pretend to have a broken wing and move away from her young. This action distracts the predator's attention from the young so that they will remain safe.

Defensive behavior also helps animals protect themselves from predators. One way animals avoid predators is to make themselves hard to see. For example, a rabbit often stands still so that its color blends into a background of shrubs or grass. But once a predator is aware of its prey, the prey needs another way to defend itself. Rabbits also try to outrun predators. As seen in **Figure 3,** skunks spray irritating chemicals at predators. Has an animal ever defended itself against you?

✓ **Reading Check** What are two ways a rabbit can defend itself?

Courtship

Animals need to find mates to reproduce. Reproduction is essential for the survival of an individual's genes. Animals have special behaviors that help them find a mate. These behaviors are referred to as *courtship*. Some birds and fish build nests to attract a mate. Other animals use special movements and sounds to attract a mate. **Figure 4** shows two cranes performing a courtship display.

Figure 3 *Skunks spray irritating chemicals at attackers to protect themselves.*

Figure 4 *These Japanese ground cranes use an elaborate courtship dance to tell each other when they are ready to mate.*

Figure 5 *Adult killer whales teach their young how to hunt in the first years of life.*

Parenting

Some animals, such as caterpillars, begin life with the ability to take care of themselves. But many young animals depend on their parents for survival. Some adult birds bring food to their young because they cannot feed themselves when they hatch. Other animals, such as the killer whales in **Figure 5,** spend years teaching their young how to hunt for food.

Seasonal Behavior

Humans bundle up when it is cold outside. Many other animals have to deal with bitter cold during the winter, too. Frogs hide from the cold by burrowing in mud. Other animals may face winter food shortages. Squirrels store food to prepare for winter. Seasonal behaviors help animals adapt to the environment.

Migration

Many animals avoid cold weather by traveling to warmer places. These animals migrate to find food, water, or safe nesting grounds. To *migrate* is to travel from one place to another. Whales, salmon, bats, and even chimpanzees migrate. Each winter, the monarch butterflies shown in **Figure 6** migrate to central Mexico from all over North America. And each fall, birds in the Northern Hemisphere fly south thousands of kilometers. In the spring, they return north to nest.

If you were planning a trip, you would probably use a map. But how do animals know which way to go when they migrate? For short trips, many animals use landmarks to find their way. *Landmarks* are fixed objects that an animal uses to find its way. Birds use landmarks such as mountain ranges, rivers, and coastlines to find their way.

Figure 6 *When monarch butterflies gather in Mexico for the winter, there can be as many as 4 million butterflies per acre!*

Figure 7 *Bears slow down for the winter, but they do not enter deep hibernation.*

hibernation a period of inactivity and lowered body temperature that some animals undergo in winter as a protection against cold weather and lack of food

estivation a period of inactivity and lowered body temperature that some animals undergo in summer as a protection against hot weather and lack of food

Slowing Down

Some animals deal with food and water shortages by hibernating. **Hibernation** is a period of inactivity and decreased body temperature that some animals experience in winter. Hibernating animals survive on stored body fat. Many animals hibernate, including mice, squirrels, and skunks. While an animal hibernates, its temperature, heart rate, and breathing rate drop. Some hibernating animals drop their body temperature to a few degrees above freezing and do not wake for weeks at a time. Other animals, such as the bear in **Figure 7,** slow down but do not enter deep hibernation. Also, bears hibernate for shorter periods of time than other hibernating animals do.

Winter is not the only time that resources can be hard to find. Many desert squirrels and mice experience a similar internal slowdown in the hottest part of the summer, when they cannot easily find water and food. This period of reduced activity in the summer is called **estivation.**

✓ Reading Check Give an example of how a food shortage can affect the behavior of an animal.

A Biological Clock

Animals need to keep track of time so that they know when to store food and when to migrate. The internal control of an animal's natural cycles is called a *biological clock*. Animals may use clues such as the length of the day and the temperature to set their clocks. Some biological clocks keep track of daily cycles. These daily cycles are called *circadian rhythms*. Most animals wake up and get sleepy at about the same time each day and night. This is an example of a circadian rhythm.

Cycles of Change

Some biological clocks control long cycles. Seasonal cycles are nearly universal among animals. Many animals hibernate at certain times of the year and reproduce at other times. Reproducing during a particular season takes advantage of environmental conditions that help the young survive. Migration patterns are also controlled by seasonal cycles.

Biological clocks also control cycles of internal changes. For example, treehoppers, such as the one in **Figure 8,** go through several stages in life. They begin as an egg, then hatch as a nymph, and then develop into an adult. Finally, the adult emerges from the skin of its nymph form.

Figure 8 *The treehopper's biological clock signals the animal to shed the skin of its nymph form and emerge as an adult.*

SECTION Review

TN GLE 0807.Inq.5, GLE 0807.5.3

Summary

- Behavior may be classified as innate or learned. The potential for innate behavior is inherited. Learned behavior depends on experience.
- Behaviors that help animals survive include finding food, marking a territory, defensive action, courtship, and parenting.
- Seasonal behaviors, such as hibernation and estivation can help animals adapt to the environment.

Using Key Terms

1. Use the following pair of terms in a sentence: *estivation* and *hibernation.*

2. An animal that lives in a hot, dry environment might spend the summer
   a. hibernating.
   b. estivating.
   c. migrating to a warmer climate.
   d. None of the above

3. Bees, ants, and wasps inject a powerful acid into their predators. What is this survival behavior called?
   a. defensive behavior
   b. slowing down
   c. parenting
   d. territorial behavior

4. Do bears hibernate?

5. What is the difference between innate and learned behaviors?

6. Name five behaviors that help animals survive.

7. Compare the ability of monarch butterflies to survive in warm versus cold environments. What seasonal behavior helps monarch butterflies adapt to changing environments? ✔0807.5.3

Math Skills

8. Gray bats use two caves in Tennessee for their winter hibernation. The population in one cave was recently determined to be 519,570 bats. If 170 bats can occupy one square foot of space, how many total square feet of ceiling space did bats cover in the one cave?

Critical Thinking

9. **Applying Concepts** People who travel to different time zones often suffer from *jet lag*. Jet lag makes people have trouble waking up and going to sleep at appropriate times. Why do you think people experience jet lag?

10. **Making Inferences** Many children are born with the tendency to make babbling sounds. But few adults make these sounds. How could you explain this change in an innate behavior?

Internet Resources

For a variety of links related to this chapter, go to www.scilinks.org

Topic: Animal Behavior; Rhythms of Life

SciLinks code: HSM0069; HSM1311

Adaptations and Survival

Sea turtles are strong swimmers because they have flippers. Sea turtles are also excellent divers. Leatherback sea turtles can dive to depths of more than 1,000 m!

The characteristics described above are called *adaptations*. An **adaptation** is a characteristic that improves an individual's ability to survive and reproduce in a particular environment. The abilities to swim fast and to dive to great depths can help sea turtles escape their predators and search for food. Although sea turtles lay their eggs on land, sea turtles are aquatic animals. Therefore, sea turtles have adaptations for an aquatic environment and could not survive in only a land environment.

Adaptations for Obtaining Food

Similar to the adaptations that some sea turtles have to be able to dive to great depths to find food, almost all other organisms have adaptations to help them obtain food. For example, the chameleon in **Figure 1** uses its long, fast-moving tongue to catch unsuspecting insects. The strong, sharply-pointed beak of the woodpecker in **Figure 1** is also an adaptation. The woodpecker could not drill into a tree to search for insects without its special beak. Even humans have adaptations for obtaining food. Because of the shape and function of our hands and fingers, humans are able to do things such as pick and peel fruit and open jars.

Reading Check Give an example of an adaptation that helps an organism obtain the food it needs to survive.

What You Will Learn

- Identify three kinds of adaptations that help organisms survive.
- Describe the four parts of natural selection.
- Explain how variation occurs within a population.
- Explain why genetic variation within a population is important.
- Explain how resistance to insecticide is a survival characteristic.

Vocabulary

adaptation
natural selection

READING STRATEGY

Reading Organizer As you read this section, create an outline of the section. Use the headings from the section in your outline.

TN GLE 0807.Inq.5 Communicate scientific understanding using descriptions, explanations, and models.

GLE 0807.5.3 Analyze how structural, behavioral, and physiological adaptations within a population enable it to survive in a given environment.

GLE 0807.5.4 Explain why variation within a population can enhance the chances for group survival.

Figure 1 The chameleon (above) catches an insect with its long tongue. The woodpecker (right) uses its strong beak to drill holes into trees to find insects.

Figure 2 *The protective quills of the porcupine (left) keep predators away. The pattern of black, red, and yellow on the coral snake (right) is a warning sign to predators.*

Predator-Prey Adaptations

Many organisms have adaptations that serve as a defense against predators. Some organisms, such as the porcupine in **Figure 2,** have a protective covering. Bright markings also warn potential predators to leave an organism alone. Patterns with black stripes and red, orange, or yellow markings are common in many species of bees, wasps, skunks, snakes, and poisonous frogs. For example, the venomous coral snake in **Figure 2** has bright markings.

Another adaptation that helps both predators and prey is called *camouflage*. An organism that is camouflaged is disguised so that it is hard to see even when the organism is in view. An organism's camouflage usually disguises the organism's recognizable features. For example, the eyes are usually the most recognizable part of an organism. Therefore, some organisms have black stripes around their eyes for disguise. Some predators use their environment as camouflage. These predators often do not chase their prey. Instead, they wait for the prey to come close enough to be caught. For example, the alligator in **Figure 3** is camouflaged by duckweed. Because the alligator blends with its environment, the alligator's prey may not notice it waiting to attack.

adaptation a characteristic that improves an individual's ability to survive and reproduce in a particular environment

For another activity related to this chapter, go to **go.hrw.com** and type in the keyword **HL5HISW.**

Figure 3 *Camouflaged by duckweed, this alligator can hide and wait for its prey.*

Figure 4 *The Hawaiian honeycreeper uses its curved beak to sip nectar from a lobelia flower.*

natural selection the process by which individuals that are better adapted to their environment survive and reproduce more successfully than less well adapted individuals do

Figure 5 *Female sea turtles can lay from 50 to 160 eggs in one nest. Because of natural selection, only some baby sea turtles from each nest will survive to adulthood.*

Adaptations to Interactions

Two species can also adapt to interact with one another. For example, the honeycreeper and the lobelia (loh BEEL yuh) plant in **Figure 4,** have adapted to each other. The honeycreeper has a long, curved beak, which lets it reach the nectar at the base of the long, curved lobelia flower. As the bird sips nectar from the flower, the bird gets pollen on its head. When the bird moves to another flower, some of the pollen will rub off. Therefore, the honeycreeper helps lobelia plants reproduce. Adaptations that allow close interactions between organisms usually occur between organisms that live close together. But these adaptations happen over a very long period of time.

Natural Selection

As you have learned, adaptations help organisms survive. Organisms inherit adaptations and other characteristics from their parents. However, inherited characteristics in populations can change over time. The change in the inherited characteristics of a population over time can be explained by *natural selection*. **Natural selection** is the process by which individuals that are better adapted to their environment survive and reproduce more success-fully than less well adapted individuals do. For example, only a small percentage of the baby sea turtles from the nest in **Figure 5** will survive to reproduce. Inherited char-acteristics and environmental factors, such as predation and food availability, may influence which baby sea turtles reach adulthood and which do not.

Four Parts of Natural Selection

Natural selection affects how a population changes in response to its environment. Because of natural selection, a population will tend to be well adapted to its environment. But if the environment changes, only those individuals that have characteristics suited to the new environment are likely to survive and reproduce. The four parts of natural selection are illustrated in **Figure 6.**

✓ Reading Check What is the relationship between the process of natural selection and survival?

Figure 6 **Natural Selection in Four Steps**

1. Overproduction
More offspring are born than will live to become adults.

2. Genetic Variation Within a Population
The individuals in a population are different from one another. Some of the different characteristics improve the chances that the individual will survive and reproduce. Others lower these chances. For example, rabbits that are stronger or faster are more likely to survive and reproduce than weaker or slower rabbits.

3. Struggle to Survive
An environment might not have enough food or water for every individual born. Many individuals are killed by other organisms. And others cannot find mates. Only some individuals survive and reproduce.

4. Successful Reproduction
Successful reproduction is the key to natural selection. The individuals that have better adaptations for living in their environment and for finding mates are more likely to reproduce. Those that are not well adapted to their environment are more likely to die early or to have few offspring.

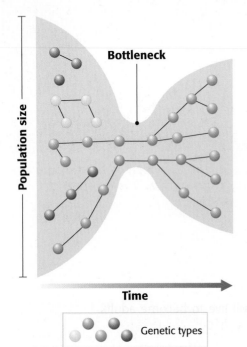

Changes in Genetic Variation

Over time, a population will be made up of more individuals with characteristics that help them survive. And for natural selection to continue, individuals within the population must be genetically different. However, if a population decreases rapidly, many characteristics may be lost entirely from a population because all of the individuals with those characteristics died. This reduced number of characteristics within a population is called a *genetic bottleneck,* as shown in **Figure 7.** If the population is able to increase again, inbreeding will cause the individuals to be genetically similar. These genetic similarities may make a population more susceptible to birth defects and genetic diseases. And many individuals would likely be affected by the same disease.

The Florida panther population is an example of a population that has experienced a genetic bottleneck. Because of isolation from other populations of panthers, habitat loss, and an overall decrease in population size, the genetic variation within the Florida panther population has decreased. As a result, many of the panthers that survived have become genetically similar. This similarity has caused inbreeding to occur within the population. Inbreeding in panthers can result in heart defects, the failure of reproductive organs, and low birth rates. However, there is a recovery program in place for the Florida panther. The program includes protecting and enlarging the panther's habitat as well as monitoring the health of the population, as shown in **Figure 8.**

Reading Check How can a decrease in genetic variation within a population affect the population?

Figure 7 *When a population is reduced to a few members, a genetic bottleneck occurs and genetic variation decreases.*

Figure 8 *These biologists have taken DNA samples from a tranquilized Florida panther. Monitoring the health of the Florida panther population is part of a program to increase the genetic variation within the population.*

Insecticide Resistance

Insecticide resistance is also a result of natural selection. Insecticides are used to kill insects. However, some individual insects within a population may be resistant to certain insecticides. These insects survive because they have genes that make them resistant to the insecticide. These survivors then reproduce and pass the insecticide-resistance genes to their offspring. Each time the insect population is sprayed with the same insecticide, the insect population changes to include more resistant members. The European corn borer in **Figure 9** is an example of an insect that is resistant to some insecticides.

Figure 9 *The European corn borer can destroy crops of corn. It is resistant to some insecticides.*

SECTION Review

TN GLE 0807.Inq.5, GLE 0807.5.3, GLE 0807.5.4

Summary

- Adaptations are characteristics that can help an organism survive.
- The four parts of natural selection are overproduction, genetic variation, competition for resources, and successful reproduction.
- Variation is due to the exchange of genetic information as it is passed from parent to offspring.
- Genetic variation allows a population to adapt to changes in the environment over time.
- When a population of insects is resistant to an insecticide, survival rates can increase.

Using Key Terms

1. Use *adaptation* and *natural selection* in separate sentences.

Understanding Key Ideas

2. Give an example of two species that have special adaptations that allow them to interact with one another.

3. Describe the four steps of natural selection.

4. What is a genetic bottleneck?

5. A chameleon can change the color of its skin to blend in with its environment. This adaptation helps it hide from predators. What is this adaptation called?
   a. camouflage
   b. resistance
   c. natural selection
   d. warning coloration

Math Skills

6. A colony of insects is sprayed with insecticide. The colony contains 1,600 insects. If 1% of the colony is resistant to the insecticide, how many insects will survive after being sprayed?

Critical Thinking

7. **Evaluating Conclusions** Why is genetic variation important to the survival of a population?

8. **Making Comparisons** Compare the adaptations of two organisms described in this section. Describe how the adaptations help increase the chances that each organism will survive and reproduce.

9. **Analyzing Processes** Many rats have become resistant to rat poison. Based on what you know about how insects become resistant to insecticides, how might rats become resistant to poisons?

10. **Making Comparisons** How does camouflage affect an organism's ability to survive in different environmental conditions?
    ✓0807.5.3

Model-Making Lab

Adaptation: It's a Way of Life

Since the beginning of life on Earth, species have had special characteristics called *adaptations* that have helped them survive changes in environmental conditions. Changes in a species' environment include climate changes, habitat destruction, or the extinction of prey. These changes can cause a species to die out unless the species has a characteristic that helps it survive. For example, a species of bird may have an adaptation for eating sunflower seeds and ants. If the ant population dies out, the bird can still eat seeds and can therefore survive.

In this activity, you will explore several adaptations and design an organism with adaptations you choose. Then, you will describe how these adaptations help the organism survive.

OBJECTIVES

Design an organism with adaptations you choose.

Describe how these adaptations help the organism survive.

MATERIALS

- arts-and-crafts materials, various
- markers, colored
- magazines for cutouts
- poster board
- scissors

SAFETY

Procedure

1. Study the chart below. Choose one adaptation from each column. For example, an organism might be a scavenger that burrows underground and has spikes on its tail!

Adaptations		
Diet	**Type of transportation**	**Special adaptation**
carnivore	flies	uses sensors to detect heat
herbivore	glides through the air	is active only at night and has excellent night vision
omnivore	burrows underground	changes colors to match its surroundings
scavenger	runs fast	has armor
decomposer	swims	has horns
	hops	can withstand extreme temperature changes
	walks	secretes a terrible and sickening scent
	climbs	has poison glands
	floats	has specialized front teeth
	slithers	has tail spikes
		stores oxygen in its cells so it does not have to breathe continuously
		one of your own invention

TN GLE 0807.Inq.2 Use appropriate tools and techniques to gather, organize, analyze, and interpret data.

GLE 0807.Inq.5 Communicate scientific understanding using descriptions, explanations, and models.

GLE 0807.5.3 Analyze how structural, behavioral and physiological adaptations within a population of organisms enable it to survive in a particular environment.

2 Design an organism that has the three adaptations you have chosen. Use poster board, colored markers, picture cutouts, or craft materials to create your organism.

3 Write a caption on your poster describing your organism. Describe its appearance, its habitat, its niche, and the way its adaptations help it survive. Give your organism a two-part "scientific" name that is based on its characteristics.

4 Display your creation in your classroom. Share with classmates how you chose the adaptations for your organism.

Analyze the Results

1 **Organizing Data** What does your imaginary organism eat?

2 **Organizing Data** In what environment or habitat would your organism be most likely to survive—in the desert, tropical rain forest, plains, icecaps, mountains, or ocean? Explain your answer.

3 **Analyzing Data** Is your creature a mammal, a reptile, an amphibian, a bird, or a fish? What modern organism (on Earth today) or ancient organism (extinct) is your imaginary organism most like? Explain the similarities between the two organisms. Do some research outside the lab, if necessary, to find out about a real organism that may be similar to your imaginary organism.

Draw Conclusions

4 **Evaluating Data** If there were a sudden climate change, such as daily downpours of rain in a desert, would your imaginary organism survive? What adaptations for surviving such a change does it have? ✔0807.Inq.5, ✔0807.5.3

Applying Your Data

Call or write to an agency such as the U.S. Fish and Wildlife Service to get a list of endangered species in your area. Choose an organism on that list. Describe the organism's niche and any special adaptations it has that help it survive. Find out why it is endangered and what is being done to protect it.

Examine the illustration of the animal at right. Based on its physical characteristics, describe its habitat and niche. Is this a real animal?

Chapter Review

TN GLE 0807.Inq.3, GLE 0807.Inq.5, GLE 0807.5.3, GLE 0807.5.4

USING KEY TERMS

For each pair of terms, explain how the meanings of the terms differ.

1 *asexual reproduction* and *sexual reproduction*

2 *external fertilization* and *internal fertilization*

3 *innate behavior* and *learned behavior*

4 *hibernation* and *estivation*

5 *adaptation* and *natural selection*

UNDERSTANDING KEY IDEAS

Multiple Choice

6 When part of a sea star breaks off, the part can develop into a new individual. What is this pattern of asexual reproduction called?

a. fragmentation

b. budding

c. external fertilization

d. internal fertilization

7 Which is NOT a pattern of asexual reproduction in plants?

a. producing runners

b. producing tubers

c. producing flowers

d. producing plantlets

8 A biological clock controls

a. circadian rhythms.

b. defensive behavior.

c. learned behavior.

d. being a consumer.

9 Which of the following statements is true about migration? ✔0807.5.3

a. It occurs only in birds.

b. It helps animals escape cold and food shortages in winter.

c. It always refers to moving southward for the winter.

d. It helps animals defend themselves.

10 Most gymnosperms have reproductive structures called *cones*. Gymnosperms have male and female cones. Where are male gametophytes found?

a. in soil

b. in eggs

c. in seeds

d. in pollen

11 Many desert animals experience an internal slowdown in the hottest part of the summer. When the availability of water and food is scarce, these animals undergo a period of inactivity and lowered body temperature. What is this seasonal behavior called? ✔0807.5.3

a. hibernation

b. estivation

c. parenting

d. circadian rhythm

Short Answer

12 Choose an organism, and describe the adaptations that help it survive.

13 What is the relationship between natural selection and reproduction?

14 What is a territory? Give an example of a territory from your environment.

15 What is pollination?

16 Concept Mapping Use the following terms to create a concept map: *asexual reproduction, external fertilization, fragmentation, reproduction, internal fertilization, budding,* and *sexual reproduction.*

17 Identifying Relationships The environment in which organisms live may change over time. For example, a wet, swampy area may gradually become a grassy area with a small pond. Explain how sexual reproduction may give species that live in a changing environment a survival advantage. ✔0807.5.3

18 Analyzing Processes What is the relationship between genetic variation and the term *genetic bottleneck*? What can happen to a population when it experiences a genetic bottleneck? ✔0807.Inq.3

CHALLENGE

19 How might coral snakes change if a new predator that was not harmed by their poison became part of the snakes' environment? ✔0807.5.3

20 Call or write to a zoo or aquarium that participates in the American Zoo and Aquarium Association's Species Survival Plan Program. Choose two species that the zoo or aquarium has in its collection. Collect information about the methods used to maintain a healthy and diverse population of these species. Analyze the methods used for each species. How are they similar? How are they different? ✔0807.5.4

INTERPRETING GRAPHICS

Germinate means "to sprout," or "grow." The graph below shows percentages of seed germination for different seed companies. Use the graph below to answer the questions that follow.

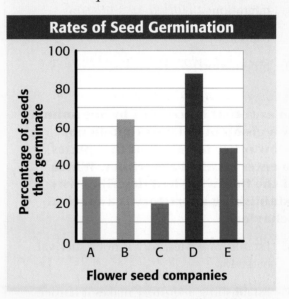

Rates of Seed Germination

Percentage of seeds that germinate

Flower seed companies

21 Which seed company had the highest percentage of seed germination? the lowest percentage of seed germination?

22 If Elaine wants to buy seeds that had a germination percentage higher than 60%, which seed companies would she buy seeds from? Why might Elaine want to buy seeds that have a higher percentage of germination?

TN SPI 0807.5.2 Analyze structural, behavioral, and physiological adaptations to predict which populations are likely to survive in a particular environment.

SPI 0807.5.3 Analyze data on levels of variation within a population to make predictions about survival under particular environmental conditions.

GLE 0807.5.3 Analyze how structural, behavioral, and physiological adaptations within a population enable it to survive in a given environment.

Multiple Choice

1. **During the winter season, animals travel to warmer places to find food, water, or safe nesting grounds. What is this seasonal behavior called?**

   A. estivation

   B. migration

   C. courtship

   D. hibernation

2. **An area that is occupied by one animal or a group of animals that do not allow other members of the species to enter is called a territory. Which of the following best describes why establishing a territory is a survival behavior?**

   A. Establishing a territory is not a survival behavior.

   B. Establishing a territory makes it harder for an animal to find a mate.

   C. Establishing a territory decreases the genetic variation of a population.

   D. Establishing a territory makes it easier for an animal to raise young and find food.

3. **An alligator is camouflaged by duckweed in a swamp. How is this an example of an adaptation?**

   A. This is not an example of an adaptation.

   B. The duckweed helps the alligator swim faster.

   C. The alligator can blend in with the duckweed and sneak up on its prey.

   D. The duckweed keeps the alligator cool during the summer.

4. **A variety of behaviors help animals survive. Some behaviors are innate. An innate behavior is inherited through genes. Some behavior is learned. A learned behavior is a type of behavior that is learned through observation. Which one of the following is an example of learned behavior?**

   A. the use of tools by chimpanzees

   B. the ability of humans to walk

   C. the courtship behavior of birds

   D. the tendency of puppies to chew

5. **Which of the following structural adaptations would be best suited for an animal living in the tree canopies of a rain forest?**

   A. short stiff tail, dog-like paws, short limbs

   B. long grasping tail, paws that can grasp, long limbs

   C. short stiff tail, paws that can grasp, short limbs

   D. long grasping tail, dog-like paws, long limbs

6. **Forms of reproduction are physiological adaptations. An animal that reproduces by external fertilization is more likely to survive in which of the following environments?**

   A. Chattanooga River basin

   B. Alaskan tundra

   C. Sonoran desert

   D. Nebraska prairie

7. **Which of the following adaptations are best suited for survival in a mild environment with predators?**

   A. hibernation

   B. estivation

   C. courtship

   D. defensive behavior

Open Response

8. **The whorled sunflower (*Helianthus verticillatus*) is a rare, giant wild sunflower. It was originally discovered in Tennessee in the late 1800s, but disappeared until specimens from an isolated stand in a Georgia wetland were reintroduced to a Tennessee wetland in the 1990s. Although the population in Georgia has several thousand plants, researchers in Tennessee recently discovered that there were only 20 to 40 genetic individuals in this population. The remaining plants are genetically identical to the plants surrounding them. Based on what you know about genetic variation in a population and plant reproduction, predict whether or not this sunflower might be able to survive in non-wetland environments. Explain your answer.**

9. **In sexual reproduction, offspring are formed when genetic information from more than one parent combines. The diagram below shows how genes mix through three generations. The child inherited genetic information from both of its parents. The child's parents inherited genetic information from their parents.**

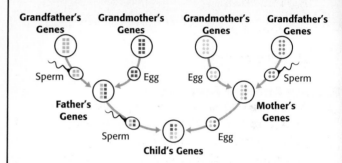

INHERITING GENES

What is an advantage of genetic variation? If the size of a population decreases drastically, how might this affect the genetic variation within a population?

Science in Action

Scientific Discoveries

Finding Another Function

T/E Has a doctor ever prescribed an antibiotic when you were sick? Antibiotics are chemicals that kill bacteria. One of the ways that antibiotics kill bacteria is by damaging its DNA. But, just as insects can become resistant to insecticides, bacteria can become resistant to antibiotics. How can bacteria become resistant to antibiotics? One way is with the help of a protein called RecA. Bacteria produce RecA, and this allows bacteria to develop new genes that may make the bacteria resistant to the antibiotic. In this case, RecA has an undesirable function. However, RecA can be an important tool in genetic engineering. Scientists can use RecA to join large pieces of DNA. This is useful because it allows scientists to study how different pieces of DNA function when they are together. **TN** GLE 0807.T/E.1

Weird Science

What's That Smell?

Imagine that you are walking through a tropical rain forest. You're surrounded by green—green leaves, green vines, and green trees. You can hear monkeys and birds calling to each other. When you touch the plants nearby, they are wet from a recent rain shower. But what's that horrible smell? You don't see any rotting garbage around, but you do see a huge flower spike. As you get closer, the smell gets stronger. Then, you realize the flower is what smells so bad! The flower is called a *corpse flower*. The corpse flower is just one plant that uses bad odors to attract pollinators.

Math ACTIVITY

Scientists measure the mass of proteins in Daltons (Da) because a protein has a very small mass. One Dalton is equal to 1.660×10^{-24} grams. If the RecA protein in bacteria has a mass of 37,842 Da, what is its mass in grams?

Social Studies ACTIVITY

The corpse flower is native to Sumatra, one of the islands of Indonesia. Find Sumatra on a map or globe. What type of climate does Sumatra have? What type of forests would you expect to find in Sumatra? Based on your discoveries, do you think that the corpse flower would survive in Tennessee? ✔0807.5.3

George Archibald

Dancing with Cranes Imagine a man flapping his arms in a dance with a whooping crane. Does this sound funny? When Dr. George Archibald danced with a crane named Tex, he wasn't joking around. To help this endangered species survive, Archibald wanted cranes to mate in captivity so that he could release cranes into the wild. But the captive cranes wouldn't do their courtship dance. Archibald's cranes had imprinted on the humans that raised them. *Imprinting* is a process in which birds learn to recognize their species by looking at their parents. The birds saw humans as their own species, and could only reproduce if a human did the courtship dance. So, Archibald decided to dance. His plan worked! After some time, Tex hatched a baby crane.

After that, Archibald found a way to help the captive cranes imprint on other cranes. He and his staff now feed baby cranes with hand puppets that look like crane heads. They play recordings of real crane sounds for the young cranes. They even wear crane suits when they are near older birds. These cranes are happy to do their courtship dance with each other instead of with Archibald.

Language Arts ACTiViTY

WRITING SKILL Imagine that you are a wildlife biologist taking care of captive cranes. Write a journal entry describing your daily responsibilities and observations of the cranes that are under your care.

To learn more about these Science in Action topics, visit go.hrw.com and type in the keyword **HT6FSRFF.**

Current Science

Check out Current Science® articles related to this chapter by visiting go.hrw.com. Just type in the keyword **HL5CS14.**

Population Changes

The Big Idea
Natural selection explains how populations change over time.

TN Tennessee Science Standards

Embedded Inquiry

GLE 0807.Inq.1 Design and conduct open-ended scientific investigations.
GLE 0807.Inq.2 Use appropriate tools and techniques to gather, organize, analyze, and interpret data. **GLE 0807.Inq.3** Synthesize information to determine cause and effect relationships between evidence and explanations. **GLE 0807.Inq.4** Recognize possible sources of bias and error, alternative explanations, and questions for further exploration.
GLE 0807.Inq.5 Communicate scientific understanding using descriptions, explanations, and models. ✔**0807.Inq.1** Design and conduct an open-ended scientific investigation to answer a question that includes a control and appropriate variables. ✔**0807.Inq.2** Identify tools and techniques needed to gather, organize, analyze, and interpret data collected from a moderately complex scientific investigation. ✔**0807.Inq.3** Use evidence from a dataset to determine cause and effect relationships that explain a phenomenon. ✔**0807.Inq.4** Review an experimental design to determine possible sources of bias or error, state alternative explanations, and identify questions for further investigation. ✔**0807.Inq.5** Design a method to explain the results of an investigation using descriptions, explanations, or models.

Embedded Technology and Engineering

GLE 0807.T/E.1 Explore how technology responds to social, political, and economic needs. **GLE 0807.T/E.3** Compare the intended benefits with the unintended consequences of a new technology. ✔**0807.T/E.3** Explore how the unintended consequences of new technologies can impact society.

Life Science

GLE 0807.5.3 Analyze how structural, behavioral, and physiological adaptations within a population enable it to survive in a given environment.
GLE 0807.5.4 Explain why variation within a population can enhance the chances for group survival. **GLE 0807.5.6** Investigate fossils in sedimentary rock layers to gather evidence of changing life forms. ✔**0807.5.3** Compare and contrast the ability of an organism to survive under different environmental conditions.
✔**0807.5.4** Collect and analyze data relating to variation within a population of organisms. ✔**0807.5.7** Create a timeline that illustrates the relative ages of fossils in sedimentary rock layers.

PRE-READING ACTIVITY

Graphic Organizer **Concept Map** Before you read the chapter, create the graphic organizer entitled "Concept Map" described in the **Study Skills** section of the Appendix. As you read the chapter, fill in the concept map with details about change over time and natural selection.

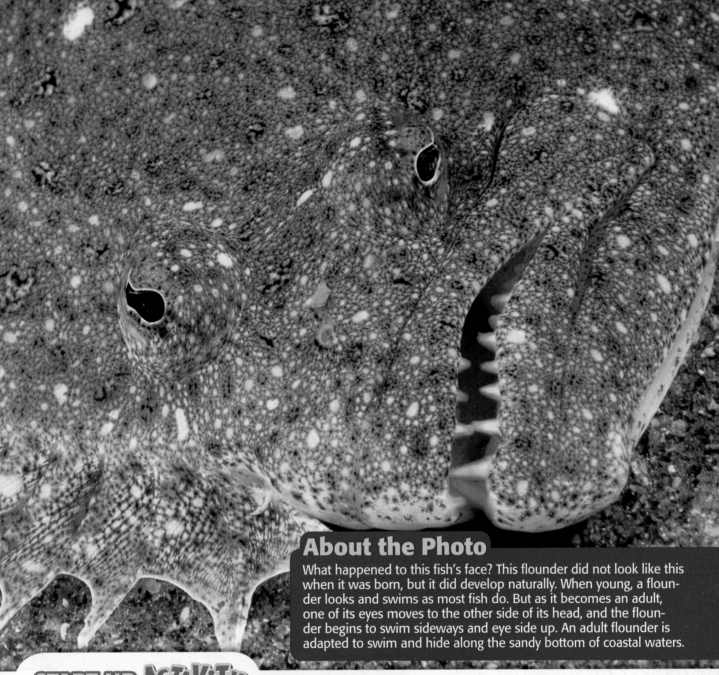

START-UP ACTiViTy

TN GLE 0807.Inq.2, GLE 0807.Inq.4, GLE 0807.5.3

Out of Sight, Out of Mind

In this activity, you will see how traits can affect the success of an organism in a particular environment.

Procedure

1. Count out **25 colored marshmallows** and **25 white marshmallows.**

2. Ask your partner to look away while you spread the marshmallows out on a **white cloth.** Do not make a pattern with the marshmallows. Now, ask your partner to turn around and pick the first marshmallow that he or she sees.

3. Repeat step 2 ten times.

Analysis

1. How many white marshmallows did your partner pick? How many colored marshmallows did he or she pick?

2. What did the marshmallows and the cloth represent in your investigation? What effect did the color of the cloth have? ✔0807.5.3

3. When an organism blends into its environment, the organism is *camouflaged*. How does this activity model camouflaged organisms in the wild? What are some weaknesses of this model? ✔0807.Inq.4, ✔0807.5.4

Change over Time

If you described a snake, you might say that a snake has a long, narrow body, has a forked tongue, and hisses. But what color skin would you say that a snake has?

Once you start to think about snakes, you realize that snakes differ in many ways. These differences set one kind of snake apart from another. The snakes in **Figures 1, 2,** and **3** look different from each other, yet they all can live in the same area.

Differences Between Organisms

As you can see, each snake has different characteristics that might help the snake survive. A characteristic that helps an organism survive and reproduce in its environment is called an **adaptation.** Some adaptations, such as a long neck or striped fur, are physical. Other adaptations are behaviors that help an organism find food, protect itself, or reproduce.

Living things that have the same characteristics may be members of the same species. A **species** is a group of organisms that can mate with one another to produce fertile offspring. For example, all eastern diamondback rattlesnakes are members of the same species. Therefore, eastern diamondback rattlesnakes can mate with each other to produce fertile eastern diamondback rattlesnakes. Groups of individuals of the same species living in the same place make up a *population.*

✓ **Reading Check** How can you tell whether organisms are members of the same species?

What You Will Learn

● Identify two kinds of evidence that show that organisms have changed over time.

● Identify how the fossil record shows that changes in the kinds of organisms in the environment have been occurring over time.

● Describe one pathway through which a modern whale could have arisen from an ancient mammal.

● Explain how comparing organisms can provide evidence that they have ancestors in common.

Vocabulary

adaptation   fossil

species   fossil record

READING STRATEGY

Reading Organizer Read this section silently. In pairs, take turns summarizing the material. Stop to discuss ideas that seem confusing.

TN **GLE 0807.Inq.5** Communicate scientific understanding using descriptions, explanations, and models.

GLE 0807.5.6 Investigate fossils in sedimentary rock layers to gather evidence of changing life forms.

Figure 2 Although the scarlet king snake is not venomous, its bright coloring warns predators to stay away.

Figure 3 The rough green snake is hard to notice because it blends into vines, bushes, and trees.

Figure 1 The eastern diamondback rattlesnake uses its venom to kill prey and uses its rattle to ward off predators.

Do Species Change over Time?

In a single square mile of rain forest, there may be dozens of species of frogs. Across Earth, there are millions of different species of organisms. The species that live on Earth today range from single-celled bacteria, which lack cell nuclei, to multicellular fungi, plants, and animals. Have these species always existed on Earth?

Scientists think that Earth has changed a great deal during its history and that living things have changed, too. Scientists estimate that the planet is 4.6 billion years old. Since life first appeared on Earth, many species have died out, and many new species have appeared. **Figure 4** shows some of the species that have existed during Earth's history.

Scientists observe that species have changed over time. They also observe that the inherited characteristics in populations change over time. Scientists think that as populations change over time, new species form. Thus, newer species descend from older species.

adaptation a characteristic that improves an individual's ability to survive and reproduce in a particular environment

species a group of organisms that are closely related and can mate to produce fertile offspring ◢TN▼ *VOCAB*

Figure 4 *This diagram shows some of the many kinds of organisms that have lived on Earth since the planet formed 4.6 billion years ago.*

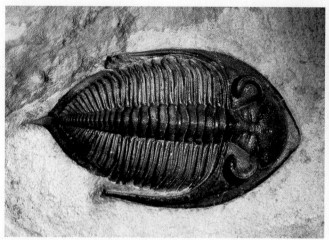

Figure 5 *The fossil on the left is of a trilobite, an ancient aquatic animal. The fossils on the right are of seed ferns.*

fossil the trace or remains of an organism that lived long ago, most commonly preserved in sedimentary rock █TN▶ *VOCAB*

fossil record a historical sequence of life indicated by fossils found in layers of Earth's crust

Evidence of Changes over Time

Evidence that organisms have changed over time is buried within Earth's crust. The layers of Earth's crust are made up of different kinds of rock and soil stacked on top of each other. These layers form when *sediments*, particles of sand, dust, or soil, are carried by wind and water and are deposited in an orderly fashion. Older layers are deposited before newer layers and are buried deeper within Earth.

Fossils

The remains or imprints of once-living organisms found in layers of rock are called **fossils.** Examples of fossils are shown in **Figure 5.** Fossils can be complete organisms, parts of organisms, or just a set of footprints. Fossils usually form when a dead organism is covered by a layer of sediment. Over time, more sediment settles on top of the organism. Minerals in the sediment may seep into the organism and gradually replace the organism with stone. If the organism rots away completely after being covered, it may leave an imprint of itself in the rock.

The Fossil Record

By studying fossils, scientists have made a timeline of life known as the **fossil record.** The fossil record organizes fossils by their estimated ages and physical similarities. Fossils found in newer layers of Earth's crust tend to be similar to present-day organisms. This similarity indicates that the fossilized organisms were close relatives of present-day organisms. Fossils from older layers are less similar to present-day organisms than fossils from newer layers are. The older fossils are of earlier life-forms, which may not exist anymore. Comparing organisms in the fossil record can reveal how organisms have changed over time.

✓ **Reading Check** What is the fossil record?

Evidence of Ancestry

The fossil record provides evidence about the order in which species have existed. Scientists observe that all living organisms have characteristics in common and inherit characteristics in similar ways. So, scientists think that all living species descended from common ancestors. Evidence of common ancestors can be found in fossils and in living organisms.

Drawing Connections

Scientists examine the fossil record to figure out the relationships between extinct and living organisms. Scientists draw models, such as the one shown in **Figure 6,** that illustrate their hypotheses. The short horizontal line at the top left in the diagram represents a species that lived in the past. Each branch in the diagram represents a group of organisms that descended from that species.

Scientists think that whales and some types of hoofed mammals have a common ancestor, as **Figure 6** shows. This ancestor was probably a land mammal that lived between 50 million and 70 million years ago. The fossil record shows that during this time period, the dinosaurs died out and a variety of mammals appeared. The first ocean-dwelling mammals appeared about 50 million years ago. Scientists think that all mammal species alive today arose from common ancestors.

Scientists have named and described hundreds of thousands of living and ancient species. Scientists use information about these species to sketch out a "tree of life" that includes all known organisms. But scientists know that their information is incomplete. For example, parts of Earth's history lack a fossil record. In fact, fossils are rare because specific conditions are necessary for fossils to form.

Sedimentary Rock Fossils are most often found in sedimentary rock. Most *sedimentary rock* forms when rock is broken into sediment by wind, water, and other means. Wind and water move the sediment around and deposit it. Over time, layers of sediment form. Lower layers are compressed and changed into rock. Find out if your area has any sedimentary rocks that contain fossils. Also, find out whether the fossils have provided scientists any information about the plants and animals that lived in your area millions of years ago. Mark the location of such rocks and fossils on a copy of a local map.

Figure 6 *This diagram is a model of the proposed relationships between ancient and modern mammals that have characteristics similar to the characteristics of whales.*

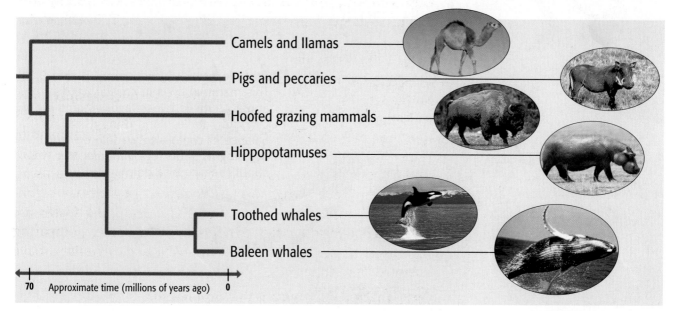

| Camels and llamas |
| Pigs and peccaries |
| Hoofed grazing mammals |
| Hippopotamuses |
| Toothed whales |
| Baleen whales |

70   Approximate time (millions of years ago)   0

Examining Organisms

Examining an organism carefully can give scientists clues about its ancestors. For example, whales seem similar to fish. But unlike fish, whales breathe air, give birth to live young, and produce milk. These traits show that whales are *mammals*. Thus, scientists think that whales arose from ancient mammals.

Case Study: Origins of the Modern Whale

Scientists think that the ancient ancestor of whales was probably a mammal that lived on land and that could run on four legs. A more recent ancestor was probably a mammal that spent time both on land and in water. Comparisons between modern whales and a large number of fossils have supported this hypothesis. **Figure 7** illustrates some of this evidence.

✓ Reading Check What evidence supports the hypothesis that the ancient ancestor of whales was a land mammal?

Figure 7   Evidence of Whale Origins

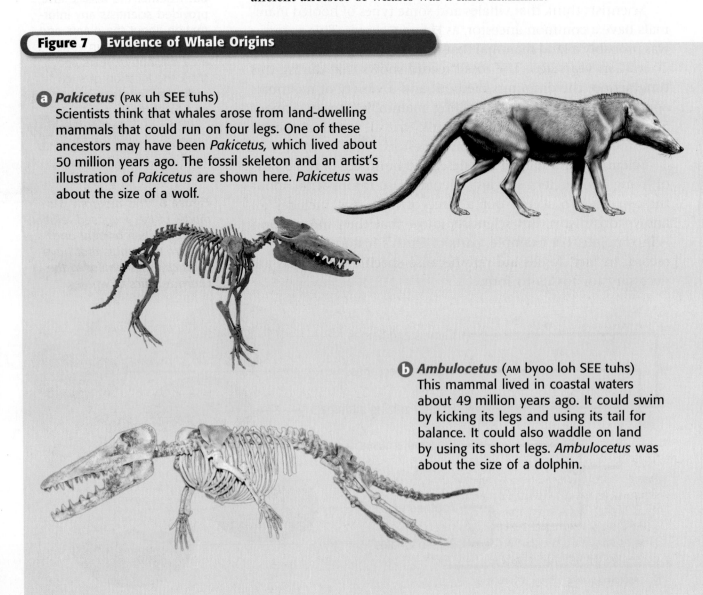

ⓐ *Pakicetus* (PAK uh SEE tuhs)
Scientists think that whales arose from land-dwelling mammals that could run on four legs. One of these ancestors may have been *Pakicetus,* which lived about 50 million years ago. The fossil skeleton and an artist's illustration of *Pakicetus* are shown here. *Pakicetus* was about the size of a wolf.

ⓑ *Ambulocetus* (AM byoo loh SEE tuhs)
This mammal lived in coastal waters about 49 million years ago. It could swim by kicking its legs and using its tail for balance. It could also waddle on land by using its short legs. *Ambulocetus* was about the size of a dolphin.

Walking Whales

The organisms in **Figure 7** form a sequence between ancient four-legged mammals and modern whales. Several pieces of evidence indicate that these species are related by ancestry. Each species shared some traits with an earlier species. However, some species had new traits that were shared with later species. Yet each species had traits that allowed it to survive in a particular time and place in Earth's history.

Further evidence can be found inside the bodies of living whales. For example, although modern whales do not have hind limbs, inside their bodies are tiny hip bones, as shown in **Figure 7**. Scientists think that these hip bones were inherited from the whales' four-legged ancestors. Scientists often look at this kind of evidence when trying to determine the relationships between organisms.

The Weight of Whales

Whales are the largest animals ever known on Earth. One reason that whales can grow so large is that they live in water, which supports their weight in a way that their bones could not. The blue whale—the largest type of whale in existence—is about 24 m long and has a mass of about 99,800 kg. Convert these measurements into feet and pounds, and round to whole numbers.

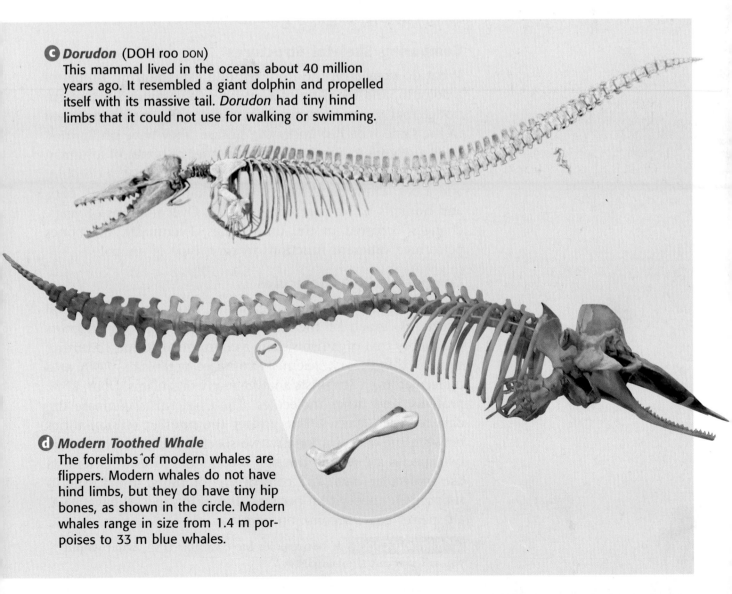

ⓒ Dorudon (DOH roo DON)
This mammal lived in the oceans about 40 million years ago. It resembled a giant dolphin and propelled itself with its massive tail. *Dorudon* had tiny hind limbs that it could not use for walking or swimming.

ⓓ Modern Toothed Whale
The forelimbs of modern whales are flippers. Modern whales do not have hind limbs, but they do have tiny hip bones, as shown in the circle. Modern whales range in size from 1.4 m porpoises to 33 m blue whales.

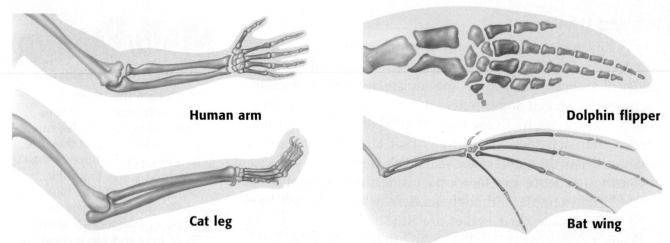

Human arm

Dolphin flipper

Cat leg

Bat wing

Figure 8 *The bones in the front limbs of these organisms are similar. Similar bones are shown in the same color. These limbs are not shown to scale.*

Comparing Organisms

Evidence that groups of organisms have common ancestry can be found by comparing the groups' DNA. Because every organism inherits DNA, every organism inherits the traits determined by DNA. Organisms contain evidence that populations and species undergo changes in traits and DNA over time.

Comparing Skeletal Structures

What do your arm, the front leg of a cat, the front flipper of a dolphin, and the wing of a bat have in common? You might notice that these structures do not look alike and are not used in the same way. But under the surface, they have similarities. Look at **Figure 8.** The structure and order of bones of a human arm are similar to those of the front limbs of a cat, a dolphin, and a bat. These similarities suggest that cats, dolphins, bats, and humans had a common ancestor. Over millions of years, changes occurred in the limb bones. Eventually, the bones performed different functions in each type of animal.

Comparing DNA Molecules

When scientists compare organisms' traits, such as skeletal structures, much of the information that they get supports the theory that organisms share a common ancestor. To further support this theory, scientists compare organisms' DNA at a molecular level. Scientists analyze many organisms' DNA, RNA, proteins, and other molecules. Then, scientists compare the data for each species. The greater the number of similarities between the data sets for any two species, the more closely the two species are related through a common ancestor. Scientists use molecular data, the comparison of traits, and fossils to support the theory that because all existing species have DNA, all species share a common ancestor.

✓ Reading Check If two species have similar DNA, what would you infer about their ancestry?

TN ⬤ GLE 0807.Inq.5, GLE 0807.5.6

Summary

⬤ The fossil record provides evidence that changes in the kinds of organisms in the environment have been occurring over time.

⬤ Evidence that organisms change over time can be found by comparing living organisms to each other. Such comparisons provide evidence of common ancestry.

⬤ Scientists think that modern whales arose from an ancient, land-dwelling mammal ancestor. Fossil organisms that support this hypothesis have been found.

⬤ Comparing DNA and inherited traits provides evidence of common ancestry among living organisms. The traits and DNA of species that have a common ancestor are more similar to each other than they are to those of distantly related species.

Using Key Terms

1. In your own words, write a definition for the term *adaptation*.

Understanding Key Ideas

2. How does the fossil record show that species have changed over time?

3. What evidence do fossils provide about the ancestors of whales?

4. Fossils are the remains or imprints of once-living organisms found in the layers of rock. What can fossils reveal about organisms in an environment?
   a. how plants supported an environment
   b. how plants and animals in an environment interacted
   c. how organisms defended themselves
   d. how organisms changed over time

5. A house cat and a tiger have similar physical characteristics. In addition, by using current DNA technology, scientists have learned that the DNA of a house cat is similar to the DNA of a tiger. Describe how DNA technology can be used to support the theory that all species share a common ancestor.

Critical Thinking

6. **Making Comparisons** Without using the examples provided in the text, name some ways in which whales differ from fishes.

7. **Forming Hypotheses** Is a person's DNA likely to be more similar to the DNA of his or her biological parents or to the DNA of one of his or her first cousins? Explain your answer.

Interpreting Graphics

8. The photograph below shows the layers of sedimentary rock exposed during the construction of a road. Imagine that a species that lived 200 million years ago is found in layer **b.** Would the species' ancestor, which lived 250 million years ago, most likely be found in layer **a** or in layer **c**? Estimate a reasonable age of the fossils that might be found in the other layer. Then create a timeline to illustrate the relative age of the fossils that would be found in these layers of rock. ✔0807.5.7

Internet Resources

For a variety of links related to this chapter, go to www.scilinks.org

Topic: Species and Adaptation; Fossil Record

SciLinks code: HSM1433; HSM0615

SECTION 2

How Do Population Changes Happen?

What You Will Learn

- Describe how some finch species of the Galápagos Islands developed adaptations in response to their environment.
- Describe the four parts of Charles Darwin's process of natural selection.
- Explain how variation in each species can occur.

Vocabulary

trait
selective breeding
natural selection

READING STRATEGY

Brainstorming The key idea of this section is natural selection. Brainstorm words and phrases related to natural selection.

TN **GLE 0807.Inq.2** Use appropriate tools and techniques to gather, organize, analyze, and interpret data.

GLE 0807.Inq.3 Synthesize information to determine cause and effect relationships between evidence and explanations.

GLE 0807.Inq.5 Communicate scientific understanding using descriptions, explanations, and models.

GLE 0807.5.3 Analyze how structural, behavioral, and physiological adaptations within a population enable it to survive in a given environment.

GLE 0807.5.4 Explain why variation within a population can enhance the chances for group survival.

Imagine that you are a scientist in the 1800s. Fossils of some very strange animals have been found. And fossils of familiar animals have been found where you would least expect them. How did seashells end up on mountaintops?

In the 1800s, geologists began to realize that Earth is much older than anyone had previously thought. Evidence showed that gradual processes had changed Earth's surface over millions of years. Some scientists saw evidence of population changes in the fossil record. However, no one had been able to explain *how* change happens—until Charles Darwin.

Charles Darwin

In 1831, 21-year-old Charles Darwin, shown in **Figure 1,** graduated from college. Like many young people just out of college, Darwin didn't know what he wanted to do with his life. His father wanted him to become a doctor, but seeing blood made Darwin sick. Although he eventually earned a degree in theology, Darwin was most interested in the study of plants and animals.

So, Darwin signed on for a five-year voyage around the world. He served as the *naturalist*—a scientist who studies nature—on the HMS *Beagle,* a British ship similar to the ship in **Figure 2.** During the trip, Darwin made observations that helped him form a theory about how change happens.

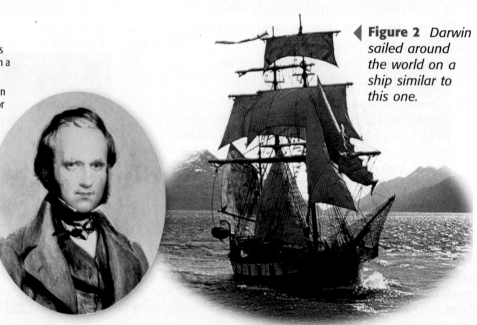

Figure 2 *Darwin sailed around the world on a ship similar to this one.*

Figure 1 *Charles Darwin wanted to understand the natural world.*

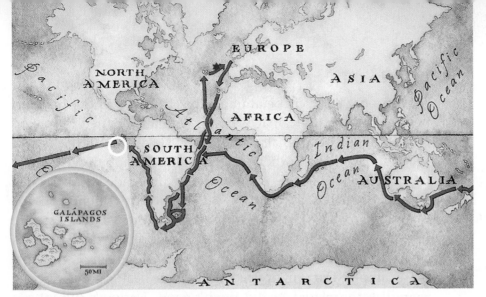

Figure 3 *The course of the HMS Beagle is shown by the red line. The journey began and ended in England.*

Darwin's Excellent Adventure

The *Beagle*'s journey is charted in **Figure 3.** Along the way, Darwin collected thousands of plant and animal samples. He kept careful notes of his observations. One interesting place that the ship visited was the Galápagos Islands. These islands are found 965 km (600 mi) west of Ecuador, a country in South America.

✔ Reading Check Where are the Galápagos Islands?

Darwin's Finches

Darwin noticed that the animals and plants on the Galápagos Islands were a lot like those in Ecuador, which is in South America. But they were not identical. For example, the finches on the Galápagos Islands differed slightly from the finches in Ecuador. And the finches on each island differed from the finches on the other islands. As **Figure 4** shows, the beak of each finch is adapted to the way the bird usually gets food.

Figure 4 Some Finches of the Galápagos Islands

The **large ground finch** has a wide, strong beak that it uses to crack open big, hard seeds. This beak works like a nutcracker.

The **cactus finch** has a tough beak that it uses for eating cactus parts and insects. This beak works like a pair of needle-nose pliers.

The **warbler finch** has a small, narrow beak that it uses to catch small insects. This beak works like a pair of tweezers.

Darwin's Thinking

Darwin puzzled over the animals that he had seen on his journey, including the Galápagos Island animals. He tried to explain why some of the animals, such as the Galápagos finches, were very similar to each other yet had unique adaptations. Darwin hypothesized that the island finches descended from South American finches. He proposed that the first finches on the islands were blown there from South America by a storm. And he suggested that over many generations, the finches developed adaptations for the various island environments. For example, Darwin noticed that finch beak size and shape were directly related to the finch's food. Darwin's hypothesis about the Galápagos finches explains his observations.

✔ **Reading Check** What structural change occurred among the finches that helped them adapt to their environment?

Ideas About Breeding

In Darwin's time, farmers and breeders had produced many kinds of farm animals and plants. These plants and animals had traits that were desired by the farmers and breeders. A **trait** is a form of a hereditary characteristic. For example, redness is a trait, and fruit color is the corresponding characteristic. The practice by which humans select plants or animals for breeding based on desired traits is **selective breeding.** Most pets, such as the dogs in **Figure 5,** have been bred for various desired traits.

trait a form of a genetically determined characteristic

selective breeding the human practice of breeding animals or plants that have certain desired traits

Figure 5 Over the past 12,000 years, dogs have been selectively bred to produce more than 150 breeds.

TN GLE 0807.Inq.3, GLE 0807.Inq.5

Population Growth Vs. Food Supply

1. Get an **egg carton** for one dozen eggs and a **teaspoon of uncooked rice.** Use a **marker** to label one row of the carton "Food supply." Then, label the second row "Human population."

2. In the "Food supply" row, place one grain of rice in the first cup. Place two grains in the second cup and three grains in the third cup. In each subsequent cup in the row, place one more grain than you placed in the previous cup. Imagine that each grain represents enough food for one person's lifetime.

3. In the "Human population" row, place one grain in the first cup, two in the second cup, and four in the third cup. In each subsequent cup, place twice as many grains as you placed in the previous cup. Each grain represents one person.

4. How many "lifetimes" of food are in the sixth cup? How many "people" are in the sixth cup? If this pattern continued, what would happen? ✔0807.Inq. 3

5. Describe how the pattern of change in the food supply differs from the pattern of change in the human population. Explain how the patterns relate to Malthus's hypothesis. ✔0807.Inq. 5

Ideas About Population

During Darwin's time, Thomas Malthus wrote *An Essay on the Principle of Population,* a famous book. Malthus noted that humans have the potential to reproduce rapidly. He warned that food supplies could not support unlimited population growth. **Figure 6** shows this relationship. However, Malthus pointed out that human populations are limited by problems such as starvation and disease.

After reading Malthus's work, Darwin realized that any species can produce many offspring. He also knew that the populations of all species are limited by starvation, disease, competition, and predation. Only a limited number of individuals live long enough to reproduce. Thus, the survivors are special. Darwin reasoned that the offspring of the survivors inherit traits that help the offspring survive in their environment.

✔ **Reading Check** Why do only a limited number of individuals of a species live long enough to reproduce?

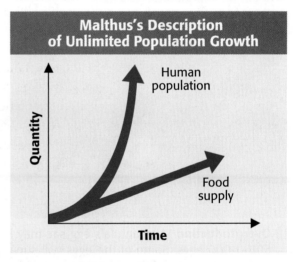

Figure 6 *Malthus thought that the human population could increase more quickly than the food supply. Such an increase would result in a worldwide food shortage.*

Ideas About Earth's History

Darwin had begun to think that species could slowly change over time. But most geologists at the time did not think that Earth was old enough to allow for slow changes. Darwin learned new ideas from *Principles of Geology,* a book by Charles Lyell. This book presented evidence that Earth had formed by natural processes over a long period of time. It became clear to Darwin that Earth was much older than anyone had imagined.

Darwin's Theory of Natural Selection

natural selection the process by which individuals that are better adapted to their environment survive and reproduce more successfully than less well adapted individuals do

After his voyage on the HMS *Beagle*, Darwin privately struggled with his ideas for about 20 years. Then, in 1858, Darwin received a letter from a naturalist named Alfred Russel Wallace. Wallace had arrived at the same ideas about change over time that Darwin had. In 1859, Darwin published a famous book called *On the Origin of Species by Means of Natural Selection*. In his book, Darwin proposed the theory that change in populations happens through *natural selection*. **Natural selection** is the process by which organisms that are better adapted to their environment survive and reproduce more successfully than less well adapted organisms do. The process has four parts and is explained in **Figure 7.**

✓ **Reading Check** What is natural selection?

Figure 7 **Four Parts of Natural Selection**

❶ **Overproduction** A tarantula's egg sac may hold 500–1,000 eggs. Some of the eggs will survive and develop into adult spiders. Some will not.

❷ **Inherited Variation** Every individual has its own combination of traits. Each tarantula is similar but not identical to its parents.

❸ **Struggle to Survive** Some tarantulas may be caught by predators, such as this wasp. Other tarantulas may starve or get a disease. Only some of the tarantulas will survive to adulthood.

❹ **Successful Reproduction** The tarantulas that are best adapted to their environment are likely to have many offspring that survive.

Genetics and Inherited Traits

Darwin knew that organisms inherit traits, but not *how* they inherit traits. He also knew that there is great variation among organisms, but not *how* that variation occurs. Today, scientists know that variation happens as a result of the exchange of genetic information as it is passed from parent to offspring. Some genes make an organism more likely to survive to reproduce. The process called *selection* happens when only organisms that carry these genes can survive to reproduce. New fossil discoveries and new information about genes add to scientists' understanding of natural selection and change over time.

Reading Check How does variation in a species happen?

SECTION
Review

TN GLE 0807.5.3, GLE 0807.5.4

Summary

- Finch species of the Galápagos Islands developed various adaptations in response to their environment.

- Natural selection is the process by which organisms that are better adapted to their environment are more likely to survive.

- The four parts of Darwin's theory of natural selection include overproduction, inherited variation, competition for resources, and successful reproduction.

- Variation in each species is due to the exchange of genetic information as it is passed from parent to offspring.

Using Key Terms

1. In your own words, write a definition for the term *trait*.

Understanding Key Ideas

2. Describe Darwin's observations about the species on the Galápagos Islands.

3. Describe the four parts of Darwin's theory of natural selection.

4. What knowledge that modern scientists now use to explain how variation occurs did Darwin lack?

5. The beak of the large ground finch of the Galápagos Islands is adapted to the way that the finch usually gets food. The beak is wide and strong. Which of the following is **most** likely the finch's main food source?

   a. small insects

   b. big, hard seeds

   c. juicy cactus parts

   d. small freshwater fish

Math Skills

6. In a sample of 80 beetles, 50 beetles had 4 spots each, and the rest had 6 spots each. What was the average number of spots per beetle?

Critical Thinking

7. **Identifying Relationships** Summarize Malthus's ideas about population. How did Darwin relate Malthus's ideas to the inheritance of survival characteristics?

8. **Predicting Consequences** Suppose that an island in the Pacific Ocean was recently formed by a volcano. Over the next million years, how might species on this island adapt?

9. **Making Hypotheses** The beak of the large ground finch of the Galápagos Islands is wide and strong, an adaptation to the finch's diet. How might this adaptation affect a finch's ability to survive if the finch's main source of food were to die out? ✔0807.5.3

Natural Selection in Action

Have you ever had to take an antibiotic medicine? The antibiotic is supposed to kill bacteria. But not all bacteria are killed by the antibiotic. Do you know why?

Through natural selection, a population of bacteria might adapt so that the bacteria survive antibiotic treatment. The process works as follows: Most of the bacteria in the population are killed by the antibiotic. But a few of the bacteria have an adaptation that makes them naturally *resistant to,* or not killed by, the antibiotic. These few bacteria survive antibiotic treatment, continue to reproduce, and pass the adaptation to their offspring. After several generations, almost all of the bacteria in the population carry the adaptation of antibiotic resistance.

Changes in Populations

The theory of natural selection explains how a population changes in response to its environment. Through ongoing natural selection, a population adapts to its environment. Well-adapted individuals will likely survive and reproduce.

Adaptation to Hunting

Changes in populations can occur when a new force affects the survival of individuals in the population. Scientists think that hunting in Uganda is affecting Uganda's elephant population. In 1930, about 99% of the male elephants in one area had tusks. Only 1% of the male elephants were born tuskless. Today, as many as 15% of the area's male elephants lack tusks. What happened?

Figure 1 shows a tusked male African elephant. Because ivory is very valuable, elephants are hunted for their tusks. So, fewer tusked elephants survive to reproduce, and more tuskless elephants survive. Tuskless elephants pass the tuskless trait to their offspring.

TN *Standards Check* How is the tuskless trait a survival characteristic for some elephants? ✔0807.5.3

Figure 1 *The ivory tusks of African elephants are very valuable. Some elephants are born without tusks.*

Figure 2 Natural Selection of Insecticide Resistance

1 An insecticide kills all but a few of the insects in a population. The survivors have genes that make them resistant to the insecticide.

2 The survivors then reproduce, passing the insecticide-resistance genes to their offspring.

3 After several generations, most of the population of insects is made up of individuals that have the insecticide-resistance genes.

4 Now, the insecticide kills only a few of the insects. Most of the insects survive because they are resistant to the insecticide.

Insecticide Resistance

To control insect pests, many people use insecticides, chemicals that kill insects. Sometimes, a few insects in a population are resistant to the chemical. These insects survive insecticide treatment and pass the resistance trait to their offspring. When this occurs, people often switch to a different insecticide. **Figure 2** shows how an insect population becomes resistant to an insecticide. More than 500 kinds of insects are resistant to some insecticides. Often, insect populations become resistant because the insects produce many offspring and have a short generation time. **Generation time** is the average time between one generation and the next.

TN *Standards Check* **Why does an insect population become resistant to an insecticide?** ✔0807.5.3

Competition for Mates

Survival of individuals does not guarantee survival of a species. For a species to survive, its members must reproduce. Natural selection works based on reproduction. For organisms that reproduce sexually, competition for mates can select for adaptations. For example, in many bird species, females prefer to mate with colorful males. So, colorful males have more offspring than noncolorful males do.

TN GLE 0807.T/E.1, GLE 0807.T/E.3

CONNECTION TO Engineering

T/E **Insecticide Genetics** Insecticide resistance has become an unintended consequence of agricultural technology. However, many crop pests are sensitive to toxins produced by the bacterium *Bacillus thuringiensis* (Bt). Agricultural scientists are using genetic engineering to insert genes from Bt into crops to make them insect-resistant. Find out if your area has any insect pests (for example, corn borers) that have become resistant to insecticides. Have corn or cotton farmers in your area planted Bt-engineered crops to combat these resistant pests? What might be an unintended consequence of this technology? ✔0807.T/E.3

generation time the period between the birth of one generation and the birth of the next generation

INTERNET ACTIVITY

For another activity related to this chapter, go to go.hrw.com, and type in the keyword **HL5EVTW**.

speciation the formation of new species as a result of change over time

Forming a New Species

Sometimes, drastic changes that can form a new species take place. In the animal kingdom, a *species* is a group of organisms that can mate with each other to produce fertile offspring. A new species may form after a group becomes separated from the original population. This group forms a new population. Over time, the new population adapts to its new environment. Eventually, the new population and the original population differ so greatly that they can no longer mate successfully. The new population may then be considered a new species. The formation of a new species as a result of change over time is called **speciation** (SPEE shee AY shuhn). **Figure 3** shows how new species of Galápagos finches may have formed. Speciation may happen in other ways as well.

Separation

Speciation often begins when a part of a population becomes separated from the rest. The process of separation can happen in several ways. For example, a newly formed canyon, mountain range, or lake can divide a population.

✓ **Reading Check** How can parts of a population become separated?

Figure 3 **The Development of Galápagos Finch Species**

❶ Some finches left the mainland and reached one of the islands (separation).

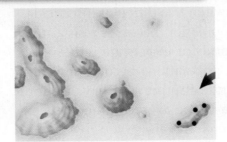

❷ The finches reproduced and adapted to the environment (adaptation).

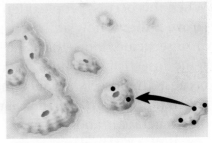

❸ Some finches flew to a second island (separation).

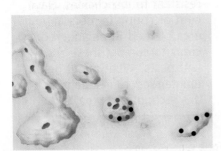

❹ These finches reproduced and adapted to the second island's environment (adaptation).

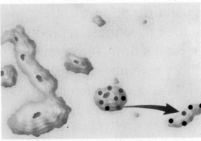

❺ Some finches flew back to the first island but could no longer interbreed with the finches there (division).

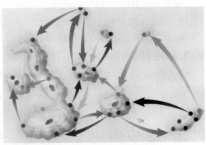

❻ This process may have occurred over and over again as the finches flew to the other islands.

Adaptation

Populations constantly undergo natural selection. After two groups have separated, natural selection continues to act on the groups. Over many generations, the groups may develop different sets of traits. If the environmental conditions for each group differ, the groups' adaptations will differ.

Division

Two separated groups of a population can become very different from each other through natural selection. Even if a geographical barrier is removed and the groups are reunited, they may no longer be able to interbreed. If they cannot interbreed, the two groups are no longer the same species. **Figure 4** shows another way that populations may stop interbreeding. Leopard frogs and pickerel frogs probably have a common ancestor. At some time in the past, a group of these ancestors began to mate at a different time of year.

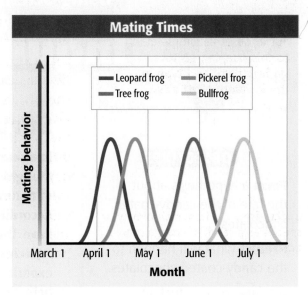

Figure 4 *The leopard frog and the pickerel frog are similar species. However, leopard frogs do not search for mates at the same time of year that pickerel frogs do.*

SECTION
Review

TN GLE 0807.T/E.3, GLE 0807.5.3, GLE 0807.5.4

Summary

● Natural selection can result in an adaptation that helps an organism survive. Two such examples are the tuskless trait in elephants and insecticide resistance in insects.

● Natural selection explains how one species changes into another. Speciation occurs as populations undergo separation, adaptation, and division.

Using Key Terms

1. In your own words, write a definition for the term *generation time.*

Understanding Key Ideas

2. How is insecticide resistance a survival characteristic?

3. Illustrate how new species of Galápagos finches may have formed.

4. In a population of frogs, male frogs croak to scare off predators. However, a few male frogs cannot croak as loudly as other male frogs do. Why are the louder male frogs more likely to survive?
   a. They will attract more mates.
   b. They will catch more insects.
   c. They will jump higher.
   d. They will escape predators.

Math Skills

5. A rusty grain beetle has a generation time of 30 days. How many generations of beetles can be produced in 5 years?

Critical Thinking

6. **Making Comparisons** Suggest an organism other than an insect that might develop an adaptation to human activities.

7. **Predicting Consequences** How might the use of a newly developed insecticide technology impact society? ✔0807.T/E.3

Internet Resources

For a variety of links related to this chapter, go to www.scilinks.org

Topic: Species and Adaptation
SciLinks code: HSM1433

Using Scientific Methods

Inquiry Lab

OBJECTIVES

Form a hypothesis about the fate of the candy-coated chocolates.

Predict what will happen to the candy-coated chocolates.

Design and conduct an experiment to test your hypothesis.

MATERIALS

- chocolates, candy-coated, small, in a variety of colors (about 100)
- items to be determined by the students and approved by the teacher

SAFETY

Survival of the Chocolates

Imagine a world populated with candy, and hold that delicious thought in your head for just a moment. Try to apply the idea of natural selection to a population of candy-coated chocolates. According to the theory of natural selection, individuals who have favorable adaptations are more likely to survive. In the "species" of candy-coated chocolates that you will study in this experiment, the characteristics of individual chocolates may help the chocolates "survive." For example, shell strength (the strength of the candy coating) could be an adaptive advantage. Plan an experiment to find out which characteristics of the chocolates are favorable "adaptations."

Ask a Question

1 What might "survival" mean for a candy-coated chocolate? What are some ways to test which chocolates are the "strongest" or "most fit" for their environment? Also, write down any other questions that you could ask about the "survival" of the chocolates.

Form a Hypothesis

2 Form a hypothesis, and make a prediction. For example, if you chose to study candy color, your prediction might be similar to this one: If the ___ colored shell is the strongest, then fewer of the chocolates with this color of shell will ___ when ___.

TN GLE 0807.Inq.1 Design and conduct open-ended scientific investigations.

GLE 0807.Inq.2 Use appropriate tools and techniques to gather, organize, analyze, and interpret data.

GLE 0807.Inq.4 Recognize possible sources of bias and error, alternative explanations, and questions for further exploration.

GLE 0807.Inq.5 Communicate scientific understanding using descriptions, explanations, and models.

GLE 0807.5.3 Analyze how structural, behavioral and physiological adaptations within a population enable it to survive in a given environment.

Test the Hypothesis

3 Design a procedure to determine which type of candy-coated chocolate is most likely to survive. In your plan, be sure to include materials and tools that you may need to complete this procedure. ✔0807.Inq.1, ✔0807.Inq.2

4 Before you begin, ask your teacher to check your experimental design. Your teacher will supply the candy and will assist you in gathering materials and tools.

5 Record your results in a data table. Be sure to organize your data in a clear and understandable way.

Analyze the Results

1 **Describing Events** Write a report that describes your experiment. Be sure to include tables and graphs of your data. ✔0807.Inq.5, ✔0807.7.5.4

Draw Conclusions

2 **Evaluating Data** In your report, explain how your data either support or do not support your hypothesis. Include possible errors and ways to improve your procedure. ✔0807.Inq.4

Applying Your Data

Can you think of another characteristic that can be tested to determine which type of chocolate is best adapted to survive? Explain your idea, and describe how you might test it. ✔0807.Inq.4

Chapter Review

USING KEY TERMS

Complete each of the following sentences by choosing the correct term from the word bank.

adaptation
species
speciation
selective breeding
natural selection

1 When a single population develops into two populations that can no longer interbreed, ___ has occurred.

2 A group of organisms that can mate with each other to produce fertile offspring is known as a(n) ___.

3 In ___, humans select organisms that have desirable traits that will be passed from one generation to another.

4 A(n) ___ makes an organism better able to survive in its environment.

UNDERSTANDING KEY IDEAS

Multiple Choice

5 Darwin observed variations between individuals within a population, but he did not know how variations occur. Which of the following causes variation in a population? ✔0807.Inq.3, ✔0807.5.4

a. interbreeding
b. differences in food
c. differences in genes
d. selective breeding

6 The fossil record is a historical sequence of life indicated by fossils found in Earth's crust. What information about organisms in an environment can the fossil record provide?

a. how natural selection occurs
b. how organisms in an environment changed over time
c. how selective breeding occurs
d. how genetic resistance occurs

7 Charles Darwin puzzled over the different species of Galápagos finches. He eventually concluded that over time, the finches adapted to various environments on the islands. On which of the following traits did Darwin base his conclusions? ✔0807.5.4

a. eye color
b. flight patterns
c. beak size and shape
d. bone structure of the wings

8 Tarantulas defend themselves by flicking hairs into the eyes of their predators. In a population of tarantulas, a few tarantulas do not have these hairs. Why are the tarantulas that have these hairs more likely to produce offspring than the hairless tarantulas are?

✔0807.Inq.3, ✔0807.5.4

a. Tarantulas that have the hairs will be better able to defend themselves.
b. Tarantulas that have the hairs will blend in with their environment.
c. The egg sacs of tarantulas that have the hairs are larger and produce more offspring.
d. Tarantulas that have the hairs will attract more mates.

Short Answer

9 Identify two ways that organisms can be compared to provide evidence that they arose from a common ancestor.

10 Describe evidence that supports the hypothesis that whales developed from land-dwelling mammals.

11 Why are some animals more likely to survive to adulthood than other animals are? ✔0807.Inq.3, ✔0807.5.3

12 Compare and contrast how natural selection enables a population to survive under different environmental conditions. ✔0807.5.3

13 Compare the intended benefits and the possible unintended consequences of a new pesticide. ✔0807.T/E.3

CRITICAL THINKING

14 Concept Mapping Use the following terms to create a concept map: *struggle to survive, theory, genetic variation, Darwin, overpopulation, natural selection,* and *successful reproduction.*

15 Forming Hypotheses In Australia, most of the mammals are marsupials, which carry their young in pouches after birth. Few kinds of marsupials are found anywhere else in the world. What is a possible explanation for the presence of so many of these mammals in Australia? ✔0807.Inq.3, ✔0807.5.3

16 Analyzing Relationships Geologists have evidence that the continents were once a single giant continent. This giant landform eventually split apart, and the individual continents moved to their current positions. What role might this drifting of continents have played in the formation of new species? ✔0807.Inq.3, ✔0807.5.3

INTERPRETING GRAPHICS

The graph on the left shows the percentage of all births by birth weight. The graph on the right shows the probability of dying at birth by birth weight. Use the graphs to answer the questions that follow.

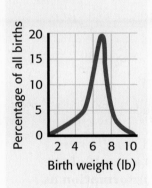

Percentage of All Births (by birth weight in pounds)

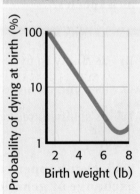

Probability of Dying at Birth (by birth weight in pounds)

17 What is the most common birth weight?

18 At which birth weight is an infant most likely to survive?

19 How do the principles of natural selection help explain why there are more deaths among babies whose birth weights are low than among babies whose birth weights are average? ✔0807.Inq.3

TN **SPI 0807.T/E.3** Distinguish between the intended benefits and the unintended consequences of a new technology.

SPI 0807.5.2 Analyze structural, behavioral, and physiological adaptations to predict which populations are likely to survive in a particular environment.

SPI 0807.5.3 Analyze data on levels of variation within a population to make predictions about survival under particular environmental conditions.

Multiple Choice

1. **A cat's leg, a dolphin's flipper, and a bat's wing contain similar bones. What does this suggest?**

   A. These species developed at the same time.

   B. These structures perform the same function.

   C. These species share a common ancestor.

   D. The cat is the most advanced of these species.

2. **A group of birds becomes separated from its original population. Over a period of time, the new population of birds adapted to its new environment. If this new population returned to the environment it originated from, which of the following would most likely determine its ability to survive as a species?**

   A. its beak size

   B. its ability to fly

   C. its common ancestry

   D. its ability to reproduce

3. **Variation happens as a result of the exchange of genetic information as it is passed from parent to offspring. Which of the following is true about inherited variation?**

   A. Variation can influence separation.

   B. Variation can influence selective breeding.

   C. Variation can influence the resources that are available to an organism.

   D. Variation can influence whether some organisms are more likely to survive to reproduce.

4. **Ahmed had a bronchial infection. His doctor gave him an antibiotic that made him feel better for a week. Then, he got sick again. When Ahmed went back to the doctor he was given a different antibiotic. This time, the infection went away. What survival characteristic explains why the first antibiotic did not cure Ahmed's infection?**

   A. division   C. overproduction

   B. resistance   D. selective breeding

5. **Which of the following is an example of selective breeding?**

   A. Populations of lizards with a certain trait become more numerous after a change in climate.

   B. Farmers allow only sheep that produce the best wool to breed.

   C. A population of bacteria develops resistance to an antibiotic.

   D. Female birds prefer to mate with colorful males rather than noncolorful males.

6. **A farmer uses a new insecticide to treat his crop plants. In the first year, the insecticide kills almost all of the insect pests. In the second year, the insecticide kills few insect pests. Which of the following is an unintended consequence of using the insecticide?**

   A. The farmer will grow crops that are larger in size.

   B. The farmer can raise more kinds of crops.

   C. The farmer will have insecticide-resistant pests on his crops.

   D. The farmer will make more money.

GLE 0807.5.3 Analyze how structural, behavioral, and physiological adaptations within a population enable it to survive in a given environment.

GLE 0807.5.4 Explain why variation within a population can enhance the chances for group survival.

7. There are three species of birds on an island. These three species are shown below. Bird A has a heavy bill for eating big seeds. Bird B has a sharply pointed bill for eating insects. Bird C has a sharp bill for eating insects and small seeds.

Bird A: Large Seed–Eating Bill   **Bird B: Insect-Eating Bill**   **Bird C: Seed-and Insect-Eating Bill**

If the insect populations suddenly disappeared one season, which bird or birds would probably be the least affected that season?

A. Bird A

C. Bird C

B. Bird B

D. Bird A and Bird B

8. The diagram below shows the layers of sedimentary rock exposed during an archaeological dig. These layers of rock have formed over hundreds of millions of years. Archaeologists discovered the fossil of a *Pakicetus*, a mammal that lived around 50 million years ago. They uncovered these remains from layer 2 in the diagram.

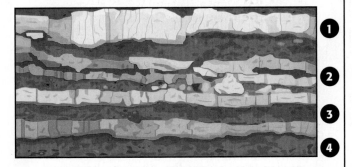

In what layer would you expect to find the remains of an *Ambulocetus*, which existed after the *Pakicetus*?

A. layer 1

C. layer 3

B. layer 2

D. layer 4

Open Response

9. Jackrabbits have long ears. The large ears help the jackrabbit shed excess body heat during hot weather. The average length of jackrabbit ears decreases the farther north the animals live. If the climate in the American southwest becomes warmer in the future, how would this affect the number of southwestern jackrabbits with very long ears?

10. Male peacocks with bigger tails attract more female mates than male peacocks with smaller tails. A peacock must be well-nourished and healthy to produce a large tail. Explain how a female's mate selection could result in peacock offspring that are more likely to survive under harsh environmental conditions.

TCAP Test Preparation

Science in Action

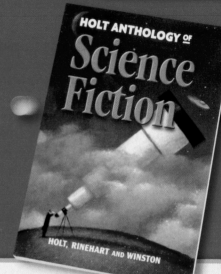

Science, Technology, and Society

Seed Banks

 All over the world, scientists are making deposits in special banks–not for money, but for seeds! Scientists know that many kinds of plants may soon disappear. Some species are vanishing before they have even been studied. Saving plant genetic material preserves plants that may someday save human lives. These plants could provide food or medicines for humans in the future. In the United States, the National Center for Genetic Resources Preservation (NCGRP) preserves seeds and plant tissues. The NCGRP keeps seeds at very cold temperatures, and low oxygen and moisture levels. **TN GLE 0807.T/E.1, GLE 0807.5.5**

Math ACTIVITY

Many drugs were originally developed from plants. Suppose that 100 plant species are used for medicines this year, but 5% of these plant species become extinct each year. How many of the medicinal plant species would be left after 1 year? after 2 years? after 3 years? Round your answers to whole numbers.

Science Fiction

"The Anatomy Lesson"
by Scott Sanders

Do you know the feeling you get when you have an important test? A medical student faces a similar situation in this story. The student needs to learn the bones of the human body for an anatomy exam the next day. The student goes to the anatomy library to study. The librarian lets him check out a box of bones that are supposed to be from a human skeleton. But something is wrong. There are too many bones. They are the wrong shape. They don't fit together correctly. Somebody must be playing a joke! Find out what's going on and why the student and the librarian will never be the same after "The Anatomy Lesson." You can read it in the *Holt Anthology of Science Fiction*.

Language Arts ACTIVITY

WRITING SKILL Before you read this story, predict what you think will happen. Write a paragraph that "gives away" the ending that you predict. After you have read the story, listen to some of the predictions made by your classmates. Discuss your opinions about the possible endings.

Raymond Pierotti

Canine Biology Raymond Pierotti thinks that it's natural that he became a biologist. He grew up exploring the desert around his home in New Mexico. He was fascinated by the abundant wildlife surviving in the bleak landscape. "One of my earliest memories is getting coyotes to sing with me from my backyard," he says.

Pierotti now studies the historical relationships between wolves, coyotes, and domestic dogs. Some of his ideas come from the traditions of the Comanche Indians. According to the Comanche story of origin, humans came from wolves. Although Pierotti doesn't believe that wolves gave rise to humans, he sees the story of origin as a suggestion that humans and wolves have developed together. "Wolves are very similar to humans in many ways," says Pierotti. "They live in family groups and hunt together. It is possible that wolves actually taught humans how to hunt in packs, and there are ancient stories of wolves and humans hunting together and sharing the food. I think it was this relationship that inspired the Comanche stories of origin."

Language Arts ACTIVITY

WRITING SKILL **T/E** Engineers have developed radio tracking systems to help biologists study wild animals. Find out how biologists use radio tracking devices in the wild to track endangered species populations as part of preservation efforts. Write a paragraph summarizing your findings.

TN GLE 0807.T/E.1

To learn more about these Science in Action topics, visit **go.hrw.com** and type in the keyword **HT6FEVFF.**

Current Science

Check out Current Science® articles related to this chapter by visiting go.hrw.com. Just type in the keyword **HL5CS07.**

5

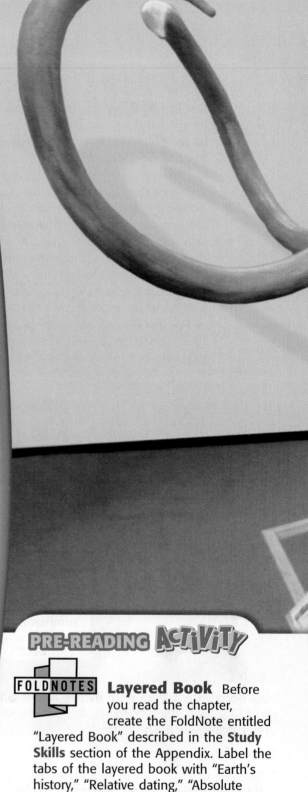

The Fossil Record

The Big Idea

The fossil record provides evidence that populations have changed over time.

PRE-READING ACTIVITY

FOLDNOTES **Layered Book** Before you read the chapter, create the FoldNote entitled "Layered Book" described in the **Study Skills** section of the Appendix. Label the tabs of the layered book with "Earth's history," "Relative dating," "Absolute dating," "Fossils," and "Geologic time." As you read the chapter, write information you learn about each category under the appropriate tab.

About the Photo

Between 12 million and 10,000 years ago, mammoths roamed North America. This skeleton of a mammoth was collected from the Aucilla River in the Florida panhandle, where the mammmouth lived during the end of the Ice Age about 16,000 years ago.

START-UP ACTIVITY

TN GLE 0807.Inq.2, GLE 0807.Inq.5

Making Fossils

How do scientists learn from fossils? In this activity, you will study models of fossils and will identify the object that made each model.

Procedure

1. You and three or four of your classmates will be given **several pieces of modeling clay** and a **paper sack** containing a few **small objects.**

2. Press each object firmly into a piece of clay. Try to leave a fossil-like imprint showing as much detail as possible.

3. After you have made an imprint of each object, exchange your fossil models with another group.

4. On a **sheet of paper,** describe the fossils that you have received. List as many details as possible. What patterns and textures do you observe?

5. Work as a group to identify each fossil, and check your results. Were you right?

Analysis

1. What kinds of details were important in identifying the fossil models that you received? What kinds of details were not preserved in the imprints? For example, can you tell from what materials the objects are made or what color the objects are?

2. Explain how scientists follow similar methods when they study fossils.

Geologic History

How do mountains form? How is new rock created? How old is Earth? Have you ever asked these questions? Nearly 250 years ago, a Scottish farmer and scientist named James Hutton did.

Searching for answers to his questions, Hutton spent more than 30 years studying rock formations in Scotland and England. His observations led to the foundation of modern geology.

The Principle of Uniformitarianism

In 1788, James Hutton collected his notes and wrote *Theory of the Earth.* In *Theory of the Earth,* he stated that the key to understanding Earth's history could be seen all around us. In other words, processes that we observe today—such as erosion and deposition—remain uniform, or do not change, over time. This assumption is now called uniformitarianism. **Uniformitarianism** is the idea that the same geologic processes that are shaping Earth today have been at work throughout Earth's history. **Figure 1** shows how Hutton developed the idea of uniformitarianism.

What You Will Learn

- Compare uniformitarianism with catastrophism.
- Describe how the science of geology has changed over the past 200 years.
- Decribe how relative dating and absolute dating are used to learn about Earth's history.

Vocabulary

uniformitarianism
catastrophism
relative age
relative dating
geologic column
absolute dating
paleontology

READING STRATEGY

Paired Summarizing Read this section silently. In pairs, take turns summarizing the material. Stop to discuss ideas that seem confusing.

TN GLE 0807.Inq.5 Communicate scientific understanding using descriptions, explanations, and models.
GLE 0807.5.6 Investigate fossils in sedimentary rock layers to gather evidence of changing life forms.

Figure 1 *Hutton observed gradual, uniform geologic change.*

1 Hutton observed that rock is broken down into smaller particles.

2 He watched as these rock particles were carried downstream.

4 Hutton thought that in time, the new rock would be raised, creating new landforms, and that the cycle would begin again.

3 He saw that rock particles are deposited and that they form new layers of sediment. He predicted that these deposits would form new rock over time.

uniformitarianism a principle that geologic processes that occurred in the past can be explained by current geologic processes

catastrophism a principle that states that geologic change occurs suddenly

Uniformitarianism Versus Catastrophism

Hutton's theories sparked a scientific debate by suggesting that Earth was much older than scientists previously thought. In Hutton's time, most people thought that Earth was only a few thousand years old. The gradual geologic processes that Hutton described could not have shaped our planet in a few thousand years. The rocks that he observed at Siccar Point, shown in **Figure 2,** were deposited and folded, which indicated a long geologic history. Most scientists supported catastrophism as the explanation of Earth's history. **Catastrophism** is the principle that states that all geologic change occurs suddenly. Supporters of catastrophism thought that Earth's features—such as mountains, canyons, and seas—formed during rare, sudden events called *catastrophes*. These unpredictable events caused rapid geologic change over large areas—sometimes even globally.

✔ **Reading Check** Compare the rates of geologic change that are proposed by uniformitarianism and catastrophism.

A Victory for Uniformitarianism

Despite Hutton's work, catastrophism remained the guiding principle of geology for decades. Only after the work of British geologist Charles Lyell did people seriously consider uniformitarianism as geology's guiding principle.

From 1830 to 1833, Lyell published three volumes, collectively titled *Principles of Geology,* in which he reintroduced uniformitarianism. Armed with Hutton's notes and new evidence of his own, Lyell successfully challenged the principle of catastrophism. Lyell saw no reason to doubt that major geologic change happened at the same rate in the past as it happens in the present—gradually.

TN GLE 0807.Inq.5, GLE 0807.T/E.1

CONNECTION TO Engineering

WRITING SKILL T/E **Geological Engineering**

Geological engineering brings together the fields of geology and engineering. Geological engineers study Earth's long geological history to learn how humans can safely and efficiently use resources such as coal, gas, oil, metals, and minerals. Research possible career opportunities for geological engineers. Write a short report summarizing your findings. Be sure to include information about how the current use of Earth's resources is affecting the careers of geological engineers.

Figure 3 *Today, scientists think that sudden events are responsible for some changes during Earth's past. For example, an asteroid may have hit Earth about 65 million years ago, which would have led to the extinction of the dinosaurs.*

Modern Geology—A Happy Medium

During the late 20th century, the scientist Stephen J. Gould and other scientists challenged Lyell's principle of uniformitarianism. They believed that catastrophes sometimes do play an important role in shaping Earth's history.

Today, scientists realize that neither uniformitarianism nor catastrophism accounts for all geologic change throughout Earth's history. Although most geologic change is gradual and uniform, catastrophes that cause geologic change have occurred during Earth's long history. For example, huge craters have been found where asteroids and comets are thought to have struck Earth in the past. Some scientists think one such asteroid strike, approximately 65 million years ago, may have caused the dinosaurs to become extinct. **Figure 3** is an imaginary re-creation of the asteroid strike that is thought to have caused the extinction of the dinosaurs. The impact of this asteroid is thought to have thrown debris into the atmosphere. The debris may have spread around the entire planet and rained down on Earth for decades. This global debris cloud may have blocked the sun's rays, which would have caused major changes in the global climate and doomed the dinosaurs.

Reading Check How can modern geology be described as a combination of uniformitarianism and catastrophism?

Relative Dating

Scientists can use two methods to determine the age of objects in sedimentary rocks. One of these methods is known as *relative dating*.

Layers of sedimentary rock have different thicknesses. Thickness generally varies by the rate at which sediments are deposited. The bottom layers of rock are usually the oldest layers. The top layers are usually the youngest layers. Scientists can use the order of these rock layers to determine the **relative age** of objects within the layers. For example, fossils in the bottom layers are usually older than fossils in the top layers. So, scientists can use a fossil's position to determine if the fossil is older or younger than other fossils. Estimating the age of rock layers in this way is called **relative dating.**

The Geologic Column

To make the job of relative dating easier, geologists combine data from all of the known rock sequences around the world. These rock sequences have not been disturbed by geologic processes. From this information, geologists create the geologic column, as illustrated in **Figure 4.** The **geologic column** is an ideal sequence of rock layers that contains all of the known fossils and rock formations on Earth. These layers are arranged from oldest to youngest. Geologists use the geologic column to interpret rock sequences.

SCHOOL to HOME

Rock Layers

At your home, collect six or more books. The books should all be different, and all of the books should have different thicknesses. Stack the books so that the spines face you. How do the stacked books resemble the rock layers in the assembled geologic column? Which book represents the oldest layer? Which book represents the youngest layer? Hypothesize about which types of geologic processes could have formed the different layers.

ACTIVITY

relative age the approximate age of fossils or other objects in rock layers determined by comparing whether the surrounding rock layers are younger or older ▬TN▬ *VOCAB*

relative dating any method of determining whether an event or object is older or younger than other events or objects

geologic column an ordered arrangement of rock layers that is based on the relative ages of the rocks and in which the oldest rocks are at the bottom

---

Figure 4 · Constructing the Geologic Column

Here, you can see three rock sequences (A, B, and C) from three different locations. Some rock layers appear in more than one sequence. Geologists construct the geologic column by piecing together different rock sequences from all over the world.

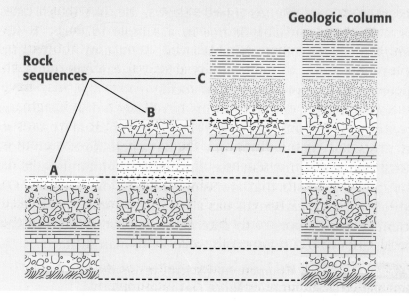

Geologic column

Rock sequences

C

B

A

Figure 5 Using Half-Lives to Date Fossils

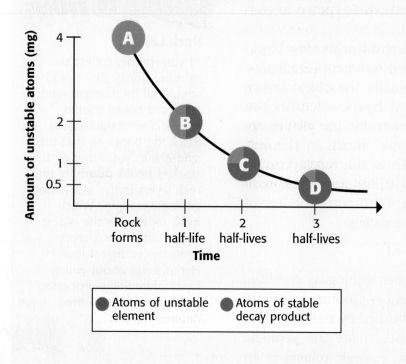

Atoms of unstable element

Atoms of stable decay product

Ⓐ The unstable atoms in this sample of rock have a half-life of 1.3 billion years. The sample contained 4 mg of unstable atoms when it formed.

Ⓑ After 1.3 billion years (one half-life for this type of unstable atom), 2 mg of the unstable atoms have decayed to become stable atoms, and 2 mg of unstable atoms remain.

Ⓒ After 2.6 billion years (two half-lives for these unstable atoms), the rock sample has 3 mg of stable atoms and 1 mg of unstable atoms.

Ⓓ After three half-lives, only 0.5 mg of unstable atoms remains in the rock sample. This mass is equal to one-eighth of the original mass.

Absolute Dating

absolute dating any method of measuring the age of an event or object in years

Scientists can use absolute dating to more precisely determine the age of a fossil or rock. **Absolute dating** is a method that measures the age of fossils or rocks in years. In absolute dating, scientists examine atoms. *Atoms* are the particles that make up all matter. Atoms, in turn, are made of smaller particles. Some atoms are unstable and will decay by releasing energy, particles, or both. When an atom decays, it becomes a different and more stable kind of atom. Each kind of unstable atom decays at its own rate. As **Figure 5** shows, the time that it takes for half of the unstable atoms in a sample to decay is the *half-life* of that type of unstable atom. By measuring the ratio of unstable atoms to stable atoms, scientists can determine the approximate age of a sample of rock.

Some kinds of unstable atoms have long half-lives. Others have relatively short half-lives. These differences are useful to scientists. For example, uranium-238 has a half-life of 4.5 billion years. So, a scientist can use the decay of uranium-238 to date rocks or fossils that are many millions of years old. On the other hand, carbon-14 has a half-life of only 5,780 years. Scientists use carbon-14 to date fossils and other objects that are less than 50,000 years old, such as human artifacts.

✓ Reading Check Compare how scientists use absolute dating and relative dating to learn about Earth's history.

Paleontology—The Study of Past Life

The science involved with the study of past life is called **paleontology.** Scientists who study past life are called *paleontologists.* The data that paleontologists use are fossils. Fossils are the remains of organisms preserved by geologic processes. Some paleontologists specialize in the study of particular organisms. Invertebrate paleontologists study animals that do not have backbones, whereas vertebrate paleontologists study animals that do have backbones. Paleobotanists study fossils of plants. Other paleontologists reconstruct past ecosystems, study the traces that animals left behind, and piece together the conditions under which fossils formed. As you see, the study of past life is as varied and complex as Earth's history itself.

paleontology the scientific study of fossils

SECTION Review

TN GLE 0807.Inq.5, GLE 0807.5.6

Summary

- Uniformitarianism assumes that geologic change is gradual. Catastrophism assumes that geologic change is sudden.

- Geology used to be based on catastrophism. Modern geology is based on the idea that gradual geologic change is interrupted by catastrophes.

- Relative dating is any method of determining whether an object or event is older or younger than other objects or events.

- Absolute dating is any method of measuring the age of an object or event in years.

- Paleontology is a science that uses fossils to study past life.

Using Key Terms

1. Use *uniformitarianism, catastrophism,* and *paleontology* in separate sentences.

Understanding Key Ideas

2. Compare uniformitarianism with catastrophism.

3. Describe how the science of geology has changed.

4. Which of the following best describes relative dating?

   a. Relative dating is used to determine the exact age of fossils.
   b. In relative dating, the deepest rock layers are the youngest layers.
   c. In relative dating, the deepest rock layers are the oldest layers.
   d. Relative dating uses the half-lives of rock layers to determine the age of fossils.

5. Explain how scientists construct the geologic column.

6. Explain the process by which scientists use half-lives to determine the age of an object.

7. Explain the role of paleontology in the study of Earth's history.

8. Describe the work of three types of paleontologists.

Math Skills

9. Rubidium-87 is an unstable atom that scientists use to date rocks that are more than 10 million years old. The half-life of rubidium-87 is approximately 49 billion years. How much rubidium-87 would remain in an object that is 147 billion years old?

Critical Thinking

10. **Analyzing Ideas** Why is uniformitarianism considered to be the foundation of modern geology?

11. **Applying Concepts** Give an example of a type of recent catastrophe.

Internet Resources

For a variety of links related to this chapter, go to www.scilinks.org
Topic: Earth's Story
SciLinks code: HSM0450

Looking at Fossils

Descending from the top of a ridge in the badlands of Argentina, your expedition team suddenly stops. You look down and realize that you are walking on eggshells—dinosaur eggshells!

A paleontologist named Luis Chiappe had this experience. He had found an enormous dinosaur nesting ground.

Fossilized Organisms

The remains or physical evidence of an organism preserved by geologic processes is called a **fossil.** Fossils are most often preserved in sedimentary rock. But as you will see, other materials can also preserve evidence of past life.

Fossils in Rocks

When an organism dies, it either immediately begins to decay or is consumed by other organisms. Sometimes, however, organisms die and are quickly buried by sediment. This sediment slows their rate of decay. Hard parts of organisms, such as shells and bones, are more resistant to decay than soft tissues are. So, when sediments become rock, the hard parts of animals are preserved much more often than soft tissues are.

Fossils in Amber

Imagine that an insect is caught in soft, sticky tree sap. Suppose that more sap covers the insect and quickly hardens. The insect is now preserved inside this sap. Hardened tree sap is called *amber.* Some of our best insect fossils are found in amber, as shown in **Figure 1.** Frogs and lizards have also been found in amber.

✓ *Reading Check* Describe how organisms are preserved in amber.

What You Will Learn

- Describe five ways in which different types of fossils form.
- List three types of fossils that are not part of organisms.
- Explain how fossils can be used to determine the history of changes in environments and organisms.
- Explain how index fossils can be used to date rock layers.

Vocabulary

fossil
trace fossil
mold
cast
index fossil

READING STRATEGY

Reading Organizer As you read this section, create an outline of the section. Use the headings from the section in your outline.

🔵 **GLE 0807.Inq.2** Use appropriate tools and techniques to gather, organize, analyze, and interpret data.

GLE 0807.Inq.4 Recognize possible sources of bias and error, alternative explanations, and questions for further exploration.

GLE 0807.Inq.5 Communicate scientific understanding using descriptions, explanations, and models.

GLE 0807.5.6 Investigate fossils in sedimentary rock layers to gather evidence of changing life forms.

fossil the trace or remains of an organism that lived long ago, most commonly preserved in sedimentary rock. ▰🔵 *VOCAB*

Figure 1 *These insects are preserved in amber.*

Figure 2 *Scientist Vladimir Eisner studies the upper molars of a 20,000-year-old woolly mammoth that was found in Siberia, Russia. The almost perfectly preserved male mammoth was excavated from a block of ice in October 1999.*

Petrifaction

Another way that organisms are preserved is by petrifaction. *Petrifaction* is a process in which minerals replace an organism's tissues. One form of petrifaction is called permineralization. *Permineralization* is a process in which the pore space in an organism's hard tissue—for example, bone or wood—is filled up with mineral. Another form of petrifaction is called replacement. *Replacement* is a process in which minerals completely replace the tissues of an organism. For example, minerals have completely replaced all of the wood in some specimens of petrified wood.

Fossils in Asphalt

In some places, asphalt wells up and forms thick, sticky pools at Earth's surface. For example, the La Brea asphalt deposits have been in Los Angeles, California, for at least 38,000 years. During this time, these pools of asphalt have trapped and preserved many kinds of organisms. From these fossils, scientists have learned about the past environment in southern California.

Frozen Fossils

In October 1999, scientists removed a 20,000-year-old woolly mammoth that was frozen in the Siberian tundra. The remains of this mammoth are shown in **Figure 2.** Woolly mammoths, relatives of modern elephants, became extinct approximately 10,000 years ago. Because cold temperatures slow down decay, many types of frozen fossils are preserved from the lastice age. Scientists hope to find out more about the mammoth and the environment in which it lived.

CONNECTION TO Environmental Science

WRITING SKILL **Preservation in Ice** Subfreezing climates contain almost no decomposing bacteria. The well-preserved body of John Torrington, a member of an expedition that explored the Northwest Passage in Canada in the 1840s, was uncovered in 1984. His body appeared much as it did at the time he died, more than 160 years earlier. Research another well-preserved discovery, and write a report for your class.

Figure 3 *These dinosaur tracks are located in Arizona. They leave a trace of a dinosaur that had longer legs than humans do.*

trace fossil a fossilized mark that formed in sedimentary rock by the movement of an animal on or within soft sediment

mold a mark or cavity made in a sedimentary surface by a shell or other body

cast a type of fossil that forms when sediments fill in the cavity left by a decomposed organism

Other Types of Fossils

Besides their hard parts—and, in rare cases, their soft parts—do organisms leave behind any other clues about their existence? What other evidence of past life do paleontologists look for?

Trace Fossils

Any naturally preserved evidence of animal activity is called a **trace fossil.** Tracks, such as the ones shown in **Figure 3,** are a fascinating example of a trace fossil. These fossils form when animal footprints fill with sediment and are preserved in rock. Tracks reveal a lot about the animal that made them, including the size and speed of the animal. Parallel trackways showing dinosaurs moving in the same direction have led paleontologists to hypothesize that dinosaurs moved in herds.

Burrows are another trace fossil. Burrows are shelters made by animals that bury themselves in sediment, such as clams. Like tracks, burrows are preserved when they fill with sediment and are buried quickly. A *coprolite* (KAHP roh LIET), a third type of trace fossil, is preserved animal dung.

Molds and Casts

Molds and casts are two more examples of fossils. A cavity in rock where a plant or animal was buried is called a **mold.** A **cast** is an object that is created when sediment fills a mold and becomes rock. A cast shows what the outside of the organism looked like. **Figure 4** shows an internal mold and an external mold of the same organism.

✓ **Reading Check** Explain how casts and molds form in sedimentary rock.

Figure 4 *The internal mold on the left formed when the shell of an ammonite filled with sediment and later dissolved away. The external mold on the right preserves the external features of the ammonite's shell.*

Using Fossils to Interpret the Past

Think about your favorite outdoor place. Now, imagine that you are a paleontologist at the same site 65 million years from now. What types of fossils would you dig up? Using the fossils that you would find, how would you reconstruct this place?

The Information in the Fossil Record

The fossil record offers only a rough sketch of the history of life on Earth. Some parts of this history are more complete than others. For example, scientists know more about organisms that had hard body parts than about organisms that had soft body parts. Scientists also know more about organisms that lived in environments that favored fossilization. The fossil record is incomplete because most organisms never became fossils. And of course, many fossils have yet to be discovered.

History of Environmental Changes

Would you expect to find marine fossils on the mountaintop shown in **Figure 5**? The presence of marine fossils means that the rocks of these mountaintops in Canada formed in a totally different environment—at the bottom of an ocean.

The fossil record reveals a history of environmental change. For example, marine fossils help scientists reconstruct ancient coastlines and the deepening and shallowing of ancient seas. Scientists can use the fossils of plants and land animals to reconstruct past climates. Scientists can tell whether the climate of an area was cooler or wetter than that climate is now.

TN GLE 0807.Inq.2, GLE 0807.Inq.5

Quick Lab

Happy Trails

1. Find an area of **soft ground** or a **sandbox**. Have your partner walk across it.

2. Observe each print closely. Is the toe print deeper than the heel print? Using a **meterstick**, measure the distance between each print. Do taller people have longer strides?

3. With a **protractor**, measure the step angle using the diagram shown below as a reference.

4. Repeat steps 2 and 3 with different walking styles. What does each set of prints tell you about the organism that left them? Try this activity with your family or even your pets!

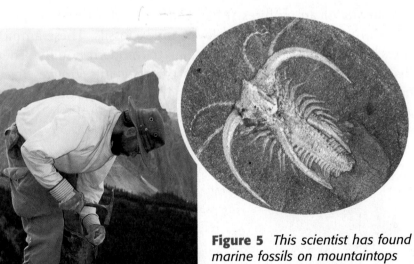

Figure 5 *This scientist has found marine fossils on mountaintops in the Yoho National Park in Canada. This fossil of an organism of the genus* Marrella, *which is shown above, tells the scientist that these rocks were pushed up from below sea level millions of years ago.*

Fossil Hunt

Go on a fossil hunt with your family. Find out what kinds of rocks in your local area might contain fossils. Take pictures or draw sketches of your trip and any fossils that you find.

index fossil a fossil that is used to establish the age of a rock layer because the fossil is distinct, abundant, and widespread and the species that formed that fossil existed for only a short span of geologic time

History of Changing Organisms

Scientists study the relationships between fossils to interpret how life has changed over time. For example, the organisms found in older rock layers often differ from the organisms found in younger rock layers.

Only a small fraction of the organisms that have existed in Earth's history have been fossilized. Because the fossil record is incomplete, it does not provide paleontologists with a continuous record of change. Instead, they look for similarities between fossils, or between a fossilized organism and its closest living relative, and try to fill in the blanks in the fossil record.

✓ Reading Check Explain how the fossil record provides paleontologists with a history of changes in organisms.

Using Fossils to Date Rocks

Scientists have found that particular types of fossils appear only in certain layers of rock. By dating the rock layers above and below these fossils, scientists can determine the time span in which the organisms that formed the fossils lived. If a type of organism existed for only a short period of time, its fossils would show up in a limited range of rock layers. These types of fossils are called index fossils. **Index fossils** are fossils of organisms that lived for a relatively short, well-defined geologic time span. To be index fossils, these fossils must be found in rock layers throughout the world.

Ammonites

The fossils of ammonites (AM uh NIETS) of the genus *Tropites*, shown in **Figure 6**, are examples of index fossils. These ammonites were marine mollusks similar to modern squids. They lived in coiled shells. Ammonites of the genus *Tropites* lived between 230 million and 208 million years ago. Fossils of these ammonites are index fossils for that time period.

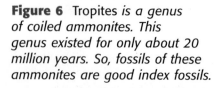

Figure 6 Tropites *is a genus of coiled ammonites. This genus existed for only about 20 million years. So, fossils of these ammonites are good index fossils.*

Trilobites

The fossils of trilobites (TRIE loh BIETS) of the genus *Phacops* are also examples of index fossils. Trilobites are extinct. Their closest living relative is the horseshoe crab. Through the dating of rock, paleontologists have determined that trilobites of the genus *Phacops* lived approximately 400 million years ago. So, when scientists find fossils of trilobites in rock layers anywhere on Earth, they assume that these rock layers are also approximately 400 million years old. An example of a fossil of a trilobite is shown in **Figure 7.**

✓ Reading Check Explain how fossils of trilobites of the genus *Phacops* help paleontologists establish the age of rock layers.

Figure 7 *Paleontologists assume that any rock layer containing a fossil of a trilobite is about 400 million years old.*

SECTION Review

TN GLE 0807.Inq.4, GLE 0807.5.6

Summary

- Fossils are the remains or physical evidence of an organism preserved by geologic processes.

- Fossils can be preserved in rock, amber, asphalt, and ice and by petrifaction.

- Trace fossils are any naturally preserved evidence of animal activity. Tracks, burrows, and coprolites are examples of trace fossils.

- Scientists study fossils to determine how environments and organisms have changed over time.

- An index fossil is a fossil of an organism that lived for a relatively short, well-defined time span. Index fossils can be used to establish the age of rock layers.

Using Key Terms

1. Use *fossil, trace fossil,* and *index fossil* in the same sentence.

Understanding Key Ideas

2. Identify five ways in which different types of fossils form.

3. Describe three types of trace fossils.

4. Explain why the fossil record is an incomplete record of the history of life on Earth.

5. Paleontologists can use the fossil record to prove which of the following statements?

   a. Fossils of all organisms that have lived on Earth have been discovered.

   b. The environment on Earth has changed little during Earth's history.

   c. Organisms have been changing over time.

   d. Hard-bodied organisms have been more common than soft-bodied organisms during the history of life on Earth.

6. Explain how fossils can be used to determine the history of changes in environments and organisms.

7. Explain how an index fossil can be used to date rock.

Math Skills

8. If a scientist finds the remains of a plant between a rock layer that contains 400 million-year-old *Phacops* fossils and a rock layer that contains 230 million-year-old *Tropites* fossils, how old could the plant fossil be?

Critical Thinking

9. **Making Inferences** If you are in a desert and you find rock layers containing fish fossils, what can you infer about the history of the desert?

10. **Identifying Bias** Because information in the fossil record is incomplete, scientists are left with certain biases about fossil preservation. Explain two of these biases. ✓0807.Inq.4

Internet Resources

For a variety of links related to this chapter, go to www.scilinks.org

Topic: Looking at Fossils

SciLinks code: HSM0886

What You Will Learn

● Explain how geologic time is recorded in layers of sedimentary rock.

● Explain how the geologic time scale illustrates the occurrence of processes on Earth.

● Identify two kinds of environmental changes that may result in a decrease in the number of species that exist.

● Explain how the fossil record provides evidence of changes that have taken place in organisms over time.

Vocabulary

geologic time scale   period
eon   epoch
era   extinction

READING STRATEGY

Brainstorming The key idea of this section is the geologic time scale. Brainstorm words and phrases related to the geologic time scale.

TN **GLE 0807.Inq.5** Communicate scientific understanding using descriptions, explanations, and models.

GLE 0807.5.4 Explain why variation within a population can enhance the chances for group survival.

GLE 0807.5.6 Investigate fossils in sedimentary rock layers to gather evidence of changing life forms.

Time Marches On

How old is Earth? Well, if Earth celebrated its birthday every million years, there would be 4,600 candles on its birthday cake! Humans have been around only long enough to light the last candle on the cake.

Suppose you could fast-forward through Earth's history. If you watched Earth change at this speed, you would see mountains rise up like wrinkles in fabric and quickly wear away. You would see life-forms appear and then go extinct. In this section, you will learn that geologists must "fast-forward" through Earth's history when they write or talk about it. You will also learn about some incredible events in the history of life on Earth.

Geologic Time

Figure 1 shows the rock wall at the Dinosaur Quarry Visitor Center in Dinosaur National Monument in Utah. Contained within this wall are approximately 1,500 fossil bones that have been excavated by paleontologists. These fossil bones are the remains of dinosaurs that inhabited the area about 150 million years ago. This number of years seems to be an incredibly long period of time. However, in terms of Earth's history, 150 million years is little more than 3% of the time our planet has existed. It is a little less than 4% of the time represented by Earth's oldest known rocks.

Figure 1 *Fossils of dinosaurs that lived about 150 million years ago are exposed in the quarry wall at Dinosaur National Monument in Utah.*

Figure 2 *Well-preserved plant and animal fossils are common in the Green River formation. Clockwise from the upper right are fossils of a leaf, a snake, a fish, and a turtle.*

The Rock Record and Geologic Time

One of the best places in North America to see Earth's history recorded in rock layers is Grand Canyon National Park, which is located in northwestern Arizona. The Colorado River has cut the Grand Canyon nearly 2 km deep in some places. Over the course of 6 million years, the river has eroded countless layers of rock. These layers represent almost half, or nearly 2 billion years, of Earth's history.

Reading Check Explain how geologic history is recorded in the sedimentary rock of the Grand Canyon.

INTERNET ACTIVITY

For another activity related to this chapter, go to **go.hrw.com,** and type in the keyword **HZ5FOSW.**

The Fossil Record and Geologic Time

Figure 2 shows sedimentary rocks that belong to the Green River formation. These rocks, which are found in parts of Wyoming, Utah, and Colorado, are thousands of meters thick. The rocks were once part of a system of ancient lakes that existed for a period of millions of years. Fossils of plants and animals are common in these rocks and are very well preserved. Burial in the fine-grained lake-bed sediments preserved even the most delicate structures.

Phanerozoic eon

(542 million years ago to the present)
The rock and fossil record represents mainly the Phanerozoic eon, which is the eon in which we live.

Proterozoic eon

(2.5 billion years ago to 542 million years ago)
The first organisms with well-developed cells appeared during this eon.

Archean eon

(3.8 billion years ago to 2.5 billion years ago)
The earliest known rocks on Earth formed during this eon.

Hadean eon

(4.6 billion years ago to 3.8 billion years ago)
The only rocks that scientists have found from this eon are meteorites and rocks from the moon.

Era	Period	Epoch	Millions of years ago
Cenozoic	Quaternary	Holocene	0.01
		Pleistocene	1.8
	Tertiary	Pliocene	5.3
		Miocene	23
		Oligocene	33.9
		Eocene	55.8
		Paleocene	65.5
Mesozoic	Cretaceous		146
	Jurassic		200
	Triassic		251
Paleozoic	Permian		299
	Pennsylvanian		318
	Mississippian		359
	Devonian		416
	Silurian		444
	Ordovician		488
	Cambrian		542

PHANEROZOIC EON

PROTEROZOIC EON — 2,500

ARCHEAN EON — 3,800

HADEAN EON — 4,600

Figure 3 *The geologic time scale accounts for Earth's entire history. The scale is divided into four major parts called* eons. *The dates of intervals on the geologic time scale are estimates.*

The Geologic Time Scale

The geologic column represents the billions of years that have passed since the first rocks formed on Earth. Geologists study a total of 4.6 billion years of Earth's history! To make their job easier, geologists have created the geologic time scale. The **geologic time scale,** which is shown in **Figure 3,** is a scale that divides Earth's 4.6 billion–year history into distinct intervals of time.

Reading Check Identify the approximate amount of time that the geologic column represents.

Divisions of Time

Geologists have divided Earth's history into sections of time, as shown on the geologic time scale in **Figure 3.** The largest divisions of geologic time are **eons** (EE AHNZ). The four eons are the Hadean eon, the Archean eon, the Proterozoic eon, and the Phanerozoic eon. The Phanerozoic eon is divided into three **eras,** which are the second-largest divisions of geologic time. The three eras are further divided into **periods,** which are the third-largest divisions of geologic time. Periods are divided into **epochs** (EP uhks), which are the fourth-largest divisions of geologic time.

The boundaries between some geologic time intervals are marked by the disappearance of index fossil species. Other boundaries are recognized only by detailed paleontological studies.

The Appearance and Disappearance of Species

At certain times during Earth's history, the number of species has increased or decreased dramatically. *Hallucigenia sparsa* appeared during the Cambrian period, when the number of marine species greatly increased. **Figure 4** shows a fossil of *Hallucigenia sparsa.* The number of species often changes as a result of either a relatively sudden increase or a relatively sudden decrease in competition between species. During a mass extinction event, the number of species greatly decreases over a relatively short period of time. **Extinction** is the death of every member of a species. Gradual events such as global climate change and changes in ocean currents can cause mass extinctions.

Reading Check What events can lead to a change in the number of species on Earth?

geologic time scale the standard method used to divide Earth's long natural history into manageable parts

eon the largest division of geologic time

era a unit of geologic time that includes two or more periods

period a unit of geologic time that is longer than an epoch but shorter than an era

epoch a subdivision of geologic time that is longer than an age but shorter than a period

extinction the death of every member of a species 🔺 *VOCAB*

Figure 4 Hallucigenia sparsa, *named for its "bizarre and dreamlike quality," was one of numerous marine organisms to make its appearance during the early Cambrian period.*

Figure 5 *Jungles were present during the Paleozoic era, but there were no birds singing in the trees and no monkeys swinging from the branches. Birds and mammals did not develop until much later.*

The Paleozoic Era—Old Life

The Paleozoic era lasted from about 543 million to 248 million years ago. It is the first era well represented by fossils.

Marine life flourished at the beginning of the Paleozoic era. The oceans became home to a diversity of life. However, there were few land organisms. By the middle of the Paleozoic era, all modern groups of land plants had appeared. By the end of the era, amphibians and reptiles lived on the land, and insects were abundant. **Figure 5** shows what Earth might have looked like in the late Paleozoic era. The Paleozoic era came to an end with the largest mass extinction in Earth's history. Some scientists believe that ocean changes were a likely cause of this extinction. This event killed nearly 90% of all marine species.

Reading Check Describe the change in the kinds of animals that lived during the Paleozoic era.

The Mesozoic Era—The Age of Reptiles

The Mesozoic era began about 248 million years ago. The Mesozoic era is known as the *Age of Reptiles* because reptiles, such as the dinosaurs shown in **Figure 6,** inhabited the land.

During this time, reptiles dominated. Small mammals appeared about the same time that dinosaurs did, and birds appeared in the late Mesozoic era. Many scientists think that birds developed directly from a type of dinosaur. At the end of the Mesozoic era, about 15% to 20% of all species on Earth, including the dinosaurs, became extinct. Global climate change may have caused this extinction.

Figure 6 *Dinosaurs, such as the creatures pictured in this scene, dominated the Mesozoic era.*

The Cenozoic Era—The Age of Mammals

The Cenozoic era, depicted in **Figure 7**, began about 65 million years ago and continues to the present. This era is known as the *Age of Mammals*. During the Mesozoic era, mammals had to compete with dinosaurs and other animals for food and habitat. After the mass extinction at the end of the Mesozoic era, mammals flourished. Unique traits may have helped these mammals survive the environmental changes that probably caused the extinction of the dinosaurs. These traits include regulating body temperature internally and bearing young that develop inside the mother.

Figure 7 *Thousands of species of mammals appeared during the Cenozoic era. The species shown in this scene of the early Cenozoic era are now extinct.*

SECTION
Review

TN GLE 0807.Inq.5, GLE 0807.5.4, GLE 0807.5.6

Summary

● Layers of sedimentary rock forms around the remains of plants and animals, creating a record of many of the organisms that have lived on Earth.

● The geologic time scale divides the 4.6 billion–year history of Earth into distinct intervals of time. The divisions of geologic time are eons, eras, periods, and epochs.

● The boundaries between geologic time intervals represent visible changes that have taken place on Earth.

● At certain times in Earth's history, the number of life-forms has increased or decreased dramatically.

Using Key Terms

1. Use *era*, *period*, and *epoch* in the same sentence.

Understanding Key Ideas

2. Explain how geologic time is recorded in rock layers.

3. Identify the major time intervals that the geologic time scale represents.

4. Identify two kinds of environmental changes that cause mass extinctions.

5. A mass extinction event occcurs when there is a significant decrease in the number of species in a relatively short period of time. Which of the following conditions has been the most frequent cause of mass extinction events?

   a. competition between species for resources
   b. the regular pattern of extinctions
   c. gradual events such as global climate changes
   d. local events such as changes in an ecosystem

6. Explain how the number of animal species has both increased and decreased during Earth's history.

7. Identify two unique traits that may have helped mammals survive the mass extinction at the end of the Mesozoic era. ✔0807.5.3

Math Activity

8. The Earth formed 4.6 billion years ago. Modern humans have existed for about 160,000 years. Simple worms have existed for at least 500 million years. For what fraction of the history of Earth have humans existed? have worms existed?

Critical Thinking

9. **Making Inferences** How can you use the relative ages of fossils in sedimentary rock layers to create a timeline? ✔0807.5.7

10. **Identifying Relationships** How might a decrease in competition between species lead to the sudden appearance of many new species?

Internet Resources

For a variety of links related to this chapter, go to www.scilinks.org
Topic: Geologic Time
SciLinks code: HSM0668

Inquiry Lab

Mystery Footprints

Rocks preserve evidence of the activities of organisms that lived thousands to millions of years ago. Sometimes, scientists find this evidence, such as preserved footprints that provide important information about an organism. Imagine that a group of scientists has asked your class to help study some human footprints. These footprints were found embedded in rocks in an area just outside of your town.

OBJECTIVES

Form hypotheses to explain observations of traces left by other organisms.

Design and **conduct** an experiment to test one of these hypotheses.

Analyze and **communicate** the results in a scientific way.

MATERIALS

- box, at least 1 m² or large enough to contain 3 to 4 footprints
- ruler, metric, or meterstick
- sand, slightly damp

SAFETY

Ask a Question

1. Your teacher will give you some mystery footprints in sand. Examine the mystery footprints. Brainstorm what you may learn about the people who walked on this patch of sand.

Form a Hypothesis

2. As a class, formulate several testable hypotheses about the people who left the footprints. Form groups of three people, and choose one hypothesis for your group to investigate.

Test the Hypothesis

3. Draw a table in which you can record your data. For example, if you have two sets of mystery footprints, your table might look similar to the one below.

Mystery Footprints		
	Footprint set 1	**Footprint set 2**
Length		
Width		
Depth of toe		
Depth of heel		
Length of stride		

DO NOT WRITE IN BOOK

TN GLE 0807.Inq.1 Design and conduct open-ended scientific investigations.

GLE 0807.Inq.2 Use appropriate tools and techniques to gather, organize, analyze, and interpret data.

GLE 0807.Inq.3 Synthesize information to determine cause and effect relationships between evidence and explanations.

GLE 0807.Inq.4 Recognize possible sources of bias and error, alternative explanations, and questions for further exploration.

GLE 0807.Inq.5 Communicate scientific understanding using descriptions, explanations, and models.

4. To help you draw conclusions about the mystery footprints, you may want to first analyze your own footprints. For example, have others in the group use a meterstick to measure your stride when you are running. Is your stride different when you are walking? What part of your foot touches the ground first when you are running? When you are running, which part of your footprint is deeper?

5. Make a list of the kind of footprint that each activity produces. For example, you may write, "When I am running, my footprints are deep near the toe area and 110 cm apart."

Analyze the Results

1. **Classifying** Compare the data from your footprints with the data from the mystery footprints. How are the footprints alike? How are they different?

2. **Identifying Patterns** How many people do you think made the mystery footprints? Explain your interpretation.

3. **Analyzing Data** Can you tell if the mystery footprints were made by men, women, children, or a combination? Can you tell if the people were standing still, were walking, or were running? Explain your interpretation. ✔0807.Inq.3

Draw Conclusions

4. **Drawing Conclusions** Do your data support your hypothesis? Explain your answer.

5. **Evaluating Methods** How could you improve your experiment? ✔0807.Inq.4

Communicating Your Data

WRITING SKILL Summarize your group's conclusions in a report for the scientists who asked for your help. Begin by stating your hypothesis. Then, summarize the methods that you used to study the footprints. Include the comparisons that you made between your footprints and the mystery footprints. Add pictures if you wish. State your conclusions. Finally, offer some suggestions about how you could improve your investigation. ✔0807.Inq.4, ✔0807.Inq.5

Chapter Review

TN GLE 0807.Inq.3, GLE 0807.Inq.5, GLE 0807.5.4, GLE 0807.5.6

USING KEY TERMS

For each pair of terms, explain how the meanings of the terms differ.

1. *uniformitarianism* and *catastrophism*

2. *relative dating* and *absolute dating*

3. *trace fossil* and *index fossil*

4. *cast* and *mold*

5. *geologic column* and *geologic time scale*

UNDERSTANDING KEY IDEAS

Multiple Choice

6. Which of the following terms does NOT describe catastrophic change?

 a. widespread

 b. sudden

 c. rare

 d. gradual

7. A scientist would use the relative dating method to

 a. reconstruct past climates.

 b. determine the causes of extinction.

 c. measure the age of a fossil in years.

 d. determine whether one rock layer is older than another rock layer.

8. Fossils are preserved most often in which of the following substances?

 a. ice

 b. sedimentary rock

 c. asphalt

 d. amber

9. Which of the following is a trace fossil?

 a. an insect preserved in amber

 b. a mammoth frozen in ice

 c. wood replaced by minerals

 d. a dinosaur trackway

10. A paleontologist is collecting many fossils from different rock layers that represent millions of years of history. Which of the following fossils is the paleontologist most likely to use to date these rock layers?

 a. a fossil that occurs in many rock layers

 b. a fossil that occurs in few rock layers

 c. a fossil that is common throughout all rock layers

 d. a fossil that is rare throughout all rock layers

11. Geologic time is organized into large divisions. Each of those large divisinons is divided into smaller divisions. What are the largest divisions of geologic time called?

 a. periods

 b. eras

 c. eons

 d. epochs

12. The fossil record shows that reptiles were once the dominant land animals on Earth. Which animals flourished after the extinction of the dinosaurs?

 a. birds

 b. amphibians

 c. insects

 d. mammals

Short Answer

13 Describe three processes that form fossils.

14 Identify the role of uniformitarianism in Earth science.

15 What are some events that can lead to the extinction of a species?

16 Describe two ways in which scientists use fossils to determine environmental change.

Math Skills

17 If Earth's history spans 4.6 billion years and the Phanerozoic eon lasted 543 million years, what percentage of Earth's history does the Phanerozoic eon represent?

CRITICAL THINKING

18 **Concept Mapping** Use the following terms to create a concept map: *Earth's history, geologic time scale, geologic column, eons, eras, periods,* and *epochs.*

19 **Applying Concepts** Identify how changes in environmental conditions can affect the survival of a species. Give two examples. ✔0807.5.3

20 **Identifying Relationships** Why do paleontologists know more about hard-bodied organisms than about soft-bodied organisms?

21 **Analyzing Processes** Why is a 100 million-year-old fossilized tree not made of wood?

INTERPRETING GRAPHICS

Use the diagram and table below to answer questions 22 and 23.

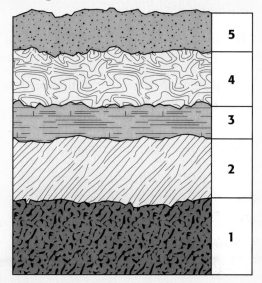

Fossil	Rock layer where fossil was found
A	1
B	5
C	4
D	2
E	3

22 Create a timeline to illustrate the relative ages of the fossils in the sedimentary rock layers. ✔0807.5.7

23 Suppose another very thin rock layer was discovered between layers 3 and 4. How would the relative ages of the fossils in your timeline change? ✔0807.Inq.3

SPI 0807.Inq.4 Draw a conclusion that establishes a cause and effect relationship supported by evidence.

SPI 0807.5.5 Compare fossils found in sedimentary rock to determine their relative age.

GLE 0807.Inq.2 Use appropriate tools and techniques to gather, organize, analyze, and interpret data.

Multiple Choice

1. The fossil record can reveal changes in the environment over time. Scientists have found fossils of marine animals on the tops of mountains in Canada. What does this tell us about the history of the environment in that area?

    A. The mountains were once sediment at the bottom of an ocean.

    B. The ancient environment in the area did not favor fossilization.

    C. The ancient environment in the area was much drier that it is today.

    D. The mountains formed before the animals died, and their remains were fossilized.

Use the graph below to answer question 2.

HOW UNSTABLE ELEMENTS CHANGE OVER TIME

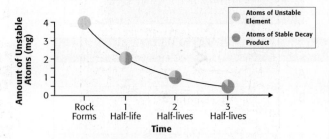

2. The graph above shows how radioactive decay occurs in a 4-milligram (mg) rock sample that contains fossils. The unstable atoms in the sample have a half-life of 1.3 billion years. When the rock forms, the atoms are all unstable. After one half-life, the atoms of 2 mg of the sample are unstable. How much time will have passed after three half-lives?

    A. 0 years
    C. 2.6 billion years

    B. 650 million years
    D. 3.9 billion years

3. At Utah's Dinosaur National Monument, paleontologists have excavated many fossils of dinosaurs that lived about 150 million years ago. What percentage of Earth's history does 150 million years represent?

    A. approximately 3%

    B. approximately 30%

    C. approximately 75%

    D. approximately 90%

4. A paleontologist is studying fossils of ferns from the Cenozoic era. Species A is abundant in older rock layers. In younger rock layers, however, Species A disappears and other species of ferns become abundant. Which is the best hypothesis for why Species A disappeared?

    A. Ferns became less abundant during the Cenozoic era.

    B. Ferns did not have the resources they needed during the Cenozoic era.

    C. Species A disappeared after a mass extinction event caused the extinction of all ferns.

    D. Species A became extinct because of increased competition from other species of ferns.

GLE 0807.Inq.5 Communicate scientific understanding using descriptions, explanations, and models.

GLE 0807.5.6 Investigate fossils in sedimentary rock layers to gather evidence of changing life forms.

Use the figure below to answer question 5.

5. **The illustration above shows *Tropites*, marine mollusks similar to squids that lived between 230 and 208 million years ago. Fossils of these mollusks are now found in rock layers throughout the world. Why are *Tropites* particularly useful to geologists and paleontologists?**

   A. They existed for a relatively long period of geologic time, and they can be used as index fossils.

   B. They existed for a relatively short period of geologic time, and they can be used as index fossils.

   C. They existed for a relatively long period of geologic time, and they can be used as examples of Cenozoic era fossils.

   D. They existed for a relatively short period of geologic time, and they can be used as examples of Paleozoic era fossils.

6. **Which of the following organisms will most likely become a fossil?**

   A. a plant covered by a lava flow

   B. a small lizard covered by tree sap

   C. a deer killed and eaten by predators

   D. a bacterium dead on the bottom of the ocean

7. **A scientist is trying to determine the age of a fossil. If the scientist wants to find the fossil's age in years, which method should she use?**

   A. The scientist should examine the rock layers.

   B. The scientist should examine atoms in the rock.

   C. The scientist should examine the fossil's position in the rock.

   D. The scientist should examine how deep in the rock the fossil was located.

Open Response

8. **Three fossils were found in the rock layers shown above. Fossil A was found in the largest rock layer, and Fossil B was found in the smallest rock layer. What is the relative age of the fossils? If Fossil C were found in the other layer, how would the age of Fossil C compare to the ages of Fossil A and Fossil B?**

9. **What fossil evidence indicates a mass extinction?**

Science in Action

Residents of this neighborhood in Jerusalem, Israel, objected when anthropologists started to dig in the area.

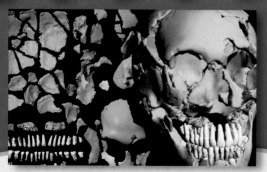

Scientific Discoveries

Using Computers to Examine Fossils

T/E Paleontologists want to examine fossils without taking them apart or damaging them. They can use a technology called *computerized axial tomography,* or *CAT scanning,* which provides views inside objects without touching them. A narrow beam of X-rays repeatedly sweeps across an object and is recorded by a detector. The X-ray beam changes slightly as it travels through each different part of an object, providing a series of detailed cross-section pictures of the object. A computer assembles these pictures, or "slices," to create a three-dimensional picture of the entire object. Computer graphic programs can also be used to move pictures of fossil pieces around to see how the pieces fit together. The fossil skull above was reconstructed using CAT scans and computers.

TN GLE 0807.T/E.1

Language Arts ACTIVITY

T/E **WRITING SKILL** CAT scanning can be used to view body organs and soft tissues that cannot be seen in a normal X-ray. Research how CAT scanning has improved the way doctors diagnose and treat patients. Write a report summarizing your findings. **TN** ✓0807.T/E.4

Scientific Debate

Who Owns the Past?

Does a piece of land include all the layers below it? If you dig, you may find evidence of past life, including valuable fossils that hold important scientific information. In areas that have been inhabited by human ancestors, you may find artifacts that they left behind. But who has the right to dig up these "leftovers" from the past? And who owns them?

In areas that contain many remains of the past, digging up land often leads to conflicts. Landowners may want to build on their own land. But if rare fossils are found, scientists may wish to investigate further. And when remains of ancient human cultures are found, living relatives of these cultures may lay claim to the remains. Scientists are often caught in the middle, because they want to study and preserve evidence of past life.

Math ACTIVITY

An adult male African lion's upper canine tooth is about 6.35 cm long. An adult male saber-toothed cat's upper canine was about 20.3 cm long. What is the ratio of the length of the lion's canine to the length of the saber-toothed cat's canine?

Lizzie May

Amateur Paleontologist For Lizzie May, summer vacations mean trips into the Alaskan wilderness with her stepfather, geologist/paleontologist Kevin May. Having fun is not the purpose of these trips. Instead, the Mays have been exploring the Alaskan wilderness for the remains of ancient life—dinosaurs, in particular.

At age 18, Lizzie May has gained the reputation of being Alaska's most famous teenage paleontologist. Her reputation is well deserved. To date, Lizzie has collected hundreds of dinosaur bones and located important sites of dinosaur, bird, and mammal tracks. In her honor and as a result of her hard work, scientists have given the name "Lizzie" to the skeleton of a dinosaur that the Mays discovered. "Lizzie" is a duckbill dinosaur, or hadrosaur, that lived approximately 90 million years ago. "Lizzie" is the oldest dinosaur ever found in Alaska and is one of the earliest known duckbill dinosaurs in North America.

The Mays have made other, equally exciting discoveries. On one summer trip, they located six dinosaur and bird track sites that were 97 million to 144 million years old. On another trip, the Mays found a fossil marine reptile—an ichthyosaur—that is more than 200 million years old. The fossil had to be removed with the help of a military helicopter. You have to wonder what other exciting adventures are in store for the Mays!

Social Studies ACTIVITY

WRITING SKILL Lizzie May is not the only young person to make a mark in dinosaur paleontology. Use the Internet or another source to research other young people who made contributions to the field of dinosaur study, such as Bucky Derflinger, Johnny Maurice, Brad Riney, and Wendy Sloboda. Write a short essay summarizing your findings.

To learn more about these Science in Action topics, visit go.hrw.com and type in the keyword **HT6FFOSF.**

Current Science

Check out Current Science® articles related to this chapter by visiting go.hrw.com. Just type in the keyword HZ5CS06.

6

Environmental Problems and Solutions

The Big Idea

Human activities affect the environment in positive and negative ways.

TN Tennessee Science Standards

Embedded Inquiry

GLE 0807.Inq.2 Use appropriate tools and techniques to gather, organize, analyze, and interpret data.

GLE 0807.Inq.3 Synthesize information to determine cause and effect relationships between evidence and explanations.

GLE 0807.Inq.4 Recognize possible sources of bias and error, alternative explanations, and questions for further exploration.

GLE 0807.Inq.5 Communicate scientific understanding using descriptions, explanations, and models.

✔**0807.Inq.3** Use evidence from a dataset to determine cause and effect relationships that explain a phenomenon.

✔**0807.Inq.4** Review an experimental design to determine possible sources of bias or error, state alternative explanations, and identify questions for further investigation.

✔**0807.Inq.5** Design a method to explain the results of an investigation using descriptions, explanations, or models.

Embedded Technology and Engineering

GLE 0807.T/E.1 Explore how technology responds to social, political, and economic needs.

GLE 0807.T/E.2 Know that the engineering design process involves an ongoing series of events that incorporate design constraints, model building, testing, evaluating, modifying, and retesting.

GLE 0807.T/E.3 Compare the intended benefits with the unintended consequences of a new technology.

✔**0807.T/E.2** Apply the engineering design process to construct a prototype that meets certain specifications.

✔**0807.T/E.3** Explore how the unintended consequences of new technologies can impact society.

Life Science

GLE 0807.5.5 Describe the importance of maintaining the earth's biodiversity.

✔**0807.5.5** Prepare a poster that illustrates the major factors responsible for reducing the amount of global biodiversity.

✔**0807.5.6** Prepare graphs that demonstrate how the amount of biodiversity has changed in a particular continent or biome.

PRE-READING ACTIVITY

FOLDNOTES **Two-Panel Flip Chart**
Before you read the chapter, create the FoldNote entitled "Two-Panel Flip Chart" described in the **Study Skills** section of the Appendix. Label the flaps of the two-panel flip chart with "Environmental problems" and "Environmental solutions." As you read the chapter, write information you learn about each category under the appropriate flap.

About the Photo

After an oil spill, volunteers try to capture oil-covered penguins. The oil affects the penguins' ability to float. So, oil-covered penguins often won't go into the water to get food. The penguins may also swallow oil, harming their stomach, kidneys, and lungs. Once captured, the penguins are fed activated charcoal. The charcoal helps the penguins get rid of any oil they have swallowed. Then, the birds are washed to remove oil from their feathers.

START-UP ACTIVITY

TN GLE 0807.Inq.2, GLE 0807.Inq.5

Recycling Paper

In this activity, you will be making paper without cutting down trees. You will be reusing paper that has already been made.

Procedure

1. Tear **two sheets of old newspaper** into small pieces, and put them in a **blender.** Add **1 L of water.** Cover and blend until the mixture is soupy.

2. Fill a **square pan** with **water** to a depth of 2 cm to 3 cm. Place a **wire screen** in the pan. Pour 250 mL of the paper mixture onto the screen, and spread the mixture evenly.

3. Lift the screen out of the water with the paper on it. Drain excess water into the pan.

4. Place the screen inside a **section of newspaper.** Close the newspaper, and turn it over so that the screen is on top of the paper mixture.

5. Cover the newspaper with a **flat board.** Press on the board to squeeze out excess water.

6. Open the newspaper, and let your paper mixture dry overnight. Use your recycled paper to write a note to a friend!

Analysis

1. How is your paper like regular paper? How is it different?

2. What could you do to improve your papermaking methods? ✓0807.Inq.4

Environmental Problems

Maybe you've heard warnings about dirty air, water, and soil. Or you've heard about the destruction of rain forests. Do these warnings mean our environment is in trouble?

In the late 1700s, the Industrial Revolution began. People started to rely more and more on machines. As a result, more harmful substances entered the air, water, and soil.

What You Will Learn

- List five kinds of pollutants.
- Distinguish between renewable and nonrenewable resources.
- Describe the impact of exotic species.
- Explain why human population growth has increased.
- Describe how habitat destruction affects biodiversity.
- Give two examples of how pollution affects humans.

Vocabulary

pollution   overpopulation
renewable   biodiversity
   resource
nonrenewable
   resource

READING STRATEGY

Reading Organizer As you read this section, make a concept map by using the terms above.

TN **GLE 0807.Inq.3** Synthesize information to determine cause and effect relationships between evidence and explanations.

GLE 0807.T/E.1 Explore how technology responds to social, political, and economic needs.

GLE 0807.T/E.3 Compare the intended benefits with the unintended consequences of a new technology.

GLE 0807.5.5 Describe the importance of maintaining the earth's biodiversity.

pollution an unwanted change in the environment caused by substances or forms of energy

Pollution

Today, machines don't produce as much pollution as they once did. But there are more sources of pollution today than there once were. **Pollution** is an unwanted change in the environment caused by substances, such as wastes, or forms of energy, such as radiation. Anything that causes pollution is called a *pollutant*. Some pollutants are produced by natural events, such as volcanic eruptions. Many pollutants are human-made. Pollutants may harm plants, animals, and humans.

Garbage

The average American throws away more trash than the average person in any other nation—about 12 kg of trash a week. This trash often goes to a landfill like the one in **Figure 1.** Other landfills contain medical waste, lead paint, and other hazardous wastes. *Hazardous waste* includes wastes that can catch fire; corrode, or eat through metal; explode; or make people sick. Many industries, such as paper mills and oil refineries, produce hazardous wastes.

✓ *Reading Check* What is hazardous waste?

Figure 1 *Every year, Americans throw away about 200 million metric tons of garbage.*

Figure 2 *Fertilizer promotes the growth of algae. As dead algae decompose, oxygen in the water is used up. So, fish die because they cannot get oxygen.*

Chemicals

People need and use many chemicals. Some chemicals are used to treat diseases. Other chemicals are used in plastics and preserved foods. Sometimes, the same chemicals that help people may harm the environment. As shown in **Figure 2,** fertilizers and pesticides may pollute soil and water.

CFCs and PCBs are two groups of harmful chemicals. Ozone protects Earth from harmful ultraviolet light. CFCs destroy ozone. CFCs were used in aerosols, refrigerators, and plastics. The second group, PCBs, was once used in appliances and paints. PCBs are poisonous and may cause cancer. Today, the use of CFCs and PCBs is banned. But CFCs are still found in the atmosphere. And PCBs are still found in even the most remote areas on Earth.

High-Powered Wastes

Nuclear power plants provide electricity to many homes and businesses. The plants also produce radioactive wastes. *Radioactive wastes* are hazardous wastes that give off radiation. Some of these wastes take thousands of years to become harmless.

Gases

Earth's atmosphere is made up of a mixture of gases, including carbon dioxide. The atmosphere acts as a protective blanket. It keeps Earth warm enough for life to exist. Since the Industrial Revolution, however, the amount of carbon dioxide in the atmosphere has increased. Carbon dioxide and other air pollutants act like a greenhouse, trapping heat around the Earth. Many scientists think the increase in carbon dioxide has increased global temperatures. If temperatures continue to rise, the polar icecaps could melt. Then, the level of the world's oceans would rise. Coastal areas could flood as a result.

TN GLE 0807.Inq.3, GLE 0807.T/E.3

CONNECTION TO Chemistry

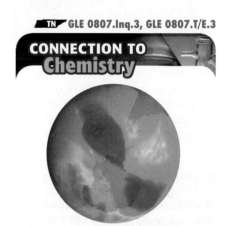

Ozone Holes This image of two holes in the ozone layer (the purple areas over Antarctica) was taken in 2002. Ozone in the stratosphere absorbs most of the ultraviolet light that comes from the sun. Ozone is destroyed by CFCs, which are part of products such as refrigerators and air conditioners. The U.S. and many other countries have found less harmful substitutes for CFCs, but CFCs are still being released into the atmosphere. Research how CFCs destroy ozone. Make a model demonstrating this process. Then compare the benefits and unintended consequences of CFCs. ✔0807.T/E.3

ACTiViTY

MATH PRACTICE

Water Depletion

In one day, millions of liters of water are removed from a water supply. Of this volume, 30 million liters cannot be replaced naturally. Today, the water supply has 60 billion liters of water. In years, how long would the water supply last if water continued to be removed at this rate? If water were removed at the same rate as it was replaced, how long would the water supply last?

renewable resource a natural resource that can be replaced at the same rate at which the resource is consumed

nonrenewable resource a resource that forms at a rate that is much slower than the rate at which it is consumed

Figure 3 *This area has been mined for iron using a method called* strip mining.

Noise

Some pollutants affect the senses. These pollutants include loud noises. Too much noise is not just annoying. Noise pollution affects your ability to hear and think clearly. And it may damage your hearing. People who work in noisy environments, such as in construction zones, must protect their ears.

Resource Depletion

Some of Earth's resources are renewable. But other resources are nonrenewable. A **renewable resource** is one that can be replaced at the same rate at which the resource is used. Solar and wind energy are renewable resources, as are some kinds of trees. A **nonrenewable resource** is one that cannot be replaced or that can be replaced only over thousands or millions of years. Most minerals and fossil fuels, such as oil and coal, are nonrenewable resources.

Nonrenewable resources cannot last forever. These resources will become more expensive as they become harder to find. The removal of some materials from the Earth also carries a high price tag. This removal may lead to oil spills, loss of habitat, and damage from mining, as shown in **Figure 3.**

Renewable or Nonrenewable?

Some resources once thought to be renewable are becoming nonrenewable. For example, scientists used to think that fresh water was a renewable resource. However, in some areas, water supplies are being used faster than they are being replaced. Eventually, these areas may run out of fresh water. So, scientists are working on ways to keep these water supplies from being used up.

Exotic Species

People are always on the move. Without knowing it, people carry other species with them. Plant seeds, animal eggs, and adult organisms are carried from one part of the world to another. An organism that makes a home for itself in a new place outside its native home is an *exotic species*. Exotic species often thrive in new places. One reason is that they are free from the predators found in their native homes.

Exotic species can become pests and compete with native species. In 2002, the northern snakehead fish was found in a Maryland pond. This fish, shown in **Figure 4,** is from Asia. Scientists are concerned because the northern snakehead eats other fish, amphibians, small birds, and some mammals. It can also move across land. The northern snakehead could invade more lakes and ponds.

✓ *Reading Check* What are exotic species?

Human Population Growth

Look at **Figure 5.** In 1800, there were 1 billion people on Earth. By 2000, there were more than 6 billion people. Advances in medicine, such as immunizations, and advances in farming have made human population growth possible. Overall, these advances are beneficial. But some people argue that there may eventually be too many people on Earth. **Overpopulation** happens when the number of individuals becomes so large that the individuals can't get the resources they need to survive. However, many scientists think that human population growth will slow down or level off before it reaches that point.

Figure 4 *Northern snakehead fish can move across land in search of water. These fish can survive out of water for up to four days!*

overpopulation the presence of too many individuals in an area for the available resources

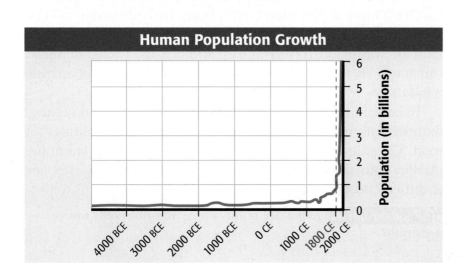

Human Population Growth

Population (in billions)

4000 BCE 3000 BCE 2000 BCE 1000 BCE 0 CE 1000 CE 1800 CE 2000 CE

Figure 5 *Recently, the human population has been doubling every few decades.*

Figure 6 *Deforestation can leave soil exposed to erosion.*

biodiversity the number and variety of organisms in a given area during a specific period of time

TN GLE 0807.Inq.3

CONNECTION TO Social Studies

Wood Identify a country that is a major exporter of wood. List some of the ways this wood is used. Research the impact this exportation is having on that country's forests. Make a poster describing your findings. ✔0807.Inq.3

ACTiViTY

Habitat Destruction

People need homes. People also need food and building materials. But when land is cleared for construction, crops, mines, or lumber, the topsoil may erode. Chemicals may pollute nearby streams and rivers. The organisms that were living in these areas may be left without food and shelter. These organisms may die.

An organism's *habitat* is where it lives. Every habitat has its own number and variety of organisms, or **biodiversity.** If a habitat is damaged or destroyed, biodiversity is lost.

Forest Habitats

Trees provide humans with oxygen, lumber, food, rubber, and paper. For some of these products, such as lumber and paper, trees must be cut down. *Deforestation* is the clearing of forest lands, as shown in **Figure 6.** At one time, many of these cleared forests were not replanted. Today, lumber companies often plant new trees to replace the trees that were cut down. However, some biodiversity is still lost.

Tropical rain forests, the most diverse habitats on Earth, are sometimes cleared for farmland, roads, and lumber. But after a tropical rain forest is cleared, the area cannot grow to be as diverse as it once was. Also, thin tropical soils are often badly damaged.

Marine Habitats

Many people think of oil spills when they think of pollution in marine habitats. This is an example of *point-source pollution,* or pollution that comes from one source. Spilled oil pollutes both open waters and coastal habitats.

A second kind of water pollution is *nonpoint-source pollution.* This kind of pollution comes from many different sources. Nonpoint-source pollution often happens when chemicals on land are washed into rivers, lakes, and oceans. These chemicals can harm or kill many of the organisms that live in marine habitats.

In addition to oil and chemicals, plastics are also sometimes dumped into marine habitats. Animals may mistake plastics for food. Or animals may become tangled in plastics. Dumping plastics into the ocean is against the law. However, this law is difficult to enforce.

✔ **Reading Check** What are point-source and nonpoint-source pollution?

Effects on Humans

Trees and marine life are not the only organisms affected by pollution and habitat destruction. Pollution and habitat destruction affect humans, too. Sometimes, the effect is immediate. Polluted air affects people with respiratory problems. If you drink polluted water, you may get sick. Sometimes, the damage is not apparent right away. Some chemicals cause cancers many years after a person is exposed to them. Over time, natural resources may be hard to find or used up. Your children or grandchildren may have to deal with these problems.

Anything that harms other organisms may eventually harm people, too. Caring for the environment means being aware of what is happening now and looking ahead to the future.

SECTION Review

TN GLE 0807.Inq.3, GLE 0807.Inq.5, GLE 0807.T/E.3, GLE 0807.5.5

Summary

- Pollutants include garbage, chemicals, high-energy wastes, gases, and noise.

- Renewable resources can be used over and over. Nonrenewable resources cannot be replaced or are replaced over thousands or millions of years.

- Exotic species can become pests and compete with native species.

- Overpopulation happens when a population is so large that it can't get what it needs to survive.

- Habitat destruction can lead to soil erosion, water pollution, and decreased biodiversity.

- In addition to harming the environment, pollution can harm humans.

Using Key Terms

The statements below are false. For each statement, replace the underlined term to make a true statement.

1. Coal is a <u>renewable resource</u>.

2. <u>Overpopulation</u> is the number and variety of organisms in an area.

Understanding Key Ideas

3. Which of the following can cause pollution? ✔0807.Inq.3
   a. noise
   b. garbage
   c. chemicals
   d. All of the above

4. Pollution
   a. does not affect humans.
   b. can make humans sick.
   c. makes humans sick only after many years.
   d. None of the above

5. Compare renewable and nonrenewable resources.

6. Why has human population growth increased?

7. What is an exotic species?

8. How does habitat destruction affect biodiversity? ✔0807.Inq.3

Math Skills

9. Jodi's family produces 48 kg of garbage each week. What is the percentage decrease if they reduce the amount of garbage to 40 kg per week? ✔0807.Inq.3

Critical Thinking

10. **Applying Concepts** Explain how each of the following technologies can help people but can also harm the environment due to unintended consequences: fertilizers, pesticides, and old refrigerators. ✔0807.T/E.3

11. **Making Inferences** Explain how human population growth is related to pollution problems.

12. **Predicting Consequences** Describe how reducing habitat destruction is important in maintaining biodiversity. ✔0807.T/E.3

Internet Resources

For a variety of links related to this chapter, go to www.scilinks.org
Topic: Air Pollution; Resource Depletion
SciLinks code: HSM0033; HSM1304

Environmental Solutions

As the human population grows, it will need more resources. People will need food, healthcare, transportation, and waste disposal. What does this mean for the Earth?

All of these needs will have an impact on the Earth. If people don't use resources wisely, people will continue to pollute the air, soil, and water. More natural habitats could be lost. Many species could die out as a result. But there are many things people can do to protect the environment.

Conservation

One way to care for the Earth is conservation (KAHN suhr VAY shuhn). **Conservation** is the preservation and wise use of natural resources. You can ride your bike to conserve fuel. At the same time, you prevent air pollution. You can use organic compost instead of chemical fertilizer in your garden. Doing so conserves the resources needed to make the fertilizer. Also, you may reduce soil and water pollution.

Practicing conservation means using fewer natural resources. Conservation helps reduce waste and pollution. Also, conservation can help prevent habitat destruction. The three Rs are shown in **Figure 1.** They describe three ways to conserve resources: Reduce, Reuse, and Recycle.

Reading Check What are the three Rs?

What You Will Learn

- Explain the importance of conservation.
- Describe the three Rs.
- Explain how biodiversity can be maintained.
- List five environmental strategies.

Vocabulary

conservation
recycling

READING STRATEGY

Discussion Read this section silently. Write down questions that you have about this section. Discuss your questions in a small group.

TN GLE 0807.Inq.3 Synthesize information to determine cause and effect relationships between evidence and explanations.

GLE 0807.T/E.1 Explore how technology responds to social, political, and economic needs.

GLE 0807.T/E.2 Know that the engineering design process involves an ongoing series of events that incorporate design constraints, model building, testing, evaluating, modifying, and retesting.

GLE 0807.T/E.3 Compare the intended benefits with the unintended consequences of a new technology.

GLE 0807.5.5 Describe the importance of maintaining the earth's biodiversity.

Figure 1 By reducing, reusing, and recycling, these teens are conserving resources.

Reduce

What is the best way to conserve the Earth's natural resources? Use less of them! Doing so also helps reduce pollution.

Reducing Waste and Pollution

As much as one-third of the waste produced by some countries is packaging material. Products can be wrapped in less paper and plastic to reduce waste. For example, fast-food restaurants used to serve sandwiches in large plastic containers. Today, sandwiches are usually wrapped in thin paper instead. This paper is more biodegradable than plastic. Something that is *biodegradable* can be broken down by living organisms, such as bacteria. Scientists, such as the ones in **Figure 2,** are working to make biodegradable plastics.

Many people and companies are using less-hazardous materials in making their products. For example, some farmers don't use synthetic chemicals on their crops. Instead, they practice organic farming. They use mulch, compost, manure, and natural pest control. Agricultural specialists are also working on farming techniques that are better for the environment.

Reducing the Use of Nonrenewable Resources

Some scientists are looking for sources of energy that can replace fossil fuels. For example, solar energy can be used to power homes, such as the home shown in **Figure 3.** Scientists are studying power sources such as wind, tides, and falling water. Car companies have developed electric and hydrogen-fueled automobiles. Driving these cars uses fewer fossil fuels and produces less pollution than driving gas-fueled cars does.

Figure 2 *These scientists are studying ways to make biodegradable plastics.*

conservation the preservation and wise use of natural resources

Figure 3 *The people who live in this home use solar panels to get energy from the sun.*

Figure 4 *This home was built with reused tires and aluminum cans.*

TN GLE 0807.T/E.1, GLE 0807.T/E.2

CONNECTION TO Engineering

T/E **Wastewater Treatment Plants** Wastewater treatment plants remove pollutants from wastewater so it can be returned to the environment safely. The operator is usually a certified, professional engineer who knows how to apply engineering processes to water treatment. Research wastewater treatment plants. Write three paragraphs about how the testing, evaluating, modifying, and retesting steps from the engineering design cycle are used to develop the equipment and to troubleshoot processes in such a plant.

ACTIVITY

Reuse

Do you get hand-me-down clothes from an older sibling? Do you try to fix broken sports equipment instead of throwing it away? If so, you are helping conserve resources by *reusing* products.

Reusing Products

Every time you reuse a plastic bag, one bag fewer needs to be made. Reusing the plastic bag at the grocery store is just one way to reuse the bag. Reusing products is an important way to conserve resources.

You might be surprised at how many materials can be reused. For example, building materials can be reused. Wood, bricks, and tiles can be used in new structures. Old tires can be reused, too. They can be reused for playground surfaces. As shown in **Figure 4,** some tires are even reused to build new homes!

Reusing Water

About 100 billion liters of water are used each day in American homes. Most of this water goes down the drain. Many communities are experiencing water shortages. Some of these communities are experimenting with reusing, or reclaiming, wastewater.

One way to reclaim water is to use organisms to clean the water. These organisms include plants and filter-feeding animals, such as clams. Often, reclaimed water isn't pure enough to drink. But it can be used to water crops, lawns, and golf courses, such as the one shown in **Figure 5.** Sometimes, reclaimed water is returned to underground water supplies.

✓ *Reading Check* **Describe how water is reused.**

Figure 5 *This golf course is being watered with reclaimed water.*

TO CONSERVE OUR NATURAL RESOURCES THIS GOLF COURSE IS IRRIGATED WITH TREATED EFFLUENT

Recycle

Another example of reuse is recycling. **Recycling** is the recovery of materials from waste. Sometimes, recyclable items, such as paper, are used to make the same kinds of products. Other recyclable items are made into different products. For example, yard clippings can be recycled into a natural fertilizer.

Recycling Trash

Plastics, paper, aluminum, wood, glass, and cardboard are examples of materials that can be recycled. Every week, about half a million trees are used to make Sunday newspapers. Recycling newspapers could save millions of trees. Recycling aluminum saves 95% of the energy needed to change raw ore into aluminum. Glass can be recycled over and over again to make new bottles and jars.

Many communities make recycling easy. Some cities provide containers for glass, plastic, aluminum, and paper. People can leave these containers on the curb. Each week, the materials are picked up for recycling, as shown in **Figure 6.** Other cities have centers where people can take materials for recycling.

Recycling Resources

Waste that can be burned can also be used to generate electricity. Electricity is generated in waste-to-energy plants, such as the one shown in **Figure 7.** Using garbage to make electricity is an example of *resource recovery*. Some companies are beginning to make electricity with their own waste. Doing so saves the companies money and conserves resources.

About 16% of the solid waste in the United States is burned in waste-to-energy plants. But some people are concerned that these plants pollute the air. Other people worry that the plants reduce recycling.

recycling the process of recovering valuable or useful materials from waste or scrap

Figure 6 *In some communities, recyclable materials are picked up each week.*

Figure 7 *A waste-to-energy plant can provide electricity to many homes and businesses.*

Figure 8 *What could happen if a fungus attacks a banana field? Biodiversity is low in fields of crops such as bananas.*

TN GLE 0807.5.5

CONNECTION TO Environmental Science

Biodiversity Every continent on Earth is experiencing a loss of biodiversity. Research the major factors responsible for reducing the amount of biodiversity on Earth. Prepare a poster that illustrates these factors. Include graphs to show the amount of change in biodiversity for at least one area, such as Madagascar.

✔0807.Inq.3, ✔0807.5.5, ✔0807.5.6

Maintaining Biodiversity

You know the three Rs. What else can you do to help the environment? You can help maintain biodiversity! So, how does biodiversity help the environment?

Imagine a forest with only one kind of tree. If a disease hit that species, the entire forest might die. Now, imagine a forest with 10 species of trees. If a disease hits one species, 9 other species will remain. Bananas, shown in **Figure 8,** are an important crop. But banana fields are not very diverse. Fungi threaten the survival of bananas. Farmers often use chemicals to control fungi. Growing other plants among the bananas, or increasing biodiversity, can also prevent the spread of fungi.

Biodiversity is also important because each species has a unique role in an ecosystem. Losing one species could disrupt an entire ecosystem. For example, if an important predator is lost, its prey will multiply. The prey might eat the plants in an area, keeping other animals from getting food. Eventually, even the prey won't have food. So, the prey will starve.

Protecting Species

One way to maintain biodiversity is to protect individual species. In the United States, a law called the *Endangered Species Act* was designed to do just that. Endangered species are put on a special list. The law forbids activities that would harm a species on this list. The law also requires the development of recovery programs for each endangered species. Some endangered species, such as the California condor in **Figure 9,** are now increasing in number.

Anyone can ask the government to add a species to or remove a species from the endangered species list. This process can take years to complete. The government must study the species and its habitat before making a decision.

Figure 9 *Thanks to captive-breeding programs, the California condor population is increasing.*

Protecting Habitats

Waiting until a species is almost extinct to begin protecting it is like waiting until your teeth are rotting to begin brushing them. Scientists want to prevent species from becoming endangered and from becoming extinct.

Plants, animals, and microorganisms depend on each other. Each organism is part of a huge, interconnected web of organisms. The entire web should be protected to protect these organisms. To protect the web, complete habitats, not just individual species, must be preserved. Nature preserves, such as the one shown in **Figure 10,** are one way to protect entire habitats.

Figure 10 *Setting aside public lands for wildlife is one way to protect habitats.*

Environmental Strategies

Laws have been passed to help protect the Earth's environment. By following those laws, people can help the environment. People can also use the following environmental strategies:

- **Reduce pollution.** Recycle as much as possible, and buy recycled products. Don't dump wastes on farmland, in forests, or into rivers, lakes, and oceans. Participate in a local cleanup project.

- **Reduce pesticide use.** Use only pesticides that are targeted specifically for harmful insects. Avoid pesticides that might harm beneficial insects, such as ladybugs or spiders. Use natural pesticides that interfere with how certain insects grow, develop, and reproduce.

- **Protect habitats.** Preserve entire habitats. Conserve wetlands. Reduce deforestation. Use resources at a rate that allows them to be replenished naturally.

- **Learn about local issues.** Attend local meetings about laws and projects that may affect your local environment. Research the impact of the project, and let people know about your concerns.

- **Develop alternative energy sources.** Increase the use of renewable energy, such as solar power and wind power.

The *Environmental Protection Agency* (EPA) is a government organization that helps protect the environment. The EPA works to help people have a clean environment in which to live, work, and play. The EPA keeps people informed about environmental issues and helps enforce environmental laws.

✓ Reading Check What is the EPA?

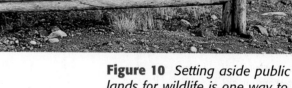

TN ▶ GLE 0807.T/E.1

CONNECTION TO Technology

Controlling Tree Pests
Deforestation is sometimes the result of human activity. Pine forests in North America are being destroyed by something much smaller than humans: pine beetles. Research pine beetles and ways scientists might use bioengineering to control them. Write a short report proposing a design for an adaptive prototype to control pine beetles. Include a way to test the effectiveness of the prototype. ✔0807.T/E.4, ✔0807.T/E.5

ACTIVITY

INTERNET ACTIVITY

For another activity related to this chapter, go to **go.hrw.com** and type in the keyword **HL5ENVW.**

What You Can Do

Reduce, reuse, and recycle. Protect the Earth. These are jobs for everyone. Children as well as adults can help clean up the Earth. By doing so, people can improve their environment. And they can improve their quality of life.

The list in **Figure 11** offers some suggestions for how *you* can help. How many of these things do you already do? What can you add to the list?

Figure 11 How You Can Help the Environment

1. Volunteer at a local preserve or nature center, and help other people learn about conservation.
2. Give away your old toys.
3. Use recycled paper.
4. Fill up both sides of a sheet of paper.
5. Start an environmental awareness club at your school or in your neighborhood.
6. Recycle glass, plastics, paper, aluminum, and batteries.
7. Don't buy any products made from an endangered plant or animal.
8. Turn off electrical devices when you are not using them.
9. Wear hand-me-downs.
10. Share books with friends, or use the library.
11. Walk, ride a bicycle, or use public transportation.
12. Carry a reusable cloth shopping bag to the store.
13. Use a lunch box, or reuse your paper lunch bags.
14. Turn off the water while you brush your teeth.
15. Buy products made from biodegradable and recycled materials.
16. Use cloth napkins and kitchen towels.
17. Buy things in packages that can be recycled.
18. Use rechargeable batteries.
19. Make a compost heap.

THIS BAG IS BIODEGRADABLE

TN GLE 0807.Inq.3, GLE 0807.Inq.5,
GLE 0807.T/E.1, GLE 0807.5.5

Summary

- Conservation is the preservation and wise use of natural resources. Conservation helps reduce pollution, ensures that resources will be available in the future, and protects habitats.

- The three Rs are Reduce, Reuse, and Recycle. Reducing means using fewer resources. Reusing means using materials and products over and over. Recycling is the recovery of materials from waste.

- Biodiversity is vital for maintaining healthy ecosystems. A loss of one species can affect an entire ecosystem.

- Biodiversity can be preserved by protecting endangered species and entire habitats.

- Environmental strategies include reducing pollution, reducing pesticide use, protecting habitats, enforcing the Endangered Species Act, and developing alternative energy resources.

Using Key Terms

1. Use each of the following terms in a separate sentence: *conservation* and *recycling*.

Understanding Key Ideas

2. Which of the following is NOT a strategy to protect the environment?
   a. preserving entire habitats
   b. using pesticides that target all insects
   c. reducing deforestation
   d. increasing the use of solar power

3. Conservation
   a. has little effect on the environment.
   b. is the use of more natural resources.
   c. involves using more fossil fuels.
   d. can prevent pollution.

4. Describe the three Rs.

5. Describe why Earth's biodiversity is important. How can Earth's biodiversity be maintained?
   ✔0807.Inq.3

Critical Thinking

6. **Applying Concepts** Liza rode her bike to the store. She bought items that had little packaging and put her purchases into her backpack. Describe how Liza practiced conservation.

7. **Identifying Relationships** How does conservation of resources reduce pollution, protect habitats, and maintain biodiversity? ✔0807.Inq.3

Interpreting Graphics

Use the pie graph below to answer the questions that follow.

Land Use in the United States

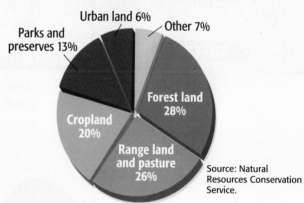

Urban land 6%
Other 7%
Parks and preserves 13%
Forest land 28%
Cropland 20%
Range land and pasture 26%

Source: Natural Resources Conservation Service.

8. If half of the forest land were made into preserves, what percentage of total land would be parks and preserves?

9. If 10% of the cropland were not planted, what percentage of land would be used for crops?

Internet Resources

For a variety of links related to this chapter, go to www.scilinks.org
Topic: Recycling; Maintaining Biodiversity
SciLinks code: HSM1277; HSM0902

Inquiry Lab

OBJECTIVES

Examine biodiversity in your community.

Identify which areas in your community have the greatest biodiversity.

MATERIALS

- items to be determined by the students and approved by the teacher (Possible field equipment includes a meterstick, binoculars, a magnifying lens, and forceps.)
- stakes (4)
- twine

SAFETY

Biodiversity—What a Disturbing Thought!

Biodiversity is important for the stability of an ecosystem. Microorganisms, plants, and animals all have a role in an ecosystem. In this activity, you will investigate areas outside your school to determine which areas contain the greatest biodiversity.

Ask a Question

1 Based on your understanding of biodiversity, do you expect a forest or an area planted with crops to be more diverse?

Form a Hypothesis

2 Select an area that is highly disturbed (such as a yard) and an area that is relatively undisturbed (such as a vacant lot). Make a hypothesis about which area contains the greater biodiversity. Get your teacher's approval of your selected locations.

Test the Hypothesis

3 Design a procedure to determine which area contains the greater biodiversity. Have your plan approved by your teacher before you begin.

TN GLE 0807.Inq.2 Use appropriate tools and techniques to gather, organize, analyze, and interpret data.
GLE 0807.Inq.3 Synthesize information to determine cause and effect relationships between evidence and explanations.

GLE 0807.Inq.4 Recognize possible sources of bias and error, alternative explanations, and questions for further exploration.
GLE 0807.Inq.5 Communicate scientific understanding using descriptions, explanations, and models. GLE 0807.5.5 Describe the importance of maintaining the earth's biodiversity.

Prairie

Wheat Field

4 To discover smaller organisms, measure off a square meter, set stakes at the corners, and mark the area with twine. Use a magnifying lens to observe organisms. When you record your observations, refer to organisms in the following way: Ant A, Ant B, and so on. Make note of any visits by larger organisms.

5 Create any data tables that you might need for recording your data. If you observe your areas on more than one occasion, make data tables for each observation period. Organize your data into clear and understandable categories.
✔0807.Inq.5, ✔0807.5.6

Analyze the Results

1 **Explaining Events** What factors did you consider before deciding which habitats were disturbed or undisturbed?

2 **Constructing Maps** Draw a map of the land around your school. Label areas of high biodiversity and those of lower biodiversity.

3 **Analyzing Data** What problems did you have while making observations and recording data for each habitat? How did you solve these problems?

Draw Conclusions

4 **Drawing Conclusions** Review your hypothesis. Did your data support your hypothesis? Explain your answer.

5 **Evaluating Methods** Describe possible errors in your investigation. Review the design of your procedure and determine ways you could improve your procedure to eliminate errors.
✔0807.Inq.4

6 **Applying Conclusions** Do you think that the biodiversity around your school increased or decreased since the school was built? Explain your answer.

Inquiry

Using what you've learned in this lab, think of an area that is less disturbed than the yard, such as a local woods or park. Design an investigation to evaluate biodiversity in this area. Identify tools you would use to collect and organize your data. How would you communicate your findings?
✔0807.Inq.2, ✔0807.Inq.5

Chapter Review

TN GLE 0807.Inq.3, GLE 0807.Inq.5, GLE 0807.T/E.3, GLE 0807.5.5

USING KEY TERMS

Complete each of the following sentences by choosing the correct term from the word bank.

conservation pollution
recycling biodiversity
overpopulation
renewable resource
nonrenewable resource

1 A(n) ___ is a resource that is replaced at a much slower rate than it is used.

2 The presence of too many individuals in a population for available resources is called ___.

3 ___ is an unwanted change in the environment caused by wastes. ✔0807.Inq.3

4 The preservation and wise use of natural resources is called ___.

5 ___ is the number and variety of organisms in an area.

UNDERSTANDING KEY IDEAS

Multiple Choice

6 Preventing habitat destruction is important because ✔0807.Inq.3

a. organisms do not live independently of each other.

b. protection of habitats is a way to promote biodiversity.

c. the balance of nature could be disrupted if habitats were destroyed.

d. All of the above

7 A renewable resource

a. is a natural resource that can be replaced as quickly as it is used.

b. is a natural resource that takes thousands or millions of years to be replaced.

c. includes fossil fuels, such as coal or oil.

d. will eventually run out.

Short Answer

8 Describe how you can use the three Rs to conserve resources.

9 What are five kinds of pollutants?

10 List three ways that technology responds to social, political, and economic needs by making it easier to reduce, reuse, or recycle. ✔0807.T/E.1

11 What are two things that can be done to maintain biodiversity? ✔0807.Inq.3

CRITICAL THINKING

12 **Concept Mapping** Use the following terms to create a concept map: *pollution, radioactive wastes, gases, pollutants, CFCs, PCBs, hazardous wastes, chemicals, noise,* and *garbage.*

13 **Analyzing Ideas** How may deforestation have contributed to the extinction of some species? ✔0807.Inq.3

14 **Predicting Consequences** It is convenient to buy water in plastic bottles. Describe how the unintended consequences of buying bottled water can impact society. ✔0807.T/E.3

15 Evaluating Conclusions A scientist thinks that farms should be planted with many different kinds of crops instead of a single crop. Based on what you learned about biodiversity, evaluate the scientist's conclusion. What unintended consequences might this cause? ✔0807.T/E.3

16 Applying Concepts Imagine that a new species has moved into a local habitat. The species feeds on some of the same plants that the native species do, but it has no natural predators. Describe what might happen to local habitats as a result. ✔0807.Inq.3

17 Making Inferences Many scientists think that forests are nonrenewable resources. Explain why they might have this opinion.

Creating Graphs

18 To study biodiversity, Caleb counted organisms A, B, and C for two years in the park. Use the data below to prepare two circle graphs that show how the biodiversity of organisms A, B, and C changed. ✔0808.5.6

Number of Organisms	A	B	C
Year 1	10	60	30
Year 2	20	50	30

The line graph below shows the concentration of carbon dioxide in the atmosphere between 1958 and 1990. Use this graph to answer the questions that follow.

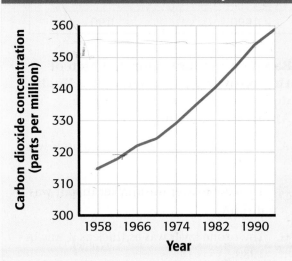

Carbon Dioxide in the Atmosphere

19 What was the concentration of carbon dioxide in parts per million in 1960? in 1990?

20 What is the average change in carbon dioxide concentration every 4 years?

21 If the concentration of carbon dioxide continues to change at the rate shown in the graph, what will the concentration be in 2010?

TN SPI 0807.Inq.2 Select tools and procedures needed to conduct a moderately complex experiment.

SPI 0807.Inq.4 Draw a conclusion that establishes a cause and effect relationship supported by evidence.

SPI 0807.T/E.3 Distinguish between the intended benefits and the unintended consequences of a new technology.

Multiple Choice

Use the table below to answer question 1.

October Ozone Levels Above Halley Bay, Antarctica, in Dobson Units (DU)	
Year	Ozone level (DU)
1960	300
1970	280
1980	235
1990	190

1. **Based on the table above, which of the following statements most likely describes the ozone layer above Antarctica in 2000?**

    A. The ozone layer was thinner than it was in 1990.

    B. The ozone layer was thicker than it was in 1960.

    C. The ozone layer was as thick as it was in 1980.

    D. The ozone layer was nonexistent over Antarctica.

2. **Which of the following would be the best way for students and teachers to decrease the amount of paper they use in their science class? They could**

    A. share handouts of class notes.

    B. use both sides of each sheet of paper.

    C. recycle sheets of paper when they are finished with them.

    D. use blackboards and overhead projectors instead of handouts of class notes.

3. **If there were a massive increase in the amount of carbon circulating in the carbon cycle, it would**

    A. cause no change.

    B. decrease the number of plants.

    C. affect photosynthesis and respiration.

    D. only affect living things that have carbon in their bodies.

4. **You are investigating the biodiversity in a local stream. You need to identify materials to use for collecting your water samples. Which of the following is the most environmentally friendly product to use?**

    A. one 1-L paper carton of water

    B. two 1-L plastic bottles of water

    C. four half-liter plastic bottles of water

    D. two refillable 1-L glass bottles of water

5. **An exotic species often thrives in its new environment because it**

    A. hunts prey.

    B. helps native species thrive.

    C. doesn't affect the existing ecosystem.

    D. is free from the predators in its native habitat.

6. **Which of the following is a reason for maintaining biodiversity?**

    A. to maintain ecosystems

    B. to reduce diseases of species

    C. to preserve habitats

    D. all of the above

Use the diagram below to answer question 7.

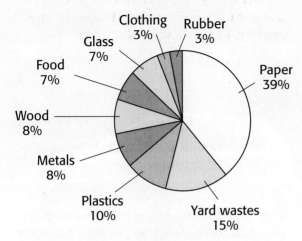

Clothing
3%

Rubber
3%

Glass
7%

Food
7%

Paper
39%

Wood
8%

Metals
8%

Plastics
10%

Yard wastes
15%

7. **Ross performed a field investigation on his local landfill and created the pie chart above, which shows the types and amounts of wastes in the landfill. How much space in this landfill could be saved if people recycled all of their glass and plastic?**

   A. 17%

   B. 25%

   C. 30%

   D. 59%

8. **A certain object is biodegradable. How does that benefit the environment?**

   A. It can be recycled, reducing the use of resources.

   B. It is readily broken down, so it doesn't take up space in a landfill.

   C. It increases the use of renewable resources, which can be quickly replaced.

   D. It releases chemicals that are less harmful than chemicals released by other items.

9. **A new fertilizer helps produce more wheat per acre. Some fertilizers can be pollutants. Which of the following statements describes a possible unintended consequence of the new fertilizer?**

   A. It gives off radiation, which harms organisms.

   B. It traps heat around Earth.

   C. It destroys the ozone that protects Earth.

   D. It can cause oxygen depletion in water, killing fish.

10. **The loss of any habitat can affect biodiversity. The loss of which of the following habitats will have the greatest effect on biodiversity?**

    A. rain forest

    B. wheat field

    C. coniferous forest

    D. banana plantation

Open Response

11. **The gray bat is an endangered species that lives in caves. Discuss 2 ways the gray bat could be protected.**

12. **Marine habitats are affected by both point and nonpoint-source pollution. Explain the difference between these kinds of pollution. Give an example of each point and nonpoint-source pollution and its effect on marine habitats.**

TCAP Test Preparation

Science in Action

Scientific Debate

Are Waste-to-Energy Plants Worthwhile?

T/E As landfill space decreases, other methods of waste disposal are being developed. One method is burning waste in a plant that produces heat energy or electricity. Supporters say that burning waste reduces trash and its transportation. Opponents say that waste-to-energy plants release pollutants into the air and water. While technology has improved the effectiveness of antipollution devices, such as scrubbers, opponents think that emissions are still too dangerous. In addition, the best materials for burning are the ones that could be recycled, such as paper. Burning these materials could actually cause a decline in the number of people who reduce, reuse, and recycle. As technology improves, the debate is likely to continue.

TN GLE 0807.T/E.1, GLE 0807.T/E.2, GLE 0807.T/E.3

Math ACTiViTY

If burning 2,000 kilograms of garbage generates the equivalent heat energy of 500 kilograms of coal, how many kilograms of coal are saved if 5,000 kilograms of garbage is burned?

Science, Technology, and Society

Hydrogen-Fueled Automobiles

T/E Can you imagine a car that purrs quieter than a kitten and gives off water vapor instead of harmful pollutants? These cars may sound like science fiction. But such cars already exist! They run on one of the most common elements in the world—hydrogen. Some car companies are already speculating that one day all cars will run on hydrogen. The U.S. government has also taken notice. In 2003, President George W. Bush promised $1.2 billion to help research and develop hydrogen-fueled cars. Oak Ridge National Laboratory, in Oak Ridge, Tennessee, is a leader in the development of hydrogen delivery and fuel cells for cars.

TN GLE 0807.T/E.1, GLE 0807.T/E.2

Language Arts ACTiViTY

WRITING SKILL Research hydrogen-fueled cars. Then, write a letter to a car company, your senator, or the President expressing your opinion about the development of hydrogen-fueled cars.

Phil McCrory

Hairy Oil Spills Phil McCrory, a hairdresser in Huntsville, Alabama, asked a brilliant question when he saw an otter whose fur was drenched with oil from the *Exxon Valdez* oil spill. If the otter's fur soaked up all the oil, why wouldn't human hair do the same? McCrory gathered hair from the floor of his salon and took it home to perform his own experiments. He stuffed hair into a pair of his wife's pantyhose and tied the ankles together to form a bagel-shaped bundle. McCrory floated the bundle in his son's wading pool and poured used motor oil into the center of the ring. When he pulled the ring closed, not a drop of oil remained in the water!

McCrory approached the National Aeronautics and Space Administration (NASA) with his discovery. Based on tests performed by NASA, scientists estimated that 64 million kilograms of hair in reusable mesh pillows could have cleaned up all of the oil spilled by the *Exxon Valdez* within a week! Unfortunately, the $2 billion spent on the cleanup removed only about 12% of the oil.

TN GLE 0807.T/E.2

Social Studies ACTiViTY

Make a map of an oil spill. Show the areas that were affected. Indicate some of the animal populations affected by the spill, such as grebes.

go.hrw.com

To learn more about these Science in Action topics, visit go.hrw.com and type in the keyword **HL5ENVF**.

Current Science

Check out Current Science® articles related to this chapter by visiting go.hrw.com. Just type in the keyword **HL5CS21**.

UNIT 2

TIMELINE

Physical Science

In this unit, you will learn ways to describe matter and the changes it goes through. You will learn about the atom—the building block of all matter—and its structure. You will learn how atoms react to form compounds. You will also learn how electricity and magnetism interact, and how electronic technology has changed the world. This timeline shows some of the events and discoveries that have occurred as scientists seek to understand the nature of matter.

1661

Robert Boyle, a chemist in England, determines that elements are substances that cannot be broken down into anything simpler by chemical processes.

1712

Thomas Newcomen invents the first practical steam engine.

1937

The *Hindenburg* explodes while docking in Lakehurst, New Jersey. To make it lighter than air, the airship was filled with flammable hydrogen gas.

1971

The first commercially available "pocket" calculator is introduced. It has a mass of nearly 1 kg and a price of about $400, hardly the kind of pocket calculator that exists today.

1766
English chemist Henry Cavendish discovers and describes the properties of a highly flammable substance now known as hydrogen gas.

1800
Current from an electric battery is used to separate water into the elements hydrogen and oxygen for the first time.

1920
American women win the right to vote with the ratification of the 19th Amendment to the Constitution.

1950
Silly Putty® is sold in a toy store for the first time. The soft, gooey substance quickly becomes popular because of its strange properties, including the ability to "pick up" the print from a newspaper page.

1957
The space age begins when the Soviet Union launches *Sputnik I*, the first artificial satellite to circle the Earth.

1989
An oil tanker strikes a reef in Prince William Sound, Alaska, and spills nearly 11 million gallons of oil. The floating oil injures or kills thousands of marine mammals and seabirds and damages the Alaskan coastline.

2000
The World's Fair, an international exhibition featuring exhibits and participants from around the world, is held in Hanover, Germany. The theme is "Humankind, Nature, and Technology."

2003
Sally Ride, the first American woman in space, is inducted into the Astronaut Hall of Fame.

7

The Properties of Matter

The Big Idea

Matter is described by its properties and may undergo changes.

TN Tennessee Science Standards

Embedded Inquiry

GLE 0807.Inq.2 Use appropriate tools and techniques to gather, organize, analyze, and interpret data.

GLE 0807.Inq.3 Synthesize information to determine cause and effect relationships between evidence and explanations.

GLE 0807.Inq.5 Communicate scientific understanding using descriptions, explanations, and models.

✔**0807.Inq.2** Identify tools and techniques needed to gather, organize, analyze, and interpret data collected from a moderately complex scientific investigation.

✔**0807.Inq.3** Use evidence from a dataset to determine cause and effect relationships that explain a phenomenon.

✔**0807.Inq.5** Design a method to explain the results of an investigation using descriptions, explanations, or models.

Embedded Technology and Engineering

GLE 0807.T/E.1 Explore how technology responds to social, political, and economic needs.

✔**0807 T/E.1** Use appropriate tools to test for strength, hardness, and flexibility of materials.

✔**0807.T/E.3** Explore how the unintended consequences of new technologies can impact society.

✔**0807.T/E.4** Research bioengineering technologies that advance health and contribute to improvements in our daily lives.

Physical Science

GLE 0807.9.3 Interpret data from an investigation to differentiate between physical and chemical changes.

GLE 0807.12.4 Identify factors that influence the amount of gravitational force between objects.

✔**0807.9.3** Measure or calculate the mass, volume, and temperature of a given substance.

✔**0807.9.4** Calculate the density of various objects.

✔**0807.9.6** Differentiate between physical and chemical changes.

✔**0807.12.5** Explain the difference between mass and weight.

✔**0807.12.6** Identify factors that influence the amount of gravitational force between objects.

PRE-READING ACTIVITY

FOLDNOTES **Booklet** Before you read the chapter, create the FoldNote entitled "Booklet" described in the **Study Skills** section of the Appendix. Label each page of the booklet with a main idea from the chapter. As you read the chapter, write what you learn about each main idea on the appropriate page of the booklet.

About the Photo

This giant ice dragon began as a 1,700 kg block of ice! Making the blocks of ice takes six weeks. Then, the ice blocks are stored at −30°C until the sculpting begins. The artist has to work at −10°C to keep the ice from melting. An ice sculptor has to be familiar with the many properties of water, including its melting point.

START-UP ACTIVITY

TN GLE 0807.Inq.2, GLE 0807.Inq.5

Sack Secrets

In this activity, you will test your skills in determining an object's identity based on the object's properties.

Procedure

1. You and two or three of your classmates will receive a **sealed paper sack** containing a **mystery object.** Do not open the sack!

2. For five minutes, make as many observations about the object as you can without opening the sack. You may touch, smell, shake, or listen to the object through the sack. Record your observations.

Analysis

1. At the end of five minutes, discuss your findings with your partners.

2. List the object's properties that you can identify. Make another list of properties that you cannot identify. Make a conclusion about the object's identity.

3. Share your observations, your list of properties, and your conclusion with the class. Then, open the sack.

4. Did you properly identify the object? If so, how? If not, why not? Record your answers.

What Is Matter?

What do you have in common with a toaster, a steaming bowl of soup, or a bright neon sign?

You are probably thinking that this is a trick question. It is hard to imagine that a person has anything in common with a kitchen appliance, hot soup, or a glowing neon sign.

Matter

From a scientific point of view, you have at least one characteristic in common with these things. You, the toaster, the bowl, the soup, the steam, the glass tubing of a neon sign, and the glowing gas are made of matter. But exactly what is matter? **Matter** is anything that has mass and takes up space. It's that simple! Every object in the universe is made up of some type of matter.

Matter and Volume

All matter takes up space. The amount of space taken up, or occupied, by an object is known as the object's **volume.** Your fingernails, the Statue of Liberty, the continent of Africa, and a cloud have volume. And because these things have volume, they cannot share the same space at the same time. Even the tiniest speck of dust takes up space. Another speck of dust cannot fit into that space without somehow bumping the first speck out of the way. **Figure 1** shows an example of how one object cannot share with another object the same space at the same time. Try the Quick Lab on the next page to see for yourself that matter takes up space.

What You Will Learn

- Describe the two properties of all matter.
- Identify the units used to measure volume and mass.
- Compare mass and weight.
- Explain the relationship between mass and inertia.

Vocabulary

matter	mass
volume	weight
meniscus	inertia

READING STRATEGY

Prediction Guide Before reading this section, write the title of each heading in this section. Next, under each heading, write what you think you will learn.

TN GLE 0807.Inq.2 Use appropriate tools and techniques to gather, organize, analyze, and interpret data.

GLE 0807.Inq.3 Synthesize information to determine cause and effect relationships between evidence and explanations.

GLE 0807.12.4 Identify factors that influence the amount of gravitational force between objects.

matter anything that has mass and takes up space

volume a measure of the size of a body or region in three-dimensional space **TN** *VOCAB*

Figure 1 *Because CDs are made of matter, they have volume. Once your CD storage rack is filled with CDs, you cannot fit another CD in the rack.*

Quick Lab

Space Case

1. Crumple a **piece of paper.** Fit it tightly in the bottom of a **clear plastic cup** so that it won't fall out.

2. Turn the cup upside down. Lower the cup straight down into a **bucket** half-filled with **water.** Be sure that the cup is completely underwater.

3. Lift the cup straight out of the water. Turn the cup upright, and observe the paper. Record your observations.

4. Use the point of a **pencil** to punch a small hole in the bottom of the cup. Repeat steps 2 and 3.

5. How do the results show that air has volume? Explain your answer.

Liquid Volume

Lake Erie, the smallest of the Great Lakes, has a volume of approximately 483 trillion (that's 483,000,000,000,000) liters of water. Can you imagine that much water? Think of a 2-liter bottle of soda. The water in Lake Erie could fill more than 241 trillion 2-liter soda bottles. That's a lot of water! On a smaller scale, a can of soda has a volume of only 355 milliliters, which is about one-third of a liter. You can check the volume of the soda by using a large measuring cup from your kitchen.

Liters (L) and milliliters (mL) are the units used most often to express the volume of liquids. The volume of any amount of liquid, from one raindrop to a can of soda to an entire ocean, can be expressed in these units.

TN *Standards Check* What are two units used to measure volume? ✔0807.9.3

Measuring the Volume of Liquids

In your science class, you'll probably use a graduated cylinder instead of a measuring cup to measure the volume of liquids. Graduated cylinders are used to measure the liquid volume when accuracy is important. The surface of a liquid in any container, including a measuring cup or a large beaker, is curved. The curve at the surface of a liquid is called a **meniscus** (muh NIS kuhs). To measure the volume of most liquids, such as water, you must look at the bottom of the meniscus, as shown in **Figure 2.** Note that you may not be able to see a meniscus in a large beaker. The meniscus looks flat because the liquid is in a wide container.

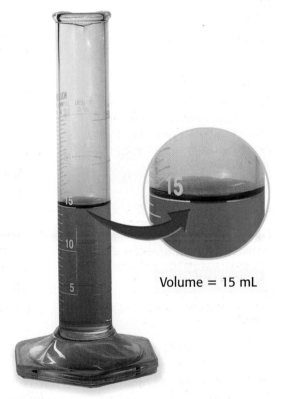

Volume = 15 mL

Figure 2 *To measure volume correctly, read the scale of the lowest part of the meniscus (as shown) at eye level.*

meniscus the curve at a liquid's surface by which one measures the volume of the liquid

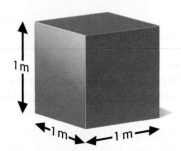

Figure 3 *A cubic meter (1 m³) is a cube that has a length, width, and height of 1 m.*

Volume of a Regularly Shaped Solid Object

The volume of any solid object is expressed in cubic units. The word *cubic* means "having three dimensions." In science, cubic meters (m³) and cubic centimeters (cm³) are the units most often used to express the volume of solid things. The 3 in these unit symbols shows that three quantities, or dimensions, were multiplied to get the final result. You can see the three dimensions of a cubic meter in **Figure 3.** There are formulas to find the volume of regularly shaped objects. For example, to find the volume of a cube or a rectangular object, multiply the length, width, and height of the object, as shown in the following equation:

$$volume = length \times width \times height$$

Volume of an Irregularly Shaped Solid Object

How do you find the volume of a solid that does not have a regular shape? For example, to find the volume of a 12-sided object, you cannot use the equation given above. But you can measure the volume of a solid object by measuring the volume of water that the object displaces. In **Figure 4,** when a 12-sided object is added to the water in a graduated cylinder, the water level rises. The volume of water displaced by the object is equal to its volume. Because 1 mL is equal to 1 cm³, you can express the volume of the water displaced by the object in cubic centimeters. Although volumes of liquids can be expressed in cubic units, volumes of solids should not be expressed in liters or milliliters.

Figure 4 *The 12-sided object displaced 15 mL of water. Because 1 mL = 1 cm³, the volume of the object is 15 cm³.*

TN *Standards Check* **Explain how you would measure the volume of an apple.** ✔0807.9.3

Volume of a Rectangular Solid What is the volume of a box that has a length of 5 cm, a width of 1 cm, and a height of 2 cm?

Step 1: Write the equation for volume.

$$volume = length \times width \times height$$

Step 2: Replace the variables with the measurements given to you, and solve.

$$volume = 5 \text{ cm} \times 1 \text{ cm} \times 2 \text{ cm} = 10 \text{ cm}^3$$

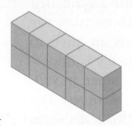

Now It's Your Turn

1. A book has a length of 25 cm, a width of 18 cm, and a height of 4 cm. What is its volume?
2. What is the volume of a suitcase that has a length of 95 cm, a width of 50 cm, and a height of 20 cm?
3. A CD case is 14.2 cm long, 12.4 cm wide, and 1 cm deep. What is its volume?

Matter and Mass

Another characteristic of all matter is mass. **Mass** is the amount of matter in an object. For example, you and a peanut are made of matter. But you are made of more matter than a peanut is, so you have more mass. The mass of an object is the same no matter where in the universe the object is located. The only way to change the mass of an object is to change the amount of matter that makes up the object.

The Difference Between Mass and Weight

The terms *mass* and *weight* are often used as though they mean the same thing, but they don't. **Weight** is a measure of the gravitational (GRAV i TAY shuh nuhl) force exerted on an object. Gravitational force keeps objects on Earth from floating into space. The gravitational force between an object and the Earth depends partly on the object's mass. The more mass an object has, the greater the gravitational force on the object and the greater the object's weight. But an object's weight can change depending on its location in the universe. An object would weigh less on the moon than it does on Earth because the moon has less gravitational force than Earth does. **Figure 5** explains the differences between mass and weight.

mass a measure of the amount of matter in an object

weight a measure of the gravitational force exerted on an object; its value can change with the location of the object in the universe **TN VOCAB**

Figure 5 **Differences Between Mass and Weight**

Mass

- Mass is a measure of the amount of matter in an object.
- Mass is always constant for an object no matter where the object is located in the universe.
- Mass is measured by using a balance (shown below).
- Mass is expressed in kilograms (kg), grams (g), and milligrams (mg).

Weight

- Weight is a measure of the gravitational force on an object.
- Weight varies depending on where the object is in relation to the Earth (or any large body in the universe).
- Weight is measured by using a spring scale (shown at right).
- Weight is expressed in newtons (N).

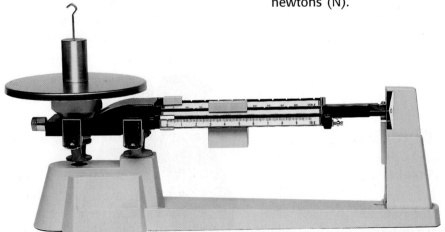

Measuring Mass and Weight

The brick and the sponge in **Figure 6** have the same volume. But because the brick has more mass, a greater gravitational force is exerted on the brick than on the sponge. As a result, the brick weighs more than the sponge.

The SI unit of mass is the kilogram (kg), but mass is often expressed in grams (g) and milligrams (mg), too. These units can be used to express the mass of any object in the universe.

Weight is a measure of gravitational force and is expressed in the SI unit of force, the *newton* (N). One newton is about equal to the weight of an object that has a mass of 100 g on Earth. So, if you know the mass of an object, you can calculate the object's weight on Earth. Weight is a good estimate of the mass of an object because, on Earth, gravity doesn't change.

✓ **Reading Check** What units are often used to measure mass? weight?

Figure 6 *The brick and the sponge take up the same amount of space. But the brick has more matter in it, so its mass—and thus its weight—is greater.*

Inertia

Imagine kicking a soccer ball that has the mass of a bowling ball. It would be not only painful but also very difficult to get the ball moving in the first place! The reason is inertia (in UHR shuh). **Inertia** is the tendency of an object to resist a change in motion. So, an object at rest will remain at rest until something causes the object to move. Also, a moving object will keep moving at the same speed and in the same direction unless something acts on the object to change its speed or direction.

inertia the tendency of an object to resist being moved or, if the object is moving, to resist a change in speed or direction until an outside force acts on the object

 *VOCAB*

MATH FOCUS

Converting Mass to Weight   A student weighs 450 newtons (N). What is this student's mass in grams?

Step 1: Write the information given to you.

450 N

Step 2: Write the conversion factor to change newtons into grams.

1 N = 100 g

Step 3: Write the equation so that newtons will cancel.

450 N x 100 g/1 N = 45,000 g

Now It's Your Turn
1. What is the mass of a car that weighs 13,620 N?
2. Your pair of boots weighs 8.50 N. If each boot has exactly the same weight, what is the mass of each boot?

Mass: The Measure of Inertia

Mass is a measure of inertia. An object that has a large mass is harder to get moving and harder to stop than an object that has less mass. The reason is that the object with the large mass has greater inertia. For example, imagine that you are going to push a grocery cart that has only one potato in it. Pushing the cart is easy because the mass and inertia are small. But suppose the grocery cart is stacked with potatoes, as in **Figure 7.** Now the total mass—and the inertia—of the cart full of potatoes is much greater. It will be harder to get the cart moving. And once the cart is moving, stopping the cart will be harder.

Figure 7 *Because of inertia, moving a cart full of potatoes is more difficult than moving a cart that is empty.*

SECTION Review

TN GLE 0807.Inq.3, GLE 0807.Inq.5, GLE 0807.12.4

Summary

- Two properties of matter are volume and mass.
- Volume is the amount of space taken up by an object.
- The SI unit of volume is the liter (L).
- Mass is the amount of matter in an object.
- The SI unit of mass is the kilogram (kg).
- Weight is a measure of the gravitational force on an object, usually in relation to the Earth.
- Inertia is the tendency of an object to resist being moved or, if the object is moving, to resist a change in speed or direction. The more massive an object is, the greater its inertia.

Using Key Terms

1. Use the following terms in the same sentence: *volume* and *meniscus.*

2. In your own words, write a definition for each of the following terms: *mass, weight,* and *inertia.*

Understanding Key Ideas

3. Which of the following is matter?
   a. dust
   b. the moon
   c. strand of hair
   d. All of the above

4. A graduated cylinder is used to measure ✔0807.9.3
   a. volume.
   b. weight.
   c. mass.
   d. inertia.

5. The volume of a solid is measured in
   a. liters.
   b. grams.
   c. cubic centimeters.
   d. All of the above

6. Mass is measured in
   a. liters.
   b. centimeters.
   c. newtons.
   d. kilograms.

7. Explain the difference between mass and weight. ✔0807.12.5

Math Skills

8. A nugget of gold is placed in a graduated cylinder that contains 80 mL of water. The water level rises to 225 mL after the nugget is added to the cylinder. What is the volume of the gold nugget? ✔0807.9.3

9. One newton equals about 100 g on Earth. If a football weighs 4 N, what is its mass? ✔0807.9.3

Critical Thinking

10. **Identifying Relationships** Do objects with large masses always have large weights? Explain. ✔0807.12.6

11. **Applying Concepts** Would an elephant weigh more or less on the moon than it would weigh on Earth? Explain your answer. ✔0807.Inq.3, ✔0807.12.6

Internet Resources

For a variety of links related to this chapter, go to www.scilinks.org
Topic: What Is Matter?
SciLinks code: HSM1662

Physical Properties

Have you ever played the game 20 Questions? The goal of this game is to figure out what object another person is thinking of by asking 20 yes/no questions or less.

If you can't figure out the object's identity after asking 20 questions, you may not be asking the right kinds of questions. What kinds of questions should you ask? You may want to ask questions about the physical properties of the object. Knowing the properties of an object can help you find out what it is.

Physical Properties

The questions in **Figure 1** help someone gather information about color, odor, mass, and volume. Each piece of information is a physical property of matter. A **physical property** of matter can be observed or measured without changing the matter's identity. For example, you don't have to change an apple's identity to see its color or to measure its volume.

Other physical properties, such as magnetism, the ability to conduct electric current, strength, and flexibility, can help someone identify how to use a substance. For example, think of a scooter with an electric motor. The magnetism produced by the motor is used to convert energy stored in a battery into energy that will turn the wheels.

✓ **Reading Check** List four physical properties.

What You Will Learn

- Identify six examples of physical properties of matter.
- Describe how density is used to identify substances.
- List six examples of physical changes.
- Explain what happens to matter during a physical change.

Vocabulary

physical property
density
physical change

READING STRATEGY

Mnemonics As you read this section, create a mnemonic device to help you remember examples of physical properties.

TN **GLE 0807.Inq.2** Use appropriate tools and techniques to gather, organize, analyze, and interpret data.

GLE 0807.Inq.3 Synthesize information to determine cause and effect relationships between evidence and explanations.

GLE 0807.Inq.5 Communicate scientific understanding using descriptions, explanations, and models.

GLE 0807.T/E.1 Explore how technology responds to social, political, and economic needs.

GLE 0807.9.3 Interpret data from an investigation to differentiate between physical and chemical changes.

Figure 1 *Asking questions about the physical properties of an object can help you identify it.*

Could I hold it in my hand? **Yes.**
Does it have an odor? **Yes.**
Is it safe to eat? **Yes.**
Is it orange? **No.**
Is it yellow? **No.**
Is it red? **Yes.**
Is it an apple? **Yes!**

Figure 2 Examples of Physical Properties

Thermal conductivity (KAHN duhk TIV uh tee) is the rate at which a substance transfers heat. Plastic foam is a poor conductor.

State is the physical form in which a substance exists, such as a solid, liquid, or gas. Ice is water in the solid state.

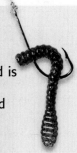

Density is the mass per unit volume of a substance. Lead is very dense, so it makes a good sinker for a fishing line.

Solubility (SAHL yoo BIL uh tee) is the ability of a substance to dissolve in another substance. Flavored drink mix dissolves in water.

Ductility (duhk TIL uh tee) is the ability of a substance to be pulled into a wire. Copper is often used to make wiring because it is ductile.

Malleability (MAL ee uh BIL uh tee) is the ability of a substance to be rolled or pounded into thin sheets. Aluminum can be rolled into sheets to make foil.

Identifying Matter

You use physical properties every day. For example, physical properties help you determine if your socks are clean (odor), if your books will fit into your backpack (volume), or if your shirt matches your pants (color). **Figure 2** gives more examples of physical properties.

Density

Density is a physical property that describes the relationship between mass and volume. **Density** is the amount of matter in a given space, or volume. A golf ball and a table-tennis ball, such as those in **Figure 3**, have similar volumes. But a golf ball has more mass than a table-tennis ball does. So, the golf ball has a greater density.

physical property a characteristic of a substance that does not involve a chemical change, such as density, color, or hardness

density the ratio of the mass of a substance to the volume of the substance ▰TN▰ *VOCAB*

mass = 46 g

mass = 2 g

Figure 3 *A golf ball is denser than a table-tennis ball because the golf ball contains more matter in a similar volume.*

Liquid Layers

What do you think causes the liquid in **Figure 4** to look the way it does? Is it trick photography? No, it is differences in density! There are six liquids in the graduated cylinder. Each liquid has a different density. If the liquids are carefully poured into the cylinder, they can form six layers because of the differences in density. The densest layer is on the bottom. The least dense layer is on top. The order of the layers shows the order of increasing density. Yellow is the least dense, followed by the colorless layer, red, blue, green, and brown (the densest).

Density of Solids

Which would you rather carry around all day: a kilogram of lead or a kilogram of feathers? At first, you might say feathers. But both the feathers and the lead have the same mass, just as the cotton balls and the tomatoes have the same mass, as shown in **Figure 5.** So, the lead would be less awkward to carry around than the feathers would. The feathers are much less dense than the lead. So, it takes a lot of feathers to equal the same mass of lead.

Figure 4 *This graduated cylinder contains six liquids. From top to bottom, they are corn oil, water, shampoo, dish detergent, antifreeze, and maple syrup.*

Knowing the density of a substance can also tell you if the substance will float or sink in water. If the density of an object is less than the density of water, the object will float. Likewise, a solid object whose density is greater than the density of water will sink when the object is placed in water.

✓ **Reading Check** What will happen to an object placed in water if the object's density is less than water's density?

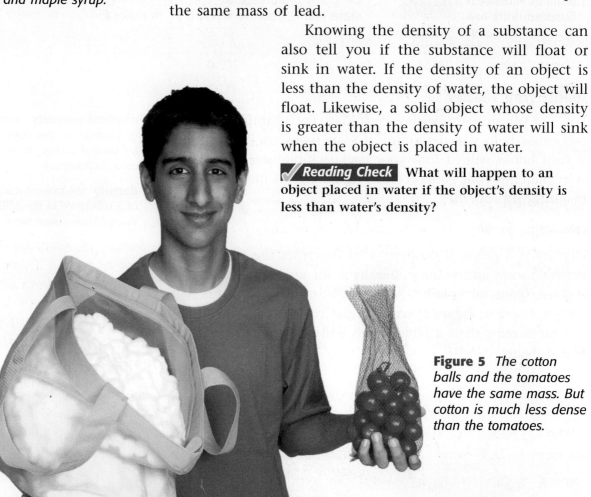

Figure 5 *The cotton balls and the tomatoes have the same mass. But cotton is much less dense than the tomatoes.*

Solving for Density

To find an object's density (D), first measure its mass (m) and volume (V). Then, use the equation below.

$$D = \frac{m}{V}$$

Units for density consist of a mass unit divided by a volume unit. Some units for density are g/cm^3, g/mL, kg/m^3, and kg/L. Remember that the volume of a solid is often given in cubic centimeters or cubic meters. So, the density of a solid should be given in units of g/cm^3 or kg/m^3.

Using Density to Identify Substances

Density is a useful physical property for identifying substances. Each substance has a density that differs from the densities of other substances. And the density of a substance is always the same at a given temperature and pressure. Look at **Table 1** to compare the densities of several common substances.

Table 1 Densities of Common Substances*

Substance	Density* (g/cm^3)	Substance	Density* (g/cm^3)
Helium (gas)	0.0001663	Zinc (solid)	7.13
Oxygen (gas)	0.001331	Silver (solid)	10.50
Water (liquid)	1.00	Lead (solid)	11.35
Pyrite (solid)	5.02	Mercury (liquid)	13.55

*at 20°C and 1.0 atm

Calculating Density What is the density of an object whose mass is 25 g and whose volume is 10 cm³?

Step 1: Write the equation for density.

$$D = \frac{m}{V}$$

Step 2: Replace m and V with the measurements given in the problem, and solve.

$$D = \frac{25 \text{ g}}{10 \text{ cm}^3} = 2.5 \text{ g/cm}^3$$

The equation for density can also be rearranged to find mass and volume, as shown.

$m = D \times V$ (Rearrange by multiplying by V.)

$V = \frac{m}{D}$ (Rearrange by dividing by D.)

Now It's Your Turn

1. Find the density of a substance that has a mass of 45 kg and a volume of 43 m³. (Hint: Make sure your answer's units are units of density.)
2. Suppose you have a lead ball whose mass is 454 g. What is the ball's volume? (Hint: Use **Table 1** above.)
3. What is the mass of a 15 mL sample of mercury?

Figure 6 Examples of Physical Changes

Changing from a solid to a liquid is a physical change. All changes of state are physical changes.

This aluminum can has gone through the physical change of being crushed. The properties of the can are the same.

Physical Changes Do Not Form New Substances

A **physical change** is a change that affects one or more physical properties of a substance. Imagine that a piece of silver is pounded and molded into a heart-shaped pendant. This change is a physical one because only the shape of the silver has changed. The piece of silver is still silver. Its properties are the same. **Figure 6** shows more examples of physical changes.

physical change a change of matter from one form to another without a change in chemical properties

✓ **Reading Check** What is a physical change?

Examples of Physical Changes

Freezing water to make ice cubes and sanding a piece of wood are examples of physical changes. These changes do not change the identities of the substances. Ice is still water. And sawdust is still wood. Another interesting physical change takes place when certain substances dissolve in other substances. For example, when you dissolve sugar in water, the sugar seems to disappear. But if you heat the mixture, the water evaporates. Then, you will see that the sugar is still there. The sugar went through a physical change when it dissolved.

TN GLE 0807.T/E.1, GLE 0807.Inq 2

CONNECTION TO Engineering

Rivers The melting of snow is a physical change. Melting snow can move into rivers quickly and cause floods. Engineers work to reduce flooding along rivers. Research ways that engineers work to reduce flooding on the Mississippi River. Write a one-page report about your findings.

ACTIVITY

Matter and Physical Changes

Physical changes do not change the identity of the matter involved. A stick of butter can be melted and poured over a bowl of popcorn, as shown in **Figure 7.** Although the shape of the butter has changed, the butter is still butter, so a physical change has occurred. In the same way, if you make a figure from a lump of clay, you change the clay's shape and cause a physical change. But the identity of the clay does not change. The properties of the figure are the same as those of the lump of clay.

Figure 7 *Melting butter for popcorn involves a physical change.*

SECTION Review

TN GLE 0807.Inq.2, GLE 0807.Inq.3, GLE 0807.Inq.5, GLE 0807.9.3

Summary

- Physical properties of matter can be observed without changing the identity of the matter.
- Examples of physical properties are conductivity, state, malleability, ductility, solubility, and density.
- Density is the amount of matter in a given space.
- The density of a substance is always the same at a given pressure and temperature.
- When a substance undergoes a physical change, its identity stays the same.
- Examples of physical changes are freezing, cutting, bending, dissolving, and melting.

Using Key Terms

1. Use each of the following terms in a separate sentence: *physical property* and *physical change.* ✔0807.9.6

Understanding Key Ideas

2. The units of density for a rectangular piece of wood are
   a. grams per milliliter.
   b. cubic centimeters.
   c. kilograms per liter.
   d. grams per cubic centimeter.

3. Explain why a golf ball is heavier than a table-tennis ball even though the balls are the same size.

4. Describe what happens to a substance when it goes through a physical change. ✔0807.9.6

5. Identify six examples of physical properties.

6. List six physical changes that matter can go through. ✔0807.9.6

Math Skills

7. What is the density of an object that has a mass of 350 g and a volume of 95 cm³? Would this object float in water? Explain. ✔0807.Inq.3, ✔0807.9.4

8. The density of an object is 5 g/cm³, and the volume of the object is 10 cm³. What is the mass of the object? ✔0807.9.3

Critical Thinking

9. **Applying Concepts** How can you determine that a coin is not pure silver if you know the mass and volume of the coin?

10. **Identifying Relationships** What physical property do the following substances have in common: water, oil, mercury, and alcohol?

11. **Analyzing Processes** Explain how you would find the density of an unknown liquid if you have all of the laboratory equipment that you need. ✔0807.Inq.2,

Internet Resources

For a variety of links related to this chapter, go to www.scilinks.org
Topic: Describing Matter; Physical Changes
SciLinks code: HSM0391; HSM1142

Chemical Properties

How would you describe a piece of wood before and after it is burned? Has it changed color? Does it have the same texture? The original piece of wood changed, and physical properties alone can't describe what happened to it.

What You Will Learn

- Describe two examples of chemical properties.
- Explain what happens during a chemical change.
- Distinguish between physical and chemical changes.

Vocabulary

chemical property
chemical change

READING STRATEGY

Reading Organizer As you read this section, create an outline of the section. Use the headings from the section in your outline.

TN **GLE 0807.Inq.2** Use appropriate tools and techniques to gather, organize, analyze, and interpret data.

GLE 0807.T/E.1 Explore how technology responds to social, political, and economic needs.

GLE 0807.9.2 Explain that matter has properties that are determined by the structure and arrangement of atoms.

GLE 0807.9.3 Interpret data from an investigation to differentiate between physical and chemical changes.

Chemical Properties

Physical properties are not the only properties that describe matter. **Chemical properties** describe matter based on its ability to change into new matter that has different properties. For example, when wood is burned, ash and smoke are created. These new substances have very different properties than the original piece of wood had. Wood has the chemical property of flammability. *Flammability* is the ability of a substance to burn. Ash and smoke cannot burn, so they have the chemical property of nonflammability.

Another chemical property is reactivity. *Reactivity* is the ability of two or more substances to combine and form one or more new substances. The photo of the old car in **Figure 1** illustrates reactivity and nonreactivity.

✓ *Reading Check* **What does the term *reactivity* mean?**

Figure 1 **Reactivity with Oxygen**

The iron used in this old car has the chemical property of **reactivity with oxygen**. When iron is exposed to oxygen, it rusts.

The bumper on this car still looks new because it is coated with chromium. Chromium has the chemical property of **nonreactivity with oxygen.**

Figure 2 Physical Versus Chemical Properties

Physical property	Chemical property

Shape Bending an iron nail will change its shape.	**Reactivity with Oxygen** An iron nail can react with oxygen in the air to form iron oxide, or rust.

State Rubbing alcohol is a clear liquid at room temperature.	**Flammability** Rubbing alcohol is able to burn easily.

Comparing Physical and Chemical Properties

How do you tell a physical property from a chemical property? You can observe physical properties without changing the identity of the substance. For example, you can find the density and hardness of wood without changing anything about the wood.

Chemical properties, however, aren't as easy to observe. For example, you can see that wood is flammable only while it is burning. And you can observe that gold is nonflammable only when it won't burn. But a substance always has chemical properties. A piece of wood is flammable even when it's not burning. **Figure 2** shows examples of physical and chemical properties.

Characteristic Properties

The properties that are most useful in identifying a substance are *characteristic properties*. These properties are always the same no matter what size the sample is. Characteristic properties can be physical properties, such as density and solubility, as well as chemical properties, such as flammability and reactivity. Scientists rely on characteristic properties to identify and classify substances.

TN GLE 0807.Inq.5, GLE 0807.T/E.1

CONNECTION TO Technology

WRITING SKILL **T/E** **The Right Stuff** When choosing materials to use in manufacturing, engineers must make sure the properties are suitable for the purpose. For example, false teeth can be made from acrylic plastic, porcelain, or gold. According to legend, George Washington wore false teeth made of wood. Do research and find what Washington's false teeth were really made of. In your **science journal,** write a paragraph about what you have learned. Include information about the advantages of the materials used in modern false teeth.

ACTIVITY

chemical property a property of matter that describes a substance's ability to participate in chemical reactions

Quick Lab

Changing Change

1. Place a folded **paper towel** in a small **pie plate.**

2. Pour **vinegar** into the pie plate until the entire paper towel is damp.

3. Place three shiny **pennies** on top of the paper towel.

4. Put the pie plate in a safe place. Wait 24 hours.

5. Describe and explain the change that took place. ✔0807.9.6

Chemical Changes and New Substances

A **chemical change** happens when one or more substances are changed into new substances that have new and different properties. Chemical changes and chemical properties are not the same. Chemical properties of a substance describe which chemical changes will occur and which chemical changes will not occur. But chemical changes are the process by which substances actually change into new substances. You can learn about the chemical properties of a substance by looking at the chemical changes that take place.

You see chemical changes more often than you may think. For example, a chemical reaction happens every time a battery is used. Chemicals failing to react results in a dead battery. Chemical changes also take place within your body when the food you eat is digested. **Figure 3** describes other examples of chemical changes.

✔ **Reading Check** How does a chemical change differ from a chemical property?

Figure 3 Examples of Chemical Changes

Soured milk smells bad because bacteria have formed new substances in the milk.

Effervescent tablets bubble when the citric acid and baking soda in them react in water.

The **hot gas** formed when hydrogen and oxygen join to make water helps blast the space shuttle into orbit.

The **Statue of Liberty** is made of orange-brown copper but it looks green from the metal's interaction with moist air. New copper compounds formed and these chemical changes made the statue turn green over time.

Figure 4 *Each of the original ingredients has different physical and chemical properties than the final product, the cake, does!*

What Happens During a Chemical Change?

A fun way to see what happens during chemical changes is to bake a cake. You combine eggs, flour, sugar, and other ingredients, as shown in **Figure 4.** When you bake the batter, you end up with something completely different. The heat of the oven and the interaction of the ingredients cause a chemical change. The result is a cake that has properties that differ from the properties of the ingredients.

Signs of Chemical Changes

Look back at **Figure 3.** In each picture, at least one sign indicates a chemical change. Other signs that indicate a chemical change include a change in color or odor, production of heat, fizzing and foaming, and sound or light being given off.

In the cake example, you would smell the cake as it baked. You would also see the batter rise and begin to brown. When you cut the finished cake, you would see the air pockets made by gas bubbles that formed in the batter. These signs show that chemical changes have happened.

Matter and Chemical Changes

Chemical changes change the identity of the matter involved. So, most of the chemical changes that occur in your daily life, such as a cake baking, would be hard to reverse. Imagine trying to unbake a cake. However, some chemical changes can be reversed by more chemical changes. For example, the water formed in the space shuttle's rockets could be split into hydrogen and oxygen by using an electric current.

chemical change a change that occurs when one or more substances change into entirely new substances with different properties

For another activity related to this chapter, go to **go.hrw.com** and type in keyword **HP5MATW.**

Figure 5 Physical and Chemical Changes

Change in Texture Grinding baking soda into a fine, powdery substance is a physical change.

Reactivity with Vinegar Gas bubbles are produced when vinegar is poured into baking soda.

Physical Versus Chemical Changes

The most important question to ask when trying to decide if a physical or chemical change has happened is, Did the composition change? The *composition* of an object is the type of matter that makes up the object and the way that the matter is arranged in the object. **Figure 5** shows both a physical and a chemical change.

A Change in Composition

Physical changes do not change the composition of a substance. For example, water is made of two hydrogen atoms and one oxygen atom. Whether water is a solid, liquid, or gas, its composition is the same. But chemical changes do alter the composition of a substance. For example, through a process called *electrolysis,* water is broken down into hydrogen and oxygen gases. The composition of water has changed, so you know that a chemical change has taken place.

TN GLE 0807.T/E.1

CONNECTION TO Environmental Science

T/E **Acid Rain** When fossil fuels are burned, a chemical change takes place. Sulfur from fossil fuels and oxygen from the air combine to produce sulfur dioxide, a gas. When sulfur dioxide enters the atmosphere, it undergoes another chemical change by interacting with water and oxygen. Research this chemical reaction and its effect on the environment. Make a poster describing the reaction and how technology helps reduce its effects on the environment.

TN GLE 0807.Inq.2, GLE 0807.Inq.5

Physical or Chemical Change?

1. Watch as your teacher places a burning **wooden stick** into a **test tube.** Record your observations.

2. Place a mixture of **powdered sulfur** and **iron filings** on a **sheet of paper.** Place a **bar magnet** underneath the paper, and try to separate the iron from the sulfur.

3. Drop an **effervescent tablet** into a **beaker of water.** Record your observations.

4. Identify whether each change is a physical change or a chemical change. Explain your answers. ✔0807.9.6

Reversing Changes

Can physical and chemical changes be reversed? Many physical changes are easily reversed. They do not change the composition of a substance. For example, if an ice cube melts, you could freeze the liquid water to make another ice cube. But composition does change in a chemical change. So, most chemical changes are not easily reversed. Look at **Figure 6.** The chemical changes that happen when a firework explodes would be almost impossible to reverse, even if you collected all of the materials made in the chemical changes.

Figure 6 *This display of fireworks represents many chemical changes happening at the same time.*

SECTION
Review

TN▶ GLE 0807.Inq.2, GLE 0807.Inq.3,
GLE 0807.Inq.5, GLE 0807.9.3

Summary

- Chemical properties describe a substance based on its ability to change into a new substance that has different properties.

- Chemical properties can be observed only when a chemical change might happen.

- Examples of chemical properties are flammability and reactivity.

- New substances form as a result of a chemical change.

- Unlike a chemical change, a physical change does not alter the identity of a substance.

Using Key Terms

1. In your own words, write a definition for each of the following terms: *chemical property* and *chemical change.*

Understanding Key Ideas

2. Rusting is an example of a ✔0807.9.6
   a. physical property.
   b. physical change.
   c. chemical property.
   d. chemical change.

3. Which of the following is a characteristic property?
   a. density
   b. chemical reactivity
   c. solubility in water
   d. All of the above

4. Write two examples of chemical properties and explain what they are.

5. The Statue of Liberty was originally a copper color. After being exposed to the air, she turned a greenish color. What kind of change happened? Explain your answer. ✔0807.Inq.3, ✔0807.9.6

6. Explain how to tell the difference between a physical and a chemical property.

Math Skills

7. The temperature of an acid solution is 25°C. A strip of magnesium is added, and the temperature rises 2°C each minute for the first 3 min. After another 5 min, the temperature has risen two more degrees. What is the final temperature?
   ✔0807.Inq.2, ✔0807.9.3

Critical Thinking

8. **Making Comparisons** Describe the difference between physical and chemical changes in terms of what happens to the matter involved in each kind of change.
   ✔0807.9.6

9. **Applying Concepts** Identify two physical properties and two chemical properties of a bag of microwave popcorn before popping and after.

Internet Resources

For a variety of links related to this chapter, go to www.scilinks.org
Topic: Chemical Changes
SciLinks code: HSM0266

Skills Practice Lab

White Before Your Eyes

You have learned how to describe matter based on its physical and chemical properties. You have also learned some signs that can help you determine whether a change in matter is a physical change or a chemical change. In this lab, you'll use what you have learned to describe four substances based on their properties and the changes that they undergo.

Procedure

1. Copy Table 1 and Table 2 shown on the next page. Be sure to leave plenty of room in each box to write down your observations.

2. Using a spatula, place a small amount of baking powder into three cups of your egg carton. Use just enough baking powder to cover the bottom of each cup. Record your observations about the baking powder's appearance, such as color and texture, in the "Unmixed" column of Table 1.

OBJECTIVES

Describe the physical properties of four substances.

Identify physical and chemical changes.

Classify four substances by their chemical properties.

MATERIALS

- baking powder
- baking soda
- carton, egg, plastic-foam
- cornstarch
- eyedroppers (3)
- iodine solution
- spatulas (4)
- stirring rod
- sugar
- vinegar
- water

SAFETY

TN GLE 0807.Inq.2 Use appropriate tools and techniques to gather, organize, analyze, and interpret data.

GLE 0807.9.3 Interpret data from an investigation to differentiate between physical and chemical changes.

③ Use an eyedropper to add 60 drops of water to the baking powder in the first cup. Stir with the stirring rod. Record your observations in Table 1 in the column labeled "Mixed with water." Clean your stirring rod.

④ Use a clean dropper to add 20 drops of vinegar to the second cup of baking powder. Stir. Record your observations in Table 1 in the column labeled "Mixed with vinegar." Clean your stirring rod.

⑤ Use a clean dropper to add five drops of iodine solution to the third cup of baking powder. Stir. Record your observations in Table 1 in the column labeled "Mixed with iodine solution." Clean your stirring rod. **Caution:** Be careful when using iodine. Iodine will stain your skin and clothes.

⑥ Repeat steps 2–5 for each of the other substances (baking soda, cornstarch, and sugar). Use a clean spatula for each substance.

Analyze the Results

① **Examining Data** What physical properties do all four substances share?

② **Analyzing Data** In Table 2, write the type of change—physical or chemical—that you observed for each substance. State the property that the change demonstrates. ✔0807.9.6

Draw Conclusions

③ **Evaluating Results** Classify the four substances by the chemical property of reactivity. For example, which substances are reactive with vinegar (acid)? ✔0807.9.6

Table 1 Observations				
Substance	Unmixed	Mixed with water	Mixed with vinegar	Mixed with iodine solution
Baking powder				
Baking soda				
Cornstarch				
Sugar				

Table 2 Changes and Properties						
	Mixed with water		Mixed with vinegar		Mixed with iodine solution	
Substance	Change	Property	Change	Property	Change	Property
Baking powder						
Baking soda						
Cornstarch						
Sugar						

Chapter Review

TN GLE 0807.Inq.2, GLE 0807.Inq.3, GLE 0807.Inq.5, GLE 0807.9.3, GLE 0807.12.4

USING KEY TERMS

1 Use each of the following terms in a separate sentence: *physical property*, *chemical property*, *physical change*, and *chemical change*.   ✔0807.9.6

For each pair of terms, explain how the meanings of the terms differ.

2 *mass* and *weight*

3 *inertia* and *mass*

4 *volume* and *density*

UNDERSTANDING KEY IDEAS

Multiple Choice

5 Which of the following properties is NOT a chemical property?

   a. reactivity with oxygen

   b. malleability

   c. flammability

   d. reactivity with acid

6 The volume of a liquid can be expressed in all of the following units EXCEPT

   a. grams.

   b. liters.

   c. milliliters.

   d. cubic centimeters.

7 The SI unit for the mass of a substance is the

   a. gram.

   b. liter.

   c. milliliter.

   d. kilogram.

8 The best way to measure the volume of an irregularly shaped solid is to ✔0807.Inq.2

   a. use a ruler to measure the length of each side of the object.

   b. weigh the solid on a balance.

   c. use the water displacement method.

   d. use a spring scale.

9 Which of the following statements about weight is true?   ✔0807.12.6

   a. Weight is a measure of the gravitational force on an object.

   b. Weight varies depending on where the object is located in relation to the Earth.

   c. Weight is measured by using a spring scale.

   d. All of the above

10 Which of the following statements does NOT describe a physical property of a piece of chalk?

   a. Chalk is a solid.

   b. Chalk can be broken into pieces.

   c. Chalk is white.

   d. Chalk will bubble in vinegar.

11 Which of the following statements about density is true?

   a. Density is expressed in grams.

   b. Density is mass per unit volume.

   c. Density is expressed in milliliters.

   d. Density is a chemical property.

Short Answer

12 In one or two sentences, explain how the process of measuring the volume of a liquid differs from the process of measuring the volume of a solid.

        ✔0807.Inq.2, ✔0807.9.3

13 What is the formula for calculating density?

14 List three characteristic properties of matter.

15 Describe the difference between mass and weight. ✔0807.12.5

Math Skills

16 What is the volume of a book that has a width of 10 cm, a length that is 2 times the width, and a height that is half the width? Remember to express your answer in cubic units. ✔0807.9.3

17 A jar contains 30 mL of glycerin (whose mass is 37.8 g) and 60 mL of corn syrup (whose mass is 82.8 g). Calculate the density of each liquid. Which liquid is on top? Show your work, and explain your answer. ✔0807.Inq.3, ✔0807.9.4

CRITICAL THINKING

18 Concept Mapping Use the following terms to create a concept map: *matter, mass, inertia, volume, milliliters, cubic centimeters, weight,* and *gravity.*

19 Applying Concepts Develop a set of questions that would be useful when identifying an unknown substance. The substance may be a liquid, a gas, or a solid.

20 Analyzing Processes You made scrambled eggs for your friend Filbert. He asked, "Would you please poach these eggs instead?" What scientific reason would you give Filbert for not changing his eggs? ✔0807.9.6

21 Identifying Relationships You look out your bedroom window and see your new neighbor moving in. Your neighbor bends over to pick up a small cardboard box, but he cannot lift it. What can you conclude about the item(s) in the box? Use the terms *mass* and *inertia* to explain how you came to your conclusion.

22 Analyzing Ideas You may sometimes hear on the radio or on TV that astronauts are weightless in space. Explain why this statement is not true.

INTERPRETING GRAPHICS

Use the photograph below to answer the questions that follow.

23 List three physical properties of this aluminum can.

24 When this can was crushed, did it undergo a physical change or a chemical change? ✔0807.9.6

25 How does the density of the metal in the crushed can compare with the density of the metal before the can was crushed?

26 Can you tell what the chemical properties of the can are by looking at the picture? Explain your answer.

TCAP Test Preparation

TN SPI 0807.Inq.1 Design a simple experimental procedure with an identified control and appropriate variables.

SPI 0807.Inq.2 Select tools and procedures needed to conduct a moderately complex experiment.

SPI 0807.Inq.4 Draw a conclusion that establishes a cause and effect relationship that is supported by evidence.

SPI 0807.T/E.1 Identify the tools and procedures needed to test the design features of a prototype.

SPI 0807.9.2 Identify the common outcome of all chemical changes.

SPI 0807.9.7 Apply an equation to determine the density of an object based on its mass and volume.

Multiple Choice

Use the chart below to answer questions 1–2.

Substance	State*	Density* (g/cm³)	Color
Helium	Gas	0.0001663	Colorless
Iron pyrite	Solid	5.02	Metallic Yellow
Mercury	Liquid	13.55	Metallic Gray
Oxygen	Gas	0.001331	Colorless
Gold	Solid	19.32	Metallic Yellow
Water	Liquid	1.00	Colorless

*at 20°C and 1.0 atm

1. **Which statement is true of mercury?**

   A. It is the densest substance listed.

   B. Its density is less than the density of water.

   C. It is a solid at 20°C and 1.0 atm.

   D. It is the densest liquid listed in the chart.

2. **A substance has a mass of 10 g and a volume of 10 cm³. Based on the chart above, what is the substance? (Hint: the density equation is $D = m/V$.)**

   A. mercury   C. water

   B. oxygen   D. helium

3. **Lee exposed iron nails to oxygen gas and found that iron oxide formed. Which statement about the experiment is correct?**

   A. This is a physical change.

   B. This is a chemical change.

   C. Iron and iron oxide have the same properties.

   D. Oxygen and iron have similar properties.

4. **What is a common outcome of chemical changes?**

   A. One or more substances become new substances with different chemical properties.

   B. One or more substances become new substances with the same chemical properties.

   C. One or more substances stay the same with the same properties.

   D. One or more substances stay the same with different properties.

5. **Sara tested the characteristics of a substance. Which observation represents a physical change in the substance?**

   A. It burns in the presence of oxygen.

   B. It melts at 100°C.

   C. It bubbles in water.

   D. It turns green when exposed to moisture.

6. **Which is a chemical change?**

   A. Clear water turns red after a dye is added.

   B. Ice melts.

   C. Salt dissolves in water.

   D. Milk sours.

7. **A spring scale measures in newtons. Which of the following does a spring scale measure?**

   A. temperature

   B. weight

   C. liquid volume

   D. mass

SPI 0807.9.8 Interpret the results of an investigation to determine whether a physical or chemical change has occurred.

SPI 0807.12.4 Distinguish between mass and weight using appropriate measuring instruments and units.

Use the diagram below to answer questions 8–9.

Before   **After**

8. An irregular object's volume is determined by displacement of water, as shown above. What is the volume of the object?

A. 15 mL

B. 40 mL

C. 55 mL

D. 95 mL

9. Jonathan finds the mass of the submerged object shown above to be 13.07 g. What can you conclude about the measurement?

A. The measurement cannot be used to determine density without also knowing the force of gravity.

B. The measurement is accurate because the resulting density is 0.87 g/mL, a common density of irregular objects.

C. The measurement can be used to determine density because the object is not completely submerged in the water.

D. The measurement is likely inaccurate because the resulting density, 0.87 g/mL, is less than that of water, 1.0 g/mL, which means it would float.

10. Max drops one effervescent tablet into a beaker of water and places a second tablet on the lab table. He observes bubbles of gas form on the surface of the tablet. The bubbles rise and break on the surface of the water. After several minutes, no more bubbles form and no tablet is visible in the water. The tablet on the lab table is unchanged. What conclusion should Max draw from his observations?

A. The solid tablet changes directly into a gas through a physical change.

B. The tablet breaks down when exposed to light and forms a gas through a chemical change.

C. The tablet causes dissolved gases in the water to be released through a physical change.

D. The tablet interacts with water to form a gas through a chemical change.

Open Response

11. Ella thinks that vinegar will undergo a chemical change if baking soda or sugar is added to it. Design an investigation that would let Ella test this hypothesis. Be sure to include an experimental control and appropriate variables.

12. Engineers developed a baking sheet that is made out of a new material. Describe a procedure that they might use to determine if the material's properties are good for baking food.

TCAP Test Preparation

Science in Action

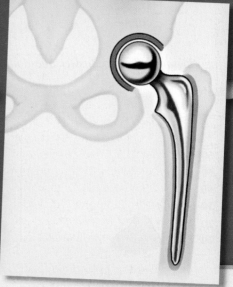

Scientific Debate

Paper or Plastic?

T/E What do you choose at the grocery store: paper or plastic? There are advantages and disadvantages to both choices. Plastic bags are waterproof and take up less space. You can use them to line waste cans and to pack lunches. Some places will recycle plastic bags. But making 1 ton of plastic bags uses 11 barrels of oil, which can't be replaced, and produces polluting chemicals. On the other hand, making 1 ton of paper bags destroys 13 to 17 trees, which take years to replace. Paper bags, too, can be reused for lining waste cans and wrapping packages. Recycling paper pollutes less than recycling plastic does. What is the answer? Maybe we should reuse both! **TN** GLE 0807.T/E.3

Science, Technology, and Society

Building a Better Body

T/E Have you ever broken a bone? If so, you probably wore a cast while the bone healed. But what happens if the bone is too damaged to heal? Sometimes, a false bone made from titanium can replace the damaged bone. Titanium appears to be a great bone-replacement material. It is a lightweight but strong metal. It can attach to existing bone and resists chemical changes. But, friction can wear away titanium bones. Research has found that implanting a form of nitrogen on the titanium makes the metal last longer.

Language Arts ACTiViTY

WRITING SKILL T/E There are benefits and unintended consequences in making and using each kind of bag. Write a one-page essay defending which bag you would choose and why. Support your choice. ✓0807.T/E.3

Social Studies ACTiViTY

T/E Are titanium bone replacement products the result of adaptive or assistive bioengineering? To answer the question, do some research on the history of bone replacement and how this technology affects people's daily lives. Design a poster that presents your answer to the question and that shows a timeline of events leading up to current technology. GLE 0807.T/E.4, ✓0807.T/E.4

Mimi So

Gemologist and Jewelry Designer A typical day for gemologist and jewelry designer Mimi So involves deciding what materials to work with. When she chooses a gemstone for a piece of jewelry, she must consider the size, hardness, color, grade, and cut of the stone. When choosing a metal to use as a setting for a stone, she must look at the hardness, melting point, color, and malleability of the metal. She needs to choose a metal that not only looks good with a particular stone but also has physical properties that will work with that stone. For example, Mimi So says emeralds are soft and fragile. A platinum setting would be too hard and could damage the emerald. So, emeralds are usually set in a softer metal, such as 18-karat gold.

The chemical properties of stones must also be considered. Heating can burn or discolor some gemstones. Mimi So says, "If you are using pearls in a design that requires heating the metal, the pearl is not a stone, so you cannot heat the pearl, because it would destroy the pearl."

Math ACTiViTY

Pure gold is 24-karat (24K). Gold that contains 18 parts gold and 6 parts other metals is 18-karat gold. The percentage of gold in 18K gold is found by dividing the amount of gold by the total amount of the material and then multiplying by 100%. For example, (18 parts gold)/(24 parts total) equals $0.75 \times 100\% = 75\%$ gold. Find the percentage of gold in 10K and 14K gold.

To learn more about these Science in Action topics, visit go.hrw.com and type in the keyword **HP5MATF**.

Current Science

Check out Current Science® articles related to this chapter by visiting go.hrw.com. Just type in the keyword **HP5CS02**.

States of Matter

The Big Idea

Matter exists in various physical states, which are determined by the movement of the matter's particles.

TN Tennessee Science Standards

Embedded Inquiry

GLE 0807.Inq.2 Use appropriate tools and techniques to gather, organize, analyze, and interpret data.

GLE 0807.Inq.3 Synthesize information to determine cause and effect relationships between evidence and explanations.

GLE 0807.Inq.5 Communicate scientific understanding using descriptions, explanations, and models.

✔**0807.Inq.2** Identify tools and techniques needed to gather, organize, analyze, and interpret data collected from a moderately complex scientific investigation.

✔**0807.Inq.3** Use evidence from a dataset to determine cause and effect relationships that explain a phenomenon.

✔**0807.Inq.5** Design a method to explain the results of an investigation using descriptions, explanations, or models.

Embedded Technology and Engineering

GLE 0807.T/E.2 Know that the engineering design process involves an ongoing series of events that incorporate design constraints, model building, testing, evaluating, modifying, and retesting.

GLE 0807.T/E.3 Compare the intended benefits with the unintended consequences of a new technology.

✔**0807.T/E.2** Apply the engineering design process to construct a prototype that meets certain specifications.

✔**0807.T/E.3** Explore how the unintended consequences of new technologies can impact society.

Physical Science

GLE 0807.9.1 Understand that all matter is made up of atoms.

GLE 0807.9.2 Explain that matter has properties that are determined by the structure and arrangement of its atoms.

✔**0807.9.2** Illustrate the particle arrangement and type of motion associated with different states of matter.

✔**0807.9.3** Measure or calculate the mass, volume, and temperature of a given substance.

PRE-READING ACTIVITY

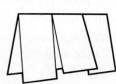

FOLDNOTES **Three-Panel Flip Chart**
Before you read the chapter, create the FoldNote entitled "Three-Panel Flip Chart" described in the **Study Skills** section of the Appendix. Label the flaps of the three-panel flip chart with "Solid," "Liquid," and "Gas." As you read the chapter, write information you learn about each category under the appropriate flap.

About the Photo

This beautiful glass creation by artist Dale Chihuly is entitled "Mille Fiori" (A Thousand Flowers). The pieces that form the sculpture were not always solid and unchanging. Each individual piece started as a blob of melted glass on the end of a hollow pipe. The artist worked with his assistants to quickly form each shape before the molten glass cooled and became a solid again.

START-UP ACTIVITY

TN GLE 0807.Inq.2, GLE 0807.Inq.3

Vanishing Act

In this activity, you will use isopropyl alcohol (rubbing alcohol) to investigate a change of state.

Procedure

1. Pour **rubbing alcohol** into a **small plastic cup** until the alcohol just covers the bottom of the cup.

2. Moisten the tip of a **cotton swab** by dipping it into the alcohol in the cup.

3. Rub the cotton swab on the palm of your hand. Make sure there are no cuts or abrasions on your hands.

4. Record your observations.

5. Wash your hands thoroughly.

Analysis

1. Explain what happened to the alcohol after you rubbed the swab on your hand.

2. Did you feel a sensation of hot or cold? If so, how do you explain what you observed? ✔0807.Inq.3

3. Record your answers.

Three States of Matter

What You Will Learn

● Describe the properties shared by particles of all matter.
● Describe three states of matter.
● Explain the differences between the states of matter.

Vocabulary

states of matter
solid
liquid
surface tension
viscosity
gas

READING STRATEGY

Paired Summarizing Read this section silently. In pairs, take turns summarizing the material. Stop to discuss ideas that seem confusing.

TN **GLE 0807.Inq.2** Use appropriate tools and techniques to gather, organize, analyze and interpret data.

GLE 0807.Inq.3 Synthesize information to determine cause and effect relationships between evidence and explanations.

GLE 0807.Inq.5 Communicate scientific understanding using descriptions, explanations, and models.

GLE 0807.9.2 Explain that matter has properties that are determined by the structure and arrangement of its atoms.

You've just walked home on one of the coldest days of the year. A fire is blazing in the fireplace. And there is a pot of water on the stove to make hot chocolate.

The water begins to bubble. Steam rises from the pot. You make your hot chocolate, but it is too hot to drink. You don't want to wait for it to cool down. So, you add an ice cube. You watch the ice melt in the hot liquid until the drink is at just the right temperature. Then, you enjoy your hot drink while warming yourself by the fire.

The scene described above has examples of the three most familiar states of matter: solid, liquid, and gas. The **states of matter** are the physical forms in which a substance can exist. For example, water commonly exists in three states of matter: solid (ice), liquid (water), and gas (steam).

Particles of Matter

Matter is made up of tiny particles called *atoms* and *molecules* (MAHL i kyoolz). These particles are too small to see without a very powerful microscope. Atoms and molecules are always in motion and are always bumping into one another. The particles interact with each other, and the way they interact with each other helps determine the state of the matter. **Figure 1** describes three states of matter—solid, liquid, and gas—in terms of the speed and attraction of the particles.

Figure 1 **Models of a Solid, a Liquid, and a Gas**

Particles of a solid do not move fast enough to overcome the strong attraction between them. So, they are close together and vibrate in place.

Particles of a liquid move fast enough to overcome some of the attraction between them. The particles are close together but can slide past one another.

Particles of a gas move fast enough to overcome almost all of the attraction between them. The particles are far apart and move independently of one another.

Solids

Imagine dropping a marble into a bottle. Would anything happen to the shape or size of the marble? Would the shape or size of the marble change if you put it in a larger bottle?

Solids Have Definite Shape and Volume

Even in a bottle, a marble keeps its original shape and volume. The marble's shape and volume stay the same no matter what size bottle you drop it into because the marble is a solid. A **solid** is the state of matter that has a definite shape and volume.

The particles of a substance in a solid state are very close together. The attraction between them is stronger than the attraction between the particles of the same substance in the liquid or gaseous state. The particles in a solid move, but they do not move fast enough to overcome the attraction between them. Each particle vibrates in place. Therefore, each particle is locked in place by the particles around it.

There Are Two Kinds of Solids

There are two kinds of solids—*crystalline* (KRIS tuhl in) and *amorphous* (uh MAWR fuhs). Crystalline solids have a very orderly, three-dimensional arrangement of particles. The particles of crystalline solids are arranged in a repeating pattern. Iron, diamond, and ice are examples of crystalline solids.

Amorphous solids are made of particles that do not have a special arrangement. So, each particle is in one place, but the particles are not arranged in a pattern. Examples of amorphous solids are glass, rubber, and wax. **Figure 2** shows a photo of quartz (a crystalline solid) and glass (an amorphous solid).

TN *Standards Check* How are the particles in a crystalline solid arranged? ✔0807.9.2

states of matter the physical forms of matter, which include solid, liquid, and gas

solid the state of matter in which the volume and shape of a substance are fixed

TN GLE 0807.Inq.2, GLE 0807.Inq.3, GLE 0807.Inq.5

CONNECTION TO Physics

Is Glass a Liquid? At one time, there was a theory that glass was a liquid. This theory came about because of the observation that ancient windowpanes were often thicker at the bottom than at the top. People thought that the glass had flowed to the bottom of the pane, so glass must be a liquid. Research this theory. Present your research to your class in an oral presentation.
✔0807.Inq.3, ✔0807.Inq.5

ACTIVITY

Figure 2 Crystalline and Amorphous Solids

The particles of crystalline solids, such as this quartz crystal, have an orderly three-dimensional pattern.

Glass, an amorphous solid, is made of particles that are not arranged in any particular pattern.

Figure 3 *Although their shapes are different, the beaker and the graduated cylinder each contain 350 mL of juice.*

liquid the state of matter that has a definite volume but not a definite shape

surface tension the force that acts on the surface of a liquid and that tends to minimize the area of the surface

viscosity the resistance of a gas or liquid to flow

gas a form of matter that does not have a definite volume or shape

Figure 4 *Water forms spherical drops as a result of surface tension.*

Liquids

What do you think would change about orange juice if you poured the juice from a can into a glass? Would the volume of juice be different? Would the taste of the juice change?

Liquids Change Shape but Not Volume

The only thing that would change when the juice is poured into the glass is the shape of the juice. The shape changes because juice is a liquid. **Liquid** is the state of matter that has a definite volume but takes the shape of its container. The particles in liquids move fast enough to overcome some of the attractions between them. The particles slide past each other until the liquid takes the shape of its container.

Although liquids change shape, they do not easily change volume. A can of juice contains a certain volume of liquid. That volume stays the same if you pour the juice into a large container or a small one. **Figure 3** shows the same volume of liquid in two different containers.

Liquids Have Unique Characteristics

A special property of liquids is surface tension. **Surface tension** is a force that acts on the particles at the surface of a liquid. Surface tension causes some liquids to form spherical drops, like the beads of water shown in **Figure 4.** Different liquids have different surface tensions. For example, gasoline has a very low surface tension and forms flat drops.

Another important property of liquids is viscosity. **Viscosity** is a liquid's resistance to flow. Usually, the stronger the attractions between the molecules of a liquid, the more viscous the liquid is. For example, honey flows more slowly than water. So, honey has a higher viscosity than water.

TN *Standards Check* **What makes a liquid more viscous?**
✔0807.9.2

Gases

Would you believe that one small tank of helium can fill almost 700 balloons? How is this possible? After all, the volume of a tank is equal to the volume of only about five filled balloons. The answer has to do with helium's state of matter.

Gases Change in Both Shape and Volume

Helium is a gas. **Gas** is the state of matter that has no definite shape or volume. The particles of a gas move quickly. So, they can break away completely from one another. There is less attraction between particles of a gas than between particles of the same substance in the solid or liquid state.

The amount of empty space between gas particles can change. Look at **Figure 5.** The particles of helium in the balloons are farther apart than the particles of helium in the tank. The particles spread out as helium fills the balloon. So, the amount of empty space between the gas particles increases.

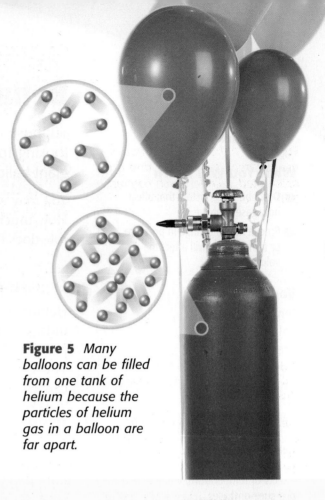

Figure 5 *Many balloons can be filled from one tank of helium because the particles of helium gas in a balloon are far apart.*

SECTION Review

TN GLE 0807.Inq.2, GLE 0807.Inq.5, GLE 0807.9.1, GLE 0807.9.2

Summary

- The three most familiar states of matter are solid, liquid, and gas.
- All matter is made of tiny particles called atoms and molecules that attract each other and move constantly.
- A solid has a definite shape and volume.
- A liquid has a definite volume but not a definite shape.
- A gas does not have a definite shape or volume.

Using Key Terms

1. Use each of the following terms in a separate sentence: *viscosity* and *surface tension*.

Understanding Key Ideas

2. One property that all particles of matter have in common is they ✔0807.9.2

   a. never move in solids.

   b. only move in gases.

   c. move constantly.

   d. None of the above

3. Describe solids, liquids, and gases in terms of shape and volume.

Critical Thinking

4. **Applying Concepts** Classify each substance according to its state of matter: apple juice, bread, a textbook, and steam.

5. **Applying Concepts** Use what you know about particles to explain why the volume of a gas can change when the gas is compressed. ✔0807.9.2

Interpreting Graphics

Use the image below to answer the questions that follow.

6. Identify the state of matter shown in the jar. ✔0807.9.2

7. Discuss how the particles in the jar are attracted to each other.

Internet Resources

For a variety of links related to this chapter, go to www.scilinks.org

Topic: Solids, Liquids, and Gases

SciLinks code: HSM1420

Behavior of Gases

What You Will Learn

● Describe three factors that affect how gases behave.

● Predict how a change in pressure or temperature will affect the volume of a gas.

Vocabulary

temperature
volume
pressure
Boyle's Law
Charles's Law

READING STRATEGY

Reading Organizer As you read this section, make a table comparing the effects of temperature, volume, and pressure on gases.

TN **GLE 0807.Inq.3** Synthesize information to determine cause and effect relationships between evidence and explanations.

GLE 0807.Inq.5 Communicate scientific understanding using descriptions, explanations, and models.

GLE 0807.T/E.2 Know that the engineering design process involves an ongoing series of events that incorporate design constraints, model building, testing, evaluating, modifying, and retesting.

GLE 0807.9.2 Explain that matter has properties that are determined by the structure and arrangement of its atoms.

Suppose you are watching a parade that you have been looking forward to for weeks. You may be fascinated by the giant balloons floating high overhead.

You may wonder how the balloons were arranged for the parade. How much helium was needed to fill all of the balloons? What role does the weather play in getting the balloons to float?

Describing Gas Behavior

Helium is a gas. Gases behave differently from solids or liquids. Unlike the particles that make up solids and liquids, gas particles have a large amount of empty space between them. The space that gas particles occupy is the gas's volume, which can change because of temperature and pressure.

Temperature

How much helium is needed to fill a parade balloon, like the one in **Figure 1**? The answer depends on the outdoor temperature. **Temperature** is a measure of how fast the particles in an object are moving. The faster the particles are moving, the more energy they have. So, on a hot day, the particles of gas are moving faster and hitting the inside walls of the balloon harder. Thus, the gas is expanding and pushing on the walls of the balloon with greater force. If the gas expands too much, the balloon will explode. But, what will happen if the weather is cool on the day of the parade? The particles of gas in the balloon will have less energy. And, the particles of gas will not push as hard on the walls of the balloon. So, more gas must be used to fill the balloons.

temperature a measure of how hot (or cold) something is; specifically, a measure of the movement of particles

Figure 1 *To properly inflate a helium balloon, you must consider the temperature outside of the balloon.*

Volume

Volume is the amount of space that an object takes up. But because the particles of a gas spread out, the volume of any gas depends on the container that the gas is in. For example, have you seen inflated balloons that were twisted into different shapes? Shaping the balloons was possible because particles of gas can be compressed, or squeezed together, into a smaller volume. But, if you tried to shape a balloon filled with water, the balloon would probably explode. It would explode because particles of liquids can't be compressed as much as particles of gases.

Pressure

The amount of force exerted on a given area of surface is called **pressure.** You can think of pressure as the number of times the particles of a gas hit the inside of their container.

The balls in **Figure 2** are the same size, which means they can hold the same volume of air, which is a gas. Notice, however, that there are more particles of gas in the basketball than in the beach ball. So, more particles hit the inside surface of the basketball than hit the inside surface of the beach ball. When more particles hit the inside surface of the basketball, the force on the inside surface of the ball increases. This increased force leads to greater pressure, which makes the basketball feel harder than the beach ball.

TN *Standards Check* Why is the pressure greater in a basketball than in a beach ball? ✔0807.9.2

volume a measure of the size of a body or region in three-dimensional space ▰TN▸ *VOCAB*

pressure the amount of force exerted per unit area of a surface

INTERNET ACTIVITY

For another activity related to this chapter, go to **go.hrw.com** and type in the keyword **HP5STAW**.

Figure 2 Gas and Pressure

High pressure

Low pressure

The basketball has a higher pressure because there are more particles of gas in it, and they are closer together. The particles collide with the inside of the ball at a faster rate.

The beach ball has a lower pressure because there are fewer particles of gas, and they are farther apart. The particles in the beach ball collide with the inside of the ball at a slower rate.

CONNECTION TO Technology

T/E Car Engines In a car's engine, the gases formed during gasoline combustion expand rapidly, causing the parts in the engine to move. The energy stored in the gasoline is changed into energy that can move the car. Research how gasoline powers car engines. Draw a simple diagram that models the cycle in the engine. The diagram should show how gasoline is ignited and how the volume of the gases changes during one engine cycle.

ACTIVITY

Boyle's law the law that states that the volume of a gas is inversely proportional to the pressure of a gas when temperature is constant

Charles's law the law that states that the volume of a gas is directly proportional to the temperature of a gas when pressure is constant

Gas Behavior Laws

Scientists found that the temperature, pressure, and volume of a gas are linked. Changing one of the factors changes the other two factors. The relationships between temperature, pressure, and volume are described by gas laws.

Boyle's Law

Imagine that a diver 10 m below the surface of a lake blows a bubble of air. When the bubble reaches the surface, the bubble's volume has doubled. The difference in pressure between the surface and 10 m below the surface caused this change.

The relationship between the volume and pressure of a gas was first described by Robert Boyle, a 17th-century Irish chemist. The relationship is now known as Boyle's law. **Boyle's law** states that for a fixed amount of gas at a constant temperature, the volume of the gas is inversely related to the pressure. So, as the pressure of a gas increases, the volume decreases by the same amount, as shown in **Figure 3.**

Charles's Law

If you blow air into a balloon and leave it in the hot sun, the balloon might pop. **Charles's law** states that for a fixed amount of gas at a constant pressure, the volume of the gas changes in the same way that the temperature of the gas changes. So, if the temperature increases, the volume of gas also increases by the same amount. Charles's law is shown by the model in **Figure 4.**

✓ Reading Check State Charles's law in your own words.

Figure 3 Boyle's Law

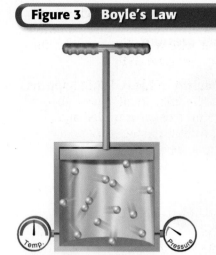

Lifting the piston lets the particles of gas spread far apart. The volume of the gas increases as the pressure decreases.

Releasing the piston allows the particles of gas to return to their original volume and pressure.

Pushing the piston forces the gas particles close together. The volume of the gas decreases as the pressure increases.

216 Chapter 8 States of Matter

Figure 4   Charles's Law

Decreasing the temperature of the gas causes the particles to move more slowly. The gas particles hit the piston less often and with less force. So, the volume of the gas decreases.

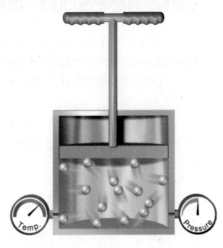

Increasing the temperature of the gas causes the particles to move more quickly. The gas particles hit the piston more often and with greater force. So, the volume of the gas increases.

SECTION Review

TN GLE 0807.Inq.3,
GLE 0807.Inq.5, GLE 0807.9.2

Summary

- Temperature measures how fast the particles in an object are moving.

- Gas pressure increases as the number of collisions of gas particles increases.

- Boyle's law states that if the temperature doesn't change, the volume of a gas increases as the pressure decreases.

- Charles's law states that if the pressure doesn't change, the volume of a gas increases as the temperature increases.

Using Key Terms

1. Use each of the following terms in the same sentence: *temperature, pressure, volume,* and *Charles's law.*

Understanding Key Ideas

2. Boyle's law describes the relationship between
   a. volume and pressure.
   b. temperature and pressure.
   c. temperature and volume.
   d. All of the above

3. What are the effects of a warm temperature on gas particles?
   ✔0807.9.2

Math Skills

4. You have 3 L of gas at a certain temperature and pressure. What would the volume of the gas be if the temperature doubled and the pressure stayed the same?
   ✔0807.9.3

Critical Thinking

5. **Applying Concepts** What happens to the volume of a balloon that is taken outside on a cold winter day? Explain.
   ✔0807.Inq.3

6. **Making Inferences** When scientists record a gas's volume, they also record its temperature and pressure. Why?

7. **Analyzing Ideas** What happens to the pressure of a gas if the volume of gas is tripled at a constant temperature?
   ✔0807.Inq.3, ✔0807.9.3

Internet Resources

For a variety of links related to this chapter, go to www.scilinks.org
Topic: Gas Laws
SciLinks code: HSM0637

Changes of State

It can be tricky to eat a frozen juice bar outside on a hot day. In just minutes, the juice bar will start to melt. Soon the solid juice bar becomes a liquid mess.

As the juice bar melts, it goes through a change of state. In this section, you will learn about the four changes of state shown in **Figure 1** as well as a fifth change of state called *sublimation* (SUHB luh MAY shuhn).

Energy and Changes of State

A **change of state** is the change of a substance from one physical form to another. All changes of state are physical changes. In a physical change, the identity of a substance does not change. In **Figure 1,** the ice, liquid water, and steam are all the same substance—water.

The particles of a substance move differently depending on the state of the substance. The particles also have different amounts of energy when the substance is in different states. For example, particles in liquid water have more energy than particles in ice. But particles of steam have more energy than particles in liquid water. So, to change a substance from one state to another, you must add or remove energy.

✓ **Reading Check** What is a change of state?

What You Will Learn

● Describe how energy is involved in changes of state.
● Describe what happens during melting and freezing.
● Compare evaporation and condensation.
● Explain what happens during sublimation.
● Identify the two changes that can happen when a substance loses or gains energy.

Vocabulary

change of
  state
melting
evaporation
boiling
condensation
sublimation

READING STRATEGY

Mnemonics As you read this section, create a mnemonic device to help you remember the five changes of state.

TN GLE 0807.Inq.2 Use appropriate tools and techniques to gather, organize, analyze, and interpret data.

GLE 0807.Inq.3 Synthesize information to determine cause and effect relationships between evidence and explanations.

GLE 0807.Inq.5 Communicate scientific understanding using descriptions, explanations, and models.

GLE 0807.9.2 Explain that matter has properties that are determined by the structure and arrangement of its atoms.

GLE 0807.9.3 Interpret data from an investigation to differentiate between physical and chemical changes.

change of state the change of a substance from one physical state to another

Figure 1 Changes of State

The terms in the arrows are changes of state. Water commonly goes through the changes of state shown here.

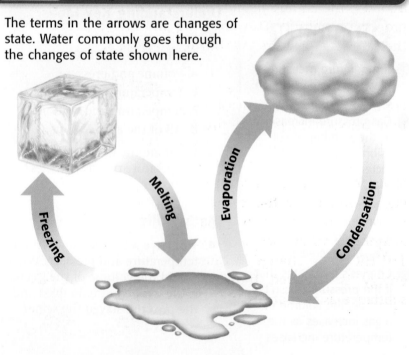

Freezing   Melting   Evaporation   Condensation

Melting: Solid to Liquid

One change of state that happens when you add energy to a substance is melting. **Melting** is the change of state from a solid to a liquid. This change of state is what happens when ice melts. Adding energy to a solid increases the temperature of the solid. As the temperature increases, the particles of the solid move faster. When a certain temperature is reached, the solid will melt. The temperature at which a substance changes from a solid to a liquid is the *melting point* of the substance. Melting point is a physical property. Different substances have different melting points. For example, gallium melts at about 30°C. Because your normal body temperature is about 37°C, gallium will melt in your hand! This is shown in **Figure 2**. Table salt, however, has a melting point of 801°C, so it will not melt in your hand.

Figure 2 *Even though gallium is a metal, it would not be very useful as jewelry!*

Adding Energy

For a solid to melt, particles must overcome some of their attractions to each other. When a solid is at its melting point, any energy added to it is used to overcome the attractions that hold the particles in place. Melting is an *endothermic* (EN doh THUHR mik) change because energy is gained by the substance as it changes state.

melting the change of state in which a solid becomes a liquid by adding energy

Freezing: Liquid to Solid

The change of state from a liquid to a solid is called *freezing*. The temperature at which a liquid changes into a solid is the liquid's *freezing point*. Freezing is the reverse process of melting. Thus, freezing and melting occur at the same temperature, as shown in **Figure 3**.

Removing Energy

For a liquid to freeze, the attractions between the particles must overcome the motion of the particles. Imagine that a liquid is at its freezing point. Removing energy will cause the particles to begin locking into place. Freezing is an *exothermic* (EK so THUHR mik) change because energy is removed from the substance as it changes state.

Figure 3 *Liquid water freezes at the same temperature at which ice melts—0°C.*

If energy is added at 0°C, the ice will melt.

If energy is removed at 0°C, the liquid water will freeze.

Evaporation: Liquid to Gas

One way to experience evaporation is to iron a shirt using a steam iron. You will notice steam coming up from the iron as the wrinkles disappear. This steam forms when the liquid water in the iron becomes hot and changes to gas.

Boiling and Evaporation

Evaporation (ee VAP uh RAY shuhn) is the change of a substance from a liquid to a gas. Evaporation can occur at the surface of a liquid that is below its boiling point. For example, when you sweat, your body is cooled through evaporation. Your sweat is mostly water. Water absorbs energy from your skin as the water evaporates. You feel cooler because your body transfers energy to the water. Evaporation also explains why water in a glass on a table disappears after several days.

Figure 4 explains the difference between boiling and evaporation. **Boiling** is the change of a liquid to a vapor, or gas, throughout the liquid. Boiling occurs when the pressure inside the bubbles, which is called *vapor pressure*, equals the outside pressure on the bubbles, or atmospheric pressure. The temperature at which a liquid boils is called its *boiling point*. No matter how much of a substance is present, neither the boiling point nor the melting point of a substance change. For example, 5 mL and 5 L of water both boil at 100°C.

Reading Check What is evaporation?

evaporation the change of a substance from a liquid to a gas

boiling the conversion of a liquid to a vapor when the vapor pressure of the liquid equals the atmospheric pressure

---

Figure 4 Boiling and Evaporation

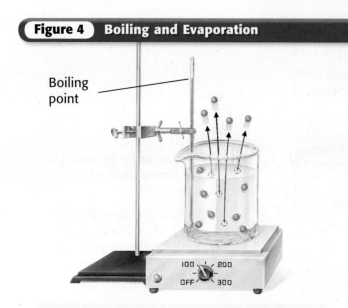

Boiling point

Boiling occurs in a liquid at its boiling point. As energy is added to the liquid, particles throughout the liquid move faster. When they move fast enough to break away from other particles, they evaporate and become a gas.

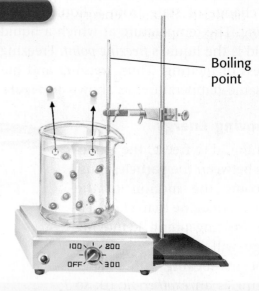

Boiling point

Evaporation can also occur in a liquid below its boiling point. Some particles at the surface of the liquid move fast enough to break away from the particles around them and become a gas.

Effects of Pressure on Boiling Point

Earlier, you learned that water boils at 100°C. In fact, water boils at 100°C only at sea level, because of atmospheric pressure. Atmospheric pressure is caused by the weight of the gases that make up the atmosphere.

Atmospheric pressure varies depending on where you are in relation to sea level. Atmospheric pressure is lower at higher elevations. The higher you go above sea level, the fewer air particles there are above you. So, the atmospheric pressure is lower. Imagine boiling water at the top of a mountain. The boiling point would be lower than 100°C. For example, Denver, Colorado, is 1.6 km above sea level. In Denver, water boils at about 95°C.

Condensation: Gas to Liquid

Look at the dragonfly in **Figure 5.** Notice the beads of water that have formed on the wings. They form because of condensation of gaseous water in the air. **Condensation** is the change of state from a gas to a liquid. Condensation and evaporation are the reverse of each other. The *condensation point* of a substance is the temperature at which the gas becomes a liquid. And the condensation point is the same temperature as the boiling point at a given pressure.

For a gas to become a liquid, large numbers of particles must clump together. Particles clump together when the attraction between them overcomes their motion. For this to happen, energy must be removed from the gas to slow the movement of the particles. Because energy is removed, condensation is an exothermic change.

condensation the change of state from a gas to a liquid

Figure 5 *Beads of water form when water vapor in the air contacts a cool surface, such as the wings of this dragonfly.*

Sublimation: Solid to Gas

The solid in **Figure 6** is dry ice. Dry ice is carbon dioxide in a solid state. It is called *dry ice* because instead of melting into a liquid, it goes through sublimation. **Sublimation** is the change of state in which a solid changes directly into a gas. Dry ice is much colder than ice made from water.

For a solid to change directly into a gas, the particles of the substance must move from being very tightly packed to being spread far apart. So, the attractions between the particles must be completely overcome. The substance must gain energy for the particles to overcome their attractions. Thus, sublimation is an endothermic change because energy is gained by the substance as it changes state.

Figure 6 *Dry ice changes directly from a solid to a gas. This change of state is called* sublimation.

sublimation the process in which a solid changes directly into a gas

Change of Temperature Vs. Change of State

When most substances lose or gain energy, one of two things happens to the substance: its temperature changes or its state changes. The temperature of a substance is related to the speed of the substance's particles. So, when the temperature of a substance changes, the speed of the particles also changes. But the temperature of a substance does not change during the change of state. For example, the temperature of boiling water stays at 100°C until it has all evaporated. In **Figure 7,** you can see what happens to ice as energy is added to the ice.

✔ **Reading Check** What happens to the temperature of a substance as it changes state?

TN GLE 0807.Inq.2, GLE 0807.Inq.3

Boiling Water Is Cool

1. Remove the cap from a **syringe.**
2. Place the tip of the syringe in the **warm water** that is provided by your teacher. Pull the plunger out until you have 10 mL of water in the syringe.
3. Tighten the cap on the syringe.
4. Hold the syringe, and slowly pull the plunger out.
5. Observe any changes you see in the water. Record your observations.
6. Why are you not burned by the water in the syringe?

✔0807.Inq.3

Figure 7 **Changing the State of Water**

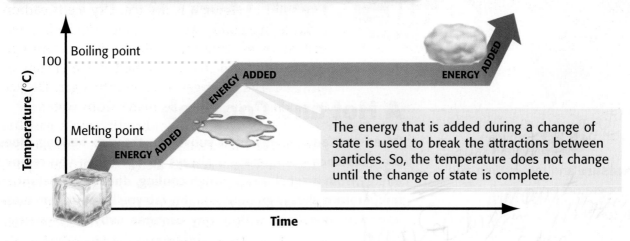

The energy that is added during a change of state is used to break the attractions between particles. So, the temperature does not change until the change of state is complete.

SECTION Review

TN GLE 0807.Inq.3, GLE 0807.Inq.5, GLE 0807.9.2

Summary

- A change of state is the conversion of a substance from one physical form to another.

- Energy is added during endothermic changes. Energy is removed during exothermic changes.

- The freezing point and the melting point of a substance are the same temperature.

- Both boiling and evaporation result in a liquid changing to a gas.

- Condensation is the change of a gas to a liquid. It is the reverse of evaporation.

- The temperature of a substance does not change during a change of state.

Using Key Terms

For each pair of terms, explain how the meanings of the terms differ.

1. *melting* and *freezing*

2. *condensation* and *evaporation*

Understanding Key Ideas

3. The change from a solid directly to a gas is called
   a. evaporation. **c.** melting.
   b. boiling. **d.** sublimation.

4. Describe how the motion and arrangement of particles in a substance change as the substance freezes. ✔0807.9.2

5. Explain what happens to the temperature of an ice cube as it melts.

6. How are evaporation and boiling different? How are they similar? ✔0807.9.2

Math Skills

7. The volume of a substance in the gaseous state is about 1,000 times the volume of the same substance in the liquid state. How much space would 18 mL of water take up if it evaporated? ✔0807.9.3

Critical Thinking

8. **Evaluating Data** The temperature of water in a beaker is 25°C. After adding a piece of magnesium to the water, the temperature increases to 28°C. Is this an exothermic or endothermic reaction? Explain your answer.

9. **Applying Concepts** Solid crystals of iodine were placed in a flask. The top of the flask was covered with aluminum foil. The flask was gently heated. Soon, the flask was filled with a reddish gas. What change of state took place? Explain your answer. ✔0807.Inq.3, ✔0807.9.2

10. **Predicting Consequences** Would using dry ice in your holiday punch cause it to become watery after several hours? Why or why not? ✔0807.Inq.3

Internet Resources

For a variety of links related to this chapter, go to www.scilinks.org
Topic: Changes of State
SciLinks code: HSM0254

Skills Practice Lab

A Hot and Cool Lab

When you add energy to a substance through heating, does the substance's temperature always go up? When you remove energy from a substance through cooling, does the substance's temperature always go down? In this lab you'll investigate these important questions with a very common substance—water.

Procedure

1. Fill the beaker about one-third to one-half full with water.

2. Put on heat-resistant gloves. Turn on the hot plate, and put the beaker on it. Put the thermometer in the beaker. **Caution:** Be careful not to touch the hot plate.

3. Make a copy of Table I. Record the temperature of the water every 30 seconds. Continue doing this until about one-fourth of the water boils away. Note the first temperature reading at which the water is steadily boiling. ✔0807.9.3

Table 1							
Time (s)	30	60	90	120	150	180	210	etc.
Temperature (°C)	DO NOT WRITE IN BOOK						

4. Turn off the hot plate.

5. While the beaker is cooling, make a graph of temperature (y-axis) versus time (x-axis). Draw an arrow pointing to the first temperature at which the water was steadily boiling. ✔0807.Inq.2

TN GLE 0807.Inq.2 Use appropriate tools and techniques to gather, organize, analyze, and interpret data.

GLE 0807.Inq.3 Synthesize information to determine cause and effect relationships between evidence and explanations.

GLE 0807.Inq.5 Communicate scientific understanding using descriptions, explanations, and models.

GLE 0807.9.2 Explain that matter has properties that are determined by the structure and arrangement of its atoms.

6 After you finish the graph, use heat-resistant gloves to pick up the beaker. Pour the warm water out, and rinse the warm beaker with cool water.
Caution: Even after cooling, the beaker is still too warm to handle without gloves.

7 Put approximately 20 mL of water in the graduated cylinder.

8 Put the graduated cylinder in the coffee can, and fill in around the graduated cylinder with crushed ice. Pour rock salt on the ice around the graduated cylinder. Place the thermometer and the wire-loop stirring device in the graduated cylinder.

9 As the ice melts and mixes with the rock salt, the level of ice will decrease. Add ice and rock salt to the can as needed.

10 Make another copy of Table I. Record the temperature of the water in the graduated cylinder every 30 seconds. Stir the water with the stirring device.
Caution: Do not stir with the thermometer.

11 Once the water begins to freeze, stop stirring. Do not try to pull the thermometer out of the solid ice in the cylinder.

12 Note the temperature when you first notice ice crystals forming in the water. Continue taking readings until the water in the graduated cylinder is completely frozen.

13 Make a graph of temperature (*y*-axis) versus time (*x*-axis). Draw an arrow to the temperature reading at which the first ice crystals form in the water in the graduated cylinder.

Analyze the Results

1 **Describing Events** What happens to the temperature of boiling water when you continue to add energy through heating?
✔0807.Inq.3, ✔0807.9.3

2 **Describing Events** What happens to the temperature of freezing water when you continue to remove energy through cooling?
✔0807.Inq.3, ✔0807.9.3

3 **Analyzing Data** What does the slope of each graph represent?

4 **Analyzing Results** How does the slope of the graph that shows water boiling compare with the slope of the graph before the water starts to boil? Why is the slope different for the two periods?

5 **Analyzing Results** How does the slope of the graph showing water freezing compare with the slope of the graph before the water starts to freeze? Why is the slope different for the two periods?

Draw Conclusions

6 **Evaluating Data** The particles that make up solids, liquids, and gases are in constant motion. Adding or removing energy causes changes in the movement of these particles. Using this idea, explain why the temperature graphs of the two experiments look the way they do.
✔0807.Inq.3, ✔0807.Inq.5, ✔0807.9.2

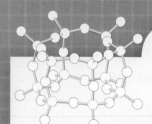

Chapter Review

USING KEY TERMS

For each pair of terms, explain how the meanings of the terms differ.

1 *solid* and *liquid*

2 *Boyle's law* and *Charles's law*

3 *evaporation* and *boiling*

4 *condensation* and *sublimation*

UNDERSTANDING KEY IDEAS

Multiple Choice

5 Which of the following statements best describes the particles of a liquid? ✔0807.9.2

  a. The particles are far apart and moving fast.

  b. The particles are close together but moving past each other.

  c. The particles are far apart and moving slowly.

  d. The particles are closely packed and vibrating in place.

6 Which of the following statements describes what happens as the temperature of a gas in a balloon increases? ✔0807.9.2

  a. The speed of the particles decreases.

  b. The volume of the gas increases, and the speed of the particles increases.

  c. The volume of the gas decreases.

  d. The pressure of the gas decreases.

7 Boiling points and freezing points are examples of ✔0807.9.6

  a. chemical properties. **c.** energy.

  b. physical properties. **d.** matter.

8 Dew collecting on a spider web in the early morning is an example of

  a. condensation. **c.** sublimation.

  b. evaporation. **d.** melting.

9 During which change of state do atoms or molecules become more ordered? ✔0807.9.2

  a. boiling **c.** melting

  b. condensation **d.** sublimation

10 Which of the following changes of state is exothermic?

  a. evaporation **c.** freezing

  b. melting **d.** All of the above

11 The atoms and molecules in matter ✔0807.9.1, ✔0807.9.2

  a. are attracted to one another.

  b. are constantly moving.

  c. move faster at higher temperatures.

  d. All of the above

Short Answer

12 In terms of particles, explain why liquid water takes the shape of its container but an ice cube does not. ✔0807.9.2

13 Rank solids, liquids, and gases in order of particle speed from the highest speed to the lowest speed. ✔0807.9.2

Math Skills

14 Kate placed 100 mL of water in five different pans, placed the pans on a windowsill for a week, and measured how much water evaporated from each pan. Draw a graph of her data, which is shown below. Place surface area on the *x*-axis and volume evaporated on the *y*-axis. Is the graph linear or non-linear? What does this information tell you? ✔0807.Inq.2, ✔0807.Inq.3, ✔0807.Inq.5

Pan number	1	2	3	4	5
Surface area (cm²)	44	82	20	30	65
Volume evaporated (mL)	42	79	19	29	62

CRITICAL THINKING

15 Concept Mapping Use the following terms to create a concept map: *states of matter, solid, liquid, gas, changes of state, freezing, evaporation, condensation,* and *melting.*

16 Applying Concepts After taking a shower, you notice that small droplets of water cover the mirror. Explain what causes this to happen. Be sure to describe where the water comes from and the changes it goes through. ✔0807.Inq.3

17 Analyzing Methods To protect their crops during freezing temperatures, orange growers spray water onto the trees and allow it to freeze. In terms of energy lost and energy gained, explain why this practice protects the oranges from damage. ✔0807.Inq.3

18 Making Inferences At sea level, water boils at 100°C, while methane boils at –161°C. Which of these substances has a stronger force of attraction between its particles? Explain your reasoning. ✔0807.Inq.3, ✔0807.9.2

INTERPRETING GRAPHICS

Use the graph below to answer the questions that follow.

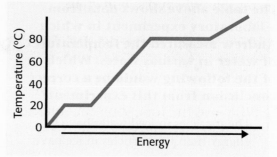

19 What is the boiling point of the substance? What is the melting point? ✔0807.9.3

20 Which state is present at 30°C?

21 How will the substance change if energy is added to the liquid at 20°C? ✔0807.Inq.3

CHALLENGE

22 Apply the engineering design process to design an inflatable ball that will stay inflated between -20 °C and 55 °C. In your design, consider the strength of the material for the skin of the ball and the range of pressures for the air inside the ball. Research materials used for balls and balloons along with the pressure and temperature ranges for which these materials are suitable. Use this information to develop your design and specifications. Design a method to present your results. ✔0807.Inq.5, ✔0807.T/E.2

TCAP Test Preparation

TN SPI 0807.Inq.1 Design a simple experimental procedure with an identified control and appropriate variables. SPI 0807.Inq.4 Draw a conclusion that establishes a cause and effect relationship supported by evidence. SPI 0807.Inq.5 Identify a faulty interpretation of data that is due to bias or experimental error. SPI 0807.T/E.1 Identify the tools and procedures needed to test the design features of a prototype. SPI 0807.9.1 Recognize that all matter consists of atoms.

Multiple Choice

Use the table below to answer question 1.

Substance	Temperature (°C)
Ice	−2
Iced water	0
Water	27
Boiling Water	100

1. **The table above shows data from a laboratory experiment in which Andrew measured the temperatures of water in various states. Which of the following would be a correct conclusion from this experiment?**

   A. The particles in iced water have less energy than the particles in ice have.

   B. The particles in ice have more energy than the particles in water have.

   C. The particles in iced water have more energy than the particles in boiling water have.

   D. The particles in boiling water have more energy than the particles in iced water have.

2. **A sealed, inflated beach ball was placed in a freezer overnight. The next day, the ball was still sealed but had shrunk. Analyze the following hypotheses to determine which is the best.**

   A. The pressure inside the ball increased, so the gas particles moved faster.

   B. The gas inside the ball escaped, which caused the ball to shrink.

   C. The temperature of the gas increased, which pushed gas out of the ball.

   D. The temperature of the gas decreased, so the particles of gas moved closer together.

3. **Which of the following could describe oxygen at room temperature?**

   A. It has a constant volume and a definite shape.

   B. It has a constant volume but takes the shape of its container.

   C. Its particles move fast enough to overcome the attraction between them.

   D. Its particles have a very orderly, three-dimensional arrangement.

4. **Kevin compared the viscosities of several fluids. Substances A, B, and C flowed at different rates, but substance D did not flow at all. Which of the following is a valid conclusion?**

   A. Substance D must be at its melting point.

   B. Substance D's particles have strong attraction for one another.

   C. Substance D is neither a liquid nor a gas.

   D. Substance D's particles have little attraction for one another.

5. **In a laboratory experiment, Joel observed water as it vaporized, froze, melted, and condensed. Which of the following is a valid conclusion?**

   A. He observed four different changes of state.

   B. He observed two different chemical changes.

   C. All of the changes required energy to be absorbed.

   D. All of the changes required energy to be released.

SPI 0807.9.6 Compare the particle arrangement and type of particle motion associated with different states of matter.

SPI 0807.9.8 Interpret the results of an investigation to determine whether a physical or chemical change has occurred.

Use the picture below to answer question 6.

6. A cup filled to the rim with water was left at room temperature overnight. The figure above shows how much water was left the next morning. Which of the following is a reasonable hypothesis for what happened to the water?

   A. The water molecules at the surface lost enough energy to evaporate.

   B. The water molecules at the surface gained enough energy to evaporate.

   C. The water molecules at the surface lost enough energy to condense.

   D. The water molecules at the surface gained enough energy to sublimate.

7. In a laboratory investigation on changes of state, Rebecca observes that the melting point of water is 0°C and that the freezing point of water is 5°C. What conclusion can Rebecca draw from these observations?

   A. Both melting and freezing are exothermic reactions.

   B. Water boils at 0°C at normal atmospheric pressure.

   C. Melting and freezing cannot occur at the same temperature.

   D. She made an error in her measurements.

8. You are asked to test the safety of a prototype for a new kind of gasoline engine. Which of the following best describes a main feature of your test?

   A. Measure the minimum work done by the engine.

   B. Measure the maximum energy provided to the engine.

   C. Measure the maximum gas pressure produced within the engine.

   D. Measure the minimum temperature at which the engine operates.

Open Response

9. Describe how the physical properties of solids, liquids, and gases affect how each state of matter behaves when placed into a new container.

10. Keisha wants to measure how the temperature of a gas affects its volume. Explain which variable she should change, which variable she should measure, and which variable she should hold constant during her experiment.

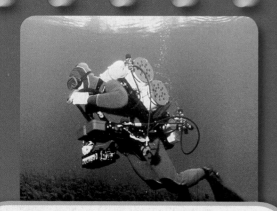

Science, Technology, and Society

Deep-sea Diving with Helium

T/E Divers who breathe air while deep in the ocean run the risk of suffering from nitrogen narcosis. Nitrogen narcosis produces an alcohol-like effect, which can cause a diver to become disoriented and to use poor judgment. To avoid nitrogen narcosis, divers who work at depths of more than 60 m breathe heliox. *Heliox* is a mixture of helium and oxygen, instead of air. The main disadvantage of heliox is that helium conducts heat about six times faster than nitrogen does, so a diver using heliox will feel cold sooner than a diver who is breathing air. **TN** GLE 0807.T/E.1

Math ACTIVITY

Dry air is mostly oxygen, nitrogen (78.03%), argon (0.94%), carbon dioxide (0.03%), and hydrogen (0.01%). If heliox contains the same amount of oxygen as air, what percentage of helium must be added to replace the other gases?

Scientific Discoveries

The Fourth State of Matter

If you heat water, it will eventually turn into a gas. But what would happen if you kept on heating the gas? Scientists only had to look to the sun for the answer. The sun, like other stars, is made of the fourth state of matter—plasma. Plasma is a superheated gas. Once a gas's temperature rises above 10,000°C to 20,000°C, its particles start to break apart and it becomes plasma. Unlike gas, plasma can create, and be affected by, electrical and magnetic fields. More than 99% of the known universe is made of plasma! Even Earth has some naturally occurring plasma. Plasma can be found in auroras, flames, and lightning. **TN** GLE 0807.9.2

Social Studies ACTIVITY

Research plasma. Find out how plasma is used in today's technology, such as plasma TVs. How will this new technology affect you and society in general? Describe your findings in a poster. **TN** GLE 0807.T/E.3, ✓0807.T/E.3

Andy Goldsworthy

Nature Artist Most of the art that Andy Goldsworthy creates will melt, decay, evaporate, or just blow away. He uses leaves, water, sticks, rocks, ice, and snow to create art. Goldsworthy observes how nature works and how it changes over time, and uses what he learns to create his art. For example, on cold, sunny mornings, Goldsworthy makes frost shadows. He stands with his back to the sun, which creates a shadow on the ground. The rising sun warms the ground and melts the frost around his shadow. When he steps away, he can see the shape of his body in the frost that is left on the ground.

In his art, Goldsworthy sometimes shows water in the process of changing states. For example, he made huge snowballs filled with branches, pebbles, and flowers. He then stored these snowballs in a freezer until summer, when they were displayed in a museum. As they melted, the snowballs slowly revealed their contents. Goldsworthy says his art reflects nature, because nature is constantly changing. Fortunately, he takes pictures of his art so we can enjoy it even after it disappears!

Language Arts ACTIVITY

WRITING SKILL Research Andy Goldsworthy's art. Write a one-page review of one of his creations. Be sure to include what you like or don't like about the art.

go.hrw.com
To learn more about these Science in Action topics, visit go.hrw.com and type in the keyword **HP5STAF.**

Current Science
Check out Current Science® articles related to this chapter by visiting go.hrw.com. Just type in the keyword **HP5CS03.**

Elements, Compounds, and Mixtures

The Big Idea

Matter can be classified into elements, compounds, and mixtures.

TN Tennessee Science Standards

Embedded Inquiry

GLE 0807.Inq.2 Use appropriate tools and techniques to gather, organize, analyze, and interpret data.

GLE 0807.Inq.3 Synthesize information to determine cause and effect relationships between evidence and explanations.

GLE 0807.Inq.4 Recognize possible sources of bias and error, alternative explanations, and questions for further exploration.

✔**0807.Inq.2** Identify tools and techniques needed to gather, organize, analyze, and interpret data collected from a moderately complex scientific investigation.

✔**0807.Inq.3** Use evidence from a dataset to determine cause and effect relationships that explain a phenomenon.

✔**0807.Inq.4** Review an experimental design to determine possible sources of bias or error, state alternative explanations, and identify questions for further investigation.

Embedded Technology and Engineering

GLE 0807.T/E.1 Explore how technology responds to social, political, and economic needs.

Physical Science

GLE 0807.9.1 Understand that all matter is made up of atoms.

GLE 0807.9.3 Interpret data from an investigation to differentiate between physical and chemical changes.

GLE 0807.9.4 Distinguish among elements, compounds, and mixtures.

GLE 0807.9.5 Apply the chemical properties of the atmosphere to illustrate a mixture of gases.

✔**0807.9.1** Identify atoms as the fundamental particles that make up matter.

✔**0807.9.6** Differentiate between physical and chemical changes.

✔**0807.9.7** Describe how the characteristics of a compound are different than the characteristics of their component parts.

✔**0807.9.9** Explain how the chemical makeup of the atmosphere illustrates a mixture of gases.

PRE-READING ACTIVITY

FOLDNOTES **Key-Term Fold** Before you read the chapter, create the FoldNote entitled "Key-Term Fold" described in the **Study Skills** section of the Appendix. Write a key term from the chapter on each tab of the key-term fold. Under each tab, write the definition of the key term.

START-UP ACTIVITY

TN GLE 0807.Inq.2, GLE 0807.Inq.3, GLE 0807.Inq.5, GLE 0807.9.3, GLE 0807.9.4

Mystery Mixture

In this activity, you will separate the different dyes found in an ink mixture.

Procedure

1. Place a **pencil** on top of a **clear plastic cup.** Tear a strip of paper (3 cm × 15 cm) from a **coffee filter.** Wrap one end of the strip around a pencil so that the other end will touch the bottom of the plastic cup. Use **tape** to attach the paper to the pencil.

2. Take the paper out of the cup. Using a **water-soluble black marker,** make a small dot in the center of the strip about 2 cm from the bottom.

3. Pour **water** in the cup to a depth of 1 cm. Lower the paper into the cup. Keep the dot above water.

4. Remove the paper when the water is 1 cm from the top. Record your observations.

Analysis

1. What happened as the paper soaked up the water?

2. Which colors make up the marker's black ink?

3. Compare your results with those of your classmates. Record your observations.

4. Is the process used to make the ink separate a physical or a chemical change? Explain. ✔0807.9.6

Elements

Imagine that you are an engineer at the Break-It-Down Company. Your job is to break down materials into simpler substances.

You haven't had any trouble breaking down materials so far. But one rainy Monday morning, you get a material that seems very hard to break down. First, you try physical changes, such as crushing and melting. But these do not change the material into something simpler. Next, you try some chemical changes, such as passing an electric current through the material. These do not change it either. What's going on?

What You Will Learn

- Describe pure substances.
- Describe the characteristics of elements, and give examples.
- Explain how elements can be identified.
- Classify elements according to their properties.

Vocabulary

element	nonmetal
pure substance	metalloid
metal	

READING STRATEGY

Reading Organizer As you read this section, make a concept map by using the terms above.

TN GLE 0807.Inq.2 Use appropriate tools and techniques to gather, organize, analyze, and interpret data.

GLE 0807.Inq.3 Synthesize information to determine cause and effect relationships between evidence and explanations.

GLE 0807.Inq.5 Communicate scientific understanding using descriptions, explanations, and models.

GLE 0807.9.1 Understand that all matter is made up of atoms.

GLE 0807.9.4 Distinguish among elements, compounds, and mixtures.

Elements, the Simplest Substances

You couldn't break down the material described above because it is an element. An **element** is a pure substance that cannot be separated into simpler substances by physical or chemical means. In this section, you'll learn about elements and the properties that help you classify them.

Only One Type of Particle

Elements are pure substances. A **pure substance** is a substance in which there is only one type of particle. So, each element contains only one type of particle. These particles, called *atoms*, are much too small for us to see. For example, every atom in a 5 g nugget of the element gold is like every other atom of gold. The particles of a pure substance are alike no matter where they are found, as shown in **Figure 1.**

TN *Standards Check* Describe the particles that elements are made of. ✔0807.9.1

Figure 1 *A meteorite might travel more than 400 million kilometers to reach Earth. But the particles of iron in a meteorite, a steel spoon, and even steel braces are alike.*

Properties of Elements

Each element can be identified by its unique set of properties. For example, each element has its own *characteristic properties.* These properties do not depend on the amount of the element present. Characteristic properties include some physical properties, such as boiling point, melting point, and density. Chemical properties, such as reactivity with acid, are also characteristic properties.

An element may share a property with another element, but other properties can help you tell the elements apart. For example, the elements helium and krypton are both unreactive gases. However, the densities (mass per unit volume) of these elements are different. Helium is less dense than air. A helium-filled balloon will float up if it is released. Krypton is denser than air. A krypton-filled balloon will sink to the ground if it is released.

Identifying Elements by Their Properties

Look at the elements shown in **Figure 2.** These three elements have some similar properties. But each element can be identified by its unique set of properties.

Notice that the physical properties shown in **Figure 2** include melting point and density. Other physical properties, such as color, hardness, and texture, could be added to the list. Chemical properties might also be useful. For example, some elements, such as hydrogen and carbon, are flammable. Other elements, such as sodium, react with oxygen at room temperature. Still other elements, including zinc, are reactive with acid.

TN GLE 0807.Inq.2, GLE 0807.Inq.3, GLE 0807.Inq.5, GLE 0807.9.4

Quick Lab

Separating Elements

1. Examine a sample of nails provided by your teacher.
2. Your sample has **aluminum nails** and **iron nails.** Try to separate the two kinds of nails. Group similar nails into piles.
3. Pass a **bar magnet** over each pile of nails. Record your results.
4. Were you successful in completely separating the two types of nails? Explain.
5. Based on your observations, explain how the properties of aluminum and iron could be used to separate cans in a recycling plant.

element a substance that cannot be separated or broken down into simpler substances by chemical means TN *VOCAB*

pure substance a sample of matter, either a single element or a single compound, that has definite chemical and physical properties

---

Figure 2 The Unique Properties of Elements

Cobalt	Iron	Nickel

Cobalt
- Melting point: 1,495°C
- Density: 8.9 g/cm³
- Conducts electric current and heat energy
- Unreactive with oxygen in the air

Iron
- Melting point: 1,535°C
- Density: 7.9 g/cm³
- Conducts electric current and heat energy
- Combines slowly with oxygen in the air to form rust

Nickel
- Melting point: 1,455°C
- Density: 8.9 g/cm³
- Conducts electric current and heat energy
- Unreactive with oxygen in the air

Figure 3 *Even though these dogs are different breeds, they have enough in common to be classified as terriers.*

Classifying Elements by Their Properties

Think about how many different breeds of dogs there are. Now, think about how you tell one breed from another. Most often, you can tell just by their appearance, or the physical properties, of the dogs. **Figure 3** shows several breeds of terriers. Many terriers are fairly small in size and have short hair. Not all terriers are alike, but they share enough properties to be classified in the same group.

Categories of Elements

Elements are also grouped into categories by the properties they share. There are three major categories of elements: metals, nonmetals, and metalloids. The elements iron, nickel, and cobalt are all metals. Not all metals are exactly alike, but they do have some properties in common. **Metals** are shiny, and they conduct heat energy and electric current. **Nonmetals** make up the second category of elements. They do not conduct heat or electric current, and solid nonmetals are dull in appearance. **Metalloids,** which have properties of both metals and nonmetals, make up the last category.

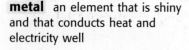 **Reading Check** What are three characteristics of metals?

Categories Are Similar

Imagine being in a music store. The CDs are categorized by type of music. If you like rock-and-roll, you would go to the rock-and-roll section. You might not know every CD, but you know that a CD has the characteristics of rock-and-roll for it to be in this section.

By knowing the category to which an unfamiliar element belongs, you can predict some of its properties. **Figure 4** shows examples of each category and describes the properties that identify elements in each category.

metal an element that is shiny and that conducts heat and electricity well

nonmetal an element that conducts heat and electricity poorly

metalloid an element that has properties of both metals and nonmetals

Figure 4 **The Three Major Categories of Elements**

Metals

Lead
Tin
Copper

Metals are elements that are shiny and are good conductors of heat and electric current. They are *malleable.* (They can be hammered into thin sheets.) They are also *ductile.* (They can be drawn into thin wires.)

Nonmetals

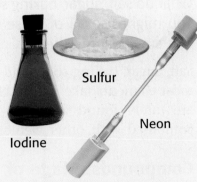

Sulfur
Neon
Iodine

Nonmetals are elements that are dull (not shiny) and that are poor conductors of heat and electric current. Solids tend to be brittle and unmalleable. Few familiar objects are made of only nonmetals.

Metalloids

Boron
Silicon
Antimony

Metalloids are also called semiconductors. They have properties of both metals and nonmetals. Some metalloids are shiny. Some are dull. Metalloids are somewhat malleable and ductile. Some metalloids conduct heat and electric current as well.

SECTION Review

TN GLE 0807.Inq.5, GLE 0807.9.1, GLE 0807.9.4

Summary

● A substance in which all of the particles are alike is a pure substance.

● An element is a pure substance that cannot be broken down into anything simpler by physical or chemical means.

● Each element has a unique set of physical and chemical properties.

● Elements are classified as metals, nonmetals, or metalloids, based on their properties.

Using Key Terms

1. Use the following terms in the same sentence: *element* and *pure substance.*

Understanding Key Ideas

2. A metalloid ✔0807.9.1
   a. may conduct electric current.
   b. is made of atoms.
   c. is also called a semiconductor.
   d. All of the above

3. What is an element? ✔0807.9.1

Math Skills

4. There are eight elements that make up 98.5% of the Earth's crust: 46.6% oxygen, 8.1% aluminum, 5.0% iron, 3.6% calcium, 2.8% sodium, 2.6% potassium, and 2.1% magnesium. The rest is silicon. What percentage of the Earth's crust is silicon?

Critical Thinking

5. **Applying Concepts** From which category of elements would you choose to make a container that wouldn't shatter if dropped during a test? Explain your answer. ✔0807.T/E.1

6. **Making Comparisons** Compare the properties of metals, nonmetals, and metalloids.

7. **Evaluating Assumptions** Your friend tells you that a shiny element has to be a metal. Do you agree? Explain.

Internet Resources

For a variety of links related to this chapter, go to www.scilinks.org
Topic: Elements
SciLinks code: HSM0496

Compounds

What do salt, sugar, baking soda, and water have in common? You might use all of these to bake bread. Is there anything else similar about them?

Salt, sugar, baking soda, and water are all compounds. Because most elements take part in chemical changes fairly easily, they are rarely found alone in nature. Instead, they are found combined with other elements as compounds.

Compounds: Made of Elements

A **compound** is a pure substance composed of two or more elements that are chemically combined. Elements combine by reacting, or undergoing a chemical change, with one another. A particle of a compound is a molecule. Molecules of compounds are formed when atoms of two or more elements join together.

In **Figure 1,** you see magnesium reacting with oxygen. A compound called *magnesium oxide* is forming. The compound is a new pure substance. It is different from the elements that make it up. Most of the substances that you see every day are compounds. **Table 1** lists some familiar examples.

The Ratio of Elements in a Compound

Elements do not randomly join to form compounds. Elements join in a specific ratio according to their masses to form a compound. For example, the ratio of the mass of hydrogen to the mass of oxygen in water is 1 to 8. This mass ratio can be written as 1:8. This ratio is always the same. Every sample of water has a 1:8 mass ratio of hydrogen to oxygen. What happens if a sample of a compound has a different mass ratio of hydrogen to oxygen? The compound cannot be water.

Table 1 Familiar Compounds

Compound	Elements combined
Table salt	sodium and chlorine
Water	hydrogen and oxygen
Vinegar	hydrogen, carbon, and oxygen
Carbon dioxide	carbon and oxygen
Baking soda	sodium, hydrogen, carbon, and oxygen

Figure 1 *As magnesium burns, it reacts with oxygen and forms the compound magnesium oxide.*

Compound Confusion

1. Measure **4 g of compound A,** and place it in a **clear plastic cup.**

2. Measure **4 g of compound B,** and place it in a **second clear plastic cup.**

3. Observe the color and texture of each compound. Record your observations.

4. Add **5 mL of vinegar** to each cup. Record your observations.

5. Baking soda reacts with vinegar. Powdered sugar does not react with vinegar. Which compound is baking soda, and which compound is powdered sugar? Explain your answer.

Properties of Compounds

As an element does, each compound has its own physical properties. Physical properties include melting point, density, and color. Compounds can also be identified by their different chemical properties. Some compounds react with acid. For example, calcium carbonate, found in chalk, reacts with acid. Other compounds, such as hydrogen peroxide, react when exposed to light.

compound a substance made up of atoms of two or more different elements joined by chemical bonds
VOCAB

Properties: Compounds Versus Elements

A compound has properties that differ from those of the elements that form it. Look at **Figure 2.** Sodium chloride, or table salt, is made of two very dangerous elements—sodium and chlorine. Sodium reacts violently with water. Chlorine is a poisonous gas. But when combined, these elements form a harmless compound with unique properties. Sodium chloride is safe to eat. It also dissolves (without exploding!) in water.

Standards Check How is a compound different from an element? ✔0807.9.7

Figure 2 Forming Sodium Chloride

Sodium is a soft, silvery white metal that reacts violently with water.

Chlorine is a poisonous, greenish yellow gas.

Sodium chloride, or table salt, is a white solid. It dissolves easily in water and is safe to eat.

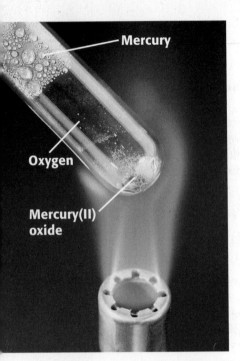

Mercury

Oxygen

Mercury(II) oxide

Figure 3 *Heating mercury(II) oxide causes a chemical change that separates it into the elements mercury and oxygen.*

Breaking Down Compounds

Some compounds can be broken down into their elements by chemical changes. Other compounds break down to form simpler compounds instead of elements. These simpler compounds can then be broken down into elements through more chemical changes. For example, carbonic acid is a compound that helps give carbonated beverages their "fizz." When you open a carbonated beverage, carbonic acid breaks down into carbon dioxide and water. Carbon dioxide and water can then be broken down into the elements carbon, oxygen, and hydrogen through chemical changes.

✓ **Reading Check** Compounds can be broken down into what two types of substances?

Methods of Breaking Down Compounds

The only way to break down a compound is through a chemical change. Sometimes, energy is needed for a chemical change to happen. Two ways to add energy to break down a compound are to apply heat and to apply an electric current. For example, heating the compound mercury(II) oxide breaks it down into the elements mercury and oxygen, as shown in **Figure 3.**

Compounds in Your World

You are surrounded by compounds. Compounds make up the food you eat, the school supplies you use, and the clothes you wear—even you!

Compounds in Industry

The compounds found in nature are not usually the raw materials needed by industry. Often, these compounds must be broken down to provide elements or other compounds that can be used as raw material. For example, aluminum is used in cans and airplanes. But aluminum is not found alone in nature. Aluminum is produced by breaking down the compound aluminum oxide. Ammonia is another important compound used in industry. It is used to make fertilizers. Ammonia is made by combining the elements nitrogen and hydrogen.

INTERNET ACTIVITY

For another activity related to this chapter, go to **go.hrw.com** and type in the keyword **HP5MIXW.**

CONNECTION TO Physics

Electrolysis The process of using electric current to break down compounds is known as *electrolysis*. For example, electrolysis can be used to separate water into hydrogen and oxygen. Research ways that electrolysis is used in industry. Make a poster of what you learn, and present a report to your class.

ACTIVITY

Compounds in Nature

Proteins are compounds found in all living things. The element nitrogen is one of the elements needed to make proteins. **Figure 4** shows how some plants get the nitrogen they need. Other plants use nitrogen compounds that are in the soil. Animals get the nitrogen they need by eating plants or by eating animals that have eaten plants. The proteins in the food are broken down as an animal digests the food. The simpler compounds that form are used by the animal's cells to make new proteins.

Another compound that plays an important role in life is carbon dioxide. You exhale carbon dioxide that was made in your body. Plants take in carbon dioxide, which is used in photosynthesis. Plants use photosynthesis to make compounds called carbohydrates. These carbohydrates can then be broken down for energy through other chemical changes by plants or animals.

Figure 4 *The bumps on the roots of this pea plant are home to bacteria that form compounds from nitrogen in the air. The pea plant makes proteins from these compounds.*

SECTION Review

TN GLE 0807.Inq.5, GLE 0807.9.4

Summary

- A compound is a pure substance composed of two or more elements.
- The elements that form a compound always combine in a specific ratio according to their masses.
- Each compound has a unique set of physical and chemical properties that differ from those of the elements that make up the compound.
- Compounds can be broken down into simpler substances only by chemical changes.

Using Key Terms

1. In your own words, write a definition for the term *compound*.

Understanding Key Ideas

2. The elements in a compound ✔0807.9.7
   a. join in a specific ratio according to their masses.
   b. combine by reacting with one another.
   c. can be separated by chemical changes.
   d. All of the above

3. What type of change is needed to break down a compound? ✔0807.9.6

Math Skills

4. Table sugar is a compound made of carbon, hydrogen, and oxygen. If sugar contains 41.86% carbon and 6.98% hydrogen, what percentage of sugar is oxygen?

Critical Thinking

5. **Applying Concepts** Iron is a solid, gray metal. Oxygen is a colorless gas. When they chemically combine, rust is made. Rust has a reddish brown color. Why is rust different from the iron and oxygen that it is made of? ✔0807.9.7

6. **Analyzing Ideas** A jar contains samples of the elements carbon and oxygen. Does the jar contain a compound? Explain your answer. ✔0807.9.7

Internet Resources

For a variety of links related to this chapter, go to www.scilinks.org
Topic: Compounds
SciLinks code: HSM0332

Mixtures

Imagine that you roll out some dough, add tomato sauce, and sprinkle some cheese on top. Then, you add green peppers, mushrooms, olives, and pepperoni! What have you just made?

A pizza, of course! But that's not all. You have also created a mixture—and a delicious one at that! In this section, you will learn about mixtures and their properties.

Properties of Mixtures

All mixtures—even pizza—share certain properties. A **mixture** is a combination of two or more substances that are not chemically combined. When two or more materials are put together, they form a mixture if they do not react to form a compound. For example, cheese and tomato sauce do not react when they are used to make a pizza. So, a pizza is a mixture.

No Chemical Changes in a Mixture

No chemical change happens when a mixture is made. So, each substance in a mixture has the same chemical makeup it had before the mixture formed. That is, each substance in a mixture keeps its identity. In some mixtures, such as the pizza in **Figure 1,** you see each of the components. In other mixtures, such as salt water, you cannot see all the components.

✓ **Reading Check** Why do substances in a mixture keep their identities? (*See the Appendix for answers to Reading Checks.*)

Separating Mixtures Through Physical Methods

You don't like mushrooms on your pizza? Just pick them off. This change is a physical change of the mixture. The identities of the substances do not change. But not all mixtures are as easy to separate as a pizza. You cannot just pick salt out of a saltwater mixture. One way to separate the salt from the water is to heat the mixture until the water evaporates. The salt is left behind. Other ways to separate mixtures are shown in **Figure 2.**

What You Will Learn

● Describe three properties of mixtures.
● Describe four methods of separating the parts of a mixture.
● Analyze a solution in terms of its solute and solvent.
● Explain how concentration affects a solution.
● Describe the particles in a suspension.
● Explain how a colloid differs from a solution and a suspension.

Vocabulary

mixture   concentration
solution   solubility
solute   suspension
solvent   colloid

READING STRATEGY

Reading Organizer As you read this section, create an outline of the section. Use the headings from the section in your outline.

TN GLE 0807.Inq.2 Use appropriate tools and techniques to gather, organize, analyze, and interpret data.

GLE 0807.Inq.5 Communicate scientific understanding using descriptions, explanations, and models.

GLE 0807.T/E.1 Explore how technology responds to social, political, and economic needs.

GLE 0807.9.3 Interpret data from an investigation to differentiate between physical and chemical changes.

GLE 0807.9.4 Distinguish among elements, compounds, and mixtures.

GLE 0807.9.5 Apply the chemical properties of the atmosphere to illustrate a mixture of gases.

mixture a combination of two or more substances that are not chemically combined

Figure 1 *You can see each topping on this mixture, which is better known as a pizza.*

Figure 2 Common Ways to Separate Mixtures

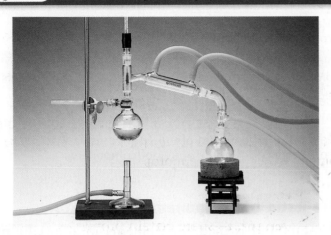

Distillation (DIS tuh LAY shuhn) is a process that separates a mixture based on the boiling points of the components. Here, pure water (at right) is being distilled from a salt-water mixture (at left). Distillation is also used to separate crude oil into components, such as gasoline and kerosene.

A **magnet** can be used to separate a mixture of the elements iron and aluminum. Iron is attracted to the magnet, but aluminum is not.

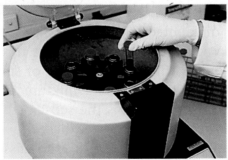

The different parts of blood are separated using a machine called a **centrifuge** (SEN truh FYOOJ). In the test tube at left, a layer of plasma rests above a layer of red blood cells. A centrifuge separates mixtures by the densities of the components.

Separating a mixture of sodium chloride (table salt) and sulfur takes more than one step.

❶ In the first step, water is added, and the mixture is stirred. Salt dissolves in water. Sulfur does not.

❷ In the second step, the mixture is poured through a filter. The filter traps the solid sulfur.

❸ In the third step, the water is evaporated. The sodium chloride is left behind.

Table 1 Mixtures and Compounds	
Mixtures	**Compounds**
Made of elements, compounds, or both	Made of elements
No change in original properties of components	Change in original properties of components
Separated by physical means	Separated by chemical means
Formed using any ratio of components	Formed using a set ratio of components

The Ratio of Components in a Mixture

A compound is made of elements in a specific mass ratio. However, the components of a mixture do not need to be mixed in a definite ratio. For example, granite is a mixture made of three minerals: feldspar, mica, and quartz. Feldspar is pink in color. Mica is black. Quartz is colorless. Look at the egg-shaped paperweights in **Figure 3.** The pink one is made from granite that has more feldspar than mica or quartz. That is why it is pink. The black one is made from granite that has more mica than the other minerals. The gray one is made from granite that has more quartz than the other minerals. Even though the proportions of the minerals change, this combination of minerals is always a mixture called *granite*. **Table 1** above summarizes the differences between mixtures and compounds.

Figure 3 *These paperweights are made of granite. They are different colors because the granite used in each has different ratios of minerals.*

Solutions

solution a homogeneous mixture of two or more substances uniformly dispersed throughout a single phase

solute in a solution, the substance that dissolves in the solvent

solvent in a solution, the substance in which the solute dissolves

A **solution** is a mixture that appears to be a single substance. A solution is composed of particles of two or more substances that are distributed evenly among each other. Solutions have the same appearance and properties throughout the mixture.

The process in which particles of substances separate and spread evenly throughout a mixture is known as *dissolving*. In solutions, the **solute** is the substance that is dissolved. The **solvent** is the substance in which the solute is dissolved. A solute must be *soluble,* or able to dissolve, in the solvent. A substance that is *insoluble,* or unable to dissolve, forms a mixture that is not a solution.

Salt water is a solution. Salt is soluble in water, meaning that salt dissolves in water. So, salt is the solute, and water is the solvent. When two liquids or two gases form a solution, the substance that is present in the largest amount is the solvent.

Table 2 Examples of Different States in Solutions

States	Examples
Gas in gas	dry air (oxygen in nitrogen)
Gas in liquid	soft drinks (carbon dioxide in water)
Liquid in liquid	antifreeze (alcohol in water)
Solid in liquid	salt water (salt in water)
Solid in solid	brass (zinc in copper)

Examples of Solutions

You may think that all solutions are liquids. And in fact, tap water, soft drinks, gasoline, and many cleaning supplies are liquid solutions. However, solutions may also be gases, such as air. Solutions may even be solids, such as steel. *Alloys* are solid solutions of metals or nonmetals dissolved in metals. Brass is an alloy of the metal zinc dissolved in copper. Steel is an alloy made of the nonmetal carbon and other elements dissolved in iron. **Table 2** lists more examples of solutions.

Reading Check What is an alloy?

Particles in Solutions

The particles in solutions are so small that they never settle out. They also cannot be removed by filtering. In fact, the particles are so small that they don't even scatter light. Both of the jars in **Figure 4** contain mixtures. The mixture in the jar on the left is a solution of table salt in water. The jar on the right holds a mixture—but not a solution—of gelatin in water.

TN GLE 0807.T/E.1, GLE 0807.9.5

CONNECTION TO Engineering

Clearing the Air The air you breathe is a mixture of gases. It contains about 78% nitrogen gas, 21% oxygen gas, and small amounts of other gases. Some gases are pollutants, such as sulfur dioxide, nitrogen oxide, and carbon monoxide, which come from factories, cars, and other human activities. Research how engineers work to control air pollution from these three pollutants. Create a poster that shows what you learn. Include a diagram that shows the mixture of gases in air with and without these pollutants.
✓0807.9.9

Figure 4 *Both of these jars contain mixtures. The mixture in the jar on the left, however, is a solution. The particles in solutions are so small that they don't scatter light. Therefore, you can't see the path of light through the solution.*

Figure 5 *The dilute solution (left) contains less solute than the concentrated solution (right).*

Concentration of Solutions

A measure of the amount of solute dissolved in a solvent is **concentration.** Concentration can be expressed in grams of solute per milliliter of solvent (g/mL).

concentration the amount of a particular substance in a given quantity of a mixture, solution, or ore
 *VOCAB*

solubility the ability of one substance to dissolve in another at a given temperature and pressure

Concentrated or Dilute?

Solutions can be described as being concentrated or dilute. In **Figure 5,** both solutions have the same amount of solvent. However, the solution on the left contains less solute than the solution on the right. The solution on the left is dilute. The solution on the right is concentrated. Keep in mind that the terms *dilute* and *concentrated* do not tell you the amount of solute that is dissolved.

Solubility

If you add too much sugar to a glass of lemonade, not all of the sugar can dissolve. Some of it sinks to the bottom. To find the maximum amount of sugar that can dissolve, you would need to know the solubility of sugar. The **solubility** of a solute is the ability of the solute to dissolve in a solvent at a certain temperature. **Figure 6** shows how the solubility of several different solid substances changes with temperature.

MATH FOCUS

Calculating Concentration What is the concentration of a solution that has 35 g of salt dissolved in 175 mL of water?

Step 1: One equation for finding concentration is the following:

$$concentration = \frac{grams\ of\ solute}{milliliters\ of\ solvent}$$

Step 2: Replace grams of solute and milliliters of solvent with the values given, and solve.

$$\frac{35\ g\ salt}{175\ mL\ water} = 0.2\ g/mL$$

Now It's Your Turn

1. What is the concentration of solution A if it has 55 g of sugar dissolved in 500 mL of water?
2. What is the concentration of solution B if it has 36 g of sugar dissolved in 144 mL of water?
3. Which solution is more concentrated?

Figure 6 Solubility of Different Solids In Water

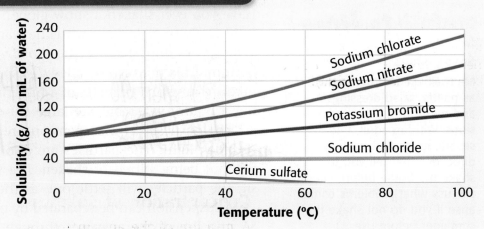

The solubility of most solids increases as the temperature gets higher. So, more solute can dissolve at higher temperatures. However, some solids, such as cerium sulfate, are less soluble at higher temperatures.

Dissolving Gases in Liquids

Most solids are more soluble in liquids at higher temperatures. But gases become less soluble in liquids as the temperature is raised. A soft drink goes flat faster when warm. The gas that is dissolved in the soft drink cannot stay dissolved when the temperature increases. So, the gas escapes, and the soft drink becomes "flat."

Reading Check How does the solubility of gases change with temperature?

Dissolving Solids Faster in Liquids

Several things affect how fast a solid will dissolve. Look at **Figure 7** to see three ways to make a solute dissolve faster. You can see why you will enjoy a glass of lemonade sooner if you stir granulated sugar into the lemonade before adding ice!

Figure 7 How to Dissolve Solids Faster

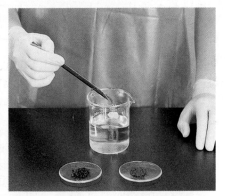

Mixing by stirring or shaking causes the solute particles to separate from one another and spread out more quickly among the solvent particles.

Heating causes particles to move more quickly. The solvent particles can separate the solute particles and spread them out more quickly.

Crushing the solute increases the amount of contact it has with the solvent. The particles of the crushed solute mix with the solvent more quickly.

suspension a mixture in which particles of a material are more or less evenly dispersed throughout a liquid or gas

colloid a mixture consisting of tiny particles that are intermediate in size between those in solutions and those in suspensions and that are suspended in a liquid, solid, or gas

Suspensions

Have you ever shaken a snow globe? If so, you have seen the solid snow particles mix with the water, as shown in **Figure 8.** When you stop shaking the globe, the snow settles to the bottom. This mixture is called a suspension. A **suspension** is a mixture in which particles of a material are dispersed throughout a liquid or gas but are large enough that they settle out.

The particles in a suspension are large enough to scatter or block light. The particles are also too large to stay mixed without being stirred or shaken. If a suspension is allowed to sit, the particles will settle out, as they do in a snow globe.

A suspension can be separated by passing it through a filter. So, the liquid or gas passes through the filter, but the solid particles are large enough to be trapped by the filter.

✓ **Reading Check** How can the particles of a suspension be separated?

Colloids

Some mixtures have properties between those of solutions and suspensions. These mixtures are known as colloids (KAHL OYDZ). A **colloid** is a mixture in which the particles are dispersed throughout but are not heavy enough to settle out. The particles in a colloid are relatively small and are fairly well mixed. You might be surprised at the number of colloids you see each day. Milk, mayonnaise, and stick deodorant—even the gelatin and whipped cream in **Figure 8**—are colloids.

The particles in a colloid are much smaller than the particles in a suspension. However, the particles are large enough to scatter light. A colloid cannot be separated by filtration. The particles are small enough to pass through a filter.

Figure 8 Properties of Suspensions and Colloids

Suspension This snow globe contains solid particles that will mix with the clear liquid when you shake it up. But the particles will soon fall to the bottom when the globe is at rest.

Colloid This dessert includes two tasty examples of colloids—fruity gelatin and whipped cream.

SECTION
Review

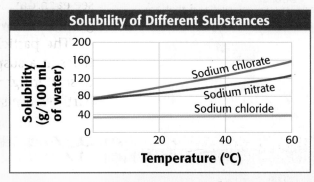

TN GLE 0807.Inq.1, GLE 0807.Inq.2, GLE 0807.Inq.5, GLE 0807.9.3, GLE 0807.9.4

Summary

- A mixture is a combination of two or more substances, each of which keeps its own characteristics.

- Mixtures can be separated by physical means, such as filtration and evaporation.

- A solution is a mixture that appears to be a single substance but is composed of a solute dissolved in a solvent.

- Concentration is a measure of the amount of solute dissolved in a solvent.

- The solubility of a solute is the ability of the solute to dissolve in a solvent at a certain temperature.

- Suspensions are mixtures that contain particles large enough to settle out or be filtered and to block or scatter light.

- Colloids are mixtures that contain particles that are too small to settle out or be filtered but are large enough to scatter light.

Using Key Terms

The statements below are false. For each statement, replace the underlined term to make a true statement.

1. The <u>solvent</u> is the substance that is dissolved.

2. A <u>suspension</u> is composed of substances that are spread evenly among each other.

3. A measure of the amount of solute dissolved in a solvent is <u>solubility</u>.

4. A <u>colloid</u> contains particles that will settle out of the mixture if left sitting.

Understanding Key Ideas

5. A mixture ✔0807.9.6
   a. has substances in it that are chemically combined.
   b. can always be separated using filtration.
   c. contains substances that are not mixed in a definite ratio.
   d. All of the above

6. List three ways to dissolve a solid faster.

Critical Thinking

7. Is the separation of a mixture a chemical or a physical change? Explain. ✔0807.9.6

8. **Applying Concepts** Design a simple experiment to separate iron filings from sawdust. Explain why your experiment works. ✔0807.Inq.1

9. **Analyzing Ideas** Identify the solute and solvent in a solution made of 15 mL of oxygen and 5 mL of helium.

Interpreting Graphics

Use the graph below to answer the questions that follow.

Solubility of Different Substances

Solubility (g/100 mL of water) vs. Temperature (°C)

Sodium chlorate
Sodium nitrate
Sodium chloride

10. At what temperature is 120 g of sodium nitrate soluble in 100 mL of water?

11. At 60°C, how much more sodium chlorate than sodium chloride will dissolve in 100 mL of water?

Skills Practice Lab

Flame Tests

Fireworks produce fantastic combinations of color when they are ignited. The different colors are the results of burning different compounds. Imagine that you are the head chemist for a fireworks company. The label has fallen off one box, and you must identify the unknown compound inside so that the fireworks may be used in the correct fireworks display. To identify the compound, you will use your knowledge that every compound has a unique set of properties.

OBJECTIVES

Observe flame colors emitted by various compounds.

Determine the composition of an unknown compound.

MATERIALS

- Bunsen burner
- chloride test solutions (4)
- hydrochloric acid, dilute, in a small beaker
- spark igniter
- tape, masking
- test tubes, small (4)
- test-tube rack
- water, distilled, in a small beaker
- wire and holder

SAFETY

Ask a Question

1 How can you identify an unknown compound by heating it in a flame?

Form a Hypothesis

2 Write a hypothesis that is a possible answer to the question above. Explain your reasoning.

Test the Hypothesis

3 Arrange the test tubes in the test-tube rack. Use masking tape to label each tube with one of the following names: calcium chloride, potassium chloride, sodium chloride, and unknown.

4 Copy the table below. Then, ask your teacher for your portions of the solutions. **Caution:** Be very careful in handling all chemicals. Tell your teacher immediately if you spill a chemical.

Test Results	
Compound	**Color of flame**
Calcium chloride	
Potassium chloride	DO NOT WRITE
Sodium chloride	IN BOOK
Unknown	

TN GLE 0807.Inq.2 Use appropriate tools and techniques to gather, organize, analyze, and interpret data.

GLE 0807.Inq.3 Synthesize information to determine cause and effect relationships between evidence and explanations.

GLE 0807.Inq.4 Recognize possible sources of bias and error, alternative explanations, and questions for further exploration.

GLE 0807.Inq.5 Communicate scientific understanding using descriptions, explanations, and models.

GLE 0807.9.4 Distinguish among elements, compounds, and mixtures.

5 Light the burner. Clean the wire by dipping it into the dilute hydrochloric acid and then into distilled water. Holding the wooden handle, heat the wire in the blue flame of the burner until the wire is glowing and it no longer colors the flame. **Caution:** Use extreme care around an open flame.

6 Dip the clean wire into the first test solution. Hold the wire at the tip of the inner cone of the burner flame. Record in the table the color given to the flame.

7 Clean the wire by repeating step 5. Then, repeat steps 5 and 6 for the other solutions.

8 Follow your teacher's instructions for cleanup and disposal.

Analyze the Results

1 **Identifying Patterns** Is the flame color a test for the metal or for the chloride in each compound? Explain your answer. ✔0807.9.7

2 **Analyzing Data** What is the identity of your unknown solution? How do you know?

Draw Conclusions

3 **Evaluating Methods** Why is it necessary to carefully clean the wire before testing each solution? ✔0807.Inq.4

4 **Making Predictions** Would you expect the compound sodium fluoride to produce the same color as sodium chloride in a flame test? Why or why not? ✔0807.Inq.3

5 **Interpreting Information** Each of the compounds you tested is made from chlorine, which is a poisonous gas at room temperature. Why is it safe to use these compounds without a gas mask? ✔0807.9.7

Chapter Review

USING KEY TERMS

Complete each of the following sentences by choosing the correct term from the word bank.

compound	element
suspension	solubility
solution	metal
nonmetal	solute

1 A(n) ___ has a definite ratio of components.

2 The ability of one substance to dissolve in another substance is the ___ of the solute.

3 A(n) ___ can be separated by filtration.

4 A(n) ___ is a pure substance that cannot be broken down into simpler substances by chemical means.

5 A(n) ___ is an element that is brittle and dull.

6 The ___ is the substance that dissolves to form a solution.

UNDERSTANDING KEY IDEAS

Multiple Choice

7 Which of the following increases the solubility of a gas in a liquid? ✓0807.Inq.3

  a. increasing the temperature of the liquid

  b. increasing the amount of gas in the liquid

  c. decreasing the temperature of the liquid

  d. decreasing the amount of liquid

8 Which of the following best describes chicken noodle soup?

  a. element   **c.** compound

  b. mixture   **d.** solution

9 Which of the following statements describes elements?

  a. All of the particles in the same element are different.

  b. Elements can be broken down into simpler substances.

  c. Elements have unique sets of properties.

  d. Elements cannot be joined together in chemical reactions.

10 A solution that contains a large amount of solute is best described as

  a. insoluble.   **c.** dilute.

  b. concentrated.   **d.** weak.

11 Which of the following substances can be separated into simpler substances only by chemical means? ✓0807.9.6

  a. sodium   **c.** water

  b. salt water   **d.** gold

12 Neon gas contains which of the following? ✓0807.9.1

  a. one kind of atom

  b. a mixture of substances

  c. air

  d. many different types of atoms

13 In which classification of matter are components chemically combined?

✔0807.9.6, ✔0807.9.9

a. a solution   **c.** a compound

b. a colloid   **d.** a suspension

Short Answer

14 How are elements, compounds, and mixtures different?   ✔0807.9.7

15 Sodium chloride is made from sodium and chlorine. Would you expect the properties of sodium chloride to be similar to sodium or chlorine? Explain.

✔0807.9.7

Math Skills

16 What is the concentration of a solution prepared by mixing 50 g of salt with 200 mL of water?

17 How many grams of sugar must be dissolved in 150 mL of water to make a solution that has a concentration of 0.6 g/mL?

CRITICAL THINKING

18 **Concept Mapping** Use the following terms to create a concept map: *matter, element, compound, mixture, solution, suspension,* and *colloid.*

19 **Forming Hypotheses** To keep the "fizz" in carbonated beverages after they have been opened, should you store them in a refrigerator or in a cabinet? Explain.   ✔0807.Inq.3

20 **Making Inferences** A light green powder is heated in a test tube. A gas is given off, and the solid becomes black. Was the change physical or chemical? Is the green powder an element, a compound, or a mixture? Explain your answer. ✔0807.9.6

21 **Predicting Consequences** Why is it desirable to know the exact concentration of solutions rather than whether they are concentrated or dilute?

22 **Applying Concepts** Describe a procedure to separate a mixture of salt, finely ground pepper, and pebbles.

✔0807.Inq.1

INTERPRETING GRAPHICS

Dr. Sol Vent did an experiment to find the solubility of a compound. The data below were collected using 100 mL of water. Use the table below to answer the questions that follow.

Temperature (°C)	10	25	40	60	95
Dissolved solute (g)	150	70	34	25	15

23 Use a computer or graph paper to construct a graph of Dr. Vent's results. Examine the graph. To increase the solubility, would you increase or decrease the temperature? Explain.

24 If 200 mL of water were used instead of 100 mL, how many grams of the compound would dissolve at 40°C?

25 Based on the solubility of this compound, is this compound a solid, liquid, or gas? Explain your answer.

TCAP Test Preparation

TN **SPI 0807.Inq.1** Design a simple experimental procedure with an identified control and appropriate variables.

SPI 0807.Inq.2 Select tools and procedures needed to conduct a moderately complex experiment.

SPI 0807.Inq.3 Interpret and translate data into a

table, graph, or diagram.

SPI 0807.Inq.4 Draw a conclusion that establishes a cause and effect relationship supported by evidence.

Multiple Choice

1. Anya found that compound A contains by mass 25.13% hydrogen and 74.87% carbon. She found that compound B contains by mass 14.37% hydrogen and 85.63% carbon. Create pie charts showing the composition of each compound. Based on your pie charts, which of the following statements is true?

   A. Compound A and compound B are the same compound.

   B. Hydrogen and carbon combine in specific but different ratios in forming compounds A and B.

   C. Although the mass compositions of compounds A and B have different percentages, the two compounds have the same mass ratio of carbon to hydrogen.

   D. The compounds hydrogen and carbon combine to form both compound A and compound B.

2. Imagine that you were asked to classify four samples of equal and known volume, each of which is made up of a single element. Which factor would be most useful for identifying them?

   A. mass

   B. shape

   C. hardness

   D. original source

Use the table below to answer question 3.

Property	Substance A	Substance B	Substance C
appearance	shiny yellow solid	powdery yellow solid	shiny gray solid
conductivity	good conductor	poor conductor	conductor
malleability	malleable	not malleable	brittle, not malleable

3. Which of the following statements is most accurate?

   A. Substances A and C are metals.

   B. Substance B is a metalloid.

   C. Substances B and C are nonmetals.

   D. Substance C is a metalloid.

4. If two poisonous elements are combined chemically, which of the following will be true of the resulting compound?

   A. The compound will be more poisonous than the original elements.

   B. The compound will be as poisonous as the original elements.

   C. The compound may or may not be poisonous.

   D. The compound will not be poisonous.

5. Which of the following processes could separate the components of a compound?

   A. dissolving, then filtering

   B. distilling at the boiling points of the compound's components

   C. using a magnet to attract the compound's metallic components

   D. applying an electric current

SPI 0807.9.1 Recognize that all matter consists of atoms.
SPI 0807.9.4 Differentiate between a mixture and a compound.

SPI 0807.9.8 Interpret the results of an investigation to determine whether a physical or chemical change has occurred.

Use the graph below to answer question 6.

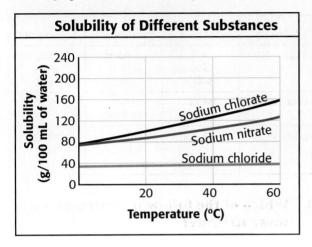

Solubility of Different Substances

9. **You are given two jars, each containing an unknown substance. Which procedure would you use to determine whether the substances are different or the same?**

   A. Compare appearances. If the substances look the same, then they are the same.

   B. Compare only physical properties. If the substances have the same density or melting point, then they are the same.

   C. Compare physical and chemical properties. If the substances perform the same in a variety of tests, then they are the same.

   D. Compare physical states. If the substances are in the same state, then they are the same.

6. **Which of the following values is the amount of sodium nitrate that can be dissolved in 100 mL of water at 40°C?**

   A. 0 g

   B. 40 g

   C. 100 g

   D. 130 g

7. **Two different atoms are chemically combined to form a new substance. What kind of substance formed?**

   A. a compound

   B. an element

   C. a mixture

   D. a solute

8. **Which procedure is a chemical change that may be used to break down a compound?**

   A. boiling

   B. freezing

   C. distillation

   D. combustion

Open Response

10. **Both vinegar and table sugar are composed of carbon, hydrogen, and oxygen atoms. Compare the properties of these two combinations of elements, and explain why the same elements can produce different substances.**

11. **Valerie placed 1.0 g of salt into one beaker, 1.0 g of soil into a second beaker, and 1.0 g of sugar into a third beaker. She then added 200 mL of water to each beaker and stirred the contents for 3 minutes. How many compounds and how many mixtures did Valerie make? Identify each. Explain whether a chemical or physical change took place in each beaker.**

12. **Describe the particles that make up all elements.**

TCAP Test Preparation

Science in Action

Science, Technology, and Society

Dry Cleaning: How Stains Are Dissolved

Sometimes, just water and detergent won't remove stains. For instance, have you ever gotten ink or something greasy on your favorite sweatshirt? Dry-cleaning technology was developed to remove these types of stains. In spite of its name, dry cleaning does involve liquids. First, the kind of stain must be determined. If the stain will dissolve in water, a stain remover for that particular stain is applied. Then, the stain is removed with a steam gun. But greasy stains won't dissolve in water. Greasy stains are treated with a liquid that can dissolve the stain. The clothing is then cleaned in a dry-cleaning machine.

 GLE 0807.T/E.1

Language Arts ACTiViTY

WRITING SKILL Imagine that you are a stained article of clothing. Write a five-paragraph short story describing how you became stained and how the stain was removed by the dry-cleaning process. You may have to research the dry-cleaning process before writing your story.

Science Fiction

"The Strange Case of Dr. Jekyll and Mr. Hyde" by Robert Louis Stevenson

Although Dr. Henry Jekyll was wild as a young man, he has become a respected doctor and scientist. Dr. Jekyll wants to understand the nature of human identity. His theory is that if he can separate his personality into "good" and "evil" parts, he can get rid of his evil side. Then, he can lead a happy, useful life.

Into Dr. Jekyll's life comes the mysterious Mr. Hyde, a man of action and anger. He sparks fear in the hearts of people he meets. Who is he? And what does he have to do with the deaths of two people? To find out more, read Stevenson's "The Strange Case of Dr. Jekyll and Mr. Hyde" in the *Holt Anthology of Science Fiction*.

Social Studies ACTiViTY

"The Strange Case of Dr. Jekyll and Mr. Hyde" was published in 1886. The story takes place in London, England. What was London like in the 1870s and 1880s? Use the library or the Internet to find information about London and its people at that time. Make a chart that compares London in the 1870s with your hometown today.

Aundra Nix

Metallurgist Aundra Nix is a chief metallurgist for a copper mine in Sahuarita, Arizona, where she supervises laboratories and other engineers. "To be able to look at rock in the ground and follow it through a process of drilling, blasting, hauling, crushing, grinding, and finally mineral separation—where you can hold a mineral that is one-third copper in your hand—is exciting."

Although she is a supervisor, Nix enjoys the flexible nature of her job. "My work environment includes office and computer work, plant work, and outdoor work. In this field you can 'get your hands into it,' which I always prefer," says Nix. "I did not want a career where it may be years before you see the results of your work." Aundra Nix enjoyed math and science, "so engineering seemed to be a natural area to study," she says. Nix's advice to students planning their own career is to learn all they can in science and technology, because that is the future.

TN GLE 0807.T/E.1

Math ACTIVITY

A large copper-mining company employed about 2,300 people at three locations in New Mexico. Because of an increase in demand for copper, 570 of these workers were hired over a period of a year. Of the 570 new workers, 115 were hired within a three-week period. What percentage of the total work force do the newly hired employees represent? Of the new workers who were hired, what percentage was hired during the three-week hiring period?

go.hrw.com

To learn more about these Science in Action topics, visit go.hrw.com and type in the keyword **HP5MIXF.**

Current Science

Check out Current Science® articles related to this chapter by visiting go.hrw.com. Just type in the keyword **HP5CS04.**

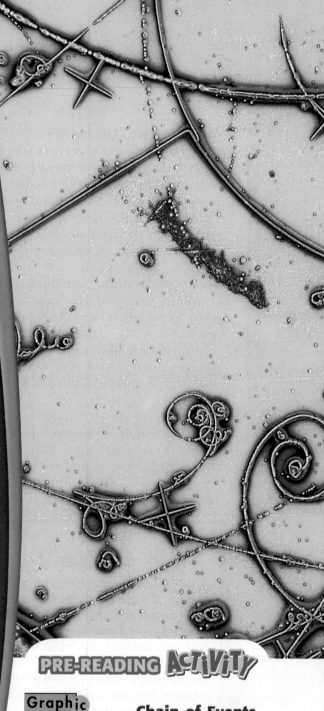

10

Introduction to Atoms

The Big Idea

Atoms are composed of small particles that determine the properties of the atom.

TN Tennessee Science Standards

Embedded Inquiry

GLE 0807.Inq.3 Synthesize information to determine cause and effect relationships between evidence and explanations.

GLE 0807.Inq.5 Communicate scientific understanding using descriptions, explanations, and models.

✓0807.Inq.3 Use evidence from a dataset to determine cause and effect relationships that explain a phenomenon.

✓0807.Inq.5 Design a method to explain the results of an investigation using descriptions, explanations, or models.

Embedded Technology and Engineering

GLE 0807.T/E.1 Explore how technology responds to social, political, and economic needs.

GLE 0807.T/E.2 Know that the engineering design process involves an ongoing series of events that incorporate design constraints, model building, testing, evaluating, modifying, and retesting.

✓0807.T/E.2 Apply the engineering design process to construct a prototype that meets certain specifications.

Physical Science

GLE 0807.9.1 Understand that all matter is made up of atoms.

GLE 0807.9.2 Explain that matter has properties that are determined by the structure and arrangement of its atoms.

GLE 0807.12.4 Identify factors that influence the amount of gravitational force between objects.

✓0807.9.1 Identify atoms as the fundamental particles that make up matter.

✓0807.9.3 Measure or calculate the mass, volume, and temperature of a given substance.

✓0807.12.6 Identify factors that influence the amount of gravitational force between objects.

PRE-READING ACTIVITY

Graphic Organizer

Chain-of-Events Chart Before you read the chapter, create the graphic organizer entitled "Chain-of-Events Chart" described in the **Study Skills** section of the Appendix. As you read the chapter, fill in the chart with details about each step in the historical development of ideas about atoms.

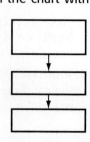

START-UP ACTIVITY

TN GLE 0807.Inq.2, GLE 0807.Inq.3

Where Is It?

Scientists have been able to gather information about atoms without actually seeing them. In this activity, you will do something similar: you will form an idea about the location and size of a hidden object by rolling marbles at it.

Procedure

1. Place a **rectangular piece of cardboard** on **four books or blocks** so that each corner of the cardboard rests on a book or block.

2. Your teacher will place an **unknown object** under the cardboard. Be sure that you cannot see the object.

3. Place a **large piece of paper** on top of the cardboard.

4. Carefully roll a **marble** under the cardboard. Record on the paper the position where the marble enters and exits. Also, record the direction it travels.

5. Keep rolling the marble from different directions to collect data about the shape and location of the object. Write down all of your observations.

Analysis

1. Form a conclusion about the object's shape, size, and location. Record your conclusion.

2. Lift the cardboard, and look at the object. Compare your conclusions with the object's actual size, shape, and location. ✔0807.Inq.4

Development of the Atomic Theory

What You Will Learn

- Describe some of the experiments that led to the current atomic theory.
- Compare the different models of the atom.
- Explain how the atomic theory has changed as scientists have discovered new information about the atom.

Vocabulary

atom   nucleus
electron   electron cloud

READING STRATEGY

Reading Organizer As you read this section, create an outline of the section. Use the headings from the section in your outline.

TN **GLE 0807.Inq.3** Synthesize information to determine cause and effect relationships between evidence and explanations.
GLE 0807.T/E.2 Know that the engineering design process involves an ongoing series of events that incorporate design constraints, model building, testing, evaluating, modifying, and retesting.
GLE 0807.9.1 Understand that all matter is made up of atoms.

Have you ever watched a mystery movie and thought you knew who the criminal was? Have you ever changed your mind because of a new fact or clue?

The same thing happens in science! Sometimes an idea or model must be changed as new information is gathered. In this section, you will see how our ideas about atoms have changed over time. Your first stop is ancient Greece.

The Beginning of Atomic Theory

Imagine that you cut something in half. Then, you cut each half in half again, and so on. Could you keep cutting the pieces in half forever? Around 440 BCE, a Greek philosopher named Democritus (di MAHK ruh tuhs) thought that you would eventually end up with a particle that could not be cut. He called this particle an atom. The word *atom* is from the Greek word *atomos,* meaning "not able to be divided." Democritus said that all atoms are small, hard particles. He thought that atoms were made of a single material formed into different shapes and sizes.

From Aristotle to Modern Science

Aristotle (AR is TAHT'l), another Greek philosopher, disagreed with Democritus's ideas. He believed that you would never end up with a particle that could not be cut. He had such a strong influence on people's ideas that for a long time, most people thought he was right.

Democritus was right, though: Matter is made of particles, which we call atoms. An **atom** is the smallest particle into which an element can be divided and still be the same substance. **Figure 1** shows a picture of aluminum atoms taken with a scanning tunneling electron microscope (STM). Long before actually being able to scan atoms, scientists had ideas about them.

Figure 1 *Aluminum cans, like all matter, are made of atoms. Aluminum atoms can be seen here as an image from a scanning tunneling electron microscope.*

Dalton's Atomic Theory Based on Experiments

By the late 1700s, scientists had learned that elements combine in certain proportions based on mass to form compounds. For example, hydrogen and oxygen always combine in the same proportion to form water. John Dalton, a British chemist and schoolteacher, wanted to know why. He experimented with different substances. His results suggested that elements combine in certain proportions because they are made of single atoms. Dalton, shown in **Figure 2,** published his atomic theory in 1803. His theory stated the following ideas:

- All substances are made of atoms. Atoms are small particles that cannot be created, divided, or destroyed.
- Atoms of the same element are exactly alike, and atoms of different elements are different.
- Atoms join with other atoms to make new substances.

✓ Reading Check Why did Dalton think that elements are made of single atoms?

Not Quite Correct

Toward the end of the 1800s, scientists agreed that Dalton's theory explained much of what they saw. However, new information was found that did not fit some of Dalton's ideas. The atomic theory was then changed to describe the atom more correctly. As you read on, you will learn how Dalton's theory has changed, step by step, into the modern atomic theory.

atom the smallest unit of an element that maintains the chemical properties of that element

Figure 2 *John Dalton developed his atomic theory from observations gathered from many experiments.*

Figure 3 Thomson's Cathode-Ray Tube Experiment

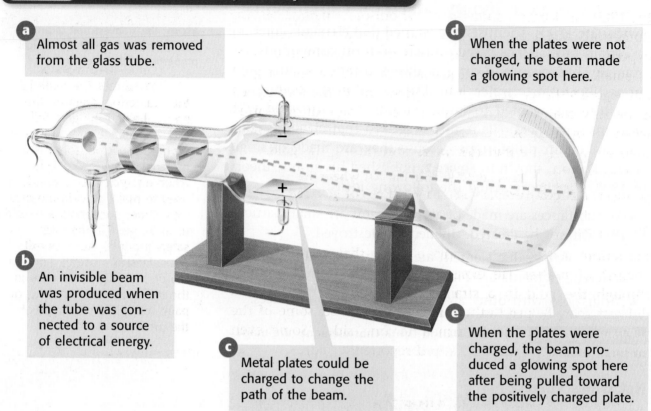

a Almost all gas was removed from the glass tube.

d When the plates were not charged, the beam made a glowing spot here.

b An invisible beam was produced when the tube was connected to a source of electrical energy.

c Metal plates could be charged to change the path of the beam.

e When the plates were charged, the beam produced a glowing spot here after being pulled toward the positively charged plate.

Thomson's Discovery of Electrons

In 1897, a British scientist named J. J. Thomson showed that there was a mistake in Dalton's theory. Thomson discovered that there are small particles *inside* the atom. This means that atoms can be divided into even smaller parts.

Thomson experimented with a cathode-ray tube like the one shown in **Figure 3.** He discovered that a positively charged plate (marked with a plus sign in the drawing) attracted the beam. Thomson concluded that the beam was made of particles that have negative electric charges. He also concluded that these negatively charged particles are present in every kind of atom. The negatively charged particles that Thomson discovered are now called **electrons.**

electron a subatomic particle that has a negative charge

Like Plums in a Pudding

After learning that atoms contain electrons, Thomson proposed a new model of the atom. This model is shown in **Figure 4.** It is sometimes called the *plum-pudding model,* after a dessert that was popular in Thomson's day. Thomson thought that electrons were mixed throughout an atom, like plums in a pudding. Today, you might call Thomson's model the *chocolate chip ice-cream model.*

Figure 4 *Thomson proposed that electrons were located throughout an atom like plums in a pudding, as shown in this model.*

Rutherford's Atomic "Shooting Gallery"

In 1909, a former student of Thomson's named Ernest Rutherford decided to test Thomson's theory. He designed an experiment to study the parts of the atom. He aimed a beam of small, positively charged particles at a thin sheet of gold foil. **Figure 5** shows Rutherford's experiment. Rutherford placed a specially coated screen around the foil. The coating glowed when hit by the positively charged particles. Rutherford could then see where the particles went after hitting the gold.

Reading Check How could Rutherford tell where the positively charged particles went after hitting the gold foil?

Surprising Results

Rutherford started with Thomson's idea that atoms are soft "blobs" of matter. He expected the particles to pass right through the gold in a straight line. Most of the particles did just that. But to Rutherford's great surprise, some of the particles were deflected (turned to one side). Some even bounced straight back. Rutherford reportedly said,

"It was quite the most incredible event that has ever happened to me in my life. It was almost as if you fired a fifteen-inch shell into a piece of tissue paper and it came back and hit you."

TN GLE 0807.T/E.2

CONNECTION TO Engineering

Glow-in-the-Dark Products The material that Rutherford used on the screen behind the gold foil was zinc sulfide. Zinc sulfide is a phosphor. A phosphor is a material that gives off light when energized. Zinc sulfide is used to make glow-in-the-dark toys. Other phosphors are used to make glow-in-the dark safety products, such as exit signs. Design a useful glow-in-the-dark product. Use glow-in-the dark powders, pigment, or paint to build a prototype of the product. ✔0807.T/E.2

ACTIVITY

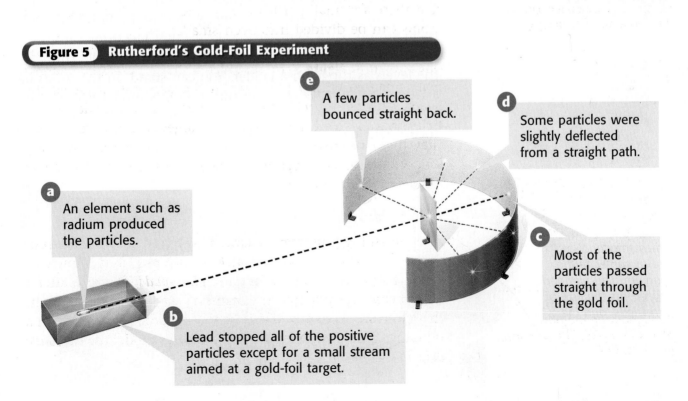

Figure 5 Rutherford's Gold-Foil Experiment

e A few particles bounced straight back.

d Some particles were slightly deflected from a straight path.

a An element such as radium produced the particles.

c Most of the particles passed straight through the gold foil.

b Lead stopped all of the positive particles except for a small stream aimed at a gold-foil target.

nucleus in physical science, an atom's central region, which is made up of protons and neutrons
━TN▶ *VOCAB*

electron cloud a region around the nucleus of an atom where electrons are likely to be found

Where Are the Electrons?

The plum-pudding model of the atom did not explain what Rutherford saw. Most of the tiny particles went straight through the gold foil, with a small number being deflected. He realized that in order to explain this, atoms must be considered mostly empty space, with a tiny part made of highly dense matter.

Far from the Nucleus

In 1911, Rutherford revised the atomic theory. He made a new model of the atom, as shown in **Figure 6.** Rutherford proposed that in the center of the atom is a tiny, extremely dense, positively charged part called the **nucleus** (NOO klee uhs). Because like charges repel, Rutherford reasoned that positively charged particles that passed close by the nucleus were pushed away by the positive charges in the nucleus. A particle that headed straight for a nucleus would be pushed almost straight back in the direction from which it came. From his results, Rutherford calculated that the diameter of the nucleus was 100,000 times smaller than the diameter of the gold atom. To get an idea of this kind of difference in size, look at **Figure 7.**

✓ **Reading Check** How did Rutherford change Thomson's model of the atom?

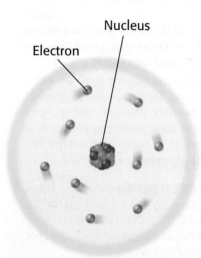

Figure 6 *Rutherford's model of the atom had electrons surrounding the nucleus at a distance. (This model does not show the true scale of sizes and distances.)*

Bohr's Electron Levels

In 1913, Niels Bohr, a Danish scientist who worked with Rutherford, studied the way that atoms react to light. Bohr's results led him to propose that electrons move around the nucleus in certain paths, or energy levels. In Bohr's model, there are no paths between the levels. But electrons can jump from a path in one level to a path in another level. Think of the levels as rungs on a ladder. You can stand on the rungs of a ladder but not *between* the rungs. Bohr's model was a valuable tool in predicting some atomic behavior, but the atomic theory still had room for improvement.

Figure 7 *The diameter of this pinhead is 100,000 times smaller than the diameter of the stadium. The pinhead represents the size of a nucleus, and the stadium represents the size of an atom.*

The Modern Atomic Theory

Many 20th-century scientists added to our current understanding of the atom. An Austrian physicist named Erwin Schrödinger (SHROH ding uhr) and a German physicist named Werner Heisenberg (HIE zuhn berkh) did especially important work. They further explained the nature of electrons in the atom. For example, electrons do not travel in definite paths as Bohr suggested. In fact, the exact path of an electron cannot be predicted. According to the current theory, there are regions inside the atom where electrons are *likely* to be found. These regions are called **electron clouds**. The electron-cloud model of the atom is shown in **Figure 8.**

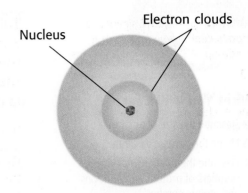

Figure 8 *In the current model of the atom, electrons surround the nucleus in electron clouds.*

SECTION Review

TN GLE 0807.Inq.5, GLE 0807.9.1

Summary

- Democritus thought that matter is composed of atoms.
- Dalton based his theory on observations of how elements combine.
- Thomson discovered electrons in atoms.
- Rutherford discovered that atoms are mostly empty space with a dense, positive nucleus.
- Bohr proposed that electrons are located in levels at certain distances from the nucleus.
- The electron-cloud model represents the current atomic theory.

Using Key Terms

The statements below are false. For each statement, replace the underlined term to make a true statement.

1. A <u>nucleus</u> is a particle with a negative electric charge.

2. The <u>electron</u> is where most of an atom's mass is located.

Understanding Key Ideas

3. What are the fundamental particles that make up matter? ✔0807.9.1

4. Which of the following scientists discovered that atoms contain electrons?
   a. Dalton
   b. Thomson
   c. Rutherford
   d. Bohr

5. What did Dalton do in developing his theory that Democritus did not do?

6. What experiment demonstrated that atoms are mostly empty space?

7. What refinements did Bohr make to Rutherford's proposed atomic theory?

Critical Thinking

8. **Making Comparisons** Compare the location of electrons in Bohr's theory with the location of electrons in the current atomic theory.

9. **Analyzing Methods** How does the design of Rutherford's experiment show what he was trying to find out?

Interpreting Graphics

10. What about the atomic model shown below was shown to be incorrect?

Internet Resources

For a variety of links related to this chapter, go to www.scilinks.org

Topic: Development of the Atomic Theory; Current Atomic Theory

SciLinks code: HSM0399; HSM0371

The Atom

Even though atoms are very small, they are made up of even smaller things. You can learn a lot about the parts that make up an atom and what holds an atom together.

In this section, you'll learn about how atoms are alike and how they are different. But first you'll find out just how small an atom really is.

How Small Is an Atom?

Think about a penny. A penny contains about 2×10^{22} atoms (which can be written as 20,000,000,000,000,000,000,000 atoms) of copper and zinc. That's 20 thousand billion billion atoms—over 3,000,000,000,000 times more atoms than there are people on Earth! If there are that many atoms in a penny, each atom must be very small.

Scientists know that aluminum is made of average-sized atoms. An aluminum atom has a diameter of about 0.00000003 cm. That's three one-hundred-millionths of a centimeter. Take a look at **Figure 1.** Even things that are very thin, such as aluminum foil, are made up of very large numbers of atoms.

What You Will Learn

- Describe the size of an atom.
- Name the parts of an atom.
- Describe the relationship between numbers of protons and neutrons and atomic number.
- State how isotopes differ.
- Calculate atomic masses.
- Describe the forces within an atom.

Vocabulary

proton
atomic mass
  unit
neutron

atomic number
isotope
mass number
atomic mass

READING STRATEGY

Reading Organizer As you read this section, make a concept map by using the terms above.

TN **GLE 0807.Inq.5** Communicate scientific understanding using descriptions, explanations, and models.

GLE 0807.T/E.2 Know that the engineering design process involves an ongoing series of events that incorporate design constraints, model building, testing, evaluating, modifying, and retesting.

GLE 0807.9.2 Explain that matter has properties that are determined by the structure and arrangement of its atoms.

GLE 0807.12.4 Identify factors that influence the amount of gravitational force between objects.

Figure 1 *This aluminum foil might seem thin to you. But it is about 50,000 atoms thick!*

Figure 2 Parts of an Atom

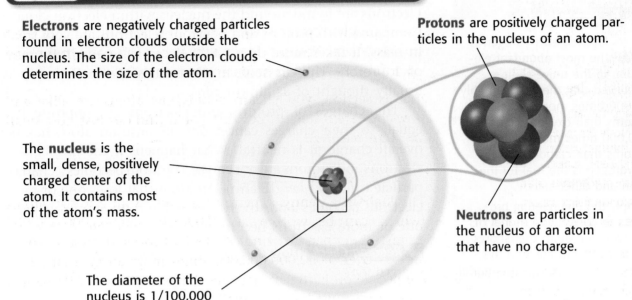

Electrons are negatively charged particles found in electron clouds outside the nucleus. The size of the electron clouds determines the size of the atom.

Protons are positively charged particles in the nucleus of an atom.

The **nucleus** is the small, dense, positively charged center of the atom. It contains most of the atom's mass.

Neutrons are particles in the nucleus of an atom that have no charge.

The diameter of the nucleus is 1/100,000 the diameter of the atom.

What Is an Atom Made Of?

As tiny as an atom is, it is made up of even smaller particles. These particles are protons, neutrons, and electrons, shown in the model in **Figure 2.** (The particles in the pictures are not shown in their correct proportions. If they were, the electrons would be too small to see.)

The Nucleus

Protons are positively charged particles in the nucleus. The mass of a proton is about 1.7×10^{-24} g. This number can also be written as 0.0000000000000000000000017 g. Because the masses of particles in atoms are so small, scientists made a new unit for them. The SI unit used to express the masses of particles in atoms is the **atomic mass unit** (amu). Each proton has a mass of about 1 amu.

Neutrons are the particles of the nucleus that have no electrical charge. Neutrons are a little more massive than protons are. But the difference in mass is so small that the mass of a neutron can be thought of as 1 amu.

Protons and neutrons are the most massive particles in an atom. But the volume of the nucleus is very small. So, the nucleus is very dense. If it were possible to have a nucleus the volume of a grape, that nucleus would have a mass greater than 9 million metric tons!

proton a subatomic particle that has a positive charge and that is found in the nucleus of an atom

atomic mass unit a unit of mass that describes the mass of an atom or molecule

neutron a subatomic particle that has no charge and that is found in the nucleus of an atom

✔ *Reading Check* Name the two kinds of particles that can be found in the nucleus.

CONNECTION TO Astronomy

Hydrogen Hydrogen is the most abundant element in the universe. It is believed that there are roughly 2,000 times more hydrogen atoms than oxygen atoms and 10,000 times more hydrogen atoms than carbon atoms. Hydrogen is the fuel for the sun and other stars.

Apply the engineering process to construct a model of a hydrogen atom that shows where the nucleus and the electron are. Explain the model to the class and describe how you could improve your model to more closely resemble a hydrogen atom. ✔ 0807.T/E.2

ACTIVITY

Outside the Nucleus

Electrons are the negatively charged particles in atoms. Electrons are found around the nucleus within electron clouds. Compared with protons and neutrons, electrons are very small in mass. It takes more than 1,800 electrons to equal the mass of 1 proton. The mass of an electron is so small that it is usually thought of as almost zero.

The charges of protons and electrons are opposite but equal, so their charges cancel out. Because an atom has no overall charge, it is neutral. What happens if the numbers of electrons and protons are not equal? The atom becomes a charged particle called an *ion* (IE ahn). An atom that loses one or more electrons becomes a positively-charged ion. An atom that gains one or more electrons becomes a negatively-charged ion.

✔ Reading Check How does an atom become a positively-charged ion?

How Do Atoms of Different Elements Differ?

There are more than 110 different elements. The atoms of each of these elements are different from the atoms of all other elements. What makes atoms different from each other? To find out, imagine that you could build an atom by putting together protons, neutrons, and electrons.

Starting Simply

It's easiest to start with the simplest atom. Protons and electrons are found in all atoms. The simplest atom is made of just one of each. It's so simple it doesn't even have a neutron. To "build" this atom, put just one proton in the center of the atom for the nucleus. Then, put one electron in the electron cloud. Congratulations! You have just made a hydrogen atom.

Now for Some Neutrons

Now, build an atom that has two protons. Both of the protons are positively charged, so they repel one another. You cannot form a nucleus with them unless you add some neutrons. For this atom, two neutrons will do. To have a neutral charge, your new atom will also need two electrons outside the nucleus. What you have is an atom of the element helium. A model of this atom is shown in **Figure 3.**

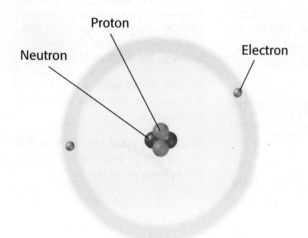

Neutron   Proton   Electron

Figure 3 *A helium nucleus must have neutrons in it to keep the protons from moving apart.*

Building Bigger Atoms

You could build a carbon atom using 6 protons, 6 neutrons, and 6 electrons. You could build an oxygen atom using 8 protons, 9 neutrons, and 8 electrons. You could even build a gold atom with 79 protons, 118 neutrons, and 79 electrons! As you can see, an atom does not have to have equal numbers of protons and neutrons.

Protons and Atomic Number

How can you tell which elements these atoms represent? The key is the number of protons. The number of protons in the nucleus of an atom is the **atomic number** of that atom. All atoms of an element have the same atomic number. Every hydrogen atom has only one proton in its nucleus, so hydrogen has an atomic number of 1. Every carbon atom has six protons in its nucleus. So, carbon has an atomic number of 6.

Isotopes

An atom that has one proton, one electron, and one neutron is shown in **Figure 4.** The atomic number of this new atom is 1, so the atom is hydrogen. However, this hydrogen atom's nucleus has two particles. Therefore, this atom has a greater mass than the hydrogen atom you made.

The new atom is another isotope (IE suh TOHP) of hydrogen. **Isotopes** are atoms that have the same number of protons but have different numbers of neutrons. Atoms that are isotopes of each other are always the same element, because isotopes always have the same number of protons. They have different numbers of neutrons, however, which gives them different masses.

INTERNET ACTIVITY

For another activity related to this chapter, go to **go.hrw.com** and type in the keyword **HP5ATSW**.

atomic number the number of protons in the nucleus of an atom; the atomic number is the same for all atoms of an element

isotope an atom that has the same number of protons (or the same atomic number) as other atoms of the same element do but that has a different number of neutrons (and thus a different atomic mass)

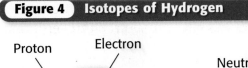

Figure 4   Isotopes of Hydrogen

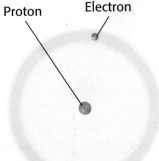

This isotope is a hydrogen atom that has one proton in its nucleus.

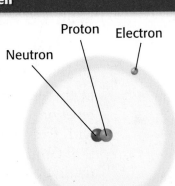

This isotope is a hydrogen atom that has one proton and one neutron in its nucleus.

Atomic Diagrams

Explain what you have learned about isotopes to an adult. Together, draw diagrams of hydrogen-2, helium-3, and carbon-14. Show the correct number and location of each type of particle. For the electrons, simply write the total number of electrons in the electron cloud. Use colored pencils or markers to represent the protons, neutrons, and electrons.

mass number the sum of the numbers of protons and neutrons in the nucleus of an atom

Properties of Isotopes

Each element has a limited number of isotopes that are found in nature. Some isotopes of an element have special properties because they are unstable. An unstable atom is an atom with a nucleus that will change over time. This type of isotope is *radioactive*. Radioactive atoms spontaneously fall apart after a certain amount of time. As they do, they give off smaller particles, as well as energy.

However, isotopes of an element share the same chemical properties and most of the same physical properties. For example, the most common oxygen isotope has 8 neutrons in the nucleus. Other isotopes of oxygen have 9 or 10 neutrons. All three isotopes are colorless, odorless gases at room temperature. Each isotope has the chemical property of combining with a substance as it burns. Different isotopes of an element even behave the same in chemical changes in your body.

Reading Check In what cases are differences between isotopes important?

Telling Isotopes Apart

You can identify each isotope of an element by its mass number. The **mass number** is the sum of the protons and neutrons in an atom. Electrons are not included in an atom's mass number because their mass is so small that they have very little effect on the atom's total mass. Look at the boron isotope models shown in **Figure 5** to see how to calculate an atom's mass number.

Figure 5 **Isotopes of Boron**

Each of these boron isotopes has five protons. But because each has a different number of neutrons, each has a different mass number.

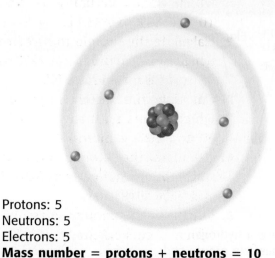

Protons: 5
Neutrons: 5
Electrons: 5
Mass number = protons + neutrons = 10

Protons: 5
Neutrons: 6
Electrons: 5
Mass number = protons + neutrons = 11

Naming Isotopes

To identify a specific isotope of an element, write the name of the element followed by a hyphen and the mass number of the isotope. A hydrogen atom with one proton and no neutrons has a mass number of 1. Its name is hydrogen-1. Hydrogen-2 has one proton and one neutron. The carbon isotope with a mass number of 12 is called carbon-12. If you know that the atomic number for carbon is 6, you can calculate the number of neutrons in carbon-12 by subtracting the atomic number from the mass number. For carbon-12, the number of neutrons is 12 − 6, or 6.

$$
\begin{array}{r}
12 \ \text{Mass number} \\
- \ 6 \ \text{Number of protons (atomic number)} \\
\hline
6 \ \text{Number of neutrons}
\end{array}
$$

Calculating the Mass of an Element

Most elements contain a mixture of two or more isotopes. For example, all copper is composed of copper-63 atoms and copper-65 atoms. The **atomic mass** of an element is the weighted average of the masses of all the naturally occurring isotopes of that element. A weighted average accounts for the percentages of each isotope that are present. Copper, including the copper in the Statue of Liberty, shown in **Figure 6,** is 69% copper-63 and 31% copper-65. The atomic mass of copper is 63.6 amu.

Figure 6 *The copper used to make the Statue of Liberty includes both copper-63 and copper-65. Copper's atomic mass is 63.6 amu.*

atomic mass the mass of an atom expressed in atomic mass units

---

MATH FOCUS

Atomic Mass Chlorine-35 makes up 76% of all the chlorine in nature, and chlorine-37 makes up the other 24%. What is the atomic mass of chlorine?

Step 1: Multiply the mass number of each isotope by its percentage abundance in decimal form.

$$(35 \times 0.76) = 26.60$$
$$(37 \times 0.24) = 8.88$$

Step 2: Add these amounts together to find the atomic mass.

$$
\begin{array}{r}
(35 \times 0.76) = 26.60 \\
(37 \times 0.24) = + \ 8.88 \\
\hline
35.48 \ \text{amu}
\end{array}
$$

Now It's Your Turn

1. Calculate the atomic mass of boron, which occurs naturally as 20% boron-10 and 80% boron-11.

2. Calculate the atomic mass of rubidium, which occurs naturally as 72% rubidium-85 and 28% rubidium-87.

3. Calculate the atomic mass of gallium, which occurs naturally as 60% gallium-69 and 40% gallium-71.

4. Calculate the atomic mass of silver, which occurs naturally as 52% silver-107 and 48% silver-109.

5. Calculate the atomic mass of silicon, which occurs naturally as 92% silicon-28, 5% silicon-29, and 3% silicon-30.

Forces in Atoms

You have seen that atoms are made of smaller particles. But what are the *forces* (the pushes or pulls between objects) acting between these particles? Four basic forces are at work everywhere, even within the atom. These forces are gravitational force, electromagnetic force, strong force, and weak force. These forces work together to give an atom its structure and properties. Look at **Figure 7** to learn about each one.

✓ **Reading Check** What are the four basic forces at work everywhere in nature?

Figure 7   Forces in the Atom

Gravitational Force Probably the most familiar of the four forces is *gravitational force*. Gravitational force acts between all objects all the time. The amount of gravitational force between objects depends on their masses and the distance between them. Gravitational force pulls objects, such as the sun, Earth, cars, and books, toward one another. However, because the masses of particles in atoms are so small, the gravitational force within atoms is very small.

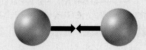

Electromagnetic Force As mentioned earlier, objects that have the same charge repel each other, while objects with opposite charge attract each other. This is due to the *electromagnetic force*. Protons and electrons are attracted to each other because they have opposite charges. The electromagnetic force holds the electrons around the nucleus.

Particles with the same charges repel each other.

Particles with opposite charges attract each other.

Strong Force Protons push away from one another because of the electromagnetic force. A nucleus containing two or more protons would fly apart if it were not for the *strong force*. At the close distances between protons and neutrons in the nucleus, the strong force is greater than the electromagnetic force, so the nucleus stays together.

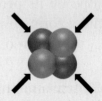

Weak Force The *weak force* is an important force in radioactive atoms. In certain unstable atoms, a neutron can change into a proton and an electron. The weak force plays a key role in this change.

TN GLE 0807.Inq.3, GLE 0807.Inq.5, GLE 0807.9.2, GLE 0807.12.4

Summary

- Atoms are extremely small. Ordinary-sized objects are made up of very large numbers of atoms.
- Atoms consist of a nucleus, which has protons and usually neutrons, and electrons, located in electron clouds around the nucleus.
- The number of protons in the nucleus of an atom is that atom's atomic number. All atoms of an element have the same atomic number.

- Different isotopes of an element have different numbers of neutrons in their nuclei. Isotopes of an element share most chemical and physical properties.
- The mass number of an atom is the sum of the atom's neutrons and protons.
- Atomic mass is a weighted average of the masses of natural isotopes of an element.
- The forces at work in an atom are gravitational force, electromagnetic force, strong force, and weak force.

Using Key Terms

1. Use the following terms in the same sentence: *proton, neutron,* and *isotope.*

Complete each of the following sentences by choosing the correct term from the word bank.

| atomic mass unit | atomic number |
| mass number | atomic mass |

2. An atom's ___ is equal to the number of protons in its nucleus.

3. An atom's ___ is equal to the weighted average of the masses of all the naturally occurring isotopes of that element.

Understanding Key Ideas

4. Which of the following particles has no electric charge?
   a. proton
   b. neutron
   c. electron
   d. ion

5. Name and describe the four forces that are at work within the nucleus of an atom.

Math Skills

6. The metal thallium occurs naturally as 30% thallium-203 and 70% thallium-205. Calculate the atomic mass of thallium.

Critical Thinking

7. **Analyzing Ideas** Why is gravitational force in the nucleus so small? ✔0807.12.6

8. **Predicting Consequences** Could a nucleus of more than one proton but no neutrons exist? Explain. ✔0807.Inq.3

Interpreting Graphics

9. Look at the two atomic models below. Do the two atoms represent different elements or different isotopes? Explain.

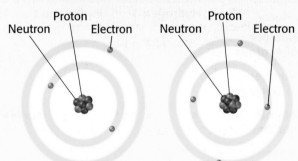

Internet Resources

For a variety of links related to this chapter, go to www.scilinks.org

Topic: Inside the Atom; Isotopes

SciLinks code: HSM0799; HSM0820

Model-Making Lab

Made to Order

Imagine that you are an employee at the Elements-4-U Company, which custom builds elements. Your job is to construct the atomic nucleus for each element ordered by your clients. You were hired for the position because of your knowledge about what a nucleus is made of and your understanding of how isotopes of an element differ from each other. Now, it's time to put that knowledge to work!

Procedure

1. Copy the table below onto another sheet of paper. Be sure to leave room to expand the table to include more elements.

2. Your first assignment is the nucleus of hydrogen-1. Pick up one proton (a white plastic-foam ball). Congratulations! You have built a hydrogen-1 nucleus, the simplest nucleus possible.

3. Count the number of protons and neutrons in the nucleus, and fill in rows 1 and 2 for this element in the table.

4. Use the information in rows 1 and 2 to determine the atomic number and mass number of the element. Record this information in the table.

OBJECTIVES

Build models of nuclei of certain isotopes.

Use the periodic table to determine the composition of atomic nuclei.

MATERIALS

- periodic table
- plastic-foam balls, blue, 2–3 cm in diameter (6)
- plastic-foam balls, white, 2–3 cm in diameter (4)
- toothpicks (20)

SAFETY

Data Collection Table						
	Hydrogen-1	Hydrogen-2	Helium-3	Helium-4	Beryllium-9	Beryllium-10
Number of protons						
Number of neutrons						
Atomic number						
Mass number						

DO NOT WRITE IN BOOK

TN GLE 0807.Inq.2 Use appropriate tools and techniques to gather, organize, analyze, and interpret data.

GLE 0807.9.2 Explain that matter has properties that are determined by the structure and arrangement of its atoms.

GLE 0807.9.6 Use the periodic table to determine the characteristics of an element.

5 Draw a picture of your model.

6 Hydrogen-2 is an isotope of hydrogen that has one proton and one neutron. Using a strong-force connector, add a neutron to your hydrogen-1 nucleus. (Remember that in a nucleus, the protons and neutrons are held together by the strong force, which is represented in this activity by the toothpicks.) Repeat steps 3–5.

7 Helium-3 is an isotope of helium that has two protons and one neutron. Add one proton to your hydrogen-2 nucleus to create a helium-3 nucleus. Each particle should be connected to the other two particles so that they make a triangle, not a line. Protons and neutrons always form the smallest arrangement possible because the strong force pulls them together. Then, repeat steps 3–5.

8 For the next part of the lab, you will need to use information from the periodic table of the elements. Look at the illustration below. It shows the periodic table entry for carbon. You can find the atomic number of any element at the top of its entry on the periodic table. For example, the atomic number of carbon is 6.

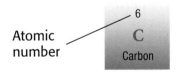

Atomic number

6
C
Carbon

9 Use the information in the periodic table to build models of the following isotopes of elements: helium-4, lithium-7, beryllium-9, and beryllium-10. Remember to put the protons and neutrons as close together as possible—each particle should attach to at least two others. Repeat steps 3–5 for each isotope. ✔0807.9.10

Analyze the Results

1 **Examining Data** What is the relationship between the number of protons and the atomic number?

2 **Analyzing Data** If you know the atomic number and the mass number of an isotope, how could you figure out the number of neutrons in its nucleus?

Draw Conclusions

3 **Applying Conclusions** Look up uranium on the periodic table. What is the atomic number of uranium? How many neutrons does the isotope uranium-235 have? ✔0807.9.10

4 **Evaluating Models** Compare your model with the models of your classmates. How are the models similar? How are they different? ✔0807.Inq.4

Applying Your Data

Combine your model with one that another student has made to create a single nucleus. Identify the element (and isotope) you have created.

275

Chapter Review

TN GLE 0807.Inq.3, GLE 0807.Inq.5, GLE 0807.9.1, GLE 0807.9.2, GLE 0807.12.4

USING KEY TERMS

The statements below are false. For each statement, replace the underlined term to make a true statement.

1 All matter is made up of <u>protons</u>.

✔0807.9.1

2 All atoms of the same element contain the same number of <u>neutrons</u>.

3 <u>Protons</u> have no electrical charge.

4 The <u>atomic number</u> of an element is the number of protons and neutrons in the nucleus.

5 The <u>mass number</u> is an average of the masses of all naturally occurring isotopes of an element.

UNDERSTANDING KEY IDEAS

Multiple Choice

6 The discovery of which particle proved that the atom is not indivisible?

a. proton

b. neutron

c. electron

d. nucleus

7 How many protons does an atom with an atomic number of 23 and a mass number of 51 have?

a. 23

b. 28

c. 51

d. 74

8 In Rutherford's gold-foil experiment, Rutherford concluded that the atom is mostly empty space with a small, massive, positively charged center because

✔0807.Inq.3

a. most of the particles passed straight through the foil.

b. some particles were slightly deflected.

c. a few particles bounced straight back.

d. All of the above

9 Which of the following determines the identity of an element?

a. atomic number

b. mass number

c. atomic mass

d. overall charge

10 Isotopes exist because atoms of the same element can have different numbers of

a. protons.

b. neutrons.

c. electrons.

d. None of the above

Short Answer

11 Would there be a stronger gravitational force acting among the particles of a helium nucleus or the particles of a uranium nucleus? Explain. ✔0807.12.6

12 Describe Thomson's plum-pudding model of the atom.

Math Skills

13 Calculate the atomic mass of gallium, which consists of 60% gallium-69 and 40% gallium-71.

14 Calculate the number of protons, neutrons, and electrons in an atom of zirconium-90 that has no overall charge and an atomic number of 40.

CRITICAL THINKING

15 **Concept Mapping** Use the following terms to create a concept map: *atom, nucleus, protons, neutrons, electrons, isotopes, atomic number,* and *mass number.*

16 **Analyzing Processes** Particle accelerators, such as the one below, are devices that speed up charged particles in order to smash them together. Scientists use these devices to modify atoms. How can scientists determine whether the atoms formed are a new element or a new isotope of a known element?

17 **Analyzing Ideas** John Dalton made a number of statements about atoms that are now known to be incorrect. Why do you think his atomic theory is still found in science textbooks?

18 **Analyzing Methods** If scientists had tried to repeat Thomson's experiment and found that they could not, would Thomson's conclusion still have been valid? Explain your answer. ✔0807.Inq.4

INTERPRETING GRAPHICS

Use the diagrams below to answer the questions that follow.

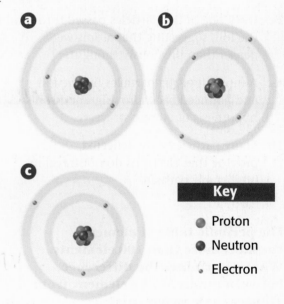

Key

● Proton

● Neutron

· Electron

19 Which diagrams represent isotopes of the same element?

20 What is the atomic number for A?

21 What is the mass number for B?

TCAP Test Preparation

TN ► SPI 0807.Inq.3 Interpret and translate data into a table, graph, or diagram.   SPI 0807.Inq.4 Draw a conclusion that establishes a cause and effect relationship supported by evidence.   SPI 0807.9.1 Recognize that all matter is made up of atoms.

Multiple Choice

Use the diagram below to answer question 1.

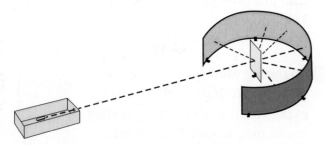

1. **In Rutherford's "shooting gallery" experiment, represented in the diagram above, what were the results?**

   A. Some particles were deflected, some passed through, and some bounced back, suggesting the existence of a nucleus.

   B. Only one of the particles passed through the foil, suggesting that atoms were denser than previously thought.

   C. Almost all of the particles hit the foil and bounced back, proving Thomson's hypothesis of atomic structure.

   D. Many particles were deflected, proving that electrons do not travel in predictable paths.

2. **The periodic table of elements contains more than 100 elements. What determines the difference between atoms of one element from atoms of other elements?**

   A. the number of electrons

   B. the number of isotopes

   C. the number of neutrons

   D. the number of protons

3. **The atoms of substance A contain 8 protons and 8 neutrons. The atoms of substance B contain 8 protons and 9 neutrons. The atoms of both substances combine with atoms of hydrogen to form water. What is the best way to classify substances A and B?**

   A. The atoms of substances A and B are isotopes.

   B. The atoms of substances A and B are radioactive.

   C. The atoms of substances A and B are atoms of different elements.

   D. The atoms of substances A and B have the same mass number.

4. **Which of the following pieces of equipment was used by J. J. Thomson to find electrons?**

   A. an electron microscope

   B. a magnifying lens

   C. a cathode-ray tube

   D. a telescope

5. **Amber has a piece of the element copper. She divides the copper in half many times. What is the smallest unit she can reach without altering the type of element she has?**

   A. electron

   B. compound

   C. atom

   D. neutron

6. **Which of the following is considered to be the basic building block of matter?**

   A. atoms

   B. compounds

   C. electrons

   D. neutrons

7. **An atom's structure determines its properties. What property of an atom is affected by the difference between the number of its protons and the number of its electrons?**

   A. atomic number

   B. atomic mass

   C. size

   D. charge

8. **All matter is made up of atoms. Which sentence correctly describes atoms?**

   A. All substances are made of the same atoms.

   B. An atom is the smallest particle of a nucleus.

   C. An atom is the smallest particle of an element.

   D. An atom is a substance that has been cut in half.

9. **What are the negatively charged particles inside an atom called?**

   A. protons

   B. neutrons

   C. nuclei

   D. electrons

Use the diagram below to answer question 10.

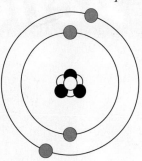

10. **The black circles in the Bohr model above represent neutrons. What do the white circles represent?**

    A. electrons

    B. isotopes

    C. nuclei

    D. protons

Open Response

11. **Erwin Schrödinger and Werner Heisenberg expanded atomic theory in the 20th century. They accepted some of the work of earlier scientists, but added to atomic theory with new ideas about electrons. Why was it possible and important for Schrödinger and Heisenberg to accept the work of earlier scientists?**

12. **The atomic mass of an element and the mass number of an atom of that element often have similar values. However, atomic mass and mass number are not the same thing. Explain the difference.**

13. **An element has 6 protons, 7 neutrons and 6 electrons. Carlos needs a colored diagram of an atom of the element. Draw the diagram for Carlos.**

TCAP Test Preparation

Science in Action

Weird Science

Mining on the Moon?

T/E Some engineers and scientists think that an isotope of helium known as *helium-3* could be used as a nonpolluting fuel for a new kind of power plant.

In the 1960s, engineers developed the technology to put a man on the moon. Later, instead of going to the moon, engineers designed space technology to go to Mars and beyond. Helium-3 is fueling new interest in returning to the moon. While helium-3 is very rare on Earth, larger amounts of the isotope can be found on the moon. How could helium-3 be brought to Earth? Some engineers imagine a robotic lunar mining operation that would harvest helium-3 and transport it to Earth.

TN GLE 0807.T/E.1

Language Arts ACTiViTY

WRITING SKILL Write a paragraph in which you rephrase the information above in your own words. Be sure to include what helium-3 is, where it can be found, and how it could be used.

Scientific Discoveries

Modern Alchemy

Hundreds of years ago, many people thought that if you treated lead with certain chemicals, it would turn into gold. People called *alchemists* often spent their whole lives trying to find a way to make gold from other metals, such as lead. We now know that the methods alchemists tried to change one element to another did not work. But in the 20th century, scientists learned that you really could change one element to another! In a nuclear reaction, small particles can be collided with atomic nuclei. This process makes the nuclei split apart to form two nuclei of different elements.

Math ACTiViTY

If you split apart an atom of lead (atomic number = 82) and one of the atoms left was gold (atomic number = 79), what would be the atomic number of the other atom that resulted from this change?

Melissa Franklin

Experimental Physicist In the course of a single day, you could find experimental physicist Melissa Franklin running a huge drill or showing her lab to a 10-year-old child. You could see her putting together a huge piece of electronic equipment or even telling a joke. Then you'd see her really get down to business—studying the smallest particles of matter in the universe.

"I am trying to understand the forces that describe how everything in the world moves—especially the smallest things," Franklin explains. Franklin and her team helped discover a particle called the top quark. (Quarks are the tiny particles that make up protons and neutrons.) "You can understand the ideas without having to be a math genius," Franklin says. "Anyone can have ideas," she says, "absolutely anyone." Franklin also has some advice for young people interested in physics. "Go and bug people at the local university. Just call up a physics person and say, 'Can I come visit you for a couple of hours?' Kids do that with me, and it's really fun."

Social Studies
ACTIVITY

WRITING SKILL **T/E** Find out about an experimental physicist who has made an important discovery since the year 1900. Write a one-page report about how that discovery led to the development of new technologies.

TN GLE 0807.T/E.1

go.hrw.com
To learn more about these Science in Action topics, visit go.hrw.com and type in the keyword **HP5ATSF**.

Current Science

Check out Current Science® articles related to this chapter by visiting go.hrw.com. Just type in the keyword HP5CS11.

The Periodic Table

The Big Idea

Elements are organized on the periodic table according to their properties.

PRE-READING ACTIVITY

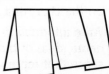

FOLDNOTES **Three-Panel Flip Chart**
Before you read the chapter, create the FoldNote entitled "Three-Panel Flip Chart" described in the **Study Skills** section of the Appendix. Label the flaps of the three-panel flip chart with "Metal," "Nonmetal," and "Metalloid." As you read the chapter, write information you learn about each category under the appropriate flap.

About the Photo

You already know or have heard about elements on the periodic table, such as oxygen, carbon, and neon. Neon gas was discovered in 1898. In 1902, a French engineer, chemist, and inventor named Georges Claude made the first neon lamp. In 1910, Claude made the first neon sign, and in 1923, he introduced neon signs to the United States. Now, artists such as Eric Ehlenberger use glass and neon to create interesting works of art, such as these neon jellyfish.

START-UP ACTiViTY

TN GLE 0807.Inq.2, GLE 0807.Inq.3, GLE 0807.Inq.5

Placement Pattern

In this activity, you will identify the pattern your teacher used to create a new classroom seating arrangement.

Procedure

1. Draw a seating chart for the new classroom arrangement that your teacher gave to you. Write the name of each of your classmates in the place on the chart that corresponds to his or her seat.

2. Write information about yourself, such as your name, date of birth, hair color, and height, in the space that represents you on the chart.

3. Gather the same information about the people near you, and write it in the spaces on the chart.

Analysis

1. From the information you gathered, identify a pattern that might explain the order of people in the chart. Collect more information if needed.
✓0807.Inq.3

2. Test your pattern by gathering information from a person you did not talk to before.

3. If the new information does not support your pattern, reanalyze your data and collect more information to determine another pattern.
✓0807.Inq.3

Arranging the Elements

Suppose you went to the video store and all the videos were mixed together. How could you tell the comedies from the action movies? If the videos were not arranged in a pattern, you wouldn't know what kind of movie you had chosen!

Scientists in the early 1860s had a similar problem. At that time, scientists knew some of the properties of more than 60 elements. However, no one had organized the elements according to these properties. Organizing the elements according to their properties would help scientists understand how elements interact with each other.

Discovering a Pattern

Dmitri Mendeleev (duh MEE tree MEN duh LAY uhf), a Russian chemist, discovered a pattern to the elements in 1869. First, he wrote the names and properties of the elements on cards. Then, he arranged his cards, as shown in **Figure 1,** by different properties, such as density, appearance, and melting point. After much thought, he arranged the elements in order of increasing atomic mass. When he did so, a pattern appeared.

✓ **Reading Check** How had Mendeleev arranged elements when he noticed a pattern?

Figure 1 *By playing "chemical solitaire" on long train rides, Mendeleev organized the elements according to their properties.*

Table 1 Properties of Germanium

	Mendeleev's predictions (1869)	Actual properties
Atomic mass	70	72.6
Density*	5.5 g/cm^3	5.3 g/cm^3
Appearance	dark gray metal	gray metal
Melting point*	high melting point	937°C

* at room temperature and pressure

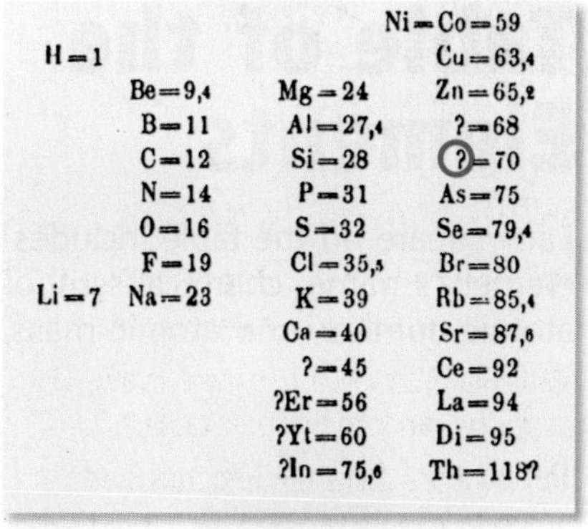

Periodic Properties of the Elements

Mendeleev saw that when the elements were arranged in order of increasing atomic mass, those that had similar properties occurred in a repeating pattern. That is, the pattern was periodic. **Periodic** means "happening at regular intervals." The days of the week are periodic. They repeat in the same order every 7 days. Similarly, Mendeleev found that the elements' properties followed a pattern that repeated every seven elements. His table became known as the *periodic table of the elements*.

Predicting Properties of Missing Elements

Figure 2 shows part of Mendeleev's first try at arranging the elements. The question marks show gaps in the pattern. Mendeleev predicted that elements yet to be found would fill these gaps. He used the pattern he found to predict their properties. **Table 1** compares his predictions for one missing element—germanium—with its actual properties. By 1886, all of the gaps had been filled. His predictions were right.

Changing the Arrangement

A few elements' properties did not fit the pattern in Mendeleev's table. Mendeleev thought that more-accurate atomic masses would fix these flaws in his table. But new atomic mass measurements showed that the masses he had used were correct. In 1914, Henry Moseley (MOHZ lee), a British scientist, determined the number of protons—the atomic number—in an atom. All elements fit the pattern in Mendeleev's periodic table when they were arranged by atomic number.

Look at the periodic table on the next two pages. All of the more than 30 elements discovered since 1914 follow the periodic law. The **periodic law** states that the repeating chemical and physical properties of elements change periodically with the elements' atomic numbers.

Reading Check What property is used to arrange elements in the periodic table?

Figure 2 *Mendeleev used question marks to mark some elements that he thought would be found later.*

periodic describes something that occurs or repeats at regular intervals

periodic law the law that states that the repeating chemical and physical properties of elements change periodically with the atomic numbers of the elements

CONNECTION TO Language Arts

WRITING SKILL **Hidden Help** You may be asked to memorize some of the chemical symbols. A story or poem that uses the symbols might be helpful. In your **science journal**, write a short story, poem, or just a few sentences in which the words correspond to and bring to mind the chemical symbols of the first 20 elements.

Periodic Table of the Elements

Each square on the table includes an element's name, chemical symbol, atomic number, and atomic mass.

The color of the chemical symbol indicates the physical state at room temperature. Aluminum is a solid.

| 13 |
| Al |
| Aluminum |
| 27.0 |

Atomic number
Chemical symbol
Element name
Average atomic mass

The background color indicates the type of element. Aluminum is a metal.

Background
Metals
Metalloids
Nonmetals

Chemical Symbol
Solid
Liquid
Gas

Period 1

| 1 |
| H |
| Hydrogen |
| 1.0 |

	Group 1	Group 2								
Period 2	3 Li Lithium 6.9	4 Be Beryllium 9.0								
Period 3	11 Na Sodium 23.0	12 Mg Magnesium 24.3	Group 3	Group 4	Group 5	Group 6	Group 7	Group 8	Group 9	
Period 4	19 K Potassium 39.1	20 Ca Calcium 40.1	21 Sc Scandium 45.0	22 Ti Titanium 47.9	23 V Vanadium 50.9	24 Cr Chromium 52.0	25 Mn Manganese 54.9	26 Fe Iron 55.8	27 Co Cobalt 58.9	
Period 5	37 Rb Rubidium 85.5	38 Sr Strontium 87.6	39 Y Yttrium 88.9	40 Zr Zirconium 91.2	41 Nb Niobium 92.9	42 Mo Molybdenum 96.0	43 Tc Technetium (98)	44 Ru Ruthenium 101.1	45 Rh Rhodium 102.9	
Period 6	55 Cs Cesium 132.9	56 Ba Barium 137.3	57 La Lanthanum 138.9	72 Hf Hafnium 178.5	73 Ta Tantalum 180.9	74 W Tungsten 183.8	75 Re Rhenium 186.2	76 Os Osmium 190.2	77 Ir Iridium 192.2	
Period 7	87 Fr Francium (223)	88 Ra Radium (226)	89 Ac Actinium (227)	104 Rf Rutherfordium (261)	105 Db Dubnium (262)	106 Sg Seaborgium (266)	107 Bh Bohrium (264)	108 Hs Hassium (277)	109 Mt Meitnerium (268)	

A row of elements is called a *period*.

A column of elements is called a *group* or *family*.

Values in parentheses are the mass numbers of those radioactive elements' most stable or most common isotopes.

These elements are placed below the table to allow the table to be narrower.

Lanthanides	58 Ce Cerium 140.1	59 Pr Praseodymium 140.9	60 Nd Neodymium 144.2	61 Pm Promethium (145)	62 Sm Samarium 150.4
Actinides	90 Th Thorium 232.0	91 Pa Protactinium 231.0	92 U Uranium 238.0	93 Np Neptunium (237)	94 Pu Plutonium (244)

Topic: **Periodic Table**
Go To: **go.hrw.com**
Keyword: **HST PERIODIC**
Visit the HRW Web site for updates on the periodic table.

This zigzag line reminds you where the metals, nonmetals, and metalloids are.

Group 10	Group 11	Group 12	Group 13	Group 14	Group 15	Group 16	Group 17	Group 18
								2 **He** Helium 4.0
			5 **B** Boron 10.8	6 **C** Carbon 12.0	7 **N** Nitrogen 14.0	8 **O** Oxygen 16.0	9 **F** Fluorine 19.0	10 **Ne** Neon 20.2
			13 **Al** Aluminum 27.0	14 **Si** Silicon 28.1	15 **P** Phosphorus 31.0	16 **S** Sulfur 32.1	17 **Cl** Chlorine 35.5	18 **Ar** Argon 39.9
28 **Ni** Nickel 58.7	29 **Cu** Copper 63.5	30 **Zn** Zinc 65.4	31 **Ga** Gallium 69.7	32 **Ge** Germanium 72.6	33 **As** Arsenic 74.9	34 **Se** Selenium 79.0	35 **Br** Bromine 79.9	36 **Kr** Krypton 83.8
46 **Pd** Palladium 106.4	47 **Ag** Silver 107.9	48 **Cd** Cadmium 112.4	49 **In** Indium 114.8	50 **Sn** Tin 118.7	51 **Sb** Antimony 121.8	52 **Te** Tellurium 127.6	53 **I** Iodine 126.9	54 **Xe** Xenon 131.3
78 **Pt** Platinum 195.1	79 **Au** Gold 197.0	80 **Hg** Mercury 200.6	81 **Tl** Thallium 204.4	82 **Pb** Lead 207.2	83 **Bi** Bismuth 209.0	84 **Po** Polonium (209)	85 **At** Astatine (210)	86 **Rn** Radon (222)
110 **Ds** Darmstadtium (271)	111 **Rg** Roentgenium (272)	112 **Uub** Ununbium (285)	113 **Uut** Ununtrium (284)	114 **Uuq** Ununquadium (289)	115 **Uup** Ununpentium (288)	116 **Uuh** Ununhexium (292)		118 **Uuo** Ununoctium (294)

The discovery of elements 112 through 116 and 118 has been reported but not confirmed.

The names and three-letter symbols of these elements are temporary. They are based on the atomic numbers of the elements. Official names and symbols will be approved by an international committee of scientists.

63 **Eu** Europium 152.0	64 **Gd** Gadolinium 157.2	65 **Tb** Terbium 158.9	66 **Dy** Dysprosium 162.5	67 **Ho** Holmium 164.9	68 **Er** Erbium 167.3	69 **Tm** Thulium 168.9	70 **Yb** Ytterbium 173.1	71 **Lu** Lutetium 175.0
95 **Am** Americium (243)	96 **Cm** Curium (247)	97 **Bk** Berkelium (247)	98 **Cf** Californium (251)	99 **Es** Einsteinium (252)	100 **Fm** Fermium (257)	101 **Md** Mendelevium (258)	102 **No** Nobelium (259)	103 **Lr** Lawrencium (262)

Quick Lab

T/E Conduction Connection

1. Fill a **plastic-foam cup** with **hot water.**

2. Stand a **piece of copper wire** and a **graphite lead** from a mechanical pencil in the water.

3. After 1 min, touch the top of each object. Record your observations.

4. Which material conducted thermal energy the best? Why?

5. Heaters often need to conduct thermal energy well. If you were an engineer designing a heater, which of these two materials would you choose? Explain. ✔ 0807.T/E.2

The Periodic Table and Classes of Elements

At first glance, you might think studying the periodic table is like trying to explore a thick jungle without a guide—you can easily get lost! However, the table itself contains a lot of information that will help you along the way.

Elements are classified as metals, nonmetals, and metalloids by their properties. The number of electrons in the outer energy level of an atom is one characteristic that helps determine which category an element belongs in. The zigzag line on the periodic table can help you recognize which elements are metals, which are nonmetals, and which are metalloids.

Metals

Most elements are metals. Metals are found to the left of the zigzag line on the periodic table. Atoms of most metals have few electrons in their outer energy level. Most metals are solid at room temperature. Mercury, however, is a liquid at room temperature. Some additional information on properties shared by most metals is shown in **Figure 3.**

✔ **Reading Check** What are four properties shared by most metals?

Figure 3 Properties of Metals

Metals tend to be **shiny.** You can see a reflection in a mirror because light reflects off the shiny surface of a thin layer of silver behind the glass.

Most metals are **ductile,** which means that they can be drawn into thin wires. All metals are **good conductors of electric current.** The wires in the electrical devices in your home are made of copper.

Most metals are **malleable,** which means that they can be flattened with a hammer and will not shatter. Aluminum is flattened into sheets to make cans and foil.

Most metals are **good conductors of thermal energy.** This iron griddle conducts thermal energy from a stove top to cook your favorite foods.

Figure 4 Properties of Nonmetals

Nonmetals are **not malleable or ductile.** In fact, solid non-metals, such as carbon in the graphite of the pencil lead, are brittle and will break or shatter when hit with a hammer.

Sulfur, like most non-metals, is **not shiny.**

Nonmetals are **poor conductors of thermal energy and electric current.** If the gap in a spark plug is too wide, the nonmetals nitrogen and oxygen in the air will stop the spark and a car's engine will not run.

Nonmetals

Nonmetals are found to the right of the zigzag line on the periodic table. Atoms of most nonmetals have an almost complete set of electrons in their outer level. Atoms of the elements in Group 18, the noble gases, have a complete set of electrons. More than half of the nonmetals are gases at room temperature. Many properties of nonmetals are the opposite of the properties of metals, as shown in **Figure 4.**

Metalloids

Metalloids, also called *semiconductors,* are the elements that border the zigzag line on the periodic table. Atoms of metalloids have about half of a complete set of electrons in their outer energy level. Metalloids have some properties of metals and some properties of nonmetals, as shown in **Figure 5.**

GLE 0807.9.6

MATH PRACTICE

Percentages
Elements are classified as metals, nonmetals, and metalloids. Use the periodic table to determine the percentage of elements in each of the three categories.

Figure 5 Properties of Metalloids

Tellurium is **shiny,** but it is **brittle** and can easily be smashed into a powder.

Boron is almost as **hard** as diamond, but it is also **very brittle.** At high temperatures, it is a **good conductor of electric current.**

period in chemistry, a horizontal row of elements in the periodic table

group a vertical column of elements in the periodic table; elements in a group share chemical properties

Decoding the Periodic Table

The periodic table may seem to be in code. In a way, it is. But the colors and symbols will help you decode the table.

Each Element Is Identified by a Chemical Symbol

Each square on the periodic table includes an element's name, chemical symbol, atomic number, and atomic mass. The names of the elements come from many sources. Some elements, such as mendelevium, are named after scientists. Others, such as californium, are named after places. Some element names vary by country. But the chemical symbols are the same worldwide. For most elements, the chemical symbol has one or two letters. The first letter is always capitalized. Any other letter is always lowercase. The newest elements have temporary three-letter symbols.

Rows Are Called *Periods*

Each horizontal row of elements (from left to right) on the periodic table is called a **period.** Look at Period 4 in **Figure 6.** The physical and chemical properties of elements in a row follow a repeating, or periodic, pattern as you move across the period. Properties such as conductivity and reactivity change gradually from left to right in each period.

Columns Are Called *Groups*

Each vertical column of elements (from top to bottom) on the periodic table is called a **group.** Elements in the same group often have similar chemical and physical properties. For this reason, a group is also called a *family.*

✓ **Reading Check** Why is a group sometimes called a family?

Figure 6 *As you move from left to right across a row, the elements become less metallic.*

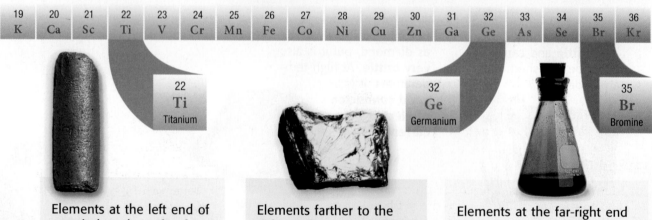

Elements at the left end of a period, such as **titanium,** are very metallic.

Elements farther to the right, such as **germanium,** are less metallic.

Elements at the far-right end of a period, such as **bromine,** are nonmetallic.

TN GLE 0807.Inq.5, GLE 0807.9.2, GLE 0807.9.6

Summary

- Mendeleev developed the first periodic table by listing the elements in order of increasing atomic mass. He used his table to predict that elements with certain properties would be discovered later.

- Properties of elements repeat in a regular, or periodic, pattern.

- Moseley rearranged the elements in order of increasing atomic number.

- The periodic law states that the repeating chemical and physical properties of elements relate to and depend on elements' atomic numbers.

- Elements in the periodic table are classified as metals, nonmetals, and metalloids.

- Each element has a chemical symbol.

- A horizontal row of elements is called a *period*.

- Physical and chemical properties of elements change across each period.

- A vertical column of elements is called a *group* or *family*.

- Elements in a group usually have similar properties.

Using Key Terms

1. In your own words, write a definition for the term *periodic*.

Understanding Key Ideas

2. Which of the following elements should be the best conductor of electric current?

   a. germanium

   b. sulfur

   c. aluminum

   d. helium

3. Compare a period and a group on the periodic table.

4. What property did Mendeleev use to position the elements on the periodic table?

5. State the periodic law.

6. Use your knowledge of atoms and the periodic table to identify the atomic number, atomic mass, number of protons, neutrons, and electrons in an atom of chromium (Cr). ✔0807.9.10

Critical Thinking

7. **Identifying Relationships** An atom that has 117 protons in its nucleus has not yet been made. Once this atom is made, to which group will element 117 belong? Explain your answer. ✔0807.9.10

8. **Applying Concepts** Are the properties of sodium, Na, more like the properties of lithium, Li, or magnesium, Mg? Explain your answer. ✔0807.9.10

Interpreting Graphics

9. The image below shows part of a periodic table. Compare the image below with the similar part of the periodic table in your book.

	1			
1	1 H 1.0079 水素			
2	3 Li 6.941 リチウム	4 Be 9.01218 ベリリウム		
3	11 Na 22.98977 ナトリウム	12 Mg 24.305 マグネシウム		
4	19 K	20 Ca	21 Sc	22 Ti

Internet Resources

For a variety of links related to this chapter, go to www.scilinks.org

Topic: Periodic Table; Metals

SciLinks code: HSM1125; HSM0947

What You Will Learn

● Explain why elements in a group often have similar properties.

● Describe the properties of the elements in the groups of the periodic table.

Vocabulary

alkali metal
alkaline-earth metal
halogen
noble gas

READING STRATEGY

Paired Summarizing Read this section silently. In pairs, take turns summarizing the material. Stop to discuss ideas that seem confusing.

TN **GLE 0807.Inq.3** Synthesize information to determine cause and effect relationships between evidence and explanations.

GLE 0807.Inq.5 Communicate scientific understanding using descriptions, explanations, and models.

GLE 0807.T/E.1 Explore how technology responds to social, political, and economic needs.

GLE 0807.T/E.2 Know that the engineering design process involves an ongoing series of events that incorporate design constraints, model building, testing, evaluating, modifying, and retesting.

GLE 0807.T/E.3 Compare the intended benefits with the unintended consequences of a new technology.

GLE 0807.9.1 Understand that all matter is made up of atoms.

GLE 0807.9.2 Explain that matter has properties that are determined by the structure and arrangement of its atoms.

GLE 0807.9.6 Use the periodic table to determine the characteristics of an element.

Grouping the Elements

You probably know a family with several members who look a lot alike. The elements in a family or group in the periodic table often—but not always—have similar properties.

The properties of the elements in a group are similar because the atoms of the elements have the same number of electrons in their outer energy level. Atoms will often take, give, or share electrons with other atoms in order to have a complete set of electrons in their outer energy level. Elements whose atoms undergo such processes are called *reactive* and can combine to form compounds.

Group 1: Alkali Metals

3 **Li** Lithium	**Group contains:** metals
11 **Na** Sodium	**Electrons in the outer level:** 1 **Reactivity:** very reactive **Other shared properties:** softness; color of silver; shininess; low density
19 **K** Potassium	
37 **Rb** Rubidium	
55 **Cs** Cesium	
87 **Fr** Francium	

Alkali metals (AL kuh LIE MET uhlz) are elements in Group 1 of the periodic table. They share physical and chemical properties, as shown in **Figure 1.** Alkali metals are the most reactive metals because their atoms can easily give away the one outer-level electron. Pure alkali metals are often stored in oil. The oil keeps them from reacting with water and oxygen in the air. Alkali metals are so reactive that in nature they are found only combined with other elements. Compounds formed from alkali metals have many uses. For example, sodium chloride (table salt) is used to flavor your food. Potassium bromide is used in photography.

Figure 1 **Properties of Alkali Metals**

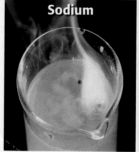
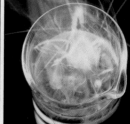

▲ Alkali metals are soft enough to be cut with a knife.

▲ Alkali metals react with water to form hydrogen gas.

Group 2: Alkaline-Earth Metals

4 Be Beryllium
12 Mg Magnesium
20 Ca Calcium
38 Sr Strontium
56 Ba Barium
88 Ra Radium

Group contains: metals
Electrons in the outer level: 2
Reactivity: very reactive but less reactive than alkali metals
Other shared properties: color of silver; higher densities than alkali metals

Alkaline-earth metals (AL kuh LIEN UHRTH MET uhlz) are less reactive than alkali metals are. Atoms of alkaline-earth metals have two outer-level electrons. It is more difficult for atoms to give two electrons than to give one when joining with other atoms. Group 2 elements and their compounds have many uses. For example, magnesium can be mixed with other metals to make low-density materials used in airplanes. And compounds of calcium are found in cement, chalk, and even you, as shown in **Figure 2.**

Figure 2 *Calcium, an alkaline-earth metal, is an important part of a compound that keeps your bones and teeth healthy.*

Groups 3–12: Transition Metals

21 Sc	22 Ti	23 V	24 Cr	25 Mn	26 Fe	27 Co	28 Ni	29 Cu	30 Zn
39 Y	40 Zr	41 Nb	42 Mo	43 Tc	44 Ru	45 Rh	46 Pd	47 Ag	48 Cd
57 La	72 Hf	73 Ta	74 W	75 Re	76 Os	77 Ir	78 Pt	79 Au	80 Hg
89 Ac	104 Rf	105 Db	106 Sg	107 Bh	108 Hs	109 Mt	110 Ds	111 Rg	112 Uub

Group contains: metals
Electrons in the outer level: 1 or 2
Reactivity: less reactive than alkaline-earth metals
Other shared properties: shininess; good conductors of thermal energy and electric current; higher densities and melting points than elements in Groups 1 and 2 (except for mercury)

alkali metal one of the elements of Group 1 of the periodic table (lithium, sodium, potassium, rubidium, cesium, and francium)

alkaline-earth metal one of the elements of Group 2 of the periodic table (beryllium, magnesium, calcium, strontium, barium, and radium)

Groups 3–12 do not have individual names. Instead, all of these groups are called *transition metals*. The atoms of transition metals do not give away their electrons as easily as atoms of the Group 1 and Group 2 metals do. So, transition metals are less reactive than alkali metals and alkaline-earth metals are.

✓ **Reading Check** Why are alkali metals more reactive than transition metals are?

Figure 3 Properties of Transition Metals

Mercury is used in thermometers. Unlike the other transition metals, mercury is liquid at room temperature.

Some transition metals, such as **titanium** in the artificial hip at right, are not very reactive. But others, such as **iron,** are reactive. The iron in the steel trowel on the left has reacted to form rust.

Many transition metals—but not all—are silver colored! This **gold** ring proves it!

Properties of Transition Metals

The properties of the transition metals vary widely, as shown in **Figure 3.** But, because these elements are metals, they share the properties of metals. Transition metals tend to be shiny and to conduct thermal energy and electric current well.

Lanthanides and Actinides

Some transition metals from Periods 6 and 7 appear in two rows at the bottom of the periodic table to keep the table from being too wide. The elements in each row tend to have similar properties. Elements in the first row follow lanthanum and are called *lanthanides*. The lanthanides are shiny, reactive metals. Some of these elements are used to make steel. An important use of a compound of one lanthanide element is shown in **Figure 4.**

Elements in the second row follow actinium and are called *actinides*. All atoms of actinides are radioactive, or unstable. The atoms of a radioactive element can change into atoms of another element. Elements listed after plutonium, element 94, do not occur in nature. They are made in laboratories. Very small amounts of americium (AM uhr ISH ee uhm), element 95, are used in some smoke detectors.

Figure 4 *Do you see red? The color red appears on a computer monitor because of a compound formed from europium that coats the back of the screen.*

✓ **Reading Check** Are lanthanides and actinides transition metals?

57
La
Lanthanum

89
Ac
Actinium

Lanthanides	58	59	60	61	62	63	64	65	66	67	68	69	70	71
	Ce	Pr	Nd	Pm	Sm	Eu	Gd	Tb	Dy	Ho	Er	Tm	Yb	Lu

Actinides	90	91	92	93	94	95	96	97	98	99	100	101	102	103
	Th	Pa	U	Np	Pu	Am	Cm	Bk	Cf	Es	Fm	Md	No	Lr

Group 13: Boron Group

5 B Boron
13 Al Aluminum
31 Ga Gallium
49 In Indium
81 Tl Thallium
113 Uut Ununtrium

Group contains: one metalloid and five metals
Electrons in the outer level: 3
Reactivity: reactive
Other shared properties: solids at room temperature

The most common element from Group 13 is aluminum. In fact, aluminum is the most abundant metal in Earth's crust. Until the 1880s, however, aluminum was considered a precious metal because the process used to make pure aluminum was very expensive. During the 1850s and 1860s, Emperor Napoleon III of France used aluminum dinnerware because aluminum was more valuable than gold.

Today, the process of making pure aluminum is easier and less expensive than it was in the 1800s. Aluminum is now an important metal used in making aircraft parts. Aluminum is also used to make lightweight automobile parts, foil, cans, and siding.

Like the other elements in the boron group, aluminum is reactive. Why can it be used in so many things? A thin layer of aluminum oxide quickly forms on aluminum's surface when aluminum reacts with oxygen in the air. This layer prevents further reaction of the aluminum.

TN GLE 0807.T/E.1

CONNECTION TO Engineering

WRITING SKILL **T/E Recycling Aluminum**

Engineering advances have helped make aluminum recycling a very successful program. Research how much energy it takes to make aluminum from its ore and how much energy it takes to process recycled aluminum. In your **science journal**, write a one-page report comparing the costs of the two processes.

ACTIVITY

Group 14: Carbon Group

6 C Carbon
14 Si Silicon
32 Ge Germanium
50 Sn Tin
82 Pb Lead
114 Uuq Ununquadium

Group contains: one nonmetal, two metalloids, and three metals
Electrons in the outer level: 4
Reactivity: varies among the elements
Other shared properties: solids at room temperature

The nonmetal carbon can be found uncombined in nature, as shown in **Figure 5.** Carbon also forms a wide variety of compounds. Some of these compounds, such as proteins, fats, and carbohydrates, are necessary for living things on Earth.

The metalloids silicon and germanium, also in Group 14, are used to make computer chips. The metal tin is useful because it is not very reactive. For example, a tin can is really made of steel coated with tin. Because the tin is less reactive than the steel is, the tin keeps the iron in the steel from rusting.

Reading Check What metalloids from Group 14 are used to make computer chips?

Figure 5 *Diamond and soot have very different properties, yet both are natural forms of carbon.*

Diamond is the hardest material known. It is used as a jewel and on cutting tools, such as saws, drills, and files.

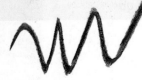

Soot is formed from burning oil, coal, and wood and is used as a pigment in paints and crayons.

Figure 6 *Simply striking a match on the side of this box causes chemicals on the match to react with phosphorus on the box and begin to burn.*

INTERNET ACTIVITY

For another activity related to this chapter, go to **go.hrw.com** and type in the keyword **HP5PRTW.**

Group 15: Nitrogen Group

7 **N** Nitrogen	
15 **P** Phosphorus	
33 **As** Arsenic	
51 **Sb** Antimony	
83 **Bi** Bismuth	
115 **Uup** Ununpentium	

Group contains: two nonmetals, two metalloids, and two metals
Electrons in the outer level: 5
Reactivity: varies among the elements
Other shared properties: solids at room temperature (except for nitrogen)

Nitrogen, which is a gas at room temperature, makes up about 80% of the air you breathe. Nitrogen removed from air can be reacted with hydrogen to make ammonia for fertilizers.

Although nitrogen is not very reactive, phosphorus is extremely reactive, as shown in **Figure 6.** In fact, in nature phosphorus is only found combined with other elements.

Group 16: Oxygen Group

8 **O** Oxygen	
16 **S** Sulfur	
34 **Se** Selenium	
52 **Te** Tellurium	
84 **Po** Polonium	
116 **Uuh** Ununhexium	

Group contains: three nonmetals, one metalloid, and one metal
Electrons in the outer level: 6
Reactivity: Reactive
Other shared properties: All but oxygen are solid at room temperature.

Oxygen makes up about 20% of air. Oxygen is necessary for substances to burn. Oxygen is also important to most living things, such as the diver in **Figure 7.** Sulfur is another commonly found member of Group 16. Sulfur can be found as a yellow solid in nature. It is used to make sulfuric acid, the most widely used compound in the chemical industry.

✓ **Reading Check** Which gases from Groups 15 and 16 make up most of the air you breathe?

Figure 7 *This diver is breathing a mixture that contains oxygen gas.*

Figure 8 **Physical Properties of Some Halogens**

Chlorine is a yellowish green gas.

Bromine is a dark red liquid.

Iodine is a dark gray solid.

Group 17: Halogens

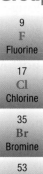

9	
F	
Fluorine	
17	
Cl	
Chlorine	
35	
Br	
Bromine	
53	
I	
Iodine	
85	
At	
Astatine	

Group contains: nonmetals
Electrons in the outer level: 7
Reactivity: very reactive
Other shared properties: poor conductors of electric current; violent reactions with alkali metals to form salts; never in uncombined form in nature

halogen one of the elements of Group 17 of the periodic table (fluorine, chlorine, bromine, iodine, and astatine); halogens combine with most metals to form salts

Halogens (HAL oh juhnz) are very reactive nonmetals because their atoms need to gain only one electron to have a complete outer level. The atoms of halogens combine readily with other atoms, especially metals, to gain that missing electron. The reaction of a halogen with a metal makes a salt, such as sodium chloride. Both chlorine and iodine are used as disinfectants. Chlorine is used to treat water. Iodine mixed with alcohol is used in hospitals.

Although the chemical properties of the halogens are similar, the physical properties are quite different, as shown in **Figure 8.**

TN GLE 0807.Inq.5, GLE 0807.T/E.1

CONNECTION TO Technology

T/E **Water Treatment** Technology has responded to the need to protect people from disease by developing the process of chlorinating water. Chlorination kills organisms in water. But there is much more to the technology of water treatment than just adding chlorine. Research how a water treatment plant purifies water for people to use. Design and construct a model of a treatment plant. Use labels to describe the role of each part of the plant in treating the water you use each day. ✔0807.Inq.5

ACTIVITY

Group 18: Noble Gases

2 **He** Helium
10 **Ne** Neon
18 **Ar** Argon
36 **Kr** Krypton
54 **Xe** Xenon
86 **Rn** Radon
118 **Uuo** Ununoctium

Group contains: nonmetals
Electrons in the outer level: 8 (except helium, which has 2)
Reactivity: unreactive
Other shared properties: colorless, odorless gases at room temperature

Noble gases are unreactive nonmetals and are in Group 18 of the periodic table. The atoms of these elements have a full set of electrons in their outer level. So, they do not need to lose or gain any electrons. Under normal conditions, they do not react with other elements. Earth's atmosphere is almost 1% argon. But all the noble gases are found in small amounts.

The unreactivity of the noble gases makes them useful. For example, ordinary light bulbs last longer when they are filled with argon. Because argon is unreactive, it does not react with the metal filament in the light bulb even when the filament gets hot. A more reactive gas might react with the filament, causing the light to burn out. The low density of helium makes blimps and weather balloons float. Another popular use of noble gases is shown in **Figure 9.**

✓ Reading Check Why are noble gases unreactive?

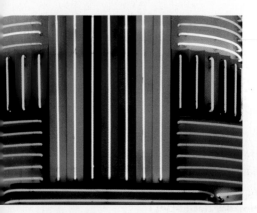

Figure 9 *In addition to neon, other noble gases can be used to make "neon" lights.*

noble gas one of the elements of Group 18 of the periodic table (helium, neon, argon, krypton, xenon, and radon); noble gases are unreactive

Hydrogen

1 **H** Hydrogen

Electrons in the outer level: 1
Reactivity: reactive
Other properties: colorless, odorless gas at room temperature; low density; explosive reactions with oxygen

The properties of hydrogen do not match the properties of any single group, so hydrogen is set apart from the other elements in the table. Hydrogen is above Group 1 because atoms of the alkali metals also have only one electron in their outer level. Atoms of hydrogen can give away one electron when they join with other atoms. However, the physical properties of hydrogen are more like those of nonmetals than those of metals. So, hydrogen really is in a group of its own. Hydrogen is found in stars. In fact, it is the most abundant element in the universe. Its reactive nature makes it useful as a fuel in rockets, as shown in **Figure 10.**

Figure 10 *Hydrogen reacts violently with oxygen. The hot water vapor that forms as a result of this reaction helps guide the space shuttle into orbit.*

TN GLE 0807.Inq.3, GLE 0807.Inq.5, GLE 0807.9.2, GLE 0807.9.6

Summary

- Alkali metals (Group 1) are the most reactive metals. Atoms of the alkali metals have one electron in their outer level.

- Alkaline-earth metals (Group 2) are less reactive than the alkali metals are. Atoms of the alkaline-earth metals have two electrons in their outer level.

- Transition metals (Groups 3–12) include most of the well-known metals and the lanthanides and actinides.

- Groups 13–16 contain the metalloids and some metals and nonmetals.

- Halogens (Group 17) are very reactive nonmetals. Atoms of the halogens have seven electrons in their outer level.

- Noble gases (Group 18) are unreactive nonmetals. Atoms of the noble gases have a full set of electrons in their outer level.

- Hydrogen is set off by itself in the periodic table. Its properties do not match the properties of any one group.

Using Key Terms

Complete each of the following sentences by choosing the correct term from the word bank.

> noble gas   alkaline-earth metal
> halogen   alkali metal

1. An atom of a(n) ___ has a full set of electrons in its outermost energy level.

2. An atom of a(n) ___ has one electron in its outermost energy level.

3. An atom of a(n) ___ tends to gain one electron when it combines with another atom.

4. An atom of a(n) ___ tends to lose two electrons when it combines with another atom.

Understanding Key Ideas

5. Which group contains elements whose atoms have six electrons in their outer level?

   a. Group 2   c. Group 16
   b. Group 6   d. Group 18

6. What are two properties of the alkali metals?

7. What causes the properties of elements in a group to be similar? ✔0807.Inq.3

8. What are two properties of the halogens?

9. Why is hydrogen set apart from the other elements in the periodic table? ✔0807.9.10

10. Which group contains elements whose atoms have three electrons in their outer level? ✔0807.9.10

Interpreting Graphics

11. Look at the model of an atom to the right. Does the model represent a metal atom or a nonmetal atom? Explain your answer.

Critical Thinking

12. **Making Inferences** Why are neither the alkali metals nor the alkaline-earth metals found uncombined in nature? ✔0807.Inq.3

13. **Making Comparisons** Compare the element hydrogen with the alkali metal sodium. ✔0807.9.10

Internet Resources

For a variety of links related to this chapter, go to www.scilinks.org

Topic: Alkali Metals; Halogens and Noble Gases

SciLinks code: HSM0043; HSM0711

Model-Making Lab

Create a Periodic Table

You probably have classification systems for many things in your life, such as your clothes, your books, and your CDs. One of the most important classification systems in science is the periodic table of the elements. In this lab, you will develop your own classification system for a collection of ordinary objects. You will analyze trends in your system and compare your system with the periodic table of the elements.

OBJECTIVES

Classify objects based on their properties.

Identify patterns and trends in data.

MATERIALS

- bag of objects
- balance, metric
- meterstick
- paper, graphing (2 sheets)
- paper, 3 × 3 cm squares (20)

Procedure

1. Your teacher will give you a bag of objects. Your bag is missing one item. Examine the items carefully. Describe the missing object in as many ways as you can. Be sure to include the reasons why you think the missing object has the characteristics you describe.

2. Lay the paper squares out on your desk or table so that you have a grid of five rows of four squares each.

3. Arrange your objects on the grid in a logical order. (You must decide what order is logical!) You should end up with one blank square for the missing object.

4. Record a description of the basis for your arrangement.

5 Measure the mass (g) and diameter (mm) of each object, and record your results in the appropriate square. Each square (except the empty one) should have one object and two written measurements on it.

6 Examine your pattern again. Does the order in which your objects are arranged still make sense? Explain.

7 Rearrange the squares and their objects if necessary to improve your arrangement. Record a description of the basis for the new arrangement.

8 Working across the rows, number the squares 1 to 20. When you get to the end of a row, continue numbering in the first square of the next row.

9 Copy your grid. In each square, be sure to list the type of object and label all measurements with appropriate units.

Analyze the Results

1 **Constructing Graphs** Make a graph of mass (y-axis) versus object number (x-axis). Label each axis, and title the graph.

2 **Constructing Graphs** Now make a graph of diameter (y-axis) versus object number (x-axis).

Draw Conclusions

3 **Analyzing Graphs** Discuss each graph with your classmates. Try to identify any important features of the graph. For example, does the graph form a line or a curve? Is there anything unusual about the graph? What do these features tell you? Record your answers.

4 **Evaluating Models** How is your arrangement of objects similar to the periodic table of the elements found in this textbook? How is your arrangement different from that periodic table?

5 **Making Predictions** Look again at your prediction about the missing object. Do you think your prediction is still accurate? Try to improve your description by estimating the mass and diameter of the missing object. Record your estimates. ✔0807.Inq.3, ✔0807.Inq.4, ✔0807.T/E.2

6 **Evaluating Methods** Mendeleev created a periodic table of elements and predicted characteristics of missing elements. How is your experiment similar to Mendeleev's work?

Chapter Review

TN GLE 0807.Inq.5, GLE 0807.9.1, GLE 0807.9.2, GLE 0807.9.6

USING KEY TERMS

Complete each of the following sentences by choosing the correct term from the word bank.

group   period
alkali metals   halogens
alkaline-earth metals   noble gases

1 Elements in the same vertical column on the periodic table belong to the same ___.

2 Elements in the same horizontal row on the periodic table belong to the same ___.

3 The most reactive metals are ___.

4 Elements that are unreactive are called ___.

UNDERSTANDING KEY IDEAS

Multiple Choice

5 Mendeleev's periodic table was useful because it

a. showed the elements arranged by atomic number.

b. had no empty spaces.

c. showed the atomic number of the elements.

d. allowed for the prediction of the properties of missing elements.

6 Most nonmetals are

a. shiny.

b. poor conductors of electric current.

c. flattened when hit with a hammer.

d. solids at room temperature.

7 Which of the following items is NOT found on the periodic table? ✔0807.9.1, ✔0807.9.10

a. the atomic number of each element

b. the name of each element

c. the date that each element was discovered

d. the atomic mass of each element

8 Which of the following statements about the periodic table is false? ✔0807.9.1, ✔0807.9.10

a. There are more metals than non-metals on the periodic table.

b. Atoms of elements in the same group have the same number of electrons in their outer level.

c. The elements at the far left of the periodic table are nonmetals.

d. Elements are arranged by increasing atomic number.

9 Which of the following statements about alkali metals is true?

a. Alkali metals are generally found in their uncombined form.

b. Alkali metals are Group 1 elements.

c. Alkali metals should be stored underwater.

d. Alkali metals are unreactive.

10 Which of the following statements about elements is true? ✔0807.9.1, ✔0807.9.10

a. Every element occurs naturally.

b. All elements are found in their uncombined form in nature.

c. Each element has a unique atomic number.

d. All of the elements exist in approximately equal quantities.

Short Answer

⓫ Use the periodic table to identify the atomic number, atomic mass, and number of protons, neutrons, and electrons in an atom of neon (Ne).

✔0807.9.10

⓬ How is the periodic table like a calendar?

Math Skills

Examine the chart of the percentages of elements in the Earth's crust below. Then, answer the questions that follow.

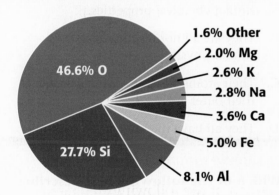

46.6% O
27.7% Si
1.6% Other
2.0% Mg
2.6% K
2.8% Na
3.6% Ca
5.0% Fe
8.1% Al

⓭ Excluding the "Other" category, what percentage of the Earth's crust are alkali metals?

⓮ Excluding the "Other" category, what percentage of the Earth's crust are alkaline-earth metals?

CRITICAL THINKING

⓯ **Concept Mapping** Use the following terms to create a concept map: *periodic table, elements, groups, periods, metals, nonmetals,* and *metalloids.*

⓰ **Forming Hypotheses** Why was Mendeleev unable to make any predictions about the noble gas elements?

⓱ Suppose that scientists synthesize a new element that has 115 protons. Will this new element be a metal, a nonmetal, or a metalloid? Use your knowledge of the periodic table to explain your answer. ✔0807.9.1, ✔0807.9.10

⓲ **Applying Concepts** Your classmate offers to give you a piece of sodium that he found on a hiking trip. What is your response? Explain.

⓳ **Applying Concepts** Use your knowledge of the period table to identify each element described below.

✔0807.9.10

a. This metal is very reactive, has properties similar to those of magnesium, and is in the same period as bromine.

b. This nonmetal is in the same group as lead.

INTERPRETING GRAPHICS

⓴ Study the diagram below to determine the pattern of the images. Predict the missing image, and draw it. Identify which properties are periodic and which properties are shared within a group.

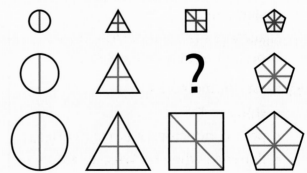

TN SPI 0807.9.1 Recognize that all matter consists of atoms.

SPI 0807.9.9 Use the periodic table to determine the properties of an element.

Multiple Choice

Use the diagram below to answer question 1.

Cobalt and Nickel Entries in Periodic Table

27	28
Co	**Ni**
Cobalt	Nickel
58.933	58.693

1. **The diagram above is an enlargement of a section of the periodic table. What is the biggest difference between an atom of cobalt (Co) and an atom of nickel (Ni) as shown in the periodic table entries?**

   A. An atom of nickel has more protons.

   B. An atom of cobalt has more electrons.

   C. An atom of cobalt has more neutrons.

   D. An atom of nickel has a higher value for atomic mass.

2. **Charles needs a very lightweight metal. Use the periodic table to determine which he would choose.**

   A. silicon

   B. magnesium

   C. iodine

   D. tungsten

3. **In what order are the regions arranged on the periodic table, reading left to right?**

   A. inert gases, metals, nonmetals, metalloids

   B. metalloids, metals, nonmetals, inert gases

   C. metals, metalloids, nonmetals, inert gases

   D. nonmetals, inert gases, metals, metalloids

4. **Fluorine, chlorine, bromine, iodine, and astatine make up Group 17, the halogens. Why are these elements grouped together?**

   A. They are all very reactive nonmetals with similar chemical properties.

   B. They are all nonreactive gases with similar physical properties.

   C. Their atoms all have eight electrons in their outer energy levels.

   D. They all have the same atomic number.

5. **Which of the following best describes the properties of metals?**

   A. hard, brittle, and unconductive

   B. liquid, dark, and conductive

   C. shiny, malleable, and conductive

   D. soft, oily, and very reactive

6. **Look at the periodic table. What is the atomic mass of cadmium (Cd)?**

   A. 12.0

   B. 35.5

   C. 58.9

   D. 112.4

7. **How are the elements in the periodic table arranged?**

   A. by their atomic mass

   B. by their chemical symbol

   C. by their chemical name

   D. by their atomic number

Use the graph below to answer question 8.

Density of Elements in the Second Period

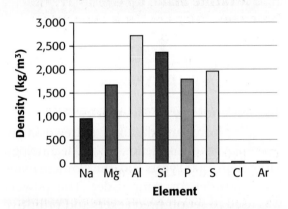

8. **The graph above shows the densities in kilograms per cubic meter (kg/m³) of the elements in Period 2 of the periodic table. Given a 100 m³ sample of each element in Period 2, which sample would have the greatest mass?**

   A. the sample of aluminum (Al)

   B. the sample of chlorine (Cl)

   C. the sample of sulphur (S)

   D. the sample of argon (Ar)

9. **Which of these does the number of electrons in the outer level indicate about the element?**

   A. its reactivity

   B. its atomic number

   C. its atomic mass

   D. its symbol

10. **According to its location on the periodic table, sodium can be described as**

    A. an alkaline-earth metal.

    B. a transition metal.

    C. an alkali metal.

    D. a metalloid.

Open Response

11. **The element hydrogen is usually placed at the top of Group 1 in the periodic table. However, hydrogen is not always considered to be a member of Group 1. Explain why hydrogen is placed in Group 1 and what properties set hydrogen apart from Group 1.**

12. **The elements in the periodic table can be classified into metals, nonmetals, and metalloids. Describe the properties of these classes, and explain where the elements that fall into these classes can be found on the periodic table.**

Science in Action

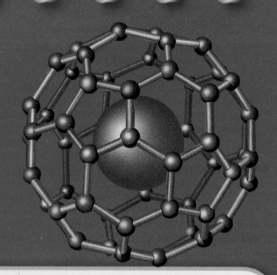

Science, Technology, and Society

The Technology of Fireworks

T/E Explosive and dazzling, a fireworks display involves science, art, and technology. More than 1,000 years ago, the Chinese made black powder, or gunpowder. The powder was used to set off firecrackers and primitive missiles. The shells of fireworks contain several different chemicals. Black powder at the bottom of the shell launches the shell into the sky. A second layer of black powder ignites the rest of the chemicals and causes an explosion that lights up the sky! Colors can be created by mixing chemicals such as strontium (for red), magnesium (for white), or copper (for blue) with the gunpowder.

TN GLE 0807.T/E.1

Math ACTIVITY

Fireworks can cost between $200 and $2,000 each. If a show uses 20 fireworks that cost $200 each, 12 fireworks that cost $500 each, and 10 fireworks that cost $1,200 each, what is the total cost for the fireworks?

Weird Science

Buckyballs

In 1985, scientists found a completely new kind of molecule! This carbon molecule has 60 carbon atoms linked together in a shape similar to that of a soccer ball. This molecule is called a buckyball. Buckyballs have also been found in the soot from candle flames. And some scientists claim to have detected buckyballs in space. Chemists have been trying to identify the molecules' properties. One property is that a buckyball can act like a cage and hold smaller substances, such as individual atoms. Buckyballs are both slippery and strong. Scientists are exploring their use in tough plastics and cutting tools.

Language Arts ACTIVITY

WRITING SKILL Imagine that you are trapped within a buckyball. Write a one-page short story describing your experience. Describe the windows in your molecular prison.

Glenn T. Seaborg

Making Elements When you look at the periodic table, you can thank Dr. Glenn Theodore Seaborg and his colleagues for many of the actinide elements. While working at the University of California at Berkeley, Seaborg and his team added a number of elements to the periodic table. His work in identifying properties of plutonium led to his working on the top-secret Manhattan Project at the University of Chicago. He was outspoken about the beneficial uses of atomic energy and, at the same time, opposed the production and use of nuclear weapons.

Seaborg's revision of the layout of the periodic table—the actinide concept—is the most significant since Mendeleev's original design. For his scientific achievements, Dr. Seaborg was awarded the 1951 Nobel Prize in Chemistry jointly with his colleague, Dr. Edwin M. McMillan. Element 106, which Seaborg neither discovered nor created, was named seaborgium in his honor. This was the first time an element had been named after a living person.

Social Studies
Activity

WRITING SKILL **T/E** A beneficial use of atomic energy is generating electricity people use to power their homes. Write a newspaper editorial that discusses unintended consequences of generating power using atomic energy. Take a stand for or against using atomic energy this way and support your position with facts. **TN** ✓0807.T/E.3

To learn more about these Science in Action topics, visit **go.hrw.com** and type in the keyword **HP5PRTF.**

Current Science

Check out Current Science® articles related to this chapter by visiting **go.hrw.com.** Just type in the keyword **HP5CS12.**

12

Chemical Bonding

The Big Idea

Atoms combine by forming ionic, covalent, and metallic bonds.

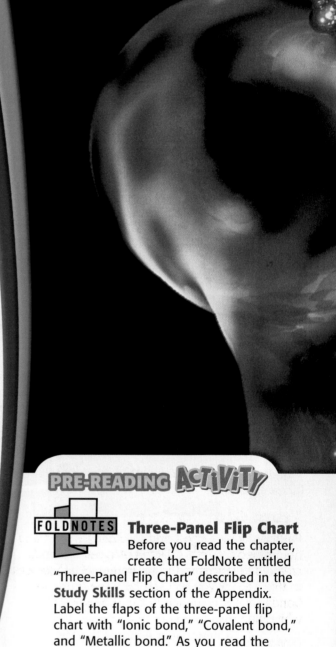

TN Tennessee Science Standards

Embedded Inquiry

GLE 0807.Inq.2 Use appropriate tools and techniques to gather, organize, and interpret data.

GLE 0807.Inq.5 Communicate scientific understanding using descriptions, explanations, and models.

✓**0807.Inq.5** Design a method to explain the results of an investigation using descriptions, explanations, or models.

Embedded Technology and Engineering

GLE 0807.T/E.1 Explore how technology responds to social, political, and economic needs.

GLE0807.T/E.2 Know that the engineering design process involves an ongoing series of events that incorporate design constraints, model building, testing, evaluating, modifying, and retesting.

GLE 0807.T/E.3 Compare the intended benefits with the unintended consequences of a new technology.

✓**0807.T/E.1** Use appropriate tools to test for strength, hardness, and flexibility of materials.

Physical Science

GLE 0807.9.1 Understand that all matter is made up of atoms.

GLE 0807.9.2 Explain that matter has properties that are determined by the structure and arrangement of its atoms.

GLE 0807.9.4 Distinguish among elements, compounds, and mixtures.

GLE 0807.9.6 Use the periodic table to determine the characteristics of an element.

✓**0807.9.1** Identify atoms as the fundamental particles that make up matter.

✓**0807.9.7** Describe how the characteristics of a compound are different than the characteristics of their component parts.

✓**0807.9.8** Determine the types of interactions between substances that result in a chemical change.

PRE-READING ACTIVITY

FOLDNOTES **Three-Panel Flip Chart**
Before you read the chapter, create the FoldNote entitled "Three-Panel Flip Chart" described in the **Study Skills** section of the Appendix. Label the flaps of the three-panel flip chart with "Ionic bond," "Covalent bond," and "Metallic bond." As you read the chapter, write information you learn about each category under the appropriate flap.

About the Photo

What looks like a fantastic "sculpture" is really a model of deoxyribonucleic acid (DNA). DNA is one of the most complex molecules in living things. In DNA, atoms are bonded together in two very long spiral strands. These strands join to form a double spiral. The DNA in living cells has all the coding for passing on the traits of that cell and that organism.

START-UP ACTIVITY

TN GLE 0807.Inq.2

From Glue to Goop

Particles of glue can bond to other particles and hold objects together. Different types of bonds create differences in the properties of substances. In this activity, you will see how the formation of bonds causes a change in the properties of white glue.

Procedure

1. Fill a **small paper cup** 1/4 full of **white glue**. Record the properties of the glue.

2. Fill a **second small paper cup** 1/4 full of **borax solution.**

3. Pour the borax solution into the cup of white glue, and stir well using a **plastic spoon** or a **wooden craft stick.**

4. When the material becomes too thick to stir, remove it from the cup and knead it with your fingers. Record the properties of the material.

Analysis

1. Compare the properties of the glue with those of the new material.

2. The properties of the material resulted from bonds between the borax and the glue. Predict the properties of the material if less borax is used.

Electrons and Chemical Bonding

Have you considered that by using only the 26 letters of the alphabet, you make all your everyday words?

Although the number of letters is limited, combining the letters in different ways allows you to make a huge number of words. In the same way that words can be formed by combining letters, chemists form new substances by combining atoms in new ways.

Combining Atoms Through Chemical Bonding

Look at **Figure 1.** Now, look around the room. Everything you see—desks, pencils, paper, and even your friends—is made of atoms of elements. All substances are made of atoms of one or more of the approximately 100 elements. For example, the atoms of carbon, hydrogen, and oxygen combine in different patterns to form sugar, alcohol, and citric acid. **Chemical bonding** is the joining of atoms to form new substances. The properties of these new substances are different from the properties of the original elements. An interaction that holds two atoms together is called a **chemical bond.** When chemical bonds form, electrons are shared, gained, or lost.

Discussing Bonding Using Theories and Models

We cannot see atoms and chemical bonds with the unaided eye. For more than 150 years, scientists have done many experiments that have led to a theory of chemical bonding. Remember that a theory is an explanation for some phenomenon that is based on observation, experimentation, and reasoning. The use of models helps people discuss the theory of how and why atoms form bonds.

Figure 1 *Everything you see in this photo is formed by combining atoms.*

Figure 2   Electron Arrangement in an Atom

a The **first energy level** is closest to the nucleus and can hold up to 2 electrons.

b Electrons will begin filling the **second energy level** only after the first level is full. The second energy level can hold up to 8 electrons.

c The **third energy level** in this model of a chlorine atom has only 7 electrons, so the atom has a total of 17 electrons. This outer level of the atom is not full.

Electron Number and Organization

To understand how atoms form chemical bonds, you need to know about the electrons in an atom. The number of electrons in an atom can be determined from the atomic number of the element. The *atomic number* is the number of protons in an atom. But atoms have no charge. So, the atomic number also represents the number of electrons in the atom.

Electrons in an atom are organized in energy levels. **Figure 2** shows a model of the arrangement of electrons in a chlorine atom. This model and models like it are useful for counting electrons in energy levels of atoms. But, these models do not show the true structure of atoms.

Outer-Level Electrons and Bonding

Not all of the electrons in an atom make chemical bonds. Most atoms form bonds using only the electrons in the outermost energy level. An electron in the outermost energy level of an atom is a **valence electron** (VAY luhns ee LEK TRAHN). The models in **Figure 3** show the valence electrons for two atoms.

TN *Standards Check*   Which electrons are used to form bonds?
✔0807.9.8

chemical bonding the combining of atoms to form molecules or ionic compounds

chemical bond an interaction that holds atoms or ions together

valence electron an electron that is found in the outermost shell of an atom and that determines the atom's chemical properties

Figure 3   Counting Valence Electrons

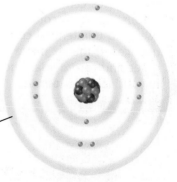

Oxygen
Electron total: 8
First level: 2 electrons
Second level: 6 electrons

An oxygen atom has 6 valence electrons.

Sodium
Electron total: 11
First level: 2 electrons
Second level: 8 electrons
Third level: 1 electron

A sodium atom has 1 valence electron.

Figure 4 Determining the Number of Valence Electrons

Atoms of elements in **Groups 1 and 2** have the same number of valence electrons as their group number.

Atoms of elements in **Groups 13–18** have 10 fewer valence electrons than their group number. However, helium atoms have only 2 valence electrons.

Atoms of elements in **Groups 3–12** do not have a rule relating their valence electrons to their group number.

1	2	3	4	5	6	7	8	9	10	11	12	13	14	15	16	17	18
H																	He
Li	Be											B	C	N	O	F	Ne
Na	Mg											Al	Si	P	S	Cl	Ar
K	Ca	Sc	Ti	V	Cr	Mn	Fe	Co	Ni	Cu	Zn	Ga	Ge	As	Se	Br	Kr
Rb	Sr	Y	Zr	Nb	Mo	Tc	Ru	Rh	Pd	Ag	Cd	In	Sn	Sb	Te	I	Xe
Cs	Ba	La	Hf	Ta	W	Re	Os	Ir	Pt	Au	Hg	Tl	Pb	Bi	Po	At	Rn
Fr	Ra	Ac	Rf	Db	Sg	Bh	Hs	Mt	Ds	Rg	Uub	Uut	Uuq	Uup	Uuh		Uuo

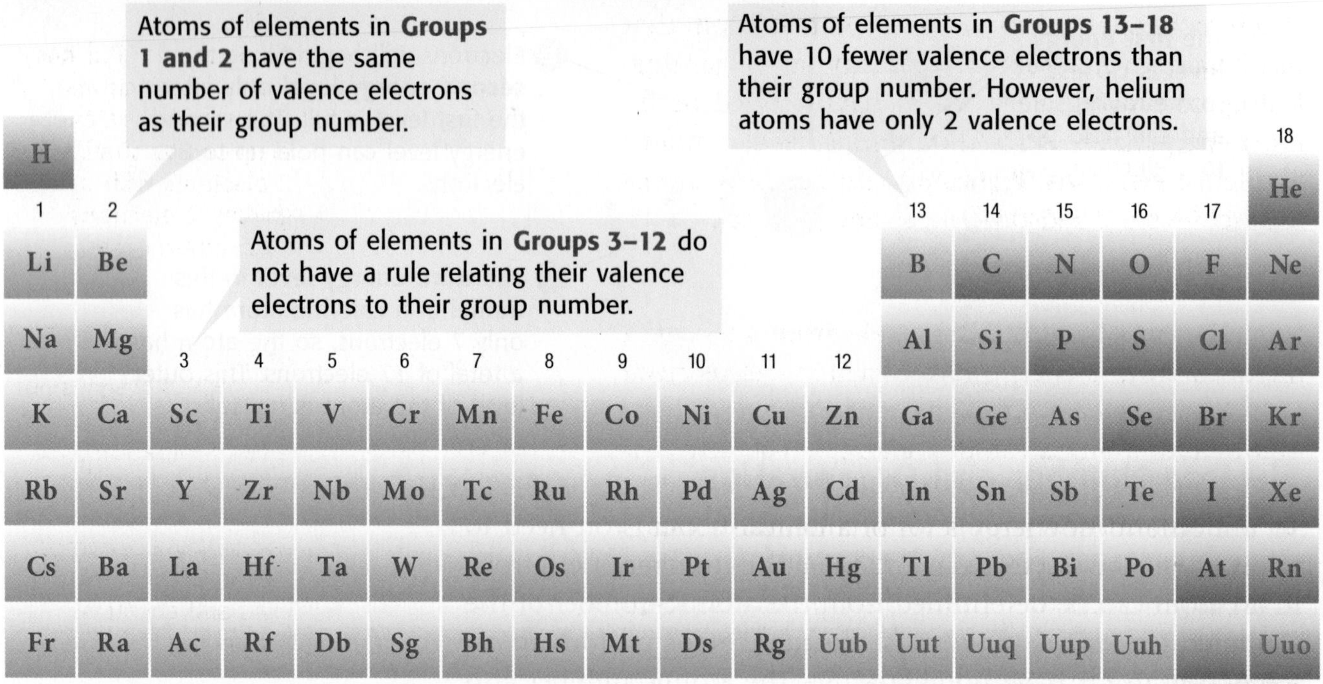

Valence Electrons and the Periodic Table

You can use a model to determine the number of valence electrons of an atom. But what would you do if you didn't have a model? You can use the periodic table to determine the number of valence electrons for atoms of some elements.

Elements are grouped based on similar properties. Within a group, or family, the atoms of each element have the same number of valence electrons. So, the group numbers can help you determine the number of valence electrons for some atoms, as shown in **Figure 4.**

To Bond or Not to Bond

Not all atoms bond in the same manner. In fact, some atoms rarely bond at all! The number of electrons in the outermost energy level of an atom determines whether an atom will form bonds.

Atoms of the noble gases (Group 18) do not usually form chemical bonds. Atoms of Group 18 elements (except helium) have 8 valence electrons. Having 8 valence electrons is a special condition. In fact, atoms that have 8 electrons in their outermost energy level do not usually form bonds. The outermost energy level of an atom is considered to be full if the energy level contains 8 electrons.

✓ **Reading Check** The atoms of which group in the periodic table rarely form chemical bonds?

TN GLE 0807.T/E.1, GLE 0807.T/E.3

CONNECTION TO Engineering

WRITING SKILL **T/E** **Uses of Noble Gases**

Because noble gases are stable and non-flammable, engineers use them for many purposes. However, some noble gases can also be dangerous. Research common uses and unintended consequences of the six noble gases and record your findings in your **science journal.**

Filling The Outermost Level

An atom that has fewer than 8 valence electrons is much more likely to form bonds than an atom that has 8 valence electrons is. Atoms bond by gaining, losing, or sharing electrons to have a filled outermost energy level. A filled outermost level contains 8 valence electrons. **Figure 5** describes how atoms can achieve a filled outermost energy level.

Is Two Electrons a Full Set?

Not all atoms need 8 valence electrons to have a filled outermost energy level. Helium atoms need only 2 valence electrons. The outermost energy level in a helium atom is the first energy level. The first energy level of any atom can hold only 2 electrons. So, the outermost energy level of a helium atom is full if the energy level has only 2 electrons. Atoms of hydrogen and other Group 1 elements also form bonds by gaining, losing, or sharing electrons to achieve 2 electrons in the first energy level.

Figure 5 Filling Outermost Energy Levels

Sulfur
An atom of sulfur has 6 valence electrons. It can have 8 valence electrons by sharing 2 electrons with or gaining 2 electrons from other atoms.

Magnesium
An atom of magnesium has 2 valence electrons. It can have a full outer level by losing 2 electrons. The second energy level becomes the outermost energy level and contains 8 electrons.

SECTION Review

TN GLE 0807.9.1, GLE 0807.9.2, GLE 0807.9.6

Summary

- Chemical bonding is the joining of atoms to form new substances. A chemical bond holds two atoms together.

- A valence electron is an electron in the outermost energy level of an atom.

- Most atoms form bonds by gaining, losing, or sharing electrons until they have 8 valence electrons. Atoms of some elements need only 2 electrons to fill their outermost level.

Using Key Terms

1. Use the following terms in a sentence about a type of inter-action that results in a chemical change: *chemical bond* and *valence electron.* ✔0807.9.8

Understanding Key Ideas

2. Which of the following atoms do not usually form bonds? ✔0807.9.1

   a. calcium   **c.** hydrogen
   b. neon   **d.** oxygen

3. Describe chemical bonding. ✔0807.9.8

4. Explain how to use the valence electrons in an atom to predict if the atom will form bonds. ✔0807.9.8

Critical Thinking

5. **Making Inferences** How can an atom that has 5 valence electrons achieve a full set of valence electrons? ✔0807.9.8

6. **Applying Concepts** Identify the number of valence electrons in a barium atom. ✔0807.9.8

Interpreting Graphics

7. Look at the model below. How many valence electrons are in a fluorine atom? Will fluorine atoms form bonds? Explain.

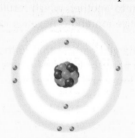

Fluorine

Internet Resources

For a variety of links related to this chapter, go to www.scilinks.org

Topic: The Electron; Periodic Table
SciLinks code: HSM0489; HSM1125

Ionic Bonds

Have you ever accidentally tasted sea water? If so, you probably didn't enjoy it. What makes sea water taste different from the water in your home?

Sea water tastes different because salt is dissolved in it. One of the salts in sea water is the same as the salt that you eat. The chemical bonds in salt are ionic (ie AHN ik) bonds.

Forming Ionic Bonds

An **ionic bond** is a bond that forms when electrons are transferred from one atom to another atom. During ionic bonding, one or more valence electrons are transferred from one atom to another. Like all chemical bonds, ionic bonds form so that the outermost energy levels of the atoms in the bonds are filled. **Figure 1** shows another substance that contains ionic bonds.

Charged Particles

An atom is neutral because the number of electrons in an atom equals the number of protons. So, the charges of the electrons and protons cancel each other. A transfer of electrons between atoms changes the number of electrons in each atom. But the number of protons stays the same in each atom. The negative charges and positive charges no longer cancel out, and the atoms become ions. **Ions** are charged particles that form when atoms gain or lose electrons. An atom normally cannot gain electrons without another atom nearby to lose electrons (or cannot lose electrons without a nearby atom to gain them). But it is easier to study the formation of ions one at a time.

✓ **Reading Check** Why are atoms neutral?

What You Will Learn

● Explain how ionic bonds form.
● Describe how positive ions form.
● Describe how negative ions form.
● Explain why ionic compounds are neutral.

Vocabulary

ionic bond
ion
crystal lattice

TN GLE 0807.T/E.1 Explore how technology responds to social, political, and economic needs.

GLE 0807.9.2 Explain that matter has properties that are determined by the structure and arrangement of its atoms.

GLE 0807.9.4 Distinguish among elements, compounds, and mixtures.

ionic bond a bond that forms when electrons are transferred from one atom to another, which results in a positive ion and a negative ion

ion a charged particle that forms when an atom or group of atoms gains or loses one or more electrons

Figure 1 *Calcium carbonate in this snail's shell contains ionic bonds.*

Figure 2　Forming Positive Ions

Here's How It Works: During chemical changes, a sodium atom can lose its 1 electron in the third energy level to another atom. The filled second level becomes the outermost level, so the resulting sodium ion now has 8 electrons in its outermost energy level.

Here's How It Works: During chemical changes, an aluminum atom can lose its 3 electrons in the third energy level to another atom. The filled second level becomes the outermost level, so the resulting aluminum ion now has 8 electrons in its outermost energy level.

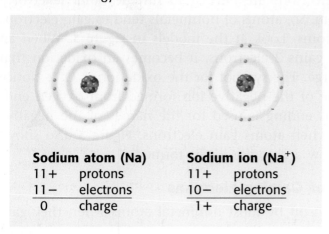

Sodium atom (Na)		Sodium ion (Na$^+$)	
11+	protons	11+	protons
11−	electrons	10−	electrons
0	charge	1+	charge

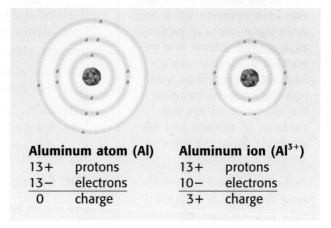

Aluminum atom (Al)		Aluminum ion (Al^{3+})	
13+	protons	13+	protons
13−	electrons	10−	electrons
0	charge	3+	charge

Forming Positive Ions

Ionic bonds form during chemical changes when atoms pull electrons away from other atoms. The atoms that lose electrons form ions that have fewer electrons than protons. Because the positive charges outnumber the negative charges, these ions have a positive charge.

Metal Atoms and the Loss of Electrons

Atoms of most metals have few valence electrons. Metal atoms tend to lose these valence electrons and form positive ions. Look at the models in **Figure 2.** When a sodium atom loses its only valence electron to another atom, the sodium atom becomes a sodium ion. A sodium ion has 1 more proton than it has electrons. So, the sodium ion has a 1+ charge. The chemical symbol for this ion is written as Na$^+$. Notice that the charge is written to the upper right of the chemical symbol. **Figure 2** also shows a model for the formation of an aluminum ion.

The Energy Needed to Lose Electrons

Energy is needed to pull electrons away from atoms. Only a small amount of energy is needed to take electrons from metal atoms. In fact, the energy needed to remove electrons from atoms of elements in Groups 1 and 2 is so small that these elements react very easily. The energy needed to take electrons from metals comes from the formation of negative ions.

TN GLE 0807.T/E.1

CONNECTION TO Engineering

WRITING SKILL **T/E** **Desalination** In countries where the drinking water supply is limited, engineers employ a process called *desalination*. Desalination allows people to drink seawater by removing the salt. Research three countries that desalinate and the methods they use. Record your findings in your **science journal.**

ACTIVITY

Forming Negative Ions

Some atoms gain electrons from other atoms during chemical changes. The ions that form have more electrons than protons. So, these ions have a negative charge.

Nonmetal Atoms Gain Electrons

The outermost energy level of nonmetal atoms is almost full. Only a few electrons are needed to fill the outer level of a nonmetal atom. So, atoms of nonmetals tend to gain electrons from other atoms. Look at the models in **Figure 3.** When an oxygen atom gains 2 electrons, it becomes an oxide ion that has a 2− charge. The symbol for the oxide ion is O^{2-}. Notice that the name of the negative ion formed from oxygen ends with -*ide*. This ending is used for the names of the negative ions formed when atoms gain electrons. **Figure 3** also shows a model of how a chloride ion is formed.

The Energy of Gaining Electrons

Energy is given off by most nonmetal atoms when they gain electrons. The more easily an atom gains an electron, the more energy the atom releases. Atoms of Group 17 elements give off the most energy when they gain an electron. These elements are very reactive. An ionic bond will form between a metal and a nonmetal if the nonmetal releases more energy than is needed to take electrons from the metal.

✓ **Reading Check** Atoms of which group on the periodic table give off the most energy when forming negative ions?

Figure 3   Forming Negative Ions

Here's How It Works: During chemical changes, an oxygen atom gains 2 electrons in the second energy level from another atom. An oxide ion that has 8 valence electrons is formed. Thus, its outermost energy level is filled.

Here's How It Works: During chemical changes, a chlorine atom gains 1 electron in the third energy level from another atom. A chloride ion that has 8 valence electrons is formed. Thus, its outermost energy level is filled.

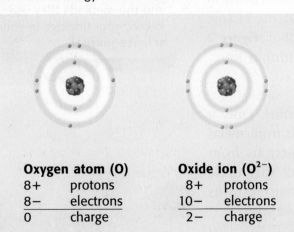

Oxygen atom (O)	
8+	protons
8−	electrons
0	charge

Oxide ion (O^{2-})	
8+	protons
10−	electrons
2−	charge

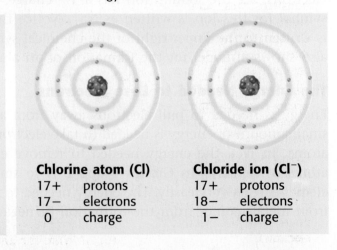

Chlorine atom (Cl)	
17+	protons
17−	electrons
0	charge

Chloride ion (Cl^-)	
17+	protons
18−	electrons
1−	charge

Ionic Compounds

When ionic bonds form, the number of electrons lost by the metal atoms equals the number gained by the nonmetal atoms. The ions that bond are charged, but the compound formed is neutral because the charges of the ions cancel each other. When ions bond, they form a repeating three-dimensional pattern called a **crystal lattice** (KRIS tuhl LAT is), like the one shown in **Figure 4.** The strong attraction between ions in a crystal lattice gives ionic compounds certain properties, which include brittleness, high melting points, and high boiling points.

crystal lattice the regular pattern in which a crystal is arranged

Figure 4 *This model of the crystal lattice of sodium chloride, or table salt, shows a three-dimensional view of the bonded ions. In the model, the sodium ions are pink and the chloride ions are green.*

SECTION Review

TN GLE 0807.9.2, GLE 0807.9.4

Summary

- An ionic bond is a bond that forms when electrons are transferred from one atom to another. During ionic bonding, the atoms become oppositely charged ions.

- Ionic bonding usually occurs between atoms of metals and atoms of nonmetals.

- Energy is needed to remove electrons from metal atoms. Energy is released when most nonmetal atoms gain electrons.

Using Key Terms

1. Use the following terms in the same sentence: *ion* and *ionic bond.* ✔0807.9.8

2. In your own words, write a definition for the term *crystal lattice.*

Understanding Key Ideas

3. Which types of atoms usually become negative ions? ✔0807.9.8
   a. metals
   b. nonmetals
   c. noble gases
   d. All of the above

4. How does an atom become a positive ion? a negative ion? ✔0807.9.8

5. What are two properties of ionic compounds? ✔0807.9.8

Math Skills

6. What is the charge of an ion that has 12 protons and 10 electrons? Write the ion's symbol.

Critical Thinking

7. **Applying Concepts** Which group of elements gains two valence electrons when the atoms form ionic bonds? ✔0807.9.8

8. **Identifying Relationships** Explain why ionic compounds are neutral even though they are made up of charged particles. ✔0807.9.8

9. **Making Comparisons** Compare the formation of positive ions with the formation of negative ions in terms of energy changes. ✔0807.9.8

Internet Resources

For a variety of links related to this chapter, go to www.scilinks.org
Topic: Types of Chemical Bonds
SciLinks code: HSM1565

Covalent and Metallic Bonds

Imagine bending a wooden coat hanger and a wire coat hanger. The wire one would bend easily, but the wooden one would break. Why do these things behave differently?

One reason is that the bonds between the atoms of each object are different. The atoms of the wooden hanger are held together by covalent bonds (KOH VAY luhnt BAHNDZ). But the atoms of the wire hanger are held together by metallic bonds. Read on to learn about the difference between these kinds of chemical bonds.

Covalent Bonds

Most things around you, such as water, sugar, oxygen, and wood, are held together by covalent bonds. Substances that have covalent bonds tend to have low melting and boiling points and are brittle in the solid state. For example, oxygen has a low boiling point, which is why it is a gas at room temperature. And wood is brittle, so it breaks when bent.

A **covalent bond** forms when atoms share one or more pairs of electrons. When two atoms of nonmetals bond, a large amount of energy is needed for either atom to lose an electron. So, two nonmetals don't transfer electrons to fill the outermost energy levels of their atoms. Instead, two nonmetal atoms bond by sharing electrons with each another, as shown in the model in **Figure 1.**

TN *Standards Check* What is a covalent bond? ✔0807.9.8

What You Will Learn

● Explain how covalent bonds form.
● Describe molecules.
● Explain how metallic bonds form.
● Describe the properties of metals.

Vocabulary

covalent bond
molecule
metallic bond

READING STRATEGY

Reading Organizer As you read this section, create an outline of the section. Use the headings from the section in your outline.

TN GLE 0807.Inq.2 Use appropriate tools and techniques to gather, organize, and interpret data.

GLE 0807.Inq.5 Communicate scientific understanding using descriptions, explanations, and models.

GLE 0807.T/E.1 Explore how technology responds to social, political, and economic needs.

GLE 0807.T/E.2 Know that the engineering design process involves an ongoing series of events that incorporate design constraints, model building, testing, evaluating, modifying, and retesting.

GLE 0807.9.2 Explain that matter has properties that are determined by the structure and arrangement of its atoms.

GLE 0807.9.4 Distinguish among elements, compounds, and mixtures.

GLE 0807.9.6 Use the periodic table to determine the characteristics of an element.

covalent bond a bond formed when atoms share one or more pairs of electrons

Figure 1 *By sharing electrons in a covalent bond, each hydrogen atom (the smallest atom) has a full outermost energy level containing two electrons.*

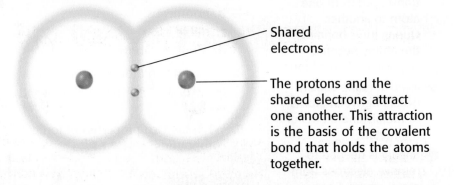

Shared electrons

The protons and the shared electrons attract one another. This attraction is the basis of the covalent bond that holds the atoms together.

Figure 2 Covalent Bonds in a Water Molecule

The oxygen atom shares one of its electrons with each of the two hydrogen atoms. It now has its outermost level filled with 8 electrons.

Each hydrogen atom shares its 1 electron with the oxygen atom. Each hydrogen atom now has an outer level filled with 2 electrons.

This electron-dot diagram for water shows only the outermost level of electrons for each atom. But you still see how the atoms share electrons.

Covalent Bonds and Molecules

Substances containing covalent bonds consist of individual particles called molecules (MAHL i KYOOLZ). A **molecule** usually consists of two or more atoms joined in a definite ratio. A hydrogen molecule is composed of two covalently bonded hydrogen atoms. However, most molecules are composed of atoms of two or more elements. The models in **Figure 2** show two ways to represent the covalent bonds in a water molecule.

One way to represent atoms and molecules is to use electron-dot diagrams. An electron-dot diagram is a model that shows only the valence electrons in an atom. Electron-dot diagrams can help you predict how atoms might bond. To draw an electron-dot diagram, write the symbol of the element and place one dot around the symbol for every valence electron in the atom, as shown in **Figure 3.** Place the first 4 dots alone on each side, and then pair up any remaining dots.

molecule the smallest unit of a substance that keeps all of the physical and chemical properties of that substance TN VOCAB

Figure 3 Using Electron–Dot Diagrams

Carbon atoms have 4 valence electrons. A carbon atom needs 4 more electrons to have a filled outermost energy level.

Oxygen atoms have 6 valence electrons. An oxygen atom needs only 2 more electrons to have a filled outermost energy level.

Krypton atoms have 8 valence electrons. Krypton is nonreactive. Krypton atoms do not need any more electrons.

This diagram represents a hydrogen molecule. The dots between the letters represent a pair of shared electrons.

Figure 4 *The water in this fishbowl is made up of many tiny water molecules. Each molecule is the smallest particle that has the chemical properties of water.*

For another activity related to this chapter, go to **go.hrw.com** and type in the keyword **HP5BNDW**.

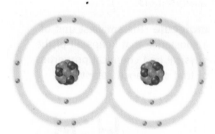

Figure 5 *Two covalently bonded fluorine atoms have filled outermost energy levels. The two electrons shared by the atoms are counted as valence electrons for each atom.*

Covalent Compounds and Molecules

An atom is the smallest particle into which an element can be divided and still be the same element. Likewise, a molecule is the smallest particle into which a covalently bonded compound can be divided and still be the same compound. Look at the three-dimensional models in **Figure 4.** They show how a sample of water is made up of many individual molecules of water. Imagine dividing water over and over. You would eventually end up with a single molecule of water. What would happen if you separated the hydrogen and oxygen atoms that make up a water molecule? Then, you would no longer have water.

The Simplest Molecules

Molecules are composed of at least two covalently bonded atoms. The simplest molecules are made up of two bonded atoms. Molecules made up of two atoms are called *diatomic molecules.* Elements that are found in nature as diatomic molecules are called *diatomic elements.* Hydrogen is a diatomic element. Oxygen, nitrogen, and the halogens fluorine, chlorine, bromine, and iodine are also diatomic elements. Look at **Figure 5.** The shared electrons are counted as valence electrons for each atom. So, both atoms of the molecule have filled outermost energy levels.

TN *Standards Check* How many atoms are in a diatomic molecule? ✔0807.9.1

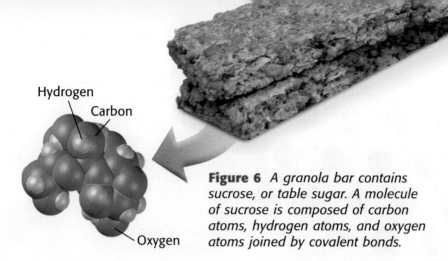

Hydrogen

Carbon

Oxygen

Figure 6 *A granola bar contains sucrose, or table sugar. A molecule of sucrose is composed of carbon atoms, hydrogen atoms, and oxygen atoms joined by covalent bonds.*

More-Complex Molecules

Diatomic molecules are the simplest molecules. They are also some of the most important molecules. You could not live without diatomic oxygen molecules. But other important molecules are much more complex. Soap, plastic bottles, and even proteins in your body are examples of complex molecules. Carbon atoms are the basis of many of these complex molecules. Each carbon atom needs to make four covalent bonds to have 8 valence electrons. These bonds can be with atoms of other elements or with other carbon atoms, as shown in the model in **Figure 6.**

Metallic Bonds

Look at the unusual metal sculptures shown in **Figure 7.** Some metal pieces have been flattened, while other metal pieces have been shaped into wires. How could the artist change the shape of the metal into all of these different forms without breaking the metal into pieces? Metal can be shaped because of the presence of a metallic bond, a special kind of chemical bond. A **metallic bond** is a bond formed by the attraction between positively charged metal ions and the electrons in the metal. Positively charged metal ions form when metal atoms lose electrons.

metallic bond a bond formed by the attraction between positively charged metal ions and the electrons around them

Figure 7 *The different shapes of metal in these sculptures are possible because of the bonds that hold the metal together.*

321

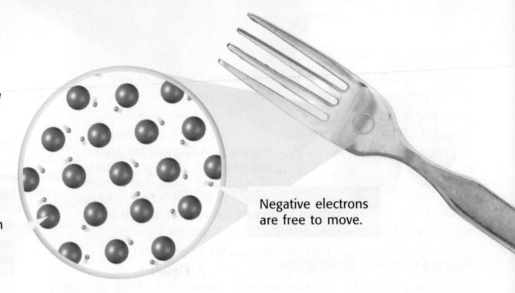

Figure 8 *Moving electrons are attracted to the metal ions, and the attraction forms metallic bonds.*

The positive metal ions are in fixed positions in the metal.

Negative electrons are free to move.

TN GLE 0807.Inq.2

Bending with Bonds

1. Straighten out a **wire paper clip.** Record your observations.

2. Bend a **piece of chalk.** Record your observations.

3. Chalk is composed of calcium carbonate, a compound containing ionic bonds. What kind of bond is present in the paper clip?

4. Explain why you could change the shape of the paper clip but could not bend the chalk without breaking it. ✔0807.T/E.2

Movement of Electrons Throughout a Metal

Bonding in metals is a result of the metal atoms being so close to one another that their outermost energy levels overlap. This overlapping allows valence electrons to move throughout the metal, as shown in **Figure 8.** You can think of a metal as being made up of positive metal ions that have enough valence electrons "swimming" around to keep the ions together. The electrons also cancel the positive charge of the ions. Metallic bonds extend throughout the metal in all directions.

Properties of Metals

Metallic bonding gives metals their particular properties, including electrical conductivity, malleability, and ductility.

Conducting Electric Current

Metallic bonding allows metals to conduct electric current. For example, when you turn on a lamp, electrons move within the copper wire that connects the lamp to the outlet. The electrons that move are the valence electrons in the copper atoms. These electrons are free to move because the electrons are not connected to any one atom.

Reshaping Metals

Because the electrons swim freely around the metal ions, the atoms in metals can be rearranged. As a result, metals can be reshaped. The properties of *ductility* (the ability to be drawn into wires) and *malleability* (the ability to be hammered into sheets) describe a metal's ability to be reshaped. For example, copper is made into wires for use in electrical cords. Aluminum can be pounded into thin sheets and made into aluminum foil.

✓ Reading Check What gives metals their physical properties, such as ductility?

Bending Without Breaking

When a piece of metal is bent, some of the metal ions are forced closer together. You might expect the metal to break because all of the metal ions are positively charged. Positively charged ions repel one another. However, positive ions in a metal are always surrounded by and attracted to the electrons in the metal—even if the metal ions move. The electrons constantly move around and between the metal ions. The moving electrons maintain the metallic bonds no matter how the shape of the metal changes. So, metal objects can be bent without being broken, as shown in **Figure 9.**

Figure 9 *Metal can be reshaped without breaking because metallic bonds occur in many directions.*

SECTION Review

TN GLE 0807.9.2, GLE 0807.9.4, GLE 0807.9.6

Summary

- In covalent bonding, two atoms share electrons. A covalent bond forms when atoms share one or more pairs of electrons.

- Covalently bonded atoms form a particle called a *molecule*. A molecule is the smallest particle of a compound that has the chemical properties of the compound.

- In metallic bonding, the valence electrons move throughout the metal. A bond formed by the attraction between positive metal ions and the electrons in the metal is a metallic bond.

- Properties of metals include conductivity, ductility, and malleability.

Using Key Terms

1. Use each of the following terms in a separate sentence: *covalent bond* and *metallic bond*. ✔0807.9.8

2. In your own words, write a definition for the term *molecule*. ✔0807.9.8

Understanding Key Ideas

3. Between which of the following atoms is a covalent bond most likely to occur? ✔0807.9.8

   a. calcium and lithium

   b. sodium and fluorine

   c. nitrogen and oxygen

   d. helium and argon

4. What happens to the electrons in covalent bonding? ✔0807.9.8

5. How many dots does an electron-dot diagram of a sulfur atom have?

6. List three properties of metals that are a result of metallic bonds.

7. Describe how the valence electrons in a metal move.

8. Explain the difference between ductility and malleability. Give an example of when each property is useful.

Critical Thinking

9. **Identifying Relationships** How do the metallic bonds in a staple allow it to function properly?

10. **Applying Concepts** Draw an electron-dot diagram for ammonia (a nitrogen atom covalently bonded to three hydrogen atoms). ✔0807.9.1, ✔0807.9.5

Interpreting Graphics

11. This electron-dot diagram is not complete. Which atom needs to form another bond? Explain. ✔0807.9.1, ✔0807.9.5

$$\begin{array}{c} \text{H} \\ \text{H} : \ddot{\text{C}} : \text{H} \end{array}$$

Model-Making Lab

Covalent Marshmallows

OBJECTIVES

Build a three-dimensional model of a water molecule.

Draw an electron-dot diagram of a water molecule.

MATERIALS

- marshmallows (two of one color, one of another color)
- toothpicks

SAFETY

A hydrogen atom has 1 electron in its outermost energy level, but 2 electrons are required to fill its outermost level. An oxygen atom has 6 electrons in its outermost level, but 8 electrons are required to fill its outermost level. To fill their outermost energy levels, two atoms of hydrogen and one atom of oxygen can share electrons, as shown below. Such a sharing of electrons to fill the outermost level of atoms is called *covalent bonding*. When hydrogen and oxygen bond in this manner, a molecule of water is formed. In this lab, you will build a three-dimensional model of water to better understand the covalent bonds formed in a water molecule.

A Model of a Water Molecule

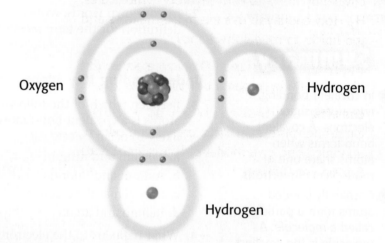

Oxygen

Hydrogen

Hydrogen

Procedure

1. Using the marshmallows and toothpicks, create a model of a water molecule. Use the diagram above for guidance in building your model.

2. Draw a sketch of your model. Be sure to label the hydrogen and oxygen atoms on your sketch.

3. Draw an electron-dot diagram of the water molecule.

TN GLE 0807.Inq.4 Recognize possible sources of bias and error, alternative explanations, and questions for further exploration.

GLE 0807.Inq.5 Communicate scientific understanding using descriptions, explanations, and models.

GLE 0807.9.4 Distinguish among elements, compounds, and mixtures.

Analyze the Results

1 Classifying What do the marshmallows represent? What do the toothpicks represent?

2 Evaluating Models Why are the marshmallows different colors?

3 Analyzing Results Compare your model with the diagram on the previous page. How might an alternative version of your model more accurately represent a water molecule? ✔0807.Inq.4

Draw Conclusions

4 Making Predictions Hydrogen in nature can covalently bond to form hydrogen molecules, H_2. How could you use the marshmallows and toothpicks to model this bond? ✔0807.Inq.5

5 Applying Conclusions Draw an electron-dot diagram of a hydrogen molecule. ✔0807.Inq.5

6 Drawing Conclusions Which do you think would be more difficult to create—a model of an ionic bond or a model of a covalent bond? Explain your answer.

Applying Your Data

Create a model of a carbon dioxide molecule, which consists of two oxygen atoms and one carbon atom. The structure is similar to the structure of water, although the three atoms bond in a straight line instead of at angles. The bond between each oxygen atom and the carbon atom in a carbon dioxide molecule is a *double bond,* so use two connections. Do the double bonds in carbon dioxide appear stronger or weaker than the single bonds in water? Explain your answer. ✔0807.Inq.5, ✔0807.9.7

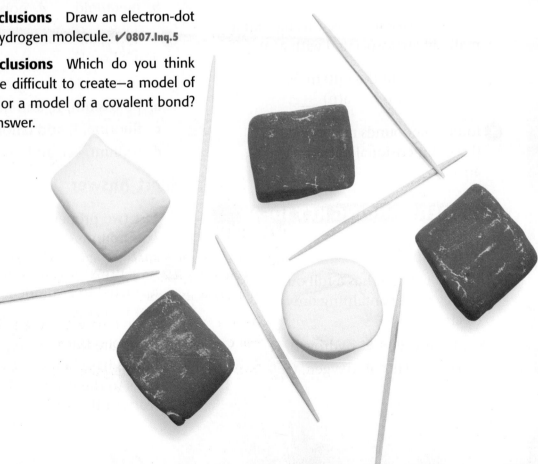

Chapter Review

TN GLE 0807.Inq.5, GLE 0807.9.1, GLE 0807.9.2, GLE 0807.9.6

USING KEY TERMS

Complete each of the following sentences by choosing the correct term from the word bank.

crystal lattice   ionic bond
molecule   chemical bond
chemical bonding   metallic bond
valence electron   ion
covalent bond

1 An interaction that holds two atoms together is a(n) ___. ✔0807.9.1

2 A charged particle that forms when an atom transfers electrons is a(n) ___. ✔0807.9.8

3 A bond formed when atoms share electrons is a(n) ___. ✔0807.9.8

4 Electrons free to move throughout a material are associated with a(n) ___.

5 An electron in the outermost energy level of an atom is a(n) ___.

6 Ionic compounds are bonded in a three-dimensional pattern called a(n) ___.

UNDERSTANDING KEY IDEAS

Multiple Choice

7 Which element has a full outermost energy level containing only two electrons?

  a. fluorine, F   **c.** hydrogen, H
  b. helium, He   **d.** oxygen, O

8 Which of the following describes what happens when an atom becomes an ion with a 2– charge?

  a. The atom gains 2 protons.
  b. The atom loses 2 protons.
  c. The atom gains 2 electrons.
  d. The atom loses 2 electrons.

9 The properties of ductility and malleability are associated with which type of bonds?

  a. ionic   **c.** metallic
  b. covalent   **d.** All of the above

10 What type of element tends to lose electrons when it forms bonds?

  a. metal   **c.** nonmetal
  b. metalloid   **d.** noble gas

11 Which pair of atoms can form an ionic bond? ✔0807.9.1

  a. sodium, Na, and potassium, K
  b. potassium, K, and fluorine, F
  c. fluorine, F, and chlorine, Cl
  d. sodium, Na, and neon, Ne

Short Answer

12 List two properties of covalent compounds. ✔0807.9.7

13 Explain why an iron ion is attracted to a sulfide ion but not to a zinc ion. ✔0807.9.8

14 Compare the three types of bonds based on what happens to the valence electrons of the atoms. ✔0807.9.8

Math Skills

15 For each atom below, write the number of electrons it must gain or lose to have 8 valence electrons. Then, calculate the charge of the ion that would form.

a. calcium, Ca

b. phosphorus, P

c. bromine, Br

d. sulfur, S

16 Concept Mapping Use the following terms to create a concept map: *chemical bonds, ionic bonds, covalent bonds, metallic bonds, molecule,* and *ions.*
✔0807.9.7, ✔0807.9.8

17 Identifying Relationships Predict the type of bond each of the following pairs of atoms would form: ✔0807.9.8

a. zinc, Zn, and zinc, Zn

b. oxygen, O, and nitrogen, N

c. phosphorus, P, and oxygen, O

d. magnesium, Mg, and chlorine, Cl

18 Applying Concepts Draw electron-dot diagrams for each of the following atoms, and state how many bonds it will have to make to fill its outer energy level. ✔0807.Inq.5

a. sulfur, S

b. nitrogen, N

c. neon, Ne

d. iodine, I

e. silicon, Si

19 Predicting Consequences Using your knowledge of valence electrons, explain the main reason so many different molecules are made from carbon atoms. ✔0807.9.7

20 Making Inferences Does the substance being hit in the photo below contain ionic or metallic bonds? Explain your answer. ✔0807.T/E.1

INTERPRETING GRAPHICS

Use the picture of a wooden pencil below to answer the questions that follow.

21 In which part of the pencil are metallic bonds found? ✔0807.9.7

22 List three materials in the pencil that are composed of molecules that have covalent bonds. ✔0807.9.7

23 Identify two differences between the properties of the material that has metallic bonds and the materials that have covalent bonds.

TCAP Test Preparation

TN **SPI 0807.Inq.4** Draw a conclusion that establishes a cause and effect relationship supported by evidence.

SPI 0807.9.1 Recognize that all matter consists of atoms.
SPI 0807.9.4 Differentiate between a mixture and a compound.

SPI 0807.9.9 Use the periodic table to determine the properties of an element.

Multiple Choice

Use the figure below to answer question 1.

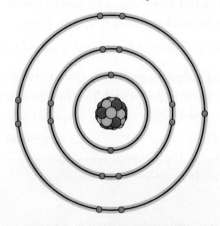

1. **What is the maximum number of electrons that can be held in the second energy level of an atom?**

   A. 2

   B. 7

   C. 8

   D. 9

2. **What happens when a nonmetal atom gains an electron from another atom? Energy is**

   A. given off by the atom losing the electron.

   B. given off by the atom gaining the electron.

   C. absorbed by the atom gaining the electron.

   D. transferred to the atom gaining the electron.

3. **An aluminum ion has 13 protons, 14 neutrons, and 10 electrons. What is the charge of an aluminum ion?**

   A. 10−

   B. 3−

   C. 1+

   D. 3+

4. **The atoms of elements in Group 17 of the periodic table are very reactive. Which of the following best describes the energy transfers that happen with the elements in this group?**

   A. The more easily an atom loses an electron, the less energy the atom releases.

   B. The more easily an atom gains an electron, the less energy the atom releases.

   C. The more easily an atom loses an electron, the more energy the atom releases.

   D. The more easily an atom gains an electron, the more energy the atom releases.

5. **Sodium chloride, or table salt, is a compound formed when a chlorine atom takes an electron from a neighboring sodium atom. Which of the following describes the force that holds the resulting chlorine particle and the resulting sodium particle together?**

   A. an ionic bond

   B. a neutral bond

   C. a metallic bond

   D. a covalent bond

Use the diagram below to answer question 6.

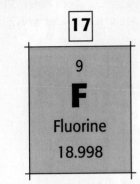

Periodic Table Listing for Fluorine

6. How many neutrons are in a typical fluorine atom?

A. 9

B. 10

C. 17

D. 19

7. What forms when atoms share one or more pairs of electrons?

A. covalent bond

B. ionic bond

C. valence electron

D. nonmetal ion

8. The ions that make up an ionic compound are bonded in a repeating three-dimensional pattern. What is this pattern called?

A. chloride lattice

B. covalent bond

C. crystal lattice

D. crystal pattern

9. What is a molecule?

A. the smallest particle of a substance that cannot be broken down any further by chemical bonding

B. a particle that forms when atoms gain or lose electrons

C. matter of particular or definite chemical composition

D. the smallest unit of a substance that keeps the physical and chemical properties of the substance

10. Juanita observes a model of two bonded atoms. She is told that the atoms are both nonmetals. She is looking at a model of

A. a covalent bond.

B. an acid.

C. an ionic bond.

D. a salt.

Open Response

11. Which of an atom's electrons are most likely to be involved in chemical bonding? Why?

12. Why don't the noble gases in Group 18 on the periodic table form chemical bonds?

Science in Action

Science, Technology, and Society

Superglue Bandages and Stitches

T/E If you aren't careful when using super-glue, you may accidentally learn that superglue quickly bonds skin together! This property of superglue led to the development of new kinds of superglue that can be used as alternatives for bandages and stitches. Using superglue to close wounds has several advantages over using bandages and stitches. For example, superglue ban-dages can cover cuts on parts of the body that are difficult to cover with regular ban-dages. And superglue stitches are less painful than regular stitches. Finally, wounds closed with superglue are easier to care for than wounds covered by bandages or closed with stitches. **GLE 0807.T/E.3**

Math ACTIVITY

A wound can be closed 3 times faster with glue than it can be with stitches. If it takes a doctor 27 min to close a wound by using stitches, how long would it take to close the same wound by using glue?

Weird Science

What Geckos Teach Scientists

T/E Geckos are known for their ability to climb up smooth surfaces. Scientists have developed a robot called Stickybot that mimics the gecko's sticky talent. Geckos have millions of microscopic hairlets on the bottom of their feet. At the end of each hair-let is a small pad. Each pad forms a *van der Waals force* with the surface on which the gecko is walking. A van der Waals force is an attraction similar to an ionic bond, but lasts only an instant and is much weaker. Because there are so many pads on a gecko's foot, the forces are strong enough to keep the gecko from falling. Stickybot has man-made fibers instead of hairlets but these also stick because of van der Waals forces. Future uses for this technology include climbing gloves and shoes, and perhaps even a rescue robot. **GLE 0807.T/E.1**

Language Arts ACTIVITY

Pick an organism that you would like to turn into a robot. What are some of the design advantages, disadvantages, and chal-lenges that would accompany your choice?

Roberta Jordan

Analytical Chemist Have you ever looked at something and wondered what chemicals it contained? That's what analytical chemists do for a living. They use tests to find the chemical makeup of a sample. Roberta Jordan is an analytical chemist at the Idaho National Engineering and Environmental Laboratory in Idaho Falls, Idaho.

Jordan's work focuses on the study of radioactive waste generated by nuclear power plants and nuclear-powered submarines. Jordan works with engineers to develop safe ways to store the radioactive waste. She tells the engineers which chemicals need to be studied and which techniques to use to study those chemicals.

Jordan enjoys her job because she is always learning new techniques. "One of the things necessary to be a good chemist is you have to be creative. You have to be able to think above and beyond the normal ways of doing things to come up with new ideas, new experiments," she explains. Jordan believes that a person interested in a career in chemistry has many opportunities. "There are a lot of things out there that need to be discovered," says Jordan.

GLE 0807.T/E.1

Social Studies ACTIVITY

Many elements in the periodic table were discovered by analytical chemists. Pick an element from the periodic table, and research its history. Make a poster about the discovery of that element.

GLE 0807.9.6

go.hrw.com

To learn more about these Science in Action topics, visit go.hrw.com and type in the keyword **HP5BNDF**.

Current Science

Check out Current Science® articles related to this chapter by visiting go.hrw.com. Just type in the keyword **HP5CS13**.

13

Chemical Reactions

The Big Idea

Substances undergo chemical reactions, which form new substances whose properties differ from the properties of the original substances.

TN Tennessee Science Standards

Embedded Inquiry

GLE 0807.Inq.1 Design and conduct open-ended scientific investigations.
GLE 0807.Inq.2 Use appropriate tools and techniques to gather, organize, analyze, and interpret data. **GLE 0807.Inq.3** Synthesize information to determine cause and effect relationships between evidence and explanations.
GLE 0807.Inq.5 Communicate scientific understanding using descriptions, explanations, and models. ✔**0807.Inq.1** Design and conduct an open-ended scientific investigation to answer a question that includes a control and appropriate variables. ✔**0807.Inq.2** Identify tools and techniques needed to gather, organize, analyze, and interpret data collected from a moderately complex scientific investigation. ✔**0807.Inq.3** Use evidence from a dataset to determine cause and effect relationships that explain a phenomenon. ✔**0807.Inq.5** Design a method to explain the results of an investigation using descriptions, explanations, or models.

Embedded Technology and Engineering

GLE 0807.T/E.1 Explore how technology responds to social, political, and economic needs. **GLE 0807.T/E.2** Know that the engineering design process involves an ongoing series of events that incorporate design constraints, model building, testing, evaluating, modifying, and retesting.
GLE 0807.T/E.3 Compare the intended benefits with the unintended consequences of a new technology.

Physical Science

GLE 0807.9.2 Explain that matter has properties that are determined by the structure and arrangement of its atoms. **GLE 0807.9.3** Interpret data from an investigation to differentiate between physical and chemical changes. **GLE 0807.9.4** Distinguish among elements, compounds, and mixtures. **GLE 0807.9.7** Explain the Law of Conservation of Mass. **GLE 0807.9.8** Interpret the events represented by a chemical equation. ✔**0807.9.5** Distinguish between elements and compounds by their symbols and formulas. ✔**0807.9.6** Differentiate between physical and chemical changes. ✔**0807.9.7** Describe how the characteristics of a compound are different than the characteristics of their component parts. ✔**0807.9.8** Determine the types of interactions between substances that result in a chemical change. ✔**0807.9.11** Use investigations of chemical and physical changes to describe the Law of Conservation of Mass. ✔**0807.9.12** Differentiate between the reactants and products of a chemical equation.

PRE-READING ACTIVITY

FOLDNOTES **Four-Corner Fold**
Before you read the chapter, create the FoldNote entitled "Four-Corner Fold" described in the **Study Skills** section of the Appendix. Label the flaps of the four-corner fold with "Chemical formulas," "Chemical equations," "Types of chemical reactions," and "Rates of chemical reactions." Write what you know about each topic under the appropriate flap. As you read the chapter, add other information that you learn.

About the Photo

Dazzling fireworks and the Statue of Liberty are great examples of chemical reactions. Chemical reactions cause fireworks to soar, explode, and light up the sky. And the Statue of Liberty has its distinctive green color because of the reaction between the statue's copper and chemicals in the air.

START-UP ACTIVITY

TN GLE 0807.Inq.2

A Model Formula

Chemicals react in very precise ways. In this activity, you will model a chemical reaction and will predict how chemicals react.

Procedure

1. You will receive **several marshmallow models.** The models are marshmallows attached by **toothpicks.** Each of these models is a Model A.

2. Your teacher will show you an example of Model B and Model C. Take apart one or more Model As to make copies of Model B and Model C.

3. If you have marshmallows left over, use them to make more Model Bs and Model Cs. If you need more parts to complete a Model B or Model C, take apart another Model A.

4. Repeat step 3 until you have no parts left over.

Analysis

1. How many Model As did you use to make copies of Model B and Model C?

2. How many Model Bs did you make? How many Model Cs did you make?

3. Suppose you needed to make six Model Bs. How many Model As would you need? How many Model Cs could you make with the leftover marshmallows?

Forming New Substances

Each fall, a beautiful change takes place when leaves turn colors. You see bright oranges and yellows that had been hidden by green all summer. What causes this change?

What You Will Learn

● Describe how chemical reactions produce new substances that have different chemical and physical properties.

● Identify four signs that indicate that a chemical reaction might be taking place.

● Explain what happens to chemical bonds during a chemical reaction.

Vocabulary

chemical reaction
precipitate

READING STRATEGY

Reading Organizer As you read this section, create an outline of the section. Use the headings from the section in your outline.

TN **GLE 0807.Inq.2** Use appropriate tools and techniques to gather, organize, analyze, and interpret data.

GLE 0807.Inq.3 Synthesize information to determine cause and effect relationships between evidence and explanations.

GLE 0807.Inq.5 Communicate scientific understanding using descriptions, explanations, and models.

GLE 0807.9.2 Explain that matter has properties that are determined by the structure and arrangement of its atoms.

GLE 0807.9.3 Interpret data from an investigation to differentiate between physical and chemical changes.

To answer this question, you need to know what causes leaves to be green. Leaves are green because they contain a green substance, or *pigment*. This pigment is called *chlorophyll* (KLAWR uh FIL). During the spring and summer, the leaves have a large amount of chlorophyll in them. But in the fall, when temperatures drop and there are fewer hours of sunlight, chlorophyll breaks down to form new substances that have no color. The green chlorophyll is no longer present to hide the other pigments. You can now see the orange and yellow colors that were present all along.

Chemical Reactions

A chemical change takes place when chlorophyll breaks down into new substances. This change is an example of a chemical reaction. A **chemical reaction** is a process in which one or more substances change to make one or more new substances. The chemical and physical properties of the new substances differ from those of the original substances. Some results of chemical reactions are shown in **Figure 1.**

Figure 1 Results of Chemical Reactions

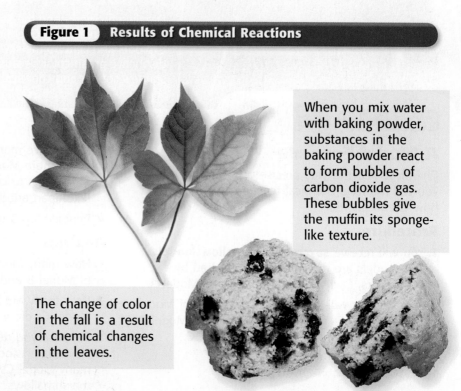

When you mix water with baking powder, substances in the baking powder react to form bubbles of carbon dioxide gas. These bubbles give the muffin its sponge-like texture.

The change of color in the fall is a result of chemical changes in the leaves.

Signs of Chemical Reactions

How can you tell when a chemical reaction is taking place? **Figure 2** shows some signs that tell you that a reaction may be taking place. In some chemical reactions, gas bubbles form. Other reactions form solid precipitates (pree SIP uh TAYTS). A **precipitate** is a solid substance that is formed in a solution. During other chemical reactions, energy is given off. This energy may be in the form of light, thermal energy, or electrical energy. Reactions often have more than one of these signs. And the more of these signs that you see, the more likely that a chemical reaction is taking place.

chemical reaction the process by which one or more substances change to produce one or more different substances

precipitate a solid that is produced as a result of a chemical reaction in solution

TN *Standards Check* What are some signs of a chemical reaction? ✔0807.9.6

Figure 2 Some Signs of Chemical Reactions

Gas Formation
The chemical reaction in the beaker has formed a brown gas, nitrogen dioxide. This gas is formed when a strip of copper is placed into nitric acid.

Solid Formation
Here you see potassium chromate solution being added to a silver nitrate solution. The dark red solid is a precipitate of silver chromate.

Energy Change
Energy is released during some chemical reactions. The fire in this photo gives off light energy and thermal energy. During some other chemical reactions, energy is taken in.

Color Change
Don't spill chlorine bleach on your jeans! The bleach reacts with the blue dye on the fabric and causes the color of the material to change.

A Change of Properties

Even though the signs we look for to see if a reaction is taking place are good signals of chemical reactions, they do not guarantee that a reaction is happening. For example, gas can be given off when a liquid boils. But this example is a physical change, not a chemical reaction.

So, how can you be sure that a chemical reaction is occurring? The most important sign is the formation of new substances that have different properties. Look at **Figure 3.** The starting materials in this reaction are sugar and sulfuric acid. Several things tell you that a chemical reaction is taking place. Bubbles form, a gas is given off, and the beaker becomes very hot. But most important, new substances form. And the properties of these substances are very different from those of the starting substances.

TN Standards Check What is the most important sign that a chemical reaction, rather than a physical change, has occurred? ✔0807.9.6

Figure 3 *The top photo shows the starting substances: table sugar and sulfuric acid, a clear liquid. The substances formed in this chemical reaction are very different from the starting substances.*

Bonds: Holding Molecules Together

A *chemical bond* is a force that holds two atoms together in a molecule. For a chemical reaction to take place, the original bonds must break and new bonds must form.

Breaking and Making Bonds

How do new substances form in a chemical reaction? First, chemical bonds in the starting substances must break. Molecules are always moving. If the molecules bump into each other with enough energy, the chemical bonds in the molecules break. The atoms then rearrange, and new bonds form to make the new substances. **Figure 4** shows how bonds break and form in the reaction between hydrogen and chlorine.

✓ Reading Check What happens to the bonds of substances during a chemical reaction?

Figure 4 Reaction of Hydrogen and Chlorine

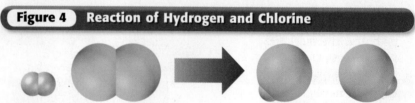

hydrogen   +   chlorine   hydrogen chloride

Breaking Bonds Hydrogen and chlorine are diatomic. Diatomic molecules are two atoms bonded together. The bonds joining these atoms must first break before the atoms can react with each other.

Making Bonds A new substance, hydrogen chloride, forms as new bonds are made between hydrogen atoms and chlorine atoms.

New Bonds, New Substances

What happens when hydrogen and chlorine are combined? A chlorine gas molecule is a diatomic (DIE uh TAHM ik) molecule. That is, a chlorine molecule is made of two atoms of chlorine. Chlorine gas has a greenish yellow color. Hydrogen gas is also a diatomic molecule. Hydrogen gas is a flammable, colorless gas. When chlorine gas and hydrogen gas react, the bond between the hydrogen atoms breaks. And the bond between the chlorine atoms also breaks. A new bond forms between each hydrogen and chlorine atom. A new substance, hydrogen chloride, is formed. Hydrogen chloride is a nonflammable, colorless gas. Its properties differ from the properties of both of the starting substances.

Let's look at another example. Sodium is a metal that reacts violently in water. Chlorine gas is poisonous. When chlorine gas and sodium react, the result is sodium chloride, or table salt, a familiar substance that almost everyone uses. The salt's properties are very different from sodium's or chlorine's. Salt is a new substance.

TN Standards Check How are the properties of salt different from the properties of of sodium and chlorine? ✔0807.9.7

TN GLE 0808.Inq.2, GLE 0807.Inq.3, GLE 0807.9.3

Reaction Ready

1. Place a **piece of chalk** in a **plastic cup**.
2. Add **5 mL of vinegar** to the cup. Record your observations.
3. What evidence of a chemical reaction do you see? ✔0807.9.6
4. What type of new substance was formed?

SECTION Review

TN GLE 0807.INQ.5, GLE 0807.9.2, GLE 0807.9.3

Summary

- A chemical reaction is a process by which substances change to produce new substances with new chemical and physical properties.
- Signs that indicate a chemical reaction has taken place are a color change, formation of a gas or a solid, and release of energy.
- During a reaction, bonds are broken, atoms are rearranged, and new bonds are formed.

Using Key Terms

1. Use the following terms in the same sentence: *chemical reaction* and *precipitate*.

Understanding Key Ideas

2. Most chemical reactions ✔0807.9.6
   a. result in substances that have different properties.
   b. do not break bonds.
   c. do not rearrange atoms.
   d. have no effects that can be seen.

3. If the chemical properties of a substance have not changed, has a chemical reaction occurred? ✔0807.9.6

Critical Thinking

4. **Analyzing Processes** Steam is escaping from a teapot. Is this a chemical or a physical change? Explain. ✔0807.9.6

5. **Applying Concepts** Explain why charcoal burning in a grill is a chemical change.

Interpreting Graphics

Use the photo below to answer the questions that follow.

6. What evidence of a chemical reaction is shown in the photo?

7. What is happening to the bonds of the starting substances?

Internet Resources

For a variety of links related to this chapter, go to www.scilinks.org

Topic: Chemical Reactions
SciLinks code: HSM0274

Chemical Formulas and Equations

What You Will Learn

- Interpret and write simple chemical formulas.
- Write and balance simple chemical equations.
- Explain how a balanced equation shows the law of conservation of mass.

Vocabulary

chemical formula
chemical equation
reactant
product
law of conservation of mass

TN GLE 0807.Inq.2 Use appropriate tools and techniques to gather, organize, analyze, and interpret data.

GLE 0807.Inq.5 Communicate scientific understanding using descriptions, explanations, and models.

GLE 0807.9.2 Explain that matter has properties that are determined by the structure and arrangement of its atoms.

GLE 0807.9.7 Explain the Law of Conservation of Mass.

GLE 0807.9.8 Interpret the events represented by a chemical equation.

chemical formula a combination of chemical symbols and numbers to represent a substance

How many words can you make using the 26 letters of the alphabet? Many thousands? Now, think of how many sentences you can make with all of those words.

Letters are used to form words. In the same way, chemical symbols are put together to make chemical formulas that describe substances. Chemical formulas can be placed together to describe a chemical reaction, just like words can be put together to make a sentence.

Chemical Formulas

All substances are formed from about 100 elements. Each element has its own chemical symbol. A **chemical formula** is a shorthand way to use chemical symbols and numbers to represent a substance. A chemical formula shows how many atoms of each kind are present in a molecule.

As shown in **Figure 1,** the chemical formula for water is H_2O. This formula tells you that one water molecule is made of two atoms of hydrogen and one atom of oxygen. The small 2 in the formula is a subscript. A *subscript* is a number written below and to the right of a chemical symbol in a formula. Sometimes, a symbol, such as O for oxygen in water's formula, has no subscript. If there is no subscript, only one atom of that element is present. Look at **Figure 1** for more examples of chemical formulas.

Figure 1   Chemical Formulas of Different Substances

Water

$$H_2O$$

Oxygen

$$O_2$$

Glucose

$$C_6H_{12}O_6$$

Water molecules are made up of 3 atoms—2 atoms of hydrogen bonded to 1 atom of oxygen.

Oxygen is a diatomic molecule. Each molecule has 2 atoms of oxygen bonded together.

Glucose molecules have 6 atoms of carbon, 12 atoms of hydrogen, and 6 atoms of oxygen.

Carbon dioxide

CO_2

The *absence of a prefix* indicates one carbon atom.

The prefix *di-* indicates two oxygen atoms.

Dinitrogen monoxide

N_2O

The prefix *di-* indicates two nitrogen atoms.

The prefix *mono-* indicates one oxygen atom.

Figure 2 *The formulas of these covalent compounds can be written by using the prefixes in the names of the compounds.*

Writing Formulas for Covalent Compounds

If you know the name of the covalent compound, you can often write the chemical formula for that compound. Covalent compounds are usually composed of two nonmetals. The names of many covalent compounds use prefixes. Each prefix represents a number, as shown in **Table 1.** The prefixes tell you how many atoms of each element are in a formula. **Figure 2** shows you how to write a chemical formula from the name of a covalent compound.

Table 1	Prefixes Used in Chemical Names		
mono-	1	hexa-	6
di-	2	hepta-	7
tri-	3	octa-	8
tetra-	4	nona-	9
penta-	5	deca-	10

Writing Formulas for Ionic Compounds

If the name of a compound contains the name of a metal and the name of a nonmetal, the compound is ionic. To write the formula for an ionic compound, make sure the compound's charge is 0. In other words, the formula must have subscripts that cause the charges of the ions to cancel out. **Figure 3** shows you how to write a chemical formula from the name of an ionic compound.

✓ *Reading Check* What kinds of elements make up an ionic compound?

Sodium chloride

NaCl

A sodium ion has a **1+ charge.**

A chloride ion has a **1− charge.**

One sodium ion and one chloride ion have an overall **charge of (1+) + (1−) = 0**

Magnesium chloride

$MgCl_2$

A magnesium ion has a **2+ charge.**

A chloride ion has a **1− charge.**

One magnesium ion and two chloride ions have an overall **charge of (2+) + 2(1−) = 0.**

Figure 3 *The formula of an ionic compound is written by using enough of each ion so that the overall charge is 0.*

Figure 4 *Like chemical symbols, the symbols on this musical score are understood around the world!*

chemical equation a representation of a chemical reaction that uses symbols to show the relationship between the reactants and the products ◼TN▶*VOCAB*

reactant a substance or molecule that participates in a chemical reaction ◼TN▶*VOCAB*

product the substance that forms in a chemical reaction ◼TN▶*VOCAB*

Chemical Equations

Think about a piece of music, such as the one in **Figure 4.** Someone writing music must tell the musician what notes to play, how long to play each note, and how each note should be played. Words aren't used to describe the musical piece. Instead, musical symbols are used. The symbols can be understood by anyone who can read music.

Describing Reactions by Using Equations

In the same way that composers use musical symbols, chemists around the world use chemical symbols and chemical formulas. Instead of changing words and sentences into other languages to describe reactions, chemists use chemical equations. A **chemical equation** uses chemical symbols and formulas as a shortcut to describe a chemical reaction. A chemical equation is short and is understood by anyone who understands chemical formulas.

From Reactants to Products

When carbon burns, it reacts with oxygen to form carbon dioxide. **Figure 5** shows how a chemist would use an equation to describe this reaction. The starting materials in a chemical reaction are **reactants** (ree AK tuhnts). The substances formed from a reaction are **products.** In this example, carbon and oxygen are reactants. Carbon dioxide is the product.

◼TN▶ **Standards Check** What is the difference between reactants and products in a chemical reaction? ✔0807.9.12

Figure 5 The Parts of a Chemical Equation

Charcoal is used to cook food on a barbecue grill. When carbon in charcoal reacts with oxygen in the air, the primary product is carbon dioxide, as shown by the chemical equation.

The formulas of the **reactants** are written before the arrow.

The formulas of the **products** are written after the arrow.

$$C + O_2 \longrightarrow CO_2$$

A **plus sign** separates the formulas of two or more reactants or products from one another.

The **arrow,** also called the *yields sign,* separates the formulas of the reactants from the formulas of the products.

Figure 6 Examples of Similar Symbols and Formulas

CO_2

The chemical formula for the compound **carbon dioxide** is CO_2. Carbon dioxide is a colorless, odorless gas that you exhale.

CO

The chemical formula for the compound **carbon monoxide** is CO. Carbon monoxide is a colorless, odorless, and poisonous gas.

Co

The chemical symbol for the element **cobalt** is Co. Cobalt is a hard, bluish gray metal.

The Importance of Accuracy

The symbol or formula for each substance in the equation must be written correctly. For a compound, use the correct chemical formula. For an element, use the proper chemical symbol. An equation that has the wrong chemical symbol or formula will not correctly describe the reaction. In fact, even a simple mistake can make a huge difference. **Figure 6** shows how formulas and symbols can be mistaken.

The Reason Equations Must Be Balanced

Atoms are never lost or gained in a chemical reaction. They are just rearranged. Every atom in the reactants becomes part of the products. When writing a chemical equation, make sure the number of atoms of each element in the reactants equals the number of atoms of those elements in the products. This is called balancing the equation.

Balancing equations comes from the work of a French chemist, Antoine Lavoisier (lah vwah ZYAY). In the 1700s, Lavoisier found that the total mass of the reactants was always the same as the total mass of the products. Lavoisier's work led to the **law of conservation of mass.** This law states that mass is neither created nor destroyed in ordinary chemical and physical changes. This law means that a chemical equation must show the same numbers and kinds of atoms on both sides of the arrow.

Counting Atoms

Some chemical formulas contain parentheses. When counting atoms, multiply everything inside the parentheses by the subscript. For example, $Ca(NO_3)_2$ has one calcium atom, two (2×1) nitrogen atoms, and six (2×3) oxygen atoms. Find the number of atoms of each element in the formulas $Mg(OH)_2$ and $Al_2(SO_4)_3$.

law of conservation of mass the law that states that mass cannot be created or destroyed in ordinary chemical and physical changes ◢**TN** ◤*VOCAB*

How to Balance an Equation

To balance an equation, you must use coefficients (кон uh FISH uhnts). A *coefficient* is a number that is placed in front of a chemical symbol or formula. For example, 2CO represents two carbon monoxide molecules. The number *2* is the coefficient.

For an equation to be balanced, all atoms must be counted. So, you must multiply the subscript of each element in a formula by the formula's coefficient. For example, $2H_2O$ contains a total of four hydrogen atoms and two oxygen atoms. Only coefficients—not subscripts—are changed when balancing equations. Changing the subscripts in the formula of a compound would change the compound. **Figure 7** shows you how to use coefficients to balance an equation.

✓ **Reading Check** If you see $4O_2$ in an equation, what is the coefficient?

CONNECTION TO Language Arts

WRITING SKILL **Diatomic Molecules** Seven of the chemical elements exist as diatomic molecules. Do research to find out which seven elements these are. Write a short report that describes each diatomic molecule. Be sure to include the formula for each molecule.

Figure 7 Balancing a Chemical Equation

Follow these steps to write a balanced equation for $H_2 + O_2 \longrightarrow H_2O$.

① **Count the atoms** of each element in the reactants and in the products. You can see that there are fewer oxygen atoms in the product than in the reactants.

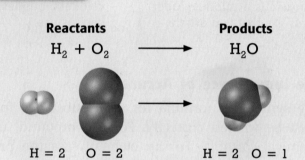

Reactants
$H_2 + O_2 \longrightarrow$

Products
H_2O

H = 2   O = 2   H = 2   O = 1

② **To balance the oxygen atoms,** place the coefficient 2 in front of H_2O. Doing so gives you two oxygen atoms in both the reactants and the products. But now there are too few hydrogen atoms in the reactants.

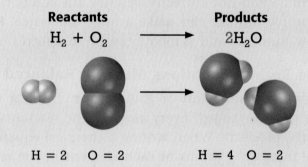

Reactants
$H_2 + O_2 \longrightarrow$

Products
$2H_2O$

H = 2   O = 2   H = 4   O = 2

③ **To balance the hydrogen atoms,** place the coefficient 2 in front of H_2. But to be sure that your answer is correct, always double-check your work!

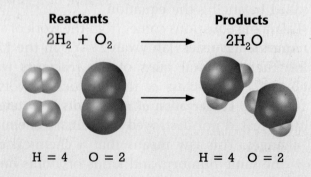

Reactants
$2H_2 + O_2 \longrightarrow$

Products
$2H_2O$

H = 4   O = 2   H = 4   O = 2

Quick Lab

Conservation of Mass

1. Place **5 g of baking soda** into a **sealable plastic bag.**

2. Place **5 mL of vinegar** into a **plastic film canister.** Put the lid on the canister.

3. Place the canister into the bag. Squeeze the air out of the bag. Seal the bag tightly.

4. Use a **balance** to measure the mass of the bag and its contents. Record the mass.

5. Keeping the bag closed, open the canister in the bag. Mix the vinegar with the baking soda. Record your observations.

6. When the reaction has stopped, measure the mass of the bag and its contents. Record the mass.

7. Compare the mass of the materials before the reaction and the mass of the materials after the reaction. Explain your observations. ✔0807.9.11

SECTION Review

TN GLE 0807.Inq.2, GLE 0807.Inq.5, GLE 0807.9.7, GLE 0807.9.8

Summary

- A chemical formula uses symbols and subscripts to represent a compound.

- Chemical formulas can often be written from the names of covalent and ionic compounds.

- A chemical equation uses chemical formulas, chemical symbols, and coefficients to describe a reaction.

- Balancing an equation requires that the same numbers and kinds of atoms be on each side of the equation.

- A balanced equation illustrates the law of conservation of mass.

Using Key Terms

The statements below are false. For each statement, replace the underlined word to make a true statement.

1. A chemical <u>formula</u> describes a chemical reaction.

2. The substances formed from a chemical reaction are <u>reactants</u>.

Understanding Key Ideas

3. The correct chemical formula for carbon tetrachloride is

   a. CCl_3. **c.** CCl.

   b. C_3Cl. **d.** CCl_4.

4. Calcium oxide is used to make soil less acidic. Its formula is

   a. Ca_2O_2. **c.** CaO_2.

   b. CaO. **d.** Ca_2O.

5. Balance the following equations by adding the correct coefficients.

   a. $Na + Cl_2 \longrightarrow NaCl$

   b. $Mg + N_2 \longrightarrow Mg_3N_2$

6. How does a balanced chemical equation illustrate that mass is never lost or gained in a chemical reaction?

7. Identify the reactants and product(s) in the following equation. $C + O_2 \rightarrow CO_2$ ✔0807.9.12

Math Skills

8. Calculate the number of atoms of each element represented in each of the following compounds: $2Na_3PO_4$, $4Al_2(SO_4)_3$, and $6PCl_5$. ✔0807.9.5

Critical Thinking

9. **Analyzing Methods** Describe how to write a formula for a covalent compound. Give an example of a covalent compound.

10. **Applying Concepts** Explain why the subscript in a formula of a chemical compound cannot be changed when balancing an equation.

Internet Resources

For a variety of links related to this chapter, go to www.scilinks.org

Topic: Chemical Formulas; Chemical Equations

SciLinks code: HSM0271; HSM0269

Types of Chemical Reactions

What You Will Learn

● Describe four types of chemical reactions.

● Classify a chemical equation as one of four types of chemical reactions.

Vocabulary

synthesis reaction
decomposition reaction
single-displacement reaction
double-displacement reaction

READING STRATEGY

Mnemonics As you read this section, create a mnemonic device to help you remember the four types of chemical reactions.

TN **GLE 0807.Inq.2** Use appropriate tools and techniques to gather, organize, analyze, and interpret data.

GLE 0807.Inq.5 Communicate scientific understanding using descriptions, explanations, and models.

GLE 0807.T/E.1 Explore how technology responds to social, political, and economic needs.

GLE 0807.T/E.3 Compare the intended benefits with the unintended consequences of a new technology.

GLE 0807.9.3 Interpret data from an investigation to differentiate between physical and chemical changes.

GLE 0807.9.4 Distinguish among elements, compounds, and mixtures.

GLE 0807.9.8 Interpret the events represented by a chemical equation.

There are thousands of known chemical reactions. Can you imagine having to memorize even 50 of them?

Remembering all of them would be impossible! But fortunately, there is help. In the same way that the elements are divided into groups based on their properties, reactions can be classified based on what occurs during the reaction.

Most reactions can be placed into one of four categories: synthesis (SIN thuh sis), decomposition, single-displacement, and double-displacement. Each type of reaction has a pattern that shows how reactants become products. One way to remember what happens in each type of reaction is to imagine people at a dance. As you learn about each type of reaction, study the models of students at a dance. The models will help you recognize each type of reaction.

Synthesis Reactions

A **synthesis reaction** is a reaction in which two or more substances combine to form one new compound. For example, a synthesis reaction takes place when sodium reacts with chlorine. This synthesis reaction produces sodium chloride, which you know as table salt. A synthesis reaction would be modeled by two people pairing up to form a dancing couple, as shown in **Figure 1.**

TN *Standards Check* What is a synthesis reaction? ✔0807.9.8

$$2Na + Cl_2 \longrightarrow 2NaCl$$

Figure 1 *Sodium reacts with chlorine to form sodium chloride in this synthesis reaction.*

$$H_2CO_3 \longrightarrow H_2O + CO_2$$

Figure 2 *In this decomposition reaction, carbonic acid, H_2CO_3, decomposes to form water and carbon dioxide.*

Decomposition Reactions

A **decomposition reaction** is a reaction in which a single compound breaks down to form two or more simpler substances. Decomposition is the reverse of synthesis. The dance model for a decomposition reaction would be a couple that finishes a dance and separates, as shown in **Figure 2.**

TN *Standards Check* How is a decomposition reaction different from a synthesis reaction? ✔0807.9.8

Single-Displacement Reactions

Sometimes, an element replaces another element that is a part of a compound. This type of reaction is called a **single-displacement reaction.** The products of single-displacement reactions are a new compound and a different element. The dance model for a single-displacement reaction would show a person cutting in on a couple who is dancing. A new couple is formed. And a different person is left alone, as shown in **Figure 3.**

synthesis reaction a reaction in which two or more substances combine to form a new compound

decomposition reaction a reaction in which a single compound breaks down to form two or more simpler substances

single-displacement reaction a reaction in which one element or radical takes the place of another element or radical in a compound

Figure 3 *Zinc replaces the hydrogen in hydrochloric acid to form zinc chloride and hydrogen gas in this single-displacement reaction.*

$$Zn + 2HCl \longrightarrow ZnCl_2 + H_2$$

Figure 4 **Reactivity of Elements**

Cu + 2AgNO₃ ⟶ 2Ag + Cu(NO₃)₂ **Ag + Cu(NO₃)₂ ⟶ no reaction**
Copper is more reactive than silver.   Silver is less reactive than copper.

 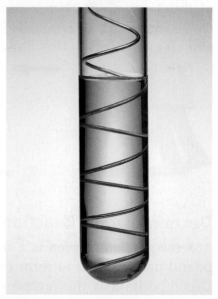

Reactivity of Elements

In a single-displacement reaction, a more reactive element can displace a less reactive element in a compound. For example, **Figure 4** shows that copper is more reactive than silver. Copper (Cu) can replace the silver (Ag) ion in the compound silver nitrate. But the opposite reaction does not occur, because silver is less reactive than copper.

The elements in Group 1 of the periodic table are the most reactive metals. Very few nonmetals are involved in single-displacement reactions. In fact, only Group 17 nonmetals participate in single-displacement reactions.

TN *Standards Check* Why can one element sometimes replace another element in a single-displacement reaction? ✔0807.9.8

INTERNET ACTIVITY

For another activity related to this chapter, go to **go.hrw.com** and type in the keyword **HP5REAW.**

TN GLE 0807.Inq.5, GLE 0807.9.8

Identifying Reactions

1. Study each of the following equations:

    4Na + O₂ ⟶ 2Na₂O   P₄ + 5O₂ ⟶ 2P₂O₅

    2Ag₃N ⟶ 6Ag + N₂   Zn + 2HCl ⟶ ZnCl₂ + H₂

2. Build models of each of these reactions using **colored clay.** Choose a different color of clay to represent each kind of atom.

3. Identify each type of reaction as a synthesis, decomposition, or single-displacement reaction. ✔0807.9.8

Double-Displacement Reactions

A **double-displacement reaction** is a reaction in which ions from two compounds exchange places. One of the products of this type of reaction is often a gas or a precipitate. A dance model of a double-displacement reaction would be two couples dancing and then trading partners, as shown in **Figure 5.**

double-displacement reaction
a reaction in which a gas, a solid precipitate, or a molecular compound forms from the exchange of ions between two compounds

$$NaCl + AgF \longrightarrow NaF + AgCl$$

Figure 5 *A double-displacement reaction occurs when sodium chloride reacts with silver fluoride to form sodium fluoride and silver chloride (a precipitate).*

SECTION Review

TN GLE 0807.Inq.5, GLE 0807.9.4, GLE 0807.9.8

Summary

- A synthesis reaction is a reaction in which two or more substances combine to form a compound.
- A decomposition reaction is a reaction in which a compound breaks down to form two or more simpler substances.
- A single-displacement reaction is a reaction in which an element takes the place of another element that is part of a compound.
- A double-displacement reaction is a reaction in which ions in two compounds exchange places.

Using Key Terms

1. In your own words, write a definition for each of the following terms: *synthesis reaction* and *decomposition reaction.*

Understanding Key Ideas

2. What type of reaction does the following equation represent? ✔0807.9.8

    $$FeS + 2HCl \longrightarrow FeCl_2 + H_2S$$

    a. synthesis reaction
    b. double-displacement reaction
    c. single-displacement reaction
    d. decomposition reaction

3. Describe the difference between single- and double-displacement reactions. ✔0807.9.8

Math Skills

4. Write the balanced equation in which potassium iodide, KI, reacts with chlorine to form potassium chloride, KCl, and iodine. ✔0807.9.12

Critical Thinking

5. **Analyzing Processes** The first reaction below is a single-displacement reaction that could occur in a laboratory. Explain why the second combination results in no reaction.

    $$CuCl_2 + Fe \longrightarrow FeCl_2 + Cu$$
    $$CaS + Al \longrightarrow no\ reaction$$

6. **Making Inferences** When two white compounds are mixed in a solution, a yellow solid forms. What kind of reaction has taken place? Explain your answer. ✔0807.9.8

Internet Resources

For a variety of links related to this chapter, go to www.scilinks.org

Topic: Reaction Types
SciLinks code: HSM1272

Energy and Rates of Chemical Reactions

What You Will Learn

● Compare exothermic and endothermic reactions.
● Explain activation energy.
● Interpret an energy diagram.
● Describe five factors that affect the rate of a reaction.

Vocabulary

exothermic reaction
endothermic reaction
law of conservation of energy
activation energy
inhibitor
catalyst

TN GLE 0807.Inq.2 Use appropriate tools and techniques to gather, organize, analyze, and interpret data.

GLE 0807.Inq.3 Synthesize information to determine cause and effect relationships between evidence and explanations.

GLE 0807.Inq.5 Communicate scientific understanding using descriptions, explanations, and models.

GLE 0807.T/E.1 Explore how technology responds to social, political, and economic needs.

GLE 0807.9.4 Distinguish among elements, compounds, and mixtures.

GLE 0807.9.8 Interpret the events represented by a chemical equation.

exothermic reaction a chemical reaction in which heat is released to the surroundings **TN** *VOCAB*

What is the difference between eating a meal and running a mile? You could say that a meal gives you energy, while running "uses up" energy.

Chemical reactions can be described in the same way. Some reactions release energy, and other reactions absorb energy.

Reactions and Energy

Chemical energy is part of all chemical reactions. Energy is needed to break chemical bonds in the reactants. As new bonds form in the products, energy is released. By comparing the chemical energy of the reactants with the chemical energy of the products, you can decide if energy is released or absorbed in the overall reaction.

Exothermic Reactions

A chemical reaction in which energy is released is called an **exothermic reaction.** *Exo* means "go out" or "exit." *Thermic* means "heat" or "energy." Exothermic reactions can give off energy in several forms, as shown in **Figure 1.** The energy released in an exothermic reaction is often written as a product in a chemical equation, as in this equation:

$$2Na + Cl_2 \longrightarrow 2NaCl + energy$$

Figure 1 Types of Energy Released in Exothermic Reactions

Light energy is released in the exothermic reaction that is taking place in these light sticks.

Electrical energy is released in the exothermic reaction that will take place in this battery.

Light and thermal energy are released in the exothermic reaction taking place in this campfire.

Endothermic Reactions

A chemical reaction in which energy is taken in is called an **endothermic reaction.** *Endo* means "go in." The energy that is taken in during an endothermic reaction is often written as a reactant in a chemical equation. Energy as a reactant is shown in the following equation:

$$2H_2O + energy \longrightarrow 2H_2 + O_2$$

An example of an endothermic process is photosynthesis. In photosynthesis, plants use light energy from the sun to produce glucose. Glucose is a simple sugar that is used for nutrition. The equation that describes photosynthesis is the following:

$$6CO_2 + 6H_2O + energy \longrightarrow C_6H_{12}O_6 + 6O_2$$

Reading Check What is an endothermic reaction?

endothermic reaction a chemical reaction that requires heat ▰ℕ▰ *VOCAB*

law of conservation of energy the law that states that energy cannot be created or destroyed but can be changed from one form to another

The Law of Conservation of Energy

Neither mass nor energy can be created or destroyed in chemical reactions. The **law of conservation of energy** states that energy cannot be created or destroyed. However, energy can change forms. And energy can be transferred from one object to another in the same way that a baton is transferred from one runner to another runner, as shown in **Figure 2.**

The energy released in exothermic reactions was first stored in the chemical bonds in the reactants. And the energy taken in during endothermic reactions is stored in the products. If you could measure all the energy in a reaction, you would find that the total amount of energy (of all types) is the same before and after the reaction.

Figure 2 *Energy can be transferred from one object to another object in the same way that a baton is transferred from one runner to another runner in a relay race.*

TN GLE 0807.Inq.2, GLE 0807.9.3

Endo Alert

1. Fill a **plastic cup** half full with **calcium chloride solution.**
2. Measure the temperature of the solution by using a **thermometer.**
3. Carefully add **1 tsp of baking soda.**
4. Record your observations.
5. When the reaction has stopped, record the temperature of the solution.
6. What evidence that an endothermic reaction took place did you observe? ✔0807.9.8

Figure 3 *Chemical reactions need energy to get started in the same way that a bowling ball needs a push to get rolling.*

Rates of Reactions

A reaction takes place only if the particles of reactants collide. But there must be enough energy to break the bonds that hold particles together in a molecule. The speed at which new particles form is called the *rate of a reaction*.

Activation Energy

Before the bowling ball in **Figure 3** can roll down the alley, the bowler must first put in some energy to start the ball rolling. A chemical reaction must also get a boost of energy before the reaction can start. This boost of energy is called activation energy. **Activation energy** is the smallest amount of energy that molecules need to react.

Another example of activation energy is striking a match. Before a match can be used to light a campfire, the match has to be lit! A strike-anywhere match has all the reactants it needs to burn. The chemicals on a match react and burn. But, the chemicals will not light by themselves. You must strike the match against a surface. The heat produced by this friction provides the activation energy needed to start the reaction.

activation energy the minimum amount of energy required to start a chemical reaction

✓ *Reading Check* What is activation energy?

Sources of Activation Energy

Friction is one source of activation energy. In the match example, friction provides the energy needed to break the bonds in the reactants and allow new bonds to form. An electric spark in a car's engine is another source of activation energy. This spark begins the burning of gasoline. Light can also be a source of activation energy for a reaction. **Figure 4** shows how activation energy relates to exothermic reactions and endothermic reactions.

TN ▶ GLE 0807.T/E.1

CONNECTION TO Technology

WRITING SKILL **T/E** **The Strike-Anywhere Match** Research the invention of the strike-anywhere match. Find out who invented it, who patented it, and when the match was introduced to the public. In your **science journal,** write a short report about what you learn from your research.

Figure 4 Energy Diagrams

Exothermic Reaction Once an exothermic reaction starts, it can continue. The energy given off as the product forms continues to supply the activation energy needed for the substances to react.

Endothermic Reaction An endothermic reaction continues to absorb energy. Energy must be used to provide the activation energy needed for the substances to react.

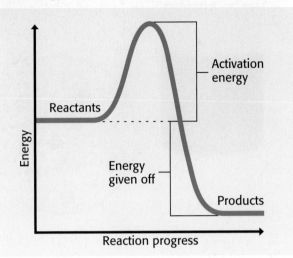

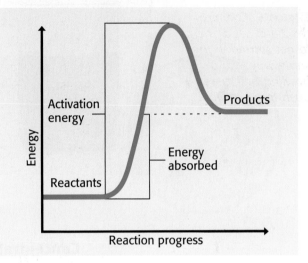

Factors Affecting Rates of Reactions

The rate of a reaction is a measure of how fast the reaction takes place. Recall that the rate of a reaction depends on how fast new particles form. There are four factors that affect the rate of a reaction. These factors are: temperature, concentration, surface area, and the presence of an inhibitor or catalyst.

Temperature

A higher temperature causes a faster rate of reaction, as shown in **Figure 5**. At high temperatures, particles of reactants move quickly. The rapid movement causes the particles to collide often and with a lot of energy. So, many particles have the activation energy to react. And many reactants can change into products in a short time.

Figure 5 *The light stick on the right glows brighter than the one on the left because the one on the right is warmer. The higher temperature causes the rate of the reaction to increase.*

TN GLE 0807.Inq.2

Which Is Quicker?

1. Fill a **clear plastic cup** with **250 mL of warm water.** Fill a **second clear plastic cup** with **250 mL of cold water.**

2. Place **one-quarter of an effervescent tablet** in each of the two cups of water at the same time. Using a **stopwatch,** time each reaction.

3. Observe each reaction, and record your observations.

4. In which cup did the reaction occur at a faster rate?

Figure 6 **Concentration of Solutions**

▼ When the amount of copper sulfate crystals dissolved in water is **small,** the concentration of the copper sulfate solution is **low.**

▼ When the amount of copper sulfate crystals dissolved in water is **large,** the concentration of the copper sulfate solution is **high.**

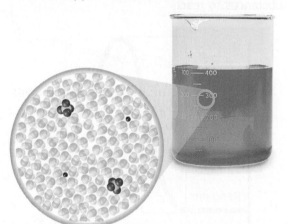

TN GLE 0807.Inq.5, GLE 0807.T/E.1

CONNECTION TO Biology

Enzymes and Inhibitors Enzymes are proteins that speed up reactions in your body. Sometimes, chemicals called *inhibitors* stop the action of enzymes. Research how inhibitors are beneficial in reactions in the human body. Make a poster or a model that explains what you have learned, and present it to your class.

ACTIVITY

inhibitor a substance that slows down or stops a chemical reaction

catalyst a substance that changes the rate of a chemical reaction without being used up or changed very much

Concentration

In general, a high concentration of reactants causes a fast rate of a reaction. *Concentration* is a measure of the amount of one substance dissolved in another substance, as shown in **Figure 6.** When the concentration is high, there are many reactant particles in a given volume. So, there is a small distance between particles. The particles run into each other often. Thus, the particles react faster.

✓ **Reading Check** How does a high concentration of reactants increase the rate of a reaction?

Surface Area

Surface area is the amount of exposed surface of a substance. Increasing the surface area of solid reactants increases the rate of a reaction. Grinding a solid into a powder makes a larger surface area. Greater surface area exposes more particles of the reactant to other reactant particles. This exposure to other particles causes the particles of the reactants to collide with each other more often. So, the rate of the reaction is increased.

Inhibitors

An **inhibitor** is a substance that slows down or stops a chemical reaction. Slowing down or stopping a reaction may sometimes be useful. For example, preservatives are added to foods to slow down the growth of bacteria and fungi. The preservatives prevent bacteria and fungi from producing substances that can spoil food. Some antibiotics are examples of inhibitors. For example, penicillin prevents certain kinds of bacteria from making a cell wall. So, the bacteria die.

Catalysts

Some chemical reactions would be too slow to be useful without a catalyst (KAT uh LIST). A **catalyst** is a substance that speeds up a reaction without being permanently changed. Because it is not changed, a catalyst is not a reactant. A catalyst lowers the activation energy of a reaction, which allows the reaction to happen more quickly. Catalysts called *enzymes* speed up most reactions in your body. Catalysts are even found in cars, as seen in **Figure 7**. The catalytic converter decreases air pollution. It does this by increasing the rate of reactions that involve the harmful products given off by cars.

Figure 7 *This catalytic converter contains platinum and palladium. These two catalysts increase the rate of reactions that make the car's exhaust less harmful.*

SECTION Review

TN GLE 0807.Inq.3, GLE 0807.Inq.5, GLE 0807.9.3

Summary

- Energy is given off in exothermic reactions.
- Energy is absorbed in an endothermic reaction.
- The law of conservation of energy states that energy is neither created nor destroyed.
- Activation energy is the energy needed for a reaction to occur.
- The rate of a chemical reaction is affected by temperature, concentration, surface area, and the presence of an inhibitor or catalyst.

Using Key Terms

The statements below are false. For each statement, replace the underlined term to make a true statement.

1. An <u>exothermic</u> reaction absorbs energy.

2. The rate of a reaction can be increased by adding <u>an inhibitor</u>.

Understanding Key Ideas

3. Which of the following will not increase the rate of a reaction?
✔0807.Inq.3

   a. adding a catalyst
   b. increasing the temperature of the reaction
   c. decreasing the concentration of reactants
   d. grinding a solid into powder

4. How does the concentration of a solution affect the rate of reaction? ✔0807.Inq.3

Critical Thinking

5. **Making Comparisons** Compare exothermic and endothermic reactions. ✔0807.9.8

6. **Applying Concepts** Explain how chewing your food thoroughly can help your body digest food.

Interpreting Graphics

Use the diagram below to answer the questions that follow.

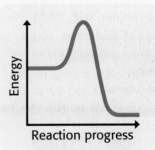

7. Does this energy diagram show an exothermic or an endothermic reaction? How can you tell?
✔0807.Inq.3, ✔0807.9.8

8. A catalyst lowers the amount of activation energy needed to get a reaction started. What do you think the diagram would look like if a catalyst were added?

Internet Resources

For a variety of links related to this chapter, go to www.scilinks.org

Topic: Exothermic and Endothermic Reactions

SciLinks code: HSM0555

Skills Practice Lab

OBJECTIVES

Describe how the surface area of a solid affects the rate of a reaction.

Explain how concentration of reactants will speed up or slow down a reaction.

MATERIALS

- funnels (2)
- graduated cylinders, 10 mL (2)
- hydrochloric acid, concentrated
- hydrochloric acid, dilute
- strips of aluminum, about 5 cm x 1 cm each (6)
- scissors
- test-tube rack
- test tubes, 30 mL (6)

SAFETY

Speed Control

The reaction rate (how fast a chemical reaction happens) is an important factor to control. Sometimes, you want a reaction to take place rapidly, such as when you are removing tarnish from a metal surface. Other times, you want a reaction to happen very slowly, such as when you are depending on a battery as a source of electrical energy.

In this lab, you will discover how changing the surface area and concentration of the reactants affects reaction rate. In this lab, you can estimate the rate of reaction by observing how fast bubbles form.

Part A: Surface Area

Ask a Question

1 How does changing the surface area of a metal affect reaction rate?

Form a Hypothesis

2 Write a statement that answers the question above. Explain your reasoning.

Test the Hypothesis

3 Use three identical strips of aluminum. Put one strip into a test tube. Place the test tube in the test-tube rack. **Caution:** The strips of metal may have sharp edges.

TN GLE 0807.Inq.2 Use appropriate tools and techniques to gather, organize, analyze, and interpret data.
GLE 0807.Inq.3 Synthesize information to determine cause and effect relationships between evidence and explanations.

GLE 0807.Inq.5 Communicate scientific understanding using descriptions, explanations, and models.

4. Carefully fold a second strip in half and then in half again. Use a textbook or other large object to flatten the folded strip as much as possible. Place the strip in a second test tube in the test-tube rack.

5. Use scissors to cut a third strip of aluminum into the smallest possible pieces. Place all of the pieces into a third test tube, and place the test tube in the test-tube rack.

6. Use a funnel and a graduated cylinder to pour 10 mL of concentrated hydrochloric acid into each of the three test tubes. **Caution:** Hydrochloric acid is corrosive. If any acid should spill on you, immediately flush the area with water and notify your teacher.

7. Observe the rate of bubble formation in each test tube. Record your observations.

Analyze the Results

1. **Organizing Data** Which form of aluminum had the greatest surface area? the smallest surface area?

2. **Analyzing Data** The amount of aluminum and the amount of acid were the same in all three test tubes. Which form of the aluminum seemed to react the fastest? Which form reacted the slowest? Explain your answers.

3. **Analyzing Results** Do your results support the hypothesis you made? Explain.

Draw Conclusions

4. **Making Predictions** Would powdered aluminum react faster or slower than the forms of aluminum you used? Explain your answer.

Part B: Concentration

Ask a Question

1. How does changing the concentration of acid affect the reaction rate?

Form a Hypothesis

2. Write a statement that answers the question above. Explain your reasoning.

Test the Hypothesis

3. Place one of the three remaining aluminum strips in each of the three clean test tubes. (Note: Do not alter the strips.) Place the test tubes in the test-tube rack.

4. Using the second funnel and graduated cylinder, pour 10 mL of water into one of the test tubes. Pour 10 mL of dilute acid into the second test tube. Pour 10 mL of concentrated acid into the third test tube.

5. Observe the rate of bubble formation in the three test tubes. Record your observations.

Analyze the Results

1. **Explaining Events** In this set of test tubes, the strips of aluminum were the same, but the concentration of the acid was different. Was there a difference between the test tube that contained water and the test tubes that contained acid? Which test tube formed bubbles the fastest? Explain. ✔0807.Inq.3

2. **Analyzing Results** Do your results support the hypothesis you made? Explain. ✔0807.Inq.3

Draw Conclusions

3. **Applying Conclusions** Why should spilled hydrochloric acid be diluted with water before it is wiped up?

Chapter Review

TN GLE 0807.Inq.3, GLE 0807.Inq.5, GLE 0807.9.2, GLE 0807.9.3, GLE 0807.9.4, GLE 0807.9.7, GLE.0807.9.8

USING KEY TERMS

Complete each of the following sentences by choosing the correct term from the word bank.

subscript   exothermic reaction

inhibitor   synthesis reaction

product   reactant

1 Adding a(n) ___ will slow down a chemical reaction.

2 A chemical reaction that gives off heat is called a(n) ___.   ✔0807.9.8

3 A chemical reaction that forms one compound from two or more substances is called a(n) ___.   ✔0807.9.8

4 The 2 in the formula Ag_2S is a(n) ___.

UNDERSTANDING KEY IDEAS

Multiple Choice

5 Balancing a chemical equation so that the same number of atoms of each element is found in both the reactants and the products is an example of   ✔0807.9.11

  a. activation energy.

  b. the law of conservation of energy.

  c. the law of conservation of mass.

  d. a double-displacement reaction.

6 Which of the following is the correct chemical formula for dinitrogen tetroxide?   ✔0807.9.5

  a. N_4O_2 **c.** N_2O_2

  b. NO_2 **d.** N_2O_4

7 In which type of reaction do ions in two compounds switch places? ✔0807.9.8

  a. a synthesis reaction

  b. a decomposition reaction

  c. a single-displacement reaction

  d. a double-displacement reaction

8 Which of the following actions is an example of the use of activation energy?

  a. plugging in an iron

  b. playing basketball

  c. holding a lit match to paper

  d. eating

9 Enzymes in your body act as catalysts. Thus, the role of enzymes is   ✔0807.Inq.3

  a. to increase the rate of chemical reactions.

  b. to decrease the rate of chemical reactions.

  c. to help you breathe.

  d. to inhibit chemical reactions.

Short Answer

10 Name the type of reaction that each of the following equations represents.   ✔0807.9.8

  a. $2Cu + O_2 \rightarrow 2CuO$

  b. $2Na + MgSO_4 \rightarrow Na_2SO_4 + Mg$

  c. $Ba(CN)_2 + H_2SO_4 \rightarrow BaSO_4 + 2HCN$

11 Describe what happens to chemical bonds during a chemical reaction.

12 Name four ways that you can change the rate of a chemical reaction.   ✔0807.Inq.3

13 Describe four clues that signal that a chemical reaction is taking place. ✔0807.9.6

Math Skills

14 Write balanced equations for the following: ✔0807.9.12

   a. $Fe + O_2 \rightarrow Fe_2O_3$

   b. $Al + CuSO_4 \rightarrow Al_2(SO_4)_3 + Cu$

   c. $Mg(OH)_2 + HCl \rightarrow MgCl_2 + H_2O$

15 Calculate the number of atoms of each element shown in the formulas below: ✔0807.9.5

   a. $CaSO_4$ **c.** $Fe(NO_3)_2$

   b. $4NaOCl$ **d.** $2Al_2(CO_3)_3$

CRITICAL THINKING

16 Concept Mapping Use the following terms to create a concept map: *products, chemical reaction, chemical equation, chemical formulas, reactants, coefficients,* and *subscripts.*

17 Evaluating Assumptions Your friend is very worried by rumors that he has heard about a substance called *dihydrogen monoxide* in the city's water system. What could you say to your friend to calm his fears? (Hint: Write the formula of the substance.)

18 Analyzing Ideas As long as proper safety precautions have been taken, why can explosives be transported long distances without exploding?

19 Applying Concepts You measured the mass of a steel pipe before leaving it outdoors. One month later, the pipe had rusted, and its mass had increased. Does this change violate the law of conservation of mass? Explain your answer. ✔0807.9.11

20 Applying Concepts Acetic acid, a compound found in vinegar, reacts with baking soda to produce carbon dioxide, water, and sodium acetate. Without writing an equation, identify the reactants and the products of this reaction. ✔0807.9.12

INTERPRETING GRAPHICS

Use the photo below to answer the questions that follow.

21 What evidence in the photo supports the claim that a chemical reaction is taking place? ✔0807.9.6

22 Is this reaction an exothermic or endothermic reaction? Explain your answer.

23 Draw and label an energy diagram of both an exothermic and endothermic reaction. Identify the diagram that describes the reaction shown in the photo above. ✔0807.Inq.5

TCAP Test Preparation

TN SPI 0807.Inq.4 Draw a conclusion that establishes a cause and effect relationship supported by evidence. **SPI 0807.9.1** Recognize that all matter consists of atoms. **SPI 0807.9.2** Identify the common outcome of all chemical changes. **SPI 0807.9.3** Classify common substances as elements or compounds based on their symbols or formulas. **SPI 0807.9.8** Interpret the results of an investigation to determine whether a physical or chemical change has occurred. **SPI 0807.9.10** Identify the reactants and products of a chemical reaction.

Multiple Choice

Use the picture below to answer question 1.

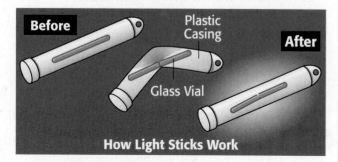

Before
Plastic Casing
After
Glass Vial
How Light Sticks Work

1. **The picture above shows a light stick. Light sticks begin to glow when the vial inside the stick is broken. Chemicals inside the vial mix with chemicals outside of the vial. Which of the following statements best supports the idea that a chemical reaction, rather than a physical change, is occurring?**

   A. The vial is broken into smaller pieces.

   B. Energy is released in the form of light.

   C. Two different substances are combined.

   D. The substances are in a flexible container.

2. **Which chemical equation best illustrates the law of conservation of mass?**

   A. $2Al + CuO \rightarrow Al_2O_3 + 3Cu$

   B. $2Al + 3CuO \rightarrow Al_2O_3 + Cu$

   C. $2Al + 3CuO \rightarrow Al_2O_3 + 3Cu$

   D. $3Al + 2CuO \rightarrow Al_2O_3 + 2Cu$

3. **Some spoons are made with the element silver (Ag). Over time, these spoons will turn black if it is not cleaned with a special solution. Which of the following statements best explains why the element silver in the spoons turns black?**

   A. It absorbs energy when exposed to warm food.

   B. It breaks down into smaller and smaller particles.

   C. It reacts with substances in the air to form a new substance.

   D. It changes from one phase of matter into another phase of matter.

4. **Which of the following contains one oxygen atom?**

   A. H_2O

   B. CO_2

   C. $2N_2O$

   D. Co

5. **Which process causes substances to react to form one or more new substances?**

   A. chemical change

   B. physical change

   C. evaporation

   D. freezing

SPI 0807.9.11 Recognize that in a chemical reaction the mass of the reactants is equal to the mass of the products (Law of Conservation of Mass).

Use the graph below to answer question 6.

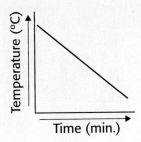

6. **The graph above shows the change in temperature over time in a chemical reaction. According to the graph, how would this reaction be described?**

   A. endothermic

   B. exothermic

   C. unbalanced

   D. combustion

7. **Which chemical equation correctly shows the formation of water from hydrogen and oxygen?**

   A. $H_2 + O_2 = H_2O$

   B. $2H_2 + O_2 = 2H_2O$

   C. $H_2 + 2O = H_2O$

   D. $H + O_2 = H_2O$

8. **A scientist carries out a reaction in a test tube. After the bubbling stops, she notices that the test tube is very warm. What might she conclude about the reaction?**

   A. The reaction happened very quickly.

   B. The reaction is endothermic.

   C. The reaction is exothermic.

   D. No reaction took place.

9. **A substance that is used to speed up a chemical reaction is called**

   A. a reactant.

   B. an inhibitor.

   C. a precipitate.

   D. a catalyst.

10. **During a laboratory experiment, Tran applied the law of conservation of energy. Which of the following did he assume to be true?**

    A. Energy is not changed.

    B. Energy is not created or destroyed.

    C. The total energy of the reactants is greater than the total energy of the products.

    D. The total energy of the reactants is less than the total mass of the products.

Open Response

11. **Identify all reactants and products in the following chemical reaction.**

    $$CaCl_2 + 2AgNO_3 \longrightarrow 2AgCl + Ca(NO_3)_2$$

12. **Compare synthesis and decomposition reactions, and give an example of each.**

Science in Action

Science, Technology, and Society

Bringing Down the House!

T/E Have you ever watched a building being demolished? It takes only minutes to demolish it, but a lot of time was spent planning the demolition. And it takes time to remove hazardous chemicals from the building. For example, asbestos, which is found in insulation, can cause lung cancer. Mercury found in thermostats can cause brain damage, birth defects, and death. It is important to remove these substances because most of the rubble is sent to a landfill. If hazardous chemicals are not removed, they could leak into the groundwater and enter the water supply. **TN** GLE 0807.T/E.3

Math ACTIVITY

A city produces 4 million tons of waste in 1 year. Of this waste, 82% is solid waste. If 38% of the solid waste comes from the construction and demolition of buildings, how many tons of waste does this represent?

Weird Science

Light Sticks

T/E Have you ever seen light sticks at a concert? Your family may even keep them in the car for emergencies. They also can provide light when the power goes out. Light sticks are used by the U.S. military, the Department of Homeland Security, and even by deep-sea divers! But how do light sticks work? To activate the light stick, you have to bend it. Most light sticks are made of a plastic tube that contains a mixture of two chemicals. Also inside the tube is a thin glass vial, which contains hydrogen peroxide. As long as the glass vial is unbroken, the two chemicals are kept separate. But bending the ends of the tube breaks the glass vial. This action releases the hydrogen peroxide into the other chemicals and a chemical reaction occurs, which makes the light stick glow. **TN** GLE 0807.T/E.1

Social Studies ACTIVITY

Who invented light sticks? What was their original purpose? Research the answers to these questions. Make a poster that shows what you have learned.

Larry McKee

T/E **Arson Investigator** Once a fire dies down, you might see an arson investigator like Lt. Larry McKee on the scene. "After the fire is out, I can investigate the fire scene to determine where the fire started and how it started," says McKee, who questions witnesses and firefighters about what they have seen. He knows that the color of the smoke can indicate certain chemicals. He also has help detecting chemicals from an accelerant-sniffing dog, Nikki. Nikki has been trained to detect about 11 different chemicals. If Nikki finds one of these chemicals, she begins to dig. McKee takes a sample of the suspicious material to the laboratory. He treats the sample so that any chemicals present will dissolve in a liquid. A sample of this liquid is placed into an instrument called a *gas chromatograph* and tested. The results of this test are printed out in a graph, from which the suspicious chemical is identified. Next, McKee begins to search for suspects. By combining detective work with scientific evidence, fire investigators can help find clues that can lead to the conviction of the arsonist. **TN** GLE 0807.T/E.1

Language Arts ACTIVITY

WRITING SKILL Write a one-page story about an arson investigator. Begin the story at the scene of a fire. Take the story through the different steps that you think an investigator would have to go through to solve the crime.

go.hrw.com

To learn more about these Science in Action topics, visit go.hrw.com and type in the keyword **HP5REAF.**

Current Science

Check out Current Science® articles related to this chapter by visiting go.hrw.com. Just type in the keyword **HP5CS14.**

14

Chemical Compounds

The Big Idea

Chemical compounds are classified into groups based on their bonds and on their properties.

TN Tennessee Science Standards

Embedded Inquiry

GLE 0807.Inq.1 Design and conduct open-ended scientific investigations.
GLE 0807.Inq.2 Use appropriate tools and techniques to gather, organize, analyze, and interpret data. **GLE 0807.Inq.3** Synthesize information to determine cause and effect relationships between evidence and explanations. **GLE 0807.Inq.5** Communicate scientific understanding using descriptions, explanations, and models. ✔**0807.Inq.1** Design and conduct an open-ended scientific investigation to answer a question that includes a control and appropriate variables. ✔**0807.Inq.2** Identify tools and techniques needed to gather, organize, analyze, and interpret data collected from a moderately complex scientific investigation. ✔**0807.Inq.3** Use evidence from a dataset to determine cause and effect relationships that explain a phenomenon. ✔**0807.Inq.5** Design a method to explain the results of an investigation using descriptions, explanations, or models.

Embedded Technology and Engineering

GLE 0807.T/E.1 Explore how technology responds to social, political, and economic needs. **GLE 0807.T/E.3** Compare the intended benefits with the unintended consequences of a new technology. ✔**0807.T/E.3** Explore how the unintended consequences of new technologies can impact society. ✔**0807.T/E.4** Research bioengineering technologies that advance health and contribute to improvements in our daily lives.

Physical Science

GLE 0807.9.2 Explain that matter has properties that are determined by the structure and arrangement of its atoms. **GLE 0807.9.4** Distinguish among elements, compounds, and mixtures. **GLE 0807.9.8** Interpret the events represented by a chemical equation. **GLE 0807.9.9** Explain the basic difference between acids and bases. ✔**0807.9.2** Illustrate the particle arrangement and type of motion associated with different states of matter. ✔**0807.9.5** Distinguish between elements and compounds by their symbols and formulas. ✔**0807.9.7** Describe how the characteristics of a compound are different than the characteristics of their component parts. ✔**0807.9.8** Determine the types of interactions between substances that result in a chemical change. ✔**0807.9.12** Differentiate between the reactants and products of a chemical equation. ✔**0807.9.13** Determine whether a substance is an acid or a base by its reaction to an indicator.

PRE-READING ACTIVITY

FOLDNOTES **Layered Book** Before you read the chapter, create the FoldNote entitled "Layered Book" described in the **Study Skills** section of the Appendix. Label the tabs of the layered book with "Ionic and covalent compounds," "Acids and bases," "Solutions of acids and bases," and "Organic compounds." As you read the chapter, write information you learn about each category under the appropriate tab.

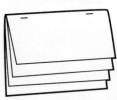

About the Photo

The bean weevil feeds on bean seeds, which are rich in chemical compounds such as proteins, carbohydrates, and lipids. The bean weevil begins life as a tiny grub that lives in the seed where it eats starch and protein. The adult then cuts holes in the seed coat and crawls out, as you can see in this photo.

START-UP ACTIVITY

TN GLE 0807.Inq.2, GLE 0807.Inq.3

Sticking Together

In this activity, you will demonstrate the force that keeps particles together in some compounds.

Procedure

1. Rub **two balloons** with a **wool cloth.** Move the balloons near each other. Describe what you see.

2. Put one balloon against a wall. Record your observations.

Analysis

1. The balloons are charged by rubbing them with the wool cloth. Like charges repel each other. Opposite charges attract each other. Do the balloons have like or opposite charges? Explain.

2. If the balloon that was placed against the wall has a negative charge, what is the charge on the wall? Explain your answer.

3. The particles that make up compounds are attracted to each other in the same way that the balloon is attracted to the wall. What can you infer about the particles that make up such compounds? ✓0807.Inq.3

Ionic and Covalent Compounds

What You Will Learn

● Describe the properties of ionic and covalent compounds.

● Classify compounds as ionic or covalent based on their properties.

Vocabulary
chemical bond
ionic compound
covalent compound

READING STRATEGY

Reading Organizer As you read this section, create an outline of the section. Use the headings from the section in your outline.

TN **GLE 0807.Inq.2** Use appropriate tools and techniques to gather, organize, analyze, and interpret data.

GLE 0807.Inq.3 Synthesize information to determine cause and effect relationships between evidence and explanations.

GLE 0807.T/E.1 Explore how technology responds to social, political, and economic needs.

GLE 0807.9.2 Explain that matter has properties that are determined by the structure and arrangement of its atoms.

GLE 0807.9.4 Distinguish among elements, compounds, and mixtures.

chemical bond the combining of atoms to form molecules or compounds

ionic compound a compound made of oppositely charged ions

When ions or molecules combine, they form compounds. Because there are millions of compounds, it is helpful to organize them into groups. But how can scientists tell the difference between compounds?

One way to group compounds is by the kind of chemical bond they have. A **chemical bond** is the combining of atoms to form molecules or compounds. Bonding can occur between valence electrons of different atoms. *Valence electrons* are electrons in the outermost energy level of an atom. The behavior of valence electrons determines if an ionic compound or a covalent compound is formed.

Ionic Compounds and Their Properties

The properties of ionic compounds are a result of strong attractive forces called ionic bonds. An *ionic bond* is an attraction between oppositely charged ions. Compounds that contain ionic bonds are called **ionic compounds.** Ionic compounds can be formed by the reaction of a metal with a nonmetal. Metal atoms become positively charged ions when electrons are transferred from the metal atoms to the nonmetal atoms. This transfer of electrons also causes the nonmetal atom to become a negatively charged ion. Sodium chloride, commonly known as *table salt,* is an ionic compound.

Brittleness

Ionic compounds tend to be brittle solids at room temperature. So, they usually break apart when hit. This property is due to the arrangement of ions in a repeating three-dimensional pattern called a *crystal lattice,* shown in **Figure 1.** Each ion in a lattice is surrounded by ions of the opposite charge. And each ion is bonded to the ions around it. When an ionic compound is hit, the pattern of ions shifts. Ions that have the same charge line up and repel one another, which causes the crystal to break.

Figure 1 *The sodium ions, shown in purple, and the chloride ions, shown in green, are bonded in the crystal lattice structure of sodium chloride.*

Figure 2 Melting Points of Some Ionic Compounds

Potassium dichromate
Melting point: 398°C

Magnesium oxide
Melting point: 2,800°C

Nickel(II) oxide
Melting point: 1,984°C

High Melting Points

Because of the strong ionic bonds that hold ions together, ionic compounds have high melting points. These high melting points are the reason that most ionic compounds are solids at room temperature. For example, solid sodium chloride must be heated to 801°C before it will melt. The melting points of three other ionic compounds are given in **Figure 2.**

Solubility and Electrical Conductivity

Many ionic compounds are highly soluble. So, they dissolve easily in water. Water molecules attract each of the ions of an ionic compound and pull the ions away from one another. The solution that forms when an ionic compound dissolves in water can conduct an electric current, as shown in **Figure 3.** The solution can conduct an electric current because the ions are charged and are able to move freely past one another. However, an undissolved crystal of an ionic compound does not conduct an electric current.

Reading Check Why do solutions of ionic compounds dissolved in water conduct an electric current?

INTERNET ACTIVITY

For another activity related to this chapter, go to **go.hrw.com** and type in the keyword **HP5CMPW.**

Figure 3 *The pure water does not conduct an electric current. However, the solution of salt water conducts an electric current, so the bulb lights up.*

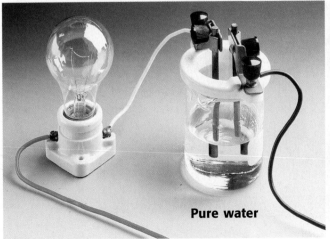

Pure water

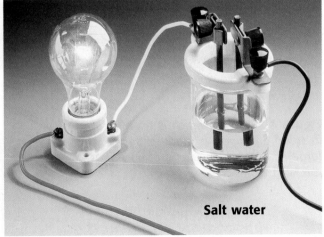

Salt water

Covalent Compounds and Their Properties

Most compounds are covalent compounds. **Covalent compounds** are compounds that form when a group of atoms shares electrons. This sharing of electrons forms a covalent bond. A *covalent bond* is a weaker attractive force than an ionic bond is. The group of atoms that make up a covalent compound is called a molecule. A *molecule* is the smallest particle into which a covalently bonded compound can be divided and still be the same compound. Properties of covalent compounds are very different from the properties of ionic compounds.

Low Solubility

Many covalent compounds are not soluble in water, which means that they do not dissolve well in water. You may have noticed this if you have ever left off the top of a soda bottle. The carbon dioxide gas that gives the soda its fizz eventually escapes, and your soda pop goes "flat." The attraction between water molecules is much stronger than their attraction to the molecules of most other covalent compounds. So, water molecules stay together instead of mixing with the covalent compounds. If you have ever made salad dressing, you probably know that oil and water don't mix. Oils, such as the oil in the salad dressing in **Figure 4,** are made of covalent compounds.

✓ **Reading Check** Why won't most covalent compounds dissolve in water?

TN GLE 0807.T/E.1

CONNECTION TO Language Arts

WRITING SKILL **Electrolyte Solutions** Ionic compounds that conduct electricity when they are dissolved in water are called *electrolytes*. Some electrolytes play important roles in the functioning of living cells. Electrolytes can be lost by the body during intense physical activity or illness and must be replenished for cells to work properly. Technology has responded to this need with the development of electrolyte replacement products. Research electrolyte replacement products. Find out what they are and how they help the body during physical activity or illness. Present your findings in a one-page research paper. ✓0807.Inq.3

Figure 4 *Olive oil, which is used in salad dressings, is made of very large covalent molecules that do not mix with water.*

Low Melting Points

The forces of attraction between molecules of covalent compounds are much weaker than the bonds holding ionic solids together. Less heat is needed to separate the molecules of covalent compounds, so these compounds have much lower melting and boiling points than ionic compounds do.

Electrical Conductivity

Although most covalent compounds don't dissolve in water, some do. Most of the covalent compounds that dissolve in water form solutions that have uncharged molecules. Sugar is a covalent compound that dissolves in water and that does not form ions. So, a solution of sugar and water does not conduct an electric current, as shown in **Figure 5.** However, some covalent compounds do form ions when they dissolve in water. Many acids, for example, form ions in water. These solutions, like ionic solutions, conduct an electric current.

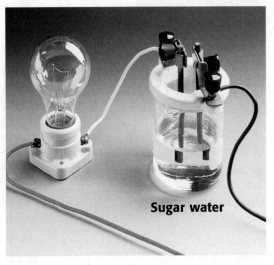

Sugar water

Figure 5 *This solution of sugar, a covalent compound, and water does not conduct an electric current because the molecules of sugar are not charged.*

SECTION Review

TN GLE 0807.Inq.3, GLE 0807.9.2, GLE 0807.9.4

Summary

- Ionic compounds have ionic bonds between ions of opposite charges.

- Ionic compounds are usually brittle, have high melting points, dissolve in water, and often conduct an electric current.

- Covalent compounds have covalent bonds and consist of particles called molecules.

- Covalent compounds have low melting points, don't dissolve easily in water, and do not conduct an electric current.

Using Key Terms

1. Use each of the following terms in a separate sentence: *ionic compound, covalent compound,* and *chemical bond.*

Understanding Key Ideas

2. Which of the following describes an ionic compound? ✔0807.9.8
   a. It has a low melting point.
   b. It consists of shared electrons.
   c. It conducts electric current in water solutions.
   d. It consists of two nonmetals.

3. List two physical properties of covalent compounds. ✔0807.9.8

Math Skills

4. A compound contains 39.37% chromium, 38.10% oxygen, and potassium. What percentage of the compound is potassium?

Critical Thinking

5. **Making Inferences** Solid crystals of ionic compounds do not conduct an electric current. But when the crystals dissolve in water, the solution conducts an electric current. Explain. ✔0807.Inq.3

6. **Applying Concepts** Some white solid crystals are dissolved in water. If the solution does not conduct an electric current, is the solid an ionic compound or a covalent compound? Explain.

Internet Resources

For a variety of links related to this chapter, go to www.scilinks.org

Topic: Ionic Compounds; Covalent Compounds

SciLinks code: HSM0817; HSM0365

Acids and Bases

Would you like a nice, refreshing glass of acid? This is just what you get when you have a glass of lemonade.

Lemons contain a substance called an *acid*. One property of acids is a sour taste. In this section, you will learn about the properties of acids and bases.

Acids and Their Properties

A sour taste is not the only property of an acid. Have you noticed that when you squeeze lemon juice into tea, the color of the tea becomes lighter? This change happens because acids cause some substances to change color. An **acid** is any compound that increases the number of hydronium ions, H_3O^+, when dissolved in water. Hydronium ions form when a hydrogen ion, H^+, separates from the acid and bonds with a water molecule, H_2O, to form a hydronium ion, H_3O^+.

✓ **Reading Check** How is a hydronium ion formed?

Acids Have a Sour Flavor

Have you ever taken a bite of a lemon or lime? If so, like the boy in **Figure 1,** you know the sour taste of an acid. The taste of lemons, limes, and other citrus fruits is a result of citric acid. However, taste, touch, or smell should NEVER be used to identify an unknown chemical. Many acids are *corrosive,* which means that they destroy body tissue, clothing, and many other things. Most acids are also poisonous.

What You Will Learn

● Describe four properties of acids.
● Identify four uses of acids.
● Describe four properties of bases.
● Identify four uses of bases.

Vocabulary

acid
indicator
base

READING STRATEGY

Reading Organizer As you read this section, make a table comparing acids and bases.

TN GLE 0807.Inq.2 Use appropriate tools and techniques to gather, organize, analyze, and interpret data.

GLE 0807.Inq.3 Synthesize information to determine cause and effect relationships between evidence and explanations.

GLE 0807.Inq.5 Communicate scientific understanding using descriptions, explanations, and models.

GLE 0807.T/E.1 Explore how technology responds to social, political, and economic needs.

GLE 0807.9.2 Explain that matter has properties that are determined by the structure and arrangement of its atoms.

GLE 0807.9.8 Interpret the events represented by a chemical equation.

GLE 0807.9.9 Explain the basic difference between acids and bases.

acid any compound that increases the number of hydronium ions when dissolved in water

NEVER touch or taste a concentrated solution of a strong acid.

Figure 1 *Foods that have a sour taste usually contain acids.*

Figure 2 Detecting Acids with Indicators

The indicator, bromthymol blue, is pale blue in water.

When acid is added, the color changes to yellow because of the presence of the indicator.

indicator a compound that can reversibly change color depending on conditions such as pH

Acids Change Colors in Indicators

A substance that changes color in the presence of an acid or base is an **indicator.** Look at **Figure 2.** The flask on the left contains water and an indicator called *bromthymol blue* (BROHM THIE MAWL BLOO). Acid has been added to the flask on the right. The color changes from pale blue to yellow because the indicator detects the presence of an acid.

Another indicator commonly used in the lab is litmus. Paper strips containing litmus are available in both blue and red. When an acid is added to blue litmus paper, the color of the litmus changes to red.

Acids React with Metals

Acids react with some metals to produce hydrogen gas. For example, hydrochloric acid reacts with zinc metal to produce hydrogen gas, as shown in **Figure 3.** The equation for the reaction is the following:

$$2HCl + Zn \longrightarrow H_2 + ZnCl_2$$

In this reaction, zinc displaces hydrogen in the compound, hydrochloric acid. This displacement happens because zinc is an active metal. But if the element silver were put into hydrochloric acid, nothing would happen. Silver is not an active metal, so no reaction would take place.

Figure 3 *Bubbles of hydrogen gas form when zinc metal reacts with hydrochloric acid.*

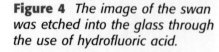
Acids Conduct Electric Current

When acids are dissolved in water, they break apart and form ions in the solution. The ions make it possible for the solution to conduct an electric current. A car battery is one example of how an acid can be used to produce an electric current. The sulfuric acid in the battery conducts electricity to help start the car's engine.

Uses of Acids

Acids are used in many areas of industry and in homes. Sulfuric acid is the most widely made industrial chemical in the world. It is used to make many products, including paper, paint, detergents, and fertilizers. Nitric acid is used to make fertilizers, rubber, and plastics. Hydrochloric acid is used to make metals from their ores by separating the metals from the materials with which they are combined. It is also used in swimming pools to help keep them free of algae. Hydrochloric acid is even found in your stomach, where it aids in digestion. Hydrofluoric acid is used to etch glass, as shown in **Figure 4.** Citric acid and ascorbic acid (Vitamin C) are found in orange juice. And carbonic acid and phosphoric acid help give a sharp taste to soft drinks.

✓ **Reading Check** What are three uses of acids?

Figure 4 *The image of the swan was etched into the glass through the use of hydrofluoric acid.*

Figure 5 **Examples of Bases**

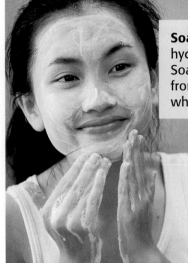

Soaps are made from sodium hydroxide, which is a base. Soaps remove dirt and oils from skin and feel slippery when you touch them.

Baking soda is a very mild base. It is used in toothpastes and mouthwashes to neutralize acids, which can produce unpleasant odors.

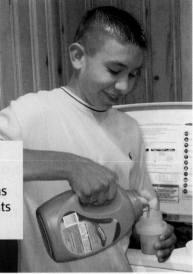

Bleach and detergents contain bases and are used for removing stains from clothing. Detergents feel slippery like soap.

Bases and Their Properties

A **base** is any compound that increases the number of hydroxide ions, OH⁻, when dissolved in water. For example, sodium hydroxide breaks apart to form sodium ions and hydroxide ions as shown below.

$$NaOH \longrightarrow Na^+ + OH^-$$

Hydroxide ions give bases their properties. **Figure 5** shows examples of bases that you are probably familiar with.

base any compound that increases the number of hydroxide ions when dissolved in water

Bases Have a Bitter Flavor and a Slippery Feel

The properties of a base solution include a bitter taste and a slippery feel. If you have ever accidentally tasted soap, you know the bitter taste of a base. Soap will also have the slippery feel of a base. However, taste, touch or smell should NEVER be used to identify an unknown chemical. Like acids, many bases are corrosive. If your fingers feel slippery when you are using a base in an experiment, you may have gotten the base on your hands. You should immediately rinse your hands with large amounts of water and tell your teacher.

NEVER touch or taste a concentrated solution of a strong base.

Figure 6 Detecting Bases with Indicators

The indicator, bromthymol blue, is pale blue in water.

When a base is added to the indicator, the indicator turns dark blue.

Bases Change Color in Indicators

Like acids, bases change the color of an indicator. Most indicators turn a different color in the presence of bases than they do in the presence of acids. For example, bases change the color of red litmus paper to blue. And the indicator, bromthymol blue, turns blue when a base is added to it, as shown in **Figure 6.**

Bases Conduct Electric Current

Solutions of bases conduct an electric current because bases increase the number of hydroxide ions, OH^-, in a solution. A hydroxide ion is actually a hydrogen atom and an oxygen atom bonded together. The extra electron gives the hydroxide ion a negative charge.

GLE 0807.Inq.2, GLE 0807.9.9

Blue to Red—Acid!

1. Pour about 5 mL of **test solution** into a **spot plate.** Test the solution using **red litmus paper** and **blue litmus paper** by dipping a **stirring rod** into it and then touching the rod to a piece of litmus paper.

2. Record any color changes. Clean the stirring rod.

3. Repeat the above steps with each solution. Use new pieces of litmus paper as needed.

4. Explain which solution is acidic and which is basic. ✔0807.9.13

Uses of Bases

Like acids, bases have many uses. Sodium hydroxide is a base used to make soap and paper. It is also used in oven cleaners and in products that unclog drains. Calcium hydroxide, $Ca(OH)_2$, is used to make cement and plaster. Ammonia is found in many household cleaners and is used to make fertilizers, and magnesium hydroxide and aluminum hydroxide are used in antacids to treat heartburn. **Figure 7** shows some of the many products that contain bases. Carefully follow the safety instructions when using these products. Remember that bases can harm your skin.

Reading Check What three ways can bases be used at home?

Figure 7 *Bases are common around the house. They are useful as cleaning agents, as cooking aids, and as medicines.*

SECTION Review

TN GLE 0807.Inq.3,
GLE 0807.T/E.1, GLE 0807.9.2,
GLE 0807.9.8, GLE 0807.9.9

Summary

- An acid is a compound that increases the number of hydronium ions in solution.

- Acids taste sour, turn blue litmus paper red, react with metals to produce hydrogen gas, and may conduct an electric current when in solution.

- Acids are used for industrial purposes and in household products.

- A base is a compound that increases the number of hydroxide ions in solution.

- Bases taste bitter, feel slippery, and turn red litmus paper blue. Most solutions of bases conduct an electric current.

- Bases are used in cleaning products and acid neutralizers.

Using Key Terms

1. In your own words, write a definition for each of the following terms: *acid, base,* and *indicator.* ✔0807.9.13

Understanding Key Ideas

2. A base is a substance that ✔0807.9.13
   a. feels slippery.
   b. tastes sour.
   c. reacts with metals to produce hydrogen gas.
   d. turns blue litmus paper red.

3. Acids are important in
   a. making antacids.
   b. preparing detergents.
   c. keeping algae out of swimming pools.
   d. manufacturing cement.

4. What happens to red litmus paper when it touches a base? ✔0807.Inq.3, ✔0807.9.13

Math Skills

5. A cake recipe calls for 472 mL of milk. You don't have a metric measuring cup at home, so you need to convert milliliters to cups. You know that 1 L equals 1.06 quarts and that there are 4 cups in 1 quart. How many cups of milk will you need to use?

Critical Thinking

6. **Analyzing Processes** Is NaOH in the reaction $NaOH \rightarrow Na^+ + OH^-$ an acid or a base? How do you know? ✔0807.9.8, ✔0807.9.12

7. **Applying Concepts** Why would it be useful for a gardener or a vegetable farmer to use litmus paper to test soil samples? ✔0807.9.13

8. **Analyzing Processes** Suppose that your teacher gives you a solution of an unknown chemical. The chemical is either an acid or a base. You know that touching or tasting acids and bases is not safe. What two tests could you perform on the chemical to determine whether it is an acid or a base? What results would help you decide if the chemical is an acid or a base? ✔0807.Inq.1, ✔0807.Inq.2, ✔0807.9.13

Solutions of Acids and Bases

Suppose that at your friend's party, you ate several large pieces of pepperoni pizza followed by cake and ice cream. Now, you have a terrible case of indigestion.

If you have ever had an upset stomach, you may have felt very much like the boy in **Figure 1.** And you may have taken an antacid. But do you know how antacids work? An antacid is a weak base that neutralizes a strong acid in your stomach. In this section, you will learn about the strengths of acids and bases. You will also learn about reactions between acids and bases.

Strengths of Acids and Bases

Acids and bases can be strong or weak. The strength of an acid or a base is not the same as the concentration of an acid or a base. The concentration of an acid or a base is the amount of acid or base dissolved in water. But the strength of an acid or a base depends on the number of molecules that break apart when the acid or base is dissolved in water.

Strong Versus Weak Acids

As an acid dissolves in water, the acid's molecules break apart and produce hydrogen ions, H^+. If all of the molecules of an acid break apart, the acid is called a *strong acid*. Strong acids include sulfuric acid, nitric acid, and hydrochloric acid. If only a few molecules of an acid break apart, the acid is a weak acid. Weak acids include acetic (uh SEET ik) acid, citric acid, and carbonic acid.

✓ **Reading Check** What is the difference between a strong acid and a weak acid?

Figure 1 *Antacids may help relieve your stomachache by reacting with the acid in your stomach.*

Strong Versus Weak Bases

When all molecules of a base break apart in water to produce hydroxide ions, OH^-, the base is a strong base. Strong bases include sodium hydroxide, calcium hydroxide, and potassium hydroxide. When only a few molecules of a base break apart, the base is a weak base, such as ammonium hydroxide and aluminum hydroxide.

Acids, Bases, and Neutralization

When the base in an antacid meets stomach acid, a reaction occurs. The reaction between acids and bases is a **neutralization reaction** (NOO truhl i ZA shuhn ree AK shuhn). Acids and bases neutralize one another because the hydrogen ions (H^+), which are present in an acid, and the hydroxide ions (OH^-), which are present in a base, react to form water, H_2O, which is neutral. Other ions from the acid and base dissolve in the water. If the water evaporates, these ions join to form a compound called a *salt*.

The pH Scale

An *indicator*, such as litmus, can identify whether a solution contains an acid or base. To describe how acidic or basic a solution is, the pH scale is used. The **pH** of a solution is a measure of the hydronium ion concentration in the solution. A solution that has a pH of 7 is neutral, which means that the solution is neither acidic nor basic. Pure water has a pH of 7. Basic solutions have a pH greater than 7. Acidic solutions have a pH less than 7. **Figure 2** shows the pH values for many common materials.

TN GLE 0807.Inq.2, GLE 0807.Inq.5, GLE 0807.9.9

Quick Lab

pHast Relief!

1. Pour **vinegar** into a **small plastic cup** until the cup is half full. Test the vinegar with **red and blue litmus paper**. Record your results.

2. Crush one **antacid tablet,** and mix it with the vinegar. Test the mixture with litmus paper. Record your results.

3. Describe how the acidity of the solution before the antacid was added was different from the acidity of the solution after it was added. ✔0807.9.13

neutralization reaction the reaction of an acid and a base to form a neutral solution of water and a salt

pH a value that is used to express the acidity or basicity (alkalinity) of a system ▬TN▶ *VOCAB*

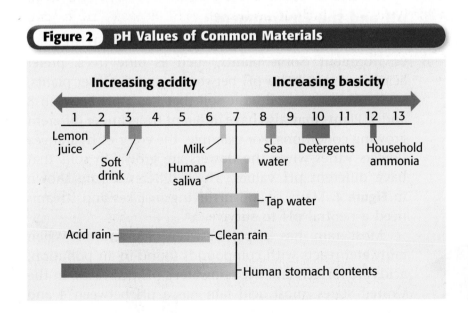

Figure 2 pH Values of Common Materials

Increasing acidity   Increasing basicity

1 2 3 4 5 6 7 8 9 10 11 12 13

Lemon juice
Soft drink
Milk
Human saliva
Sea water
Detergents
Household ammonia
Tap water
Acid rain — Clean rain
Human stomach contents

Figure 3 Using Indicators to Find pH

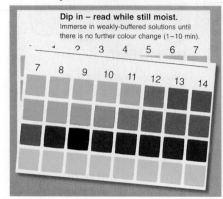

pH Indicator Scale

pH 4

pH 10

TN GLE 0807.Inq.2, GLE 0807.Inq.5, GLE 0807.T/E.1, GLE 0807.9.9

CONNECTION TO Biology

Blood and pH Human blood has a normal pH range between 7.38 and 7.42. If the blood pH is lower or higher, the body cannot function properly. Above normal range is called *acidosis.* Below normal range is called *alkalosis.* A variety of drugs and medical technologies are available to treat acidosis and alkalosis. Explore a treatment for acidosis or alkalosis. Write a one-page paper that details your findings.
✔0807.Inq.5, ✔0807.T/E.4, ✔0807.9.13

Figure 4 *To grow blue flowers, plant hydrangeas in soil that has a low pH. To grow pink flowers, use soil that has a high pH.*

Using Indicators to Determine pH

A combination of indicators can be used to find out how basic or how acidic a solution is. This can be done if the colors of the indicators are known at different pH values. **Figure 3** shows strips of pH paper, which contains several different indicators. These strips were dipped into two different solutions. The pH of each solution is found by comparing the colors on each strip with the colors on the indicator scale provided. This kind of indicator is often used to test the pH of water in pools and aquariums. Another way to find the pH of a solution is to use a pH meter. These meters can detect and measure hydronium ion concentration electronically.

TN *Standards Check* How can indicators determine pH?
✔0807.9.13

pH and the Environment

Living things depend on having a steady pH in their environment. Some plants, such as pine trees, prefer acidic soil that has a pH between 4 and 6. Other plants, such as lettuce, need basic soil that has a pH between 8 and 9. Plants may also have different traits under different growing conditions. For example, the color of hydrangea flowers varies when the flowers are grown in soils that have different pH values. These differences are shown in **Figure 4.** Many organisms living in lakes and streams need a neutral pH to survive.

Most rain has a pH between 5.5 and 6. When rainwater reacts with compounds found in air pollution, acids are formed and the rainwater's pH decreases. In the United States, most acid rain has a pH between 4 and 4.5, but some precipitation has a pH as low as 3.

Salts

When an acid neutralizes a base, a salt and water are produced. A **salt** is an ionic compound formed from the positive ion of a base and the negative ion of an acid. When you hear the word *salt*, you probably think of the table salt you use to season your food. But the sodium chloride found in your salt shaker is only one example of a large group of compounds called *salts*.

Uses of Salts

Salts have many uses in industry and in homes. You already know that sodium chloride is used to season foods. It is also used to make other compounds, including lye (sodium hydroxide) and baking soda. Sodium nitrate is a salt that is used to preserve food. And calcium sulfate is used to make wallboard, which is used in construction. Another use of salt is shown in **Figure 5.**

Figure 5 *Salts help keep roads free of ice by decreasing the freezing point of water.*

salt an ionic compound that forms when a metal atom replaces the hydrogen of an acid

SECTION Review

TN GLE 0807.Inq.2, GLE 0807.T/E.1, GLE 0807.9.2, GLE 0807.9.4, GLE 0807.9.9

Summary

● Every molecule of a strong acid or base breaks apart to form ions. Few molecules of weak acids and bases break apart to form ions.

● An acid and a base can neutralize one another to make salt and water.

● pH is a measure of hydronium ion concentration in a solution.

● A salt is an ionic compound formed in a neutralization reaction. Salts have many industrial and household uses.

Using Key Terms

1. Use the following terms in the same sentence: *neutralization reaction* and *salt.* ✔0807.9.8, ✔0807.9.12

Understanding Key Ideas

2. A neutralization reaction ✔0807.9.8, ✔0807.9.12
   a. includes an acid and a base.
   b. produces a salt.
   c. forms water.
   d. All of the above

3. Explain the difference between a strong acid and a weak acid.

Math Skills

4. For each point lower on the pH scale, the hydrogen ions in solution increase tenfold. For example, a solution of pH 3 is not twice as acidic as a solution of pH 6 but is 1,000 times as acidic. How many times more acidic is a solution of pH 2 than a solution of pH 4?

Critical Thinking

5. **Analyzing Processes** Predict what will happen to the hydrogen ion concentration and the pH of water if hydrochloric acid is added to the water. ✔0807.9.12

6. **Analyzing Relationships** Would fish be healthy in a lake that has a low pH? Explain.

7. **Applying Concepts** Soap is made from a strong base and oil. Would you expect the pH of soap to be 4 or 9? Explain.

Internet Resources

For a variety of links related to this chapter, go to www.scilinks.org
Topic: pH scale; Salts
SciLinks code: HSM1130; HSM1347

Organic Compounds

Can you believe that more than 90% of all compounds are members of a single group of compounds? It's true!

Most compounds are members of a group called organic compounds. **Organic compounds** are covalent compounds composed of carbon-based molecules. Fuel, rubbing alcohol, and sugar are organic compounds. Even cotton, paper, and plastic belong to this group. Why are there so many kinds of organic compounds? Learning about the carbon atom can help you understand why.

The Four Bonds of a Carbon Atom

All organic compounds contain carbon. Each carbon atom has four valence electrons. So, each carbon atom can make four bonds with four other atoms.

Carbon Backbones

The models in **Figure 1** are called *structural formulas*. They are used to show how atoms in a molecule of a compound are connected. Each line represents a pair of electrons that form a covalent bond. Many organic compounds are based on the types of carbon backbones shown in **Figure 1.** Some compounds have hundreds or thousands of carbon atoms as part of their backbone! Organic compounds may also contain hydrogen, oxygen, sulfur, nitrogen, and phosphorus.

TN *Standards Check* What is the purpose of structural formulas? ✔0807.9.5

What You Will Learn

● Explain why there are so many organic compounds.

● Identify and describe saturated, unsaturated, and aromatic hydrocarbons.

● Describe the characteristics of carbohydrates, lipids, proteins, and nucleic acids and their functions in the body.

Vocabulary

organic compound   lipid
hydrocarbon   protein
carbohydrate   nucleic acid

READING STRATEGY

Paired Summarizing Read this section silently. In pairs, take turns summarizing the material. Stop to discuss ideas that seem confusing.

TN **GLE 0807.Inq.2** Use appropriate tools and techniques to gather, organize, analyze, and interpret data.

GLE 0807.Inq.3 Synthesize information to determine cause and effect relationships between evidence and explanations.

GLE 0807.Inq.5 Communicate scientific understanding using descriptions, explanations, and models.

GLE 0807.T/E.1 Explore how technology responds to social, political, and economic needs.

GLE 0807.T/E.3 Compare the intended benefits with the unintended consequences of a new technology.

GLE 0807.9.2 Explain that matter has properties that are determined by the structure and arrangement of its atoms.

GLE 0807.9.4 Distinguish among elements, compounds, and mixtures.

GLE 0807.9.8 Interpret the events represented by a chemical equation.

Figure 1   **Three Models of Carbon Backbones**

Straight chain	Branched chain	Ring
▲ All carbon atoms are connected in a straight line.	▲ The chain of carbon atoms branches into different directions when a carbon atom is bonded to more than one other carbon atom.	▲ The chain of carbon atoms forms a ring.

Figure 2 Three Types of Hydrocarbons

Alkane

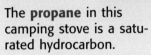

The **propane** in this camping stove is a saturated hydrocarbon.

Alkene

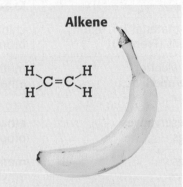

Fruits make **ethene,** which is a compound that helps ripen the fruit.

Alkyne

H–C≡C–H

Ethyne is better known as acetylene. It is burned in this miner's lamp and in welding torches.

Hydrocarbons and Other Organic Compounds

Although many organic compounds contain several kinds of atoms, some contain only two. Organic compounds that contain only carbon and hydrogen are called **hydrocarbons.**

Saturated Hydrocarbons

The propane shown in **Figure 2** is a saturated hydrocarbon. A *saturated hydrocarbon,* or *alkane,* is a hydrocarbon in which each carbon atom in the molecule shares a single bond with each of four other atoms. A single bond is a covalent bond made up of one pair of shared electrons.

Unsaturated Hydrocarbons

An *unsaturated hydrocarbon,* such as ethene or ethyne shown in **Figure 2,** is a hydrocarbon in which at least one pair of carbon atoms shares a double bond or a triple bond. A double bond is a covalent bond made up of two pairs of shared electrons. A triple bond is a covalent bond made up of three pairs of shared electrons. Hydrocarbons that contain double or triple bonds are unsaturated because these bonds can be broken and more atoms can be added to the molecules.

Compounds that contain two carbon atoms connected by a double bond are called *alkenes.* Hydrocarbons that contain two carbon atoms connected by a triple bond are called *alkynes.*

Aromatic Hydrocarbons

Most aromatic (AR uh MAT ik) compounds are based on benzene. As shown in **Figure 3,** benzene has a ring of six carbons that have alternating double and single bonds. Aromatic hydrocarbons often have strong odors.

organic compound a covalently bonded compound that contains carbon

hydrocarbon an organic compound composed only of carbon and hydrogen

Figure 3 *Benzene is the starting material for manufacturing many products, including medicines.*

Table 1 Types and Uses of Organic Compounds

Type of compound	Uses	Examples
Alkyl halides	starting material for Teflon™ refrigerant (Freon™)	chloromethane, CH_3Cl bromoethane, C_2H_5Br
Alcohols	rubbing alcohol gasoline additive antifreeze	methanol, CH_3OH ethanol, C_2H_5OH
Organic acids	food preservatives flavorings	ethanoic acid, CH_3COOH propanoic acid, C_2H_5COOH
Esters	flavorings fragrances clothing (polyester)	methyl ethanoate, CH_3COOCH_3 ethyl propanoate, $C_2H_5COOC_2H_5$

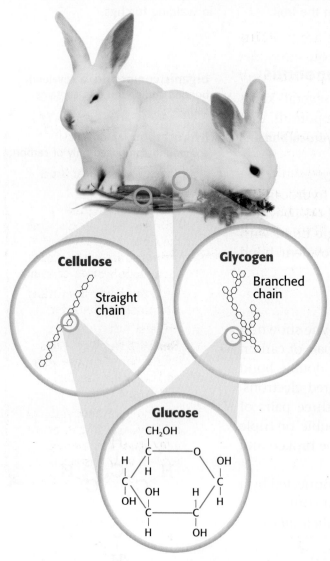

Figure 4 *Glucose molecules, represented by hexagons, can bond to form complex carbohydrates, such as cellulose and glycogen.*

Other Organic Compounds

There are many other kinds of organic compounds. Some have atoms of halogens, oxygen, sulfur, and phosphorus in their molecules. A few of these compounds and their uses are listed in **Table 1.**

Biochemicals: The Compounds of Life

Organic compounds that are made by living things are called *biochemicals.* Biochemicals are divided into four categories: carbohydrates, lipids, proteins, and nucleic acids (noo KLEE ik AS idz).

Carbohydrates

Carbohydrates are biochemicals that are composed of one or more simple sugar molecules bonded together. Carbohydrates are used as a source of energy. There are two kinds of carbohydrates: simple carbohydrates and complex carbohydrates.

Simple carbohydrates include simple sugars, such as glucose. **Figure 4** shows how glucose molecules can bond to form different complex carbohydrates. Complex carbohydrates may be made of hundreds or thousands of sugar molecules bonded together. *Cellulose* gives plant cell walls their rigid structure, and *glycogen* supplies energy to muscle cells.

Lipids

Lipids are biochemicals that do not dissolve in water. Fats, oils, and waxes are kinds of lipids. Lipids have many functions, including storing energy and making up cell membranes. Although too much fat in your diet can be unhealthy, some fat is important to good health. The foods in **Figure 5** are sources of lipids.

Lipids store excess energy in the body. Animals tend to store lipids as fats, while plants store lipids as oils. When an organism has used up most of its carbohydrates, it can obtain energy by breaking down lipids. Lipids are also used to store some vitamins.

Proteins

Most of the biochemicals found in living things are proteins. In fact, after water, proteins are the most common molecules in your cells. **Proteins** are biochemicals that are composed of "building blocks" called *amino acids*.

Amino acids are small molecules made up of carbon, hydrogen, oxygen, and nitrogen atoms. Some amino acids also include sulfur atoms. Amino acids bond to form proteins of many shapes and sizes. The shape of a protein determines the function of the protein. If even a single amino acid is missing or out of place, the protein may not function correctly or at all. Proteins have many functions. They regulate chemical activities, transport and store materials, and provide structural support.

Reading Check What are proteins made of?

carbohydrate a class of energy-giving nutrients that includes sugars, starches, and fiber; composed of one or more simple sugars bonded together

lipid a type of biochemical that does not dissolve in water; fats and steroids are lipids

protein a molecule that is made up of amino acids and that is needed to build and repair body structures and to regulate processes in the body

Food Facts

1. Select **four empty food packages.**
2. Without reading the Nutrition Facts labels, rank the items from most carbohydrate content to least carbohydrate content.
3. Rank the items from most fat content to least fat content.
4. Read the Nutrition Facts labels, and compare your rankings with the real rankings.
5. Why do you think your rankings were right, or why were they wrong? Explain your answer.

Figure 5 *Vegetable oil, meat, cheese, nuts, eggs, and milk are sources of lipids in your diet.*

Examples of Proteins

Proteins have many roles in your body and in living things. Enzymes (EN ZIEMZ) are proteins that are catalysts. *Catalysts* regulate chemical reactions in the body by increasing the rate at which the reactions occur. Some hormones are proteins. For example, insulin is a protein hormone that helps regulate your blood-sugar level. Another kind of protein, called *hemoglobin,* is found in red blood cells and delivers oxygen throughout the body. There are also large proteins that extend through cell membranes. These proteins help control the transport of materials into and out of cells. Some proteins, such as those in your hair, provide structural support. The structural proteins of silk fibers make the spider web shown in **Figure 6** strong and lightweight.

Figure 6 *Spider webs are made up of proteins that are shaped like long fibers.*

nucleic acid a molecule made up of subunits called *nucleotides*

Nucleic Acids

The largest molecules made by living organisms are nucleic acids. **Nucleic acids** are biochemicals made up of *nucleotides* (NOO klee oh TIEDZ). Nucleotides are molecules made of carbon, hydrogen, oxygen, nitrogen, and phosphorus atoms. There are only five kinds of nucleotides. But nucleic acids may have millions of nucleotides bonded together. The only reason living things differ from each other is that each living thing has a different order of nucleotides.

Nucleic acids have several functions. One function of nucleic acids is to store genetic information. They also help build proteins and other nucleic acids. Nucleic acids are sometimes called *the blueprints of life,* because they contain all the information needed for a cell to make all of its proteins.

Reading Check What are two functions of nucleic acids?

TN GLE 0807.Inq.2, GLE 0807.Inq.3, GLE 0807.T/E.1, GLE 0807.T/E.3

CONNECTION TO Engineering

T/E Bioengineering Developments in bioengineering enable scientists and engineers to add genetic material to food crops. However, some people think that bioengineering of food crops may have unintended consequences. Research the debate over bioengineering of food crops. List one benefit and one possible unintended consequence of the bioengineering of food crops. Decide whether bioengineering of food crops is adaptive or assistive and explain your reasoning. Write your findings in your **science journal.**
✔0807.Inq.2, ✔0807.Inq.3, ✔0807.T/E.3, ✔0807.T/E.4

ACTIVITY

DNA and RNA

There are two kinds of nucleic acids: DNA and RNA. A model of DNA (**d**eoxyribo**n**ucleic **a**cid) is shown in **Figure 7**. DNA is the genetic material of the cell. DNA molecules can store a huge amount of information because of their length. The DNA molecules in a single human cell have a length of about 2 m—which is more than 6 ft long! When a cell needs to make a certain protein, it copies a certain part of the DNA. The information copied from the DNA directs the order in which amino acids are bonded to make that protein. DNA also contains information used to build the second type of nucleic acid, RNA (**r**ibo**n**ucleic **a**cid). RNA is involved in the actual building of proteins.

Figure 7 *Two strands of DNA are twisted in a spiral shape. Four different nucleotides make up the rungs of the DNA ladder.*

SECTION Review

TN GLE 0807.Inq.3, GLE 0807.T/E.1, GLE 0807.9.2, GLE 0807.9.4

Summary

- Organic compounds contain carbon, which can form four bonds.
- Hydrocarbons are composed of only carbon and hydrogen.
- Hydrocarbons may be saturated, unsaturated, or aromatic hydrocarbons.
- Carbohydrates are made of simple sugars.
- Lipids store energy and make up cell membranes.
- Proteins are composed of amino acids.
- Nucleic acids store genetic information and help cells make proteins.

Using Key Terms

1. Use the following terms in the same sentence: *organic compound, hydrocarbon,* and *biochemical.*

2. In your own words, write a definition for each of the following terms: *carbohydrate, lipid, protein,* and *nucleic acid.* ✔0807.9.7

Understanding Key Ideas

3. A saturated hydrocarbon has
   a. only single bonds.
   b. double bonds.
   c. triple bonds.
   d. double and triple bonds.

4. List two functions of proteins.

5. What is an aromatic hydrocarbon?

Critical Thinking

6. **Identifying Relationships** Hemoglobin is a protein that is in blood and that transports oxygen to the tissues of the body. Information stored in nucleic acids tells a cell how to make proteins. What might happen if there is a mistake in the information needed to make hemoglobin? ✔0807.Inq.3

7. **Making Comparisons** Compare saturated hydrocarbons with unsaturated hydrocarbons.

Interpreting Graphics

Use the structural formula of this organic compound to answer the questions that follow.

$$\begin{array}{ccc} H & H & H \\ | & | & | \\ H-C-C-C-H \\ | & | & | \\ H & H & H \end{array}$$

8. What type of bonds are present in this molecule?

9. Can you determine the shape of the molecule from this structural formula? Explain your answer.

10. What elements make up this compound? ✔0807.9.5

Internet Resources

For a variety of links related to this chapter, go to www.scilinks.org

Topic: Aromatic Compounds; Organic Compounds

SciLinks code: HSM0095; HSM1078

Skills Practice Lab

Cabbage Patch Indicators

Indicators are weak acids or bases that change color due to the pH of the substance to which they are added. Red cabbage contains a natural indicator. It turns specific colors at specific pHs. In this lab you will extract the indicator from red cabbage. Then, you will use it to determine the pH of several liquids.

Procedure

1. Copy the table below. Be sure to include one line for each sample liquid.

Data Collection Table			
Liquid	Color with indicator	pH	Effect on litmus paper
Control			
		DO NOT WRITE IN BOOK	

MATERIALS

- beaker, 250 mL
- beaker tongs
- eyedropper
- hot plate
- litmus paper
- pot holder
- red cabbage leaf
- sample liquids provided by teacher
- tape, masking
- test tubes
- test-tube rack
- water, distilled

SAFETY

TN▸ GLE 0807.Inq.2 Use appropriate tools and techniques to gather, organize, analyze, and interpret data.

GLE 0807.Inq.5 Communicate scientific understanding using descriptions, explanations, and models.

GLE 0807.9.9 Explain the basic difference between acids and bases.

2. Put on protective gloves. Place 100 mL of distilled water in the beaker. Tear the cabbage leaf into small pieces. Place the pieces in the beaker.

3. Use the hot plate to heat the cabbage and water to boiling. Continue boiling until the water is deep blue. **Caution:** Use extreme care when working near a hot plate.

4. Use tongs to remove the beaker from the hot plate. Turn the hot plate off. Allow the solution to cool on a pot holder for 5 to 10 minutes.

5. While the solution is cooling, use masking tape and a pen to label the test tubes for each sample liquid. Label one test tube as the control. Place the tubes in the rack.

6. Use the eyedropper to place a small amount (about 5 mL) of the indicator (cabbage juice) in the test tube labeled as the control.

7. Pour a small amount (about 5 mL) of each sample liquid into the appropriate test tube.

8. Using the eyedropper, place several drops of the indicator into each test tube. Swirl gently. Record the color of each liquid in the table.

9. Use the chart below to the find the pH of each sample. Record the pH values in the table.

10. Litmus paper has an indicator that turns red in an acid and blue in a base. Test each liquid with a strip of litmus paper. Record the results.

Analyze the Results

1. **Analyzing Data** What purpose does the control serve? What is the pH of the control?

2. **Examining Data** What colors in your samples indicate the presence of an acid? What colors indicate the presence of a base? ✔0807.9.13

3. **Analyzing Results** Why is red cabbage juice considered a good indicator? ✔0807.9.13

Draw Conclusions

4. **Interpreting Information** Which do you think would be more useful to help identify an unknown liquid—litmus paper or red cabbage juice? Why? ✔0807.9.13

Applying Your Data

Unlike distilled water, rainwater has some carbon dioxide dissolved in it. Is rainwater acidic, basic, or neutral? To find out, place a small amount of the cabbage juice indicator (which is water-based) in a clean test tube. Use a straw to gently blow bubbles in the indicator. Continue blowing bubbles until you see a color change. What can you conclude about the pH of your "rainwater"? What is the purpose of blowing bubbles in the cabbage juice? ✔0807.9.13

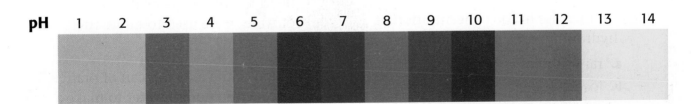

| pH | 1 | 2 | 3 | 4 | 5 | 6 | 7 | 8 | 9 | 10 | 11 | 12 | 13 | 14 |

Chapter Review

TN GLE 0807.Inq.3, GLE 0807.Inq.5, GLE 0807.9.2, GLE 0807.9.3, GLE 0807.9.4, GLE 0807.9.9

USING KEY TERMS

For each pair of terms, explain how the meanings of the terms differ.

1 *ionic compound* and *covalent compound*

2 *acid* and *base* ✔0807.9.8

3 *pH* and *indicator* ✔0807.9.8, ✔0807.9.13

4 *hydrocarbon* and *organic compound*

5 *carbohydrate* and *lipid*

6 *protein* and *nucleic acid*

UNDERSTANDING KEY IDEAS

Multiple Choice

7 Which of the following statements describes lipids?

a. Lipids are used to store energy.

b. Lipids do not dissolve in water.

c. Lipids make up part of the cell membrane.

d. All of the above

8 Ionic compounds

a. have a low melting point.

b. are often brittle.

c. do not conduct electric current in water.

d. do not dissolve easily in water.

9 An increase in the concentration of hydronium ions in solution ✔0807.Inq.3

a. raises the pH.

b. lowers the pH.

c. does not affect the pH.

d. doubles the pH.

10 The compounds that store information for building proteins are

a. lipids.

b. hydrocarbons.

c. nucleic acids.

d. carbohydrates.

Short Answer

11 What type of compound would you use to neutralize a solution of potassium hydroxide? ✔0807.9.8

12 Explain why the reaction of an acid with a base is called *neutralization*. ✔0807.9.8

13 What characteristic of carbon atoms helps to explain the wide variety of organic compounds? ✔0807.9.7

14 What kind of ions are produced when an acid is dissolved in water and when a base is dissolved in water? ✔0807.9.8

Math Skills

15 Most of the vinegar used to make pickles is 5% acetic acid. So, in 100 mL of vinegar, 5 mL is acid diluted with 95 mL of water. If you bought a 473 mL bottle of 5% vinegar, how many milliliters of acetic acid would be in the bottle? How many milliliters of water were used to dilute the acetic acid?

16 If you dilute a 75 mL can of orange juice with enough water to make a total volume of 300 mL, what is the percentage of juice in the mixture?

CRITICAL THINKING

17 Concept Mapping Use the following terms to create a concept map: *acid*, *base*, *salt*, *neutral*, and *pH*.

18 Applying Concepts Fish give off the base, ammonia, NH_3, as waste. How does the release of ammonia affect the pH of the water in the aquarium? What can be done to correct the pH of the water? ✔0807.Inq.3

19 Analyzing Methods Many insects, such as fire ants, inject formic acid, a weak acid, when they bite or sting. Describe the type of compound that should be used to treat the bite. ✔0807.9.8

20 Making Comparisons Organic compounds are also covalent compounds. What properties would you expect organic compounds to have as a result?

21 Applying Concepts Farmers have been known to taste their soil to determine whether the soil has the correct acidity for their plants. How would taste help the farmer determine the acidity of the soil? ✔0807.9.13

22 Analyzing Ideas A diet that includes a high level of lipids is unhealthy. Why is a diet containing no lipids also unhealthy?

INTERPRETING GRAPHICS

Use the structural formulas below to answer the questions that follow.

a.

b.

c.

d.

23 A saturated hydrocarbon is represented by which structural formula(s)? ✔0807.9.5

24 An unsaturated hydrocarbon is represented by which structural formula(s)? ✔0807.9.5

25 An aromatic hydrocarbon is represented by which structural formula(s)? ✔0807.9.5

TN SPI 0807.Inq.4 Draw a conclusion that establishes a cause and effect relationship supported by evidence.

SPI 0807.9.3 Classify common substances as elements or compounds based on their symbols or formulas.

SPI 0807.9.4 Differentiate between a mixture and a compound.

Multiple Choice

Use the table below to answer question 1.

Properties of Some Compounds

Compound	Melting point	Solubility	Electrical conductivity in solution
A	801°C	high	yes
B	398°C	low	yes
C	20°C	low	no
D	1,200°C	high	yes

1. Which of the compounds in the table above is most likely a covalent compound?

   A. compound A

   B. compound B

   C. compound C

   D. compound D

2. Akeem reads the following description of the results of an investigation: "clear liquid, boiling point of 78°C, flammable, soluble in water." Which of the properties listed is a chemical property?

   A. clear liquid

   B. boiling point of 78°C

   C. flammable

   D. soluble in water

3. A compound dissolved in water turns red litmus paper blue and changes the indicator bromthymol blue to dark blue. What kind of compound is it?

   A. an acid

   B. water

   C. table salt

   D. a base

4. What type of compound increases the number of hydronium ions (H^+) when dissolved in water?

   A. an acid

   B. a base

   C. an indicator

   D. hydrogen gas

5. Which of the following is a kind of biochemical that does not dissolve in water and that is found in cell walls, fats, oils, and waxes?

   A. glycogen

   B. carbohydrate

   C. lipid

   D. cellulose

6. Jacques is going to perform a laboratory experiment with organic compounds. He can conclude that all the organic compounds he will study must contain a certain element. What is that element?

   A. hydrogen

   B. carbon

   C. oxygen

   D. nitrogen

SPI 0807.9.10 Identify the reactants and
products of a chemical reaction.
SPI 0807.9.12 Identify the basic properties of
acids and bases.

Use the figure below to answer questions 7 and 8.

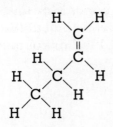

7. **The figure above shows the structural
    formula of a covalent compound.
    Which of the following statements is
    true about the compound?**

    A. The compound has ionic bonds.

    B. The compound may be an organic
        compound.

    C. The compound may be a salt.

    D. The compound has metallic bonds.

8. **The compound in question 7 is made
    of which two elements?**

    A. helium and carbon

    B. hydrogen and calcium

    C. hydrogen and carbon

    D. helium and calcium

9. **During a laboratory experiment,
    Martin observes a substance with a
    high melting point. This substance
    also dissolves in water easily. Which
    of the following is a valid conclusion?**

    A. He is looking at a substance with a
        covalent bond.

    B. He is looking at an acid.

    C. He is looking at a substance with an
        ionic bond.

    D. He is looking at a substance with a
        metallic bond.

10. **The ions in an ionic compound
    are arranged in a repeating, three-
    dimensional pattern. What is this
    pattern called?**

    A. ionic solution

    B. chemical bond

    C. valence electron

    D. crystal lattice

11. **What factor does the pH scale
    measure?**

    A. the degree of neutralization between
        acids and bases

    B. the concentration of hydroxide ions in a
        solution

    C. the number of salt molecules present in a
        solution

    D. the concentration of hydronium ions in
        a solution

Open Response

12. **Acids and bases are two kinds of
    chemical compounds. Compare and
    contrast at least four chemical and
    physical properties of acids and bases.**

13. **Alexa is writing a report about
    biochemicals. Describe the four
    categories of biochemicals that Alexa
    should include in her report. Give an
    example of each kind of biochemical.**

TCAP Test Preparation

Science, Technology, and Society

Molecular Photocopying

T/E To learn about our human ancestors, scientists can use DNA from mummies. Well-preserved DNA can be copied using a technique called polymerase chain reaction (PCR). PCR uses enzymes called *polymerases,* which make new strands of DNA using old strands as templates. Thus, PCR is called molecular photocopying. However, scientists have to be very careful when using this process. If just one of their own skin cells falls into the PCR mixture, it will contaminate the ancient DNA with their own DNA.

TN GLE 0807.T/E.1

Social Studies ACTiViTY

WRITING SKILL DNA analysis of mummies is helping archaeologists study human history. Write a research paper about what scientists have learned about human history through DNA analysis.

Weird Science

Silly Putty™

T/E During World War II, the supply of natural rubber was very low. So, James Wright, at General Electric, tried to make a synthetic rubber. The putty he made could be molded, stretched, and bounced. But it did not work as a rubber substitute and was ignored. Then, Peter Hodgson, a consultant for a toy company, had a brilliant idea. He marketed the putty as a toy in 1949. It was an immediate success. Hodgson created the name Silly Putty™. Although Silly Putty™ was invented more than 50 years ago, it has not changed much. It did not deliver the intended benefit as a substitute for rubber. However, its unintentional use as a toy packaged in a plastic "egg" was great fun for kids and very profitable for its creator. More than 300 million eggs of Silly Putty have been sold since 1950. **TN** GLE 0807.T/E.3

Math ACTiViTY

In 1949, Mr. Hodgson bought 9.5 kg of putty for $147. The putty was divided into balls, each having a mass of 14 g. What was his cost for one 14 g ball of putty?

Jeannie Eberhardt

T/E **Forensic Scientist** Jeannie Eberhardt says that her job as a forensic scientist is not really as glamorous as it may seem on popular TV shows. "If they bring me a garbage bag from the crime scene, then my job is to dig through the trash and look for evidence," she laughs. Jeannie Eberhardt explains that her job is to "search for, collect, and analyze evidence from crime scenes." Eberhardt says that one of the most important qualities a forensic scientist can have is the ability to be unbiased. She says that she focuses on the evidence and not on any information she may have about the alleged crime or the suspect. Eberhardt advises students who think they might be interested in a career as a forensic scientist to talk to someone who works in the field. She also recommends that students develop a broad science background. And she advises students that most of these jobs require extensive background checks. "Your actions now could affect your ability to get a job later on," she points out. **TN** GLE 0807.T/E.1

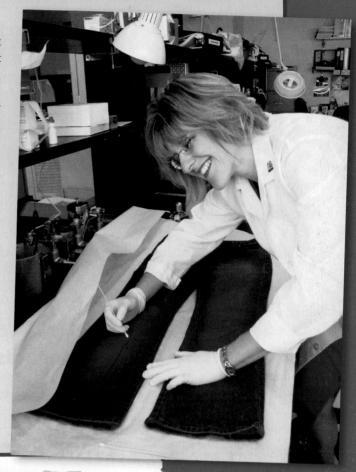

Language Arts ACTIVITY

WRITING SKILL Jeannie Eberhardt says that it is very important to be unbiased when analyzing a crime scene. Write a one-page essay explaining why it is necessary to focus on the evidence in a crime and not on personal feelings or news reports.

go.hrw.com

To learn more about these Science in Action topics, visit **go.hrw.com** and type in the keyword **HP5CMPF**

Current Science

Check out Current Science® articles related to this chapter by visiting go.hrw.com. Just type in the keyword **HP5CS15**

15

Formation of the Solar System

The Big Idea

The way in which stars, planets, and solar systems form is controlled by gravity and pressure.

TN Tennessee Science Standards

Embedded Inquiry

GLE 0807.Inq.2 Use appropriate tools and techniques to gather, organize, analyze, and interpret data.

GLE 0807.Inq.3 Synthesize information to determine cause and effect relationships between evidence and explanations.

GLE 0807.Inq.4 Recognize possible sources of bias and error, alternative explanations, and questions for further exploration.

GLE 0807.Inq.5 Communicate scientific understanding using descriptions, explanations, and models.

✓0807.Inq.2 Identify tools and techniques needed to gather, organize, analyze, and interpret data collected from a moderately complex scientific investigation.

✓0807.Inq.3 Use evidence from a dataset to determine cause and effect relationships that explain a phenomenon.

✓0807.Inq.4 Review an experimental design to determine possible sources of bias or error, state alternative explanations, and identify questions for further investigation.

Embedded Technology and Engineering

GLE 0807.T/E.1 Explore how technology responds to social, political, and economic needs.

Physical Science

GLE 0807.9.1 Understand that all matter is made up of atoms.

GLE 0807.9.5 Apply the chemical properties of the atmosphere to illustrate a mixture of gases.

GLE 0807.9.6 Use the periodic table to determine the characteristics of an element.

GLE 0807.12.4 Identify factors that influence the amount of gravitational force between objects.

GLE 0807.12.5 Recognize that gravity is the force that controls the motion of objects in the solar system.

✓0807.9.9 Explain how the chemical makeup of the atmosphere illustrates a mixture of gases.

✓0807.12.6 Identify factors that influence the amount of gravitational force between objects.

✓0807.12.7 Explain how the motion of objects in the solar system is affected by gravity.

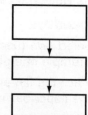

PRE-READING ACTIVITY

Graphic Organizer

Chain-of-Events Chart Before you read the chapter, create the graphic organizer entitled "Chain-of-Events Chart" described in the **Study Skills** section of the Appendix. As you read the chapter, fill in the chart with details about each step of the formation of the solar system.

About the Photo

The Orion Nebula, a vast cloud of dust and gas that is 35 trillion miles wide, is part of the familiar Orion constellation. Here, swirling clouds of dust and gas give birth to systems like our own solar system.

START-UP ACTIVITY

TN GLE 0807.Inq.2, GLE 0807.Inq.3, GLE 0807.Inq.5

Strange Gravity

If you drop a heavy object, will it fall faster than a lighter one? According to the law of gravity, the answer is no. In 1971, *Apollo 15* astronaut David Scott stood on the moon and dropped a feather and a hammer. Television audiences were amazed to see both objects strike the moon's surface at the same time. Now, you can perform a similar experiment.

Procedure

1. Select **two pieces of identical notebook paper.** Crumple one piece of paper into a ball.
2. Place the flat piece of paper on top of a **book** and the paper ball on top of the flat piece of paper.
3. Hold the book waist high, and then drop it to the floor.

Analysis

1. Which piece of paper reached the bottom first? Did either piece of paper fall slower than the book? Explain your observations. ✓0807.Inq.3
2. Now, hold the crumpled paper in one hand and the flat piece of paper in the other. Drop both pieces of paper at the same time. Besides gravity, what affected the speed of the falling paper? Record your observations. ✓0807.Inq.3

A Solar System Is Born

As you read this sentence, you are traveling at a speed of about 30 km/s around an incredibly hot star shining in the vastness of space!

Earth is not the only planet orbiting the sun. In fact, Earth has many fellow travelers in its cosmic neighborhood. The solar system includes a star we call the sun, the planets, and many moons and small bodies that travel around the sun. For almost 5 billion years, planets have been orbiting the sun. But how did the solar system come to be?

The Solar Nebula

All of the ingredients for building planets, moons, and stars are found in the vast, seemingly empty regions of space between the stars. Just as there are clouds in the sky, there are clouds in space. These clouds are called nebulas. **Nebulas** (or nebulae) are mixtures of gases—mainly hydrogen and helium—and dust made of elements such as carbon and iron. Although nebulas are normally dark and invisible to optical telescopes, they can be seen when nearby stars illuminate them. So, how can a cloud of gas and dust such as the Horsehead Nebula, shown in **Figure 1,** form planets and stars? To answer this question, you must explore two forces that interact in nebulas—gravity and pressure.

Gravity Pulls Matter Together

The gas and dust that make up nebulas are made of matter. The matter of a nebula is held together by the force of gravity. In most nebulas, there is a lot of space between the particles. In fact, nebulas are less dense than air! Thus, the gravitational attraction between the particles in a nebula is very weak. The force is just enough to keep the nebula from drifting apart.

TN *Standards Check* What is one factor that influences the amount of gravitational force between particles in a nebula?
✓0807.12.6

nebula a large cloud of gas and dust in interstellar space; a region in space where stars are born or where stars explode at the end of their lives

Figure 1 *The Horsehead Nebula is a cold, dark cloud of gas and dust. But observations suggest that it is also a site where stars form.*

Figure 2 **Gravity and Pressure in a Nebula**

❶ Gravity causes the particles in a nebula to be attracted to each other.

❷ As particles move closer together, collisions cause pressure to increase and particles are pushed apart.

❸ If the inward force of gravity is balanced by outward pressure, the nebula becomes stable.

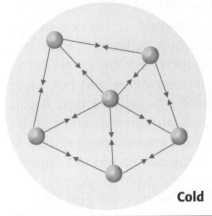

Cold

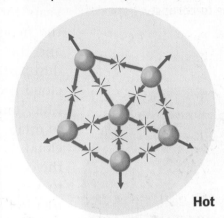

Hot

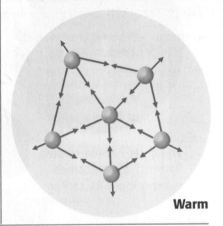

Warm

Pressure Pushes Matter Apart

If gravity pulls on all of the particles in a nebula, why don't nebulas slowly collapse? The answer has to do with the relationship between temperature and pressure in a nebula. *Temperature* is a measure of the average kinetic energy, or the energy of motion, of the particles in an object. If the particles in a nebula have little kinetic energy, they move slowly and the temperature of the cloud is very low. If the particles move fast, the temperature of the cloud is high. As particles move around, they sometimes crash into each other. As shown in **Figure 2,** these collisions cause particles to push away from each other, which creates *pressure*. If you have ever blown up a balloon, you understand how pressure works—pressure keeps a balloon from collapsing. In a nebula, outward pressure balances the inward gravitational pull and keeps the cloud from collapsing.

Upsetting the Balance

The balance between gravity and pressure in a nebula can be upset if two nebulas collide or a nearby star explodes. These events compress, or push together, small regions of a nebula called *globules,* or gas clouds. Globules can become so dense that they contract under their own gravity. As the matter in a globule collapses inward, the temperature increases and the stage is set for stars to form. The **solar nebula**—the cloud of gas and dust that formed our solar system—may have formed in this way.

solar nebula the cloud of gas and dust that formed our solar system

✓ *Reading Check* **What is the solar nebula?**

Figure 3 The Formation of the Solar System

1 The young solar nebula begins to collapse.

2 The solar nebula rotates, flattens, and becomes warmer near its center.

3 Planetesimals begin to form within the swirling disk.

4 As the largest planetesimals grow in size, their gravity attracts more gas and dust.

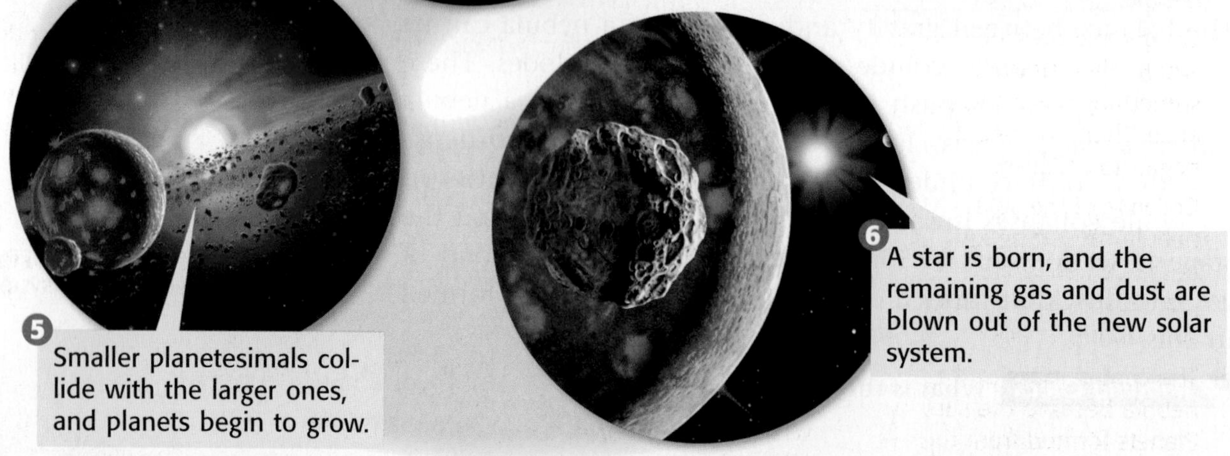

5 Smaller planetesimals collide with the larger ones, and planets begin to grow.

6 A star is born, and the remaining gas and dust are blown out of the new solar system.

How the Solar System Formed

The events that may have led to the formation of the solar system are shown in **Figure 3.** After the solar nebula began to collapse, it took about 10 million years for the solar system to form. As the nebula collapsed, it became denser and the attraction between the gas and dust particles increased. The center of the cloud became very dense and hot. Over time, much of the gas and dust began to rotate slowly around the center of the cloud. While the tremendous pressure at the center of the nebula was not enough to keep the cloud from collapsing, this rotation helped balance the pull of gravity. Over time, the solar nebula flattened into a rotating disk. All of the planets still follow this rotation.

From Planetesimals to Planets

As bits of dust circled the center of the solar nebula, some collided and stuck together to form golf ball–sized bodies. These bodies eventually drifted into the solar nebula, where further collisions caused them to grow to kilometer-wide bodies. As more collisions happened, some of these bodies grew to hundreds of kilometers wide. The largest of these bodies are called *planetesimals*, or small planets. Some of these planetesimals are part of the cores of current planets, while others collided with forming planets to create enormous craters.

Gas Giant or Rocky Planet?

The largest planetesimals formed near the outside of the rotating solar disk, where hydrogen and helium were located. These planetesimals were far enough from the solar disk that their gravity could attract the nebula gases. These outer planets grew to huge sizes and became the gas giants—Jupiter, Saturn, Uranus, and Neptune. Closer to the center of the nebula, where Mercury, Venus, Earth, and Mars formed, temperatures were too hot for gases to remain. Therefore, the inner planets in our solar system are made mostly of rocky material.

Reading Check Which planets are gas giants?

The Birth of a Star

As the planets were forming, other matter in the solar nebula was traveling toward the center. The center became so dense and hot that hydrogen atoms began to fuse, or join, to form helium. Fusion released huge amounts of energy and created enough outward pressure to balance the inward pull of gravity. At this point, when the gas stopped collapsing, our sun was born and the new solar system was complete!

CONNECTION TO
Language Arts

WRITING SKILL **Eyewitness Account** Research information on the formation of the outer planets, inner planets, and the sun. Then, imagine that you witnessed the formation of the planets and sun. Write a short story describing your experience.

SECTION Review

TN GLE 0807.Inq.3, GLE 0807.Inq.5, GLE 0807.12.4

Summary

- The solar system formed out of a vast cloud of gas and dust called the *nebula*.

- Gravity and pressure were balanced until something upset the balance. Then, the nebula began to collapse.

- Collapse of the solar nebula caused heating at the center, while planetesimals formed in surrounding space.

- The central mass of the nebula became the sun. Planets formed from the surrounding materials.

Using Key Terms

1. In your own words, write a definition for each of the following terms: *nebula* and *solar nebula*.

Understanding Key Ideas

2. What is the relationship between gravity and pressure in a nebula? ✔0807.12.6

   a. Gravity reduces pressure.

   b. Pressure balances gravity.

   c. Pressure increases gravity.

   d. None of the above

3. Describe how our solar system formed. ✔0807.12.6

4. Compare the inner planets with the outer planets.

Critical Thinking

5. **Identifying Relationships** The gravitational force between particles in the solar nebula is very weak because there is a lot of space between particles. But when globules form, the gravitational force exerted by the particles causes the globule to collapse. Explain how distance influences the amount of gravitational force between particles. ✔0807.Inq.3, ✔0807.12.6

6. **Evaluating Hypotheses** Beyond the orbit of Neptune, a field of smaller bodies orbits the sun. Some scientists think these objects are the remains of material that formed the early solar system. Use what you know about how solar systems form to evaluate this hypothesis. ✔0807.Inq.3

7. **Making Inferences** Why do all of the planets go around the sun in the same direction, and why do the planets lie on a relatively flat plane? ✔0807.Inq.3

Internet Resources

For a variety of links related to this chapter, go to www.scilinks.org
Topic: The Planets
SciLinks code: HSM1152

The Sun: Our Very Own Star

Can you imagine what life on Earth would be like if there were no sun? Without the sun, life on Earth would be impossible!

Energy from the sun lights and heats Earth's surface. Energy from the sun even drives the weather. Making up more than 99% of the solar system's mass, the sun is the dominant member of our solar system. The sun is basically a large ball of gas made mostly of hydrogen and helium held together by gravity. But what does the inside of the sun look like?

The Structure of the Sun

Although the sun may appear to have a solid surface, it does not. When you see a picture of the sun, you are really seeing through the sun's outer atmosphere. The visible surface of the sun starts at the point where the gas becomes so thick that you cannot see through it. As **Figure 1** shows, the sun is made of several layers.

What You Will Learn

● Describe the basic structure and composition of the sun.
● Explain how the sun generates energy.
● Describe the surface activity of the sun, and identify how this activity affects Earth.

Vocabulary

nuclear fusion
sunspot

READING STRATEGY

Reading Organizer As you read this section, create an outline of the section. Use the headings from the section in your outline.

TN **GLE 0807.Inq.3** Synthesize information to determine cause and effect relationships between evidence and explanations.

GLE 0807.Inq.5 Communicate scientific understanding using descriptions, explanations, and models.

GLE 0807.9.1 Understand that all matter is made up of atoms.

GLE 0807.9.6 Use the periodic table to determine the characteristics of an element.

Figure 1 The Structure and Atmosphere of the Sun

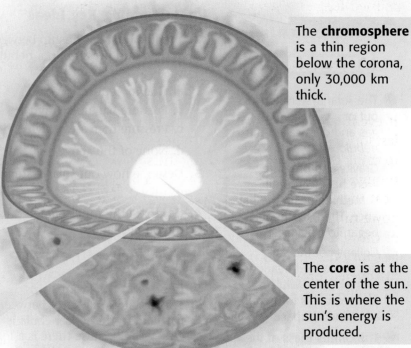

The **corona** forms the sun's outer atmosphere.

The **chromosphere** is a thin region below the corona, only 30,000 km thick.

The **photosphere** is the visible part of the sun that we can see from Earth.

The **convective zone** is a region about 200,000 km thick where gases circulate.

The **radiative zone** is a very dense region about 300,000 km thick.

The **core** is at the center of the sun. This is where the sun's energy is produced.

At first, some type of burning fuel was thought to be the source of the sun's energy.

A shrinking sun was another explanation for solar energy.

Figure 2 *Ideas about the source of the sun's energy have changed over time.*

Energy Production in the Sun

The sun has been shining on Earth for about 4.6 billion years. How can the sun stay hot for so long? And what makes it shine? **Figure 2** shows two theories that were proposed to answer these questions. Many scientists thought that the sun burned fuel to generate its energy. But the amount of energy that is released by burning would not be enough to power the sun. If the sun were simply burning, it would last for only 10,000 years.

Burning or Shrinking?

It eventually became clear to scientists that burning wouldn't last long enough to keep the sun shining. Then, scientists began to think that gravity was causing the sun to slowly shrink. They thought that perhaps gravity would release enough energy to heat the sun. While the release of gravitational energy is more powerful than burning, it is not enough to power the sun. If all of the sun's gravitational energy were released, the sun would last for only 45 million years. However, fossils that have been discovered prove that dinosaurs roamed the Earth more than 65 million years ago, so this couldn't be the case. Therefore, something even more powerful than gravity was needed.

✓ Reading Check Why isn't energy from gravity enough to power the sun?

Helium

Nucleus

Electron(−)

Neutron

Proton(+)

CONNECTION TO
Chemistry

Atoms An atom consists of a nucleus surrounded by one or more electrons. Electrons have a negative charge. In most elements, the atom's nucleus is made up of two types of particles: *protons,* which have a positive charge, and *neutrons,* which have no charge. The protons in the nucleus are usually balanced by an equal number of electrons. The number of protons and electrons gives the atom its chemical identity. A helium atom, shown at left, has two protons, two neutrons, and two electrons. Use a Periodic Table to find the chemical identity of the following atoms: nitrogen, oxygen, and carbon. ✔0807.9.10

Nuclear Fusion

At the beginning of the 20th century, Albert Einstein showed that matter and energy are interchangeable. Matter can change into energy according to his famous formula: $E = mc^2$. (E is energy, m is mass, and c is the speed of light.) Because c is such a large number, tiny amounts of matter can produce a huge amount of energy. With this idea, scientists began to understand a very powerful source of energy.

Nuclear fusion is the process by which two or more low-mass nuclei join together, or fuse, to form another nucleus. In this way, four hydrogen nuclei can fuse to form a single nucleus of helium. During the process, energy is produced. Scientists now know that the sun gets its energy from nuclear fusion. Einstein's equation, shown in **Figure 3,** changed ideas about the sun's energy source by equating mass and energy.

nuclear fusion the combination of the nuclei of small atoms to form a larger nucleus; releases energy

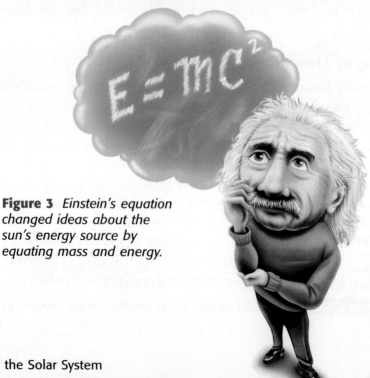

Figure 3 *Einstein's equation changed ideas about the sun's energy source by equating mass and energy.*

Fusion in the Sun

During fusion, under normal conditions, the nuclei of hydrogen atoms never get close enough to combine. The reason is that they are positively charged. Like charges repel each other, as shown in **Figure 4.** In the center of the sun, however, the temperature and pressure are very high. As a result, the hydrogen nuclei have enough energy to overcome the repulsive force, and hydrogen fuses into helium, as shown in **Figure 5.**

The energy produced in the center, or core of the sun takes millions of years to reach the sun's surface. The energy passes from the core through a very dense region called the *radiative zone*. The matter in the radiative zone is so crowded that the light and energy are blocked and sent in different directions. Eventually, the energy reaches the *convective zone*. Gases circulate in the convective zone, which is about 200,000 km thick. Hot gases in the convective zone carry the energy up to the *photosphere*, the visible surface of the sun. From there, the energy leaves the sun as light, which takes only 8.3 min to reach Earth.

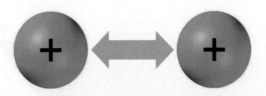

Figure 4 *Like charges repel just as similar poles on a pair of magnets do.*

✓ **Reading Check** What causes the nuclei of hydrogen atoms to repel each other?

Figure 5   Fusion of Hydrogen in the Sun

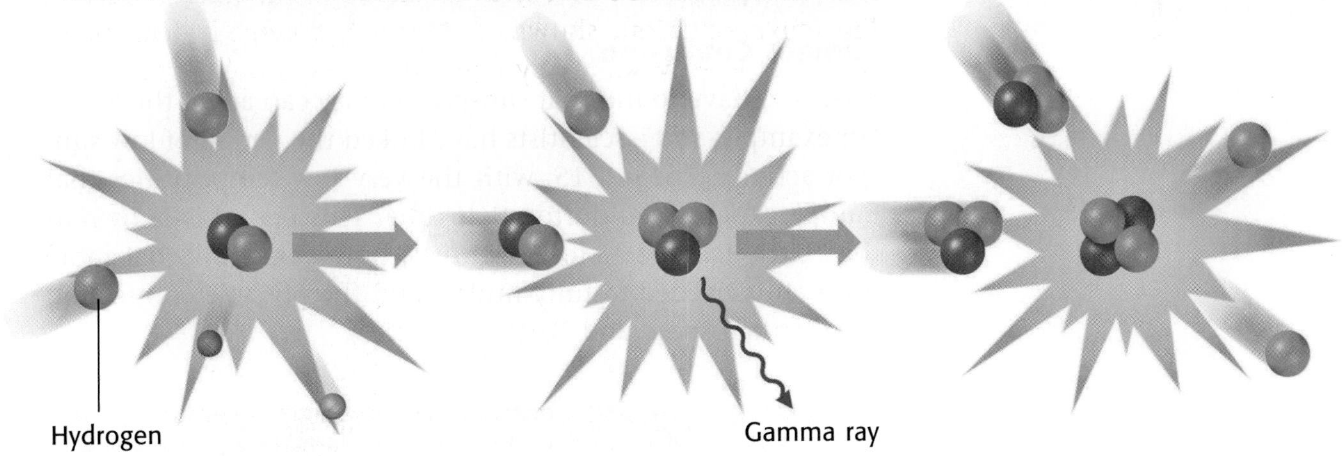

Hydrogen

Gamma ray

❶ **Deuterium** Two hydrogen nuclei (protons) collide. One proton emits particles and energy and then becomes a neutron. The proton and neutron combine to produce a heavy form of hydrogen called *deuterium*.

❷ **Helium-3** Deuterium combines with another hydrogen nucleus to form a variety of helium called *helium-3*. More energy, as well as gamma rays, is released.

❸ **Helium-4** Two helium-3 atoms then combine to form ordinary helium-4, which releases more energy and a pair of hydrogen nuclei.

Solar Activity

The photosphere is an ever-changing place. Thermal energy moves from the sun's interior by the circulation of gases in the convective zone. This movement of energy causes the gas in the photosphere to boil and churn. This circulation, combined with the sun's rotation, creates magnetic fields that reach far out into space.

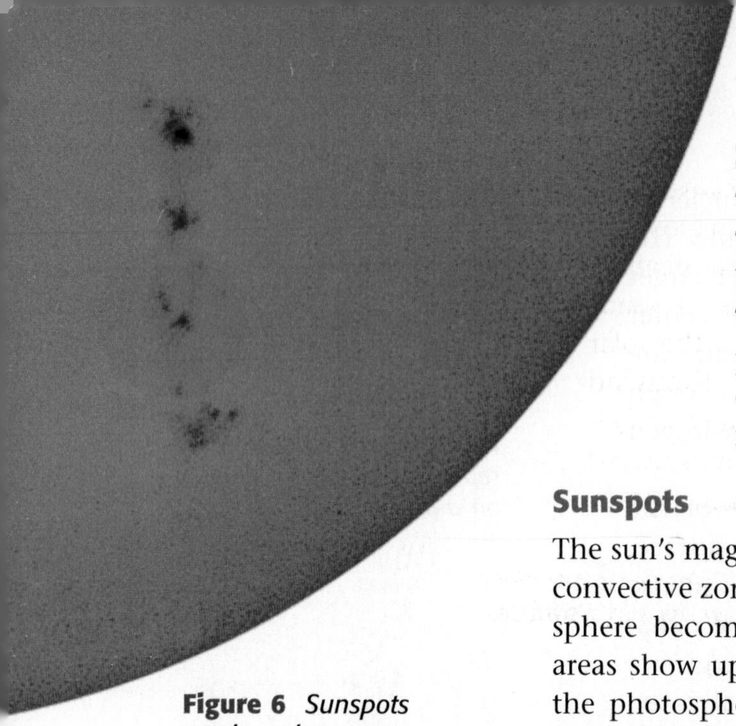

Sunspots

The sun's magnetic fields tend to slow down the activity in the convective zone. When activity slows down, areas of the photosphere become cooler than surrounding areas. These cooler areas show up as sunspots. **Sunspots** are cooler, dark spots of the photosphere of the sun, as shown in **Figure 6.** Sunspots can vary in shape and size. Some sunspots can be as large as 50,000 miles in diameter.

The numbers and locations of sunspots on the sun change in a regular cycle. Scientists have found that the sunspot cycle lasts about 11 years. Every 11 years, the amount of sunspot activity in the sun reaches a peak intensity and then decreases. **Figure 7** shows the sunspot cycle since 1610, excluding the years 1645–1715, which was a period of unusually low sunspot activity.

✓ Reading Check What are sunspots? What causes sunspots to occur?

Climate Confusion

Scientists have found that sunspot activity can affect the Earth. For example, some scientists have linked the period of low sunspot activity, 1645–1715, with the very low temperatures that Europe experienced during that time. This period is known as the "Little Ice Age." Most scientists, however, think that more research is needed to fully understand the possible connection between sunspots and Earth's climate.

Figure 6 *Sunspots mark cooler areas on the sun's surface. They are related to changes in the magnetic properties of the sun.*

sunspot a dark area of the photosphere of the sun that is cooler than the surrounding areas and that has a strong magnetic field

Figure 7 *This graph shows the number of sunspots that have occurred each year since Galileo's first observation in 1610.*

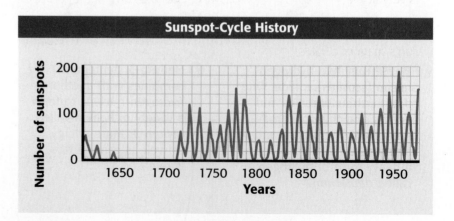

Solar Flares

The magnetic fields that cause sunspots also cause solar flares. *Solar flares,* as shown in **Figure 8,** are regions of extremely high temperature and brightness that develop on the sun's surface. When a solar flare erupts, it sends huge streams of electrically charged particles into the solar system. Solar flares can extend upward several thousand kilometers within minutes. Solar flares are usually associated with sunspots and can interrupt radio communications on Earth and in orbit. Scientists are trying to find ways to give advance warning of solar flares.

Figure 8 *Solar flares are giant eruptions on the sun's surface.*

SECTION Review

TN GLE 0807.Inq.3, GLE 0807.Inq.5, GLE 0807.9.1

Summary

- The sun is a large ball of gas made mostly of hydrogen and helium. The sun consists of many layers.
- The sun's energy comes from nuclear fusion that takes place in the center of the sun.
- The visible surface of the sun, or the photosphere, is very active.
- Sunspots and solar flares are the result of the sun's magnetic fields that reach space.
- Sunspot activity may affect Earth's climate, and solar flares can interact with Earth's atmosphere.

Using Key Terms

1. In your own words, write a definition for each of the following terms: *sunspot* and *nuclear fusion.*

Understanding Key Ideas

2. Which of the following statements describes how energy is produced in the sun? ✔0807.Inq.3

    a. The sun burns fuels to generate energy.

    b. As hydrogen changes into helium deep inside the sun, a great deal of energy is made.

    c. Energy is released as the sun shrinks because of gravity.

    d. None of the above

3. Describe the composition of the sun.

4. Name and describe the layers of the sun.

5. In which area of the sun do sunspots appear?

6. Explain how sunspots form. ✔0807.Inq.3

7. Describe how sunspots can affect the Earth. ✔0807.Inq.3

8. What are solar flares, and how do they form? ✔0807.Inq.3

Math Skills

9. If the equatorial diameter of the sun is 1.39 million kilometers, how many kilometers is the sun's radius?

Critical Thinking

10. **Applying Concepts** If nuclear fusion in the sun's core suddenly stopped today, would the sky be dark in the daytime tomorrow? Explain. ✔0807.Inq.3

11. **Making Comparisons** Compare the theories that scientists proposed about the source of the sun's energy with the process of nuclear fusion in the sun.

The Earth Takes Shape

In many ways, Earth seems to be a perfect place for life.

We live on the third planet from the sun. The Earth, shown in **Figure 1,** is mostly made of rock, and nearly three-fourths of its surface is covered with water. It is surrounded by a protective atmosphere of mostly nitrogen and oxygen and smaller amounts of other gases. But Earth has not always been such an oasis in the solar system.

Formation of the Solid Earth

The Earth formed as planetesimals in the solar system collided and combined. From what scientists can tell, the Earth formed within the first 10 million years of the collapse of the solar nebula!

The Effects of Gravity

When a young planet is still small, it can have an irregular shape, somewhat like a potato. But as the planet gains more matter, the force of gravity increases. When a rocky planet, such as Earth, reaches a diameter of about 350 km, the force of gravity becomes greater than the strength of the rock. As the Earth grew to this size, the rock at its center was crushed by gravity and the planet started to become round.

The Effects of Heat

As the Earth was changing shape, it was also heating up. Planetesimals continued to collide with the Earth, and the energy of their motion heated the planet. Radioactive material, which was present in the Earth as it formed, also heated the young planet. After Earth reached a certain size, the temperature rose faster than the interior could cool, and the rocky material inside began to melt. Today, the Earth is still cooling from the energy that was generated when it formed. Volcanoes, earthquakes, and hot springs are effects of this energy trapped inside the Earth. As you will learn later, the effects of heat and gravity also helped form the Earth's layers when the Earth was very young.

✓ **Reading Check** What factors heated the Earth during its early formation?

Figure 1 *When Earth is seen from space, one of its unique features—the presence of water—is apparent.*

How the Earth's Layers Formed

Have you ever watched the oil separate from vinegar in a bottle of salad dressing? The vinegar sinks because it is denser than oil. The Earth's layers formed in much the same way. As rocks melted, denser materials, such as nickel and iron, sank to the center of the Earth and formed the core. Less dense materials floated to the surface and became the crust. This process is shown in **Figure 2.**

The **crust** is the thin, outermost layer of the Earth. It is 5 to 100 km thick. Crustal rock is made of materials that have low densities, such as oxygen, silicon, and aluminum. The **mantle** is the layer of Earth beneath the crust. It extends 2,900 km below the surface. Mantle rock is made of materials such as magnesium and iron and is denser than crustal rock. The **core** is the central part of the Earth below the mantle. It contains the densest materials (nickel and iron) and extends to the center of the Earth—almost 6,400 km below the surface.

crust the thin and solid outermost layer of the Earth above the mantle

mantle the layer of rock between the Earth's crust and core

core the central part of the Earth below the mantle

Figure 2 **The Formation of Earth's Layers**

❶ All materials in the early Earth are randomly mixed.

❷ Rocks melt, and denser materials sink toward the center. Less dense elements rise and form layers.

❸ According to composition, the Earth is divided into three layers: the crust, the mantle, and the core.

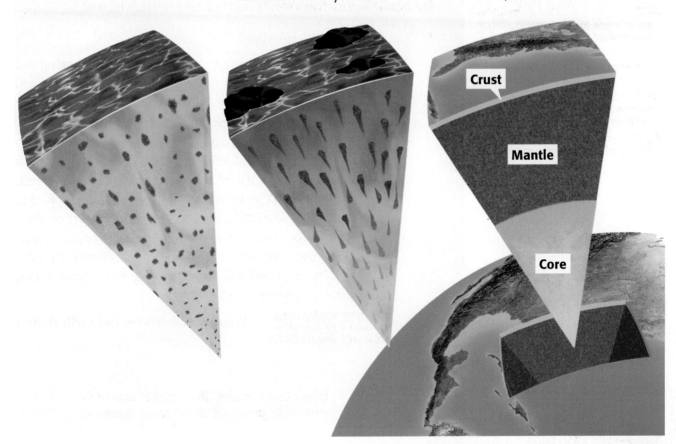

Crust

Mantle

Core

CONNECTION TO
Environmental Science

WRITING SKILL **The Greenhouse Effect** Carbon dioxide is a greenhouse gas. Greenhouse gases are gases that absorb thermal energy and radiate it back to Earth. This process is called the greenhouse effect because the gases function like the walls and roof of a greenhouse, which allow solar energy to enter but prevent thermal energy from escaping. Do research to find the percentage of carbon dioxide that is thought to make up Earth's early atmosphere. Write a report, and share your findings with your class. ✔0807.9.9

Formation of the Earth's Atmosphere

Today, Earth's atmosphere is a mixture of 78% nitrogen and 21% oxygen. The remaining 1% is a mixture of argon, water vapor, carbon dioxide, ozone, and other gases. Did you know that the Earth's atmosphere did not always contain the oxygen that you need to live? The Earth's atmosphere has changed over time. Scientists think that Earth's earliest atmosphere was very different than it is today.

Earth's Early Atmosphere

Scientists think that Earth's early atmosphere was a mixture of gases that were released as Earth cooled. During the final stages of the Earth's formation, its surface was very hot—even molten in places—as shown in **Figure 3.** The molten rock released large amounts of carbon dioxide and water vapor. Therefore, scientists think that Earth's early atmosphere was a steamy mixture of carbon dioxide and water vapor.

TN **Standards Check** Describe Earth's early atmosphere. ✔0807.9.9

Figure 3 *This artwork is an artist's view of what Earth's surface may have looked like shortly after the Earth formed.*

Figure 4 *As this volcano in Hawaii shows, a large amount of gas is released during an eruption.*

Earth's Changing Atmosphere

As the Earth cooled and its layers formed, the Earth's atmosphere changed again. This atmosphere probably formed from volcanic gases. Volcanoes, such as the one in **Figure 4,** released chlorine, nitrogen, and sulfur in addition to large amounts of carbon dioxide and water vapor. Some of this water vapor may have condensed to form the Earth's first oceans.

Comets, which are planetesimals made of ice, also may have contributed to this change of Earth's atmosphere. As comets crashed into the Earth, they brought in a range of elements, such as carbon, hydrogen, oxygen, and nitrogen. Comets also may have brought some of the water that helped form the oceans.

The Role of Life

How did this change of Earth's atmosphere become the air you are breathing right now? The answer is related to the appearance of life on Earth.

Ultraviolet Radiation

Scientists think that ultraviolet (UV) radiation, the same radiation that causes sunburns, helped produce the conditions necessary for life. Because UV light has a lot of energy, it can break apart molecules in your skin and in the air. Today, we are shielded from most of the sun's UV rays by Earth's protective ozone layer. But Earth's early atmosphere probably did not have ozone, so many molecules in the air and at Earth's surface were broken apart. Over time, this material collected in the Earth's waters. Water offered protection from the effects of UV radiation. In these sheltered pools of water, chemicals may have combined to form the complex molecules that made life possible. The first life-forms were very simple and did not need oxygen to live.

Comets and Meteors

What is the difference between a comet and a meteor? With a parent or guardian, research the difference between comets and meteors. Then, find out if you can view meteor showers in your area!

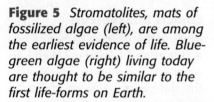
Figure 5 *Stromatolites, mats of fossilized algae (left), are among the earliest evidence of life. Blue-green algae (right) living today are thought to be similar to the first life-forms on Earth.*

The Source of Oxygen

Sometime before 3.4 billion years ago, organisms that produced food by photosynthesis appeared. *Photosynthesis* is the process of absorbing energy from the sun and carbon dioxide from the atmosphere to make food. During the process of making food, these organisms released oxygen—a gas that was not abundant in the atmosphere at that time. Scientists think that the descendants of these early life-forms are still around today, as shown in **Figure 5.**

Photosynthetic organisms helped change Earth's atmosphere into the mixture of gases you breathe today. Over hundreds of millions of years, more oxygen was added to the atmosphere and carbon dioxide was removed. As oxygen levels increased, energy from sunlight caused oxygen molecules in the atmosphere to react with each other. This reaction created a layer of ozone in the stratosphere. This ozone blocked most of the UV radiation and made it possible for life, in the form of simple plants, to move onto land about 2.2 billion years ago.

TN Standards Check How did photosynthesis change the mixture of gases in Earth's early atmosphere? ✓0807.9.9

Formation of Oceans and Continents

Scientists think that the oceans probably formed during Earth's second atmosphere, when the Earth was cool enough for rain to fall and remain on the surface. After millions of years of rainfall, water began to cover the Earth. By 4 billion years ago, a global ocean covered the planet.

For the first few hundred million years of Earth's history, there may not have been any continents. Given the composition of the rocks that make up the continents, scientists know that these rocks have melted and cooled many times in the past. Each time the rocks melted, the heavier elements sank and the lighter ones rose to the surface.

The Growth of Continents

After a while, some of the rocks were light enough to pile up on the surface. These rocks were the beginning of the earliest continents. The continents gradually thickened and slowly rose above the surface of the ocean. These scattered young continents did not stay in the same place, however. The slow transfer of thermal energy in the mantle pushed them around. Approximately 2.5 billion years ago, continents really started to grow. And by 1.5 billion years ago, the upper mantle had cooled and had become denser and heavier. At this time, it was easier for the cooler parts of the mantle to sink. These conditions made it easier for the continents to move in the same way that they do today.

INTERNET ACTIVITY

For another activity related to this chapter, go to **go.hrw.com** and type in the keyword **HZ5SOLW**.

SECTION Review

TN GLE 0807.Inq.3, GLE 0807.Inq.5, GLE 0807.9.5

Summary

- The effects of gravity and heat created the shape and structure of Earth.
- The Earth is divided into three main layers based on composition: the crust, mantle, and core.
- The presence of life dramatically changed Earth's atmosphere by adding free oxygen.
- Earth's oceans formed shortly after the Earth did, when it had cooled off enough for rain to fall. Continents formed when lighter materials gathered on the surface and rose above sea level.

Using Key Terms

1. Use each of the following terms in a separate sentence: *crust*, *mantle*, and *core*.

Understanding Key Ideas

2. Earth's first atmosphere was mostly a mixture of ✔0807.9.9
   a. nitrogen and oxygen.
   b. chlorine, nitrogen, and sulfur.
   c. carbon dioxide and water vapor.
   d. water vapor and oxygen.

3. Describe the structure of the Earth.

4. Why did the Earth separate into distinct layers?

5. Describe how Earth's atmosphere developed into a mixture of gases. ✔0807.9.9

6. Explain how Earth's oceans and continents formed. ✔0807.Inq.3

Critical Thinking

7. **Applying Concepts** How did the effects of gravity help shape the Earth? ✔0807.Inq.3

8. **Making Inferences** How would the removal of forests affect the Earth's atmosphere? ✔0807.Inq.3

Interpreting Graphics

Use the illustration below to answer the questions that follow.

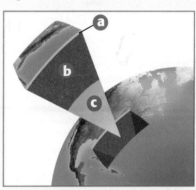

9. Which of the layers is composed mostly of the elements magnesium and iron?

10. Which of the layers is composed mostly of the elements iron and nickel?

Planetary Motion

Why do the planets revolve around the sun? Why don't they fly off into space? Does something hold them in their paths?

What You Will Learn

● Explain the difference between rotation and revolution.
● Describe three laws of planetary motion.
● Describe how distance and mass affect gravitational attraction.

Vocabulary

rotation
orbit
revolution

READING STRATEGY

Paired Summarizing Read this section silently. In pairs, take turns summarizing the material. Stop to discuss ideas that seem confusing.

TN GLE 0807.Inq.2 Use appropriate tools and techniques to gather, organize, analyze, and interpret data.

GLE 0807.Inq.3 Synthesize information to determine cause and effect relationships between evidence and explanations.

GLE 0807.Inq.5 Communicate scientific understanding using descriptions, explanations, and models.

GLE 0807.12.4 Identify factors that influence the amount of gravitational force between objects.

GLE 0807.12.5 Recognize that gravity is the force that controls the motion of objects in the solar system.

To answer these questions, you need to go back in time to look at the discoveries made by the scientists of the 1500s and 1600s. Danish astronomer Tycho Brahe (TIE koh BRAH uh) carefully observed the positions of planets for more than 25 years. When Brahe died in 1601, a German astronomer named Johannes Kepler (yoh HAHN uhs KEP luhr) continued Brahe's work. Kepler set out to understand the motions of planets and to describe the solar system.

A Revolution in Astronomy

Each planet spins on its axis. The spinning of a body, such as a planet, on its axis is called **rotation.** As the Earth rotates, only one-half of the Earth faces the sun. The half facing the sun is light (day). The half that faces away from the sun is dark (night).

The path that a body follows as it travels around another body in space is called the **orbit.** One complete trip along an orbit is called a **revolution.** The amount of time a planet takes to complete a single trip around the sun is called a *period of revolution.* Each planet takes a different amount of time to circle the sun. Earth's period of revolution is about 365.25 days (a year), but Mercury orbits the sun in only 88 days. **Figure 1** illustrates the orbit and revolution of the Earth around the sun as well as the rotation of the Earth on its axis.

Figure 1 *A planet rotates on its own axis and revolves around the sun in a path called an* orbit.

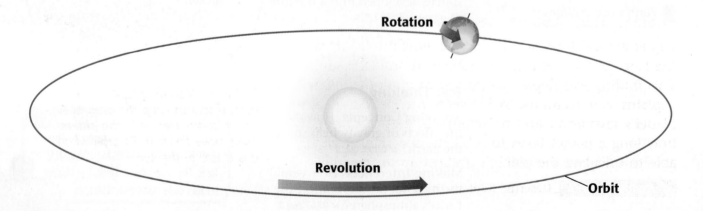

Rotation

Revolution

Orbit

Figure 2 Parts of an Ellipse

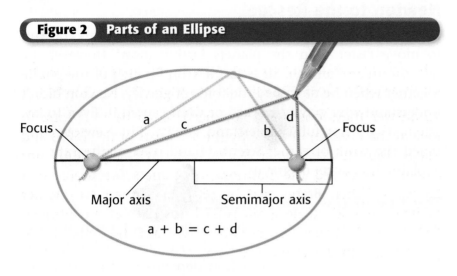

Kepler's Formula

Kepler's third law can be expressed with the formula

$$P^2 = a^3$$

where P is the period of revolution and a is the semimajor axis of an orbiting body. For example, Mars's period is 1.88 years, and its semimajor axis is 1.523 AU. Thus, $1.88^2 = 1.523^3 = 3.53$. Calculate a planet's period of revolution if the semimajor axis is 5.74 AU.

Kepler's First Law of Motion

Kepler's first discovery came from his careful study of Mars. Kepler discovered that Mars did not move in a circle around the sun but moved in an elongated circle called an *ellipse*. This finding became Kepler's first law of motion. An ellipse is a closed curve in which the sum of the distances from the edge of the curve to two points inside the ellipse is always the same, as shown in **Figure 2.** An ellipse's maximum length is called its *major axis*. Half of this distance is the *semimajor axis,* which is usually used to describe the size of an ellipse. The semimajor axis of Earth's orbit—the maximum distance between Earth and the sun—is about 150 million kilometers.

Kepler's Second Law of Motion

Kepler's second discovery, or second law of motion, was that the planets seemed to move faster when they are close to the sun and slower when they are farther away. To understand this idea, imagine that a planet is attached to the sun by a string, as modeled in **Figure 3.** When the string is shorter, the planet must move faster to cover the same area.

Kepler's Third Law of Motion

Kepler noticed that planets that are more distant from the sun, such as Saturn, take longer to orbit the sun. This finding was Kepler's third law of motion, which explains the relationship between the period of a planet's revolution and its semimajor axis. Knowing how long a planet takes to orbit the sun, Kepler was able to calculate the planet's distance from the sun.

Reading Check Describe Kepler's third law of motion.

rotation the spin of a body on its axis

orbit the path that a body follows as it travels around another body in space

revolution the motion of a body that travels around another body in space; one complete trip along an orbit

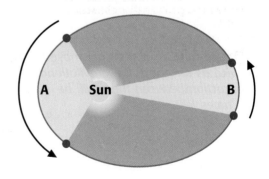

Figure 3 *According to Kepler's second law, to keep the area of* A *equal to the area of* B, *the planet must move faster in its orbit when it is closer to the sun.*

Newton to the Rescue!

Kepler wondered what caused the planets closest to the sun to move faster than the planets farther away. However, he never found an answer. Sir Isaac Newton finally put the puzzle together when he described the force of gravity. Newton didn't understand why gravity worked or what caused it. Even today, scientists do not fully understand gravity. But Newton combined the work of earlier scientists and used mathematics to explain the effects of gravity.

The Law of Universal Gravitation

Newton reasoned that an object falls toward Earth because Earth and the object are attracted to each other by gravity. He discovered that this attraction depends on the masses of the objects and the distance between the objects.

Newton's *law of universal gravitation* states that the force of gravity depends on the product of the masses of the objects divided by the square of the distance between the objects. The larger the masses of two objects and the closer together the objects are, the greater the force of gravity between the objects. For example, if two objects are moved twice as far apart, the gravitational attraction between them will decrease by 2×2 (a factor of 4), as shown in **Figure 4.** If two objects are moved 10 times as far apart, the gravitational attraction between them will decrease by 10×10 (a factor of 100).

Both Earth and the moon are attracted to each other. Although it may seem as if Earth does not orbit the moon, Earth and the moon actually orbit each other.

TN Standards Check Explain Newton's law of universal gravitation. ✔0807.12.6

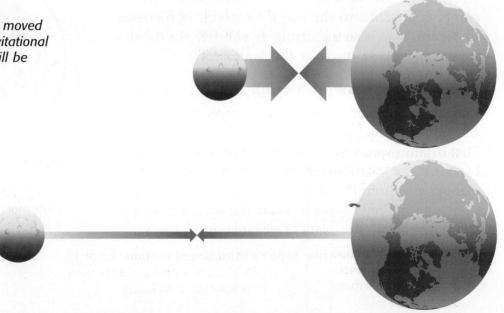

Figure 4 *If two objects are moved twice as far apart, the gravitational attraction between them will be 4 times less.*

Orbits Falling Down and Around

If you drop a rock, it falls to the ground. So, why doesn't the moon come crashing into the Earth? The answer has to do with the moon's inertia. *Inertia* is an object's resistance in speed or direction until an outside force acts on the object. In space, there isn't any air to cause resistance and slow down the moving moon. Therefore, the moon continues to move, but gravity keeps the moon in orbit, as **Figure 5** shows.

Imagine twirling a ball on the end of a string. As long as you hold the string, the ball will orbit your hand. As soon as you let go of the string, the ball will fly off in a straight path. This same principle applies to the moon. Gravity keeps the moon from flying off in a straight path. This principle holds true for all bodies in orbit, including the Earth and other planets in our solar system.

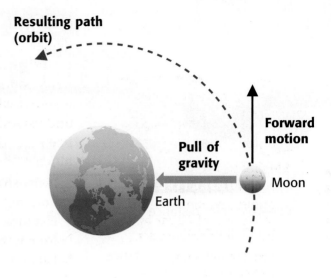

Figure 5 *Gravity causes the moon to fall toward the Earth and changes a straight-line path into a curved orbit.*

SECTION Review

TN GLE 0807.Inq.3, GLE 0807.Inq.5, GLE 0807.12.4, GLE 0807.12.5

Summary

- Rotation is the spinning of a planet on its axis, and revolution is one complete trip along an orbit.

- Planets move in an ellipse around the sun. The closer they are to the sun, the faster they move. The period of a planet's revolution depends on the planet's semimajor axis.

- Gravitational attraction decreases as distance increases and as mass decreases.

Using Key Terms

1. In your own words, write a definition for each of the following terms: *revolution* and *rotation*.

Understanding Key Ideas

2. Kepler discovered that planets move faster when they
   a. are farther from the sun.
   b. are closer to the sun.
   c. have more mass.
   d. rotate faster.

3. On what properties does the force of gravity between two objects depend? ✔0807.12.6

4. How does gravity keep a planet moving in an orbit around the sun? ✔0807.Inq.3, ✔0807.12.6, ✔0807.12.7

Math Skills

5. The Earth's period of revolution is 365.25 days. Convert this period of revolution into hours.

Critical Thinking

6. **Applying Concepts** If a planet had two moons and one moon was twice as far from the planet as the other, which moon would complete a revolution of the planet first? Explain your answer. ✔0807.Inq.3, ✔0807.12.7

7. **Making Comparisons** Describe the three laws of planetary motion. How is each law related to the other laws? ✔0807.12.6, ✔0807.12.7

Internet Resources

For a variety of links related to this chapter, go to www.scilinks.org

Topic: Kepler's Laws
SciLinks code: HSM0827

Skills Practice Lab

OBJECTIVES

Create a solar-distance measuring device.

Calculate the Earth's distance from the sun.

MATERIALS

- aluminum foil, 5 cm × 5 cm
- card, index
- meterstick
- poster board
- ruler, metric
- scissors
- tape, masking
- thumbtack

SAFETY

How Far Is the Sun?

It doesn't slice, it doesn't dice, but it can give you an idea of how big our universe is! You can build your very own solar-distance measuring device from household items. Amaze your friends by figuring out how many metersticks can be placed between the Earth and the sun.

Ask a Question

1 How many metersticks could I place between the Earth and the sun?

Form a Hypothesis

2 Write a hypothesis that answers the question above.

Test the Hypothesis

3 Measure and cut a 4 cm × 4 cm square from the middle of the poster board. Tape the foil square over the hole in the center of the poster board.

4 Using a thumbtack, carefully prick the foil to form a tiny hole in the center. Congratulations! You have just constructed your very own solar-distance measuring device!

5 Tape the device to a window facing the sun so that sunlight shines directly through the pinhole. **Caution:** Do not look directly into the sun.

6 Place one end of the meterstick against the window and beneath the foil square. Steady the meterstick with one hand.

7 With the other hand, hold the index card close to the pinhole. You should be able to see a circular image on the card. This image is an image of the sun.

8 Move the card back until the image is large enough to measure. Be sure to keep the image on the card sharply focused. Reposition the meterstick so that it touches the bottom of the card.

TN GLE 0807.Inq.2 Use appropriate tools and techniques to gather, organize, analyze, and interpret data.

GLE 0807.Inq.3 Synthesize information to determine cause and effect relationships between evidence and explanations.

GLE 0807.Inq.4 Recognize possible sources of bias and error, alternative explanations, and questions for further exploration.

GLE 0807.Inq.5 Communicate scientific understanding using descriptions, explanations, and models.

Analyze the Results

1. **Analyzing Results** According to your calculations, how far from the Earth is the sun? Don't forget to convert your measurements to meters.

Draw Conclusions

2. **Evaluating Data** You could put 150 billion metersticks between the Earth and the sun. Compare this information with your result in step 11. Do you think that this activity was a good way to measure the Earth's distance from the sun? Support your answer. ✓0807.Inq.3, ✓0807.Inq.4

9. Ask your partner to measure the diameter of the image on the card by using the metric ruler. Record the diameter of the image in millimeters.

10. Record the distance between the window and the index card by reading the point at which the card rests on the meterstick.

11. Calculate the distance between Earth and the sun by using the following formula:

$$\text{distance between the sun and Earth} = \text{sun's diameter} \times \frac{\text{distance to the image}}{\text{image's diameter}}$$

1 cm = 10 mm
1 m = 100 cm
1 km = 1,000 m

(Hint: The sun's diameter is 1,392,000,000 m.)

Chapter Review

TN GLE 0807.Inq.3, GLE 0807.Inq.5, GLE 0807.9.5, GLE 0807.12.4, GLE 0807.12.5

USING KEY TERMS

Complete each of the following sentences by choosing the correct term from the word bank.

nebula   crust
mantle   solar nebula

1 A ___ is a large cloud of gas and dust in interstellar space.

2 The ___ lies between the core and the crust of the Earth.

For each pair of terms, explain how the meanings of the terms differ.

3 *nebula* and *solar nebula*

4 *crust* and *mantle*

5 *rotation* and *revolution*

6 *sunspot* and *solar flare*

UNDERSTANDING KEY IDEAS

Multiple Choice

7 To determine a planet's period of revolution, you must know its   ✔0807.12.7
a. size.
b. mass.
c. orbit.
d. All of the above

8 During Earth's formation, materials such as nickel and iron sank to the
a. mantle.
b. core.
c. crust.
d. All of the above

9 Planetary orbits are shaped like
a. orbits.
b. spirals.
c. ellipses.
d. periods of revolution.

10 Impacts in the early solar system
a. brought new materials to the planets.
b. released energy.
c. dug craters.
d. All of the above

11 The two factors that influence the amount of gravitational force between objects are   ✔0807.12.6
a. pressure and gravity.
b. mass and velocity.
c. mass and distance.
d. distance and gravity.

12 Which of the following planets has the shortest period of revolution?
✔0807.12.7
a. Mars   c. Mercury
b. Earth   d. Jupiter

13 Which gas in Earth's atmosphere suggests that there is life on Earth?
✔0807.9.9
a. hydrogen   c. carbon dioxide
b. oxygen   d. nitrogen

14 Which layer of the Earth has the lowest density?
a. the core
b. the mantle
c. the crust
d. None of the above

15 What is the measure of the average kinetic energy of particles in an object?

a. temperature   c. gravity

b. pressure   d. force

Short Answer

16 Explain how the chemical makeup of the atmosphere illustrates a mixture of gases.   ✔0807.9.9

17 Describe how the Earth's oceans and continents formed.

18 Explain how pressure and gravity may have become unbalanced in the solar nebula.   ✔0807.12.6

19 Define *nuclear fusion* in your own words. Describe how nuclear fusion generates the sun's energy.

CRITICAL THINKING

20 **Concept Mapping** Use the following terms to create a concept map: *solar nebula, solar system, planetesimals, sun, photosphere, core, nuclear fusion, planets,* and *Earth.*

21 **Making Comparisons** How did Newton's law of universal gravitation help explain the work of Johannes Kepler?   ✔0807.12.6, ✔0807.12.7

22 **Predicting Consequences** Using what you know about the relationship between living things and the development of Earth's atmosphere, explain how the formation of ozone holes in Earth's atmosphere could affect living things.   ✔0807.Inq.3

23 **Identifying Relationships** Describe Kepler's three laws of motion in your own words. Describe how each law relates to either the revolution, rotation, or orbit of a planetary body.   ✔0807.12.6, ✔0807.12.7

INTERPRETING GRAPHICS

Use the illustration below to answer the questions that follow.

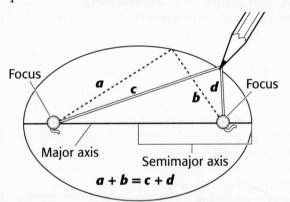

Focus   Focus

a   *c*   *b*   *d*

Major axis   Semimajor axis

$a + b = c + d$

24 Which of Kepler's laws of motion does the illustration represent?

25 How does the equation shown above support the law?

26 What is an ellipse's maximum length called?

$E = mc^2$

TCAP Test Preparation

TN SPI 0807.Inq.3 Interpret and translate data into a table, graph, or diagram.

SPI 0807.Inq.4 Draw a conclusion that establishes a cause and effect relationship supported by evidence.

SPI 0807.9.5 Describe the chemical makeup of the atmosphere.

Multiple Choice

Use the table below to answer question 1.

Gravitational Force Versus Distance Data	
Distance (meters)	Force (Newtons)
1.0	4.00
2.0	1.00
4.0	0.250
8.0	0.0625

1. **Which graph best fits the data provided in the table?**

    A.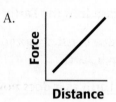

    B.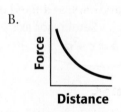

    C.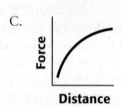

    D.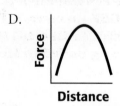

2. **Which of the following planets takes the longest time to complete one revolution of the sun?**

    A. Earth

    B. Venus

    C. Mercury

    D. Jupiter

3. **Which of the following will most likely occur inside a cold nebula?**

    A. Rapid collisions will push particles far apart.

    B. Particles will move closer to one another due to gravity.

    C. Gravity and pressure will push particles rapidly together.

    D. No forces will act on the particles, and the particles will drift apart.

4. **Which of the following statements about the gases in Earth's atmosphere is true?**

    A. The gases in the atmosphere are nonreactive.

    B. Most of the ozone in the atmosphere is located in the photosphere.

    C. 78% of Earth's atmosphere is nitrogen, 21% is oxygen, and the rest is other gases.

    D. Oxygen was one of the gases in Earth's very early atmosphere.

SPI 0807.12.5 Determine the relationship among the mass of objects, the distance between these objects, and the amount of gravitational attraction.

SPI 0807.12.6 Illustrate how gravity controls the motion of objects in the solar system.

5. **How has photosynthesis changed the mixture of gases in Earth's atmosphere? During photosynthesis, plants take in**

   A. carbon dioxide from the atmosphere and release oxygen.

   B. oxygen from the atmosphere and release nitrogen.

   C. nitrogen from the atmosphere and release carbon dioxide.

   D. sulfur from the atmosphere and release nitrogen.

Use the diagram below to answer questions 6–7.

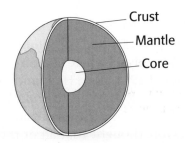

Crust
Mantle
Core

6. **Pam made the sketch of Earth's layers shown above. What is the most likely location of the densest elements?**

   A. crust

   B. mantle

   C. core

   D. all layers

7. **Pam made a second sketch of the Earth as it looked during the early period of planetary accretion. How would Pam's new sketch compare with the sketch above? The new sketch would**

   A. look about the same as the one above.

   B. have more layers than the sketch above.

   C. have only the mantle and core layers.

   D. show materials that are randomly mixed.

8. **A student swings a ball attached to a string to model the moon's orbit around the Earth. What force does the string represent?**

   A. inertia

   B. pressure

   C. gravity

   D. momentum

9. **If there were no gravitational forces acting on the moon, the moon would**

   A. quickly crash into the Earth.

   B. continue at a constant speed in a straight line through space.

   C. still orbit Earth as it does now.

   D. remain stationary, at a fixed distance from Earth.

Open Response

10. **In 2011, NASA's MESSENGER spacecraft is expected to decrease its forward velocity and begin orbiting the planet Mercury as it enters Mercury's gravitational field. Draw a diagram to illustrate how the gravity of Mercury will begin to control the motion of the MESSENGER spacecraft. Explain why MESSENGER will orbit Mercury instead of being pulled to Mercury's surface by gravity.**

11. **Two objects are near each other in space. If the objects are moved farther apart, how would the amount of gravitational attraction between the two objects be affected? If the objects are moved closer together, how would the amount of gravitational attraction between them be affected? Explain your answers.**

TCAP Test Preparation

Science in Action

Science, Technology, and Society

Far-Sighted

T/E Have you ever noticed that you see more stars at night when you are away from the city? "Light pollution" from city lights makes it hard to see stars and planets. Astronomers face the same problem when studying galaxies. Light from bright stars near Earth make it difficult to detect fainter light from distant galaxies using a telescope. Sending telescopes into space helps solve this problem.

The Spitzer Space Telescope, launched in 2003, has provided new information about how our solar system was formed. The Spitzer telescope also detects and analyzes the infrared light emitted by objects in space. It detected a star 450 light-years away in the UX Tau A system. Scientists think that the star could have planets around it. Scientists hope to use more sensitive space telescopes to search for planets in the UX Tau A system.

TN GLE 0807.T/E.1

Scientific Discoveries

The Oort Cloud

Have you ever wondered where comets come from? In 1950, Dutch astronomer Jan Oort decided to find out where comets originated. Oort studied 19 comets. He found that none of these comets had orbits indicating that the comets had come from outside the solar system. Oort thought that all of the comets had come from an area at the far edge of the solar system. In addition, he believed that the comets had entered the planetary system from different directions. These conclusions led Oort to theorize that the area from which comets come surrounds the solar system like a sphere and that comets can come from any point within the sphere. Today, this spherical zone at the edge of the solar system is called the *Oort Cloud*. Astronomers believe that billions or even trillions of comets may exist within the Oort Cloud.

Math ACTiViTY

Scientists measure distances in space in *light-years*. A light-year is the distance light travels in one year. The star system UX Tau A is 450 light-years from Earth. Light travels at 3.00×10^8 meters per second. If there are 3.15×10^7 seconds in a year, how many kilometers from Earth is UX Tau A?

Social Studies ACTiViTY

WRITING SKILL Before astronomers understood the nature of comets, comets were a source of much fear and misunderstanding among humans. Research some of the myths that humans have created about comets. Summarize your findings in a short essay.

Subrahmanyan Chandrasekhar

From White Dwarfs to Black Holes You may be familiar with the *Chandra X-Ray Observatory*. Launched by NASA in July 1999 to search for X-Ray sources in space, the observatory is the most powerful X-Ray telescope that has ever been built. However, you may not know how the observatory got its name. The *Chandra X-Ray Observatory* was named after the Indian American astrophysicist Subrahmanyan Chandrasekhar (SOOB ruh MAHN yuhn CHUHN druh SAY kuhr).

One of the most influential astrophysicists of the 20th century, Chandrasekhar was simply known as "Chandra" by his fellow scientists. Chandrasekhar made many contributions to physics and astrophysics. The contribution for which Chandrasekhar is best known was made in 1933, when he was a 23-year-old graduate student at Cambridge University in England. At the time, astrophysicists thought that all stars eventually became planet-sized stars known as *white dwarfs*. But from his calculations, Chandrasekhar believed that not all stars ended their lives as white dwarfs. He determined that the upper limit to the mass of a white dwarf was 1.4 times the mass of the sun. Stars that were more massive would collapse and would become very dense objects. These objects are now known as *black holes*. Chandrasekhar's ideas revolutionized astrophysics. In 1983, at the age of 73, Chandrasekhar was awarded the Nobel Prize in physics for his work on the stars.

Language Arts ACTIVITY

WRITING SKILL Using the Internet or another source, research the meaning of the word *chandra*. Write a paragraph describing your findings.

go.hrw.com

To learn more about these Science in Action topics, visit go.hrw.com and type in the keyword **HZ5SOLF.**

Current Science

Check out Current Science® articles related to this chapter by visiting go.hrw.com. Just type in the keyword **HZ5CS20.**

Electromagnetism

The Big Idea

Forces of attraction and repulsion result from magnetic and electric fields.

TN Tennessee Science Standards

Embedded Inquiry

GLE 0807.Inq.2 Use appropriate tools and techniques to gather, organize, analyze, and interpret data. **GLE 0807.Inq.3** Synthesize information to determine cause and effect relationships between evidence and explanations. **GLE 0807.Inq.4** Recognize possible sources of bias and error, alternative explanations, and questions for further exploration. **GLE 0807.Inq.5** Communicate scientific understanding using descriptions, explanations, and models. ✔**0807.Inq.1** Design and conduct an open-ended scientific investigation to answer a question that includes a control and appropriate variables. ✔**0807.Inq.2** Identify tools and techniques needed to gather, organize, analyze, and interpret data collected from a moderately complex scientific investigation. ✔**0807.Inq.3** Use evidence from a dataset to determine cause and effect relationships that explain a phenomenon. ✔**0807.Inq.4** Review an experimental design to determine possible sources of bias or error, state alternative explanations, and identify questions for further investigation. ✔**0807.Inq.5** Design a method to explain the results of an investigation using descriptions, explanations, or models.

Embedded Technology and Engineering

GLE 0807.T/E.1 Explore how technology responds to social, political, and economic needs. **GLE 0807.T/E.2** Know that the engineering design process involves an ongoing series of events that incorporate design constraints, model building, testing, evaluating, modifying, and retesting. **GLE 0807.T/E.3** Compare the intended benefits with the unintended consequences of a new technology. ✔**0807.T/E.2** Apply the engineering design process to construct a prototype that meets certain specifications.

Physical Science

GLE 0807.9.1 Understand that all matter is made up of atoms. **GLE 0807.9.2** Explain that matter has properties that are determined by the structure and arrangement of its atoms. **GLE 0807.12.1** Investigate the relationship between magnetism and electricity. **GLE 0807.12.2** Design an investigation to change the strength of an electromagnet. **GLE 0807.12.3** Compare and contrast the earth's magnetic field to that of a magnet and an electromagnet. ✔**0807.9.1** Identify atoms as the fundamental particles that make up matter. ✔**0807.12.1** Create a diagram to explain the relationship between electricity and magnetism. ✔**0807.12.2** Produce an electromagnet using a bar magnet and a wire coil. ✔**0807.12.3** Experiment with an electromagnet to determine how to vary its strength. ✔**0807.12.4** Create a chart to distinguish among the earth's magnetic field, and fields that surround a magnet and an electromagnet.

PRE-READING ACTIVITY

Graphic Organizer

Comparison Table Before you read the chapter, create the graphic organizer entitled "Comparison Table" described in the **Study Skills** section of the Appendix. Label the columns with "Motor" and "Generator." Label the rows with "Energy in" and "Energy out." As you read the chapter, fill in the table with details about the energy conversion that happens in each device.

GLE 0807.Inq.2, GLE 0807.Inq.3

About the Photo

Superhot particles at millions of degrees Celsius shoot out of the sun. But they do not escape. They loop back and crash into the sun's surface at more than 100 km/s (223,000 mi/h). The image of Earth has been added to show how large these loops can be. What directs the particles? The particles follow along the path of the magnetic field lines of the sun. You depend on magnetic fields in electric motors and generators. And you can use them to show off a good report card on the refrigerator.

START-UP ACTIVITY

Magnetic Attraction

In this activity, you will investigate ways you can use a magnet to lift steel.

Procedure

1. Put **5 steel paper clips** on your desk. Touch the clips with an **unmagnetized iron nail.** Record the number of clips that stick to it.

2. Touch the clips with the end of a **strong bar magnet.** Record the number of clips that stick to the magnet.

3. While holding the magnet against the head of the nail, touch the tip of the nail to the paper clips. Record the number of paper clips that stick to the nail.

4. Remove the magnet from the end of the nail. Recall the number of paper clips that you counted in step 3 and compare this with your observations when you removed the magnet.

5. Drag one end of the bar magnet down the nail 50 times. Drag the magnet in only one direction.

6. Set the magnet aside. Touch the nail to the clips. Record the number of clips that stick to it.

Analysis

1. What caused the difference between the number of paper clips that you picked up in step 1 and in step 3? ✔0807.Inq.3

2. What effect did the magnet have on the nail in step 5? ✔0807.Inq.3

Magnets and Magnetism

You've probably seen magnets stuck to a refrigerator door. These magnets might be holding notes or pictures. Or they might be just for looks.

If you have ever experimented with magnets, you know that they stick to each other and to some kinds of metals. You also know that magnets can stick to things without directly touching them—such as a magnet used to hold a piece of paper to a refrigerator door.

Properties of Magnets

More than 2,000 years ago, the Greeks discovered a mineral that attracted things made of iron. Because this mineral was found in a part of Turkey called Magnesia, the Greeks called it magnetite. Today, any material that attracts iron or things made of iron is called a **magnet.** All magnets have certain properties. For example, all magnets have two poles. Magnets exert forces on each other and are surrounded by a magnetic field.

✓ **Reading Check** What is a magnet?

Magnetic Poles

The magnetic effects are not the same throughout a magnet. What would happen if you dipped a bar magnet into a box of paper clips? Most of the clips would stick to the ends of the bar, as shown in **Figure 1.** This shows that the strongest effects are near the ends of the bar magnet. Each end of the magnet is a magnetic pole. As you will see, **magnetic poles** are points on a magnet that have opposite magnetic qualities.

Figure 1 *More paper clips stick to the ends, or magnetic poles, of a magnet because the magnetic effects are strongest there.*

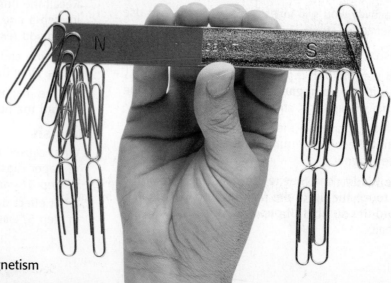

What You Will Learn

● Describe the properties of magnets.
● Explain why some materials are magnetic and some are not.
● Describe four kinds of magnets.
● Give two examples of the effect of Earth's magnetic field.

Vocabulary

magnet
magnetic pole
magnetic force

READING STRATEGY

Prediction Guide Before reading this section, predict whether each of the following statements is true or false:

- Every magnet has a north pole and a south pole.
- The magnetic pole near the South Pole in Antarctica is a north pole.

TN GLE 0807.Inq.2 Use appropriate tools and techniques to gather, organize, analyze, and interpret data.

GLE 0807.Inq.3 Synthesize information to determine cause and effect relationships between evidence and explanations.

GLE 0807.Inq.5 Communicate scientific understanding using descriptions, explanations, and models.

GLE 0807.9.1 Understand that all matter is made up of atoms.

GLE 0807.9.2 Explain that matter has properties that are determined by the structure and arrangement of its atoms.

GLE 0807.12.1 Investigate the relationship between magnetism and electricity.

GLE 0807.12.3 Compare and contrast the earth's magnetic field to that of a magnet and an electromagnet.

North and South

Suppose you hang a magnet by a string so that the magnet can spin. You will see that one end of the magnet always ends up pointing to the north, as shown in **Figure 2.** The pole of a magnet that points to the north is called the magnet's *north pole*. The opposite end of the magnet points to the south. It is called the magnet's *south pole*. Magnetic poles are always in pairs. You will never find a magnet that has only a north pole or only a south pole.

Figure 2 *The needle in a compass is a magnet that is free to rotate.*

Magnetic Forces

When you bring two magnets close together, each magnet exerts a **magnetic force** on the other magnet. These magnetic forces result from spinning electric charges in the magnets. The force can either push the magnets apart or pull them together. The magnetic force is a universal force. It is always present when magnetic poles come near one another.

Think of the last time you worked with magnets. If you held two magnets in a certain way, they pulled together. When you turned one of the magnets around, they pushed apart. Why? The magnetic force between magnets depends on how the poles of the magnets line up. Like poles repel, and opposite poles attract, as shown in **Figure 3.**

✓ Reading Check If two magnets push each other away, what can you conclude about their poles?

magnet any material that attracts iron or materials containing iron

magnetic pole one of two points, such as the ends of a magnet, that have opposing magnetic qualities

magnetic force the force of attraction or repulsion generated by moving or spinning electric charges

Figure 3 Magnetic Force Between Magnets

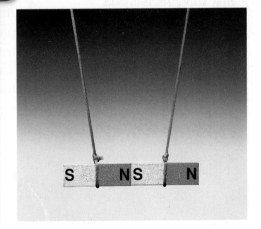

▲ If you hold the north poles of two magnets close together, the magnetic force will push the magnets apart. The same is true if you hold the south poles close together.

▲ If you hold the north pole of one magnet close to the south pole of another magnet, the magnetic force will pull the magnets together.

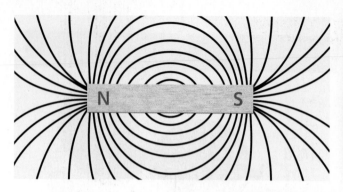

Figure 4 *Magnetic field lines show the shape of a magnetic field around a magnet. You can model magnetic field lines by sprinkling iron filings around a magnet.*

Magnetic Fields

A *magnetic field* exists in the region around a magnet in which magnetic forces can act. The shape of a magnetic field can be shown with lines drawn from the north pole of a magnet to the south pole, as shown in **Figure 4.** These lines map out the magnetic field and are called *magnetic field lines*. The closer together the field lines are, the stronger the magnetic field is. The lines around a magnet are closest together at the poles, where the magnetic force on an object is strongest.

The Cause of Magnetism

Some materials are magnetic. Some are not. For example, a magnet can pick up paper clips and iron nails. But it cannot pick up paper, plastic, pennies, or aluminum foil. What causes the difference? Whether a material is magnetic or not depends on the material's atoms.

Atoms and Domains

All matter is made of atoms. Electrons are negatively charged particles of atoms. As an electron moves around, it makes, or induces, a magnetic field. The atom will then have a north and a south pole. In most materials, such as copper and aluminum, the magnetic fields of the individual atoms cancel each other out. Therefore, these materials are not magnetic.

But in materials such as iron, nickel, and cobalt, groups of atoms are in tiny areas called *domains*. The north and south poles of the atoms in a domain line up and make a strong magnetic field. Domains are like tiny magnets of different sizes within an object. The arrangement of domains in an object determines whether the object is magnetic. **Figure 5** shows how the arrangement of domains works.

TN *Standards Check* Which element has atoms whose magnetic fields do not cancel each other out: copper or iron? ✔0807.9.1

CONNECTION TO Biology

WRITING SKILL **Animal Compasses**
Scientists think that birds and other animals may use Earth's magnetic field to help them navigate. Write a one-page paper in your **science journal** that tells which animals might find their way using Earth's magnetic field. Include evidence scientists have found that supports the idea.

Figure 5 Arrangement of Domains in an Object

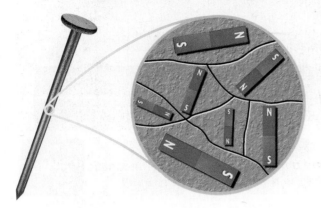

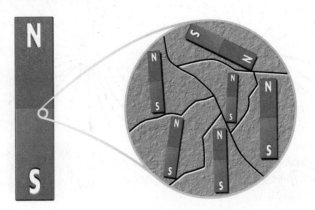

If the domains in an object are randomly arranged, the magnetic fields of the individual domains cancel each other out, and the object has no magnetic properties.

If most of the domains in an object are aligned, the magnetic fields of the individual domains combine to make the whole object magnetic.

Losing Alignment

The domains of a magnet may not always stay lined up. When domains move, the magnet is demagnetized, or loses its magnetic properties. Dropping a magnet or hitting it too hard can move the domains. Putting the magnet in a strong magnetic field that is opposite to its own can also move domains. Increasing the temperature of a magnet can also demagnetize it. At higher temperatures, atoms in the magnet vibrate faster. As a result, the atoms in the domains may no longer line up.

✓ **Reading Check** Describe two ways a magnet can lose its magnetic properties.

Making Magnets

You can make a magnet from something made of iron, cobalt, or nickel. You just need to line up the domains in it. For example, you can magnetize an iron nail if you rub it in one direction with one pole of a magnet. The domains in the nail line up with the magnetic field of the magnet. So, the domains in the nail become aligned. As more domains line up, the magnetic field of the nail grows stronger. The nail will become a magnet, as shown in **Figure 6.**

The process of making a magnet also explains how a magnet can pick up an unmagnetized object, such as a paper clip. When a magnet is close to a paper clip, some domains in the paper clip line up with the field of the magnet. So, the paper clip becomes a temporary magnet. The north pole of the paper clip points toward the south pole of the magnet. The paper clip is attracted to the magnet. When the magnet is removed, the domains of the paper clip become scrambled again.

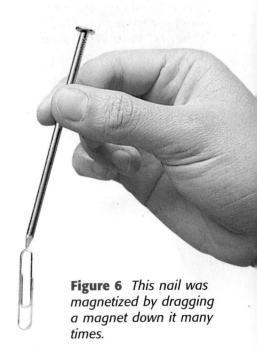

Figure 6 *This nail was magnetized by dragging a magnet down it many times.*

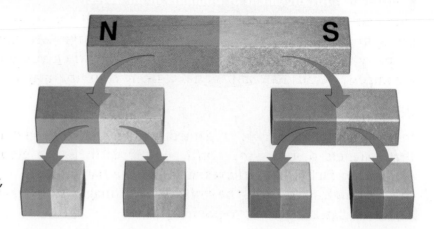

Figure 7 *If you cut a magnet in pieces, each piece will still be a magnet with two poles.*

Cutting a Magnet

What do you think would happen if you cut a magnet in half? You might think that you would end up with one north-pole piece and one south-pole piece. But that's not what happens. When you cut a magnet in half, you end up with two magnets. Each piece has its own north pole and south pole, as shown in **Figure 7**. A magnet has poles because its domains are lined up. Each domain within a magnet is like a tiny magnet with a north pole and a south pole. Even the smallest pieces of a magnet have two poles.

Kinds of Magnets

There are different ways to describe magnets. Some magnets are made of iron, nickel, cobalt, or mixtures of those metals. Magnets made with these metals have strong magnetic properties and are called *ferromagnets*. Look at **Figure 8**. The mineral magnetite is an example of a naturally occurring ferromagnet. Another kind of magnet is the *electromagnet*. This is a magnet made by an electric current. An electromagnet usually has an iron core.

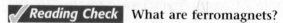 **Reading Check** What are ferromagnets?

Temporary and Permanent Magnets

Magnets can also be described as temporary magnets or permanent magnets. *Temporary magnets* are made from materials that are easy to magnetize. But they tend to lose their magnetization easily. Soft iron is iron that is not mixed with any other materials. It can be made into temporary magnets. *Permanent magnets* are difficult to magnetize. But they tend to keep their magnetic properties longer than temporary magnets do. Some permanent magnets are made with alnico (AL ni KOH)—an alloy of aluminum, nickel, cobalt, and iron.

Figure 8 *Magnetite attracts objects containing iron and is a ferromagnet.*

Earth as a Magnet

One end of every magnet points to the north if the magnet can spin. For more than 2,000 years, travelers have used this property to find their way. In fact, you use this when you use a compass, because a compass has a freely spinning magnet.

One Giant Magnet

In 1600, an English physician named William Gilbert suggested that magnets point to the north because Earth is one giant magnet. In fact, Earth behaves as if it has a bar magnet running through its center. The poles of this imaginary magnet are located near Earth's geographic poles.

Poles of a Compass Needle

If you put a compass on a bar magnet, the marked end of the needle points to the south pole of the magnet. Does that surprise you? Opposite poles of magnets attract each other. A compass needle is a small magnet. And the tip that points to the north is the needle's north pole. Therefore, the point of a compass needle is attracted to the south pole of a magnet.

South Magnetic Pole near North Geographic Pole

Look at **Figure 9.** A compass needle points north because the magnetic pole of Earth that is closest to the geographic North Pole is a magnetic *south* pole. A compass needle points to the north because its north pole is attracted to a very large magnetic south pole.

GLE 0807.Inq.2, GLE 0807.Inq.5

Quick Lab

Model of Earth's Magnetic Field

1. Place a **bar magnet** on a **sheet of butcher paper.** Draw a circle on the paper with a diameter larger than the bar magnet. This represents the surface of the Earth. Label Earth's North Pole and South Pole.

2. Place the bar magnet under the butcher paper, and line up the bar magnet with the poles.

3. Sprinkle some **iron filings** lightly around the perimeter of the circle. Describe and sketch the pattern you see.

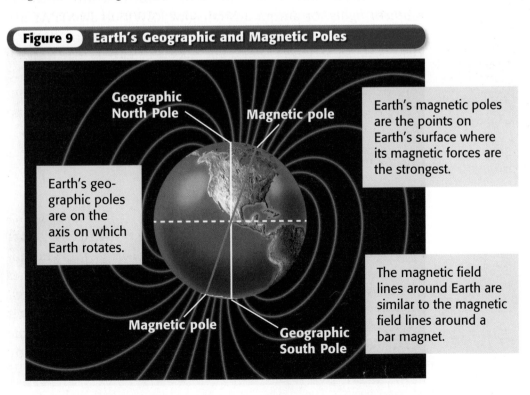

Figure 9   Earth's Geographic and Magnetic Poles

Geographic North Pole

Magnetic pole

Earth's magnetic poles are the points on Earth's surface where its magnetic forces are the strongest.

Earth's geographic poles are on the axis on which Earth rotates.

Magnetic pole

Geographic South Pole

The magnetic field lines around Earth are similar to the magnetic field lines around a bar magnet.

History of the Compass
Records from the first century BCE found in China show that people knew that the mineral lodestone (magnetite) would align to the north. But not until about 1,200 years later were floating compasses used for navigation. Research early compasses, and build a working model of one. Demonstrate to your class how it works.
✔0807.Inq.5, ✔0807.T/E.2

ACTIVITY

The Core of the Matter

Although you can think of Earth as having a giant bar magnet through its center, there isn't really a magnet there. The temperature of Earth's core (or center) is very high. The atoms in it move too violently to stay lined up in domains.

Scientists think that Earth's magnetic field is made by the movement of electric charges in the Earth's core. The Earth's core is made mostly of iron and nickel. The inner core is solid because it is under great pressure. The outer core is liquid because the pressure is not as high. As Earth rotates, the liquid in the core flows. Electric charges move, which makes a magnetic field.

Reading Check What do scientists think causes Earth's magnetic field?

A Magnetic Light Show

Look at **Figure 10.** The beautiful curtain of light is called an *aurora* (aw RAWR uh). Earth's magnetic field plays a part in making auroras. An aurora is formed when charged particles from the sun hit oxygen and nitrogen atoms in the air. The atoms become excited and then give off light of many colors.

Earth's magnetic field blocks most of the charged particles from the sun. But the field bends inward at the magnetic poles. As a result, the charged particles can crash into the atmosphere at and near the poles. Auroras seen near Earth's North Pole are called the *northern lights,* or aurora borealis (aw RAWR uh BAWR ee AL is). Auroras seen near the South Pole are called the *southern lights,* or aurora australis (aw RAWR uh aw STRAY lis).

Figure 10 *An aurora is an amazing light show in the sky.*

TN GLE 0807.Inq.3, GLE 0807.Inq.5,
GLE 0807.12.3

Summary

- All magnets have two poles. The north pole will always point to the north if allowed to rotate freely. The other pole is called the south pole.

- Like magnetic poles repel each other. Opposite magnetic poles attract.

- Every magnet is surrounded by a magnetic field. The shape of the field can be shown with magnetic field lines.

- A material is magnetic if its domains line up.

- Magnets can be classified as ferromagnets, electromagnets, temporary magnets, and permanent magnets.

- Earth acts as if it has a big bar magnet through its core. Compass needles and the north poles of magnets point to Earth's magnetic south pole, which is near Earth's geographic North Pole.

- Auroras are most commonly seen near Earth's magnetic poles because Earth's magnetic field bends inward at the poles.

Using Key Terms

1. Use the following terms in the same sentence: *magnet, magnetic force,* and *magnetic pole.*

Understanding Key Ideas

2. What metal is used to make ferromagnets?

   a. iron

   b. cobalt

   c. nickel

   d. All of the above

3. Name three properties of magnets.

4. Why are some iron objects magnetic and others not magnetic? ✔0807.Inq.3, ✔0807.9.1

5. How are temporary magnets different from permanent magnets?

Critical Thinking

6. **Forming Hypotheses** Why are auroras more commonly seen in places such as Alaska and Australia than in places such as Florida and Mexico? ✔0807.Inq.3

7. **Applying Concepts** Explain how you could use magnets to make a small object appear to float in air. ✔0807.Inq.3

8. **Making Inferences** Earth's moon has no atmosphere and has a cool, solid core. Would you expect to see auroras on the moon? Explain your answer. ✔0807.Inq.3

Interpreting Graphics

The image below shows a model of Earth as a large magnet. Use the image below to answer the questions that follow.

9. Which magnetic pole is closest to the geographic North Pole?

10. Is the magnetic field of Earth stronger near the middle of Earth (in Mexico) or at the bottom of Earth (in Antarctica)? Explain your answer. ✔0807.Inq.3

Internet Resources

For a variety of links related to this chapter, go to www.scilinks.org

Topic: Magnetism; Types of Magnets

SciLinks code: HSM0900; HSM1566

Magnetism from Electricity

Most of the trains you see roll on wheels on top of a track. But engineers have developed trains that have no wheels. The trains actually float above the track.

They float because of magnetic forces between the track and the train cars. Such trains are called maglev trains. The name *maglev* is short for magnetic levitation. To levitate, maglev trains use a kind of magnet called an electromagnet. Electromagnets can make strong magnetic fields. In this section, you will learn how electricity and magnetism are related and how electromagnets are made.

The Discovery of Electromagnetism

Danish physicist Hans Christian Oersted (UHR STED) discovered the relationship between electricity and magnetism in 1820. During a lecture, he held a compass near a wire carrying an electric current. Oersted noticed that when the compass was close to the wire, the compass needle no longer pointed to the north. The result surprised Oersted. A compass needle is a magnet. It moves from its north-south orientation only when it is in a magnetic field different from Earth's. Oersted tried a few experiments with the compass and the wire. His results are shown in **Figure 1.**

What You Will Learn

- Identify the relationship between an electric current and a magnetic field.
- Compare solenoids and electromagnets.
- Describe how electromagnetism is involved in the operation of doorbells, electric motors, and galvanometers.

Vocabulary

electromagnetism
solenoid
electromagnet
electric motor

READING STRATEGY

Reading Organizer As you read this section, make a table comparing solenoids and electromagnets.

TN **GLE 0807.Inq.2** Use appropriate tools and techniques to gather, organize, analyze, and interpret data.

GLE 0807.Inq.3 Synthesize information to determine cause and effect relationships between evidence and explanations.

GLE 0807.Inq.4 Recognize possible sources of bias and error, alternative explanations, and questions for further exploration.

GLE 0807.Inq.5 Communicate scientific understanding using descriptions, explanations, and models.

GLE 0807.T/E.1 Explore how technology responds to social, political, and economic needs.

GLE 0807.T/E.3 Compare the intended benefits with the unintended consequences of a new technology.

GLE 0807.12.1 Investigate the relationship between magnetism and electricity.

GLE 0807.12.2 Design an investigation to change the strength of an electromagnet.

Figure 1 **Oersted's Experiment**

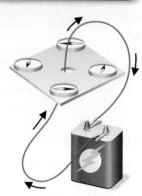

ⓐ If no electric current exists in the wire, the compass needles point in the same direction.

ⓑ Electric current in one direction in the wire causes the compass needles to deflect in a clockwise direction.

ⓒ Electric current in the opposite direction makes the compass needles deflect in a counterclockwise direction.

More Research

From his experiments, Oersted concluded that an electric current produces a magnetic field. He also found that the direction of the field depends on the direction of the current. The French scientist André-Marie Ampère heard about Oersted's findings. Ampère did more research with electricity and magnetism. Their work was the first research in electromagnetism. **Electromagnetism** is the interaction between electricity and magnetism.

✓ Reading Check What is electromagnetism?

Using Electromagnetism

The magnetic field generated by an electric current in a wire can move a compass needle. But the magnetic field is not strong enough to be very useful. However, two devices, the solenoid and the electromagnet, strengthen the magnetic field made by a current-carrying wire. Both devices make electromagnetism more useful.

Solenoids

A single loop of wire carrying a current does not have a very strong magnetic field. But suppose you form many loops into a coil. The magnetic fields of the individual loops will combine to make a much stronger field. A **solenoid** is a coil of wire that produces a magnetic field when carrying an electric current. In fact, the magnetic field around a solenoid is very similar to the magnetic field of a bar magnet, as shown in **Figure 2.** The strength of the magnetic field of a solenoid increases as more loops per meter are used. The magnetic field also becomes stronger as the current in the wire is increased.

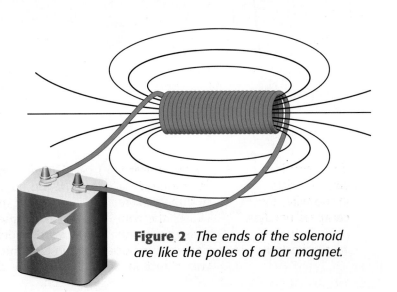

Figure 2 *The ends of the solenoid are like the poles of a bar magnet.*

electromagnetism the interaction between electricity and magnetism

solenoid a coil of wire with an electric current in it

INTERNET ACTIVITY

For another activity related to this chapter, go to **go.hrw.com** and type in the keyword **HP5EMGW.**

CONNECTION TO Engineering

Maglev Trains Use the Internet to research magnetic levitation. Write an explanation of the advantages of maglev trains as compared to conventional trains. Using what you have learned about magnetic levitation and maglev trains, describe how you think that engineers might use a maglev system to launch a rocket. ✔0807.Inq.3

ACTIVITY

Quick Lab

Electromagnets

1. Tightly wrap an **insulated copper wire** around a **large iron nail,** and leave 10 cm of wire loose at each end.

2. Use **electrical tape** to attach the bare ends of the wire against the top and bottom of a **D-cell battery.** ✔0807.12.2

3. Hold the end of the nail near some **paper clips,** and try to lift them up.

4. While holding the clips up, remove the wires from the cell. Then, record your observations.

5. What happens to the strength of the electromagnet if you reduce the number of coils? ✔0807.12.3

6. What happens to the strength of the electromagnet if you change from a D-cell battery to a 9-volt battery? ✔0807.12.3

7. What advantage of electromagnets did you see? ✔0807.Inq.3

electromagnet a coil that has a soft iron core and that acts as a magnet when an electric current is in the coil

Electromagnets

An **electromagnet** is made up of a solenoid wrapped around an iron core. The magnetic field of the solenoid makes the domains inside the iron core line up. The magnetic field of the electromagnet is the field of the solenoid plus the field of the magnetized core. As a result, the magnetic field of an electromagnet may be hundreds of times stronger than the magnetic field of just the solenoid.

You can make an electromagnet even stronger. You can increase the number of loops per meter in the solenoid. You can also increase the electric current in the wire. Some electromagnets are strong enough to lift a car or levitate a train! Maglev trains levitate because strong magnets on the cars are pushed away by powerful electromagnets in the rails.

✔ Reading Check What happens to the magnetic field of an electromagnet if you increase the current in the wire?

Turning Electromagnets On and Off

Electromagnets are very useful because they can be turned on and off as needed. The solenoid has a field only when there is electric current in it. So, electromagnets attract things only when a current exists in the wire. When there is no current in the wire, the electromagnet is turned off. **Figure 3** shows an example of how this property can be useful.

Figure 3 *Electromagnets used in salvage yards are turned on to pick up metal objects and turned off to put them down again.*

Applications of Electromagnetism

Electromagnetism is useful in your everyday life. You already know that electromagnets can be used to lift heavy objects containing iron. But did you know that you use a solenoid whenever you ring a doorbell? Or that there are electromagnets in motors? Keep reading to learn how electromagnetism makes these things work.

Doorbells

Look at **Figure 4.** Have you ever noticed a doorbell button that has a light inside? Have you noticed that when you push the button, the light goes out? Two solenoids in the doorbell allow the doorbell to work. Pushing the button opens the circuit of the first solenoid. The current stops, causing the magnetic field to drop and the light to go out. The change in the field causes a current in the second solenoid. This current induces a magnetic field that pushes an iron rod that sounds the bell.

Magnetic Force and Electric Current

An electric current can cause a compass needle to move. The needle is a small magnet. The needle moves because the electric current in a wire creates a magnetic field that exerts a force on the needle. If a current-carrying wire causes a magnet to move, can a magnet cause a current-carrying wire to move? **Figure 5** shows that the answer is yes. This property is useful in electric motors.

✓ **Reading Check** Why does a current-carrying wire cause a compass needle to move?

Figure 4 *Ringing this doorbell requires two solenoids.*

Figure 5 Magnetic Force on a Current-Carrying Wire

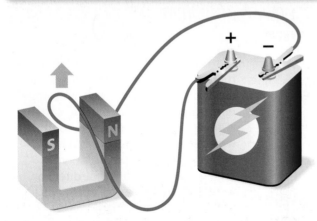

ⓐ When a current-carrying wire is placed between two poles of a magnet, the wire will jump up.

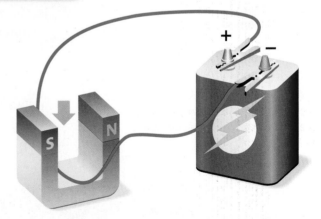

ⓑ Switching the wires at the battery reverses the direction of the current, and the wire is pushed down.

Electric Motors

electric motor a device that converts electrical energy into mechanical energy

An **electric motor** is a device that changes electrical energy into mechanical energy. All electric motors have an *armature*—a loop or coil of wire that can rotate. The armature is mounted between the poles of a permanent magnet or electromagnet.

In electric motors that use direct current, a device called a *commutator* is attached to the armature to reverse the direction of the electric current in the wire. A commutator is a ring that is split in half and connected to the ends of the armature. Electric current enters the armature through brushes that touch the commutator. Every time the armature and the commutator make a half turn, the direction of the current in the armature is reversed. **Figure 6** shows how a direct-current motor works.

Figure 6 **A Direct-Current Electric Motor**

Getting Started An electric current in the armature causes the magnet to exert a force on the armature. Because of the direction of the current on either side of the armature, the magnet pulls up on one side and down on the other side. This pulling turns the armature one half turn.

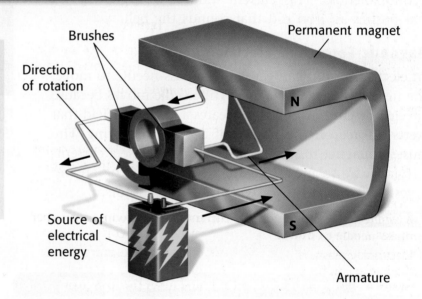

Brushes

Direction of rotation

Permanent magnet

N

Source of electrical energy

S

Armature

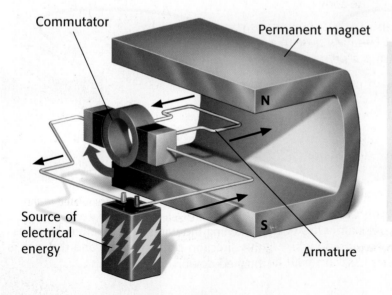

Commutator

Permanent magnet

N

S

Source of electrical energy

Armature

Running the Motor As the armature rotates, the commutator causes the electric current in the coil to change directions. When the electric current is reversed, the side of the coil that was pulled up is pulled down and the side that was pulled down is pulled up. This change of direction turns the armature the other half turn.

Galvanometers

A galvanometer (GAL vuh NAHM uht uhr) measures current. A galvanometer has a small electromagnet and needle on a pivot between the poles of a permanent magnet. When current passes through the electromagnet, its poles are pushed away from the poles of the permanent magnet. The greater the current, the more the electromagnet and needle pivot. Galvanometers are sometimes found in equipment used by electricians, such as voltmeters and ammeters, as shown in **Figure 7.**

Figure 7 *This ammeter uses a galvanometer to measure electric current.*

✓ **Reading Check** What does a galvanometer measure?

SECTION Review

TN GLE 0807.Inq.3, GLE 0807.Inq.4, GLE 0807.Inq.5, GLE 0807.12.1, GLE 0807.12.2

Summary

- Oersted discovered that a wire carrying a current makes a magnetic field.

- Electromagnetism is the interaction between electricity and magnetism.

- An electromagnet is a solenoid that has an iron core.

- A magnet can exert a force on a wire carrying a current.

- A doorbell, an electric motor, and a galvanometer all make use of electromagnetism.

Using Key Terms

For each pair of terms, explain how the meanings of the terms differ.

1. *electromagnet* and *solenoid*

Understanding Key Ideas

2. Which of the following actions will decrease the strength of the magnetic field of an electromagnet? ✓0807.Inq.3, ✓0807.12.3

   a. using fewer loops of wire per meter in the coil

   b. decreasing the current in the wire

   c. removing the iron core

   d. All of the above

3. Describe what happens when you hold a compass close to a wire carrying a current. ✓0807.Inq.3

4. What is the relationship between an electric current and a magnetic field? ✓0807.Inq.3

5. What makes the armature in an electric motor rotate? ✓0807.Inq.3

Critical Thinking

6. **Applying Concepts** What do Hans Christian Oersted's experiments have to do with a galvanometer? Explain your answer.

7. **Making Comparisons** Compare the structures and magnetic fields of solenoids with those of electromagnets.

Interpreting Graphics

8. Look at the image below. Your friend says that the image shows an electromagnet because there are loops with a core in the middle. Did your friend produce an electromagnet? Explain your reasoning. ✓0807.Inq.4, ✓0807.12.2

Internet Resources

For a variety of links related to this chapter, go to www.scilinks.org

Topic: Electromagnetism

SciLinks code: HSM0483

Electricity from Magnetism

When you use an electrical appliance or turn on a light in your home, you probably don't think about where the electrical energy comes from.

For most people, an electric power company supplies their home with electrical energy. In this section, you'll learn how a magnetic field can cause an electric current to flow and how power companies use this process to supply electrical energy.

Electric Current from a Changing Magnetic Field

Hans Christian Oersted discovered that an electric current is surrounded by a magnetic field. Soon after, scientists wondered if a magnetic field could cause an electric current to flow. In 1831, two scientists each solved this problem. Joseph Henry, of the United States, made the discovery first. Michael Faraday, from Great Britain, published his results first. Faraday also reported his results in great detail, so they are better known.

Faraday's Experiment

Faraday used a setup like the one shown in **Figure 1.** Faraday hoped that the magnetic field of the electromagnet would make—or induce—an electric current in the second wire. But no matter how strong the electromagnet was, he could not make an electric current in the second wire.

✓ **Reading Check** What did Faraday try to do in his experiment?

What You Will Learn

● Explain how a magnetic field can induce an electric current.
● Explain how electromagnetic induction is used in a generator.
● Compare step-up and step-down transformers.

Vocabulary

electromagnetic induction
electric generator
transformer

READING STRATEGY

Paired Summarizing Read this section silently. In pairs, take turns summarizing the material. Stop to discuss ideas that seem confusing.

TN GLE 0807.Inq.3 Synthesize information to determine cause and effect relationships between evidence and explanations.

GLE 0807.Inq.5 Communicate scientific understanding using descriptions, explanations, and models.

GLE 0807.12.1 Investigate the relationship between magnetism and electricity.

Figure 1 **Faraday's Experiment with Magnets and Induction**

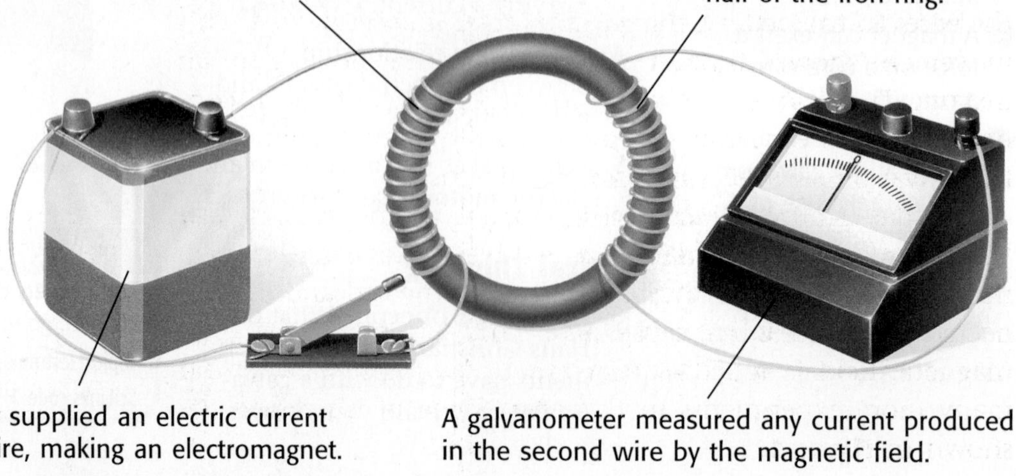

One wire was wound around one half of an iron ring.

A second wire was wound around the other half of the iron ring.

A battery supplied an electric current to the wire, making an electromagnet.

A galvanometer measured any current produced in the second wire by the magnetic field.

Figure 2 Factors that Affect an Induced Current

a An electric current is induced when you move a magnet through a coil of wire because the magnetic field is changing relative to the coil of wire.

b A greater electric current is induced if you move the magnet faster through the coil because the magnetic field is changing faster.

c A greater electric current is induced if you add more loops of wire. This magnet is moving at the same speed as the magnet in **b.**

d The induced electric current reverses direction if the magnet is pulled out rather than pushed in.

Success for an Instant

As Faraday experimented with the electromagnetic ring, he noticed something interesting. At the instant he connected the wires to the battery, the galvanometer pointer moved. This movement showed that an electric current was flowing for an instant. The pointer moved again at the instant he disconnected the battery. But when the battery stayed connected, the galvanometer measured no electric current.

Faraday realized that electric current in the second wire flowed only when the magnetic field was changing. The magnetic field changed as the battery was connected and disconnected. The process that causes an electric current in a changing magnetic field is called **electromagnetic induction.** Faraday did many more experiments in this area. Some of his results are shown in **Figure 2.**

electromagnetic induction the process of creating a current in a circuit by changing a magnetic field

Inducing Electric Current

Faraday's experiments also showed that moving either the magnet or the wire changes the magnetic field around the wire. An electric current is induced when a magnet moves in a coil of wire or when a wire moves between the poles of a magnet.

Consider the magnetic field lines between the poles of the magnet. An electric current is induced only when a wire moves the magnetic field lines, as shown in **Figure 3.** An electric current is induced because a magnetic force can cause electric charges to move. But the charges move in a wire only when the wire moves through the magnetic field.

Electric Generators

Electromagnetic induction is very important for the generation of electrical energy. An **electric generator** uses electromagnetic induction to change mechanical energy into electrical energy. **Figure 4** shows the parts of a simple generator. **Figure 5** explains how the generator works.

✓ **Reading Check** What energy change happens in an electric generator?

Figure 3 *As the wire moves between the poles of the magnet, it moves through magnetic field lines, and an electric current is induced.*

electric generator a device that converts mechanical energy into electrical energy

---

Figure 4 **Parts of a Simple Generator**

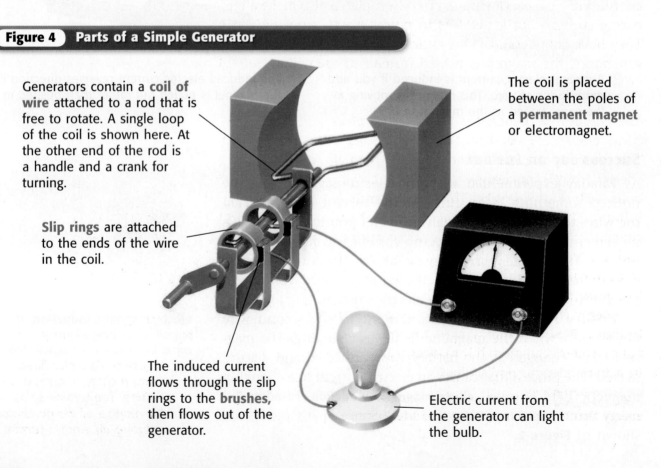

Generators contain a **coil of wire** attached to a rod that is free to rotate. A single loop of the coil is shown here. At the other end of the rod is a handle and a crank for turning.

The coil is placed between the poles of a **permanent magnet** or electromagnet.

Slip rings are attached to the ends of the wire in the coil.

The induced current flows through the slip rings to the **brushes,** then flows out of the generator.

Electric current from the generator can light the bulb.

Figure 5 **How a Generator Works**

1 As the crank is turned, the rotating coil crosses the magnetic field lines of the magnet, and an electric current is induced in the wire.

2 When the coil is not crossing the magnetic field lines, no electric current is induced.

3 As the coil continues to rotate, the magnetic field lines are crossed in a different direction. An electric current is induced in the opposite direction.

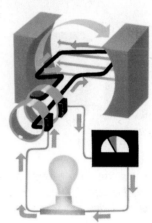

Alternating Current

The electric current produced by the generator shown in **Figure 5** changes direction each time the coil makes a half turn. Because the electric current changes direction, it is an alternating current. Generators in power plants also make alternating current. But generators in power plants are very large. They have many coils of wire instead of just one. In most large generators, the magnet is turned instead of the coils.

Generating Electrical Energy

The energy that generators convert into electrical energy comes from different sources. The source in nuclear power plants is thermal energy from a nuclear reaction. The energy boils water into steam. The steam turns a turbine. The turbine turns the magnet of the generator, which induces an electric current and generates electrical energy. Other kinds of power plants burn fuel such as coal or gas to release thermal energy.

Energy from wind can also be used to turn turbines. **Figure 6** shows how the energy of falling water is converted into electrical energy in a hydroelectric power plant.

✓ **Reading Check** What are three sources of energy that are used to generate electrical energy?

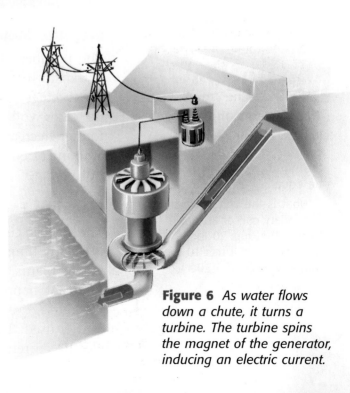

Figure 6 *As water flows down a chute, it turns a turbine. The turbine spins the magnet of the generator, inducing an electric current.*

Figure 7 **How Transformers Change Voltage**

The primary coil of a **step-up transformer** has fewer loops than the secondary coil. So, the voltage of the electric current in the secondary coil is higher than the voltage of the electric current in the primary coil. Therefore, voltage is increased.

The primary coil of a **step-down transformer** has more loops than the secondary coil. So, the voltage of the electric current in the secondary coil is lower than the voltage of the electric current in the primary coil. Therefore, voltage is decreased.

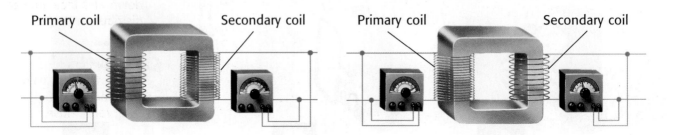

Primary coil   Secondary coil   Primary coil   Secondary coil

transformer a device that increases or decreases the voltage of alternating current

Transformers

Another device that relies on induction is a transformer. A **transformer** increases or decreases the voltage of alternating current. A simple transformer is made up of two coils of wire wrapped around an iron ring. The primary coil gets alternating current from an electrical energy source. The current makes the ring an electromagnet. But the current in the primary coil is alternating. The magnetic field of the electromagnet changes as the direction of the current changes. The changing magnetic field in the iron ring induces a current in the secondary coil.

✓ **Reading Check** What does a transformer do?

Step-Up, Step-Down

The number of loops in the primary and secondary coils of a transformer determines whether it increases or decreases the voltage, as shown in **Figure 7.** A step-up transformer increases voltage and decreases current. A step-down transformer decreases voltage and increases current. However, the amount of energy going into and out of the transformer does not change.

Electrical Energy for Your Home

The electric current that brings electrical energy to your home is usually transformed three times, as shown in **Figure 8.** At the power plants, the voltage is increased. This decreases power loss that happens as the energy is sent over long distances. Of course, the voltage must be decreased again before the current is used. Two step-down transformers are used before the electric current reaches your house.

Transformers and Voltage

In a transformer, for each coil, the voltage divided by the number of loops must be equal.

What is the voltage in the secondary coil of a transformer that has 20 loops if the primary coil has 10 loops and a voltage of 1,200 V?

Figure 8 Getting Energy to Your Home

❶ The voltage is stepped up thousands of times at the power plant.

❷ The voltage is stepped down at a local power distribution center.

❸ The voltage is stepped down again at a transformer near your house.

SECTION Review

TN GLE 0807.Inq.3, GLE 0807.Inq.5, GLE 0807.12.1

Summary

- Electromagnetic induction is the process of making an electric current by changing a magnetic field.

- An electric generator converts mechanical energy into electrical energy through electromagnetic induction.

- A step-up transformer increases the voltage of an alternating current. A step-down transformer decreases the voltage.

- The side of a transformer that has the greater number of loops has the higher voltage.

Using Key Terms

For each pair of terms, explain how the meanings of the terms differ.

1. *electric generator* and *transformer*

Understanding Key Ideas

2. Which of the following will induce an electric current in a wire? ✔0807.Inq.3

   a. moving a magnet into a coil of wire

   b. moving a wire between the poles of a magnet

   c. turning a loop of wire between the poles of a magnet

   d. All of the above

3. How does a generator produce an electric current?

4. Compare a step-up transformer with a step-down transformer based on the number of loops in the primary and secondary coils.

Math Skills

5. A transformer has 500 loops in its primary coil and 5,000 loops in its secondary coil. What is the voltage in the primary coil if the voltage in the secondary coil is 20,000 V?

6. A transformer has 3,000 loops in its primary coil and 1,500 loops in its secondary coil. What is the voltage in the secondary coil if the voltage in the primary coil is 120 V?

Critical Thinking

7. **Analyzing Ideas** One reason that electric power plants do not send out electrical energy as direct current is that direct current cannot be transformed. Explain why not. ✔0807.Inq.3

8. **Analyzing Processes** Explain why rotating either the coil or the magnet in a generator induces an electric current. ✔0807.Inq.3

9. **Applying Concepts** Create a diagram to show the relationship between electricity and magnetism. ✔0807.12.1

Internet Resources

For a variety of links related to this chapter, go to www.scilinks.org

Topic: Electromagnetic Induction
SciLinks code: HSM0481

Model-Making Lab

OBJECTIVES

Build a model of an electric motor.

Analyze the workings of the parts of a motor.

MATERIALS

- battery, 4.5 V
- cup, plastic-foam
- magnet, disc (4)
- magnet wire, 100 cm
- marker, permanent
- paper clips, large (2)
- sandpaper
- tape
- tube, cardboard
- wire, insulated, with alligator clips, approximately 30 cm long (2)

SAFETY

Build a DC Motor

Electric motors can be used for many things. Hair dryers, CD players, and even some cars and buses are powered by electric motors. In this lab, you will build a direct current electric motor—the basis for the electric motors you use every day.
✓0807.T/E.2

Procedure

1 To make the armature for the motor, wind the wire around the cardboard tube to make a coil like the one shown below. Wind the ends of the wire around the loops on each side of the coil. Leave about 5 cm of wire free on each end.

2 Hold the coil on its edge. Sand the enamel from only the top half of each end of the wire. This acts like a commutator, except that it blocks the electric current instead of reversing it during half of each rotation.

3 Partially unfold the two paper clips from the middle. Make a hook in one end of each paper clip to hold the coil, as shown below.

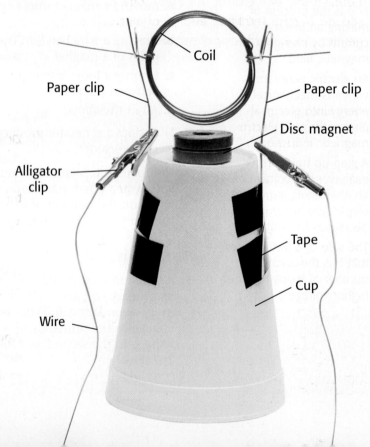

Coil

Paper clip

Paper clip

Disc magnet

Alligator clip

Tape

Cup

Wire

TN GLE 0807.Inq.2 Use appropriate tools and techniques to gather, organize, analyze, and interpret data.
GLE 0807.Inq.3 Synthesize information to determine cause and effect relationships between evidence and explanations.
GLE 0807.Inq.4 Recognize possible sources of bias and error, alternative explanations, and questions for further exploration.
GLE 0807.Inq.5 Communicate scientific understanding using descriptions, explanations, and models.

GLE 0807.T/E.2 Know that the engineering design process involves an ongoing series of events that incorporate design constraints, model building, testing, evaluating, modifying, and retesting.
GLE 0807.12.1 Investigate the relationship between magnetism and electricity.

④ Place two disc magnets in the bottom of the cup, and place the other magnets on the outside of the bottom of the cup. The magnets should remain in place when the cup is turned upside down.

⑤ Tape the paper clips to the sides of the cup. The hooks should be at the same height, and should keep the coil from hitting the magnet.

⑥ Test your coil. Flick the top of the coil lightly with your finger. The coil should spin freely without wobbling or sliding to one side.

⑦ Make adjustments to the ends of the wire and the hooks until your coil spins freely.

⑧ Use the alligator clips to attach one wire to each paper clip.

⑨ Attach the free end of one wire to one terminal of the battery.

⑩ Connect the free end of the other wire to the second battery terminal, and give your coil a gentle spin. Record your observations.

⑪ Stop the coil, and give it a gentle spin in the opposite direction. Record your observations.

⑫ If the coil does not keep spinning, check the ends of the wire. Bare wire should touch the paper clips during half of the spin, and only enamel should touch the paper clips for the other half of the spin.

⑬ If you removed too much enamel, color half of the wire with a permanent marker.

⑭ Switch the connections to the battery, and repeat steps 10 and 11.

Analyze the Results

❶ **Describing Events** Did your motor always spin in the direction you started it? Explain. ✔0807.Inq.4

❷ **Explaining Events** Why was the motor affected by switching the battery connections? ✔0807.Inq.3

❸ **Explaining Events** Some electric cars run on solar power. Which part of your model would be replaced by the solar panels? ✔0807.Inq.4

Draw Conclusions

❹ **Drawing Conclusions** Some people claim that electric-powered cars produce less pollution than gasoline-powered cars do. Why might this be true? ✔0807.Inq.4

❺ **Evaluating Models** List some reasons that electric cars are not ideal. ✔0807.T/E.3

❻ **Applying Conclusions** How could your model be used to help design a hair dryer? ✔0807.Inq.4

❼ **Applying Conclusions** List at least three items that could be powered by an electric motor like the one you built. ✔0807.Inq.4

Chapter Review

TN GLE 0807.Inq.3, GLE 0807.Inq.5, GLE 0807.T/E.3, GLE 0807.9.1, GLE 0807.12.1, GLE 0807.12.2, GLE 0807.12.3

USING KEY TERMS

Complete each of the following sentences by choosing the correct term from the word bank.

electric motor   transformer
magnetic force   electric generator
magnetic pole   electromagnetism
electromagnetic induction

1 Each end of a bar magnet is a(n) ___.

2 A(n) ___ converts mechanical energy into electrical energy.

3 ___ occurs when an electric current is made by a changing magnetic field.

✔0807.Inq.3

4 The relationship between electricity and magnetism is called ___.

UNDERSTANDING KEY IDEAS

Multiple Choice

5 In the region around a magnet in which magnetic forces act exists the

a. magnetic field.   **c.** pole.
b. domain.   **d.** solenoid.

6 An electric fan has an electric motor inside to change   ✔0807.Inq.3

a. mechanical energy into electrical energy.

b. thermal energy into electrical energy.

c. electrical energy into thermal energy.

d. electrical energy into mechanical energy.

7 The marked end of a compass needle always points directly to

a. Earth's geographic South Pole.

b. Earth's geographic North Pole.

c. a magnet's south pole.

d. a magnet's north pole.

8 A device that increases the voltage of an alternating current is called a(n)

✔0807.Inq.3

a. electric motor.

b. galvanometer.

c. step-up transformer.

d. step-down transformer.

9 The magnetic field of a solenoid can be increased by   ✔0807.Inq.3, ✔0807.12.3

a. adding more loops per meter.

b. increasing the current.

c. putting an iron core inside the coil to make an electromagnet.

d. All of the above

10 What do you end up with if you cut a magnet in half?

a. one north-pole piece and one south-pole piece

b. two unmagnetized pieces

c. two pieces each with a north pole and a south pole

d. two north-pole pieces

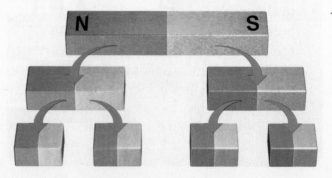

Short Answer

⑪ Explain why auroras are seen mostly near the North Pole and South Pole.

✔0807.Inq.3

⑫ Compare the function of an electric generator with the function of an electric motor.

⑬ Explain why some pieces of iron are more magnetic than others are.

✔0807.9.1

Math Skills

⑭ A step-up transformer increases voltage 20 times. If the voltage of the primary coil is 1,200 V, what is the voltage of the secondary coil?

CRITICAL THINKING

⑮ **Concept Mapping** Use the following terms to create a concept map: *electromagnetism, electricity, magnetism, electromagnetic induction, generators,* and *transformers.*

✔0807.12.1

⑯ **Applying Concepts** You win a hand-powered flashlight as a prize in your school science fair. The flashlight has a clear plastic case, so you can look inside to see how it works. When you press the handle, a gray ring spins between two coils of wire. The ends of the wire are connected to the light bulb. So, when you press the handle, the light bulb glows. Explain how an electric current is produced to light the bulb. (Hint: Paper clips are attracted to the gray ring.)

✔0807.Inq.3, ✔0807.Inq.4

INTERPRETING GRAPHICS

⑰ Look at the solenoids and electromagnets shown below. Identify which of them has the strongest magnetic field and which has the weakest magnetic field. Explain your reasoning.

✔0807.Inq.3, ✔0807.12.3

ⓐ
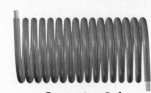
Current = 2 A

ⓑ

Current = 2 A

ⓒ

Current = 4 A

ⓓ

Current = 4 A

Challenge

⑱ Create a chart to show the similarities and differences between the Earth's magnetic field and the fields that surround a magnet and an electromagnet.

✔0807.12.4

TN SPI 0807.Inq.3 Interpret and translate data into a table, graph, or diagram.

SPI 0807.Inq.4 Draw a conclusion that establishes a cause and effect relationship supported by evidence.

SPI 0807.12.1 Recognize that electricity can be produced using a magnet and wire coil.

Multiple Choice

1. **Putting two north poles or two south poles of two magnets together makes the magnets push each other apart. Putting a north pole with a south pole makes the magnets stick together. For which of the following could the magnets serve as a simple model?**

   A. parallel circuit

   B. voltage

   C. law of electric charges

   D. potential difference

Use the diagram below to answer question 2.

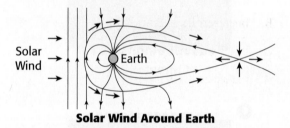

Solar Wind → Earth

Solar Wind Around Earth

2. **Charged particles in the solar wind bombard Earth constantly. The image above shows how the paths of these charged particles are bent as they approach Earth. What causes the charged particles in the solar wind to change course as they approach Earth?**

   A. Earth's gravity

   B. Earth's radiation

   C. Earth's electric field

   D. Earth's magnetic field

3. **Which powerline would most likely have the highest voltage?**

   A. The one supplying a residential area.

   B. The one near a power distribution center.

   C. The one near a power plant.

   D. The one along a highway.

4. **A junkyard electromagnet is strong enough to pick up cars, but not trucks. How could it be upgraded to lift larger vehicles?**

   A. The electric current and the number of coils in the solenoid could be increased.

   B. The electric current could be increased and the number of coils in the solenoid decreased.

   C. The electric current and the number of coils in the solenoid could be decreased.

   D. The electric current could be decreased and the number of coils in the solenoid increased.

5. **How could engineers remodeling a hydroelectric plant increase power output from the plant without replacing its magnet?**

   A. increase the current flowing to the magnet and the turbine.

   B. increase the height of the dam so that water will flow faster.

   C. add more electrical wires coming from the generator.

   D. heat the water before it enters the generator.

SPI 0807.12.2 Describe the basic principles of an electromagnet.

SPI 0807.12.3 Distinguish among the Earth's magnetic field, a magnet, and the fields that surround a magnet and an electromagnet.

6. **Electric outlets in the United States provide 120 volts of alternating current, while those in England provide 230 volts. What device is needed to run an American hair dryer in a British hotel?**

   A. galvanometer

   B. step-up transformer

   C. commutator

   D. step-down transformer

Use the following description to answer questions 7–8.

John created a device to power his television made out of a stationary bike, a thick rubber band, a magnet, a coil, and wire.

7. **What kind of device did John create?**

   A. electric motor

   B. electric generator

   C. electromagnet

   D. solenoid

8. **Which form of energy was converted to electrical energy?**

   A. thermal energy

   B. mechanical energy

   C. light energy

   D. chemical energy

Use the table below to answer question 9.

Power Lines	Voltage
Line A	24,000 V
Line B	12,750 V
Line C	7,200 V
Line D	4,000 V

9. **The table shows typical voltages carried by power lines. A distribution station has a transformer that uses 3 loops of wire for every volt. The transformer's primary coil contains 38,250 loops. Its secondary coil contains 21,600 loops. Where is the station located?**

   A. between lines A and B

   B. between lines B and C

   C. between lines C and D

   D. between lines B and D

Open Response

10. **Elise tells her friends that the Earth is like a giant bar magnet or an electromagnet. Is she right? Explain your answer.**

11. **Draw and label a simple device that could induce an electric current. Describe how your device could produce an alternating current.**

Science in Action

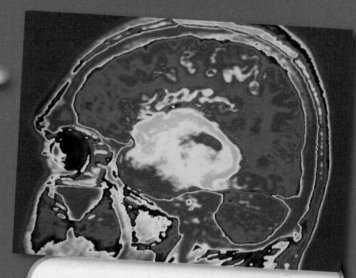

Weird Science

Electromagnets and Particle Accelerators

Physicists create subatomic particles by smashing atoms at speeds near the speed of light. To get the atoms to these high speeds, they use particle accelerators. Essentially, particle accelerators are a series of electromagnets that apply stronger and stronger forces to move electrically charged particles, such as electrons and ions, within atoms to higher and higher velocities. One such accelerator, called the Spallation Neutron Source, or SNS, is at Oak Ridge National Laboratory in Oak Ridge, Tennessee. The SNS produces neutrons for scientific research and industrial activities. **TN GLE 0807.T/E.1**

Social Studies ACTiViTY

Research the SNS at Oak Ridge National Laboratory. Find out what the neutrons produced by the SNS are used for. Write a one-page report on your findings.

Science, Technology, and Society

Magnets in Medicine

T/E Like X rays, magnetic resonance imaging (MRI) creates pictures of a person's internal organs and skeleton. But MRI produces clearer pictures than X rays do, and MRI does not expose the body to the potentially harmful radiation of X rays. Instead, MRI uses powerful electromagnets and radio waves to create images. MRI allows doctors to find small tumors, see subtle changes in the brain, locate blockages in blood vessels, and observe damage to the spinal cord. **TN GLE 0807.T/E.1**

Language Arts ACTiViTY

WRITING SKILL Write a two-page story about a student who undergoes an MRI scan. In your story, include the reason he or she must have the scan, a description of the procedure, and the information the doctor can determine by looking at the scan.

James Clerk Maxwell

Magnetic Math James Clerk Maxwell was a Scottish mathematician who lived in the 1800s. Maxwell's research led to advances in electromagnetism and in many other areas of science. He proposed that light is an electromagnetic wave—a wave that consists of electric and magnetic fields that vibrate at right angles to each other. His work on electromagnetic fields provided the foundation for Einstein's theory of relativity.

After college, Maxwell decided to study the work of Michael Faraday. Many physicists of the time thought that Faraday's work was not scientific enough. Faraday described his experiments but did not try to apply any scientific or mathematical theory to the results. Maxwell felt that this was a strength. He decided not to read any of the mathematical descriptions of electricity and magnetism until he had read all of Faraday's work. The first paper Maxwell wrote about electricity, called "On Faraday's Lines of Force," brought Faraday's experimental results together with a mathematical analysis of the magnetic field surrounding a current. This paper described a few simple mathematical equations that could be used to describe the interactions between electric and magnetic fields. Maxwell continued to work with Faraday's results and to publish papers that gave scientific explanations of some of Faraday's most exciting observations.

Social Studies ACTiViTY

Study the life of James Clerk Maxwell. Make a timeline that shows major events in his life. Include three or four historic events that happened during his lifetime.

Electronic Technology

The Big Idea

Electronic technology uses electrical energy to store and handle information.

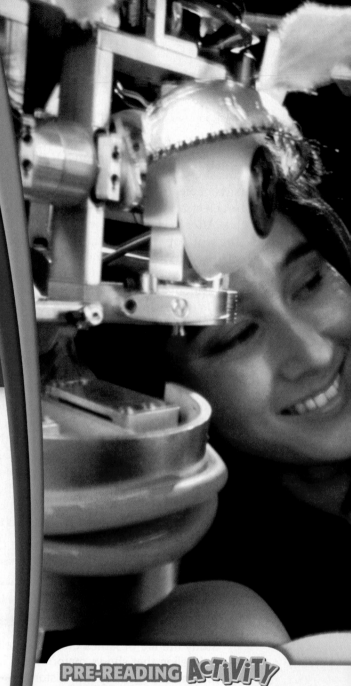

TN Tennessee Science Standards

Embedded Inquiry

GLE 0807.Inq.2 Use appropriate tools and techniques to gather, organize, analyze, and interpret data.

GLE 0807.Inq.3 Synthesize information to determine cause and effect relationships between evidence and explanations.

GLE 0807.Inq.4 Recognize possible sources of bias and error, alternative explanations, and questions for further exploration.

GLE 0807.Inq.5 Communicate scientific understanding using descriptions, explanations, and models.

✓0807.Inq.3 Use evidence from a dataset to determine cause and effect relationships that explain a phenomenon.

✓0807.Inq.4 Review an experimental design to determine possible sources of bias or error, state alternative explanations, and identify questions for further investigation.

✓0807.Inq.5 Design a method to explain the results of an investigation using descriptions, explanations, or models.

Embedded Technology and Engineering

GLE 0807.T/E.1 Explore how technology responds to social, political, and economic needs.

GLE 0807.T/E.2 Know that the engineering design process involves an ongoing series of events that incorporate design constraints, model building, testing, evaluating, modifying, and retesting.

GLE 0807.T/E.4 Describe and explain adaptive and assistive bioengineered products.

✓0807.T/E.2 Apply the engineering design process to construct a prototype that meets certain specifications.

✓0807.T/E.4 Research bioengineering technologies that advance health and contribute to improvements in our daily lives.

Physical Science

GLE 0807.9.1 Understand that all matter is made up of atoms.

GLE 0807.9.2 Explain that matter has properties that are determined by the structure and arrangement of its atoms.

✓0807.9.1 Identify atoms as the fundamental particles that make up matter.

PRE-READING ACTIVITY

FOLDNOTES **Booklet** Before you read the chapter, create the FoldNote entitled "Booklet" described in the **Study Skills** section of the Appendix. Label each page of the booklet with a main idea from the chapter. As you read the chapter, write what you learn about each main idea on the appropriate page of the booklet.

About the Photo

Can you read the expression on Kismet's face? This robot's expression can be sad, happy, angry, interested, surprised, disgusted, or just plain calm. Kismet was developed by MIT researchers to interact with humans. Electronic devices in cameras, motors, and computers allow Kismet to change its expression as it responds to its surroundings.

START-UP ACTiViTY

TN GLE 0807.Inq.2, GLE 0807.Inq.3, GLE 0807.Inq.5

Talking Long Distance

In this activity, you'll build a model of a telephone.

Procedure

1. Thread one end of a **piece of string** through the hole in the bottom of one **empty food can.**

2. Tie a knot in the end of the string inside the can. The knot should be large enough to keep the string in place. The rest of the string should come out of the bottom of the can.

3. Repeat steps 1 and 2 with **another can** and the other end of the string.

4. Hold one can, and have a classmate hold the other. Walk away from each other until the string is fairly taut.

5. Speak into your can while your classmate holds the other can at his or her ear. Switch roles.

Analysis

1. Describe what you heard.

2. Compare your model with a real telephone.

3. How are signals sent back and forth along the string? ✓0807.Inq.3

4. Why do you think it was important to pull the string taut?

Electronic Devices

Electronic devices use electrical energy. But they do not use electrical energy in the same way that machines do.

Some machines can change electrical energy into other forms of energy in order to do work. Electronic devices use it to handle information.

Inside an Electronic Device

For example, a remote control sends information to a television. **Figure 1** shows the inside of a remote control. The large green board is a circuit board. A **circuit board** is a collection of many circuit parts on a sheet of insulating material. A circuit board connects the parts of the circuit to supply electric current and send signals to the parts of an electronic device.

Sending Information to Your Television

To change the channel or volume on the television, you push buttons on the remote control. When you push a button, you send a signal to the circuit board. The components of the circuit board process the signal to send the correct information to the television. The information is sent to the television in the form of infrared light by a tiny bulb called a *light-emitting diode* (DIE OHD), or LED. In this section, you'll learn about diodes and other components and learn about how they work.

What You Will Learn

● Identify the role of a circuit board in an electronic device.

● Describe semiconductors and how their conductivity can be changed.

● Describe diodes and how they are used in circuits.

● Describe transistors and how they are used in circuits.

● Explain how integrated circuits have influenced electronic technology.

Vocabulary

circuit board

semiconductor

doping

diode

transistor

integrated circuit

READING STRATEGY

Reading Organizer As you read this section, make a concept map by using the terms above.

TN **GLE 0807.Inq.3** Synthesize information to determine cause and effect relationships between evidence and explanations.

GLE 0807.Inq.5 Communicate scientific understanding using descriptions, explanations, and models.

GLE 0807.T/E.1 Explore how technology responds to social, political, and economic needs.

GLE 0807.9.1 Understand that all matter is made up of atoms.

GLE 0807.9.2 Explain that matter has properties that are determined by the structure and arrangement of its atoms.

circuit board a sheet of insulating material that carries circuit elements and that is inserted in an electronic device

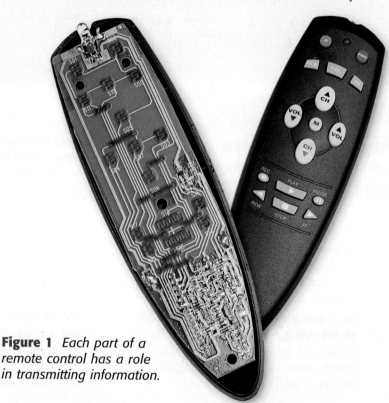

Figure 1 *Each part of a remote control has a role in transmitting information.*

Semiconductors

Semiconductors (SEM i kuhn DUHK tuhrz) are used in many electronic components. A **semiconductor** is a substance that conducts an electric current better than an insulator does but not as well as a conductor does. Semiconductors have allowed people to make incredible advances in electronic technology.

How Do Semiconductors Work?

The way a semiconductor conducts electric current is based on how its electrons are arranged. Silicon, Si, is a widely used semiconductor. As shown in **Figure 2,** when silicon atoms bond, they share all of their valence electrons. There are no electrons free to make much electric current. So, why are semiconductors such as silicon used? They are used because their conductivity can be changed.

Doping

You can change the conductivity of a semiconductor through doping (DOHP eeng). **Doping** is the addition of an impurity to a semiconductor. Adding the impurity changes the arrangement of electrons. A few atoms of the semiconductor are replaced with a few atoms of another element that has a different number of electrons, as shown in **Figure 3.**

TN *Standards Check* What is the result of doping a semiconductor with atoms of another element? ✔**0807.9.1**

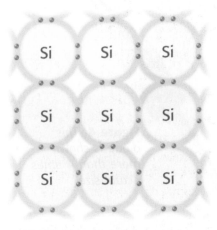

Figure 2 *Each silicon atom shares its four valence electrons with other silicon atoms.*

semiconductor an element or compound that conducts electric current better than an insulator does but not as well as a conductor does

doping the addition of an impurity element to a semiconductor

Figure 3 **Types of Doped Semiconductors**

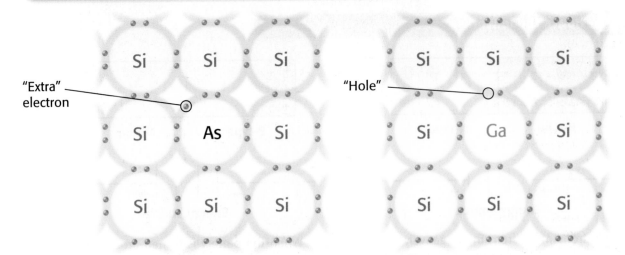

"Extra" electron

"Hole"

N-Type Semiconductor An atom of arsenic, As, has five electrons in its outermost energy level. Replacing a silicon atom with an arsenic atom results in an "extra" electron.

P-Type Semiconductor An atom of gallium, Ga, has three electrons in its outermost energy level. Replacing a silicon atom with a gallium atom results in a "hole" where an electron could be.

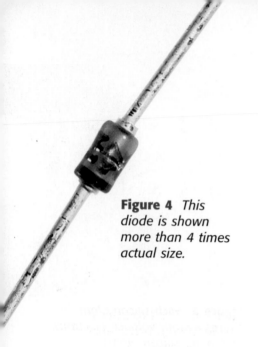

Diodes

Layers of semiconductors can be put together like sandwiches to make electronic components. Joining an n-type semiconductor with a p-type semiconductor forms a diode. A **diode** is an electronic component that allows electric charge to move mainly in one direction. Look at **Figure 4.** Each wire joins to one of the layers in the diode.

Figure 4 *This diode is shown more than 4 times actual size.*

The Flow of Electrons in Diodes

Where the two layers in a diode meet, some "extra" electrons move from the n-type layer to fill some "holes" in the p-type layer. This change gives the n-type layer a positive charge and the p-type layer a negative charge. If a diode is connected to a source of electrical energy, such as a battery, so that the positive terminal is closer to the p-type layer, a current is made. If the connections are switched so that the negative terminal is closer to the p-type layer, there is no current. **Figure 5** shows how a diode works.

diode an electronic device that allows electric charge to move more easily in one direction than in the other

Using Diodes to Change AC to DC

Power plants send electrical energy to homes by means of alternating current (AC). But many things, such as radios, use direct current (DC). Diodes can help change AC to DC. Alternating current switches direction many times each second. The diodes in an AC adapter block the current in one direction. Other components average the current in the direction that remains. As a result, AC is changed to DC.

✓ **Reading Check** Why can a diode change AC to DC?

Figure 5 **How a Diode Works**

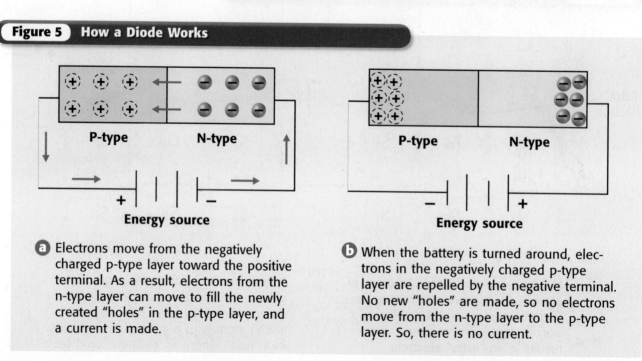

a Electrons move from the negatively charged p-type layer toward the positive terminal. As a result, electrons from the n-type layer can move to fill the newly created "holes" in the p-type layer, and a current is made.

b When the battery is turned around, electrons in the negatively charged p-type layer are repelled by the negative terminal. No new "holes" are made, so no electrons move from the n-type layer to the p-type layer. So, there is no current.

Transistors

What do you get when you sandwich three layers of semiconductors together? You get a transistor! A **transistor** is an electronic component that amplifies, or increases, current. It can be used in many circuits, including an amplifier and a switch. Transistors can be NPN or PNP transistors. An NPN transistor has a p-type layer between two n-type layers. A PNP transistor has an n-type layer between two p-type layers. Look at **Figure 6.** Each wire joins to one of the layers in the transistor.

✓ Reading Check Name two kinds of transistors made from semiconductors.

Transistors as Amplifiers

A microphone does not make a current that is large enough to run a loudspeaker. But a transistor can be used in an amplifier to make a larger current. Look at **Figure 7.** In the circuit, there is a small electric current in the microphone. This current triggers the transistor to allow a larger current in the loudspeaker. The electric current can be larger because of a large source of electrical energy in the loudspeaker side of the circuit.

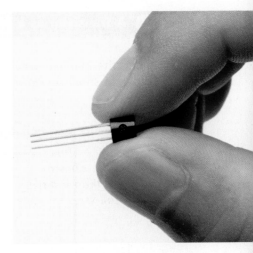

Figure 6 *This transistor is smaller than a pencil eraser!*

transistor a semiconductor device that can amplify current and that is used in amplifiers, oscillators, and switches

---

Figure 7 **A Transistor as an Amplifier**

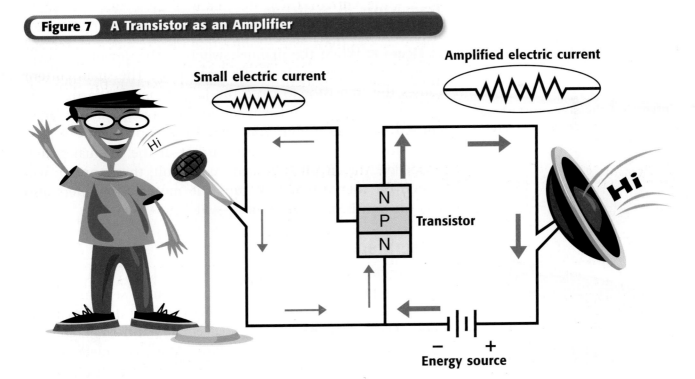

① Sound waves from your voice enter the microphone. As a result, a small electric current is made in the microphone side of the circuit.

② A transistor allows the small electric current to control a larger electric current that operates the loudspeaker.

③ The current in the loudspeaker is larger than the current produced by the microphone. Otherwise, the two currents are identical.

Figure 8   A Transistor as a Switch

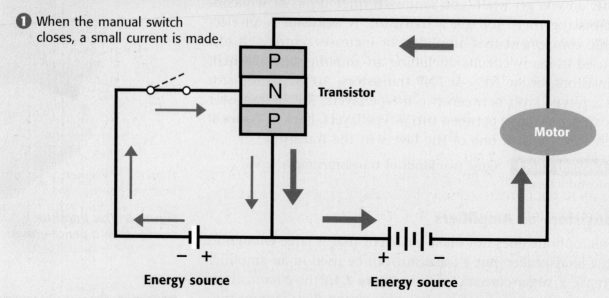

1 When the manual switch closes, a small current is made.

Transistor

Motor

Energy source

Energy source

2 The small current in the transistor causes the transistor to close the right side of the circuit. A larger current can then run the motor.

Transistors in Switches

Remote-controlled toy cars use transistors in switches. Look at **Figure 8.** When the manual switch in the circuit is closed, a small current is made in the small loop. The small current causes the transistor to close the large loop on the right. As a result, a larger current is made in the large loop. The larger current runs the motor. You switch on a small current. The transistor switches on a larger current. If the manual switch is opened, the circuit is broken. As a result, the transistor will switch off the current that runs the motor. Computers also rely on transistors that work in switches.

Integrated Circuits

An **integrated circuit** (IN tuh GRAYT id SUHR kit) is an entire circuit that has many components on a single semiconductor. The parts of the circuit are made by carefully doping certain spots. Look at **Figure 9.** Integrated circuits and circuit boards have helped shrink electronic devices. Many complete circuits can fit into one integrated circuit. So, complicated electronic systems can be made very small. Because the circuits are so small, the electric charges moving through them do not have to travel very far. Devices that use integrated circuits can run at very high speeds.

integrated circuit a circuit whose components are formed on a single semiconductor

Figure 9 *This integrated circuit contains many electronic components, yet its dimensions are only about 1 cm × 3 cm!*

✓ *Reading Check* Describe two benefits of using integrated circuits in electronic devices.

Smaller and Smarter Devices

Before transistors and semiconductor diodes were made, vacuum tubes, like the one in **Figure 10,** were used. Vacuum tubes can amplify electric current and change AC to DC. But vacuum tubes are much larger than semiconductor components are. They also get hotter and don't last as long. Early radios had to be large. Space was needed to hold the vacuum tubes and to keep them from overheating. Modern radios are very small. They use transistors and integrated circuits. And your radio might have other features, such as a clock or a CD player. But even more importantly than waking you up to your favorite music, integrated circuits have changed the world through their use in computers.

Figure 10 *Vacuum tubes are much larger than the transistors used today. So, radios that used the tubes were very large also.*

SECTION Review

TN GLE 0807.Inq.3, GLE 0807.Inq.5, GLE 0807.9.1, GLE 0807.9.2

Summary

- Circuit boards contain circuits that supply current to different parts of electronic devices.
- Semiconductors are often used in electronic devices because their conductivity can be changed by doping.
- Diodes allow current in one direction and can change AC to DC.
- Transistors are used in amplifiers and switches.
- Integrated circuits have made smaller, smarter electronic devices possible.

Using Key Terms

For each pair of terms, explain how the meanings of the terms differ.

1. *circuit board* and *integrated circuit*
2. *semiconductor* and *doping*
3. *diode* and *transistor*

Understanding Key Ideas

4. Which element forms the basis for semiconductors?
   a. oxygen   c. arsenic
   b. gallium   d. silicon

5. Describe how p-type and n-type semiconductors are made. ✓0807.Inq.3, ✓0807.9.1

6. Explain how a diode changes AC to DC. ✓0807.Inq.3

7. What are two purposes transistors serve?

Math Skills

8. An integrated circuit that was made in 1974 contained 6,000 transistors. An integrated circuit that was made in 2000 contained 42,000,000 transistors. How many times more transistors did the circuit made in 2000 have?

Critical Thinking

9. **Making Comparisons** How might an electronic system that uses vacuum tubes be different from one that uses integrated circuits?

10. **Applying Concepts** Would modern computers be possible without integrated circuits? Explain. ✓0807.Inq.3

Interpreting Graphics

11. The graph below represents electric current in a series circuit. Does the circuit contain a diode? Explain your reasoning.

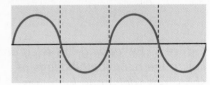

Internet Resources

For a variety of links related to this chapter, go to www.scilinks.org

Topic: Transistors
SciLinks code: HSM1550

Communication Technology

What electronic devices do you use to send or receive information? Your answer might include telephones, radios, or televisions.

In this section, you'll study these and other electronic devices that are used for communication. You'll also learn about two kinds of signals used to send and store information.

What You Will Learn

- Identify how signals transmit information.
- Describe analog signals and their use in telephones and records.
- Describe digital signals and their use in compact discs.
- Describe how information is transmitted and received in radios and televisions.

Vocabulary

analog signal
digital signal

READING STRATEGY

Discussion Read this section silently. Write down questions that you have about this section. Discuss your questions in a small group.

TN **GLE 0807.Inq.2** Use appropriate tools and techniques to gather, organize, analyze, and interpret data.

GLE 0807.Inq.3 Synthesize information to determine cause and effect relationships between evidence and explanations.

GLE 0807.Inq.5 Communicate scientific understanding using descriptions, explanations, and models.

Communicating with Signals

One of the first electronic communication devices was the telegraph. It was invented in the 1830s. It used an electric current to send messages between places joined by wires. People sent messages in Morse code through the wires. **Table 1** shows the patterns of dots and dashes that stand for each letter and number in Morse code. The message was sent by tapping a telegraph key, like the one in **Figure 1.** This tapping closed a circuit, causing "clicks" at the receiving end of the telegraph.

Signals and Carriers

Electronic communication devices, including the telegraph, send information by using signals. A *signal* is anything, such as a movement, a sound, or a set of numbers and letters, that can be used to send information. Often, one signal is sent using another signal called a *carrier*. Electric current is the carrier of the signals made by tapping a telegraph key. Two kinds of signals are analog signals and digital signals.

Figure 1 *By tapping this telegraph key in the right combinations of short taps (dots) and long taps (dashes), people could send messages over long distances.*

Table 1	International Morse Code						
A	·–	I	··	R	·–·	1	·––––
B	–···	J	·–––	S	···	2	··–––
C	–·–·	K	–·–	T	–	3	···––
D	–··	L	·–··	U	··–	4	····–
E	·	M	––	V	···–	5	·····
F	··–·	N	–·	W	·––	6	–····
G	––·	O	–––	X	–··–	7	––···
H	····	P	·––·	Y	–·––	8	–––··
		Q	––·–	Z	––··	9	––––·
						0	–––––

Analog Signals

An **analog signal** (AN uh LAWG SIG nuhl) is a signal whose properties change without a break or jump between values. Think of a dimmer switch on a light. You can continuously change the brightness of the light using the dimmer switch.

The changes in an analog signal are based on changes in the original information. For example, when you talk on the phone, the sound of your voice is changed into changing electric current in the form of a wave. This wave is an analog signal that is similar to the original sound wave. But remember that sound waves do not travel down your phone line!

✓ Reading Check What is an analog signal?

Talking on the Phone

Look at the telephone in **Figure 2.** You talk into the transmitter. You listen to the receiver. The transmitter changes the sound waves made when you speak into an analog signal. This signal moves through phone wires to the receiver of another phone. The receiver changes the analog signal back into the sound of your voice. Sometimes, the analog signals are changed to digital signals and back again before they reach the other person. You will learn about digital signals later in this section.

analog signal a signal whose properties can change continuously in a given range

🏷 TN GLE 0807.Inq.2, GLE 0807.Inq.5, GLE 0807.T/E.1

CONNECTION TO Technology

Seismograms One instrument that scientists use to study earthquakes is the seismograph. A *seismograph* is a device that was developed to record waves made by earthquakes. It makes a *seismogram*—wavy lines on paper that record ground movement. Draw an example of a seismogram that shows changes in the wave, and explain why this is an example of an analog signal.

ACTIVITY

Figure 2 How a Telephone Works

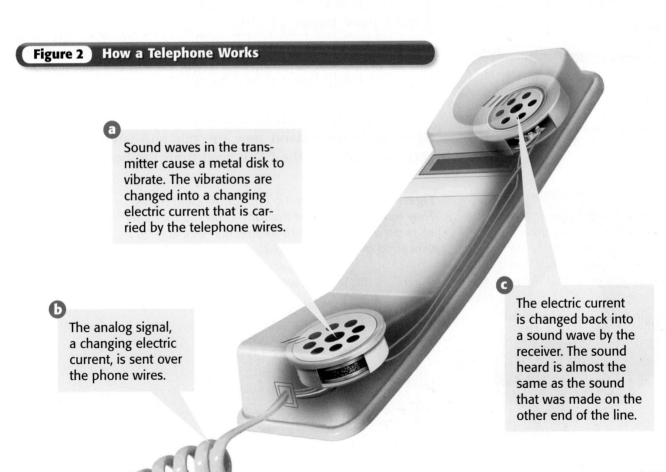

a Sound waves in the transmitter cause a metal disk to vibrate. The vibrations are changed into a changing electric current that is carried by the telephone wires.

b The analog signal, a changing electric current, is sent over the phone wires.

c The electric current is changed back into a sound wave by the receiver. The sound heard is almost the same as the sound that was made on the other end of the line.

Analog Recording

If you want to save a sound, you can store an analog signal of the sound wave. In vinyl records, the signal is made into grooves on a plastic disk. The sound's properties are represented by the number and depth of the contours in the disk.

Playing a Record

Figure 3 shows a record being played. The stylus (STIE luhs), or needle, makes an electromagnet vibrate. The vibrating electromagnet induces an electric current that is used to make sound. Analog recording makes sound that is very close to the original. But unwanted sounds are sometimes recorded and are not easy to remove. Also, the stylus touches the record to play it. So, the record wears out, and the sound changes over time.

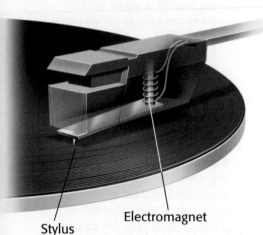

Stylus   Electromagnet

Figure 3 *As the stylus rides in the record's grooves, it causes an electromagnet to vibrate.*

digital signal a signal that can be represented as a sequence of discrete values

Digital Signals

A **digital signal** is a signal that is represented as a sequence of separate values. It does not change continuously. Think of a regular light switch. It can be either on or off. Information in a digital signal is represented as binary (BIE nuh ree) numbers. *Binary* means "two." Numbers in binary are made up of only two digits, 1 and 0. Each digit is a *bit*, which is short for *binary digit*. Computers process digital signals that are in the form of a pattern of electric pulses. Each pulse stands for a 1. Each missing pulse stands for a 0.

Digital Storage on a CD

You've probably heard digital sound from a compact disc, or CD. Sound is recorded to a CD by means of a digital signal. A CD stores the signals in a thin layer of aluminum. Look at **Figure 4.** To understand how the pits and lands are named, keep in mind that the CD is read from the bottom.

Figure 4 *Pits stand for 1s, and lands stand for 0s. They form a tight spiral from the center to the outer edge on a CD. They store information that can be converted by a CD player into sound.*

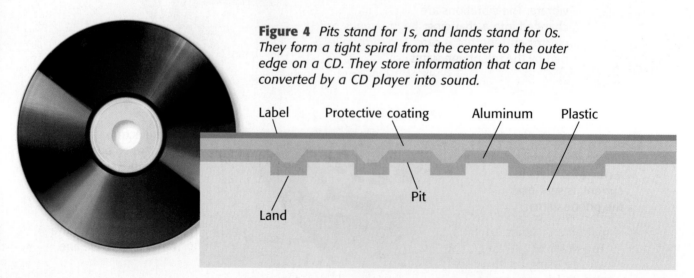

Label   Protective coating   Aluminum   Plastic

Pit

Land

Digital Recording

In a digital recording, the sound wave is measured many times each second. **Figure 5** shows how these sample values represent the original sound. These numbers are then changed into binary values using 1s and 0s. The 1s and 0s are stored as pits and lands on a CD.

In digital recording, the sample values don't exactly match the original sound wave. So, the number of samples taken each second is important to make sure the recording sounds the way it should sound. Taking more sample values each second makes a digital sound that is closer to the original sound.

✓ Reading Check How can a digital recording be made to sound more like the original sound?

Playing a CD

In a CD player, the CD spins around while a laser shines on the CD from below. As shown in **Figure 6,** light reflected from the CD enters a detector. The detector changes the pattern of light and dark into a digital signal. The digital signal is changed into an analog signal, which is used to make a sound wave. Because only light touches the CD, the CD doesn't wear out. But errors can happen from playing a dirty or scratched CD.

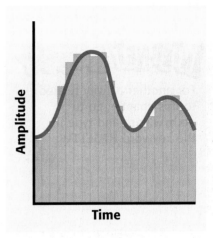

Figure 5 *Each of the bars represent a digital sample of the sound wave.*

Figure 6 **How a CD Player Works**

Different sequences and sizes of pits and lands will register different patterns of numbers that are converted into different sounds.

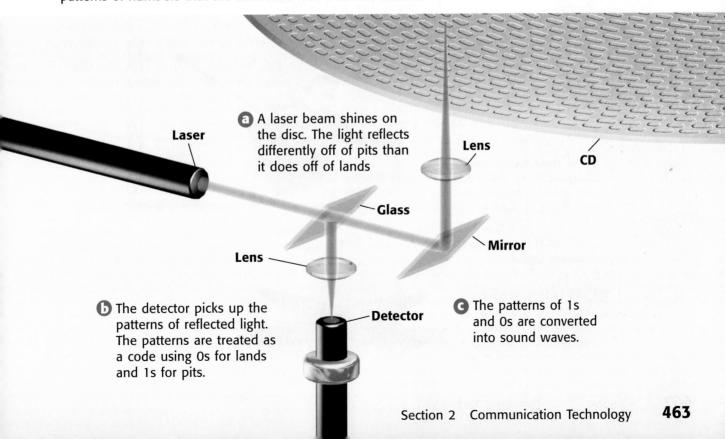

a A laser beam shines on the disc. The light reflects differently off of pits than it does off of lands

b The detector picks up the patterns of reflected light. The patterns are treated as a code using 0s for lands and 1s for pits.

c The patterns of 1s and 0s are converted into sound waves.

Radio and Television

You hear or see shows on your radio or television that are broadcast from a station that may be many kilometers away. The radio and TV signals can be either analog or digital. An *electromagnetic* (EM) *wave* is a wave that consists of changing electric and magnetic fields. EM waves are used as carriers.

Radio

Radio waves are one kind of EM wave. Radio stations use radio waves to carry signals that represent sound. Look at **Figure 7.** Radio waves are transmitted by a radio tower. They travel through the air and are picked up by a radio antenna.

INTERNET ACTIVITY

For another activity related to this chapter, go to **go.hrw.com** and type in the keyword **HP5ELTW.**

Figure 7 **How a Radio Works**

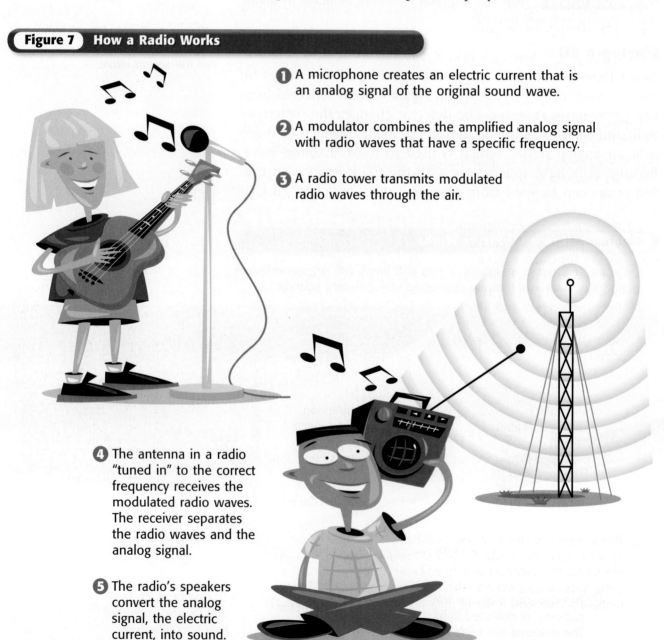

① A microphone creates an electric current that is an analog signal of the original sound wave.

② A modulator combines the amplified analog signal with radio waves that have a specific frequency.

③ A radio tower transmits modulated radio waves through the air.

④ The antenna in a radio "tuned in" to the correct frequency receives the modulated radio waves. The receiver separates the radio waves and the analog signal.

⑤ The radio's speakers convert the analog signal, the electric current, into sound.

Television

The pictures you see on your television are made by beams of electrons hitting the screen, as described in **Figure 8.** Video signals hold the information to make a picture. Audio signals hold the information to make the sound. These signals can be sent as analog or digital signals to your television. The signals can be broadcast using EM waves as carriers. The signals can be sent through cables or from satellites or broadcast towers.

More and more, television programs are going digital. This means that they are filmed using digital cameras and transmitted to homes as digital signals. You can watch digital shows on an analog TV. However, on a digital display, the images and sound of these programs are much clearer than on a television made for analog broadcasts.

✓ *Reading Check* **What kinds of signals can be picked up by a color television?**

TN GLE 0807.Inq.2, GLE 0807.Inq.5

SCHOOL to HOME

TV Screen

With an adult, use a magnifying lens to look at a television screen. How are the fluorescent materials arranged? Hold the lens at various distances from the screen. What effects do you see? How does the screen's changing picture affect what you see?

ACTIVITY

Figure 8 Images on a Color Television

❶ Video signals transmitted from a TV station are received by the antenna of a TV receiver.

❷ Electronic circuits divide the video signal into separate signals for each of three electron beams. The beams, one for each primary color of light (red, green, and blue), strike the screen in varying strengths determined by the video signal.

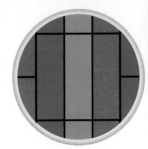

❸ The screen has stripes or dots of three fluorescent (FLOO uh RES uhnt) materials. These materials glow when hit by electrons. The electron beams sweep the screen 30 times every second and activate the fluorescent materials. These materials then emit colored light that is viewed as a picture.

Plasma Display

Standard televisions must be deep enough so that the electron beams can reach all parts of the screen. So, televisions are bulky and heavy. A newer kind of screen, called a *plasma display,* is much thinner. It can be as thin as 15 cm. So, it is not much thicker than a painting on the wall!

Figure 9 shows how a plasma display works. Plasma displays do not use electron tubes. Instead, they have thousands of tiny cells with gases in them. A computer charges the cells, making a current in the gases. The current generates colored lights. Each light can be red, green, blue, or a combination. As in a regular television, these three colors are combined to make every picture on the screen.

✔ Reading Check Why is a plasma display thinner than a regular television?

Figure 9 How a Plasma Display Works

❶ Video signals transmitted from a TV station are received by a device, such as a VCR, that has a television tuner in it. The signals are then sent to the plasma display.

❷ The signal includes commands to charge conductors on either side of small wells in the screen. The atoms of gas in the wells become charged and form a plasma.

❸ Each well contains one of three fluorescent materials. The materials give off red, blue, or green light after absorbing energy given off by the plasma.

❹ The colored light from each group of three wells blends together and makes a small dot of light in the picture on the screen.

TN ▸ GLE 0807.Inq.3, GLE 0807.Inq.5

Summary

- Signals transmit information in electronic devices. Signals can be transmitted using a carrier. Signals can be analog or digital.

- Analog signals have continuous values. Telephones, record players, radios, and regular TV sets use analog signals.

- In a telephone, a transmitter changes sound waves to electric current. The current is sent across a phone line. The receiving telephone converts the signal back into a sound wave.

- Analog signals of sounds are used to make vinyl records. Changes in the groove reflect changes in the sound.

- Digital signals have discrete values, such as 0 and 1. CD players use digital signals.

- Radios and televisions use electromagnetic waves. These waves travel through the atmosphere. In a radio, the signals are converted to sound waves. In a television, electron beams convert the signals into images on the screen.

Using Key Terms

1. In your own words, write a definition for each of the following terms: *analog signal* and *digital signal*.

Understanding Key Ideas

2. Which of the following objects changes sound waves into an electric current in order to transmit information? ✓0807.Inq.3

   a. telephone

   b. radio

   c. television

   d. telegraph

3. Why are carriers used to transmit signals?

4. What is an early example of an electrical device used for sending information over long distances? How did this device work? ✓0807.Inq.3

Critical Thinking

5. **Applying Concepts** Is Morse code an example of an analog signal or a digital signal? Explain your reasoning.

6. **Making Comparisons** Compare how a telephone and a radio tower transmit information.

7. **Making Inferences** Does a mercury thermometer provide information in an analog or digital way? Explain your reasoning.

Interpreting Graphics

8. Look at the graphs below. They represent a sound wave that is being changed into a digital signal. Each bar represents a digital sample of the sound wave. Which graph represents the digital signal that is closer to the original sound wave? Explain your reasoning. ✓0807.Inq.3

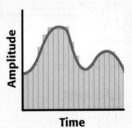

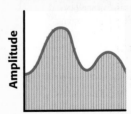

Internet Resources

For a variety of links related to this chapter, go to www.scilinks.org

Topic: Telephone Technology; Television Technology

SciLinks code: HSM1499; HSM1501

Computers

Did you use a computer to wake up this morning?

You might think of a computer as something you use to send e-mail or to surf the Internet. But computers are around you all the time. Computers are in automobiles, VCRs, and telephones. Even an alarm clock is an example of a simple computer!

What Is a Computer?

A **computer** is an electronic device that performs tasks by following instructions given to it. A computer does a task when it is given a command and has the instructions necessary to carry out that command. Computers can do tasks very quickly.

Basic Functions

The basic functions of a computer are shown in **Figure 1.** The information you give to a computer is called *input*. The computer *processes* the input. Processing could mean adding a list of numbers, making a drawing, or even moving a piece of equipment. Input doesn't have to be processed right away. It can be stored until it is needed. The computer *stores* information in its memory. *Output* is the final result of the job done by the computer.

✓ **Reading Check** What are the basic functions of a computer?

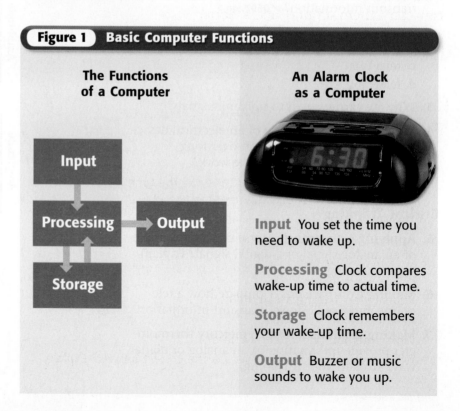

Figure 1 Basic Computer Functions

The Functions of a Computer

Input → Processing → Output
Processing → Storage

An Alarm Clock as a Computer

Input You set the time you need to wake up.

Processing Clock compares wake-up time to actual time.

Storage Clock remembers your wake-up time.

Output Buzzer or music sounds to wake you up.

The First Computers

Your pocket calculator is a simple computer. But computers were not always so small and easy to use. The first computers were huge! They were made up of large pieces of equipment that could fill a room. The first general-purpose computer is shown in **Figure 2.** This is the ENIAC. ENIAC stands for Electronic Numerical Integrator and Computer. It was made in 1946 by the U.S. Army. The ENIAC was made up of thousands of vacuum tubes. As a result, it had to be cooled while in use. It also cost a lot to build and to run.

Figure 2 *Fast for its time, the ENIAC could add 5,000 numbers per second.*

Modern Computers

Computers have become much smaller because of integrated circuits. Computers today use microprocessors. A **microprocessor** is a single chip that controls and carries out a computer's instructions. The first widely available microprocessor had only 4,800 transistors. But microprocessors made today may have more than 40 million transistors. Computers are now made so small that we can carry them around like a book!

computer an electronic device that can accept data and instructions, follow the instructions, and output the results

microprocessor a single semiconductor chip that controls and executes a microcomputer's instructions

Reading Check What is a microprocessor?

TN GLE 0807.Inq.2

The Speed of a Simple Computer

1. With a partner, use a **clock** to measure the time it takes each of you to solve the following items by hand.
   a. (108 ÷ 9) + 231 − 19
   b. 1 × 2 × 3 × 4 × 5
   c. (4 × 6 × 8) ÷ 2
   d. 3 × (5 + 12) − 2
2. Repeat step 1 using a **calculator.**
3. Which method was faster?
4. Which method was more accurate?
5. Will the calculator always give you the correct answer? Explain.
   ✔0807.Inq.4, ✔0807.Inq.5

Computer Hardware

hardware the parts or pieces of equipment that make up a computer

Different parts of a computer do different jobs. **Hardware** is the parts or pieces of equipment that make up a computer. As you read about each piece of hardware, look at **Figure 3** and **Figure 4** to see what the hardware looks like.

Input Devices

An *input device* gives information, or input, to the computer. You can enter information into a computer using a keyboard, a mouse, a scanner, or a digitizing pad and pen. You can even enter information using a microphone.

Central Processing Unit

A computer does tasks in the *central processing unit,* or CPU. In a personal computer, the CPU is a microprocessor. Input goes through the CPU for processing on the spot or for storage in memory. In the CPU, the computer does calculations, solves problems, and carries out instructions given to it.

✓ **Reading Check** What does *CPU* stand for?

🌐 GLE 0807.T/E.1

CONNECTION TO Social Studies

WRITING SKILL **ENIAC** ENIAC was developed for use by the U.S. Army during World War II. Research what ENIAC was to be used for in the war and what plans were made for ENIAC after the war. Write a one-page report in your **science journal** to report your findings.

Figure 3 Computer Hardware

Microphone
Monitor
Keyboard
Mouse
Speaker
Modem port
RAM
CPU
ROM
CD-ROM drive
Floppy drive
Hard disk

Memory

Information can be stored in the computer's memory until it is needed. Hard disks inside a computer and floppy disks or CDs that are put into a computer have memory to store information. Two other types of memory are *ROM* (read-only memory) and *RAM* (random-access memory).

ROM is permanent. It handles jobs such as start-up, maintenance, and hardware management. ROM normally cannot be added to or changed. It also cannot be lost when the computer is turned off. RAM is temporary. RAM stores information only while it is being used. RAM is sometimes called *working memory*. Information in RAM is lost if the power is shut off. So, it is a good habit to save your work to a hard drive or to a disk every few minutes.

Output Devices

Once a computer does a job, it shows the results on an *output device*. Monitors, printers, and speaker systems are all examples of output devices.

Modems and Interface Cards

Computers can exchange information if they are joined by modems or interface cards. Modems send information through telephone lines. Modems convert information from a digital signal to an analog signal and vice versa. Interface cards use cables or wireless connections.

Computer Memory

Suppose you download a document from the Internet that uses 25 kilobytes of memory. How many of those documents could you fit on a disk that has 1 gigabyte of memory? A kilobyte is 1,024 bytes, and a gigabyte is 1,073,741,824 bytes.

Figure 4 Additional Computer Hardware

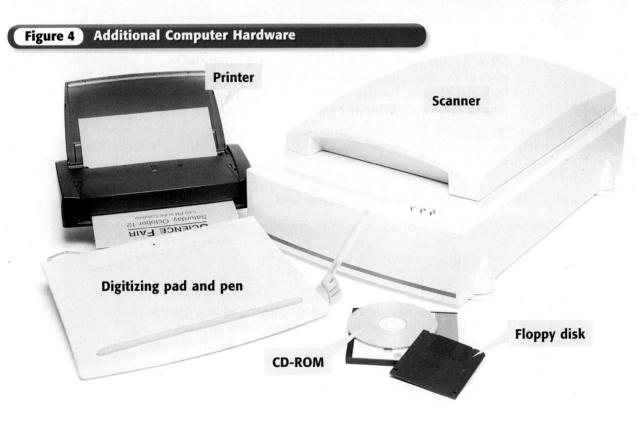

Printer

Scanner

Digitizing pad and pen

CD-ROM

Floppy disk

CONNECTION TO Engineering

T/E Night-Vision Goggles
To see in the dark, emergency personal could use a product such as a night-vision device, which uses a lens to capture infrared light. The light is intensified, and the image is projected on a small screen. When you use a night-vision device, you are not looking through the device at the objects, but at the objects projected on the screen. Research night-vision devices and what they are used for. Explain how night-vision goggles are an adaptive or assistive product. Write a one-page report on your findings. ✔0807.T/E.4

ACTIVITY

Compact Discs

Today, you can use a CD burner to make your own compact discs. A CD can hold about 500 times more information than a floppy disk. It can store digital photos, music files, and any other type of computer file.

Burning and Erasing CDs

The first kind of CD that you could put information onto, or "burn," is a CD-recordable (CD-R) disc. CD-R discs use a dye to block light. When the dye is heated, light cannot pass through to reflect off the aluminum. To burn a CD, a special laser heats some places and not others. This burning creates a pattern of "on" and "off" spots on the CD-R. These spots store information just as the pits and lands do on a regular CD. You can burn a CD-R disc only once.

A CD-rewritable (CD-RW) disc can be used more than once. CD-RW discs use a special compound that can be erased and written over again. CD-RW discs cost more than CD-R discs. But CD-RW discs cannot be read by all CD players. Look at **Figure 5** to see how CD-R and CD-RW discs work.

Figure 5 How CD-R and CD-RW Discs Work

Label   Aluminum   Dye   Darkened dye   Plastic

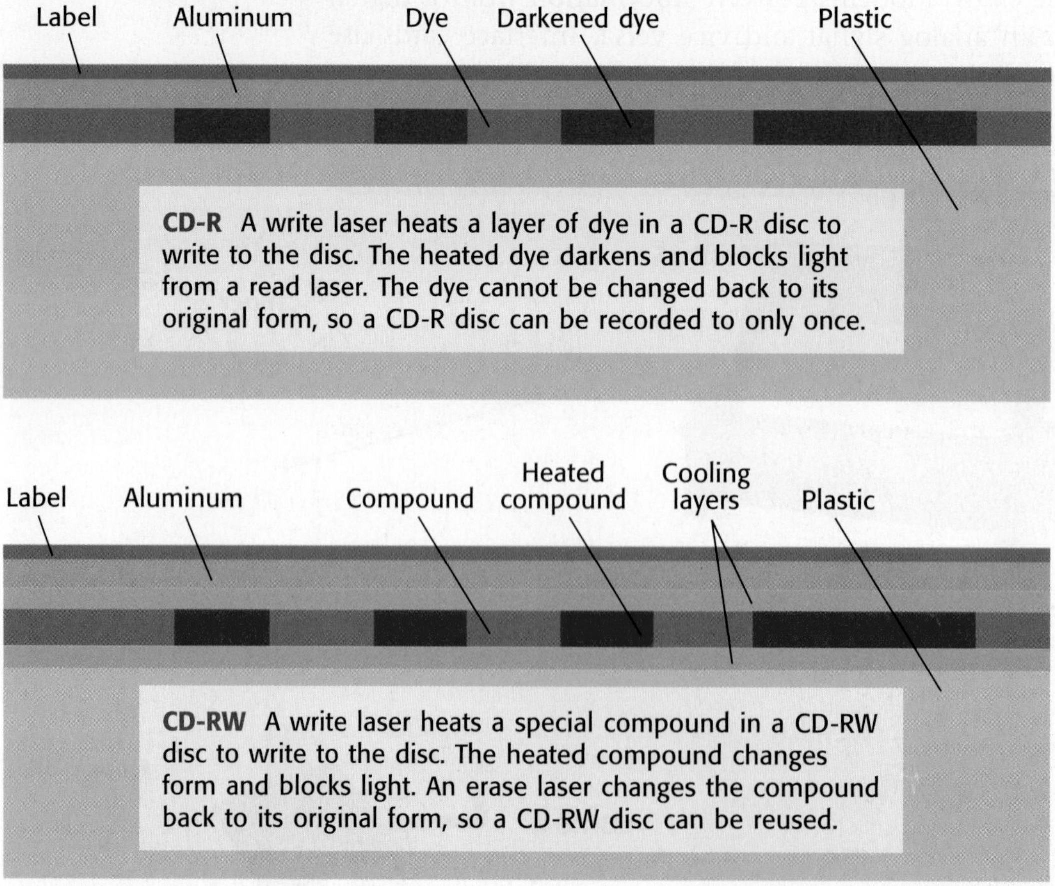

CD-R A write laser heats a layer of dye in a CD-R disc to write to the disc. The heated dye darkens and blocks light from a read laser. The dye cannot be changed back to its original form, so a CD-R disc can be recorded to only once.

Label   Aluminum   Compound   Heated compound   Cooling layers   Plastic

CD-RW A write laser heats a special compound in a CD-RW disc to write to the disc. The heated compound changes form and blocks light. An erase laser changes the compound back to its original form, so a CD-RW disc can be reused.

Computer Software

Computers need instructions before they can do any given task. **Software** is a set of instructions or commands that tells a computer what to do. A computer program is software.

Kinds of Software

Software can be split into two kinds: operating-system software and application software. Operating-system software handles basic operations needed by the computer. It helps the software and hardware communicate. It also handles commands from an input device. It can find programming instructions on a hard disk to be loaded into memory.

Application software tells the computer to run a utility, such as the ones shown in **Figure 6.** The pages in this book were made using many kinds of application software!

Reading Check What are the two main kinds of software?

software a set of instructions or commands that tells a computer what to do; a computer program

Figure 6 Common Types of Computer Software

Word Processing

Video Games

Interactive Instruction

Graphics

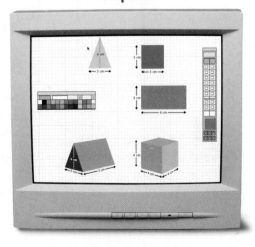

Computer Networks

By using modems and software, many computers can be connected, which allows them to communicate with one another. The **Internet** is a huge computer network made up of millions of computers that can all share information.

Internet a large computer network that connects many local and smaller networks all over the world

The Internet

Figure 7 shows some ways computers can be connected. Computers can connect on the Internet by using modems to dial into an Internet Service Provider, or ISP. A home computer often connects to an ISP over a phone or cable line. Computers in a school or business can be joined in a Local Area Network, or LAN. These computers connect to an ISP through only one line. ISPs around the world are connected by fiber optic cables.

The World Wide Web

The part of the Internet that people know best is called the *World Wide Web*. When you use a Web browser to look at pages on the Internet, you are on the World Wide Web. Web pages share a format that is simple enough that any computer can view them. They are grouped into Web sites. Clicking on a link takes you from one page or site to another. You can use a search engine to find Web pages on a topic for a report or to find out about your favorite movie!

✓ **Reading Check** Describe the World Wide Web.

Figure 7 *Internet Service Providers allow computers in your home or school to connect to large routing computers that are linked around the world.*

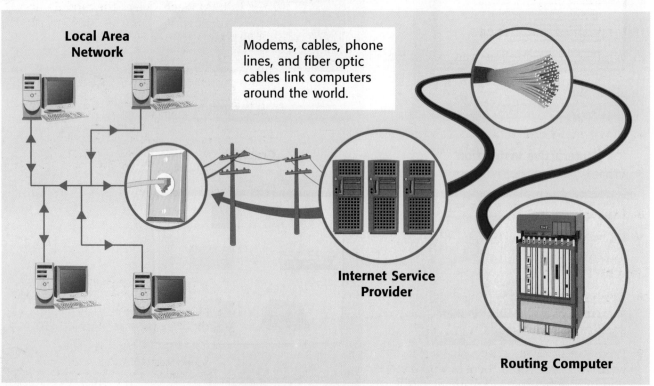

Local Area Network

Modems, cables, phone lines, and fiber optic cables link computers around the world.

Internet Service Provider

Routing Computer

SECTION
Review

TN GLE 0807.Inq.3, GLE 0807.Inq.5

Summary

- All computers have four basic functions: input, processing, storage, and output.

- The first general-purpose computer, ENIAC, was made of thousands of vacuum tubes and filled an entire room. Microprocessors have made it possible to have computers the size of notebooks.

- Computer hardware includes input devices, the CPU, memory, output devices, and modems.

- CD burners can store information on recordable CDs, or CD-Rs. Rewritable CDs, or CD-RWs, can be erased and reused. Both use patterns of light and dark spots.

- Computer software is a set of instructions that tell a computer what to do. The two main types are operating systems and applications. Applications include word processors, spreadsheets, and games.

- The Internet is a huge network that allows millions of computers to share information.

Using Key Terms

The statements below are false. For each statement, replace the underlined term to make a true statement.

1. A word-processing application is an example of hardware.

2. An ISP allows you to connect to the microprocessor.

Understanding Key Ideas

3. Which of the following is an example of hardware used for input?

   a. monitor   **c.** printer

   b. keyboard   **d.** speaker

4. How are modern computers different from ENIAC? How are they the same?

5. What is the difference between hardware and software?

6. Explain how a CD burner works.

7. What is the Internet?

Critical Thinking

8. **Applying Concepts** Using the terms *input, output, processing,* and *store,* explain how you use a pocket calculator to add numbers.

9. **Predicting Consequences** If no phone lines were working, would there be any communication on the Internet? Explain. ✔0807.Inq.3

Math Skills

10. How many 800 KB digital photos could you burn onto a CD-R disc that can hold 700 MB of information? (Note: 1,024 KB = 1 MB)

Interpreting Graphics

11. Look at the image of a RAM module below. Each of the black rectangles on the module is 32 MB of RAM. Each side of the module has the same number of rectangles. How much total RAM does the module have?

Internet Resources

For a variety of links related to this chapter, go to www.scilinks.org

Topic: Computer Technology; Internet

SciLinks code: HSM0334; HSM0808

Skills Practice Lab

Sending Signals

With a telegraph, you can use electric current to send signals between two telegraph keys connected by wires. In this lab, you will build a model of a telegraph that allows you to use Morse code to transmit messages to a friend.

OBJECTIVES

Build a working model of a telegraph key.

Send a message in Morse code by using your model.

Receive a message in Morse code by using your model.

MATERIALS

- battery, 6 V
- flashlight bulb with bulb holder
- paper clip (3)
- thumbtack (2)
- wire, insulated, with ends stripped, 15 cm (4)
- wood block, small

SAFETY

Procedure

1 Build a switch on the wood block, as shown below. Use a thumbtack to tack down a paper clip so that one end of the paper clip hangs over the edge of the wood block.

2 Unfold a second paper clip so that it looks like an *s*. Use the second thumbtack to tack down one end of the open paper clip on top of the remaining paper clip. The free end of the closed paper clip should hang off of the edge of the wood block opposite the first paper clip. The free end of the open paper clip should touch the thumbtack below it when pushed down.

3 Build the rest of the circuit, as shown below. Use a wire to connect one terminal of the battery to one of the paper clips that hangs over the edge of the wood block.

4 Use a second wire to connect the other paper clip that hangs over the edge of the wood block to the bulb holder.

5 Use a third wire to connect the other side of the bulb holder with the second terminal of the battery.

6 Test your circuit by gently pressing down on the open paper clip so that it touches the thumbtack below it. The light bulb should light. This is your model of a telegraph key.

7 Connect your model to another team's model. Use the remaining wire in each team's materials to connect the bulb holders, as shown on the next page. Test your circuit by closing each switch one at a time.

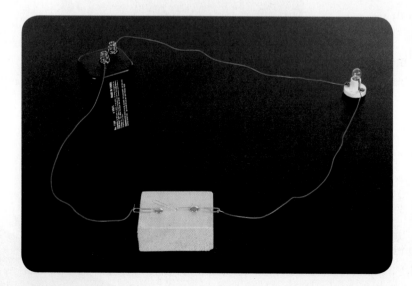

TN GLE 0807.Inq.2 Use appropriate tools and techniques to gather, organize, analyze, and interpret data.

GLE 0807.Inq.3 Synthesize information to determine cause and effect relationships between evidence and explanations.

GLE 0807.Inq.4 Recognize possible sources of bias and error, alternative explanations, and questions for further exploration.

GLE 0807.Inq.5 Communicate scientific understanding using descriptions, explanations, and models.

⑧ Write a short, four- or five-word message in Morse code. Take turns sending messages to the other team using the telegraph. To send a dot, press the paper clip down for two seconds. To send a dash, hold the clip down for four seconds. Decode the message you receive, and check to see if you got the correct message.

⑨ Remove one of the batteries. Test your circuit again by closing each switch one at a time.

Analyze the Results

① **Describing Events** When both batteries are attached, what happens to the flashlight bulbs when you close your switch?

② **Describing Events** When both batteries are attached, what happens to the flashlight bulbs when the other team closes their switch?

③ **Describing Events** How does removing one of the batteries change the way you can send or receive messages on the telegraph?

④ **Analyzing Results** Did you receive the correct message from the other team? If not, what problems did you have? ✔0807.Inq.3, ✔0807.Inq.4, ✔0807.T/E.2

Draw Conclusions

⑤ **Drawing Conclusions** When the two models are connected, are the flashlight bulbs part of a series circuit or a parallel circuit?

⑥ **Making Predictions** Describe how using a telegraph to transmit messages overseas might be difficult. ✔0807.Inq.4

Table 1 International Morse Code			
A ·−	J ·−−−	S ···	2 ··−−−
B −···	K −·−	T −	3 ···−−
C −·−·	L ·−··	U ··−	4 ····−
D −··	M −−	V ···−	5 ·····
E ·	N −·	W ·−−	6 −····
F ··−·	O −−−	X −··−	7 −−···
G −−·	P ·−−·	Y −·−−	8 −−−··
H ····	Q −−·−	Z −−··	9 −−−−·
I ··	R ·−·	1 ·−−−−	0 −−−−−

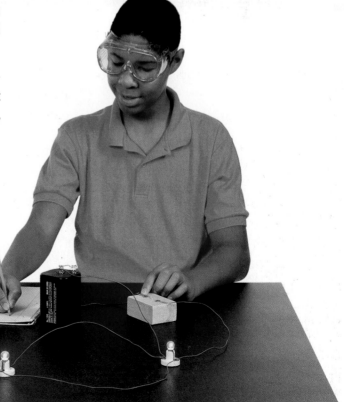

Chapter Review

TN GLE 0807.Inq.3, GLE 0807.Inq.5, GLE 0807.T/E.1, GLE 0807.9.1, GLE 0807.9.2

USING KEY TERMS

For each pair of terms, explain how the meanings of the terms differ.

1 *semiconductor* and *integrated circuit*

2 *transistor* and *doping*

3 *analog signal* and *digital signal*

4 *computer* and *microprocessor*

5 *hardware* and *software*

UNDERSTANDING KEY IDEAS

Multiple Choice

6 All electronic devices transmit information using

  a. signals.

  b. electromagnetic waves.

  c. radio waves.

  d. modems.

7 Semiconductors are used to make

  ✔0807.9.1

  a. transistors.

  b. integrated circuits.

  c. diodes.

  d. All of the above

8 In a semiconductor, what arrangement does doping change?   ✔0807.9.1

  a. protons

  b. neutrons

  c. electrons

  d. gluons

9 A monitor, a printer, and a speaker are examples of

  a. input devices.

  b. memory.

  c. computers.

  d. output devices.

10 Record players play sounds that were recorded in the form of

  a. digital signals.

  b. electric currents.

  c. analog signals.

  d. radio waves.

11 Memory in a computer that is permanent and cannot be changed is called

  a. RAM.

  b. ROM.

  c. CPU.

  d. None of the above

12 Beams of electrons that shine on fluorescent materials are used in

  ✔0807.9.1

  a. telephones.

  b. telegraphs.

  c. televisions.

  d. radios.

Short Answer

13 How is an electronic device different from other machines that use electrical energy?

14 In one or two sentences, describe how a television works.

15 Give three examples of how computers are used in your everyday life.

16 Explain the advantages that transistors have over vacuum tubes.

Math Skills

17 How many bits can be stored on a 20 GB hard disk? (Hint: 1 GB = 1,073,741,824 bytes; 1 byte = 8 bits.)

CRITICAL THINKING

18 **Concept Mapping** Use the following terms to create a concept map: *electronic devices, radio waves, electric current, signals,* and *information.*

19 **Applying Concepts** Your friend is preparing an oral report on the history of radio and finds the photograph shown below. He asks you why the radio is so large. Using what you know about electronic devices, how do you explain the size of this vintage radio?

20 **Making Comparisons** Using what you know about the differences between analog signals and digital signals, compare the sound from a record player to the sound from a CD player.

21 **Making Comparisons** What do Morse code and digital signals have in common?

INTERPRETING GRAPHICS

The diagram below shows a circuit that contains a transistor. Use the diagram below to answer the questions that follow. ✔0807.Inq.3

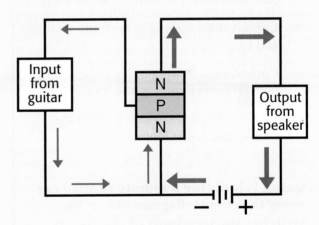

22 What purpose does the transistor serve in this diagram?

23 Compare the current in the left side of the circuit with the current in the right side of the circuit.

24 Compare the sound from the speaker with the sound from the guitar.

TN SPI 0807.Inq.2 Select tools and procedures needed to conduct a moderately complex experiment.

SPI 0807.Inq.3 Interpret and translate data into a table, graph, or diagram.

SPI 0807.Inq.4 Draw a conclusion that establishes a cause and effect relationship supported by evidence.

Multiple Choice

Use the diagram below to answer questions 1–2.

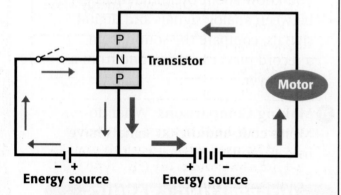

1. In the diagram above, what happens to the current in the circuit if the manual switch is opened?

A. Current stops flowing in the smaller loop but continues to flow in the larger loop.

B. Current stops flowing in both the smaller and larger loops.

C. Current stops flowing in the larger loop but continues to flow in the smaller loop.

D. Current continues to flow in both the smaller and larger loops.

2. Quinn is building a remote-control car using the circuit diagram above. She switches the terminals of the energy source in the smaller loop so that the positive terminal is on the left. What else would she have to do to make the car run?

A. Nothing. The position of the terminals does not affect how the energy flows within the circuit.

B. She would have to switch the terminals of the energy source in the larger loop.

C. She would have to use an NPN transistor and switch the terminals in the larger loop.

D. She would have to move the manual switch so that it controlled the larger loop.

3. Dan needs an analog device to test a system. Which of the following is most likely to work in an analog way?

A. remote control for a television

B. volume control dial on a stereo

C. programmable thermostat

D. light switch

4. Jake hears a sound that has 3 pulses, 2 beats of silence, and 5 alternating pulses and silences. How would Jake represent the sound using digital notation?

A. 0001101010

B. 1110101011

C. 0100001010

D. 1110010101

5. Which of these electronic devices most likely contains a solenoid?

A. record player

B. CD player

C. television set

D. remote control

6. Electronic technology helps make bioengineered products smaller. Which of the following is an example of assistive bioengineering that uses electronic technology?

A. implantable pacemaker

B. drought-resistant hybrid seeds

C. night-vision goggles

D. replacement knee joint

SPI 0807.T/E.4 Differentiate between adaptive and assistive bioengineered products (e.g., food, biofuels, medicines, integrated pest management).

SPI 0807.9.1 Recognize that all matter consists of atoms.

7. **Dawn wants to burn songs to a CD. Each song takes up between 3.96 and 4.54 megabytes. What is the maximum number of songs she can fit on a 700 megabyte CD?**

   A. 154

   B. 164

   C. 176

   D. 189

8. **Laptop computers are thin, light, and portable. How does a laptop screen produce images?**

   A. Electron beams sweep the screen and cause fluorescent materials to glow.

   B. Laser beams shine behind the screen and create patterns of reflected light.

   C. Vibrations in thousands of electron tubes transfer energy to wells of colored light.

   D. Charged atoms of gas in wells on the screen transfer energy to fluorescent materials.

9. **Cecily uses a remote control to turn on her DVD player. Which of the following performs a similar function as the remote control?**

   A. vacuum tube

   B. computer mouse

   C. modem

   D. CD burner

Use the table below to answer question 9.

Element	Number of Electrons in Outermost Energy Level
Boron	3
Germanium	4
Phosphorus	5
Selenium	6

10. **Which element in the table above could be used with silicon to make a p-type semiconductor (the type that contains a "hole")?**

    A. boron

    B. germanium

    C. phosphorus

    D. selenium

Open Response

11. **Would a diode containing two p-type semiconductors create a current? Explain your answer.**

12. **Describe how a transistor radio picks up a radio signal and converts it to sound. Then, draw and label the circuit that allows the radio to amplify sound.**

TCAP Test Preparation

Science in Action

Science, Technology, and Society

Wearable Computers

T/E Today's thin, portable laptop computers are extremely tiny compared to the first general-purpose computer, ENIAC, which filled an entire room. But today's laptops may look bulky next to the computers of tomorrow. In the future, you might wear your computer! A wearable computer is always with you, like clothing or eyeglasses. It is easy to operate. You can even use it while moving around. You might use a wearable computer to take notes in class, look up a phone number, check e-mail, or browse the Internet. Doctors can monitor diagnostic data and records of patients wearing computer-enabled clothing. Firefighters who have temporary vision loss due to smoke, and people who have long-term or permanent blindness could benefit from this technology. **TN** GLE 0807.Inq.5, GLE 0807.T/E.1, GLE 0807.T/E.4

Social Studies ACTIVITY

An important technology used in wearable computers is an *organic light emitting diode* (OLED). Like semiconductors, OLEDs are doped. Use the Internet to research OLEDs and write a brief explanation of how they work and how they might impact society. **TN** ✔0807.Inq.5

Science Fiction

"There Will Come Soft Rains" by Ray Bradbury

Ticktock, seven o'clock, time to get up, seven o'clock. The voice clock in the living room sent out the wake-up message, gently calling to the family to get up and begin their new day. A few minutes later, the automatic stove in the kitchen began the family breakfast. A soft rain was falling outside, so the weather box by the front door suggested that raincoats were necessary today.

But no family sounds come from the house. The house goes on talking to itself as if it were keeping itself company. Why doesn't anyone answer? Find out when you read Ray Bradbury's "There Will Come Soft Rains" in the *Holt Anthology of Science Fiction.*

Language Arts ACTIVITY

WRITING SKILL The story described above takes place in 2026. The author has imagined how the future world might be. Write a short story about how you think life will be different in the year 2050.

HOLT ANTHOLOGY OF Science Fiction

HOLT, RINEHART AND WINSTON

Agnes Riley

Computer Technician Some people take it for granted how smoothly a computer works—until it breaks down. When that happens, you may need to call in an expert, such as Agnes Riley. Agnes is a computer technician from Budapest, Hungary. When a computer isn't working properly, she will take it apart, find the problem, and fix it.

Many people go to school to learn about computer repair, but Agnes taught herself. In Hungary, the company she worked for had a set of old, run-down computers. Agnes started experimenting, trying to repair them. The more she tinkered, the more she learned.

When Agnes moved to New York City in 1999, she wanted to become a computer technician. She started out as a computer salesperson. Eventually, she got the technician training materials. Her earlier experimenting and her studying paid off. She passed the exam to become a licensed technician. Agnes enjoys solving problems and likes helping people. If you are the same type of person, you might want to become a computer technician, too!

Social Studies ACTiViTY

WRITING SKILL Agnes Riley is from Budapest, Hungary. What might you see if you visited Budapest? Do some research to find out, and then design a travel brochure to encourage tourists to visit the city. You might include information about local points of interest or Budapest's history.

To learn more about these Science in Action topics, visit go.hrw.com and type in the keyword HP5ELTF.

Current Science

Check out Current Science® articles related to this chapter by visiting go.hrw.com. Just type in the keyword HP5CS19.

Contents

Voyage of the *USS Adventure*

You are a crew member on the *USS Adventure*. The *Adventure* has been on a 5-year mission to collect life-forms from outside the solar system. On the voyage back to Earth, your ship went through a meteor shower, which ruined several of the compartments containing the extraterrestrial life-forms. Now it is necessary to put more than one life-form in the same compartment.

Life-form 1

   You have only three undamaged compartments in your starship. You and your crewmates must stay in one compartment, and that compartment should be used for extraterrestrial life-forms only if absolutely necessary. You and your crewmates must decide which of the life-forms could be placed together. It is thought that similar life-forms will have similar needs. You can use only observable characteristics to group the life-forms.

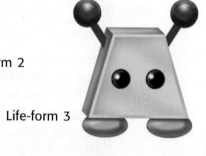
Life-form 2

Life-form 3

Procedure

1. Make a data table similar to the one below. Label each column with as many characteristics of the various life-forms as possible. Leave enough space in each square to write your observations. The life-forms are pictured on this page.

Life-form 4

Life-form Characteristics				
	Color	Shape	Legs	Eyes
Life-form 1				
Life-form 2	DO NOT WRITE IN BOOK			
Life-form 3				
Life-form 4				

2. Describe each characteristic as completely as you can. Based on your observations, determine which of the life-forms are most alike.

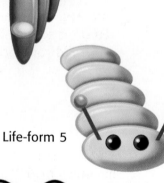
Life-form 5

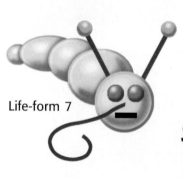
Life-form 7

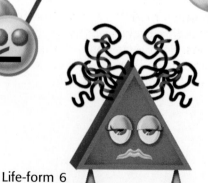
Life-form 6

3 Make a data table like the one below. Fill in the table according to the decisions you made in step 2. State your reasons for the way you have grouped your life-forms. ✔0807.5.2

Life-form Room Assignments		
Compartment	Life-forms	Reasons
1		
2		
3		*DO NOT WRITE IN BOOK*

4 The USS *Adventure* has to make one more stop before returning home. On planet X437 you discover the most interesting life-form ever found outside of Earth—the CC9, shown at right. Make a decision, based on your previous grouping of life-forms, about whether you can safely include CC9 in one of the compartments for the trip to Earth.

Analyze the Results

1 Describe the life-forms in compartment 1. How are they similar? How are they different?

2 Describe the life-forms in compartment 2. How are they similar? How do they differ from the life-forms in compartment 1?

3 Are there any life-forms in compartment 3? If so, describe their similarities. In which compartment will you and your crewmates remain for the journey home?

CC9

Draw Conclusions

4 Are you able to transport life-form CC9 safely back to Earth? If so, in which compartment will it be placed? How did you decide?

Applying Your Data

In 1831, Charles Darwin sailed from England on a ship called the HMS *Beagle*. You have studied the finches that Darwin observed on the Galápagos Islands. What were some of the other unusual organisms he found there? For example, find out about the Galápagos tortoise.

Wet, Wiggly Worms!

Earthworms have been digging in the Earth for more than 100 million years! Earthworms fertilize the soil with their waste and loosen the soil when they tunnel through the moist dirt of a garden or lawn. Worms are food for many animals, such as birds, frogs, snakes, rodents, and fish. Some say they are good food for people, too!

In this activity, you will observe the behavior of a live earthworm. Remember that earthworms are living animals that deserve to be handled gently. Be sure to keep your earthworm moist during this activity. The skin of the earthworm must stay moist so that the worm can get oxygen. If the earthworm's skin dries out, the worm will suffocate and die. Use a spray bottle to moisten the earthworm with water.

MATERIALS

- celery leaves
- clock
- dissecting pan
- earthworm, live
- flashlight
- paper towels
- probe
- ruler, metric
- shoe box, with lid
- soil
- spray bottle
- water

SAFETY

Procedure

1 Place a wet paper towel in the bottom of a dissecting pan. Put a live earthworm on the paper towel, and observe how the earthworm moves. Record your observations.

2 Use the probe to carefully touch the anterior end (head) of the worm. Gently touch other areas of the worm's body with the probe. Record the kinds of responses you observe.

3 Place celery leaves at one end of the pan. Record how the earthworm responds to the presence of food.

4 Shine a flashlight on the anterior end of the earthworm. Record the earthworm's reaction to the light.

5 Line the bottom of the shoe box with a damp paper towel. Cover half of the shoe box with the box top.

6 Place the worm on the uncovered side of the shoe box in the light. Record your observations of the worm's behavior for 3 min.

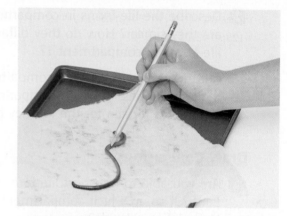

7 Place the worm in the covered side of the box. Record your observations for 3 min.

8 Repeat steps 6–7 three times.

9 Spread some loose soil evenly in the bottom of the shoe box so that the soil is about 4 cm deep. Place the earthworm on top of the soil. Observe and record the earthworm's behavior for 3 min.

10 Dampen the soil on one side of the box, and leave the other side dry. Place the earthworm in the center of the box between the wet and dry soil. Cover the box, and wait 3 min. Uncover the box, and record your observations. Repeat this procedure three times. (You may need to search for the worm!)

Analyze the Results

1 How did the earthworm respond to being touched? Were some areas more sensitive than others?

2 How did the earthworm respond to the presence of food?

Draw Conclusions

3 How is the earthworm's behavior influenced by light? Based on your observations, describe how an animal's response to a stimulus might provide protection for the animal.

4 When the worm was given a choice of wet or dry soil, which did it choose? Explain this result.

Communicating Your Data

Based on your observations of an earthworm's behavior, prepare a poster showing where you might expect to find earthworms. Draw a picture with colored markers, or cut out pictures from magazines. Include all the variables that you used in your experiment, such as soil or no soil, wet or dry soil, light or dark, and food. Write a caption at the bottom of your poster describing where earthworms might be found in nature. ✔0807.Inq.5

Skills Practice Lab

TN GLE 0807.Inq.2, GLE 0807.Inq.3, GLE 0807.Inq.5

The Half-life of Pennies

Carbon-14 is a special unstable element used in the absolute dating of material that was once alive, such as fossil bones. Every 5,730 years, half of the carbon-14 in a fossil specimen decays or breaks down into a more stable element. In the following experiment you will see how pennies can show the same kind of "decay."

MATERIALS

- container with a cover, large
- pennies (100)

Procedure

1. Place 100 pennies in a large, covered container. Shake the container several times, and remove the cover. Carefully empty the container on a flat surface making sure the pennies don't roll away.

2. Remove all the coins that have the "head" side of the coin turned upward. Record the number of pennies removed and the number of pennies remaining in a data table similar to the one at right.

3. Repeat the process until no pennies are left in the container. Remember to remove only the coins showing "heads."

4. Draw a graph similar to the one at right. Label the *x*-axis "Number of shakes," and label the *y*-axis "Pennies remaining." Using data from your data table, plot the number of coins remaining at each shake on your graph.

Analyze the Results

1. Examine the "Half-life of Carbon-14" graph at right. Compare the graph you have made for pennies with the one for carbon-14. Explain any similarities that you see.

2. Recall that the probability of landing "heads" in a coin toss is 1/2. Use this information to explain why the remaining number of pennies is reduced by about half each time they are shaken and tossed. ✔0807.Inq.3

Shake number	Number of coins remaining	Number of coins removed
1		
2	DO NOT WRITE IN BOOK	
3		

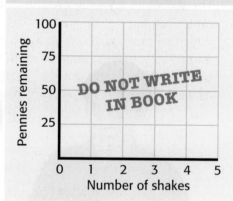

Half-life of Pennies

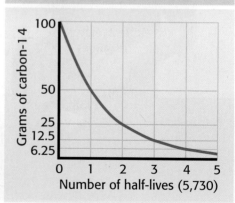

Half-life of Carbon-14

Skills Practice Lab

Deciding About Environmental Issues

You make hundreds of decisions every day. Some of them are complicated, but many of them are very simple, such as what to wear or what to eat for lunch. Deciding what to do about an environmental issue can be very difficult. There are many different factors that must be considered. How will a certain solution affect people's lives? How much will it cost? Is it ethically right?

In this activity, you will analyze an issue in four steps to help you make a decision about it. Find out about environmental issues that are being discussed in your area. Examine newspapers, magazines, and other publications to find out what the issues are. Choose one local issue to evaluate. For example, you could evaluate whether the city should spend the money to provide recycling bins and special trucks for picking up recyclable trash.

MATERIALS

- newspapers, magazines, and other publications containing information about environmental issues

A Four-Step Decision-Making Model

Gather Information
↓
Consider Values
↓
Explore Consequences
↓
Make a Decision

Procedure

1. Write a statement about an environmental issue.

2. Read about your issue in several publications. On a separate sheet of paper, summarize important facts.

3. The values of an issue are the things that you consider important. Examine the diagram below. Several values are given. Which values do you think apply most to the environmental issue you are considering? Are there other values that you believe will help you make a decision about the issue? Consider at least four values in making your decision. ✔0807.Inq.3

4 Consequences are the things that result from a certain course of action. Create a table similar to the one below. Use your table to organize your thoughts about consequences related to your environmental issue. List your values at the top. Fill in each space with the consequences for each value. ✔0807.Inq.3, ✔0807.T/E.3

Consequences Table				
Consequences	**Values**			
Positive short-term consequences				
Negative short-term consequences		*DO NOT WRITE IN BOOK*		
Positive long-term consequences				
Negative long-term consequences				

5 Thoroughly consider all of the consequences you have recorded in your table. Evaluate how important each consequence is. Make a decision about what course of action you would choose on the issue. ✔0807.Inq.4

Analyze the Results

1 In your evaluation, did you consider short-term consequences or long-term consequences to be more important? Why? ✔0807.Inq.4, ✔0807.T/E.3

2 Which value or values had the greatest influence on your final decision? Explain your reasoning.

Communicating Your Data

Compare your table with your classmates' tables. Did you all make the same decision about a similar issue? If not, form teams, and organize a formal classroom debate of a specific environmental issue. ✔0807.Inq.4, ✔0807.Inq.5

Volumania!

You have learned how to measure the volume of a solid object that has square or rectangular sides. But there are lots of objects in the world that have irregular shapes. In this lab activity, you'll learn some ways to find the volume of objects that have irregular shapes.

Part A: Finding the Volume of Small Objects

Procedure

1. Fill a graduated cylinder half full with water. Read and record the volume of the water. Be sure to look at the surface of the water at eye level and to read the volume at the bottom of the meniscus, as shown below.

Read volume here

2. Carefully slide one of the objects into the tilted graduated cylinder, as shown below.

3. Read the new volume, and record it.

4. Subtract the old volume from the new volume. The resulting amount is equal to the volume of the solid object.

5. Use the same method to find the volume of the other objects. Record your results.

Analyze the Results

1. What changes do you have to make to the volumes you determine in order to express them correctly?

2. Do the heaviest objects always have the largest volumes? Why or why not?

MATERIALS

Part A

- graduated cylinder
- water
- various small objects supplied by your teacher

Part B

- bottle, plastic (or similar container), 2 L, bottom half
- funnel
- graduated cylinder
- pan, aluminum pie
- paper towels
- water

SAFETY

Part B: Finding the Volume of Your Hand

Procedure

1. Completely fill the container with water. Put the container in the center of the pie pan. Be sure not to spill any of the water into the pie pan.

2. Make a fist, and put your hand into the container up to your wrist.

3. Remove your hand, and let the excess water drip into the container, not the pie pan. Dry your hand with a paper towel.

4. Use the funnel to pour the overflow water into the graduated cylinder. Measure the volume. This measurement is the volume of your hand. Record the volume. (Remember to use the correct unit of volume for a solid object.)

5. Repeat this procedure with your other hand.

Analyze the Results

1. Was the volume the same for both of your hands? If not, were you surprised? What might account for a person's hands having different volumes? ✔0807.Inq.3, ✔0807.9.3

2. Would it have made a difference if you had placed your open hand into the container instead of your fist? Explain your reasoning. ✔0807.Inq.3, ✔0807.9.3

3. Compare the volume of your right hand with the volume of your classmates' right hands. Create a class graph of right-hand volumes. What is the average right-hand volume for your class? ✔0807.Inq.3, ✔0807.Inq.5, ✔0807.9.3

Inquiry

Design an experiment to determine the volume of a person's body. Plan to test your procedure by trying it on an object whose volume you can calculate. In your plans, be sure to include the materials needed for the experiment and the procedures that must be followed. Include a sketch that shows how your materials and methods would be used in this experiment.

Using an encyclopedia, the Internet, or other reference materials, find out how the volumes of very large samples of matter—such as an entire planet—are determined. ✔0807.Inq.1, ✔0807.Inq.2, ✔0807.9.3

Skills Practice Lab

Determining Density

The density of an object is its mass divided by its volume. But how does the density of a small amount of a substance relate to the density of a larger amount of the same substance? In this lab, you will calculate the density of one marble and of a group of marbles. Then, you will confirm the relationship between the mass and volume of a substance.

MATERIALS

- balance, metric
- graduated cylinder, 100 mL
- marbles, glass (8–10)
- paper, graph
- paper towels
- water

SAFETY

Procedure

1 Copy the table below. Include one row for each marble.

Mass of marble (g)	Total mass of marbles (g)	Total volume (mL)	Volume of marbles (mL) (total volume minus 50.0 mL)	Density of marbles (g/mL) (total mass divided by volume)
		DO NOT WRITE IN BOOK		

2 Fill the graduated cylinder with 50 mL of water. If you put in too much water, twist one of the paper towels, and use it to absorb excess water.

3 Measure the mass of a marble as accurately as you can (to at least .01 g). Record the mass in the table.

4 Carefully drop the marble in the tilted cylinder, and measure the total volume. Record the volume in the third column.

5 Measure and record the mass of another marble. Add the masses of the marbles together, and record this value in the second column of the table.

6 Carefully drop the second marble in the graduated cylinder. Complete the row of information in the table.

7 Repeat steps 5 and 6. Add one marble at a time. Stop when you run out of marbles, the water no longer completely covers the marbles, or the graduated cylinder is full.

Analyze the Results

1 Examine the data in your table. As the number of marbles increases, what happens to the total mass of the marbles? What happens to the volume of the marbles? What happens to the density of the marbles? ✔0807.Inq.3

2 Graph the total mass of the marbles (y-axis) versus the volume of the marbles (x-axis). Is the graph a straight line? ✔0807.Inq.3

Draw Conclusions

3 Does the density of a substance depend on the amount of substance present? Explain how your results support your answer.

Applying Your Data

Calculate the slope of the graph. How does the slope compare with the values in the column titled "Density of marbles"? Explain.

Skills Practice Lab

TN GLE 0807.Inq.2, GLE 0807.Inq.3

Layering Liquids

You have learned that liquids form layers according to the densities of the liquids. In this lab, you'll discover whether it matters in which order you add the liquids.

Ask a Question

1 Does the order in which you add liquids of different densities to a container affect the order of the layers formed by those liquids?

Form a Hypothesis

2 Write a possible answer to the question above.

Test the Hypothesis

3 Using the graduated cylinders, add 10 mL of each liquid to the clear container. Remember to read the volume at the bottom of the meniscus, as shown below. Record the order in which you added the liquids.

4 Observe the liquids in the container. Sketch what you see. Be sure to label the layers and the colors.

5 Add 10 mL more of liquid C. Observe what happens, and record your observations.

6 Add 20 mL more of liquid A. Observe what happens, and record your observations.

Analyze the Results

1 Which of the liquids has the greatest density? Which has the least density? How can you tell?

2 Did the layers change position when you added more of liquid C? Explain your answer. ✔0807.Inq.3

3 Did the layers change position when you added more of liquid A? Explain your answer. ✔0807.Inq.3

MATERIALS

- beaker (or other small, clear container)
- funnel (3)
- graduated cylinder, 10 mL (3)
- liquid A
- liquid B
- liquid C

SAFETY

4 Find out in what order your classmates added the liquids to the container. Compare your results with those of a classmate who added the liquids in a different order. Were your results different? Explain why or why not.

Draw Conclusions

5 Based on your results, evaluate your hypothesis from step 2.

Skills Practice Lab

 GLE 0807.Inq.2, GLE 0807.Inq.3, GLE 0807.Inq.4, GLE 0807.Inq.5

Full of Hot Air!

Why do hot-air balloons float gracefully above Earth, but balloons you blow up fall to the ground? The answer has to do with the density of the air inside the balloon. *Density* is mass per unit volume, and volume is affected by changes in temperature. In this experiment, you will investigate the relationship between the temperature of a gas and its volume. Then, you will be able to determine how the temperature of a gas affects its density.

MATERIALS

- balloon
- beaker, 250 mL
- gloves, heat-resistant
- hot plate
- ice water
- pan, aluminum (2)
- ruler, metric
- water

SAFETY

Ask a Question

1. How does an increase or decrease in temperature affect the volume of a balloon?

Form a Hypothesis

2. Write a hypothesis that answers the question above.

Test the Hypothesis

3. Fill an aluminum pan with water about 4 cm to 5 cm deep. Put the pan on the hot plate, and turn the hot plate on.

4. Fill the other pan 4 cm to 5 cm deep with ice water.

5. Blow up a balloon inside the 500 mL beaker, as shown. The balloon should fill the beaker but should not extend outside the beaker. Tie the balloon at its opening.

6. Place the beaker and balloon in the ice water. Observe what happens. Record your observations.

7. Remove the balloon and beaker from the ice water. Observe the balloon for several minutes. Record any changes.

8. Put on heat-resistant gloves. When the hot water begins to boil, put the beaker and balloon in the hot water. Observe the balloon for several minutes, and record your observations.

9. Turn off the hot plate. When the water has cooled, carefully pour it into a sink.

Analyze the Results

1. Summarize your observations of the balloon. Relate your observations to Charles's law.

2. Was your hypothesis from step 2 supported? If not, revise your hypothesis. ✔0807.Inq.4

Draw Conclusions

3. Based on your observations, how is the density of a gas affected by an increase or decrease in temperature? ✔0807.Inq.3

Can Crusher

Condensation can occur when gas particles come near the surface of a liquid. The gas particles slow down because they are attracted to the liquid. This reduction in speed causes the gas particles to condense into a liquid. In this lab, you'll see that particles that have condensed into a liquid don't take up as much space and therefore don't exert as much pressure as they did in the gaseous state.

MATERIALS

- beaker, 1 L
- can, aluminum (2)
- gloves, heat-resistant
- hot plate
- tongs
- water

SAFETY

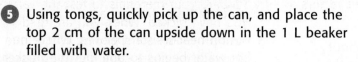

Procedure

1. Fill the beaker with room-temperature water.

2. Place just enough water in an aluminum can to slightly cover the bottom.

3. Put on heat-resistant gloves. Place the aluminum can on a hot plate turned to the highest temperature setting.

4. Heat the can until the water is boiling. Steam should be rising vigorously from the top of the can.

5. Using tongs, quickly pick up the can, and place the top 2 cm of the can upside down in the 1 L beaker filled with water.

6. Describe your observations.

Analyze the Results

1. The can was crushed because the atmospheric pressure outside the can became greater than the pressure inside the can. Explain what happened inside the can to cause the difference in pressure. ✔0807.Inq.3

Draw Conclusions

2. Inside every popcorn kernel is a small amount of water. When you make popcorn, the water inside the kernels is heated until it becomes steam. Explain how the popping of the kernels is the opposite of what you saw in this lab. Be sure to address the effects of pressure in your explanation. ✔0807.Inq.3

Inquiry

Try the experiment again, but redesign it to use ice water instead of room-temperature water. Explain your results in terms of the effects of temperature. ✔0807.Inq.1

Skills Practice Lab

TN GLE 0807.Inq.1, GLE 0807.Inq.2, GLE 0807.Inq.3, GLE 0807.Inq.4, GLE 0807.Inq.5

A Sugar Cube Race!

If you drop a sugar cube into a glass of water, how long will it take to dissolve? What can you do to speed up the rate at which it dissolves? Should you change something about the water, the sugar cube, or the process? In other words, what variable should you change? Before reading further, make a list of variables that could be changed in this situation. Record your list.

MATERIALS

- beakers or other clear containers (2)
- clock or stopwatch
- graduated cylinder
- sugar cubes (2)
- water
- other materials approved by your teacher

SAFETY

Ask a Question

① Write a question you can test about factors that affect the rate sugar dissolves.
✔0807.Inq.1

Form a Hypothesis

② Choose one variable to test. Record your choice, and predict how changing your variable will affect the rate of dissolving.
✔0807.Inq.1

Test the Hypothesis

③ Pour 150 mL of water into one of the beakers. Add one sugar cube, and use the stopwatch to measure how long it takes for the sugar cube to dissolve. You must not disturb the sugar cube in any way! Record this time.

④ Be sure to get your teacher's approval before you begin. You may need additional equipment.

⑤ Prepare your materials to test the variable you have picked. When you are ready, start your procedure for speeding up the rate at which the sugar cube dissolves. Use the stopwatch to measure the time. Record this time. ✔0807.Inq.1, ✔0807.Inq.2

Analyze the Results

① Compare your results with the prediction you made in step 2. Was your prediction correct? Why or why not? ✔0807.Inq.4

Draw Conclusions

② Why was it necessary to observe the sugar cube dissolving on its own before you tested the variable? ✔0807.Inq.3

③ Do you think changing more than one variable would speed up the rate of dissolving even more? Explain your reasoning.
✔0807.Inq.3, ✔0807.Inq.4

④ Discuss your results with a group that tested a different variable. Which variable had a greater effect on the rate of dissolving?
✔0807.Inq.3

Making Butter

A colloid is an interesting substance. It has properties of both solutions and suspensions. Colloidal particles are not heavy enough to settle out, so they remain evenly dispersed throughout the mixture. In this activity, you will make butter—a very familiar colloid—and observe the characteristics that classify butter as a colloid.

MATERIALS

- clock or stopwatch
- container with lid, small, clear
- heavy cream
- marble

SAFETY

Procedure

1. Place a marble inside the container, and fill the container with heavy cream. Put the lid tightly on the container.

2. Take turns shaking the container vigorously and constantly for 10 min. Record the time when you begin shaking. Every minute, stop shaking the container, and hold it up to the light. Record your observations.

3. Continue shaking the container, taking turns if necessary. When you see, hear, or feel any changes inside the container, note the time and change.

4. After 10 min of shaking, you should have a lump of "butter" surrounded by liquid inside the container. Describe both the butter and the liquid in detail.

5. Let the container sit for about 10 min. Observe the butter and liquid again, and record your observations.

Analyze the Results

1. When you noticed the change inside the container, what did you think was happening at that point?
✔0807.Inq.3

2. Based on your observations, explain why butter is classified as a colloid.

3. What kind of mixture is the liquid that is left behind? Explain.
✔0807.Inq.3

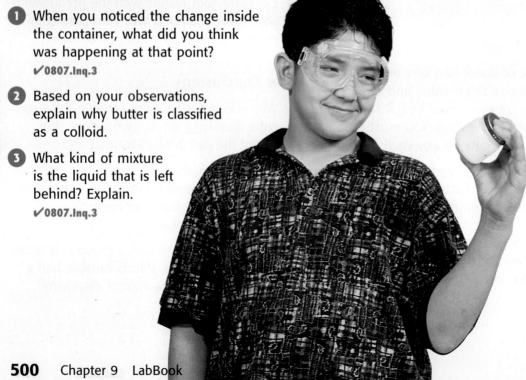

Model-Making Lab

Unpolluting Water

In many cities, the water supply comes from a river, lake, or reservoir. This water may include several mixtures, including suspensions (with suspended dirt, oil, or living organisms) and solutions (with dissolved chemicals). To make the water safe to drink, your city's water supplier must remove impurities. In this lab, you will model the procedures used in real water treatment plants.

Part A: Untreated Water

Procedure

1. Measure 100 mL of "polluted" water into a graduated cylinder. Be sure to shake the bottle of water before you pour so your sample will include all the impurities.

2. Pour the contents of the graduated cylinder into one of the beakers.

3. Copy the table below, and record your observations of the water in the "Before treatment" row.

MATERIALS

- beaker, 250 mL (4)
- charcoal, activated, washed
- cup, plastic-foam, 8 oz (2)
- graduated cylinder
- nail, small
- paper, filter (2 pieces)
- rubber band
- ruler, metric
- sand, fine, washed
- scissors
- spoon, plastic (2)
- water, "polluted"

SAFETY

Observations						
	Color	Clearness	Odor	Any layers?	Any solids?	Water volume
Before treatment						
After oil separation						
After sand filtration			*DO NOT WRITE IN BOOK*			
After charcoal						

Part B: Settling In

If a suspension is left standing, the suspended particles will settle to the top or bottom. You should see a layer of oil at the top.

Procedure

1. Separate the oil by carefully pouring the oil into another beaker. You can use a plastic spoon to get the last bit of oil from the water. Record your observations.

Part C: Filtration

Cloudy water can be a sign of small particles still in suspension. These particles can usually be removed by filtering. Water treatment plants use sand and gravel as filters.

Procedure

1 Make a filter as follows:

   a. Use the nail to poke 5 to 10 small holes in the bottom of one of the cups.

   b. Cut a circle of filter paper to fit inside the bottom of the cup. (This filter will keep the sand in the cup.)

   c. Fill the cup to 2 cm below the rim with wet sand. Pack the sand tightly.

   d. Set the cup inside an empty beaker.

2 Pour the polluted water on top of the sand, and let the water filter through. Do not pour any of the settled mud onto the sand. (Dispose of the mud as instructed by your teacher.) In your table, record your observations of the water collected in the beaker.

Part D: Separating Solutions

Something that has been dissolved in a solvent cannot be separated using filters. Water treatment plants use activated charcoal to absorb many dissolved chemicals.

Procedure

1 Place activated charcoal about 3 cm deep in the unused cup. Pour the water collected from the sand filtration into the cup, and stir with a spoon for 1 min.

2 Place a piece of filter paper over the top of the cup, and fasten it in place with a rubber band. With the paper securely in place, pour the water through the filter paper and back into a clean beaker. Record your observations in your table.

Analyze the Results

1 Is your unpolluted water safe to drink? Why or why not?
✓0807.Inq.3

2 When you treat a sample of water, do you get out exactly the same amount of water that you put in? Explain your answer.
✓0807.Inq.3

3 Some groups may still have cloudy water when they finish. Explain a possible cause for this. ✓0807.Inq.4

Model-Making Lab

Finding a Balance

Usually, balancing a chemical equation involves just writing. But in this activity, you will use models to practice balancing chemical equations, as shown below. By following the rules, you will soon become an expert equation balancer!

MATERIALS

- envelopes, each labeled with an unbalanced equation

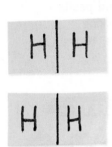

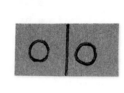

Example

$$\_H_2 + \_O_2 \rightarrow \_H_2O$$

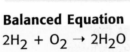

Balanced Equation

$$2H_2 + O_2 \rightarrow 2H_2O$$

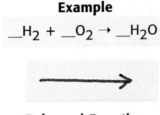

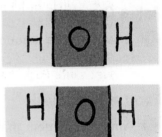

Procedure

1. The rules are as follows:
   a. Reactant-molecule models may be placed only to the left of the arrow.
   b. Product-molecule models may be placed only to the right of the arrow.
   c. You may use only complete molecule models.
   d. At least one of each of the reactant and product molecules shown in the equation must be included in the model when you are finished.

2. Select one of the labeled envelopes. Copy the unbalanced equation written on the envelope.

3. Open the envelope, and pull out the molecule models and the arrow. Place the arrow in the center of your work area.

4. Put one model of each molecule that is a reactant on the left side of the arrow and one model of each product on the right side.

5. Add one reactant-molecule or product-molecule model at a time until the number of each of the different-colored squares on each side of the arrow is the same. Remember to follow the rules.

6. When the equation is balanced, count the number of each of the molecule models you used. Write these numbers as coefficients, as shown in the balanced equation above.

7. Select another envelope, and repeat the steps until you have balanced all of the equations.

Analyze the Results

1. The rules specify that you are allowed to use only complete molecule models. How are these rules similar to what occurs in a real chemical reaction?

2. In chemical reactions, energy is either released or absorbed. Devise a way to improve the model to show energy being released or absorbed. ✔0807.Inq.5, ✔0807.9.5, ✔0807.9.11

Skills Practice Lab

TN ⬛ GLE 0807.Inq.2, GLE 0807.Inq.3, GLE 0807.Inq.5

Cata-what? Catalyst!

Catalysts increase the rate of a chemical reaction without being changed during the reaction. In this experiment, hydrogen peroxide, H_2O_2, decomposes into oxygen, O_2, and water, H_2O. An enzyme present in liver cells acts as a catalyst for this reaction. You will investigate the relationship between the amount of the catalyst and the rate of the decomposition reaction.

Ask a Question

1. How does the amount of a catalyst affect reaction rate?

Form a Hypothesis

2. Write a statement that answers the question above. Explain your reasoning.

Test the Hypothesis

3. Put a small piece of masking tape near the top of each test tube, and label the tubes "1," "2," and "3."

4. Create a hot-water bath by filling the beaker half full with hot water.

5. Using the funnel and graduated cylinder, measure 5 mL of the hydrogen peroxide solution into each test tube. Place the test tubes in the hot-water bath for 5 min.

6. While the test tubes warm up, grind one liver cube with the mortar and pestle.

7. After 5 min, use the tweezers to place the cube of liver in test tube 1. Place the ground liver in test tube 2. Leave test tube 3 alone.

8. Observe the reaction rate (the amount of bubbling) in all three test tubes, and record your observations.

Analyze the Results

1. Does liver appear to be a catalyst? Explain your answer.

2. Which type of liver (whole or ground) produced a faster reaction? Why?

3. What is the purpose of test tube 3?

MATERIALS

- beaker, 600 mL
- funnel
- graduated cylinder, 10 mL
- hydrogen peroxide, 3% solution
- liver cubes, small (2)
- mortar and pestle
- tape, masking
- test tubes, 10 mL (3)
- tweezers
- water, hot

SAFETY

Draw Conclusions

4. How do your results support or disprove your hypothesis? ✔ 0807.Inq.3

5. Why was a hot-water bath used? (Hint: Look in your book for a definition of *activation energy.*)

TN GLE 0807.Inq.2, GLE 0807.Inq.3, GLE 0807.Inq.5, GLE 0807.9.7

Putting Elements Together

A synthesis reaction is a reaction in which two or more substances combine to form a single compound. The resulting compound has different chemical and physical properties than the substances from which it is composed. In this activity, you will synthesize, or create, copper(II) oxide from the elements copper and oxygen.

Procedure

1 Copy the table below.

Data Collection Table	
Object	**Mass (g)**
Evaporating dish	
Copper powder	DO NOT WRITE IN BOOK
Copper + evaporating dish after heating	
Copper(II) oxide	

2 Use the metric balance to measure the mass (to the nearest 0.1 g) of the empty evaporating dish. Record this mass in the table.

3 Place a piece of weighing paper on the metric balance, and measure approximately 10 g of copper powder. Record the mass (to the nearest 0.1 g) in the table. **Caution:** Wear protective gloves when working with copper powder.

4 Use the weighing paper to place the copper powder in the evaporating dish. Spread the powder over the bottom and up the sides as much as possible.
Discard the weighing paper.

MATERIALS

- balance, metric
- Bunsen burner (or portable burner)
- copper powder
- evaporating dish
- gauze, wire
- gloves, protective
- igniter
- paper, weighing
- ring stand and ring
- tongs

SAFETY

5 Set up the ring stand and ring. Place the wire gauze on top of the ring. Carefully place the evaporating dish on the wire gauze.

6 Place the Bunsen burner under the ring and wire gauze. Use the igniter to light the Bunsen burner. **Caution:** Use extreme care when working near an open flame.

7 Heat the evaporating dish for 10 min.

8 Turn off the burner, and allow the evaporating dish to cool for 10 min. Use tongs to remove the evaporating dish and to place it on the balance to determine the mass. Record the mass in the table.

9 Determine the mass of the reaction product—copper(II) oxide—by subtracting the mass of the evaporating dish from the mass of the evaporating dish and copper powder after heating. Record this mass in the table.

Analyze the Results

1 What evidence of a chemical reaction did you observe after the copper was heated?

2 Explain why there was a change in mass.

3 How does the change in mass support the idea that this reaction is a synthesis reaction? ✔0807.9.8

4 Explain how the change in the mass during this chemical reaction does not break the law of conservation of mass. ✔0807.9.11

Draw Conclusions

5 Why was powdered copper used rather than a small piece of copper? (Hint: How does surface area affect the rate of the reaction?)

6 Why was the copper heated? (Hint: Look in your book for the discussion of activation energy.)

7 The copper bottoms of cooking pots can turn black when used. How is that similar to the results you obtained in this lab? ✔0807.Inq.3

Applying Your Data

Rust, shown below, is iron(III) oxide—the product of a synthesis reaction between iron and oxygen. How does painting a car help prevent this type of reaction?

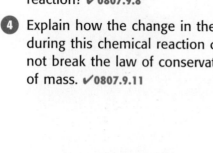

Skills Practice Lab

Making Salt

A neutralization reaction between an acid and a base produces water and a salt. In this lab, you will react an acid with a base and then let the water evaporate. You will then examine what is left for properties that tell you that it is indeed a salt.

Ask a Question

1 Write a question about reactions between acids and bases.

Form a Hypothesis

2 Write a hypothesis that may answer the question you asked in the step above.

Test the Hypothesis

3 Put on protective gloves. Carefully measure 25 mL of hydrochloric acid in a graduated cylinder, and then pour it into the beaker. Carefully rinse the graduated cylinder with distilled water to clean out any leftover acid. **Caution:** Hydrochloric acid is corrosive. If any should spill on you, immediately flush the area with water, and notify your teacher.

4 Add 3 drops of phenolphthalein indicator to the acid in the beaker. You will not see anything happen yet because this indicator won't show its color unless too much base is present. ✔0807.9.13

5 Measure 20 mL of sodium hydroxide (base) in the graduated cylinder, and add it slowly to the beaker with the acid. Use the stirring rod to mix the substances completely. **Caution:** Sodium hydroxide is also corrosive. If any should spill on you, immediately flush the area with water, and notify your teacher.

6 Use an eyedropper to add more base, a few drops at a time, to the acid-base mixture in the beaker. Be sure to stir the mixture after each few drops. Continue adding drops of base until the mixture remains colored after stirring. ✔0807.9.13

- beaker, 100 mL
- eyedroppers (2)
- evaporating dish
- gloves, protective
- graduated cylinder, 100 mL
- hydrochloric acid
- magnifying lens
- phenolphthalein solution in a dropper bottle
- stirring rod, glass
- sodium hydroxide
- water, distilled

SAFETY

7 Use another eyedropper to add acid to the beaker, 1 drop at a time, until the color just disappears after stirring.

8 Pour the mixture carefully into an evaporating dish, and place the dish where your teacher tells you to allow the water to evaporate overnight.

9 The next day, examine your evaporating dish, and with a magnifying lens, study the crystals that were left. Identify the color, shape, and other properties of the crystals.

Analyze the Results

1 The following equation is for the reaction that occurred in this experiment:

$$HCl + NaOH \longrightarrow H_2O + NaCl$$

NaCl is ordinary table salt and forms very regular cubic crystals that are white. Did you find white cubic crystals? Do you think the white crystals are the reactants or the products? ✔0807.9.7, ✔0807.9.8, ✔0807.9.12

2 The phenolphthalein indicator changes color in the presence of a base. Why did you add more acid in step 7 until the color disappeared? ✔0807.9.13

Applying Your Data

Another neutralization reaction occurs between hydrochloric acid and potassium hydroxide, KOH. The equation for this reaction is as follows:

$$HCl + KOH \longrightarrow H_2O + KCl$$

What are the products of this neutralization reaction? How do they compare with those you discovered in this experiment? ✔0807.Inq.3, ✔0807.9.8, ✔0807.9.12

Skills Practice Lab

TN GLE 0807.Inq.1, GLE 0807.Inq.2, GLE 0807.Inq.3, GLE 0807.Inq.5

Magnetic Mystery

Every magnet is surrounded by a magnetic field. Magnetic field lines show the shape of the magnetic field. These lines can be modeled by using iron filings. The iron filings are affected by the magnetic field, and they fall into lines showing the field. In this lab, you will first learn about magnetic fields, and then you will use this knowledge to identify a mystery magnet's shape and orientation based on observations of the field lines.

MATERIALS

- acetate, clear (1 sheet)
- iron filings
- magnets, different shapes (2)
- shoe box
- tape, masking

SAFETY

Ask a Question

1. Can a magnet's shape and orientation be determined without seeing the magnet?

Form a Hypothesis

2. Write a possible answer to the question above. Explain your reasoning.

Test the Hypothesis

3. Lay one of the magnets flat on a table.

4. Place a sheet of clear acetate over the magnet. Sprinkle some iron filings on the acetate to see the magnetic field lines.

5. Draw the magnet and the magnetic field lines.

6. Remove the acetate, and return the filings to the container.

7. Place your magnet so that one end is pointing up. Repeat steps 4 through 6.

8. Place your magnet on its side. Repeat steps 4 through 6.

9. Repeat steps 3 through 8 with the other magnet.

10. Remove the lid from a shoe box, and tape a magnet underneath the lid. Once the magnet is secure, place the lid on the box.

11. Exchange boxes with another team.

12. Without opening the box, use the sheet of acetate and the iron filings to determine the shape of the magnetic field.

13. Draw the magnetic field lines.

Analyze the Results

1. Use your drawings from steps 3 through 9 to find the shape and orientation of the magnet in your box. Draw a picture of your conclusion. ✔0807.Inq.5

Inquiry

Examine your drawings. Can you identify the north and south poles of a magnet from the shape of the magnetic field lines? Design a procedure that would allow you to determine the poles of a magnet. ✔0807.Inq.1, ✔0807.Inq.2, ✔0807.Inq.5

Model-Making Lab

TN GLE 0807.Inq.2, GLE 0807.Inq.3, GLE 0807.Inq.5,
✓0807.Inq.3, ✓0807.Inq.5

Tune In!

You probably have listened to radios many times in your life. Modern radios are complicated electronic devices. However, radios do not have to be so complicated. The basic parts of all radios include a diode, an inductor, a capacitor, an antenna, a ground wire, and an earphone (or a speaker and amplifier on a large radio). In this activity, you will examine each of these components one at a time as you build a working model of a radio-wave receiver.

Ask a Question

1. Write a question you can test using the procedure in this lab.

Form a Hypothesis

2. Write a possible answer to the question you wrote in the step above. Explain your reasoning.

Test the Hypothesis

3. Examine the diode. Describe it on another sheet of paper.

4. A diode carries current in only one direction. Draw the inside of a diode, and illustrate how the diode might allow current in only one direction.

5. An inductor controls the amount of electric current because of the resistance of the wire. Make an inductor by winding the insulated wire around a cardboard tube approximately 100 times. Wind the wire so that all the turns of the coil are neat and in an orderly row, as shown below. Leave about 25 cm of wire on each end of the coil. The coil of wire may be held on the tube using tape.

MATERIALS

- aluminum foil
- antenna
- cardboard, 20 cm × 30 cm
- cardboard tubes (2)
- connecting wires, 30 cm each (7)
- diode
- earphone
- ground wire
- paper (1 sheet)
- paper clips (3)
- scissors
- tape
- wire, insulated, 2 m

SAFETY

6 Now, you will construct the variable capacitor. A capacitor stores electrical energy when an electric current is applied. A variable capacitor is a capacitor in which the amount of energy stored can be changed. Cut a piece of aluminum foil to go around the tube but only half the length of the tube, as shown at right. Keep the foil as wrinkle-free as possible as you wrap it around the tube, and tape the foil to itself. Now, tape the foil to the tube.

7 Use the sheet of paper and tape to make a sliding cover on the tube. The paper should completely cover the foil on the tube with about 1 cm extra.

8 Cut another sheet of aluminum foil to wrap completely around the paper. Leave approximately 1 cm of paper showing at each end of the foil. Tape this foil sheet to the paper sleeve. If you have done this correctly, you have a paper/foil sheet that will slide up and down the tube over the stationary foil. The two pieces of foil should not touch.

9 Stand your variable capacitor on its end so that the stationary foil is at the bottom. The amount of stored energy is greater when the sleeve is down than when the sleeve is up.

10 Use tape to attach one connecting wire to the stationary foil at the end of the tube. Use tape to attach another connecting wire to the sliding foil sleeve. Be sure that the metal part of the wire touches the foil.

Cardboard tube

Paper and foil sleeve

Foil

Capacitor

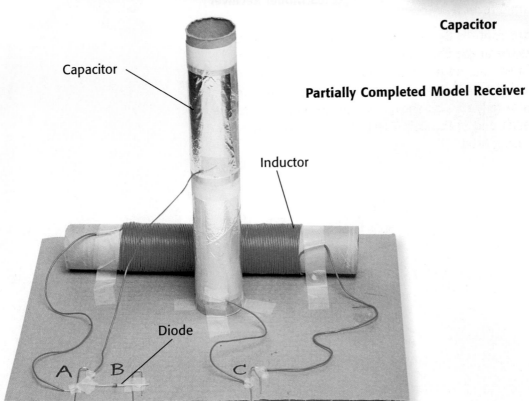

Capacitor

Partially Completed Model Receiver

Inductor

Diode

A   B   C

11 Hook three paper clips on one edge of the cardboard, as shown below. Label one paper clip "A," the second one "B," and the third one "C."

12 Lay the inductor on the piece of cardboard, and tape it to the cardboard.

13 Stand the capacitor next to the inductor, and tape the tube to the cardboard. Be sure not to tape the sleeve—it must be free to slide.

14 Use tape to connect the diode to paper clips A and B. The cathode should be closest to paper clip B. (The cathode end of the diode is the one with the dark band.) Make sure that all connections have good metal-to-metal contact.

15 Connect one end of the inductor to paper clip A and the other end to paper clip C. Use tape to hold the wires in place.

16 Connect the wire from the sliding part of the capacitor to paper clip A. Connect the other wire (from the stationary foil) to paper clip C.

17 The antenna receives radio waves transmitted by a radio station. Tape a connecting wire to your antenna. Then, connect this wire to paper clip A.

Earphone

A Completed Model Receiver

Ground Wire

Antenna

18 Use tape to connect one end of the ground wire to paper clip C. The other end of the ground wire should be connected to an object specified by your teacher.

19 The earphone will allow you to detect the radio waves you receive. Connect one wire from the earphone to paper clip B and the other wire to paper clip C.

20 You are now ready to begin listening. With everything connected and the earphone in your ear, slowly slide the paper/foil sheet of the capacitor up and down. Listen for a very faint sound. You may have to troubleshoot many of the parts to get your receiver to work. As you troubleshoot, check to be sure there is good contact between all the connections.

Analyze the Results

1 Describe the process of operating your receiver. ✔0807.Inq.5

2 Considering what you have learned about a diode, why is it important to have the diode connected the correct way? ✔0807.Inq.3

3 A function of the inductor on a radio is to "slow the current down." Why does the inductor you made slow the current down more than does a straight wire the length of your coil? ✔0807.Inq.3

4 A capacitor consists of any two conductors separated by an insulator. For your capacitor, list the two conductors and the insulator.

Draw Conclusions

5 Explain why the amount of stored energy is increased down when you slide the foil sleeve and decreased when you slide the foil sleeve up. ✔0807.Inq.3, ✔0807.Inq.5

6 Make a list of ways that your receiver is similar to a modern radio. Make a second list of ways that your receiver is different from a modern radio.

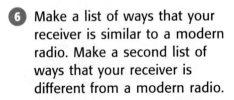

Contents

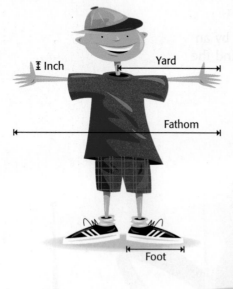

Inch

Yard

Fathom

Foot

Appendix

Study Skills

FoldNote Instructions

Have you ever tried to study for a test or quiz but didn't know where to start? Or have you read a chapter and found that you can remember only a few ideas? Well, FoldNotes are a fun and exciting way to help you learn and remember the ideas you encounter as you learn science!

FoldNotes are tools that you can use to organize concepts. By focusing on a few main concepts, FoldNotes help you learn and remember how the concepts fit together. They can help you see the "big picture." Below you will find instructions for building 10 different FoldNotes.

Pyramid

1. Place a sheet of paper in front of you. Fold the lower left-hand corner of the paper diagonally to the opposite edge of the paper.

2. Cut off the tab of paper created by the fold (at the top).

3. Open the paper so that it is a square. Fold the lower right-hand corner of the paper diagonally to the opposite corner to form a triangle.

4. Open the paper. The creases of the two folds will have created an X.

5. Using scissors, cut along one of the creases. Start from any corner, and stop at the center point to create two flaps. Use tape or glue to attach one of the flaps on top of the other flap.

Double Door

1. Fold a sheet of paper in half from the top to the bottom. Then, unfold the paper.

2. Fold the top and bottom edges of the paper to the crease.

Booklet

1. Fold a sheet of paper in half from left to right. Then, unfold the paper.

2. Fold the sheet of paper in half again from the top to the bottom. Then, unfold the paper.

3. Refold the sheet of paper in half from left to right.

4. Fold the top and bottom edges to the center crease.

5. Completely unfold the paper.

6. Refold the paper from top to bottom.

7. Using scissors, cut a slit along the center crease of the sheet from the folded edge to the creases made in step 4. Do not cut the entire sheet in half.

8. Fold the sheet of paper in half from left to right. While holding the bottom and top edges of the paper, push the bottom and top edges together so that the center collapses at the center slit. Fold the four flaps to form a four-page book.

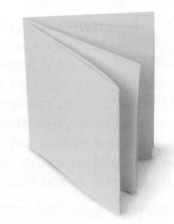

Layered Book

1. Lay one sheet of paper on top of another sheet. Slide the top sheet up so that 2 cm of the bottom sheet is showing.

2. Hold the two sheets together, fold down the top of the two sheets so that you see four 2 cm tabs along the bottom.

3. Using a stapler, staple the top of the FoldNote.

Appendix

Key-Term Fold

1. Fold a sheet of lined notebook paper in half from left to right.

2. Using scissors, cut along every third line from the right edge of the paper to the center fold to make tabs.

Four-Corner Fold

1. Fold a sheet of paper in half from left to right. Then, unfold the paper.

2. Fold each side of the paper to the crease in the center of the paper.

3. Fold the paper in half from the top to the bottom. Then, unfold the paper.

4. Using scissors, cut the top flap creases made in step 3 to form four flaps.

Three-Panel Flip Chart

1. Fold a piece of paper in half from the top to the bottom.

2. Fold the paper in thirds from side to side. Then, unfold the paper so that you can see the three sections.

3. From the top of the paper, cut along each of the vertical fold lines to the fold in the middle of the paper. You will now have three flaps.

Table Fold

1. Fold a piece of paper in half from the top to the bottom. Then, fold the paper in half again.

2. Fold the paper in thirds from side to side.

3. Unfold the paper completely. Carefully trace the fold lines by using a pen or pencil.

Two-Panel Flip Chart

1. Fold a piece of paper in half from the top to the bottom.

2. Fold the paper in half from side to side. Then, unfold the paper so that you can see the two sections.

3. From the top of the paper, cut along the vertical fold line to the fold in the middle of the paper. You will now have two flaps.

Tri-Fold

1. Fold a piece a paper in thirds from the top to the bottom.

2. Unfold the paper so that you can see the three sections. Then, turn the paper sideways so that the three sections form vertical columns.

3. Trace the fold lines by using a pen or pencil. Label the columns "Know," "Want," and "Learn."

Graphic Organizer Instructions

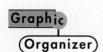

Have you ever wished that you could "draw out" the many concepts you learn in your science class? Sometimes, being able to *see* how concepts are related really helps you remember what you've learned. Graphic Organizers do just that! They give you a way to draw or map out concepts.

All you need to make a Graphic Organizer is a piece of paper and a pencil. Below you will find instructions for four different Graphic Organizers designed to help you organize the concepts you'll learn in this book.

Spider Map

1. Draw a diagram like the one shown. In the circle, write the main topic.

2. From the circle, draw legs to represent different categories of the main topic. You can have as many categories as you want.

3. From the category legs, draw horizontal lines. As you read the chapter, write details about each category on the horizontal lines.

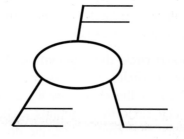

Comparison Table

1. Draw a chart like the one shown. Your chart can have as many columns and rows as you want.

2. In the top row, write the topics that you want to compare.

3. In the left column, write characteristics of the topics that you want to compare. As you read the chapter, fill in the characteristics for each topic in the appropriate boxes.

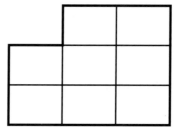

Appendix

Chain-of-Events-Chart

1. Draw a box. In the box, write the first step of a process or the first event of a timeline.

2. Under the box, draw another box, and use an arrow to connect the two boxes. In the second box, write the next step of the process or the next event in the timeline.

3. Continue adding boxes until the process or timeline is finished.

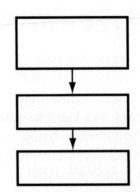

Concept Map

1. Draw a circle in the center of a piece of paper. Write the main idea of the chapter in the center of the circle.

2. From the circle, draw other circles. In those circles, write characteristics of the main idea. Draw arrows from the center circle to the circles that contain the characteristics.

3. From each circle that contains a characteristic, draw other circles. In those circles, write specific details about the characteristic. Draw arrows from each circle that contains a characteristic to the circles that contain specific details. You may draw as many circles as you want.

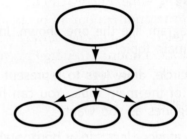

Appendix

Physical Science Laws and Principles

Law of Conservation of Mass

Mass cannot be created or destroyed during ordinary chemical or physical changes.

The total mass in a closed system is always the same no matter how many physical changes or chemical reactions occur.

Law of Conservation of Energy

Energy can be neither created nor destroyed.

The total amount of energy in a closed system is always the same. Energy can be changed from one form to another, but all of the different forms of energy in a system always add up to the same total amount of energy no matter how many energy conversions occur.

Law of Universal Gravitation

All objects in the universe attract each other by a force called *gravity*. The size of the force depends on the masses of the objects and the distance between the objects.

The first part of the law explains why lifting a bowling ball is much harder than lifting a marble. Because the bowling ball has a much larger mass than the marble does, the amount of gravity between the Earth and the bowling ball is greater than the amount of gravity between the Earth and the marble.

The second part of the law explains why a satellite can remain in orbit around the Earth. The satellite is carefully placed at a distance great enough to prevent the Earth's gravity from immediately pulling the satellite down but small enough to prevent the satellite from completely escaping the Earth's gravity and wandering off into space.

Newton's Laws of Motion

Newton's first law of motion states that an object at rest remains at rest and an object in motion remains in motion at constant speed and in a straight line unless acted on by an unbalanced force.

The first part of the law explains why a football will remain on a tee until it is kicked off or until a gust of wind blows it off.

The second part of the law explains why a bike rider will continue moving forward after the bike comes to an abrupt stop. Gravity and the friction of the sidewalk will eventually stop the rider.

Newton's second law of motion states that the acceleration of an object depends on the mass of the object and the amount of force applied.

The first part of the law explains why the acceleration of a 4 kg bowling ball will be greater than the acceleration of a 6 kg bowling ball if the same force is applied to both balls.

The second part of the law explains why the acceleration of a bowling ball will be larger if a larger force is applied to the bowling ball.

The relationship of acceleration (a) to mass (m) and force (F) can be expressed mathematically by the following equation:

$$acceleration = \frac{force}{mass}, \text{ or } a = \frac{F}{m}$$

This equation is often rearranged to the form

$$force = mass \times acceleration, \text{ or } F = m \times a$$

Newton's third law of motion states that whenever one object exerts a force on a second object, the second object exerts an equal and opposite force on the first.

This law explains that a runner is able to move forward because of the equal and opposite force that the ground exerts on the runner's foot after each step.

Law of Reflection

The law of reflection states that the angle of incidence is equal to the angle of reflection. This law explains why light reflects off a surface at the same angle that the light strikes the surface.

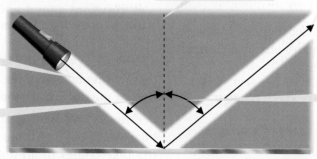

A line perpendicular to the mirror's surface is called the *normal.*

The beam of light reflected off the mirror is called the *reflected beam.*

The beam of light traveling toward the mirror is called the *incident beam.*

The angle between the incident beam and the normal is called the *angle of incidence.*

The angle between the reflected beam and the normal is called the *angle of reflection.*

Charles's Law

Charles's law states that for a fixed amount of gas at a constant pressure, the volume of the gas increases as the temperature of the gas increases. Likewise, the volume of the gas decreases as the temperature of the gas decreases.

If a basketball that was inflated indoors is left outside on a cold winter day, the air particles inside the ball will move more slowly. They will hit the sides of the basketball less often and with less force. The ball will get smaller as the volume of the air decreases.

Boyle's Law

Boyle's law states that for a fixed amount of gas at a constant temperature, the volume of a gas increases as the pressure of the gas decreases. Likewise, the volume of a gas decreases as its pressure increases.

If an inflated balloon is pulled down to the bottom of a swimming pool, the pressure of the water on the balloon increases. The pressure of the air particles inside the balloon must increase to match that of the water outside, so the volume of the air inside the balloon decreases.

Pascal's Principle

Pascal's principle states that a change in pressure at any point in an enclosed fluid will be transmitted equally to all parts of that fluid.

When a mechanic uses a hydraulic jack to raise an automobile off the ground, he or she increases the pressure on the fluid in the jack by pushing on the jack handle. The pressure is transmitted equally to all parts of the fluid-filled jacking system. As fluid presses the jack plate against the frame of the car, the car is lifed off the ground.

Archimedes' Principle

Archimedes' principle states that the buoyant force on an object in a fluid is equal to the weight of the volume of fluid that the object displaces.

A person floating in a swimming pool displaces 20 L of water. The weight of that volume of water is about 200 N. Therefore, the buoyant force on the person is 200 N.

Bernoulli's Principle

Bernoulli's principle states that as the speed of a moving fluid increases, the fluid's pressure decreases.

The lift on an airplane wing or on a Frisbee® can be explained in part by using Bernoulli's principle. Because of the shape of the Frisbee, the air moving over the top of the Frisbee must travel farther than the air below the Frisbee in the same amount of time. In other words, the air above the Frisbee is moving faster than the air below it. This faster-moving air above the Frisbee exerts less pressure than the slower-moving air below it does. The resulting increased pressure below exerts an upward force and pushes the Frisbee up.

Useful Equations

Average speed

$$average\ speed = \frac{total\ distance}{total\ time}$$

Example: A bicycle messenger traveled a distance of 136 km in 8 h. What was the messenger's average speed?

$$\frac{136\ km}{8\ h} = 17\ km/h$$

The messenger's average speed was **17 km/h.**

Average acceleration

$$\frac{average}{acceleration} = \frac{final\ velocity - starting\ velocity}{time\ it\ takes\ to\ change\ velocity}$$

Example: Calculate the average acceleration of an Olympic 100 m dash sprinter who reaches a velocity of 20 m/s south at the finish line. The race was in a straight line and lasted 10 s.

$$\frac{20\ m/s - 0\ m/s}{10s} = 2\ m/s/s$$

The sprinter's average acceleration is **2 m/s/s south.**

Net force

Forces in the Same Direction
When forces are in the same direction, add the forces together to determine the net force.

Example: Calculate the net force on a stalled car that is being pushed by two people. One person is pushing with a force of 13 N northwest, and the other person is pushing with a force of 8 N in the same direction.

$$13\ N + 8\ N = 21\ N$$

The net force is **21 N northwest.**

Forces in Opposite Directions
When forces are in opposite directions, subtract the smaller force from the larger force to determine the net force. The net force will be in the direction of the larger force.

Example: Calculate the net force on a rope that is being pulled on each end. One person is pulling on one end of the rope with a force of 12 N south. Another person is pulling on the opposite end of the rope with a force of 7 N north.

$$12\ N - 7\ N = 5\ N$$

The net force is **5 N south.**

Work

Work is done by exerting a force through a distance. Work has units of joules (J), which are equivalent to Newton-meters.

$$Work = F \times d$$

Example: Calculate the amount of work done by a man who lifts a 100 N toddler 1.5 m off the floor.

$Work = 100 \text{ N} \times 1.5 \text{ m} = 150 \text{ N} \cdot \text{m} = 150 \text{ J}$

The man did **150 J** of work.

Power

Power is the rate at which work is done. Power is measured in watts (W), which are equivalent to joules per second.

$$P = \frac{Work}{t}$$

Example: Calculate the power of a weightlifter who raises a 300 N barbell 2.1 m off the floor in 1.25 s.

$Work = 300 \text{ N} \times 2.1 \text{ m} = 630 \text{ N} \cdot \text{m} = 630 \text{ J}$

$P = \frac{630 \text{ J}}{1.25 \text{ s}} = \frac{504 \text{ J}}{\text{s}} = 504 \text{ W}$

The weightlifter has **504 W** of power.

Pressure

Pressure is the force exerted over a given area. The SI unit for pressure is the pascal (Pa).

$$pressure = \frac{force}{area}$$

Example: Calculate the pressure of the air in a soccer ball if the air exerts a force of 25,000 N over an area of 0.15 m^2.

$pressure = \frac{25,000 \text{ N}}{0.15 \text{ m}^2} = \frac{167,000 \text{ N}}{\text{m}^2} = 167,000 \text{ Pa}$

The pressure of the air inside the soccer ball is **167,000 Pa.**

Density

$$density = \frac{mass}{volume}$$

Example: Calculate the density of a sponge that has a mass of 10 g and a volume of 40 cm^3.

$\frac{10 \text{ g}}{40 \text{ cm}^3} = \frac{0.25 \text{ g}}{\text{cm}^3}$

The density of the sponge is $\frac{0.25 \text{ g}}{\text{cm}^3}$.

Concentration

$$concentration = \frac{mass \ of \ solute}{volume \ of \ solvent}$$

Example: Calculate the concentration of a solution in which 10 g of sugar is dissolved in 125 mL of water.

$\frac{10 \text{ g of sugar}}{125 \text{ mL of water}} = \frac{0.08 \text{ g}}{\text{mL}}$

The concentration of this solution is $\frac{0.08 \text{ g}}{\text{mL}}$.

Math Refresher

Science requires an understanding of many math concepts. The following pages will help you review some important math skills.

Averages

An **average,** or **mean,** simplifies a set of numbers into a single number that *approximates* the value of the set.

Example: Find the average of the following set of numbers: 5, 4, 7, and 8.

Step 1: Find the sum.
$$5 + 4 + 7 + 8 = 24$$

Step 2: Divide the sum by the number of numbers in your set. Because there are four numbers in this example, divide the sum by 4.
$$\frac{24}{4} = 6$$

The average, or mean, is **6.**

Ratios

A **ratio** is a comparison between numbers, and it is usually written as a fraction.

Example: Find the ratio of thermometers to students if you have 36 thermometers and 48 students in your class.

Step 1: Make the ratio.
$$\frac{36 \text{ thermometers}}{48 \text{ students}}$$

Step 2: Reduce the fraction to its simplest form.
$$\frac{36}{48} = \frac{36 \div 12}{48 \div 12} = \frac{3}{4}$$

The ratio of thermometers to students is **3 to 4,** or $\frac{3}{4}$. The ratio may also be written in the form 3:4.

Proportions

A **proportion** is an equation that states that two ratios are equal.
$$\frac{3}{1} = \frac{12}{4}$$

To solve a proportion, first multiply across the equal sign. This is called *cross-multiplication.* If you know three of the quantities in a proportion, you can use cross-multiplication to find the fourth.

Example: Imagine that you are making a scale model of the solar system for your science project. The diameter of Jupiter is 11.2 times the diameter of the Earth. If you are using a plastic-foam ball that has a diameter of 2 cm to represent the Earth, what must the diameter of the ball representing Jupiter be?
$$\frac{11.2}{1} = \frac{x}{2 \text{ cm}}$$

Step 1: Cross-multiply.
$$\frac{11.2}{1} \diagdown\!\!\!\!\diagup \frac{x}{2}$$
$$11.2 \times 2 = x \times 1$$

Step 2: Multiply.
$$22.4 = x \times 1$$

Step 3: Isolate the variable by dividing both sides by 1.
$$x = \frac{22.4}{1}$$
$$x = 22.4 \text{ cm}$$

You will need to use a ball that has a diameter of **22.4** cm to represent Jupiter.

Percentages

A **percentage** is a ratio of a given number to 100.

Example: What is 85% of 40?

Step 1: Rewrite the percentage by moving the decimal point two places to the left.

0.85

Step 2: Multiply the decimal by the number that you are calculating the percentage of.

$0.85 \times 40 = 34$

85% of 40 is **34.**

Decimals

To **add** or **subtract decimals,** line up the digits vertically so that the decimal points line up. Then, add or subtract the columns from right to left. Carry or borrow numbers as necessary.

Example: Add the following numbers: 3.1415 and 2.96.

Step 1: Line up the digits vertically so that the decimal points line up.

$$\begin{array}{r} 3.1415 \\ + \ 2.96 \\ \hline \end{array}$$

Step 2: Add the columns from right to left, and carry when necessary.

$$\begin{array}{r} {\scriptstyle 1 \ \ 1} \\ 3.1415 \\ + \ 2.96 \\ \hline 6.1015 \end{array}$$

The sum is **6.1015.**

Fractions

Numbers tell you how many; **fractions** tell you *how much of a whole.*

Example: Your class has 24 plants. Your teacher instructs you to put 5 plants in a shady spot. What fraction of the plants in your class will you put in a shady spot?

Step 1: In the denominator, write the total number of parts in the whole.

$$\frac{?}{24}$$

Step 2: In the numerator, write the number of parts of the whole that are being considered.

$$\frac{5}{24}$$

So, $\frac{5}{24}$ of the plants will be in the shade.

Reducing Fractions

It is usually best to express a fraction in its simplest form. Expressing a fraction in its simplest form is called *reducing* a fraction.

Example: Reduce the fraction $\frac{30}{45}$ to its simplest form.

Step 1: Find the largest whole number that will divide evenly into both the numerator and denominator. This number is called the *greatest common factor* (GCF).

Factors of the numerator 30:

1, 2, 3, 5, 6, 10, **15,** 30

Factors of the denominator 45:

1, 3, 5, 9, **15,** 45

Step 2: Divide both the numerator and the denominator by the GCF, which in this case is 15.

$$\frac{30}{45} = \frac{30 \div 15}{45 \div 15} = \frac{2}{3}$$

Thus, $\frac{30}{45}$ reduced to its simplest form is $\frac{2}{3}$.

Appendix

Adding and Subtracting Fractions

To **add** or **subtract fractions** that have the **same denominator,** simply add or subtract the numerators.

Examples:

$$\frac{3}{5} + \frac{1}{5} = ? \quad \text{and} \quad \frac{3}{4} - \frac{1}{4} = ?$$

Step 1: Add or subtract the numerators.

$$\frac{3}{5} + \frac{1}{5} = \frac{4}{} \quad \text{and} \quad \frac{3}{4} - \frac{1}{4} = \frac{2}{}$$

Step 2: Write the sum or difference over the denominator.

$$\frac{3}{5} + \frac{1}{5} = \frac{4}{5} \quad \text{and} \quad \frac{3}{4} - \frac{1}{4} = \frac{2}{4}$$

Step 3: If necessary, reduce the fraction to its simplest form.

$\frac{4}{5}$ cannot be reduced, and $\frac{2}{4} = \frac{1}{2}$.

To **add** or **subtract fractions** that have **different denominators,** first find the least common denominator (LCD).

Examples:

$$\frac{1}{2} + \frac{1}{6} = ? \quad \text{and} \quad \frac{3}{4} - \frac{2}{3} = ?$$

Step 1: Write the equivalent fractions that have a common denominator.

$$\frac{3}{6} + \frac{1}{6} = ? \quad \text{and} \quad \frac{9}{12} - \frac{8}{12} = ?$$

Step 2: Add or subtract the fractions.

$$\frac{3}{6} + \frac{1}{6} = \frac{4}{6} \quad \text{and} \quad \frac{9}{12} - \frac{8}{12} = \frac{1}{12}$$

Step 3: If necessary, reduce the fraction to its simplest form.

The fraction $\frac{4}{6} = \frac{2}{3}$, and $\frac{1}{12}$ cannot be reduced.

Multiplying Fractions

To **multiply fractions,** multiply the numerators and the denominators together, and then reduce the fraction to its simplest form.

Example:

$$\frac{5}{9} \times \frac{7}{10} = ?$$

Step 1: Multiply the numerators and denominators.

$$\frac{5}{9} \times \frac{7}{10} = \frac{5 \times 7}{9 \times 10} = \frac{35}{90}$$

Step 2: Reduce the fraction.

$$\frac{35}{90} = \frac{35 \div 5}{90 \div 5} = \frac{7}{18}$$

Dividing Fractions

To **divide fractions,** first rewrite the divisor (the number you divide by) upside down. This number is called the *reciprocal* of the divisor. Then multiply and reduce if necessary.

Example:

$$\frac{5}{8} \div \frac{3}{2} = ?$$

Step 1: Rewrite the divisor as its reciprocal.

$$\frac{3}{2} \rightarrow \frac{2}{3}$$

Step 2: Multiply the fractions.

$$\frac{5}{8} \times \frac{2}{3} = \frac{5 \times 2}{8 \times 3} = \frac{10}{24}$$

Step 3: Reduce the fraction.

$$\frac{10}{24} = \frac{10 \div 2}{24 \div 2} = \frac{5}{12}$$

Appendix

Scientific Notation

Scientific notation is a short way of representing very large and very small numbers without writing all of the place-holding zeros.

> **Example:** Write 653,000,000 in scientific notation.

Step 1: Write the number without the place-holding zeros.

653

Step 2: Place the decimal point after the first digit.

6.53

Step 3: Find the exponent by counting the number of places that you moved the decimal point.

6.53000000

The decimal point was moved eight places to the left. Therefore, the exponent of 10 is positive 8. If you had moved the decimal point to the right, the exponent would be negative.

Step 4: Write the number in scientific notation.

6.53×10^8

Area

Area is the number of square units needed to cover the surface of an object.

> **Formulas:**
>
> area of a square = side × side
> area of a rectangle = length × width
> area of a triangle = $\frac{1}{2}$ × base × height
>
> **Examples:** Find the areas.

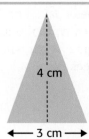

Triangle

$area = \frac{1}{2} \times base \times height$

$area = \frac{1}{2} \times 3\ cm \times 4\ cm$

$area = \textbf{6 cm}^2$

4 cm

3 cm

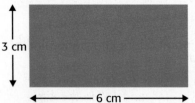

Rectangle

area = length × width

area = 6 cm × 3 cm

area = **18 cm²**

3 cm

6 cm

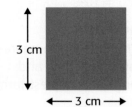

Square

area = side × side

area = 3 cm × 3 cm

area = **9 cm²**

3 cm

3 cm

Volume

Volume is the amount of space that something occupies.

> **Formulas:**
>
> volume of a cube = side × side × side
>
> volume of a prism = area of base × height
>
> **Examples:**
> Find the volume of the solids.

Cube

volume = side × side × side

volume = 4 cm × 4 cm × 4 cm

volume = **64 cm³**

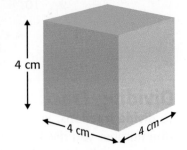

4 cm

4 cm   4 cm

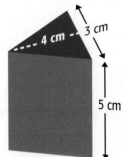

4 cm   3 cm

5 cm

Prism

volume = area of base × height

volume = (area of triangle) × height

volume = ($\frac{1}{2}$ × 3 cm × 4 cm) × 5 cm

volume = 6 cm² × 5 cm

volume = **30 cm³**

Making Charts and Graphs

Pie Charts

A pie chart shows how each group of data relates to all of the data. Each part of the circle forming the chart represents a category of the data. The entire circle represents all of the data. For example, a biologist studying a hardwood forest in Wisconsin found that there were five different types of trees. The data table at right summarizes the biologist's findings.

Wisconsin Hardwood Trees	
Type of tree	**Number found**
Oak	600
Maple	750
Beech	300
Birch	1,200
Hickory	150
Total	3,000

How to Make a Pie Chart

1 To make a pie chart of these data, first find the percentage of each type of tree. Divide the number of trees of each type by the total number of trees, and multiply by 100.

$$\frac{600 \text{ oak}}{3,000 \text{ trees}} \times 100 = 20\%$$

$$\frac{750 \text{ maple}}{3,000 \text{ trees}} \times 100 = 25\%$$

$$\frac{300 \text{ beech}}{3,000 \text{ trees}} \times 100 = 10\%$$

$$\frac{1,200 \text{ birch}}{3,000 \text{ trees}} \times 100 = 40\%$$

$$\frac{150 \text{ hickory}}{3,000 \text{ trees}} \times 100 = 5\%$$

2 Now, determine the size of the wedges that make up the pie chart. Multiply each percentage by 360°. Remember that a circle contains 360°.

$20\% \times 360° = 72°$ $\quad$ $25\% \times 360° = 90°$

$10\% \times 360° = 36°$ $\quad$ $40\% \times 360° = 144°$

$5\% \times 360° = 18°$

3 Check that the sum of the percentages is 100 and the sum of the degrees is 360.

$20\% + 25\% + 10\% + 40\% + 5\% = 100\%$

$72° + 90° + 36° + 144° + 18° = 360°$

4 Use a compass to draw a circle and mark the center of the circle.

5 Then, use a protractor to draw angles of 72°, 90°, 36°, 144°, and 18° in the circle.

6 Finally, label each part of the chart, and choose an appropriate title.

A Community of Wisconsin Hardwood Trees

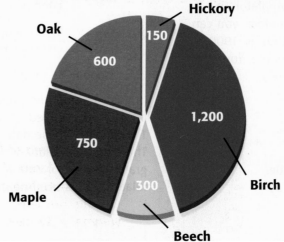

Appendix

...raphs

...s are most often used to demonstrate continuous change. For example, Mr. Smith's students analyzed the population records for their hometown, Appleton, between 1900 and 2000. Examine the data at right.

Because the year and the population change, they are the *variables*. The population is determined by, or dependent on, the year. Therefore, the population is called the **dependent variable,** and the year is called the **independent variable.** Each set of data is called a **data pair.** To prepare a line graph, you must first organize data pairs into a table like the one at right.

Population of Appleton, 1900–2000	
Year	Population
1900	1,800
1920	2,500
1940	3,200
1960	3,900
1980	4,600
2000	5,300

How to Make a Line Graph

1 Place the independent variable along the horizontal (*x*) axis. Place the dependent variable along the vertical (*y*) axis.

2 Label the *x*-axis "Year" and the *y*-axis "Population." Look at your largest and smallest values for the population. For the *y*-axis, determine a scale that will provide enough space to show these values. You must use the same scale for the entire length of the axis. Next, find an appropriate scale for the *x*-axis.

3 Choose reasonable starting points for each axis.

4 Plot the data pairs as accurately as possible.

5 Choose a title that accurately represents the data.

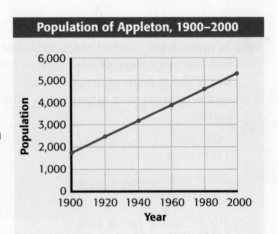

How to Determine Slope

Slope is the ratio of the change in the *y*-value to the change in the *x*-value, or "rise over run."

1 Choose two points on the line graph. For example, the population of Appleton in 2000 was 5,300 people. Therefore, you can define point *a* as (2000, 5,300). In 1900, the population was 1,800 people. You can define point *b* as (1900, 1,800).

2 Find the change in the *y*-value.
(*y* at point *a*) − (*y* at point *b*) =
5,300 people − 1,800 people =
3,500 people

3 Find the change in the *x*-value.
(*x* at point *a*) − (*x* at point *b*) =
2000 − 1900 = 100 years

4 Calculate the slope of the graph by dividing the change in *y* by the change in *x*.

$$slope = \frac{change\ in\ y}{change\ in\ x}$$

$$slope = \frac{3,500\ people}{100\ years}$$

$$slope = 35\ people\ per\ year$$

In this example, the population in Appleton increased by a fixed amount each year. The graph of these data is a straight line. Therefore, the relationship is **linear.** When the graph of a set of data is not a straight line, the relationship is **nonlinear.**

Using Algebra to Determine Slope

The equation in step 4 may also be arranged to be

$$y = kx$$

where y represents the change in the y-value, k represents the slope, and x represents the change in the x-value.

$$slope = \frac{change\ in\ y}{change\ in\ x}$$

$$k = \frac{y}{x}$$

$$k \times x = \frac{y \times x}{x}$$

$$kx = y$$

Bar Graphs

Bar graphs are used to demonstrate change that is not continuous. These graphs can be used to indicate trends when the data cover a long period of time. A meteorologist gathered the precipitation data shown here for Hartford, Connecticut, for April 1–15, 1996, and used a bar graph to represent the data.

Precipitation in Hartford, Connecticut April 1–15, 1996			
Date	Precipitation (cm)	Date	Precipitation (cm)
April 1	0.5	April 9	0.25
April 2	1.25	April 10	0.0
April 3	0.0	April 11	1.0
April 4	0.0	April 12	0.0
April 5	0.0	April 13	0.25
April 6	0.0	April 14	0.0
April 7	0.0	April 15	6.50
April 8	1.75		

How to Make a Bar Graph

1 Use an appropriate scale and a reasonable starting point for each axis.

2 Label the axes, and plot the data.

3 Choose a title that accurately represents the data.

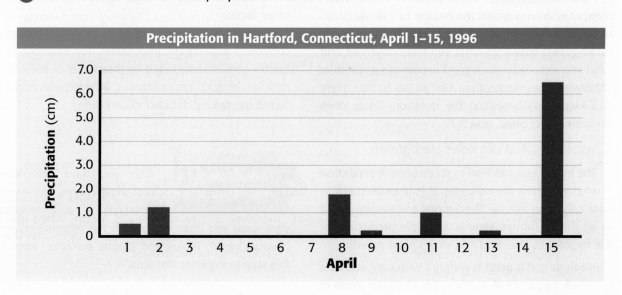

Appendix

ntific Methods

ways in which scientists answer questions and solve problems are called **scientific methods.** The same steps are often used by scientists as they look for answers. However, there is more than one way to use these steps. Scientists may use all of the steps or just some of the steps during an investigation. They may even repeat some of the steps. The goal of using scientific methods is to come up with reliable answers and solutions.

Six Steps of Scientific Methods

1 Ask a Question

Good questions come from careful **observations.** You make observations by using your senses to gather information. Sometimes, you may use instruments, such as microscopes and telescopes, to extend the range of your senses. As you observe the natural world, you will discover that you have many more questions than answers. These questions drive investigations.

Questions beginning with *what, why, how,* and *when* are important in focusing an investigation. Here is an example of a question that could lead to an investigation.

Question: How does acid rain affect plant growth?

2 Form a Hypothesis

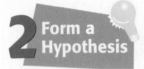

After you ask a question, you need to form a **hypothesis.** A hypothesis is a clear statement of what you expect the answer to your question to be. Your hypothesis will represent your best "educated guess" based on what you have observed and what you already know. A good hypothesis is testable. Otherwise, the investigation can go no further. Here is a hypothesis based on the question, "How does acid rain affect plant growth?"

Hypothesis: Acid rain slows plant growth.

The hypothesis can lead to predictions. A prediction is what you think the outcome of your experiment or data collection will be. Predictions are usually stated in an if-then format. Here is a sample prediction for the hypothesis that acid rain slows plant growth.

Prediction: If a plant is watered with only acid rain (which has a pH of 4), then the plant will grow at half its normal rate.

3 Test the Hypothesis

After you have formed a hypothesis and made a prediction, your hypothesis should be tested. One way to test a hypothesis is with a controlled experiment. A **controlled experiment** tests only one factor at a time. In an experiment to test the effect of acid rain on plant growth, the **control group** would be watered with normal rain water. The **experimental group** would be watered with acid rain. All of the plants should receive the same amount of sunlight and water each day. The air temperature should be the same for all groups. However, the acidity of the water will be a variable. In fact, any factor that is different from one group to another is a **variable.** If your hypothesis is correct, then the acidity of the water and plant growth are *dependant variables.* The amount a plant grows is dependent on the acidity of the water. However, the amount of water each plant receives and the amount of sunlight each plant receives are *independent variables.* Either of these factors could change without affecting the other factor.

Sometimes, the nature of an investigation makes a controlled experiment impossible. For example, the Earth's core is surrounded by thousands of meters of rock. Under such circumstances, a hypothesis may be tested by making detailed observations.

4 Analyze the Results

After you have completed your experiments, made your observations, and collected your data, you must analyze all the information you have gathered. Tables and graphs are often used in this step to organize the data.

5 Draw Conclusions

After analyzing your data, you can determine if your results support your hypothesis. If your hypothesis is supported, you (or others) might want to repeat the observations or experiments to verify your results. If your hypothesis is not supported by the data, you may have to check your procedure for errors. You may even have to reject your hypothesis and make a new one. If you cannot draw a conclusion from your results, you may have to try the investigation again or carry out further observations or experiments.

6 Communicate Results

After any scientific investigation, you should report your results. By preparing a written or oral report, you let others know what you have learned. They may repeat your investigation to see if they get the same results. Your report may even lead to another question and then to another investigation.

Scientific Methods in Action

Scientific methods contain loops in which several steps may be repeated over and over again. In some cases, certain steps are unnecessary. Thus, there is not a "straight line" of steps. For example, sometimes scientists find that testing one hypothesis raises new questions and new hypotheses to be tested. And sometimes, testing the hypothesis leads directly to a conclusion. Furthermore, the steps in scientific methods are not always used in the same order. Follow the steps in the diagram, and see how many different directions scientific methods can take you.

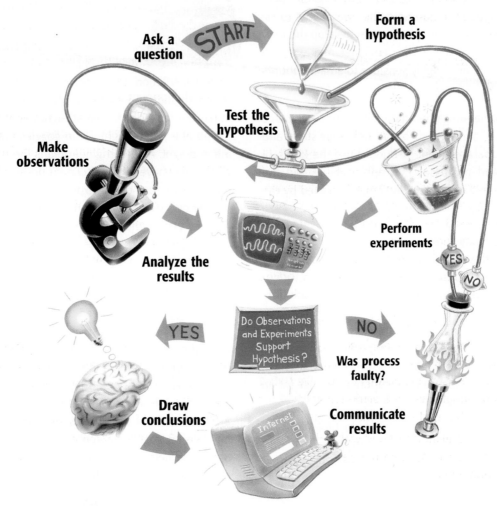

Appendix

...neering Design Process

Engineers follow the **engineering design process** when they are given a problem to solve. Engineers may be asked to design a safer elevator or a disease-resistant potato. They may be asked to design a new **technology** that would allow people to see in the dark. Regardless of the problem, engineers will use the engineering design process to research the problem, brainstorm solutions, test a **prototype** of the solution, and, when needed, modify the solution. The goal of the engineering design process is to solve a design problem or obtain an **intended benefit** in the most efficient way possible.

Five Steps of the Engineering Design Process

Step 1: ASK

The engineering design process starts by identifying a need or a problem. Consider the following question: How can a biologist observe animal behavior at night without disturbing the animals with bright lights? To solve this problem, the first thing an engineer would do is conduct research. An engineer might start by talking to possible users of the new technology. For example, the engineer would ask biologists what types of animals they would want to observe at night and what sorts of behavior they would expect to see. Engineers would also gather samples of existing technologies that may help them develop the new technology. For instance, the engineer may want to examine film that is highly sensitive to small amounts of light.

The information gathered during the research stage will be used during each of the next four steps and will allow the engineers to understand the kinds of materials and processes that are available and the kinds of people or other living things impacted by the problem.

Step 2: IMAGINE

After engineers have identified a problem, they brainstorm ideas for a solution. When brainstorming, engineers will use the information gathered during the **ASK** step to propose as many solutions as possible. This is an important step because engineers are encouraged to use creativity to solve the problem and may stumble upon a new use for an existing technology.

The engineers keep in mind how biologists can observe animal behavior at night. Knowing this, they will study the appropriate knowledge available from science. For example, they might check the current research about the electromagnetic spectrum. From there, the engineer could learn about advances in infrared, or heat-sensing, technology. The engineer could then brainstorm ways to use infrared technology to develop a camera or set of goggles that would allow a person to see objects by the heat they give off.

Engineers must keep in mind the limitations of the people or situations in which the new technology will be used but also apply their mathematical and scientific knowledge to overcome these limitations.

Step 3: PLAN

After engineers have brainstormed a list of possible solutions, they must decide which solution will be tested. To test a solution, engineers must create a prototype of the solution. An engineer who brainstormed using infrared technology to see at night might build a prototype of a pair of night-vision goggles that can sense infrared light. As the engineer plans the prototype, he or she may have to reject certain designs that are too dangerous to use or too expensive to make. The engineer knows that the final prototype must be identical in every way to the final product so that it can be accurately tested.

Step 4: CREATE

Once the engineering team has arrived at the best solution, it must actually create the prototype. The prototype is then tested and evaluated. Depending on the kind of engineering being done, many different kinds of people may become involved in the engineering design process at this point. For example, a biologist might want to try out a prototype of the night-vision goggles to see how effective the goggles are in the field. The biologist will then give feedback about the prototype to the engineer.

Step 5: IMPROVE

After testing a prototype, engineers will use what they learned to try to improve the prototype's design. During this step, engineers may try to make the product easier and safer to use or less expensive to build. Engineers might also redesign the product if they found any major **unintended consequences** or unanticipated dangers during the testing stage. For example, suppose a biologist reported that the night-vision goggles prototype seemed to disorient some animals. The engineer discovered that a beam of near-infrared light emitted by the goggles was the cause of this problem. The engineer may then work to design a second prototype of night-vision goggles that did not use a beam of near-infrared light. To do this, the engineer will return to previous steps of the engineering design process.

Engineering Design Process in Action

The engineering design process for some types of technology can be a never-ending cycle. Think about a technology that you are familiar with, such as a telephone. The telephones that people use today are much improved over the telephones of the past. The sound quality is better, for one thing. In addition, there are now cordless and cellular telephones. These changes to telephones have occurred because engineers are always looking at ways to improve telephone technology. Likewise, night-vision technology has greatly improved. The improvements occur as engineers revisit different steps of the engineering design process. As you can see in the flowchart that follows, engineers don't necessarily go through the engineering design process in the same order every time. They may backtrack and repeat steps, they may skip steps entirely, or they may repeat the entire process several times before a useable design is achieved.

Start

ASK: Identify and research problem

Do you have enough information?
NO — **Does the prototype work well?** YES → **End**

IMAGINE: Brainstorm a solution

IMPROVE: Make the prototype better

Does the prototype show promise? YES → IMPROVE; NO ↓

CREATE: Make a prototype and test it

Can you make a prototype? YES ↑; NO → IMAGINE

Do you have an idea worth trying? YES → **PLAN: Determine the solution to test**; NO ↑

Appendix

the Microscope

Parts of the Compound Light Microscope

- The **ocular lens** magnifies the image 10×.
- The **low-power objective** magnifies the image 10×.
- The **high-power objective** magnifies the image either 40× or 43×.
- The **revolving nosepiece** holds the objectives and can be turned to change from one magnification to the other.
- The **body tube** maintains the correct distance between the ocular lens and objectives.
- The **coarse-adjustment knob** moves the body tube up and down to allow focusing of the image.

- The **fine-adjustment knob** moves the body tube slightly to bring the image into sharper focus. It is usually located in the center of the coarse-adjustment knob.
- The **stage** supports a slide.
- **Stage clips** hold the slide in place for viewing.
- The **diaphragm** controls the amount of light coming through the stage.
- The light source provides a **light** for viewing the slide.
- The **arm** supports the body tube.
- The **base** supports the microscope.

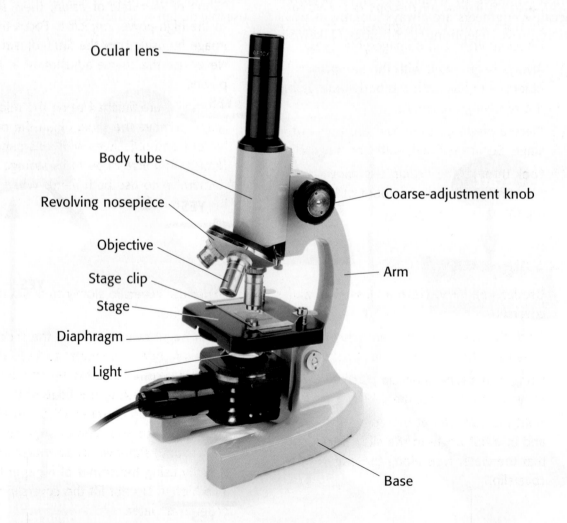

Ocular lens

Body tube

Revolving nosepiece

Objective

Stage clip

Stage

Diaphragm

Light

Coarse-adjustment knob

Arm

Base

Proper Use of the Compound Light Microscope

1. Use both hands to carry the microscope to your lab table. Place one hand beneath the base, and use the other hand to hold the arm of the microscope. Hold the microscope close to your body while carrying it to your lab table.

2. Place the microscope on the lab table at least 5 cm from the edge of the table.

3. Check to see what type of light source is used by your microscope. If the microscope has a lamp, plug it in and make sure that the cord is out of the way. If the microscope has a mirror, adjust the mirror to reflect light through the hole in the stage. **Caution:** If your microscope has a mirror, do not use direct sunlight as a light source. Direct sunlight can damage your eyes.

4. Always begin work with the low-power objective in line with the body tube. Adjust the revolving nosepiece.

5. Place a prepared slide over the hole in the stage. Secure the slide with the stage clips.

6. Look through the ocular lens. Move the diaphragm to adjust the amount of light coming through the stage.

7. Look at the stage from eye level. Slowly turn the coarse adjustment to lower the objective until the objective almost touches the slide. Do not allow the objective to touch the slide.

8. Look through the ocular lens. Turn the coarse adjustment to raise the low-power objective until the image is in focus. Always focus by raising the objective away from the slide. Never focus the objective downward. Use the fine adjustment to sharpen the focus. Keep both eyes open while viewing a slide.

9. Make sure that the image is exactly in the center of your field of vision. Then, switch to the high-power objective. Focus the image by using only the fine adjustment. Never use the coarse adjustment at high power.

10. When you are finished using the microscope, remove the slide. Clean the ocular lens and objectives with lens paper. Return the microscope to its storage area. Remember to use both hands when carrying the microscope.

Making a Wet Mount

1. Use lens paper to clean a glass slide and a coverslip.

2. Place the specimen that you wish to observe in the center of the slide.

3. Using a medicine dropper, place one drop of water on the specimen.

4. Hold the coverslip at the edge of the water and at a 45° angle to the slide. Make sure that the water runs along the edge of the coverslip.

5. Lower the coverslip slowly to avoid trapping air bubbles.

6. Water might evaporate from the slide as you work. Add more water to keep the specimen fresh. Place the tip of the medicine dropper next to the edge of the coverslip. Add a drop of water. (You can also use this method to add stain or solutions to a wet mount.) Remove excess water from the slide by using the corner of a paper towel as a blotter. Do not lift the coverslip to add or remove water.

erties of Common Minerals

	Mineral	Color	Luster	Streak	Hardness
Silicate Minerals	Beryl	deep green, pink, white, bluish green, or yellow	vitreous	white	7.5–8
	Chlorite	green	vitreous to pearly	pale green	2–2.5
	Garnet	green, red, brown, black	vitreous	white	6.5–7.5
	Hornblende	dark green, brown, or black	vitreous	none	5–6
	Muscovite	colorless, silvery white, or brown	vitreous or pearly	white	2–2.5
	Olivine	olive green, yellow	vitreous	white or none	6.5–7
	Orthoclase	colorless, white, pink, or other colors	vitreous	white or none	6
	Plagioclase	colorless, white, yellow, pink, green	vitreous	white	6
	Quartz	colorless or white; any color when not pure	vitreous or waxy	white or none	7

Native Elements

	Mineral	Color	Luster	Streak	Hardness
Nonsilicate Minerals	Copper	copper-red	metallic	copper-red	2.5–3
	Diamond	pale yellow or colorless	adamantine	none	10
	Graphite	black to gray	submetallic	black	1–2

Carbonates

Aragonite	colorless, white, or pale yellow	vitreous	white	3.5–4
Calcite	colorless or white to tan	vitreous	white	3

Halides

Fluorite	light green, yellow, purple, bluish green, or other colors	vitreous	none	4
Halite	white	vitreous	white	2.0–2.5

Oxides

Hematite	reddish brown to black	metallic to earthy	dark red to red-brown	5.6–6.5
Magnetite	iron-black	metallic	black	5.5–6.5

Sulfates

Anhydrite	colorless, bluish, or violet	vitreous to pearly	white	3–3.5
Gypsum	white, pink, gray, or colorless	vitreous, pearly, or silky	white	2.0

Sulfides

Galena	lead-gray	metallic	lead-gray to black	2.5–2.8
Pyrite	brassy yellow	metallic	greenish, brownish, or black	6–6.5

Density (g/cm³)	Cleavage, Fracture, Special Properties	Common Uses
2.6–2.8	1 cleavage direction; irregular fracture; some varieties fluoresce in ultraviolet light	gemstones, ore of the metal beryllium
2.6–3.3	1 cleavage direction; irregular fracture	
4.2	no cleavage; conchoidal to splintery fracture	gemstones, abrasives
3.0–3.4	2 cleavage directions; hackly to splintery fracture	
2.7–3	1 cleavage direction; irregular fracture	electrical insulation, wallpaper, fireproofing material, lubricant
3.2–3.3	no cleavage; conchoidal fracture	gemstones, casting
2.6	2 cleavage directions; irregular fracture	porcelain
2.6–2.7	2 cleavage directions; irregular fracture	ceramics
2.6	no cleavage; conchoidal fracture	gemstones, concrete, glass, porcelain, sandpaper, lenses
8.9	no cleavage; hackly fracture	wiring, brass, bronze, coins
3.5	4 cleavage directions; irregular to conchoidal fracture	gemstones, drilling
2.3	1 cleavage direction; irregular fracture	pencils, paints, lubricants, batteries
2.95	2 cleavage directions; irregular fracture; reacts with hydrochloric acid	no important industrial uses
2.7	3 cleavage directions; irregular fracture; reacts with weak acid; double refraction	cements, soil conditioner, whitewash, construction materials
3.0–3.3	4 cleavage directions; irregular fracture; some varieties fluoresce	hydrofluoric acid, steel, glass, fiberglass, pottery, enamel
2.1–2.2	3 cleavage directions; splintery to conchoidal fracture; salty taste	tanning hides, salting icy roads, food preservation
5.2–5.3	no cleavage; splintery fracture; magnetic when heated	iron ore for steel, pigments
5.2	no cleavage; splintery fracture; magnetic	iron ore
3.0	3 cleavage directions; conchoidal to splintery fracture	soil conditioner, sulfuric acid
2.3	3 cleavage directions; conchoidal to splintery fracture	plaster of Paris, wallboard, soil conditioner
7.4–7.6	3 cleavage directions; irregular fracture	batteries, paints
5	no cleavage; conchoidal to splintery fracture	sulfuric acid

Sky Maps

Spring

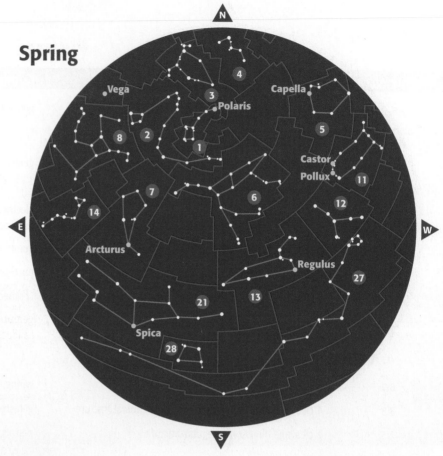

Summer

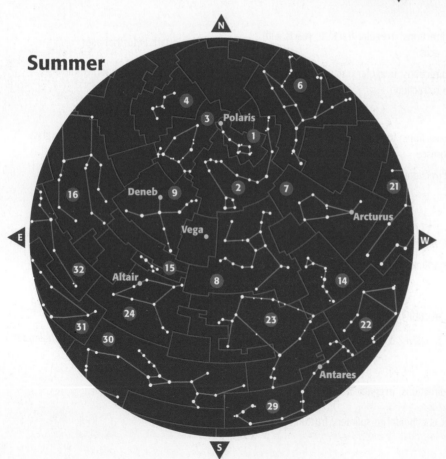

Constellations

1 Ursa Minor
2 Draco
3 Cepheus
4 Cassiopeia
5 Auriga
6 Ursa Major
7 Bootes
8 Hercules
9 Cygnus
10 Perseus
11 Gemini
12 Cancer
13 Leo
14 Serpens
15 Sagitta
16 Pegasus
17 Pisces

Autumn

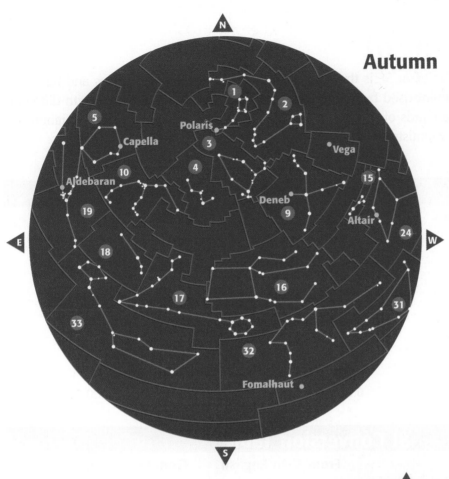

Constellations

18 **Aries**
19 **Taurus**
20 **Orion**
21 **Virgo**
22 **Libra**
23 **Ophiuchus**
24 **Aquila**
25 **Lepus**
26 **Canis Major**
27 **Hydra**
28 **Corvus**
29 **Scorpius**
30 **Sagittarius**
31 **Capricornus**
32 **Aquarius**
33 **Cetus**
34 **Columba**

Winter

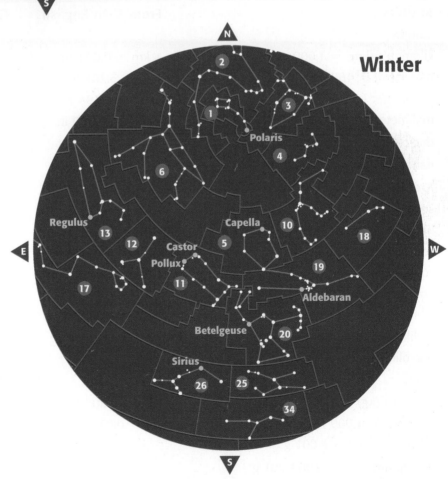

SI Measurement

The International System of Units, or SI, is the standard system of measurement used by many scientists. Using the same standards of measurement makes it easier for scientists to communicate with one another.

SI works by combining prefixes and base units. Each base unit can be used with different prefixes to define smaller and larger quantities. The table below lists common SI prefixes.

SI Prefixes

Prefix	Symbol	Factor	Example
kilo-	k	1,000	kilogram, 1 kg = 1,000 g
hecto-	h	100	hectoliter, 1 hL = 100 L
deka-	da	10	dekameter, 1 dam = 10 m
		1	meter, liter, gram
deci-	d	0.1	decigram, 1 dg = 0.1 g
centi-	c	0.01	centimeter, 1 cm = 0.01 m
milli-	m	0.001	milliliter, 1 mL = 0.001 L
micro-	μ	0.000 001	micrometer, 1 μm = 0.000 001 m

SI Conversion Table

SI units	From SI to English	From English to SI
Length		
kilometer (km) = 1,000 m	1 km = 0.621 mi	1 mi = 1.609 km
meter (m) = 100 cm	1 m = 3.281 ft	1 ft = 0.305 m
centimeter (cm) = 0.01 m	1 cm = 0.394 in.	1 in. = 2.540 cm
millimeter (mm) = 0.001 m	1 mm = 0.039 in.	
micrometer (μm) = 0.000 001 m		
nanometer (nm) = 0.000 000 001 m		
Area		
square kilometer (km^2) = 100 hectares	1 km^2 = 0.386 mi^2	1 mi^2 = 2.590 km^2
hectare (ha) = 10,000 m^2	1 ha = 2.471 acres	1 acre = 0.405 ha
square meter (m^2) = 10,000 cm^2	1 m^2 = 10.764 ft^2	1 ft^2 = 0.093 m^2
square centimeter (cm^2) = 100 mm^2	1 cm^2 = 0.155 in.^{2}	1 in.^{2} = 6.452 cm^2
Volume		
liter (L) = 1,000 mL = 1 dm^3	1 L = 1.057 fl qt	1 fl qt = 0.946 L
milliliter (mL) = 0.001 L = 1 cm^3	1 mL = 0.034 fl oz	1 fl oz = 29.574 mL
microliter (μL) = 0.000 001 L		
Mass		*Equivalent weight at Earth's surface
kilogram (kg) = 1,000 g	1 kg = 2.205 lb*	1 lb* = 0.454 kg
gram (g) = 1,000 mg	1 g = 0.035 oz*	1 oz* = 28.350 g
milligram (mg) = 0.001 g		
microgram (μg) = 0.000 001 g		

Measuring Skills

Using a Graduated Cylinder

When using a graduated cylinder to measure volume, keep the following procedures in mind:

1. Place the cylinder on a flat, level surface before measuring liquid.
2. Move your head so that your eye is level with the surface of the liquid.
3. Read the mark closest to the liquid level. On glass graduated cylinders, read the mark closest to the center of the curve in the liquid's surface.

Using a Meterstick or Metric Ruler

When using a meterstick or metric ruler to measure length, keep the following procedures in mind:

1. Place the ruler firmly against the object that you are measuring.
2. Align one edge of the object exactly with the 0 end of the ruler.
3. Look at the other edge of the object to see which of the marks on the ruler is closest to that edge. (Note: Each small slash between the centimeters represents a millimeter, which is one-tenth of a centimeter.)

Using a Triple-Beam Balance

When using a triple-beam balance to measure mass, keep the following procedures in mind:

1. Make sure the balance is on a level surface.
2. Place all of the countermasses at 0. Adjust the balancing knob until the pointer rests at 0.
3. Place the object you wish to measure on the pan. **Caution:** Do not place hot objects or chemicals directly on the balance pan.
4. Move the largest countermass along the beam to the right until it is at the last notch that does not tip the balance. Follow the same procedure with the next-largest countermass. Then, move the smallest countermass until the pointer rests at 0.
5. Add the readings from the three beams together to determine the mass of the object.
6. When determining the mass of crystals or powders, first find the mass of a piece of filter paper. Then, add the crystals or powder to the paper, and remeasure. The actual mass of the crystals or powder is the total mass minus the mass of the paper. When finding the mass of liquids, first find the mass of the empty container. Then, find the combined mass of the liquid and container. The mass of the liquid is the total mass minus the mass of the container.

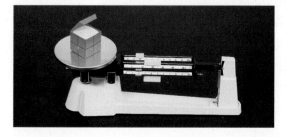

Temperature Scales

Temperature can be expressed by using three different scales: Fahrenheit, Celsius, and Kelvin. The SI unit for temperature is the kelvin (K).

Although 0 K is much colder than 0°C, a change of 1 K is equal to a change of 1°C.

Three Temperature Scales

	Fahrenheit	Celsius	Kelvin
Water boils	212°	100°	373
Body temperature	98.6°	37°	310
Room temperature	68°	20°	293
Water freezes	32°	0°	273

Temperature Conversions Table

To convert	Use this equation:	Example
Celsius to Fahrenheit °C → °F	$°F = \left(\dfrac{9}{5} \times °C\right) + 32$	Convert 45°C to °F. $°F = \left(\dfrac{9}{5} \times 45°C\right) + 32 = 113°F$
Fahrenheit to Celsius °F → °C	$°C = \dfrac{5}{9} \times (°F - 32)$	Convert 68°F to °C. $°C = \dfrac{5}{9} \times (68°F - 32) = 20°C$
Celsius to Kelvin °C → K	$K = °C + 273$	Convert 45°C to K. $K = 45°C + 273 = 318\ K$
Kelvin to Celsius K → °C	$°C = K - 273$	Convert 32 K to °C. $°C = 32K - 273 = -241°C$

Glossary

A

absolute dating any method of measuring the age of an event or object in years (132)

acid any compound that increases the number of hydronium ions when dissolved in water (368)

activation energy the minimum amount of energy required to start a chemical reaction (350)

adaptation a characteristic that improves an individual's ability to survive and reproduce in a particular environment (85, 100)

adaptive bioengineering engineering that results in a product or process that changes living organisms (28)

alkali metal (AL kuh LIE MET uhl) one of the elements of Group 1 of the periodic table (lithium, sodium, potassium, rubidium, cesium, and francium) (293)

alkaline-earth metal (AL kuh LIEN UHRTH MET uhl) one of the elements of Group 2 of the periodic table (beryllium, magnesium, calcium, strontium, barium, and radium) (293)

analog signal (AN uh LAWG SIG nuhl) a signal whose properties can change continuously in a given range (461)

Animalia a kingdom made up of complex, multicellular organisms that lack cell walls, can usually move around, and quickly respond to their environment (58)

Archaea (AHR kee uh) in a modern taxonomic system, a domain made up of prokaryotes (most of which are known to live in extreme environments) that are distinguished from other prokaryotes by differences in their genetics and in the makeup of their cell wall; the domain aligns with the traditional kingdom Archaebacteria (55)

area a measure of the size of a surface or a region (32)

asexual reproduction reproduction that does not involve the union of sex cells and in which one parent produces offspring that are genetically identical to the parent (70) TN VOCAB

assistive bioengineering engineering that results in a product or process that helps living organisms but does not change them permenently (28)

atom the smallest unit of an element that maintains the properties of that element (261)

atomic mass the mass of an atom expressed in atomic mass units (271)

atomic mass unit a unit of mass that describes the mass of an atom or molecule (267)

atomic number the number of protons in the nucleus of an atom; the atomic number is the same for all atoms of an element (269)

B

Bacteria (bak TEER ee uh) in the modern taxonomic system, a domain made up of prokaryotes that usually have a cell wall and that usually reproduce by cell division; this domain aligns with the traditional kingdom Eubacteria (55)

base any compound that increases the number of hydroxide ions when dissolved in water (371)

biodiversity the number and variety of organisms in a given area during a specific period of time (160)

bioengineering the application of engineering to living things, such as humans and plants (28)

boiling the conversion of a liquid to a vapor when the vapor pressure of the liquid equals the atmospheric pressure (220)

Boyle's law the law that states that the volume of a gas is inversely proportional to the pressure of a gas when temperature is constant (216)

C

carbohydrate a class of energy-giving nutrients that includes sugars, starches, and fiber; contains carbon, hydrogen, and oxygen (381)

cast a type of fossil that forms when sediments fill in the cavity left by a decomposed organism (136)

catalyst (KAT uh LIST) a substance that changes the rate of a chemical reaction without being used up or changed very much (352)

catastrophism a principle that states that geologic change occurs suddenly (129)

change of state the change of a substance from one physical state to another (218)

Charles's law the law that states that the volume of a gas is directly proportional to the temperature of a gas when pressure is constant (216)

chemical bond an interaction that holds atoms or ions together (311, 364)

chemical bonding the combining of atoms to form molecules or ionic compounds (311)

chemical change a change that occurs when one or more substances change into entirely new substances with different properties (197)

chemical equation a representation of a chemical reaction that uses symbols to show the relationship between the reactants and the products (340) *TN VOCAB*

chemical formula a combination of chemical symbols and numbers to represent a substance (338)

chemical property a property of matter that describes a substance's ability to participate in chemical reactions (195)

chemical reaction the process by which one or more substances change to produce one or more different substances (335)

circuit board a sheet of insulating material that carries circuit elements and that is inserted in an electronic device (454)

classification the division of organisms into groups, or classes, based on specific characteristics (48) *TN VOCAB*

colloid (KAHL oyd) a mixture consisting of tiny particles that are intermediate in size between those in solutions and those in suspensions and that are suspended in a liquid, solid, or gas (248)

compound a substance made up of atoms of two or more different elements joined by chemical bonds (239) *TN VOCAB*

computer an electronic device that can accept data and instructions, follow the instructions, and output the results (469)

concentration the amount of a particular substance in a given quantity of a mixture, solution, or ore (246) *TN VOCAB*

condensation the change of state from a gas to a liquid (221)

conservation (KAHN suhr VAY shun) the preservation and wise use of natural resources (163)

core the central part of the Earth below the mantle (405)

cost-benefit analysis the process of determining whether the cost of doing something is worth the benefit provided (24)

covalent bond (koh VAY luhnt BAHND) a bond formed when atoms share one or more pairs of electrons (318)

covalent compound a chemical compound that is formed by the sharing of electrons (366)

crust the thin and solid outermost layer of the Earth above the mantle (405)

crystal lattice (KRIS tuhl LAT is) the regular pattern in which a crystal is arranged (317)

D

data any pieces of information acquired through observation or experimentation (15)

decomposition reaction a reaction in which a single compound breaks down to form two or more simpler substances (345)

density the ratio of the mass of a substance to the volume of the substance (33, 189) *TN VOCAB*

dichotomous key (die KAHT uh muhs KEE) an aid that is used to identify organisms and that consists of the answers to a series of questions (52) *TN VOCAB*

digital signal a signal that can be represented as a sequence of discrete values (462)

diode an electronic device that allows electric charge to move more easily in one direction than in the other (456)

doping (DOHP eeng) the addition of an impurity element to a semiconductor (455)

double-displacement reaction a reaction in which a gas, a solid precipitate, or a molecular compound forms from the exchange of ions between two compounds (347)

E

electric generator a device that converts mechanical energy into electrical energy (440)

electric motor a device that converts electrical energy into mechanical energy (436)

electromagnet a coil that has a soft iron core and that acts as a magnet when an electric current is in the coil (434)

electromagnetic induction the process of creating a current in a circuit by changing a magnetic field (439)

electromagnetism the interaction between electricity and magnetism (433)

electron a subatomic particle that has a negative charge (262)

electron cloud a region around the nucleus of an atom where electrons are likely to be found (264)

element a substance that cannot be separated or broken down into simpler substances by chemical means (235) ◼TN▶ VOCAB

endothermic reaction a chemical reaction that requires heat (349) ◼TN▶ VOCAB

engineering the process of creating technology (23)

engineering design process the process engineers use to develop a new technology (24)

eon (EE AHN) the largest division of geologic time (143)

epoch a subdivision of geologic time that is longer than an age but shorter than a period (143)

era a unit of geologic time that includes two or more periods (143)

estivation a period of inactivity and lowered body temperature that some animals undergo in summer as a protection against hot weather and lack of food (82)

Eukarya in a modern taxonomic system, a domain made up of all eukaryotes; this domain aligns with the traditional kingdoms Protista, Fungi, Plantae, and Animalia (56)

evaporation (ee vap uh RAY shuhn) the change of a substance from a liquid to a gas (220)

exothermic reaction a chemical reaction in which heat is released to the surroundings (348) ◼TN▶ VOCAB

external fertilization the union of sex cells outside the bodies of the parents (72)

extinction the death of every member of a species (143) ◼TN▶ VOCAB

F

fossil the trace or remains of an organism that lived long ago, most commonly preserved in sedimentary rock (102, 134) ◼TN▶ VOCAB

fossil record a historical sequence of life indicated by fossils found in layers of Earth's crust (102)

Fungi (FUHN JIE) a kingdom made up of nongreen, eukaryotic organisms that have no means of movement, reproduce by using spores, and get food by breaking down substances in their surroundings and absorbing the nutrients (56)

G

gas a form of matter that does not have a definite volume or shape (212)

generation time the period between the birth of one generation and the birth of the next generation (115)

geologic column an arrangement of rock layers in which the oldest rocks are at the bottom (131)

geologic time scale the standard method used to divide the Earth's long natural history into manageable parts (143)

group a vertical column of elements in the periodic table; elements in a group share chemical properties (290)

H

halogen (HAL oh juhn) one of the elements of Group 17 of the periodic table (fluorine, chlorine, bromine, iodine, and statine); halogens combine with most metals to form salts (297)

hardware the parts or pieces of equipment that make up a computer (470)

hibernation a period of inactivity and lowered body temperature that some animals undergo in winter as a protection against cold weather and lack of food (82)

hydrocarbon an organic compound composed only of carbon and hydrogen (379)

hypothesis (hie PAHTH uh sis) an explanation that is based on prior scientific research or observations and that can be tested (13)

I

index fossil a fossil that is used to establish the age of a rock layer because the fossil is distinct, abundant, and widespread and the species that formed the fossil existed for only a short span of geologic time (138)

indicator a compound that can reversibly change color depending on conditions such as pH (369)

inertia (in UHR shuh) the tendency of an object to resist being moved or, if the object is moving, to resist a change in speed or direction until an outside force acts on the object (186) ◼TN▶ VOCAB

inhibitor a substance that slows down or stops a chemical reaction (352)

innate behavior an inherited behavior that does not depend on the environment or experience (79)

integrated circuit (IN tuh GRAYT id SUHR kit) a circuit whose components are formed on a single semiconductor (458)

internal fertilization fertilization of an egg by sperm that occurs inside the body of a female (72)

Internet a large computer network that connects many local and smaller networks all over the world (474)

ion a charged particle that forms when an atom or group of atoms gains or loses one or more electrons (314)

ionic bond (ie AHN ik BAHND) a bond that forms when electrons are transferred from one atom to another, which results in a positive ion and a negative ion (314)

ionic compound a compound made of oppositely charged ions (364)

isotope (IE suh TOHP) an atom that has the same number of protons (or the same atomic number) as other atoms of the same element do but that has a different number of neutrons (and thus a different atomic mass) (269)

L

law a summary of many experimental results and observations; a law tells how things work (20)

law of conservation of energy the law that states that energy cannot be created or destroyed but can be changed from one form to another (349)

law of conservation of mass the law that states that mass cannot be created or destroyed in ordinary chemical and physical changes (341) *TN VOCAB*

learned behavior a behavior that has been learned from experience (79)

lipid a type of biochemical that does not dissolve in water; fats and steroids are lipids (381)

liquid the state of matter that has a definite volume but not a definite shape (212)

M

magnet any material that attracts iron or materials containing iron (425)

magnetic force the force of attraction or repulsion generated by moving or spinning electric charges (425)

magnetic pole one of two points, such as the ends of a magnet, that have opposing magnetic qualities (425)

mantle the layer of rock between the Earth's crust and core (405)

mass a measure of the amount of matter in an object (32, 185)

mass number the sum of the numbers of protons and neutrons in the nucleus of an atom (270)

matter anything that has mass and takes up space (182)

melting the change of state in which a solid becomes a liquid by adding heat (219)

meniscus (muh NIS kuhs) the curve at a liquid's surface by which one measures the volume of the liquid (183)

metal an element that is shiny and that conducts heat and electricity well (236)

metallic bond a bond formed by the attraction between positively charged metal ions and the electrons around them (321)

metalloid elements that have properties of both metals and nonmetals (236)

meter the basic unit of length in the SI (symbol, m) (32)

microprocessor a single semiconductor chip that controls and executes a microcomputer's instructions (469)

mixture a combination of two or more substances that are not chemically combined (242)

model a pattern, plan, representation, or description designed to show the structure or workings of an object, system, or concept (18)

mold a mark or cavity made in a sedimentary surface by a shell or other body (136)

molecule (MAHL i KYOOL) the smallest unit of a substance that keeps all of the physical and chemical properties of that substance (319) *TN VOCAB*

N

natural selection the process by which individuals that are better adapted to their environment survive and reproduce more successfully than less well adapted individuals do (86, 112)

nebula a large cloud of gas and dust in interstellar space; a region in space where stars are born or where stars explode at the end of their lives (394)

neutralization reaction (NOO truhl i ZA shuhn ree AK shuhn) the reaction of an acid and a base to form a neutral solution of water and a salt (375)

neutron a subatomic particle that has no charge and that is found in the nucleus of an atom (267)

noble gas one of the elements of Group 18 of the periodic table (helium, neon, argon, krypton, xenon, and radon); noble gases are unreactive (298)

nonmetal an element that conducts heat and electricity poorly (236)

nonrenewable resource a resource that forms at a rate that is much slower than the rate at which it is consumed (158)

nuclear fusion the combination of the nuclei of small atoms to form a larger nucleus; releases energy (400)

nucleic acid (noo KLEE ik AS id) a molecule made up of subunits called *nucleotides* (382)

nucleus (NOO klee uhs) in physical science, an atom's central region, which is made up of protons and neutrons (264) ◢TN▶VOCAB

O

observation the process of obtaining information by using the senses (11)

orbit the path that a body follows as it travels around another body in space (411)

organic compound a covalently bonded compound that contains carbon (379)

overpopulation the presence of too many individuals in an area for the available resources (159)

P

paleontology the scientific study of fossils (133)

period in chemistry, a horizontal row of elements in the periodic table (290); a unit of geologic time that is longer than an epoch but shorter than an era (143)

periodic describes something that occurs or repeats at regular intervals (285)

periodic law the law that states that the repeating chemical and physical properties of elements change periodically with the atomic numbers of the elements (285)

pH a value that is used to express the acidity or basicity (alkalinity) of a system (375) ◢TN▶VOCAB

physical change a change of matter from one form to another without a change in chemical properties (192)

physical property a characteristic of a substance that does not involve a chemical change, such as density, color, or hardness (189)

Plantae a kingdom made up of complex, multicellular organisms that are usually green, have cell walls made of cellulose, cannot move around, and use the sun's energy to make sugar by photosynthesis (57)

pollination the transfer of pollen from the male reproductive structures to the female structures of seed plants (75)

pollution an unwanted change in the environment caused by substances or forms of energy (156)

precipitate (pree SIP uh TAYT) a solid that is produced as a result of a chemical reaction in solution (335)

pressure the amount of force exerted per unit area of a surface (215)

product a substance that forms in a chemical reaction (340) ◢TN▶VOCAB

protein a molecule that is made up of amino acids and that is needed to build and repair body structures and to regulate processes in the body (381)

Protista (proh TIST uh) a kingdom of mostly one-celled eukaryotic organisms that are different from plants, animals, bacteria, and fungi (56)

proton a subatomic particle that has a positive charge and that is located in the nucleus of an atom (267)

prototype a test model of a product (24)

pure substance a sample of matter, either a single element or a single compound, that has definite chemical and physical properties (235)

R

reactant (ree AK tuhnt) a substance or molecule that participates in a chemical reaction (340) ◢TN▶VOCAB

recycling the process of recovering valuable or useful materials from waste or scrap (165)

relative age the approximate age of fossils or other objects in rock layers determined by comparing whether the surrounding rock layers are younger or older (131) ◢TN▶VOCAB

relative dating any method of determining whether an event or object is older or younger than other events or objects (131)

renewable resource a natural resource that can be replaced at the same rate at which the resource is consumed (158)

revolution the motion of a body that travels around another body in space; one complete trip along an orbit (411)

rotation the spin of a body on its axis (411)

S

salt an ionic compound that forms when a metal atom replaces the hydrogen of an acid (377)

science the knowledge obtained by observing natural events and conditions in order to discover facts and formulate laws or principles that can be verified or tested (5)

scientific methods a series of steps followed to solve problems (11)

selective breeding the human practice of breeding animals or plants that have certain desired traits (110)

semiconductor (SEM i kuhn DUHK tuhr) an element or compound that conducts electric current better than an insulator does but not as well as a conductor does (455)

sexual reproduction reproduction in which the sex cells from two parents unite to produce offspring that share traits from both parents (71) TN VOCAB

single-displacement reaction a reaction in which one element takes the place of another element in a compound (345)

software a set of instructions or commands that tells a computer what to do; a computer program (473)

solar nebula the cloud of gas and dust that formed our solar system (395)

solenoid a coil of wire with an electric current in it (433)

solid the state of matter in which the volume and shape of a substance are fixed (211)

solubility the ability of one substance to dissolve in another at a given temperature and pressure (246)

solute in a solution, the substance that dissolves in the solvent (244)

solution a homogeneous mixture of two or more substances uniformly dispersed throughout a single phase (244)

solvent in a solution, the substance in which the solute dissolves (244)

speciation (spee shee AY shuhn) the formation of new species as a result of change over time (116)

species a group of organisms that are closely related and can mate to produce fertile offspring (101) TN VOCAB

states of matter the physical forms of matter, which include solid, liquid, and gas (211)

sublimation (SUHB luh MAY shuhn) the process in which a solid changes directly into a gas (222)

sunspot a dark area of the photosphere of the sun that is cooler than the surrounding areas and that has a strong magnetic field (402)

surface tension the force that acts on the surface of a liquid and that tends to minimize the area of the surface (212)

suspension a mixture in which particles of a material are more or less evenly dispersed throughout a liquid or gas (248)

synthesis reaction (SIN thuh sis ree AK shuhn) a reaction in which two or more substances combine to form a new compound (345)

T

taxonomy (taks AHN uh mee) the science of describing, naming, and classifying organisms (49)

technology the products and processes that are designed to serve our needs (6, 23)

temperature a measure of how hot (or cold) something is; specifically, a measure of the average kinetic energy of the particles in an object (34, 214)

territory an area that is occupied by one animal or a group of animals that do not allow other members of the species to enter (79)

theory an explanation that ties together many hypotheses and observations (20)

trace fossil a fossilized mark that formed in sedimentary rock by the movement of an animal on or within soft sediment (136)

trait a genetically determined characteristic (110)

transformer a device that increases or decreases the voltage of alternating current (442)

transistor a semiconductor device that can amplify current and that is used in amplifiers, oscillators, and switches (457)

U

uniformitarianism a principle that states that geologic processes that occurred in the past can be explained by current geologic processes (129)

V

valence electron (VAY luhns ee LEK TRAHN) an electron that is found in the outermost shell of an atom and that determines the atom's chemical properties (311)

viscosity the resistance of a gas or liquid to flow (212)

volume a measure of the size of a body or region in three-dimensional space (33, 182, 215) *TN VOCAB*

W

weight a measure of the gravitational force exerted on an object; its value can change with the location of the object in the universe (185) *TN VOCAB*

Spanish Glossary

A

absolute dating/datación absoluta cualquier método que sirve para determinar la edad de un suceso u objeto en años (132)

acid/ácido cualquier compuesto que aumenta el número de iones de hidrógeno cuando se disuelve en agua (368)

activation energy/energía de activación la cantidad mínima de energía que se requiere para iniciar una reacción química (350)

adaptation/adaptación una característica que mejora la capacidad de un individuo para sobrevivir y reproducirse en un determinado ambiente (85, 100)

adaptive bioengineering/bioingeniería de adaptación aplicación de la ingeniería a un producto o proceso que cambia a los organismos vivos (28)

alkali metal/metal alcalino uno de los elementos del Grupo 1 de la tabla periódica (litio, sodio, potasio, rubidio, cesio y francio) (293)

alkaline-earth metal/metal alcalinotérreo uno de los elementos del Grupo 2 de la tabla periódica (berilio, magnesio, calcio, estroncio, bario y radio) (293)

analog signal/señal análoga una señal cuyas propiedades cambian continuamente en un rango determinado (461)

Animalia/Animalia un reino formado por organismos pluricelulares complejos que no tienen pared celular, normalmente son capaces de moverse y reaccionan rápidamente a su ambiente (58)

Archaea/Archaea en un sistema taxonómico moderno, un dominio compuesto por procariotes (la mayoría de los cuales viven en ambientes extremos) que se distinguen de otros procariotes por diferencias genéticas y por la diferente composición de su pared celular; el dominio coincide con el reino tradicional Archaebacteria (55)

area/área una medida del tamaño de una superficie o región (32)

asexual reproduction/reproducción asexual reproducción que no involucra la unión de células sexuales, en la que un solo progenitor produce descendencia que es genéticamente igual al progenitor (70) TN VOCAB

assistive bioengineering/bioingeniería de asistencia aplicación de la ingeniería a un producto o proceso que ayuda a los organismos vivos pero que no los cambia de manera permanente (28)

atom/átomo la unidad más pequeña de un elemento que conserva las propiedades de ese elemento (261)

atomic mass/masa atómica la masa de un átomo, expresada en unidades de masa atómica (271)

atomic mass unit/unidad de masa atómica una unidad de masa que describe la masa de un átomo o una molécula (267)

atomic number/número atómico el número de protones en el núcleo de un átomo; el número atómico es el mismo para todos los átomos de un elemento (269)

B

Bacteria/Bacteria en un sistema taxonómico moderno, un dominio compuesto por procariotes que normalmente tienen pared celular y se reproducen por división celular; este dominio coincide con el reino tradicional Eubacteria (55)

base/base cualquier compuesto que aumenta el número de iones de hidróxido cuando se disuelve en agua (371)

biodiversity/biodiversidad el número y la variedad de organismos que se encuentran en un área determinada durante un período específico de tiempo (160)

bioengineering/bioingeniería aplicación de la ingeniería a los seres vivos, como los humanos y las plantas (28)

boiling/ebullición la conversión de un líquido en vapor cuando la presión de vapor del líquido es igual a la presión atmosférica (220)

Boyle's law/ley de Boyle la ley que establece que el volumen de un gas es inversamente proporcional a su presión cuando la temperatura es constante (216)

C

carbohydrate/carbohidrato una clase de nutrientes que proporcionan energía; incluye los azúcares, los almidones y las fibras; contiene carbono, hidrógeno y oxígeno (381)

cast/contramolde un tipo de fósil que se forma cuando un organismo descompuesto deja una cavidad que es llenada por sedimentos (136)

catalyst/catalizador una substancia que cambia la tasa de una reacción química sin consumirse ni cambiar demasiado (352)

catastrophism/catastrofismo un principio que establece que los cambios geológicos ocurren súbitamente (129)

change of state/cambio de estado el cambio de una substancia de un estado físico a otro (218)

Charles's law/ley de Charles la ley que establece que el volumen de un gas es directamente proporcional a su temperatura cuando la presión es constante (216)

chemical bond/enlace químico una interacción que mantiene unidos los átomos o los iones (311, 364)

chemical bonding/formación de un enlace químico la combinación de átomos para formar moléculas o compuestos iónicos (311)

chemical change/cambio químico un cambio que ocurre cuando una o más substancias se transforman en substancias totalmente nuevas con propiedades diferentes (197)

chemical equation/ecuación química una representación de una reacción química que usa símbolos para mostrar la relación entre los reactivos y los productos (340) **⬛TN▸VOCAB**

chemical formula/fórmula química una combinación de símbolos químicos y números que se usan para representar una substancia (338)

chemical property/propiedad química una propiedad de la materia que describe la capacidad de una substancia de participar en reacciones químicas (195)

chemical reaction/reacción química el proceso por medio del cual una o más substancia cambian para producir una o más substancias distintas (335)

circuit board/cuadro del circuito una lámina de material aislante que lleva elementos del circuito y que es insertado en un aparato electrónico (454)

classification/clasificación la división de organismos en grupos, o clases, en función de características específicas (48) **⬛TN▸VOCAB**

colloid/coloide una mezcla formada por partículas diminutas que son de tamaño intermedio entre las partículas de las soluciones y las de las suspensiones y que se encuentran suspendidas en un líquido, sólido o gas (248)

compound/compuesto una substancia formada por átomos de dos o más elementos diferentes unidos por enlaces químicos (239) **⬛TN▸VOCAB**

computer/computadora un aparato electrónico que acepta información e instrucciones, sigue instrucciones y produce una salida para los resultados (469)

concentration/concentración la cantidad de una cierta substancia en una cantidad determinada de mezcla, solución o mena (246) **⬛TN▸VOCAB**

condensation/condensación el cambio de estado de gas a líquido (221)

conservation/conservación la preservación y el uso inteligente de los recursos naturales (163)

core/núcleo la parte central de la Tierra, debajo del manto (405)

cost-benefit analysis/análisis de costos y beneficio proceso para determinar si el costo de hacer algo justifica el beneficio obtenido (24)

covalent bond/enlace covalente un enlace formado cuando los átomos comparten uno o más pares de electrones (318)

covalent compound/compuesto covalente un compuesto químico que se forma al compartir electrones (366)

crust/corteza la capa externa, delgada y sólida de la Tierra, que se encuentra sobre el manto (405)

crystal lattice/red cristalina el patrón regular en el que un cristal está ordenado (317)

D

data/datos cualquier parte de la información que se adquiere por medio de la observación o experimentación (15)

decomposition reaction/reacción de descomposición una reacción en la que un solo compuesto se descompone para formar dos o más substancias más simples (345)

density/densidad la relación entre la masa de una substancia y su volumen (33, 189) **⬛TN▸VOCAB**

dichotomous key/clave dicotómica una ayuda para identificar organismos, que consiste en las respuestas a una serie de preguntas (52) **⬛TN▸VOCAB**

digital signal/señal digital una señal que se puede representar como una secuencia de valores discretos (462)

diode/diodo un aparato electrónico que permite que la corriente eléctrica pase más fácilmente en una dirección que en otra (456)

doping/adulteración la adición de un elemento impuro a un semiconductor (455)

double-displacement reaction/reacción de doble desplazamiento una reacción en la que se forma un gas, un precipitado sólido o un compuesto molecular a partir del intercambio de iones entre dos compuestos (347)

E

electric generator/generador eléctrico un aparato que transforma la energía mecánica en energía eléctrica (440)

electric motor/motor eléctrico un aparato que transforma la energía eléctrica en energía mecánica (436)

electromagnet/electroimán una bobina que tiene un centro de hierro suave y que funciona como un imán cuando hay una corriente eléctrica en la bobina (434)

electromagnetic induction/inducción electromagnética el proceso de crear una corriente en un circuito por medio de un cambio en el campo magnético (439)

electromagnetism/electromagnetismo la interacción entre la electricidad y el magnetismo (433)

electron/electrón una partícula subatómica que tiene carga negativa (262)

electron cloud/nube de electrones una región que rodea al núcleo de un átomo en la cual es probable encontrar a los electrones (264)

element/elemento una substancia que no se puede separar o descomponer en substancias más simples por medio de métodos químicos (235) TN VOCAB

endothermic reaction/reacción endotérmica una reacción química que necesita calor (349) TN VOCAB

engineering/ingeniería el proceso de crear tecnología (23)

engineering design process/proceso de diseño de la ingeniería proceso que usan los ingenieros para desarrollar una nueva tecnología (24)

eon/eón la mayor división del tiempo geológico (143)

epoch/época una subdivisión del tiempo geológico que es más larga que una edad pero más corta que un período (143)

era/era una unidad de tiempo geológico que incluye dos o más períodos (143)

estivation/estivación un período de inactividad y menor temperatura corporal por el que pasan algunos animales durante el verano para protegerse del calor y la falta de alimento (82)

Eukarya/Eukarya en un sistema taxonómico moderno, un dominio compuesto por todos los eucariotes; este dominio coincide con los reinos tradicionales Protista, Fungi, Plantae y Animalia (56)

evaporation/evaporación el cambio de una substancia de líquido a gas (220)

exothermic reaction/reacción exotérmica una reacción química en la que se libera calor a los alrededores (348) TN VOCAB

external fertilization/fecundación externa la unión de células sexuales fuera del cuerpo de los progenitores (72)

extinction/extinción la muerte de todos los miembros de una especie (143) TN VOCAB

F

fossil/fósil los indicios o los restos de un organismo que vivió hace mucho tiempo, comúnmente preservados en las rocas sedimentarias (102, 134) TN VOCAB

fossil record/registro fósil una secuencia histórica de la vida indicada por fósiles que se han encontrado en las capas de la corteza terrestre (102)

Fungi/Fungi un reino formado por organismos eucarióticos no verdes que no tienen capacidad de movimiento, se reproducen por esporas y obtienen alimento al descomponer substancias de su entorno y absorber los nutrientes (56)

G

gas/gas un estado de la materia que no tiene volumen ni forma definidos (212)

generation time/tiempo de generación el período entre el nacimiento de una generación y el nacimiento de la siguiente generación (115)

geologic column/columna geológica un arreglo ordenado de capas de rocas que se basa en la edad relativa de las rocas y en el cual las rocas más antiguas están al fondo (131)

geologic time scale/escala de tiempo geológico el método estándar que se usa para dividir la larga historia natural de la Tierra en partes razonables (142)

group/grupo una columna vertical de elementos de la tabla periódica; los elementos de un grupo comparten propiedades químicas (290)

Spanish Glossary

H

halogen/halógeno uno de los elementos del Grupo 17 de la tabla periódica (flúor, cloro, bromo, yodo y ástato); los halógenos se combinan con la mayoría de los metales para formar sales (297)

hardware/hardware las partes o piezas de equipo que forman una computadora (470)

hibernation/hibernación un período de inactividad y disminución de la temperatura del cuerpo que algunos animales experimentan en invierno como protección contra el tiempo frío y la escasez de comida (82)

hydrocarbon/hidrocarburo un compuesto orgánico compuesto únicamente por carbono e hidrógeno (379)

hypothesis/hipótesis una explicación que se basa en observaciones o investigaciones científicas previas y que se puede probar (13)

I

index fossil/fósil guía un fósil que se usa para establecer la edad de una capa de roca debido a que puede diferenciarse bien de otros, es abundante y está extendido; la especie que formó ese fósil existió sólo por un corto período de tiempo geológico (138)

indicator/indicador un compuesto que puede cambiar de color de forma reversible dependiendo de condiciones tales como el pH (369)

inertia/inercia la tendencia de un objeto a no moverse o, si el objeto se está moviendo, la tendencia a resistir un cambio en su rapidez o dirección hasta que una fuerza externa actúe en el objeto (186) ◢TN VOCAB

inhibitor/inhibidor una substancia que desacelera o detiene una reacción química (352)

innate behavior/conducta innata una conducta heredada que no depende del ambiente ni de la experiencia (79)

integrated circuit/circuito integrado un circuito cuyos componentes están formados en un solo semiconductor (458)

internal fertilization/fecundación interna fecundación de un óvulo por un espermatozoide, la cual ocurre dentro del cuerpo de la hembra (72)

Internet/Internet una amplia red de computadoras que conecta muchas redes locales y redes más pequeñas por todo el mundo (474)

ion/ion una partícula cargada que se forma cuando un átomo o grupo de átomos gana o pierde uno o más electrones (314)

ionic bond/enlace iónico un enlace que se forma cuando los electrones se transfieren de un átomo a otro, y que produce un ion positivo y uno negativo (314)

ionic compound/compuesto iónico un compuesto formado por iones con cargas opuestas (364)

isotope/isótopo un átomo que tiene el mismo número de protones (o el mismo número atómico) que otros átomos del mismo elemento, pero que tiene un número diferente de neutrones (y, por lo tanto, otra masa atómica) (269)

L

law/ley un resumen de muchos resultados y observaciones experimentales; una ley dice cómo funcionan las cosas (20)

law of conservation of energy/ley de la conservación de la energía la ley que establece que la energía ni se crea ni se destruye, sólo se transforma de una forma a otra (349)

law of conservation of mass/ley de la conservación de la masa la ley que establece que la masa no se crea ni se destruye por cambios químicos o físicos comunes (341) ◢TN VOCAB

learned behavior/conducta aprendida una conducta que se ha aprendido por experiencia (79)

lipid/lípido un tipo de substancia bioquímica que no se disuelve en agua; las grasas y los esteroides son lípidos (381)

liquid/líquido el estado de la materia que tiene un volumen definido, pero no una forma definida (212)

M

magnet/imán cualquier material que atrae hierro o materiales que contienen hierro (425)

magnetic force/fuerza magnética la fuerza de atracción o repulsión generadas por cargas eléctricas en movimiento o que giran (425)

magnetic pole/polo magnético uno de dos puntos, tales como los extremos de un imán, que tienen cualidades magnéticas opuestas (425)

mantle/manto la capa de roca que se encuentra entre la corteza terrestre y el núcleo (405)

mass/masa una medida de la cantidad de materia que tiene un objeto (32, 185)

mass number/número de masa la suma de los números de protones y neutrones que hay en el núcleo de un átomo (270)

matter/materia cualquier cosa que tiene masa y ocupa un lugar en el espacio (182)

melting/fusión el cambio de estado en el que un sólido se convierte en líquido al añadirse calor (219)

meniscus/menisco la curva que se forma en la superficie de un líquido, la cual sirve para medir el volumen de un líquido (183)

metal/metal un elemento que es brillante y conduce bien el calor y la electricidad (236)

metallic bond/enlace metálico un enlace formado por la atracción entre iones metálicos cargados positivamente y los electrones que los rodean (321)

metalloid/metaloides elementos que tienen propiedades tanto de metales como de no metales (236)

meter/metro la unidad fundamental de longitud en el sistema internacional de unidades (símbolo: m) (32)

microprocessor/microprocesador un chip único de un semiconductor, el cual controla y ejecuta las instrucciones de una microcomputadora (469)

mixture/mezcla una combinación de dos o más substancias que no están combinadas químicamente (242)

model/modelo un diseño, plan, representación o descripción cuyo objetivo es mostrar la estructura o funcionamiento de un objeto, sistema o concepto (18)

mold/molde una marca o cavidad hecha en una superficie sedimentaria por una concha u otro cuerpo (136)

molecule/molécula la unidad más pequeña de una substancia que conserva todas las propiedades físicas y químicas de esa substancia (319) ▰TN▰ VOCAB

N

natural selection/selección natural el proceso por medio del cual los individuos que están mejor adaptados a su ambiente sobreviven y se reproducen con más éxito que los individuos menos adaptados (86, 112)

nebula/nebulosa una nube grande de gas y polvo en el espacio interestelar; una región en el espacio donde las estrellas nacen o donde explotan al final de su vida (394)

neutralization reaction/reacción de neutralización la reacción de un ácido y una base que forma una solución neutra de agua y una sal (375)

neutron/neutrón una partícula subatómica que no tiene carga y que se encuentra en el núcleo de un átomo (267)

noble gas/gas noble uno de los elementos del Grupo 18 de la tabla periódica (helio, neón, argón, criptón, xenón y radón); los gases nobles son no reactivos (298)

nonmetal/no metal un elemento que es mal conductor del calor y la electricidad (236)

nonrenewable resource/recurso no renovable un recurso que se forma a una tasa que es mucho más lenta que la tasa a la que se consume (158)

nuclear fusion/fusión nuclear combinación de los núcleos de átomos pequeños para formar un núcleo más grande; libera energía (400)

nucleic acid/ácido nucleico una molécula formada por subunidades llamadas *nucleótidos* (382)

nucleus/núcleo en ciencias físicas, la región central de un átomo, la cual está constituida por protones y neutrones (264) ▰TN▰ VOCAB

O

observation/observación el proceso de obtener información por medio de los sentidos (11)

orbit/órbita la trayectoria que sigue un cuerpo al desplazarse alrededor de otro cuerpo en el espacio (410)

organic compound/compuesto orgánico un compuesto enlazado de manera covalente que contiene carbono (379)

overpopulation/sobrepoblación la presencia de demasiados individuos en un área para los recursos disponibles (159)

P

paleontology/paleontología el estudio científico de los fósiles (133)

period/período en química, una hilera horizontal de elementos en la tabla periódica (290); una unidad de tiempo geológico que es más larga que una época pero más corta que una era (143)

periodic/periódico término que describe algo que ocurre o que se repite a intervalos regulares (285)

periodic law/ley periódica la ley que establece que las propiedades químicas y físicas repetitivas de un elemento cambian periódicamente en función del número atómico de los elementos (285)

pH/pH un valor que expresa la acidez o la basicidad (alcalinidad) de un sistema (375) ▰TN▰ VOCAB

physical change/cambio físico un cambio de materia de una forma a otra sin que ocurra un cambio en sus propiedades químicas (192)

physical property/propiedad física una característica de una substancia que no implica un cambio químico, tal como la densidad, el color o la dureza (189)

Plantae/Plantae un reino formado por organismos pluricelulares complejos que normalmente son verdes, tienen una pared celular de celulosa, no tienen capacidad de movimiento y utilizan la energía del Sol para producir azúcar mediante la fotosíntesis (57)

pollination/polinización la transferencia de polen de las estructuras reproductoras masculinas a las estructuras femeninas de las plantas con semillas (75)

pollution/contaminación un cambio indeseable en el ambiente producido por substancias o formas de energía (156)

precipitate/precipitado un sólido que se produce como resultado de una reacción química en una solución (335)

pressure/presión la cantidad de fuerza ejercida en una superficie por unidad de área (215)

product/producto una substancia que se forma en una reacción química (340) *TN▶VOCAB*

protein/proteína una molécula formada por aminoácidos que es necesaria para construir y reparar estructuras corporales y para regular procesos del cuerpo (381)

Protista/Protista un reino compuesto principalmente por organismo eucarióticos unicelulares que son diferentes de las plantas, animales, bacterias y hongos (56)

proton/protón una partícula subatómica que tiene una carga positiva y que se encuentra en el núcleo de un átomo (267)

prototype/prototipo prueba modelo de un producto (24)

pure substance/substancia pura una muestra de materia, ya sea un solo elemento o un solo compuesto, que tiene propiedades químicas y físicas definidas (235)

R

reactant/reactivo una substancia o molécula que participa en una reacción química (340) *TN▶VOCAB*

recycling/reciclar el proceso de recuperar materiales valiosos o útiles de los desechos o de la basura (165)

relative age/edad relativa la edad aproximada de los fósiles u otros objetos encontrados en las capas de la roca, que se determina al comparar si las capas circundantes de la roca son más jóvenes o más antiguas. (131) *TN▶VOCAB*

relative dating/datación relativa cualquier método que se utiliza para determinar si un acontecimiento u objeto es más viejo o más joven que otros acontecimientos u objetos (131)

renewable resource/recurso renovable un recurso natural que puede reemplazarse a la misma tasa a la que se consume (158)

revolution/revolución el movimiento de un cuerpo que viaja alrededor de otro cuerpo en el espacio; un viaje completo a lo largo de una órbita (411)

rotation/rotación el giro de un cuerpo alrededor de su eje (411)

S

salt/sal un compuesto iónico que se forma cuando un átomo de un metal reemplaza el hidrógeno de un ácido (377)

science/ciencia el conocimiento que se obtiene por medio de la observación natural de acontecimientos y condiciones con el fin de descubrir hechos y formular leyes o principios que puedan ser verificados o probados (5)

scientific methods/métodos científicos una serie de pasos que se siguen para solucionar problemas (11)

selective breeding/reproducción selectiva la práctica humana de cruzar animales o plantas que tienen ciertos caracteres deseados (110)

semiconductor/semiconductor un elemento o compuesto que conduce la corriente eléctrica mejor que un aislante, pero no tan bien como un conductor (455)

sexual reproduction/reproducción sexual reproducción en la que se unen las células sexuales de los dos progenitores para producir descendencia que comparte caracteres de ambos progenitores (71) *TN▶VOCAB*

single-displacement reaction/reacción de sustitución simple una reacción en la que un elemento toma el lugar de otro elemento en un compuesto (345)

software/software un conjunto de instrucciones o comandos que le dicen qué hacer a una computadora; un programa de computadora (473)

solar nebula/nebulosa solar la nube de gas y polvo que formó nuestro Sistema Solar (395)

solenoid/solenoide una bobina de alambre que tiene una corriente eléctrica (433)

solid/sólido el estado de la materia en el cual el volumen y la forma de una sustancia están fijos (211)

solubility/solubilidad la capacidad de una substancia de disolverse en otra a una temperatura y una presión dadas (246)

solute/soluto en una solución, la sustancia que se disuelve en el solvente (244)

solution/solución una mezcla homogénea de dos o más sustancias dispersas de manera uniforme en una sola fase (244)

solvent/solvente en una solución, la sustancia en la que se disuelve el soluto (244)

speciation/especiación la formación de especies nuevas como resultado de los cambios originados en un tiempo determinado (116)

species/especie un grupo de organismos que tienen un parentesco cercano y que pueden aparearse para producir descendencia fértil (101) **TN VOCAB**

states of matter/estados de la materia las formas físicas de la materia, que son sólida, líquida y gaseosa (211)

sublimation/sublimación el proceso por medio del cual un sólido se transforma directamente en un gas (222)

sunspot/mancha solar un área oscura en la fotosfera del Sol que es más fría que las áreas que la rodean y que tiene un campo magnético fuerte (402)

surface tension/tensión superficial la fuerza que actúa en la superficie de un líquido y que tiende a minimizar el área de la superficie (212)

suspension/suspensión una mezcla en la que las partículas de un material se encuentran dispersas de manera más o menos uniforme a través de un líquido o de un gas (248)

synthesis reaction/reacción de síntesis una reacción en la que dos o más sustancias se combinan para formar un compuesto nuevo (345)

T

taxonomy/taxonomía la ciencia de describir, nombrar y clasificar organismos (49)

technology/tecnología productos y procesos diseñados para satisfacer nuestras necesidades (6, 23)

temperature/temperatura una medida de qué tan caliente (o frío) está algo; específicamente, una medida de la energía cinética promedio de las partículas de un objeto (34, 214)

territory/territorio un área que está ocupada por un animal o por un grupo de animales que no permiten que entren otros miembros de la especie (79)

theory/teoría una explicación que relaciona muchas hipótesis y observaciones (20)

trace fossil/fósil traza una marca fosilizada que se formó en una roca sedimentaria por el movimiento de un animal sobre sedimento blando o dentro de éste (136)

trait/carácter una característica determinada genéticamente (110)

transformer/transformador un aparato que aumenta o disminuye el voltaje de la corriente alterna (442)

transistor/transistor un aparato semiconductor que puede amplificar la corriente y se usa en los amplificadores, osciladores e interruptores (457)

U

uniformitarianism/uniformitarianismo un principio que establece que es posible explicar los procesos geológicos que ocurrieron en el pasado en función de los procesos geológicos actuales (129)

V

valence electron/electrón de valencia un electrón que se encuentra en el orbital más externo de un átomo y que determina las propiedades químicas del átomo (311)

viscosity/viscosidad la resistencia de un gas o un líquido a fluir (212)

volume/volumen una medida del tamaño de un cuerpo o región en un espacio de tres dimensiones (33, 182, 215) **TN VOCAB**

W

weight/peso una medida de la fuerza gravitacional ejercida sobre un objeto; su valor puede cambiar en función de la ubicación del objeto en el universo (185) **TN VOCAB**

Index

Boldface page numbers refer to illustrative materials, such as figures, tables, margin elements, photographs, and illustrations

A

Index

Index

Index

Index

Index

Index

Index

proteins *(continued)*
  examples of, 382, **382**
Proterozoic eon, **142**
Proteus (penguin boat), 14–15, 16, 18
Protista, 56, **56**
protons, 267, **267**, 268, 400
prototype, 24–25, **24, 25**
protozoans, 56
P-type semiconductor, 455
pure substance, 235
pyramid instructions (FoldNote), 515, **515**
pyrite, 538–539

Q

quarks, 281
quartz, 244, 538–539
questions
  asking, in scientific method, 532

R

radiation, ultraviolet (UV), 407
radioactive atoms, 270
radioactive decay
  determining age by using, 132, **132**
  half-lives, 132, **132,** 490
radioactive wastes, 157
radioactive zone, 398, 401
radioactivity, half-lives in, 132, **132,** 490
radios, lab on components of, 510–513
radio waves, 464
RAM (random-access memory), 471
ratios, 525
reactants, 340
reactive, 292
reactivity, 194, **194**
  of elements, 346, **346**
reciprocals, 527
record, playing, 462
rectangle, area of, 528
recycling, 6, **6,** 165, 206
  of aluminum, 295
red cup sponge, 59, **59**
reducing fractions, 526
reflected beam, 522
reflection, 522
  law of, 522
relative dating, 131, **131**
renewable resources, 158
replacement, in fossils, 135
reproduction
  asexual, 70, **70,** 77

competition for mates, 115
fertilization, 71–72, **71**
  in mammals, 73
  natural selection and, 86–87, **86, 87**
  in plants, 74–77, **75, 76, 77**
research, 5, **5,** 13
resistance to insecticides, 89, **89**
resources
  depletion of, 158, **158**
  recycling, 6, **6,** 165, **165**
  saving, 6, **6**
reuse, 164
revolution, 410, **410**
revolving nosepiece, 536, **536**
ribonucleic acid (RNA), 383
Riley, Agnes, 483, **483**
rock layers, 131, **131**
rocks
  fossils in, 103, 134, **134**
  sedimentary, 103
ROM (read-only) memory, 471
Roosevelt, Franklin D., 16
rotation, 410, **410**
runners, 77
Rutherford, Ernest, 263–264

S

safety
  with animals, xxvii
  with chemicals, xxvi
  with electricity, xxvi
  equipment for, xxv
  eye, xxv
  neatness and, xxv
  rules on, xxiv-xxvii, 35
  sharp/pointed objects, xxv
  symbols in, xxiv, 35
salt, 315, 377
  uses of, 377, **377**
Sanders, Scott, 124
satellites, gravity's effect on, 521
saturated hydrocarbons, 379, **379**
Saturn, 397
scale, 19
  pH, 375, **375**
scanning tunneling electron microscope (STM), 260
Schrödinger, Erwin, 265
science, 4
  questions in, 4
science illustrator, 9, **9**
scientific knowledge, models in building, 20, **20**
scientific laws, 21, **21**
scientific methods, 10–16, **10,** 532
  analyzing results, 15, 532
  asking questions, 11–12, 532
  communicating results, 16, 533
  drawing conclusions, 16, 533

forming hypothesis, 13, 532
  in action, 533
  testing hypothesis, 14, 532
scientific models, 18–21, 43
  types of, 18–21, **18, 19, 20**
scientific names, 50–51, **51**
scientific notation, 528
scientists
  ecologists, 8
  geochemists, 8, **8**
  meteorologists, 7, **7**
  science illustrators, 9, **9**
  volcanologists, 8, **8**
Seaborg, Glenn T., 307, **307**
seaborgium, 307
seasonal behavior, 81–83, **81, 82, 83**
sea stars, 70, **70**
sedimentary rock, 103
sediments, 102
seedless vascular plants, 74–75, **74**
seed banks, 124, **124**
seed plants, reproduction in, 75–77, **75, 77**
seed production, 76, **76**
seismograms, 461
seismograph, 461
selective breeding, 110, **110**
semiconductor, 289, **289,** 454, **454**
sexual reproduction, 71–73
  genes in, 71, **71**
  internal and external fertilization in, 72, **72**
  in mammals, 73
  in plants, 74–77, **75, 76, 77**
shape
  of gases, 213
  of liquids, 212
  of solids, 211
sharp/pointed objects, safety with, xxv
signals, 460
  analog, 461
  audio, 465
  communicating with, 460, **460**
  digital, 462–463, **462, 463**
  lab in sending, 476–477
Silicon, 454
Silly Putty™, 390
simple carbohydrates, 380, **380**
single-displacement reactions, 345, **345**
sky maps, 540–541, **540–541**
slope, 530–531
snakes, adaptations in, 100, **100**
So, Mimi, 207, **207**
soap, 371, **371**
sodium, 337
sodium chloride, 239, **239,** 337
sodium hydroxide, 375
software, 473
solar activity, 402
solar energy, 163, **163,** 399–401, **399, 400, 401**

Index

Acknowledgments

continued from page ii

Erica C. Waggoner
Science Teacher
Neelys Bend Middle School
Madison, Tennessee

Academic Reviewers

Glenn Adelson, Ph.D.
Instructor
Department of Organismic
and Evolutionary Biology
Harvard University
Cambridge, Massachusetts

Richard H. Audet, Ed.D.
Associate Professor
School of Education
Roger Williams University
Bristol, Rhode Island

Wesley N. Colley, Ph.D.
Lecturer
Department of Astronomy
University of Virginia
Charlottesville, Virginia

Roger J. Cuffey, Ph.D.
Professor of Paleontology
Department of Geosciences
Pennsylvania State
University
University Park,
Pennsylvania

Scott Darveau, Ph.D.
*Assistant Professor of
Chemistry*
Chemistry Department
University of Nebraska at
Kearney
Kearney, Nebraska

Jim Denbow, Ph.D.
*Associate Professor of
Archaeology*
Department of
Anthropology and
Archaeology
The University of Texas at
Austin
Austin, Texas

William E. Dunscombe
*Associate Professor and
Chairman*
Biology Department
Union County College
Cranford, New Jersey

Cassandra Eagle, Ph.D.
*Professor of Organic
Chemistry*
Chemistry Department
Appalachian State
University
Boone, North Carolina

William Grisham, Ph.D.
Lecturer
Psychology Department
University of California,
Los Angeles
Los Angeles, California

David Haig, Ph.D.
Professor of Biology
Department of Organismic
and Evolutionary Biology
Harvard University
Cambridge, Massachusetts

P. Shiv Halasyamani, Ph.D.
*Associate Professor of
Chemistry*
Department of Chemistry
University of Houston
Houston, Texas

David S. Hall, Ph.D.
Assistant Professor of Physics
Department of Physics
Amherst College
Amherst, Massachusetts

David Hershey, Ph.D.
Education Consultant
Hyattsville, Maryland

William H. Ingham, Ph.D.
Professor of Physics
James Madison University
Harrisonburg, Virginia

Steven A. Jennings, Ph.D.
Associate Professor
Department of Geography
and Environmental
Studies
University of Colorado
Colorado Springs, Colorado

**Ping H. Johnson, M.D.,
Ph.D., C.H.E.S.**
*Assistant Professor of Health
Education*
Department of Health,
Physical Education and
Sport Science
Kennesaw State University
Kennesaw, Georgia

Mark N. Kobrak, Ph.D.
*Assistant Professor of
Chemistry*
Chemistry Department
Brooklyn College of the
City
University of New York
Brooklyn, New York

Daniela Kohen, Ph.D.
*Assistant Professor of
Chemistry*
Chemistry Department
Carleton College
Northfield, Minnesota

John Krenz, Ph.D.
*Associate Professor
Biological Sciences*
Minnesota State University
Mankato, Minnesota

Joel S. Leventhal, Ph.D.
*Emeritus Scientist,
Geochemistry*
U.S. Geological Survey
Lakewood, Colorado

Mark Mattson, Ph.D.
*Director, College of Science
and Mathematics Learning
Center*
James Madison University
Harrisonburg, Virginia

Richard F. Niedziela, Ph.D.
*Assistant Professor of
Chemistry*
Department of Chemistry
DePaul University
Chicago, Illinois

Eva Oberdoerster, Ph.D.
Lecturer
Department of Biology
Southern Methodist
University
Dallas, Texas

Sten Odenwald, Ph.D.
Astronomer
NASA Goddard Space Flight
Center and Raytheon
ITSS
Greenbelt, Maryland

**Enrique Peacock-López,
Ph.D.**
Professor of Chemistry
Department of Chemistry
Williams College
Williamstown,
Massachusetts

Kate Queeney, Ph.D.
*Assistant Professor of
Chemistry*
Chemistry Department
Smith College
Northampton,
Massachusetts

Michael H. Renfroe, Ph.D.
Professor of Biology
Department of Biology
James Madison University
Harrisonburg, Virginia

Laurie Santos, Ph.D.
Assistant Professor
Department of Psychology
Yale University
New Haven, Connecticut

Fred Seaman, Ph.D.
Retired Research Associate
College of Pharmacy
The University of Texas at
Austin
Austin, Texas

Daniel Z. Sui, Ph.D.
Professor
Department of Geography
Texas A&M University
College Station, Texas

Colin D. Sumrall, Ph.D.
Lecturer of Paleontology
Earth and Planetary
Sciences
The University of Tennessee
Knoxville, Tennessee

Richard S. Treptow, Ph.D.
Professor of Chemistry
Department of Chemistry
and Physics
Chicago State University
Chicago, Illinois

Richard P. Vari, Ph.D.
*Research Scientist and
Curator*
Department of Vertebrate
Zoology
National Museum of
Natural History
Washington, D.C.

John D. Wehr, Ph.D.
Associate Professor
Department of Biological
Sciences
Fordham University
Bronx, New York

Dale Wheeler
*Associate Professor of
Chemistry*
A. R. Smith Department of
Chemistry
Appalachian State
University
Boone, North Carolina

Kim Withers, Ph.D.
Research Scientist
Center for Coastal Studies
Texas A&M University at
Corpus Christi
Corpus Christi, Texas

Teacher Reviewers

Diedre S. Adams
Physical Science Instructor
West Vigo Middle School
West Terre Haute, Indiana

Barbara Gavin Akre
Teacher of Biology, Anatomy-Physiology, and Life Science
Duluth Independent School District
Duluth, Minnesota

Sarah Carver
Science Teacher
Jackson Creek Middle School
Bloomington, Indiana

Robin K. Clanton
Science Department Head
Berrien Middle School
Nashville, Georgia

Hilary Cochran
Science Teacher
Indian Crest Junior High School
Souderton, Pennsylvania

Karen Dietrich, S.S.J., Ph.D.
Principal and Biology Instructor
Mount Saint Joseph Academy
Flourtown, Pennsylvania

Randy Dye, M.S.
Science Department Head
Wood Middle School
Fort Leonard Wood, Missouri

Trisha Elliott
Science and Mathematics Teacher
Chain of Lakes Middle School
Orlando, Florida

Liza M. Guasp
Science Teacher
Celebration K–8 School
Celebration, Florida

Ronald W. Hudson
Science Teacher
Batchelor Middle School
Bloomington, Indiana

Denise Hulette
Science Teacher
Conway Middle School
Orlando, Florida

M. R. Penny Kisiah
Science Teacher and Department Chair
Fairview Middle School
Tallahassee, Florida

Debra S. Kogelman, MAed.
Science Teacher
University of Chicago Laboratory Schools
Chicago, Illinois

Tiffany Kracht
Science Teacher
Chain of Lakes Middle School
Orlando, Florida

Deborah L. Kronsteiner
Science Teacher
Spring Grove Area Middle School
Spring Grove, Pennsylvania

Jennifer L. Lamkie
Science Teacher
Thomas Jefferson Middle School
Edison, New Jersey

Rebecca Larsen
Science Teacher
Fernandina Beach Middle School
Fernandina Beach, Florida

Augie Maldonado
Science Teacher
Grisham Middle School
Round Rock, Texas

Bill Martin
Science Teacher
Southeast Middle School
Kernersville, North Carolina

Maureen Martin
Green Team Science Teacher
Jackson Creek Middle School
Bloomington, Indiana

Alyson Mike
Science Teacher
Radley Middle School
East Helena, Montana

Magdalena F. Molledo
Science Department Chair
DeLaura Middle School
Satellite Beach, Florida

Nancy Poage-Nixon
Science Teacher
Covington Middle School
Austin, Texas

Thomas Lee Reed
Science Teacher
Rising Starr Middle School
Fayetteville, Georgia

Shannon Ripple
Science Teacher
Canyon Vista Middle School
Round Rock, Texas

Elizabeth J. Rustad
Science Department Chair
Coronado Elementary
Gilbert, Arizona

Helen P. Schiller
Instructional Coach
The School District of Greenville County
Greenville, South Carolina

Mark Schnably
Science Instructor
Thomas Jefferson Middle School
Winston-Salem, North Carolina

Stephanie Snowden
Science Teacher
Canyon Vista Middle School
Austin, Texas

Marci L. Stadiem
Science Department Head
Cascade Middle School
Seattle, Washington

Martha Tedrow
Science Teacher
Thomas Jefferson Middle School
Winston-Salem, North Carolina

Martha B. Trisler
Science Teacher
Rising Starr Middle School
Fayetteville, Georgia

Sherrye Valenti
Curriculum Leader
Science Department
Wildwood Middle School
Wildwood, Missouri

Florence Vaughan
Science Teacher
University of Chicago Laboratory Schools
Chicago, Illinois

Angie Williams
Teacher
Riversprings Middle School
Crawfordville, Florida

Roberta Young
Science Teacher
Gunn Junior High School
Arlington, Texas

Lab Testing

Paul Boyle
Science Teacher
Perry Heights Middle School
Evansville, Indiana

Daniel Bugenhagen
Science Teacher
Yutan Junior-Senior High School
Yutan, Nebraska

Gladys Cherniak
Science Teacher
St. Paul's Episcopal School
Mobile, Alabama

Georgiann Delgadillo
Science Teacher
East Valley School District Continuous Curriculum School
Spokane, Washington

Alonda Droege
Science Teacher
Pioneer Middle School
Steilacom, Washington

Rebecca Ferguson
Science Teacher
North Ridge Middle School
North Richland Hills, Texas

Laura Fleet
Science Teacher
Alice B. Landrum Middle School
Ponte Vedra Beach, Florida

Susan Gorman
Science Teacher
North Ridge Middle School
North Ridge, Texas

C. John Graves
Science Teacher
Monforton Middle School
Bozeman, Montana

Dennis Hanson
Science Teacher
Big Bear Middle School
Big Bear Lake, California

Norman Holcomb
Science Teacher
Marion Elementary School
Maria Stein, Ohio

Kenneth J. Horn
Science Teacher
Fallston Middle School
Fallston, Maryland

Karma Houston-Hughes
Science Mentor
Kyrene Middle School
Tempe, Arizona

Tracy Jahn
Science Teacher
Berkshire Junior-Senior High School
Canaan, New York

Maurine Marchani
Science Teacher
Raymond Park Middle
  School
Indianapolis, Indiana

Alyson Mike
Science Teacher
Radley Middle School
East Helena, Montana

Joseph W. Price
Science Teacher
H.M. Browne Junior High
  School
Washington, D.C.

Terry Rakes
Science Teacher
Elmwood Junior High
  School
Rogers, Arkansas

Debra Sampson
Science Teacher
Booker T. Washington
  Middle School
Elgin, Texas

Rodney A. Sandefur
Science Teacher
Naturita Middle School
Naturita, Colorado

David M. Sparks
Science Teacher
Redwater Junior High
  School
Redwater, Texas

Sharon Woolf
Science Teacher
Langston Hughes Middle
  School
Reston, Virginia

Lee Yassinski
Science Teacher
Sun Valley Middle School
Sun Valley, California

Answer Checking

Hatim Belyamani
Austin, Texas

John A. Benner
Austin, Texas

Catherine Podeszwa
Duluth, Minnesota

Credits

Chapter Seven 180-181 (all), Mark Renders/Getty Images; 182 (b), Sam Dudgeon/HRW; 182 (bc), Digital Image copyright © 2005 PhotoDisc; 183 (cr), Sam Dudgeon/HRW; 184 (cl), Sam Dudgeon/HRW; 184 (cl), Victoria Smith/HRW; 185 (all), Sam Dudgeon/HRW; 186 (tl), John Langford/HRW; 186 (br), Corbis Images; 188 (b), Sam Dudgeon/HRW; 189 (tl), Victoria Smith/HRW; 189 (tr, tc, c), Sam Dudgeon/HRW; 189 (cl), Peter Van Steen/HRW; 189 (cr, bl), John Morrison/Morrison Photography; 190 (tl), Richard Megna/Fundamental Photographs; 190 (bl), Victoria Smith/HRW; 192 (tr), Lance Schriner/HRW; 192 (tl), John Langford/HRW; 193 (tr), Victoria Smith/HRW; 193 (inset), Sam Dudgeon/HRW; 194 (br), Rob Boudreau/Getty Images; 195 (cl, cr), Charlie Winters/HRW; 195 (tl, tr), Sam Dudgeon/HRW; 196 (c, cr), Morrison Photography; 196 (bl), Joseph Drivas/Getty Images; 196 (br), © SuperStock; 197 (all), Sam Dudgeon/HRW; 198 (all), Charlie Winters/HRW; 199 (tr), CORBIS Images/HRW; 200 (b), Sam Dudgeon/HRW; 202 (b), Richard Megna/Fundamental Photographs; 203 (cr), Lance Schriner/HRW; 206 (tl), © David Young-Wolff/PhotoEdit; 207 (cr), Courtesy Mimi So; 207 (b), Steve Cole/PhotoDisc/PictureQuest

Chapter Eight 208-209 (all), Teresa Nouri Rishel/Dale Chihuly Studio; 211 (bl), Digital Image copyright © 2005 PhotoDisc; 211 (br), Susumu Nishinaga/Science Photo Library/Photo Researchers, Inc.; 212 (tr), Victoria Smith/HRW; 212 (bl), © Dr. Jeremy Burgess/Photo Researchers, Inc.; 213 (tr), Scott Van Osdol/HRW; 214 (br), AP Photo/Beth Keiser; 215 (bl), Corbis Images; 215 (br), Victoria Smith/HRW; 219 (bc), Scott Van Osdol/HRW; 219 (tr), Richard Megna/Fundamental Photographs; 221 (bl), Ed Reschke/Peter Arnold, Inc.; 222 (tl), Omni Photo Communications, Inc./Index Stock Imagery, Inc.; 224 (br), Victoria Smith/HRW; 225 (br), Sam Dudgeon/HRW; 226 (bc), Sam Dudgeon/HRW; 227 (bl), Charles D. Winters/Photo Researchers, Inc.; 230 (tr), CORBIS Images/HRW; 230 (tl), Scoones/SIPA Press; 231 (cr), Susanna Frohman/San Jose Mercury News/NewsCom; 231 (bl), Chris Heillier/Corbis

Chapter Nine 232-233 (all), Scott Van Osdol/HRW; 234 (br), Jonathan Blair/Woodfin Camp & Associates, Inc.; 234 (bl), Victoria Smith/HRW; 235 (br), Russ Lappa/Photo Researchers, Inc.; 235 (bl, bc), Charles D. Winters/Photo Researchers, Inc.; 236 (tl), © Zack Burris/Zack Burris, Inc.; 236 (tcl), Yann Arthus-Bertrand/CORBIS; 236 (tcr, tr), Walter Chandoha; 237 (lead), Victoria Smith/HRW; 237 (copper, tin, sulfur), Sam Dudgeon/HRW; 237 (phosphorus), Charles D. Winters/Photo Researchers, Inc.; 237 (silicon), Joyce Photographics/Photo Researchers, Inc.; 237 (boron), Russ Lappa/Photo Researchers, Inc.; 237 (antimony), Charles D. Winters/Photo Researchers, Inc.; 237 (iodine), Larry Stepanowicz; 238 (bl), Charles D. Winters/Photo Researchers, Inc.; 239 (bl), Andrew Lambert Photography/Photo Researchers, Inc.; 239 (bc), Richard Megna/Fundamental Photographs; 239 (br), Sam Dudgeon/HRW; 240 (tl), Richard Megna/Fundamental Photographs; 241 (tr), John Kaprielian/Photo Researchers, Inc.; 242 (br), Sam Dudgeon/HRW; 243 (tl), Charles D. Winters; 243 (cl), Sam Dudgeon/HRW; 243 (bc), Charles D. Winters/Photo Researchers, Inc.; 243 (bl), Klaus Guldbrandsen/Science Photo Library/Photo Researchers, Inc.; 243 (tr, cr, br), John Langford/HRW; 244 (tl), Sam Dudgeon/HRW; 245 (bl), Richard Haynes/HRW; 246 (tr), Sam Dudgeon/HRW; 247 (all), John Langford/HRW; 248 (bl), HRW; 248 (br), Lance Schriner/HRW; 249 (tr), Sam Dudgeon/HRW; 250 (bl), © Stuart Westmoreland/Getty Images; 251 (b), Sam Dudgeon/HRW; 252 (tr), Sam Dudgeon/HRW; 252 (tl), Walter Chandoha; 253 (tr), Sam Dudgeon/HRW; 256 (tl), Peter Van Steen/HRW; 257 (tr), Courtesy of Aundra Nix; 257 (cr), Astrid & Hans-Frieder Michler/SPL/Photo Researchers, Inc.

Chapter Ten 258-259 (all), P. Loiez Cern/Science Photo Library/Photo Researchers, Inc.; 260 (bl), Victoria Smith/HRW; 260 (bc), Courtesy JEOL; 261 (b), Corbis-Bettmann; 264 (br), John Zoiner; 264 (bc), Mavournea Hay/HRW; 266 (b), Sam Dudgeon/HRW; 271 (cr), Corbis Images; 273 (b), Sam Dudgeon/HRW; 274 (br), Victoria Smith/HRW; 275 (br), Sam Dudgeon/HRW; 276 (bl), Corbis-Bettmann; 277 (bl), Fermilab; 280 (tr), NASA; 280 (tl), Giraudon/Art Resource, NY; 281 (br), Fermi National Accelerator Laboratory/CORBIS; 281 (tr), Stephen Maclone

Chapter Eleven 282-283 (all), Gerard Perrone/Courtesy of Eric Ehlenberger; 285 (tr), Sam Dudgeon/HRW; 288 (all), Sam Dudgeon/HRW; 289 (tr), Sam Dudgeon/HRW; 289 (tc), Richard Megna/Fundamental Photographs; 289 (bl), Russ Lappa/Photo Researchers, Inc.; 289 (bc), Lester V. Bergman/Corbis-Bettmann; 289 (tl), Sally Anderson-Bruce/HRW; 290 (bc, br), Richard Megna/Fundamental Photographs; 290 (bl), Tom Pantages Photography; 291 (br), HRW; 291 (tr), Sam Dudgeon/HRW; 292 (bl), Charles D. Winters/Photo Researchers, Inc.; 292 (bc, br), Richard Megna/Fundamental Photographs; 293 (tr), Sam Dudgeon/HRW; 294 (tl, cl), Sam Dudgeon/HRW; 294 (tr), ©1990 P. Petersen/Custom Medical Stock Photo; 294 (tc, bl), Victoria Smith/HRW; 295 (cr), Phillip Hayson/Photo Researchers, Inc.; 295 (br), Sam Dudgeon/HRW; 296 (tl), Sam Dudgeon/HRW; 296 (b), CORBIS Images/HRW; 297 (tl, tc), Richard Megna/Fundamental Photographs; 297 (tr), Charlie Winters/HRW; 298 (bl), NASA; 298 (tl), Spencer Grant/Photo Researchers, Inc.; 299 (tr), Sam Dudgeon/HRW; 300 (b), Sam Dudgeon/HRW; 301 (br), John Langford/HRW; 302 (tl), Sam Dudgeon/HRW; 306 (tr), CORBIS Images/HRW; 307 (cr), © Lawrence Berkeley National Laboratory/Photo Researchers, Inc.; 307 (cl), © Bettmann/CORBIS

Chapter Twelve 308-309 (all), © Doug Struthers/Getty Images; 310 (bl), Don Couch/HRW Photo; 314 (br), © Konrad Wothe/Minden Pictures; 317 (cl), Paul Silverman/Fundamental Photographs; 320 (tr), Sam Dudgeon/HRW; 321 (tc), Sam Dudgeon/HRW; 321 (bl), © Jonathan Blair/CORBIS; 322 (tr), Victoria Smith/HRW; 323 (tr), John Langford/HRW; 325 (b), Sam Dudgeon/HRW; 326 (br), Victoria Smith/HRW; 327 (cr, br), Sam Dudgeon/HRW; 327 (tc), © Konrad Wothe/Minden Pictures; 330 (tr), Peter Oxford/Nature Picture Library; 330 (tl), Diaphor Agency/Index Stock Imagery, Inc.; 330 (tl), Mark R. Cutkosky, Stanford University Center for Design Research; 331 (cr), Steve Fischbach/HRW; 331 (bl), W. & D. McIntyre/Photo Researchers, Inc.

Chapter Thirteen 332-333 (all), Corbis Images; 334 (bl), Rob Matheson/The Stock Market; 334 (br), Sam Dudgeon/HRW; 335 (cl, cr), Richard Megna/Fundamental Photographs, New York; 335 (br), Scott Van Osdol/HRW; 335 (bl), J.T. Wright/Bruce Coleman Inc./Picture Quest; 336 (all), Charlie Winters; 337 (br), Charlie Winters/HRW; 340 (tl), John Langford/HRW; 340 (bl), Richard Haynes/HRW; 341 (tr), Charles D. Winters/Photo Researchers, Inc.; 341 (tc), John Langford/HRW; 341 (tl), © Ingram Publishing; 346 (tl), Peticolas/Megna/Fundamental Photographs; 346 (tr), Richard Megna/Fundamental Photographs; 348 (bl), Victoria Smith/HRW; 348 (bc), Peter Van Steen/HRW; 348 (br), © Tom Stewart/The Stock Market; 349 (br), © David Stoecklein/CORBIS; 350 (t), Michael Newman/PhotoEdit; 351 (cr), Richard Megna/Fundamental Photographs; 352 (tl), Sam Dudgeon/HRW; 353 (tr), Dorling Kindersley Limited courtesy of the Science Museum, London/CORBIS; 353 (bl), Victoria Smith/HRW; 354 (b), Victoria Smith/HRW; 356 (tr), Richard Megna/Fundamental Photographs; 357 (cr), Richard Megna/Fundamental Photographs; 357 (br), Rob Matheson/The Stock Market; 360 (tr), Tony Freeman/PhotoEdit; 360 (tl), Henry Bargas/Amarillo Globe-News/AP/Wide World Photos; 361 (all), Bob Parker/Austin Fire Investigation

Chapter Fourteen 362-363, Dennis Kunkel Microscopy, Inc.; 364 (bl), © Andrew Syred/Microscopix Photolibrary; 365 (all), Richard Megna/Fundamental Photographs; 366 (b), Victoria Smith/HRW; 367 (tr), Richard Megna/Fundamental Photographs; 368 (br), Jack Newkirk/HRW; 369 (br), Charles D. Winters/Timeframe Photography, Inc.; 369 (tl, tr), Peter Van Steen/HRW; 370 (br), Tom Tracy/The Stock Shop/Medichrome; 371 (tc), Victoria Smith/HRW; 371 (tr), © Peter Cade/Getty Images; 371 (tl), Houghton Mifflin Harcourt; 372 (all), Peter Van Steen/HRW; 373 (tr), Peter Van Steen/HRW; 376 (bl), Digital Image copyright © 2005 PhotoDisc; 376 (tl), Victoria Smith/HRW; 376 (tc, tr), Scott Van Osdol/HRW; 377 (tr), Miro Vinton/Stock Boston/PictureQuest; 379 (tl), Sam Dudgeon/HRW; 379 (tc), John Langford/HRW; 379 (tr), Charles D. Winters/Timeframe Photography, Inc.; 380 (tc), Digital Image copyright © 2005 PhotoDisc; 381 (bl), Sam Dudgeon/HRW; 382 (tl), Hans Reinhard/Bruce Coleman, Inc.; 383 (tr), CORBIS Images/HRW; 384 (b), Sam Dudgeon/HRW; 386 (tr), Peter Van Steen/HRW; 387 (all), Digital Image copyright © 2005 PhotoDisc; 390 (tr), Dan Loh/AP/Wide World Photos; 390 (tl), AP Photo/Augustin Ochsenreiter; 391 (tr), Nicole Guglielmo; 391 (bl), Corbis Images

Chapter Fifteen 392-393, Anglo-Australian Observatory/Royal Obs. Edinburgh; 394, David Malin/Anglo-Australian Observatory/Royal Observatory, Edinburgh; 402, NASA/Mark Marten/Photo Researchers, Inc.; 403, NASA/TSADO/Tom Stack & Associates; 404, Earth Imaging/Getty Images/Stone; 407, SuperStock; 408 (l), Breck P. Kent/Animals Animals/Earth Scenes; 408 (r), John Reader/Science Photo Library/Photo Researchers, Inc; 410 (bc), Scott Van Osdol/HRW; 414, Sam Dudgeon/HRW; 416, Earth Imaging/Getty Images/Stone; 420 (b), NSO/NASA; 420 (tr), Jon Lomberg/Science Photo Library/Photo Researchers, Inc.; 420 (inset), David A. Hardy/Science Photo Library/Photo Researchers, Inc.; 420 (bl), NASA/JPL-Caltech; 421 (r), AIP/Photo Researchers, Inc.; 421 (l), AP Photo/NASA

Chapter Sixteen 422-423 (all), © NASA/Photo Researchers, Inc.; 424 (bc), Sam Dudgeon/HRW; 425 (tr, bc, br), Richard Megna/Fundamental Photographs; 425 (cr), Sam Dudgeon/HRW; 426 (tr), Richard Megna/Fundamental Photographs; 427 (br), Sam Dudgeon/HRW; 428 (cl), Sam Dudgeon/HRW; 430 (br), Pekka Parviainen/Science Photo Library/Photo Researchers, Inc.; 431 (tr), Sam Dudgeon/HRW; 434 (br), © Tom Tracy/The Stock Shop; 435 (tr), Victoria Smith/HRW; 437 (cr), Victoria Smith/HRW; 437 (tr), Sam Dudgeon/HRW; 444 (cr), Sam Dudgeon/HRW; 445 (bl), David Young Wolf/PhotoEdit; 446 (tl), Sam Dudgeon/HRW; 450 (cl), © Getty Images; 450 (tr), Howard Sochurek; 450 (tl) Photo by Larry Hamill for Oak Ridge National Laboratory; 451 (tr), © Baldwin Ward/CORBIS

Chapter Seventeen 452-453 (all), © Peter Menzel Photography; 454 (all), Sam Dudgeon/HRW; 456 (tl), Sam Dudgeon/HRW; 457 (tr), Sam Dudgeon/HRW; 458 (bl), Sam Dudgeon/HRW; 459 (all), Sam Dudgeon/HRW; 460 (bl), Digital Image copyright © 2005 PhotoDisc; 462 (bl), Digital Image copyright © 2005 PhotoDisc; 465 (inset), Corbis Images; 466 (inset), Corbis Images; 468 (br), Sam Dudgeon/HRW; 469 (tr), Corbis-Bettmann; 470 (b), Sam Dudgeon/HRW; 471 (b), Sam Dudgeon/HRW; 475 (all), Sam Dudgeon/HRW; 476 (bl), Sam Dudgeon/HRW; 477 (b), Sam Dudgeon/HRW; 478 (br), Sam Dudgeon/HRW; 479 (bl), Sam Dudgeon/HRW; 482 (tl), © Reuters NewMedia Inc./CORBIS; 483 (cr), Courtesy Agnes Riley; 483 (bl), Digital Image copyright © 2005 PhotoDisc

STAFF CREDITS

The people who contributed to *Holt Science & Technology* are listed below. They represent editorial, design, production, eMedia, permissions, and marketing.

Chris Allison, Melanie Baccus, Wesley M. Bain, Juan Baquera, Angela Beckmann, Ed Blake, Sara Buller, Marc Burgamy, Rebecca Calhoun, Kimberly Cammerata, Soojinn Choi, Eddie Dawson, Julie Dervin, Michelle Dike, Lydia Doty, Jen Driscoll, Leigh Ann García, Catherine Gnader, Diana Goetting, Tim Hovde, Wilonda Ieans, Jevara Jackson, Simon Key, Jane A. Kirschman, Cathy Kuhles, Laura Likon, Denise Mahoney, Michael Mazza, Kristen McCardel, Richard Metzger, Micah Newman, Janice Noske, Joeleen Ornt, Cathy Paré, Jenny Patton, Laura Prescott, Bill Rader, Peter D. Reid, Sara Rider, Curtis Riker, Michael Rinella, Jeff Robinson, Audrey Rozsypal, Beth Sample, Margaret Sanchez, Kay Selke, Elizabeth Simmons, Chris Smith, Dawn Marie Spinozza, Sherry Sprague, Jeff Streber, JoAnn Stringer, Roshan Strong, Jeannie Taylor, Bob Tucek, Tam Voynick, Clay Walton, Kira J. Watkins, Ken Whiteside, Holly Whittaker, David Wisnieski, Monica Yudron, Patty Zepeda